Contents

Pure Mathematics

Statistics

A-Level
Mathematics

Exam Board: AQA

If A-Level Maths was an action movie, the exams would be the big final showdown.
They won't be easy, but you do have a wise mentor to guide you — this brilliant CGP book.

It's packed with all the notes and examples you need to wipe the floor with
every topic, all fully up to date for the new course starting in 2017 and beyond.

We've also thrown in plenty of questions to help you sharpen your skills (if it helps, think
of them as the exam's evil henchmen). You can even read the whole thing online...

How to get your free Online Edition

Just go to **cgpbooks.co.uk/extras** and enter this code:

2786 8474 9842 1863

This code only works for one person. If somebody else has used
this book before you, they might have already claimed the Online Edition.

A-Level revision? It has to be CGP!

Published by CGP

Editors:
Chris Corrall, Sammy El-Bahrawy, Will Garrison, Paul Jordin, Caley Simpson, Dawn Wright

Contributors:
Andrew Ballard, Claire Jackson, Mark Moody, Garry Rowlands, Mike Smith, Chris Worth

ISBN: 978 1 78294 809 4

With thanks to Ruth Wilbourne for the proofreading.

Clipart from Corel®
Printed by Elanders Ltd, Newcastle upon Tyne.

Based on the classic CGP style created by Richard Parsons.

Mechanics

Proof

Like an annoying child who keeps asking 'But whyyyyyyyy?', sometimes the examiners expect you to prove something is true. The next two pages feature two classic maths ways of proving things, plus a bonus way to disprove stuff.

Some **Notation**

There are certain bits of **notation** that'll be **useful** not only for **proofs**, but for the **rest** of A-Level Maths too.

A **set** is just a **collection** of objects or numbers (called **elements**), shown using **curly brackets**.
A set is often represented by a capital letter — e.g. A = {0, 1, 2}. There are different ways of writing sets:
- A list of elements — e.g. {1, 3, 5, 7, 9}
- A rule — e.g. {odd numbers between 0 and 10}
- Mathematical notation — e.g. $\{x : x < 0\}$ (this means "the set of values of x such that x is less than 0")

The symbols $\Rightarrow$ and $\Leftrightarrow$ are **logic symbols** — they show when one thing **implies** another.
- '$p \Rightarrow q$' means 'p implies q' or 'if p then q'. E.g. $x = 2 \Rightarrow x^2 = 4$.
- '$p \Leftrightarrow q$' means 'p implies q and q implies p' or 'p if and only if q'. E.g. $x^2 = 4 \Leftrightarrow x = \pm 2$

'If and only if' is sometimes written as 'iff'.

There are a few variations on the **equals sign** that you need to know:
- $\neq$ means **not equal to** — e.g. $\sin 90° \neq \cos 90°$
- $\approx$ means **approximately equal to** — e.g. $1 \div 3 \approx 0.33$
- $\equiv$ is the **identity symbol**. It means that two things are **identically equal** to each other.
  So $(a + b)(a - b) \equiv a^2 - b^2$ is true for all values of a and b
  (unlike an equation like $a^2 = 9$, which is only true for certain values of a).

Proof by **Exhaustion**

In **proof by exhaustion** you break things down into two or more **cases**. You have to make sure that your cases cover **all possible situations**, then prove **separately** that the statement is true for **each case**.

Example: Prove the following statement: "For any integer x, the value of $f(x) = x^3 + x + 1$ is an odd integer."

To prove the statement, split the situation into **two cases**:
      (i) x is an **even number**,   and   (ii) x is an **odd number**

(i) If x is an **even integer**, then it can be written as $x = 2n$, for some integer n — *this is the definition of an even number.*

    Substitute $x = 2n$ into the function: $f(2n) = (2n)^3 + 2n + 1 = 8n^3 + 2n + 1$
$$= 2(4n^3 + n) + 1$$

    n is an integer $\Rightarrow (4n^3 + n)$ is an integer — *the sum or product of any integers are also integers.*
                     $\Rightarrow 2(4n^3 + n)$ is an even integer — *2 × an integer is the definition of an even number.*
                     $\Rightarrow 2(4n^3 + n) + 1$ is an **odd integer** — *since even + odd = odd.*

    So $f(x)$ is **odd** when x is **even**.

(ii) If x is an **odd integer**, then it can be written as $x = 2m + 1$, for some integer m — *this is the definition of an odd number.*

    Substitute $x = 2m + 1$ into the function:
$$f(2m + 1) = (2m + 1)^3 + (2m + 1) + 1 = (8m^3 + 12m^2 + 6m + 1) + 2m + 1 + 1$$
$$= 8m^3 + 12m^2 + 8m + 3 = 2(4m^3 + 6m^2 + 4m + 1) + 1$$

You can use the binomial expansion formula on p.51 to help you find these coefficients.

    m is an integer $\Rightarrow (4m^3 + 6m^2 + 4m + 1)$ is an integer
                     $\Rightarrow 2(4m^3 + 6m^2 + 4m + 1)$ is an even integer
                     $\Rightarrow 2(4m^3 + 6m^2 + 4m + 1) + 1$ is an **odd integer**

    So $f(x)$ is **odd** when x is **odd**.

We have shown that $f(x)$ is **odd** when x is even **and** when x is odd. As any integer x **must** be either odd or even, we have therefore shown that $f(x)$ is **odd** for **any** integer x.

Proof

Proof by **Deduction**

A **proof by deduction** (or **direct proof** or '**proof by direct argument**') is when you use **known facts** to **build up** your argument and show a statement **must** be true.

> **Example:** A definition of a rational number is: 'a number that can be written as a quotient of two integers, where the denominator is non-zero'.
> Use this definition to prove that the following statement is true:
> "The product of two rational numbers is always a rational number."

Take **any two** rational numbers, call them a and b.

By the **definition** of rational numbers you can write them in the form $a = \frac{p}{q}$ and $b = \frac{r}{s}$, where p, q, r and s are all integers, and q and s are non-zero.

The **product** of a and b is $ab = \frac{p}{q} \times \frac{r}{s} = \frac{pr}{qs}$

pr and qs are the products of integers, so they must also be integers, and because q and s are non-zero, qs must also be non-zero.

We've shown that ab is a quotient of two integers and has a non-zero denominator, so by definition, ab **is rational**.

Hence the original statement is **true**.

Disproof by **Counter-Example**

Disproof by **counter-example** is the easiest way to show a mathematical statement is **false**.
All you have to do is find **one case** where the statement doesn't hold.

> **Example:** Disprove the following statement:
> "For any pair of real numbers x and y, if $x > y$, then $x^2 + x > y^2 + y$."

To **disprove** the statement, it's enough to find just **one example** of x and y where $x > y$, but $x^2 + x \leq y^2 + y$.
Let $x = 2$ and $y = -4$.
Then $\quad 2 > -4$, so $x > y$
but $\quad x^2 + x = 2^2 + 2 = 6 \quad$ and $\quad y^2 + y = (-4)^2 + (-4) = 12$, so $x^2 + x < y^2 + y$
So when $x = 2$ and $y = -4$, the first part of the statement holds, but the second part of the statement doesn't.
So the statement is **not true**.

Practice Questions

Q1 Write out the following sets as lists of elements:
   a) {even prime numbers}   b) {factors of 28}   c) $\{x : x^2 = 1\}$

Q2 Disprove the following statements by giving a counter-example:
   a) If $\frac{x}{y} < 1$, then $x < y$ for all values of x and y b) If $x^2 + y = y^2 + x$, then $x = y$

Exam Questions

> Q1 Prove that, for any integer n, $(n + 6)^2 - (n + 1)^2$ is always divisible by 5. [3 marks]
>
> Q2 Prove that the difference between an integer and its square is always even. [3 marks]
>
> Q3 Is the following statement true or false? $(x + 2)(x - 1) > 2x - 2$ for all values of x.
> Give either a proof or a counter-example. [3 marks]

If you've exhausted all options, just stick it in a proving drawer for an hour...

When you're trying to disprove something, don't be put off if you can't find a counter-example straight away. Sometimes you have to just try a few different cases until you find one that doesn't work.

Proof by Contradiction

There's one more type of proof that you need to know for your A Level, and it's a bit of a mind-bender. Very clever though, once you get your head round it...

Proof by **Contradiction**

To prove a statement by **contradiction**, you say 'Assume the statement is **not true**...', then prove that something **impossible** would have to be true for that to be the case.

Example: Prove the following statement: "If x^2 is even, then x must be even."

We can prove the statement by contradiction.

Assume the statement is **not true**. Then there must be an **odd number** x for which x^2 is **even**.

If x is odd, then you can write x as $2k + 1$, where k is an integer — this is the definition of an odd number.

Now, $x^2 = (2k + 1)^2 = 4k^2 + 4k + 1$

$4k^2 + 4k = 2(2k^2 + 2k)$ is **even** because it is 2 × an integer — this is the definition of an even number.

$\Rightarrow 4k^2 + 4k + 1$ is **odd** — since even + odd = odd.

But this **isn't possible** if the assumption that x^2 is even is true.
We've **contradicted** the assumption that there is an odd number x for which x^2 is even.

So if x^2 is **even**, then x must be **even**, hence the original statement is **true**.

Surds are **Irrational**

You can use **proof by contradiction** to prove some **really important** facts.
For example, you can prove that the **square root** of **any** non-square number is **irrational**.

Example: Prove that $\sqrt{2}$ is irrational.

We can prove the statement by contradiction.

Start by assuming that the statement is **not true**, and that $\sqrt{2}$ can be written as $\frac{a}{b}$ with a and b both **non-zero integers** — using the definition of a rational number.

You can also assume that a and b do **not** have any **common factors.** *— cannot be simplified*

If $\sqrt{2} = \frac{a}{b}$, then $\sqrt{2}b = a$.

Squaring both sides gives you $2b^2 = a^2$ so a^2 is an **even** number — using the definition of an even number.

You saw in the previous example that if a^2 is **even**, then a must be **even** as well.
So replace a with $2k$ for some integer k:

$$2b^2 = (2k)^2 = 4k^2 \implies b^2 = 2k^2.$$

Like before, this tells you that b must be **even** (since b^2 is even).
However, you assumed at the start that a and b had **no common factors**, so you have **contradicted** your initial assumption.

Therefore $\sqrt{2}$ **cannot** be written as a fraction $\frac{a}{b}$, so it is **irrational**.

You can use the same method to prove the irrationality of **any** surd, although you need to prove the statement "If x^2 is a multiple of a prime number p, then x must also be a multiple of p", which is a bit **trickier** than the proof in the first example above.

Proof by Contradiction

You can prove there are **Infinitely Many** of something

Another use for proof by contradiction is to show that there are **infinitely many** numbers in a **certain set**.

Example: Prove by contradiction that there are infinitely many even numbers.

Assume that there are a **finite** number of even numbers, and that the biggest one can be written N, where $N = 2n$ and n is an integer.

But if you add 2 to this, you get $N + 2 = 2n + 2 = 2(n + 1)$, which is an even number **bigger** than N.

You assumed that N is the biggest even number, so you have **contradicted** your initial assumption.

So there are **infinitely many** even numbers.

You can use the same method to show that there are infinitely many **odd numbers**, or **multiples** of **5**, or **16** or **any number**. To prove that there are infinitely many **prime numbers**, you need a **slightly different** method:

Example: Prove by contradiction that there are infinitely many prime numbers.

Assume that there are a **finite** number of primes (say n), and label them $p_1 = 2, p_2 = 3, p_3 = 5, \ldots, p_{n-1}, p_n$, so p_n is the **largest** prime number.

Now **multiply** all of these together: $p_1 p_2 p_3 \ldots p_{n-1} p_n$ — call this number P.

Because of how you defined it, P is a **multiple** of **every** prime number.

Now think about $P + 1$ — if you **divide** $P + 1$ by p_1, you get:

$$(P + 1) \div p_1 = (p_1 p_2 p_3 \ldots p_{n-1} p_n + 1) \div p_1$$
$$= p_2 p_3 \ldots p_{n-1} p_n \text{ remainder } 1.$$

In fact, dividing $(P + 1)$ by any prime number gives a **remainder** of **1**.

So $(P + 1)$ **isn't divisible** by **any** of the prime numbers, so either it is **also** a prime number, or it is a **product** of some other prime numbers that aren't in the list.

Either way, there is at least one prime number that is **not** on the list, which **contradicts** the assumption that the list contained all of them, so there must be **infinitely many** prime numbers.

> Using subscripts is standard notation for writing lists of any numbers.

Practice Questions

Q1 Prove by contradiction that if x is irrational, then $-x$ is also irrational.

Q2 Prove by contradiction that there is no largest multiple of 21.

Q3 a) Prove by contradiction that there is no largest integer power of 10.

    b) Prove by contradiction that there is no smallest integer power of 10.

Proof by photograph that CGP HQ is irrational.

Exam Questions

Q1   Prove by contradiction that if $p + q$ is irrational, then at least one of p or q is irrational.   [3 marks]

Q2   For any two prime numbers p and q, where $p > 2$ and $q > 2$, prove by contradiction that pq is always odd.   [3 marks]

Proof that pantomimes are hilarious: Oh no they aren't... Oh. Yes they are...

One crucial point to remember with proofs is that you have to justify every step of your working. Make sure that you've got a mathematical rule or principle to back up each bit of the proof — you can't take anything for granted.

Laws of Indices and Surds

You use the laws of indices all the time in maths — when you're integrating, differentiating and ...er... well loads of other places. So take the time to get them sorted now.

Three mega-important *Laws of Indices*

You **must** know these three rules. I can't make it any clearer than that.

$$a^m \times a^n = a^{m+n}$$

If you **multiply** two numbers — you **add** their powers.

$a^2 a^3 = a^5$

$x^{-2} x^5 = x^3$

$p^{\frac{1}{2}} \cdot p^{\frac{1}{4}} = p^{\frac{3}{4}}$

$(a+b)^2 (a+b)^5 = (a+b)^7$

$y \cdot y^3 = y^4$ ← *Since $y = y^1$.*

$ab^3 \cdot a^2 b = a^3 b^4$

The dot just means 'multiplied by'.

Add the powers of a and b separately.

$$\frac{a^m}{a^n} = a^{m-n}$$

If you **divide** two numbers — you **subtract** their powers.

$\dfrac{x^5}{x^2} = x^3$

$\dfrac{x^{\frac{3}{4}}}{x} = x^{-\frac{1}{4}}$

$\dfrac{x^3 y^2}{xy^3} = x^2 y^{-1}$

Subtract the powers of x and y separately.

$$(a^m)^n = a^{mn}$$

If you have a **power** to the **power of something else** — **multiply** the powers together.

$(x^2)^3 = x^6$

$\{(a+b)^3\}^4 = (a+b)^{12}$

$(p^3)^{-2} = p^{-6}$

$(ab^2)^4 = a^4 (b^2)^4 = a^4 b^8$

This power applies to both bits inside the brackets.

Other important stuff about *Indices*

You can't get very far without knowing this sort of stuff. Learn it — you'll definitely be able to use it.

$$a^{\frac{1}{m}} = \sqrt[m]{a}$$

You can write **roots** as powers...

$x^{\frac{1}{5}} = \sqrt[5]{x}$

$4^{\frac{1}{2}} = \sqrt{4} = 2$

$125^{\frac{1}{3}} = \sqrt[3]{125} = 5$

$$a^{\frac{m}{n}} = \sqrt[n]{a^m} = \left(\sqrt[n]{a}\right)^m$$

A power that's a **fraction** like this is the **root of a power** — or the **power of a root**.

It's often easier to work out the root first, then raise it to the power.

$9^{\frac{3}{2}} = (9^{\frac{1}{2}})^3 = (\sqrt{9})^3 = 3^3 = 27$

$81^{\frac{3}{4}} = (81^{\frac{1}{4}})^3 = (\sqrt[4]{81})^3 = 3^3 = 27$

$$a^{-m} = \frac{1}{a^m}$$

A **negative** power means it's on the bottom line of a fraction.

$2^{-3} = \dfrac{1}{2^3} = \dfrac{1}{8}$

$(x+1)^{-1} = \dfrac{1}{x+1}$

$$a^0 = 1$$

This is true for **any** number or letter.

$x^0 = 1$

$2^0 = 1$

$(a+b)^0 = 1$

Surds are sometimes the only way to give an *Exact Answer*

If you put $\sqrt{2}$ into a calculator, you'll get something like 1.414213562...
But if you square 1.414213562, then you get 1.999999999.
And no matter how many decimal places you use, you'll never get **exactly** 2.

To write the exact, spot on value you can **use surds**.
There are three **rules** you'll need to know to be able to use surds properly.

Rules of Surds

$\sqrt{ab} = \sqrt{a}\sqrt{b}$

$\sqrt{\dfrac{a}{b}} = \dfrac{\sqrt{a}}{\sqrt{b}}$

$a = (\sqrt{a})^2 = \sqrt{a}\sqrt{a}$

Laws of Indices and Surds

Use the Three Rules to deal with Surds

Examples: a) Simplify (i) $\sqrt{12}$ (ii) $\sqrt{\frac{3}{16}}$ b) Find $(2\sqrt{5}+3\sqrt{6})^2$

a) To **simplify** a surd, make the number in the $\sqrt{\ }$ sign **smaller**, or get rid of a **fraction** in the $\sqrt{\ }$ sign.

(i) $\sqrt{12} = \sqrt{4\times3} = \sqrt{4}\times\sqrt{3} = 2\sqrt{3}$ — Using $\sqrt{ab}=\sqrt{a}\sqrt{b}$.

(ii) $\sqrt{\frac{3}{16}} = \frac{\sqrt{3}}{\sqrt{16}} = \frac{\sqrt{3}}{4}$ — Using $\sqrt{\frac{a}{b}}=\frac{\sqrt{a}}{\sqrt{b}}$.

b) Multiply surds very **carefully** — it's easy to make a silly mistake.

$$(2\sqrt{5}+3\sqrt{6})^2 = (2\sqrt{5}+3\sqrt{6})(2\sqrt{5}+3\sqrt{6})$$
$$= (2\sqrt{5})^2 + (2\times2\sqrt{5}\times3\sqrt{6}) + (3\sqrt{6})^2$$
$$= (2^2\times\sqrt{5}^2) + (2\times2\times3\times\sqrt{5}\times\sqrt{6}) + (3^2\times\sqrt{6}^2)$$
$$= 20 + 12\sqrt{30} + 54$$
$$= 74 + 12\sqrt{30}$$

$= 4\times5 = 20$ $= 12\sqrt{5}\sqrt{6} = 12\sqrt{30}$ $= 9\times6 = 54$

You might need to Rationalise the Denominator

Rationalising the denominator means getting rid of the surds from the bottom of a fraction.

Example: Show that $\frac{9}{\sqrt{3}} = 3\sqrt{3}$

Multiply the top and bottom by the denominator.

$$\frac{9}{\sqrt{3}}\times\frac{\sqrt{3}}{\sqrt{3}} = \frac{9\sqrt{3}}{\sqrt{3}\times\sqrt{3}}$$
$$= \frac{9\sqrt{3}}{3}$$
$$= 3\sqrt{3}$$

Example: Rationalise the denominator of $\frac{1}{1+\sqrt{2}}$

Multiply the top and bottom by the denominator (but change the sign in front of the surd).

$$\frac{1}{1+\sqrt{2}}\times\frac{1-\sqrt{2}}{1-\sqrt{2}}$$

This works because: $(a+b)(a-b) = a^2 - b^2$

$$= \frac{1-\sqrt{2}}{(1+\sqrt{2})(1-\sqrt{2})} = \frac{1-\sqrt{2}}{1^2-\sqrt{2}+\sqrt{2}-\sqrt{2}^2}$$
$$= \frac{1-\sqrt{2}}{1-2} = \frac{1-\sqrt{2}}{-1} = -1+\sqrt{2}$$

Practice Questions

Q1 Simplify these:

a) $x^3\cdot x^5$ b) $a^7\cdot a^8$ c) $\frac{x^8}{x^2}$ d) $(a^2)^4$ e) $(xy^2)\cdot(x^3yz)$ f) $\frac{a^2b^4c^6}{a^3b^2c}$

Q2 Work out the following: a) $16^{\frac{1}{2}}$ b) $8^{\frac{1}{3}}$ c) $16^{\frac{3}{4}}$ d) x^0 e) $49^{-\frac{1}{2}}$

Q3 Simplify: a) $\sqrt{28}$ b) $\sqrt{\frac{5}{36}}$ c) $\sqrt{18}$ d) $\sqrt{\frac{9}{16}}$

Q4 Find $(6\sqrt{3}+2\sqrt{7})^2$

Q5 Rationalise the denominator of: $\frac{2}{3+\sqrt{7}}$

Bruce lived by the sword and died by the surd.

Exam Questions

Q1 Simplify a) $(5\sqrt{3})^2$ [1 mark]
b) $(5+\sqrt{6})(2-\sqrt{6})$ [2 marks]

Q2 Given that $10000\sqrt{10} = 10^k$, find the value of k. [2 marks]

Q3 Express $\frac{5+\sqrt{5}}{3-\sqrt{5}}$ in the form $a+b\sqrt{5}$, where a and b are integers. [4 marks]

Where does Poseidon keep his powers — indices...

For lots of these questions you can check your answers on your calculator. If you ever forget the rules of surds you can even write $\sqrt{\ }$ as $^{\frac{1}{2}}$ and manipulate the indices instead — e.g. $\sqrt{ab} = (ab)^{\frac{1}{2}} = a^{\frac{1}{2}}b^{\frac{1}{2}} = \sqrt{a}\sqrt{b}$. Very sneaky.

Polynomials

A polynomial is just an expression of algebraic terms. In A-level maths you need to manipulate them all the time.

Expand brackets by Multiplying them out

Here are the basic types you have to deal with — you'll have seen them all before.

Single Brackets

$a(b + c + d) = ab + ac + ad$

Double Brackets

$(a + b)(c + d) = ac + ad + bc + bd$

Long Brackets

Write it out again with **each term** from one bracket separately multiplied by the **other bracket**.

Then **multiply out each** of these **brackets**, one at a time.

Squared Brackets

$(a + b)^2 = (a + b)(a + b) = a^2 + 2ab + b^2$

Use the middle stage until you're comfortable with it. Just **never** make this **mistake**: $(a + b)^2 = a^2 + b^2$

Difference of Two Squares

$(a + b)(a - b) = a^2 - ab + ab - b^2 = a^2 - b^2$

The difference of two squares can be applied to surds:
$(\sqrt{x} + \sqrt{y})(\sqrt{x} - \sqrt{y}) = x - y$

$(x + y + z)(a + b + c + d)$
$= x(a + b + c + d) + y(a + b + c + d) + z(a + b + c + d)$

Example: Expand and simplify $(2x^2 + 3x + 6)(4x^3 + 6x^2 + 3)$

Multiply each term in the first bracket by the second bracket:

$2x^2(4x^3 + 6x^2 + 3) + 3x(4x^3 + 6x^2 + 3) + 6(4x^3 + 6x^2 + 3)$

Multiply out each bracket individually:

$= (8x^5 + 12x^4 + 6x^2) + (12x^4 + 18x^3 + 9x) + (24x^3 + 36x^2 + 18)$

Simplify it all:

$= \mathbf{8x^5 + 24x^4 + 42x^3 + 42x^2 + 9x + 18}$

Look for Common Factors when Simplifying Expressions

Something that is in each term of an expression is a **common factor** — this can be **numbers**, **variables** or even **brackets**. If you spot a common factor you can '**take it outside**' a bracket.

Example: Simplify $(x + 1)(x - 2) + (x + 1)^2 - x(x + 1)$

There's an $(x + 1)$ factor in each term, so we can take this out as a common factor (hurrah):

$(x + 1)\{(x - 2) + (x + 1) - x\}$ ◄

The terms inside the curly bracket are the old terms with an $(x + 1)$ removed.

At this point you should check that this multiplies out to give the original expression. (You can just do this in your head, if you trust it.)

Then simplify the big bracket's innards:

$(x + 1)\{x - 2 + x + 1 - x\}$

$= (x + 1)(x - 1) = x^2 - 1$

Use the "difference of two squares" (or multiply out) to get this answer

Factorise a Quadratic by putting it into Two Brackets

Factorising a quadratic in the form $ax^2 + bx + c$ is pretty easy when $a = 1$:

Factorising Quadratics

1) Write down the two brackets:
   $(x \quad)(x \quad)$

2) Find two numbers that **multiply** to give 'c' and **add/subtract** to give 'b' (ignoring signs).

3) Put the numbers in the brackets and choose the correct **signs**.

Example: Factorise $x^2 + 4x - 21$

1) $x^2 + 4x - 21 = (x \quad)(x \quad)$

2) 1 and 21 multiply to give 21 — and add / subtract to give 22 and 20.
   3 and 7 multiply to give 21 — and add / subtract to give 10 and **4**.

3) $x^2 + 4x - 21 = (x \quad 7)(x \quad 3)$
   $= \mathbf{(x + 7)(x - 3)}$

This is the value of 'b' you're after — 3 and 7 are the right numbers.

These get much easier with practice — you might even be able to do them in your head. Make sure you always check your answer by multiplying the brackets out.

Polynomials

Use a **Similar Method** for **Factorising** a quadratic when **a ≠ 1**

Example: Factorise $3x^2 + 4x - 15$

As before, write down two brackets — but instead of having
x in each, you need two things that will multiply to give $3x^2$:
$$3x^2 + 4x - 15 = (3x \quad)(x \quad)$$

It's got to be 3x and x here.

This is where it gets a bit fiddly. You need to find two numbers that multiply together to make 15 — but which will give you 4x when you multiply them by x and 3x, and then add/subtract them:

$(3x \quad 1)(x \quad 15) \Rightarrow$ x and 45x — which then add or subtract to give 46x and 44x.
$(3x \quad 15)(x \quad 1) \Rightarrow$ 15x and 3x — which then add or subtract to give 18x and 12x.
$(3x \quad 3)(x \quad 5) \Rightarrow$ 3x and 15x — which then add or subtract to give 18x and 12x.
$(3x \quad 5)(x \quad 3) \Rightarrow$ 5x and 9x — which then add or subtract to give 14x and **4x**.

This is the value you're after — so this is the right combination.

You know the brackets must be like these... $(3x \quad 5)(x \quad 3) = 3x^2 + 4x - 15$
so all you have to do is put in the plus or minus signs:

$$(3x + 5)(x - 3) = 3x^2 - 4x - 15$$
or...
$$(3x - 5)(x + 3) = 3x^2 + 4x - 15 \quad \Longleftarrow \text{So it's this one.}$$

You've only got two choices — if you're unsure, just multiply them out to see which one's right.

'c' is negative — that means the signs in the brackets are different.

Simplify algebraic fractions by **Factorising** and **Cancelling Factors**

Algebraic fractions are a lot like normal fractions — and you can treat them in the **same way**, whether you're multiplying, dividing, adding or subtracting them. All fractions are much **easier** to deal with when they're in their **simplest form**, so the first thing to do with algebraic fractions is to **simplify** them as much as possible.

1) Look for **common factors** in the numerator and denominator — **factorise** top and bottom and see if there's anything you can **cancel**.

Examples: Simplify the following: a) $\dfrac{ax + ay}{az}$ b) $\dfrac{3x + 6}{x^2 - 4}$

a) $\dfrac{ax + ay}{az} = \dfrac{\cancel{a}(x + y)}{\cancel{a}z} = \dfrac{x + y}{z}$

b) $\dfrac{3x + 6}{x^2 - 4} = \dfrac{3\cancel{(x+2)}}{\cancel{(x+2)}(x-2)} = \dfrac{3}{x-2}$

Watch out for the difference of two squares.

2) If there's a **fraction** in the numerator or denominator (e.g. $\frac{1}{x}$), **multiply** the **whole thing** (i.e. top and bottom) by the same factor to get rid of it (e.g. for $\frac{1}{x}$, you'd multiply through by x).

Example: Simplify $\dfrac{2 + \frac{1}{2x}}{4x^2 + x}$

$$\dfrac{2 + \frac{1}{2x}}{4x^2 + x} = \dfrac{\left(2 + \frac{1}{2x}\right) \times 2x}{x(4x + 1) \times 2x} = \dfrac{4x + \cancel{1}}{2x^2 \cancel{(4x + 1)}} = \dfrac{1}{2x^2}$$

3) You **multiply** algebraic fractions in exactly the same way as normal fractions — multiply the **numerators** together, then multiply the **denominators**. It's a good idea to **cancel** any **common factors** before you multiply.

4) To **divide** by an algebraic fraction, you just **multiply** by its **reciprocal** (the reciprocal is 1 ÷ the original thing — for fractions you just turn the fraction **upside down**).

Examples: Simplify the following: a) $\dfrac{x^2 - 2x - 15}{2x + 8} \times \dfrac{x^2 - 16}{x^2 + 3x}$ b) $\dfrac{3x}{5} \div \dfrac{3x^2 - 9x}{20}$

Turn the second fraction upside down.

a) $\dfrac{x^2 - 2x - 15}{2x + 8} \times \dfrac{x^2 - 16}{x^2 + 3x} = \dfrac{(x+3)(x-5)}{2\cancel{(x+4)}} \times \dfrac{\cancel{(x+4)}(x-4)}{x\cancel{(x+3)}}$

$= \dfrac{(x-5)(x-4)}{2x} \quad \left(= \dfrac{x^2 - 9x + 20}{2x}\right)$

Factorise both fractions.

b) $\dfrac{3x}{5} \div \dfrac{3x^2 - 9x}{20} = \dfrac{\cancel{3x}}{5} \times \dfrac{20}{\cancel{3x}(x-3)}$

$= \dfrac{4}{x - 3}$

Polynomials

Add *and* Subtract *fractions by finding a* Common Denominator

You'll have come across **adding** and **subtracting fractions** before, so here's a little reminder of how to do it:

Example: Simplify $\dfrac{2y}{x(x+3)} + \dfrac{1}{y^2(x+3)} - \dfrac{x}{y}$

The individual 'bits' here are x, (x + 3) and y. But you need to use y^2 because there's a y^2 in the second fraction's denominator.

1) **Find the common denominator**
   Take all the individual 'bits' from the bottom lines and multiply them together. Only use each bit once unless something on the bottom line is raised to a power:

   common denominator = $xy^2(x+3)$

2) **Put each fraction over the common denominator**
   Make the denominator of each fraction into the common denominator. Multiply the top and bottom lines of each fraction by whatever makes the bottom line the same as the common denominator:

   $$\dfrac{y^2 \times 2y}{y^2 x(x+3)} + \dfrac{x \times 1}{xy^2(x+3)} - \dfrac{xy(x+3) \times x}{xy(x+3)y}$$

3) **Combine into one fraction**
   Once everything's over the common denominator you can just add the top lines together and simplify the numerator:

   $$= \dfrac{2y^3 + x - x^2 y(x+3)}{xy^2(x+3)} = \dfrac{2y^3 + x - x^3 y - 3x^2 y}{xy^2(x+3)}$$

All the bottom lines are the same — so you can just add the top lines.

Practice Questions

Q1 Expand the brackets and simplify the following expressions:
   a) $(x+y)(x-y)$
   b) $(x+y)(x+y)$
   c) $35xy + 25y(5y + 7x) - 100y^2$
   d) $(x + 3y + 2)(3x + y + 7)$

Q2 Show that $(\sqrt{x} + \sqrt{2})(\sqrt{x} - \sqrt{2}) = x - 2$.

Q3 Take out the common factors from the following expressions:
   a) $2x^2 y + axy + 2xy^2$
   b) $a^2 x + a^2 b^2 x^2$
   c) $16y + 8yx + 56x$
   d) $x(x-2) + 3(2-x)$

Q4 Factorise the following quadratics:
   a) $x^2 + 6x - 7$
   b) $x^2 - 4x - 12$
   c) $9x^2 - 64$
   d) $4x^2 - 11x - 20$

Q5 Simplify the following:
   a) $\dfrac{4x^2 - 25}{6x - 15}$
   b) $\dfrac{2x + 3}{x - 2} \times \dfrac{4x - 8}{2x^2 - 3x - 9}$
   c) $\dfrac{x^2 - 3x}{x + 1} \div \dfrac{x}{2}$

Exam Questions

Q1 Write $\dfrac{2x^2 - 9x - 35}{x^2 - 49}$ as a fraction in its simplest form. [3 marks]

Q2 Factorise $2x^4 - 32x^2$ completely. [2 marks]

Q3 Write each of the following polynomials as a single fraction in its simplest form.
   a) $\dfrac{x}{2x + 1} + \dfrac{3}{x^2} + \dfrac{1}{x}$ [3 marks]
   b) $\dfrac{2}{x^2 - 1} - \dfrac{3x}{x - 1} + \dfrac{x}{x + 1}$ [3 marks]

What do you call a hungry parrot? Polynomials...

Nothing on these pages should be a big shock to you — you've been using normal fractions for years, and algebraic fractions work in just the same way. They look a bit scary, but they're all warm and fuzzy inside.

Section 2 — Algebra and Functions

Algebraic Division

I'm going to spoil you with three methods for algebraic division — these can be a bit tricky so take your time with them. I know you can't wait to get stuck into them, but first you'll need to learn the Remainder Theorem.

There are some **Terms** you need to **Know**

These words will keep popping up over the next few pages, so make sure you know what they all mean.

1) **DEGREE** — the highest power of x in the polynomial (e.g. the degree of $4x^5 + 6x^2 - 3x - 1$ is 5).
2) **DIVISOR** — this is the thing you're dividing by (e.g. if you divide $x^2 + 4x - 3$ by $x + 2$, the divisor is $x + 2$).
3) **QUOTIENT** — the stuff that you get when you divide by the divisor (not including the remainder).
4) **REMAINDER** — the bit that's left over at the end (for A-level maths this will be a constant).

The **Remainder Theorem** is an easy way to work out **Remainders**

If f(x) is a **polynomial** then the **Remainder Theorem** states that:

> When you divide f(x) by $(x - a)$, the remainder is f(a).
>
> When you divide f(x) by $(ax - b)$, the remainder is $f\left(\frac{b}{a}\right)$.

Example: Find the remainder when you divide $2x^3 - 3x^2 - 3x + 7$ by $2x - 1$.

f(x) $= 2x^3 - 3x^2 - 3x + 7$. The **divisor** is $2x - 1$, so $a = 2$ and $b = 1$.

Using the Remainder Theorem, the **remainder** must be $f\left(\frac{1}{2}\right) = 2\left(\frac{1}{8}\right) - 3\left(\frac{1}{4}\right) - 3\left(\frac{1}{2}\right) + 7 = 5$

The **Factor Theorem** is just the Remainder Theorem with a **Zero Remainder**

If you get a **remainder of zero** when you divide f(x) by $(x - a)$, then $(x - a)$ must be a **factor**. That's the **Factor Theorem**:

> If f(x) is a polynomial, and f(a) = 0, then $(x - a)$ is a factor of f(x).
>
> If $f\left(\frac{b}{a}\right) = 0$, then $(ax - b)$ is a factor of f(x).
>
> In other words: If you know the roots, you also know the factors — and vice versa.

Example: Show that $(2x + 1)$ is a factor of f(x) $= 2x^3 - 3x^2 + 4x + 3$.

Use the second version of the Factor Theorem — in this case, $a = 2$ and $b = -1$.
This means that if you show that $f\left(-\frac{1}{2}\right) = 0$, then, by the Factor Theorem, $(2x + 1)$ is a factor.

$$f(x) = 2x^3 - 3x^2 + 4x + 3 \text{ and so } f\left(-\frac{1}{2}\right) = 2\left(-\frac{1}{8}\right) - 3\left(\frac{1}{4}\right) + 4\left(-\frac{1}{2}\right) + 3 = 0$$

So, by the **Factor Theorem**, $(2x + 1)$ is a factor of f(x).

Method 1 — Divide by Subtracting Multiples of the Divisor

This is the first of **three methods** I'm going to show you for dividing a polynomial by a **linear expression**.
To do **algebraic division** you can keep **subtracting** chunks of the **divisor**, $(x - k)$, until you get the **remainder**.

Algebraic Division

① Subtract a multiple of $(x - k)$ to get rid of the highest power of x.
② Repeat step 1 until you've got rid of all the powers of x.
③ Work out how many lumps of $(x - k)$, you've subtracted, and read off the remainder.

For this course you'll only have to divide by a linear expression — i.e. ax + b, where a and b are constants. This means that the remainder will always be a constant because the degree of the remainder has to be less than the degree of the divisor.

Algebraic Division

Always get **Rid** of the **Highest Power** of x

Example: Divide $(2x^3 - 3x^2 - 3x + 7)$ by $(x - 2)$

You're asked to calculate $(2x^3 - 3x^2 - 3x + 7) \div (x - 2)$.
Start with $2x^3 - 3x^2 - 3x + 7$, and subtract $2x^2$
lots of $(x - 2)$ to get rid of the x^3 term:

$(2x^3 - 3x^2 - 3x + 7) - \mathbf{2x^2}(x - 2)$
$= (2x^3 - 3x^2 - 3x + 7) - 2x^3 + 4x^2$
$= \mathbf{x^2 - 3x + 7}$ ← This is what's left — so now you have to get rid of the x^2 term.

Now start again with $x^2 - 3x + 7$.
The highest power of x is the x^2 term.
So subtract x lots of $(x - 2)$ to get rid of that:

$(x^2 - 3x + 7) - x(x - 2)$
$= (x^2 - 3x + 7) - x^2 + 2x$
$= \mathbf{-x + 7}$

All that's left now is $-x + 7$.
Get rid of the $-x$ by subtracting -1 lots of $(x - 2)$:

$(-x + 7) - (-1(x - 2))$
$= (-x + 7) + x - 2 = \mathbf{5}$ ← Check your answer with the Remainder Theorem: $2(2^3) - 3(2^2) - 3(2) + 7 = 5$

So $(2x^3 - 3x^2 - 3x + 7) \div (x - 2) = \mathbf{2x^2 + x - 1 \text{ remainder } 5}$

Method 2 — use **Algebraic Long Division**

To divide two **algebraic** expressions, you can use **long division** (using the same method you'd use for numbers).

Example: Divide $2x^3 - 7x^2 - 16x + 11$ by $x - 5$.

> If the original polynomial doesn't have an x term, for example, just put 0x where the x term should be.

① $2x^3 \div x = 2x^2$

② Multiply $(x - 5)$ by $2x^2$ to get this.

③ Subtracting gives $3x^2$, so divide this by x to get 3x.

④ Multiply $(x - 5)$ by 3x to get this, then subtract again.

⑤ Divide $-x$ by x to get -1, then multiply $(x - 5)$ by -1.

⑥ After subtracting, this term has a degree that's less than the degree of the divisor, $(x - 5)$, so it can't be divided. This is the remainder.

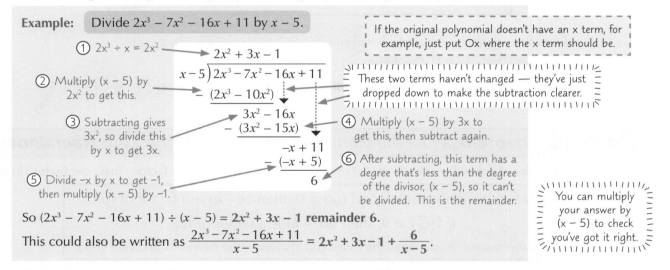

$$
\require{enclose}
\begin{array}{r}
2x^2 + 3x - 1 \\
x - 5 \enclose{longdiv}{2x^3 - 7x^2 - 16x + 11} \\
-\underline{(2x^3 - 10x^2)} \\
3x^2 - 16x \\
-\underline{(3x^2 - 15x)} \\
-x + 11 \\
-\underline{(-x + 5)} \\
6
\end{array}
$$

These two terms haven't changed — they've just dropped down to make the subtraction clearer.

> You can multiply your answer by $(x - 5)$ to check you've got it right.

So $(2x^3 - 7x^2 - 16x + 11) \div (x - 5) = \mathbf{2x^2 + 3x - 1 \text{ remainder } 6}$.

This could also be written as $\dfrac{2x^3 - 7x^2 - 16x + 11}{x - 5} = 2x^2 + 3x - 1 + \dfrac{6}{x - 5}$.

Method 3 — use the **Formula** f(x) = q(x)d(x) + r(x)

There's a **formula** you can use to do **algebraic division**. It comes from the Remainder Theorem and looks like this:

> A polynomial f(x) can be written in the form $\mathbf{f(x) \equiv q(x)d(x) + r(x)}$,
> where q(x) is the quotient, d(x) is the divisor and r(x) is the remainder.

You'll be given f(x) and d(x) in the **question**, and it's down to you to **work out** q(x) and r(x). Here's how you do it:

Using the Formula

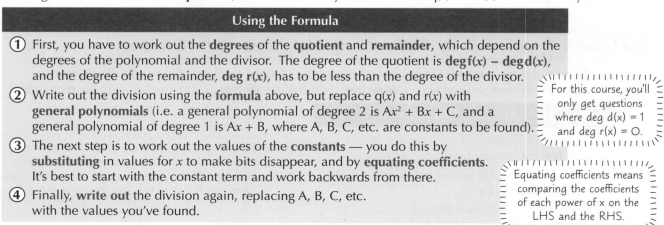

① First, you have to work out the **degrees** of the **quotient** and **remainder**, which depend on the degrees of the polynomial and the divisor. The degree of the quotient is $\mathbf{\deg f(x) - \deg d(x)}$, and the degree of the remainder, $\mathbf{\deg r(x)}$, has to be less than the degree of the divisor.

> For this course, you'll only get questions where $\deg d(x) = 1$ and $\deg r(x) = 0$.

② Write out the division using the **formula** above, but replace q(x) and r(x) with **general polynomials** (i.e. a general polynomial of degree 2 is $Ax^2 + Bx + C$, and a general polynomial of degree 1 is $Ax + B$, where A, B, C, etc. are constants to be found).

③ The next step is to work out the values of the **constants** — you do this by **substituting** in values for x to make bits disappear, and by **equating coefficients**. It's best to start with the constant term and work backwards from there.

> Equating coefficients means comparing the coefficients of each power of x on the LHS and the RHS.

④ Finally, **write out** the division again, replacing A, B, C, etc. with the values you've found.

The method looks a bit **intense**, but follow through the **example** on the next page to see how it works.

Algebraic Division

Start with the **Remainder** and **Work Backwards**

When you're using this method, you might have to use **simultaneous equations** to work out some of the coefficients.

Example: Divide $x^4 - 3x^3 - 3x^2 + 10x + 5$ by $x - 2$.

① The polynomial f(x) has degree 4 and the divisor d(x) has degree 1, which means that the quotient q(x) has degree $4 - 1 = 3$ (i.e. a **cubic**). The remainder r(x) has degree 0.

Remember, it's easiest to start by finding the constant term.

② Write out the division in the form $f(x) \equiv q(x)d(x) + r(x)$:
$$x^4 - 3x^3 - 3x^2 + 10x + 5 \equiv (Ax^3 + Bx^2 + Cx + D)(x - 2) + E$$

③ Substitute $x = 2$ into the identity to make the q(x)d(x) bit disappear. This gives the remainder as **E = 5**. Now, using this value of E and putting $x = 0$ into the identity gives the equation $5 = -2D + 5$, so **D = 0**.
Using the values of D and E you now have:
$$x^4 - 3x^3 - 3x^2 + 10x + 5 \equiv (Ax^3 + Bx^2 + Cx)(x - 2) + 5$$
$$\equiv Ax^4 + (B - 2A)x^3 + (C - 2B)x^2 - 2Cx + 5$$
Equating coefficients of x^4, x^3 and x gives **A = 1**, $B - 2A = -3$ (so **B = -1**) and $-2C = 10$ (so **C = -5**).

④ Putting these values into the original identity gives: $x^4 - 3x^3 - 3x^2 + 10x + 5 \equiv (x^3 - x^2 - 5x)(x - 2) + 5$.
So the answer is $(x^3 - x^2 - 5x)$ remainder 5.

Practice Questions

Q1 Find the remainder when $f(x) = x^4 - 3x^3 + 7x^2 - 12x + 14$ is divided by:
   a) $x + 2$ b) $2x + 4$ c) $x - 3$ d) $2x - 6$

Q2 Which of the following are factors of $f(x) = x^5 - 4x^4 + 3x^3 + 2x^2 - 2$?
   a) $x - 1$ b) $x + 1$ c) $x - 2$ d) $2x - 2$

Q3 Use algebraic long division to divide $x^3 + 2x^2 - x + 19$ by $x + 4$.

Q4 Write the following functions f(x) in the form $f(x) = (x + 2)q(x) + r(x)$, where q(x) is a quadratic:
   a) $f(x) = 3x^3 - 4x^2 - 5x - 6$,   b) $f(x) = x^3 + 2x^2 - 3x + 4$,   c) $f(x) = 2x^3 + 6x - 3$

Q5 Write $2x^3 + 8x^2 + 7x + 8$ in the form $(Ax^2 + Bx + C)(x + 3) + D$.
   Using your answer, state the result when $2x^3 + 8x^2 + 7x + 8$ is divided by $(x + 3)$.

Exam Questions

Q1 $f(x) = 2x^3 - 5x^2 - 4x + 3$
   a) Find the remainder when f(x) is divided by:
      (i) $(x - 1)$ [1 mark]
      (ii) $(2x + 1)$ [1 mark]
   b) Show using the Factor Theorem that $(x + 1)$ is a factor of f(x).   [2 marks]
   c) Factorise f(x) completely.   [3 marks]

Q2 $f(x) = (4x^2 + 3x + 1)(x - p) + 5$, where p is a constant.
   a) State the value of f(p).   [1 mark]
   b) Find the value of p, given that when f(x) is divided by $(x + 1)$, the remainder is -1.   [2 marks]
   c) Find the remainder when f(x) is divided by $(x - 1)$.   [1 mark]

Q3 Write $x^3 + 15x^2 + 43x - 30$ in the form $(Ax^2 + Bx + C)(x + 6) + D$,
   where A, B, C and D are constants to be found.   [3 marks]

Just keep repeating — divide and conquer, divide and conquer...

There's a lot to take in about algebraic division so feel free to go over it again. It's up to you which method you prefer but I'd recommend either long division or the formula — these are a bit quicker than the first method. Using the Remainder Theorem to find remainders (rather than actually dividing) can also save you time in the exam.

Partial Fractions

Partial fractions aren't mega useful, but they can be helpful with binomial expansions and integration — welcome back if you're reading Section 4 or 8 and have completely forgotten about them. That's what revision is all about.

'Expressing in Partial Fractions' is Splitting the fraction up

You can **split** a fraction with **more than one linear factor** in the denominator into **partial fractions**.

$\dfrac{7x-7}{(2x+1)(x-3)}$ can be written as **partial fractions** of the form $\dfrac{A}{(2x+1)} + \dfrac{B}{(x-3)}$.

$\dfrac{4}{(x+2)(2x-1)(x-3)}$ can be written as **partial fractions** of the form $\dfrac{A}{(x+2)} + \dfrac{B}{(2x-1)} + \dfrac{C}{(x-3)}$.

$\dfrac{3x-8}{(x+2)^2(3x-1)}$ can be written as **partial fractions** of the form $\dfrac{A}{(x+2)^2} + \dfrac{B}{(x+2)} + \dfrac{C}{(3x-1)}$.

> Watch out here — this one doesn't quite follow the pattern.

For A-level maths the **numerator** of the fraction will always be **linear** or a **constant**.
You can find A, B and C by using the **substitution method** or the **equating coefficients method**:

Example: Express $\dfrac{7x-1}{(x-3)(x-1)(x+2)}$ as partial fractions.

Write it out as partial fractions with unknown constants and put it over a common denominator:

$$\frac{7x-1}{(x-3)(x-1)(x+2)} \equiv \frac{A}{(x-3)} + \frac{B}{(x-1)} + \frac{C}{(x+2)}$$
$$\equiv \frac{A(x-1)(x+2) + B(x-3)(x+2) + C(x-3)(x-1)}{(x-3)(x-1)(x+2)}$$

Cancel the denominators from both sides:

$$7x-1 \equiv A(x-1)(x+2) + B(x-3)(x+2) + C(x-3)(x-1)$$

Substitution Method

Substitute values of x which make one of the expressions in brackets equal zero to get rid of all but one of A, B and C:

Substituting $x = 3$ gets rid of B and C
$21 - 1 = A(3-1)(3+2) + 0 + 0$
$20 = 10A \Rightarrow A = 2$

Substituting $x = 1$ gets rid of A and C:
$7 - 1 = 0 + B(1-3)(1+2) + 0$
$6 = -6B \Rightarrow B = -1$

Substituting $x = -2$ gets rid of A and B:
$-14 - 1 = 0 + 0 + C(-2-3)(-2-1)$
$-15 = 15C \Rightarrow C = -1$

OR...

Equating Coefficients Method

Equating coefficients in the numerator will give equations, which you can solve simultaneously to find A, B and C:

Compare coefficients in the numerators:
$7x - 1 \equiv A(x-1)(x+2) + B(x-3)(x+2) + C(x-3)(x-1)$
$\equiv A(x^2 + x - 2) + B(x^2 - x - 6) + C(x^2 - 4x + 3)$
$\equiv (A + B + C)x^2 + (A - B - 4C)x + (-2A - 6B + 3C)$

Equating x^2 coefficients: $0 = A + B + C$

Equating x coefficients: $7 = A - B - 4C$

Equating constant terms: $-1 = -2A - 6B + 3C$

Solving these equations simultaneously gives:
$A = 2$, $B = -1$ and $C = -1$.

Finally, replace A, B and C in the original identity:

$$\frac{7x-1}{(x-3)(x-1)(x+2)} \equiv \frac{2}{(x-3)} - \frac{1}{(x-1)} - \frac{1}{(x+2)}$$

Watch out for Difference of Two Squares Denominators

Just for added meanness, they might give you an expression like $\dfrac{4}{x^2-1}$ and tell you to express it as partial fractions.
You have to recognise that the denominator is a **difference of two squares** and write it as **two linear factors**.

Example: Express $\dfrac{12x+6}{4x^2-9}$ as partial fractions.

The denominator can be factorised: $4x^2 - 9 = (2x + 3)(2x - 3)$, so write it out as partial fractions and cancel the denominators from both sides:

$$\frac{12x+6}{(2x+3)(2x-3)} \equiv \frac{A}{(2x+3)} + \frac{B}{(2x-3)}$$
$$12x + 6 \equiv A(2x-3) + B(2x+3)$$

Substitute values of x to find A and B:

$x = \dfrac{3}{2} \Rightarrow 24 = 6B \Rightarrow B = 4$

$x = -\dfrac{3}{2} \Rightarrow -12 = -6A \Rightarrow A = 2$

> You could compare coefficients here, but you would need to solve some simultaneous equations.

Replace A and B in the original identity:

$$\frac{12x+6}{(2x+3)(2x-3)} \equiv \frac{2}{(2x+3)} + \frac{4}{(2x-3)}$$

Partial Fractions

Sometimes it's best to use *Substitution* AND *Equate Coefficients*

Now things are hotting up in the partial fractions department — here's an example involving a **repeated factor**.

Example: Express $\dfrac{5x+12}{x^2(x-3)}$ in partial fractions.

x is a repeated factor so the identity will be:

$$\frac{5x+12}{x^2(x-3)} \equiv \frac{A}{x^2} + \frac{B}{x} + \frac{C}{(x-3)}$$

$$\equiv \frac{A(x-3) + Bx(x-3) + Cx^2}{x^2(x-3)}$$

Cancel the denominators from both sides:

$$5x + 12 \equiv A(x-3) + Bx(x-3) + Cx^2$$

Substitute values of x to find A and C:

$$x = 0 \Rightarrow 12 = -3A \Rightarrow A = -4$$
$$x = 3 \Rightarrow 27 = 9C \Rightarrow C = 3$$

There's no value of x you can substitute to get rid of A and C to leave just B, so equate coefficients of x^2:

Equating x^2 coefficients: $0 = B + C$
You know $C = 3$, so $0 = B + 3 \Rightarrow B = -3$

Replace A, B and C in the original identity:

$$\frac{5x+12}{x^2(x-3)} \equiv -\frac{4}{x^2} - \frac{3}{x} + \frac{3}{(x-3)}$$

Practice Questions

Q1 Find the values of the constants A and B in the identity $\dfrac{2x-1}{x^2-x-12} \equiv \dfrac{A}{x-4} + \dfrac{B}{x+3}$.

Q2 Express the following as partial fractions:

a) $\dfrac{4x+5}{(x+4)(2x-3)}$ b) $\dfrac{-7x-7}{(3x+1)(x-2)}$

c) $\dfrac{x-18}{(x+4)(3x-4)}$ d) $\dfrac{5x}{x^2+x-6}$

Q3 Express the following as partial fractions:

a) $\dfrac{2x+2}{(x+3)^2}$ b) $\dfrac{-18x+14}{(2x-1)^2(x+2)}$

c) $\dfrac{3x}{(x-5)^2}$ d) $\dfrac{2x-1}{(x+2)^2(x-3)}$

Spot the difference of two squares
(as in, there are 2^2 to find).

Q4 Write $\dfrac{3x-4}{x^3-16x}$ in the form $\dfrac{A}{x} + \dfrac{B}{x+4} + \dfrac{C}{x-4}$.

Exam Questions

Q1 Given that, for $x \neq -\dfrac{1}{3}$, $\dfrac{5+9x}{(1+3x)^2} \equiv \dfrac{A}{(1+3x)^2} + \dfrac{B}{(1+3x)}$, where A and B are integers, find the values of A and B.   [2 marks]

Q2 Express $\dfrac{x+4}{(x-2)(x^2-1)}$ as partial fractions.   [3 marks]

Q3 Express $\dfrac{2x-9}{x(x-6)^2}$ as partial fractions.   [3 marks]

Q4 a) Use the Factor Theorem to fully factorise $f(x) = x^3 + 5x^2 - x - 5$.   [3 marks]

     b) Hence write $\dfrac{3x+1}{x^3+5x^2-x-5}$ as partial fractions.   [3 marks]

The algebra was a little dry but I was quite partial to the fractions...

It's worth learning both methods for finding the values of A, B, C etc. Sometimes one's easier to use than the other, and sometimes you might want to mix and match. Just remember the number of factors on the bottom tells you how many fractions you need and a squared term appears in two partial fractions — once squared and once just as it is.

Solving Quadratic Equations

You've probably been solving equations since before you could walk, so lots of this should be familiar.
Here, you'll be finding x for lovely quadratic equations of the form $ax^2 + bx + c = 0$.

Solve quadratic equations by **Factorising**

Factorising is probably the quickest way to solve a quadratic equation — if it looks fairly **simple**,
try to factorise it. The examples below use the methods described on pages 8-9.

> **Example:** Solve $x^2 - 8 = 2x$ by factorising.
>
> Put into $ax^2 + bx + c = 0$ form: $x^2 - 8 = 2x \Rightarrow x^2 - 2x - 8 = 0$
>
> Solve the equation by factorising: $(x + 2)(x - 4) = 0$
> $$\Rightarrow x + 2 = 0 \text{ or } x - 4 = 0$$
> $$\Rightarrow x = -2 \text{ or } x = 4$$

Watch out for '**disguised quadratics**', where there's some **function of x** instead of x. To solve quadratics of the form
$a(\text{f}(x))^2 + b(\text{f}(x)) + c$ use the **substitution** $y = \text{f}(x)$, solve to find values of y, then use these to find values of x.

> **Example:** Solve $x^{\frac{2}{3}} + 3x^{\frac{1}{3}} - 40 = 0$.
>
> $\text{f}(x) = x^{\frac{1}{3}}$, so use the substitution: $y = x^{\frac{1}{3}}$ Using $x^{\frac{2}{3}} = \left(x^{\frac{1}{3}}\right)^2 = y^2$
> $$y^2 + 3y - 40 = 0$$
>
> Solve the quadratic in y by factorising: $(y + 8)(y - 5) = 0$
> $$\Rightarrow y + 8 = 0 \text{ or } y - 5 = 0$$
> $$\Rightarrow y = -8 \text{ or } y = 5$$
>
> Use the values of y to find the values of x: $y = -8 \Rightarrow -8 = x^{\frac{1}{3}} \Rightarrow x = (-8)^3 = \textbf{-512}$
> $$y = 5 \Rightarrow 5 = x^{\frac{1}{3}} \Rightarrow x = 5^3 = \textbf{125}$$

'Disguised quadratics' might involve trig functions (see Section 5) or exponentials and logs (see Section 6).

The quadratics were becoming more cunning with their disguises.

Completing the Square puts any old quadratic in a *Special Form*

Completing the square sounds really confusing. For starters, what does "Completing the Square" **mean**?
What is the square? **Why** does it need completing? Well, there is **some** logic to it:

1) The **square** looks like this: $(x + \text{something})^2$

   It's basically the factorised equation (with two identical factors), but there's something missing...

2) ...so you need to '**complete**' it by adding a number to the square to make it equal to the original equation.

   $$(x + \text{something})^2 + ?$$

You start with something like this...   ...sort the x-coefficients...   ...and end up with something like this.

$$\boxed{2x^2 + 8x - 5} \Longrightarrow \boxed{2(x + 2)^2 + ?} \Longrightarrow \boxed{2(x + 2)^2 - 13}$$

The method below can be used to complete the square of a quadratic expression:

> ### Completing the Square of $ax^2 + bx + c$
>
> ① Take a **factor of a** out of the x^2 and x terms: $a\left(x^2 + \frac{b}{a}x\right) + c$.
>
> ② Rewrite the bit in the bracket as **one bracket squared**.
> The number in the brackets is always $\frac{b}{2a}$, so the bracket is $a\left(x + \frac{b}{2a}\right)^2$.
>
> ③ **Add d** to the bracket to complete the square and **find d** by
> setting the new and original expressions **equal** to each other:
> $$a\left(x + \frac{b}{2a}\right)^2 + d = ax^2 + bx + c$$
>
> Expanding the LHS gives:
>
> $\cancel{ax^2} + \cancel{bx} + \frac{b^2}{4a} + d = \cancel{ax^2} + \cancel{bx} + c$.
> Then cancel and rearrange to get d.
>
> ④ **Solving** this equation always gives $d = \left(c - \frac{b^2}{4a}\right)$, so:
> $$a\left(x + \frac{b}{2a}\right)^2 + \left(c - \frac{b^2}{4a}\right) = ax^2 + bx + c$$

Solving Quadratic Equations

Complete the square to find **Exact Solutions**

Completing the square probably isn't the easiest way to solve an equation but it is useful
if you are asked to **sketch a graph** or find an **exact solution** — usually this means **surds** will be involved.

Example: a) Rewrite $2x^2 - 8x + 3$ by completing the square.

You can also use the quadratic formula to find exact solutions (see p.20).

Take out a factor of 2 out of the x^2 and x terms: $2(x^2 - 4x) + 3$

Rewrite the bracket as one bracket squared: $b = -8$, so $\dfrac{b}{2a} = \dfrac{-8}{2 \times 2} = -2$, so the bracket is $2(x - 2)^2$

Add d to the bracket. Then find d by setting the new and original equation equal to each other:

$2(x - 2)^2 + d$
$2(x - 2)^2 + d = 2x^2 - 8x + 3$
$2x^2 - 8x + 8 + d = 2x^2 - 8x + 3$
$8 + d = 3 \Rightarrow d = -5$, so the completed square is $\mathbf{2(x - 2)^2 - 5}$

b) Hence find exact solutions to $2x^2 - 8x + 3 = 0$.

Set your answer from part a) equal to O and solve to find x:

$2(x - 2)^2 - 5 = 0$
$\Rightarrow (x - 2)^2 = \dfrac{5}{2}$

Using $d = c - \dfrac{b^2}{4a}$ also gives
$d = 3 - \dfrac{8^2}{4 \times 2} = 3 - 8 = -5.$

There's a positive and negative square root: $\Rightarrow x - 2 = \pm\sqrt{\dfrac{5}{2}} = \pm\dfrac{\sqrt{10}}{2}$

Rationalise the denominator
$\sqrt{\dfrac{5}{2}} = \dfrac{\sqrt{5}}{\sqrt{2}} = \dfrac{\sqrt{5}\sqrt{2}}{\sqrt{2}\sqrt{2}} = \dfrac{\sqrt{10}}{2}$

You're asked for the exact solutions so leave your answer in surd form: $x = 2 + \dfrac{\sqrt{10}}{2}$ and $x = 2 - \dfrac{\sqrt{10}}{2}$

Sometimes it's best just to use the **Formula**

Factorising or completing the square can be really messy for some equations — in which case your best bet is to use
the **quadratic formula** (see page 20). But be careful, the question probably won't tell you which method is best.

For example, if you are asked to solve $6x^2 + 87x - 144 = 0$ things can get **tricky**.

This will actually **factorise**, but there are 2 possible bracket forms to try:
$(6x \quad)(x \quad)$ or $(3x \quad)(2x \quad)$ For each of these, there are 8 possible ways of making 144 to try.

And completing the square would be much **slower** than using the formula.

Practice Questions

Q1 Solve the following equations. While you're doing this, sing a jolly song to show how much you enjoy it.
  a) $x^2 + x - 12 = 0$ b) $2 + x - x^2 = 0$ c) $4x^2 - 1 = 0$ d) $3x^2 - 15x - 14 = 4x$

Q2 Solve $3(x + 2)^2 - 17(x + 2) - 6 = 0$ by substitution.

Q3 Solve these quadratic equations by completing the square, leaving your answers in surd form where necessary.
  a) $x^2 - 6x + 5 = 0$ b) $3x^2 - 7x + 3 = 0$ c) $2x^2 - 6x - 2 = 0$ d) $x^2 + 4x + 6 = 12$

Q4 Solve the equation $5x^2 + 4x - 36 = x^2 - 3x$.

Exam Questions

Q1 a) Write $3x^2 + 2x - 2$ in completed square form. [3 marks]
   b) Hence, or otherwise, solve the equation $3x^2 + 2x - 2 = 0$. Give your answers to 2 decimal places. [1 mark]

Q2 Find the exact solutions of the equation $6x^2 = 1 - 3x$, by completing the square. [4 marks]

I'm popular with squares — they always tell me how I complete them...

Completing the square is useful when you're sketching graphs (see page 19). It's worth making sure that you're
comfortable with all the methods discussed here, they'll all come in handy at some point. If you've got a fancy
calculator it might even solve quadratic equations for you — but don't forget to write some working out in the exam.

Quadratic Functions and Graphs

If a question doesn't seem to make sense, or you can't see how to go about solving a problem, try drawing a graph.
It sometimes helps if you can actually see what the problem is, rather than just reading about it.

Quadratic graphs are **Always** u-shaped or n-shaped

The **coefficient of** x^2 tells you whether a quadratic curve (called a **parabola**) is u-shaped or n-shaped.
When sketching a graph you might have to consider the following things:

Sketching Quadratic Graphs

① **Up or down:** Decide on the shape of the curve
       — if the coefficient of x^2 is positive, then the graph is u-shaped.
       — if the coefficient of x^2 is negative, then the graph is n-shaped.

② **Axes:** Find where the curve crosses the y-axis (set $x = 0$) and x-axis (set $y = 0$).

③ **Maximum or minimum:** Find the maximum or minimum point by using the fact that it's halfway
            between the roots or by completing the square (see next page).

④ **Sketch the graph:** Make sure that you label all the bits that you need to.

> A u-shaped graph has a minimum and a n-shaped graph has a maximum.

Examples: | Sketch $y = 8 - 2x - x^2$. | Sketch $y = 2x^2 - 5x + 3$.

① **Up or Down**

$y = 8 - 2x - x^2$

The coefficient of x^2 is negative so the graph is n-shaped. → $-ve$

$y = 2x^2 - 5x + 3$

The coefficient of x^2 is positive so the graph is u-shaped. → $+ve$

② **Axes**

When $x = 0$, $y = 8 - 2(0) - 0^2 = \mathbf{8}$
When $y = 0$, $\quad 8 - 2x - x^2 = 0$
$\qquad\qquad (2 - x)(x + 4) = 0$
$\qquad\qquad x = 2 \text{ or } x = -4$

This means that the curve crosses the y-axis at (O, 8) and the x-axis at (2, O) and (−4, O).

When $x = 0$, $y = 2(0^2) - 5(0) + 3 = \mathbf{3}$
When $y = 0$, $\quad 2x^2 - 5x + 3 = 0$
$\qquad\qquad (2x - 3)(x - 1) = 0$
$\qquad\qquad x = \dfrac{3}{2} \text{ or } x = 1$

This means that the curve crosses the y-axis at (O, 3) and the x-axis at $\left(\dfrac{3}{2}, \text{O}\right)$ and (1, O).

③ **Max or Min**

The maximum value is halfway between the roots because the curve is symmetrical:
$(2 + -4) \div 2 = -1$

So the maximum value is at $x = -1$.
The maximum is $y = 8 - 2(-1) - (-1)^2 = 9$

i.e. the graph has a maximum at the point **(−1, 9)**.

The minimum value is halfway between the roots:
$\left(\dfrac{3}{2} + 1\right) \div 2 = \dfrac{5}{4}$

The minimum value is at $x = \dfrac{5}{4}$.

The minimum is $y = 2\left(\dfrac{5}{4}\right)^2 - 5\left(\dfrac{5}{4}\right) + 3 = -\dfrac{1}{8}$

i.e. the graph has a minimum at the point $\left(\dfrac{5}{4}, -\dfrac{1}{8}\right)$.

④ **Sketch**

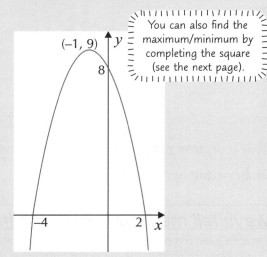

> You can also find the maximum/minimum by completing the square (see the next page).

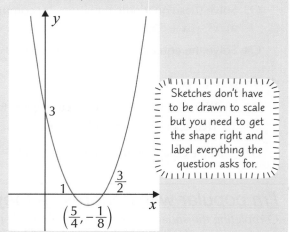

> Sketches don't have to be drawn to scale but you need to get the shape right and label everything the question asks for.

Quadratic Functions and Graphs

Completing the square can be *Useful*

Once you've completed the square, you can very quickly say **loads** about a quadratic function.
And it all relies on the fact that a squared number can **never** be less than zero... **ever**.

Example: Sketch the curve of $f(x) = 3x^2 - 6x - 7$.

Complete the square of $f(x)$ (see page 16): $\quad f(x) = 3x^2 - 6x - 7 = 3(x-1)^2 - 10$

Find where $y = f(x)$ crosses the axes:

When $x = 0$, $y = -7$, the curve crosses the y-axis at -7.

When $y = 0$, $3(x-1)^2 - 10 = 0$

$$(x-1)^2 = \frac{10}{3}$$

$$x - 1 = \pm\sqrt{\frac{10}{3}}$$

Rationalise the denominator (p.7).

$$x = 1 \pm \frac{\sqrt{30}}{3}$$

So the curve crosses the x-axis at $x = 1 + \frac{\sqrt{30}}{3}$ and $x = 1 - \frac{\sqrt{30}}{3}$

$(x-1)^2 \geq 0$ so the smallest value occurs when $(x-1) = 0$, i.e. when $x = 1$.
Find the minimum by substituting $x = 1$ into $f(x)$:

$f(x) = 3(x-1)^2 - 10$, $\Rightarrow$ $f(1) = 3(1-1)^2 - 10 = -10$ $\quad$ Now you can
So the minimum is at **(1, –10)**. $\quad\quad\quad\quad\quad\quad\quad\quad$ sketch the graph.

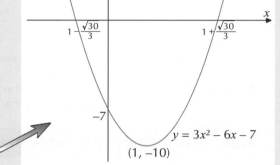

$1 - \frac{\sqrt{30}}{3}$ $\quad\quad$ $1 + \frac{\sqrt{30}}{3}$

$y = 3x^2 - 6x - 7$

$(1, -10)$

Some functions don't have *Real Roots*

By completing the square, you can also quickly tell if the graph of a quadratic function ever crosses the x-axis.
It'll only cross the x-axis if the function changes sign (i.e. goes from positive to negative or vice versa).

Example: $f(x) = x^2 + 4x + 7$. Does $f(x) = 0$ have any real roots?

To sketch a graph like this you'd need to show the correct shape, y-intercept, and coordinates of the minimum or maximum.

The smallest this bit can be is zero (at $x = -2$). $\quad\quad f(x) = (x+2)^2 + 3$

$(x+2)^2$ is never less than zero, so the minimum of $f(x)$ is 3.

This means that:
  a) $f(x)$ can never be negative.
  b) The graph of $f(x)$ never crosses the x-axis.

So the function has **no real roots**.

If the coefficient of x^2 is negative, you can do the same sort of thing to check whether $f(x)$ ever becomes positive.

Practice Questions

Q1 Sketch the following curves, labelling the maximum/minimum and the points where it crosses the axes.
  a) $y = x^2 + 4x - 5$ $\quad\quad$ b) $y = 2x^2 - 7x + 6$ $\quad\quad$ c) $y = 11x - 10 - 3x^2$ $\quad\quad$ d) $y = 25 - 4x^2$

Q2 Show that the equation $f(x) = 0$, where $f(x) = 2x^2 - 12x + 23$, has no real roots.

Exam Questions

Q1 a) $f(x) = x^2 - 14x + k$, where k is a constant. Given that one of the roots of $f(x) = 0$ is $x = 7 + 2\sqrt{6}$,
  find the value of k, and hence verify that the other root is $x = 7 - 2\sqrt{6}$. [4 marks]
  b) Sketch the curve of $y = f(x)$. Label the minimum and the points of intersection with the axes. [3 marks]

Q2 a) Rewrite $x^2 - 12x + 15$ in the form $(x-a)^2 + b$, for integers a and b. [2 marks]
  b) Find the minimum value of $x^2 - 12x + 15$ and state the value of x at which this minimum occurs. [2 marks]

Sketches really help you get to the root of the problem...

Completing the square is really useful here — you can use it to find where the curve crosses the x-axis and also to find the minimum. Sketching graphs is probably the most fun you'll have in this section, so draw away to your heart's content. And once you've had your fill of quadratics there's a load of other graphs to sketch later in the section.

The Quadratic Formula

Unlike factorising, the quadratic formula always works... no ifs, no buts, no butts, no nothing...

I shall teach you the ways of the **Formula**

If you want to solve a quadratic equation $ax^2 + bx + c = 0$, then the answers are given by the **quadratic formula**:

$$x = \frac{-b \pm \sqrt{b^2 - 4ac}}{2a}$$

Example: Solve the quadratic equation $3x^2 - 4x = 8$, leaving your answer in surd form.

Get the equation into the standard $ax^2 + bx + c = 0$ form: $\quad 3x^2 - 4x - 8 = 0$

Plug the values $a = 3$, $b = -4$, $c = -8$ into the formula (be very careful with all the minus signs):

$$x = \frac{-(-4) \pm \sqrt{(-4)^2 - 4 \times 3 \times -8}}{2 \times 3}$$

$$= \frac{4 \pm \sqrt{112}}{6} = \frac{2 \pm 2\sqrt{7}}{3}$$

Use the rules of surds (see p.6).

There are two answers (one using + and one using −): $\quad x = \dfrac{2 + 2\sqrt{7}}{3} \;$ or $\; x = \dfrac{2 - 2\sqrt{7}}{3}$

Some **calculators** have a quadratic equation solver — you just enter the values of a, b and c and hey presto. This can be quite useful for **checking** your answers but make sure you show your working in the exam.

How Many Roots? Check the $b^2 - 4ac$ bit...

$$x = \frac{-b \pm \sqrt{b^2 - 4ac}}{2a}$$

When you try to find the roots of a quadratic equation, this bit in the square root sign ($b^2 - 4ac$) can be positive, zero, or negative. It's this that tells you if a quadratic equation has **two real roots**, **one real root**, or **no real roots**.

The $b^2 - 4ac$ bit is called the **discriminant** (sometimes written D, or Δ).

It's good to be able to picture what the graphs will look like in these different cases:

$b^2 - 4ac > 0$	$b^2 - 4ac = 0$	$b^2 - 4ac < 0$
Two real roots	One real root	No real roots

The graph crosses the x-axis twice and these values are the roots:

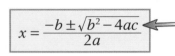

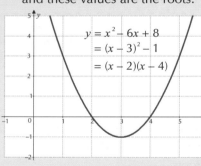

$$y = x^2 - 6x + 8$$
$$= (x - 3)^2 - 1$$
$$= (x - 2)(x - 4)$$

The graph just touches the x-axis from above (or from below if the x^2 coefficient is negative).

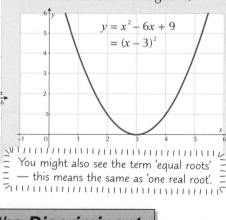

$$y = x^2 - 6x + 9$$
$$= (x - 3)^2$$

You might also see the term 'equal roots' — this means the same as 'one real root'.

The graph doesn't touch the x-axis at all.

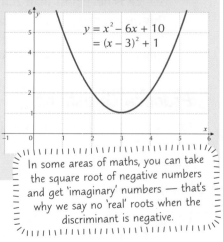

$$y = x^2 - 6x + 10$$
$$= (x - 3)^2 + 1$$

In some areas of maths, you can take the square root of negative numbers and get 'imaginary' numbers — that's why we say no 'real' roots when the discriminant is negative.

Identify **a**, **b** and **c** to find the **Discriminant**

Make sure you get them the **right way round** — it's easy to get mixed up if the quadratic's in a **different order**.

Example: Find the discriminant of $15 - x - 2x^2$. How many real roots does $15 - x - 2x^2 = 0$ have?

First identify a, b and c: $\quad a = -2$, $b = -1$ and $c = 15$ (NOT $a = 15$, $b = -1$ and $c = -2$)

Work out the discriminant: $\quad b^2 - 4ac = (-1)^2 - (4 \times -2 \times 15) = 1 + 120 = \mathbf{121}$.

The discriminant is > 0: $\quad$ so $15 - x - 2x^2 = 0$ has **two distinct real roots**.

The Quadratic Formula

a, *b* and *c* might be *Unknown*

In exam questions, you might be given a **quadratic** where one or more of *a*, *b* and *c* are given in terms of an **unknown** (such as *k*, *p* or *q*). This means that you'll end up with an **equation** or **inequality** for the discriminant **in terms of the unknown** — you might have to **solve** it to find the **value** or **range of values** of the unknown.

Example: If $f(x) = 3x^2 + 2x + k$, find the range of values of *k* for which:
a) $f(x) = 0$ has 2 distinct roots,   b) $f(x) = 0$ has 1 root,   c) $f(x) = 0$ has no real roots.

Using $a = 3$, $b = 2$ and $c = k$, work out what the discriminant is:
$$b^2 - 4ac = 2^2 - 4 \times 3 \times k = 4 - 12k$$

The only difference is the (in)equality symbol.

a) Two distinct roots means:
$$b^2 - 4ac > 0 \Rightarrow 4 - 12k > 0$$
$$\Rightarrow 4 > 12k$$
$$\Rightarrow k < \frac{1}{3}$$

b) One root means:
$$b^2 - 4ac = 0 \Rightarrow 4 - 12k = 0$$
$$\Rightarrow 4 = 12k$$
$$\Rightarrow k = \frac{1}{3}$$

c) No real roots means:
$$b^2 - 4ac < 0 \Rightarrow 4 - 12k < 0$$
$$\Rightarrow 4 < 12k$$
$$\Rightarrow k > \frac{1}{3}$$

You might have to *Solve* a *Quadratic Inequality* to find *k*

When you put your values of *a*, *b* and *c* into the formula for the **discriminant**, you might end up with a **quadratic inequality** in terms of *k*. You'll have to solve this to find the range of values of *k* — there's more on this on p.24.

Example: The equation $kx^2 + (k + 3)x + 4 = 0$ has two distinct real solutions.
Show that $k^2 - 10k + 9 > 0$, and find the set of values of *k* which satisfy this inequality.

Using $a = k$, $b = (k + 3)$ and $c = 4$, work out what the discriminant is:
$$b^2 - 4ac = (k + 3)^2 - (4 \times k \times 4) = k^2 + 6k + 9 - 16k = k^2 - 10k + 9$$

The equation has two distinct real solutions, so the discriminant must be > 0:
$$k^2 - 10k + 9 > 0$$

Now, to find the set of values for k, you have to factorise the quadratic:
$$k^2 - 10k + 9 = (k - 1)(k - 9)$$

This expression is zero when $k = 1$ and $k = 9$.
From the graph, you can see that this is a u-shaped quadratic which is > 0 when:

$$k < 1 \text{ or when } k > 9$$

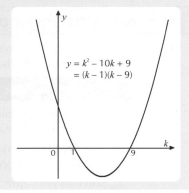

$y = k^2 - 10k + 9$
$= (k - 1)(k - 9)$

Practice Questions

Q1 For each of the following: (i) Find the discriminant and state the number of real roots of the quadratic.
                                 (ii) Find the exact values of its real roots, if it has any.
a) $4x^2 + 28x + 49 = 0$ b) $3x^2 + 3x + 1 = 0$ c) $9x^2 - 6\sqrt{2}x + 2 = 0$ d) $2x^2 + 9x - 5 = 0$

Q2 If the quadratic equation $x^2 + kx + 4 = 0$ has two distinct real roots, find the possible values of *k*.

Exam Questions

Q1   The equation $x^2 + 2kx + 4k = 0$, where *k* is a non-zero integer, has equal roots. Find the value of *k*.   [3 marks]

Q2   The equation $(p + 1)x^2 + (p + 1)x + 1 = 0$ has 2 distinct real solutions for *x* (*p* is a constant).
a) Show that $p^2 - 2p - 3 > 0$ [3 marks]
b) Hence find the range of possible values for *p*.   [3 marks]

All the best mathematicians are raised on quadratic formula...

Don't panic if you're not sure how to solve quadratic inequalities — they're covered in more detail on page 24. Although it might be tempting to hide under your exam desk and hope a discriminant question doesn't find you, there's no escaping these questions — so get practising until you can recite the quadratic formula in your sleep.

Simultaneous Equations

Solving simultaneous equations is one of those things that you'll have to do again and again — so it's definitely worth practising them until you feel really confident.

Solving **Simultaneous Equations** by **Elimination**

Solving **simultaneous equations** means finding the answers to two equations **at the same time** — i.e. finding values for x and y for which both equations are true.

Example: Solve the following equations: $3x + 5y = -4$
$$-2x + 3y = 9$$

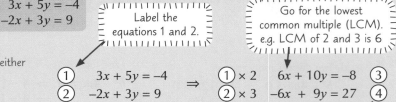

Label the equations 1 and 2.

Go for the lowest common multiple (LCM). e.g. LCM of 2 and 3 is 6

1) **Match the coefficients**

Multiply the equations by numbers that will make either the x's or the y's match in the two equations (ignoring minus signs):

①　$3x + 5y = -4$　　　①$\times 2$　$6x + 10y = -8$　③
②　$-2x + 3y = 9$　$\Rightarrow$　②$\times 3$　$-6x + 9y = 27$　④

Label these 3 and 4.

2) **Eliminate to find one variable**

The coefficients of x have different signs, so you need to add the equations (if the coefficients have the same sign, you'll need to subtract one equation from the other):

③$+$④　$6x + 10y + (-6x) + 9y = -8 + 27$
$\Rightarrow 19y = 19$
$\Rightarrow y = 1$

3) **Find the variable you eliminated**

Put y = 1 into one of the equations to find x:

$y = 1$ in ①　$3x + 5 = -4 \Rightarrow 3x = -9$
$\Rightarrow x = -3$

4) **Check your answer**

Put x = –3 and y = 1 into the other equation:

$x = -3, y = 1$ in ②　$-2(-3) + 3(1) = 9$ ✓

Use **Substitution** if one equation is **Quadratic**

Sadly elimination won't always work. Sometimes one of the equations has not just x's and y's in it — but bits with x^2 and y^2 as well. When this happens, you can **only** use the **substitution** method:

One Quadratic and One Linear Equation

1) Isolate one variable in the linear equation by rearranging to get either x or y on its **own**.

2) **Substitute** the variable into the quadratic equation (to get an equation in just one variable).

3) Solve to get values for **one variable** — either by factorising or using the quadratic formula.

4) Stick these values in the linear equation to find the **corresponding values** for the other variables.

Substitute this for your own hilarious caption.

Example: Solve $-x + 2y = 5$ and $x^2 + y^2 = 25$.

Call the linear equation L and the quadratic equation Q.

Rearrange the linear equation so that either x or y is on its own on one side of the equals sign:

Ⓛ $-x + 2y = 5 \Rightarrow x = 2y - 5$

Substitute this expression into the quadratic equation:

Ⓠ $x^2 + y^2 = 25 \Rightarrow (2y - 5)^2 + y^2 = 25$

Rearrange this into the form ax² + bx + c and then solve it:

$\Rightarrow (4y^2 - 20y + 25) + y^2 = 25$
$\Rightarrow 5y^2 - 20y = 0$
$\Rightarrow 5y(y - 4) = 0$
$\Rightarrow y = 0$ or $y = 4$

$x^2 + y^2 = 25$ is actually a circle about the origin with radius 5 (see p.38).

Finally put both these values back into the linear equation to find corresponding values of x:

When $y = 0$: Ⓛ $-x + 2(0) = 5 \Rightarrow x = -5$
When $y = 4$: Ⓛ $-x + 2(4) = 5 \Rightarrow x = 3$
So the solutions are $x = -5, y = 0$ and $x = 3, y = 4$.

Check your answers by putting them back into Ⓛ and Ⓠ:

$x = -5, y = 0 \Rightarrow -(-5) + 2 \times 0 = 5$ and $(-5)^2 + 0^2 = 25$ ✓
$x = 3, y = 4 \Rightarrow -3 + 2 \times 4 = 5$ and $3^2 + 4^2 = 25$ ✓

Simultaneous Equations

Number of **Solutions** = number of **Intersections**

When you have to interpret something **geometrically**, you have to sketch the graphs of the two functions and 'say what you see'. The number of **solutions** affects what your picture will look like:

Two Solutions	One Solution	No Solutions
The graphs meet in **two places**.	The graphs meet in **one place** — the straight line is a **tangent** to the curve.	The graphs **never meet**.

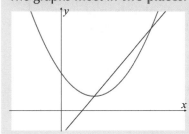

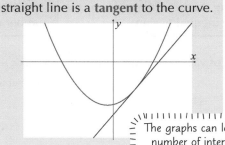

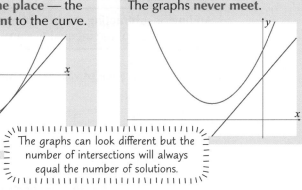

The graphs can look different but the number of intersections will always equal the number of solutions.

Example: Interpret geometrically: $y = x^2 - 4x + 5$
$\qquad\qquad\qquad\qquad y = 2x - 4$

Geometric Interpretation

Substitute the expression for y from ② into ①: $2x - 4 = x^2 - 4x + 5$

Rearrange and solve:
$$x^2 - 6x + 9 = 0$$
$$(x - 3)^2 = 0$$
$$\Rightarrow x = 3$$

Putting x = 3 in ② gives: $x = 3 \Rightarrow y = 2 \times 3 - 4 = 2$

There's only 1 solution: $x = 3, y = 2$

Since the equations have only one solution, the two graphs only meet at one point — (3, 2):

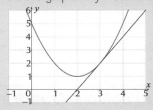

The straight line is a tangent to the curve at (3, 2).

Practice Questions

Q1 Solve these sets of simultaneous equations:
   a) $3x - 4y = 7$ and $-2x + 7y = -22$
   b) $2x - 3y = \frac{11}{12}$ and $x + y = -\frac{7}{12}$

Q2 Find where the following lines meet:
   a) $y = 3x - 4$ and $y = 7x - 5$
   b) $y = 13 - 2x$ and $7x - y - 23 = 0$
   c) $2x - 3y + 4 = 0$ and $x - 2y + 1 = 0$

Q3 Find the possible solutions to these sets of simultaneous equations. Interpret your answers geometrically.
   a) $y = x^2 - 7x + 4$
      $2x - y - 10 = 0$
   b) $y = 30 - 6x + 2x^2$
      $y = 2(x + 11)$
   c) $x^2 + 2y^2 - 3 = 0$
      $y = 2x + 4$

Exam Questions

Q1 Find the coordinates of the points of intersection of $x^2 + 2y^2 = 36$ and $x + y = 6$. [6 marks]

Q2 The line *l* has equation $y = 2x - 3$ and the curve *C* has equation $y = (x + 2)(x - 4)$.

   a) Sketch the line *l* and the curve *C* on the same axes, showing the coordinates of the x- and y- intercepts. [4 marks]

   b) Show that the x-coordinates of the points of intersection of *l* and *C* satisfy the equation $x^2 - 4x - 5 = 0$. [2 marks]

   c) Hence, or otherwise, find the points of intersection of *l* and *C*. [2 marks]

The Eliminator — a robot sent back through time to destroy one variable...

For a linear and quadratic equation you have to use substitution, but for a pair of linear equations elimination is usually the easiest method. Knowing how to sketch a graph is handy here, but there's no need to be a Van Gogh about it. Simultaneous equations pop up all over A-level maths so it's worth spending some time now to get them sorted.

Inequalities

Solving inequalities is very similar to solving equations. You've just got to be really careful that you keep the inequality sign pointing the right way.

When **Multiplying** or **Dividing** by something **Negative** flip the inequality sign

Like I said, these are pretty similar to solving equations — because whatever you do to one side, you have to do to the other. But multiplying or dividing by **negative** numbers **changes** the direction of the inequality sign.

> **Adding** or **subtracting** doesn't change the direction of the inequality sign.

> **Multiplying** or **dividing** by a **positive** number doesn't affect the inequality sign.

Examples: Find the range of values of x that satisfies: a) $x - 3 < -1 + 2x$ b) $8x + 2 \geq 2x + 17$

a) Adding 1 to both sides leaves the inequality sign pointing in the same direction.
$$x - 3 < -1 + 2x$$
$$\Rightarrow x - 2 < 2x$$
Subtracting x from both sides doesn't affect the inequality.
$$\Rightarrow -2 < x$$
so $x > -2$

b) Subtract 2, and then 2x, from both sides.
$$8x + 2 \geq 2x + 17$$
$$\Rightarrow 8x \geq 2x + 15$$
$$\Rightarrow 6x \geq 15$$
Divide both sides by 6 and simplify.
$$\Rightarrow x \geq \frac{5}{2}$$

> **Multiplying** or **dividing** an inequality by a **negative** number changes the direction of the inequality sign.

Example: Find the range of values of x that satisfies $4 - 3x \leq 16$

Subtract 4 from both sides.
$$4 - 3x \leq 16$$
Then divide both sides by -3
$$\Rightarrow -3x \leq 12$$
— but change the direction of the inequality.
$$\Rightarrow x \geq -4$$

The reason for the sign changing direction is because it's just the same as swapping everything from one side to the other:
$$-3x \leq 12 \Rightarrow -12 \leq 3x \Rightarrow x \geq -4$$

Sketch a **Graph** to solve a **Quadratic** inequality

With quadratic inequalities, you're best off sketching the **graph** and taking it from there.
You've got to be really careful when you divide by variables that might be **negative** — basically, don't do it.

Example Find the range of values of x that satisfies $36x \leq 6x^2$

Rearrange into the form f(x) ≥ O.
Start by dividing by 6:
Take 6x from both sides and rearrange:
$$36x \leq 6x^2$$
$$\Rightarrow 6x \leq x^2$$
$$\Rightarrow 0 \leq x^2 - 6x$$
So $x^2 - 6x \geq 0$

You shouldn't divide by x here because it could be negative (or zero).

The coefficient of x² is positive, so the graph of y is u-shaped.

Write the inequality as an equation: Let $y = x^2 - 6x$

Find where the curve crosses the x-axis by setting y = O and factorising:
$$x^2 - 6x = 0 \Rightarrow x(x - 6) = 0$$
So $x = 0$ and $x = 6$.

Use a sketch to find where $x^2 - 6x \geq O$:
The graph is positive to the left of $x = 0$ and to the right of $x = 6$ (inclusive).
So **$x \leq 0$ or $x \geq 6$.**

You might be asked to give your answer in **set notation**:

In set notation, the answer to the example above is $\{x : x \leq O\} \cup \{x : x \geq 6\}$.

Set Notation

- Set notation uses **curly brackets**: $\{x : x < a\}$ means 'the set of values of x such that x is less than a'.

- The **empty set**, written $\emptyset$, contains **nothing**. For example, $\{x : x^2 < 0\} = \emptyset$ (as x^2 is never < 0).

- The **union** ($\cup$) of two sets is **everything** contained in **either set**: $x < a$ or $x > b$ is written as $\{x : x < a\} \cup \{x : x > b\}$.

- The **intersection** ($\cap$) of two sets is **only** the things present in **both sets**: $x > c$ and $x < d$ is written as $\{x : x > c\} \cap \{x : x < d\}$.

- You can also use **brackets** to show an interval — **round** means the value **isn't** included, and **square** means it **is**. So (3, 5] means $3 < x \leq 5$.

Inequalities

Test **Both Sides** of a curve to find a **Region**

You might be given two (or more) inequalities and asked to find the **region** that satisfies them. All you need to do is **sketch** the curves or lines and **test** the coordinates of a point (usually the origin) in each of the inequalities. The region you're after will include the **areas** where each inequality holds **true** for any tested point.

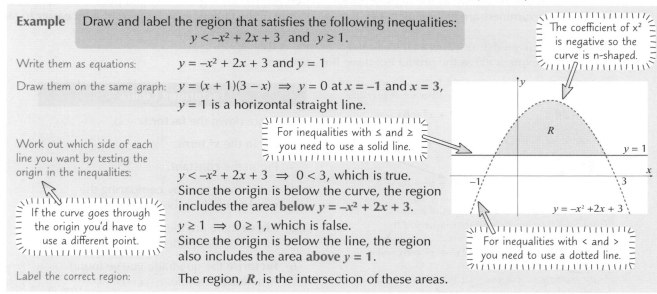

Example Draw and label the region that satisfies the following inequalities:
$y < -x^2 + 2x + 3$ and $y \geq 1$.

The coefficient of x^2 is negative so the curve is n-shaped.

Write them as equations: $y = -x^2 + 2x + 3$ and $y = 1$

Draw them on the same graph: $y = (x + 1)(3 - x) \Rightarrow y = 0$ at $x = -1$ and $x = 3$,
$y = 1$ is a horizontal straight line.

For inequalities with $\leq$ and $\geq$ you need to use a solid line.

Work out which side of each line you want by testing the origin in the inequalities:

If the curve goes through the origin you'd have to use a different point.

$y < -x^2 + 2x + 3 \Rightarrow 0 < 3$, which is true.
Since the origin is below the curve, the region includes the area **below** $y = -x^2 + 2x + 3$.

$y \geq 1 \Rightarrow 0 \geq 1$, which is false.
Since the origin is below the line, the region also includes the area **above** $y = 1$.

For inequalities with $<$ and $>$ you need to use a dotted line.

Label the correct region: The region, **R**, is the intersection of these areas.

Practice Questions

Q1 Find the ranges of x that satisfy these inequalities:
a) $x + 6 < 5x - 4$
b) $4x - 2 > x - 14$
c) $7 - x \leq 4 - 2x$

Q2 Solve: a) $7x - 4 > 2x - 42$
b) $12y - 3 \leq 4y + 4$
c) $9y - 4 \geq 17y + 2$

Q3 Find the ranges of x that satisfy the following inequalities:
a) $3x^2 - 5x - 2 \leq 0$
b) $6 - x - 2x^2 < 0$
c) $3x^2 + 7x + 4 \geq 2(x^2 + x - 1)$

Q4 Find the ranges of x that satisfy these jokers. Give your answers in set notation.
a) $x^2 + 3x - 1 \geq x + 2$
b) $2x^2 > x + 1$
c) $3x^2 - 12 < x^2 - 2x$

Q5 Draw and label the region that satisfies the following inequalities:
$y \leq 3$, $y > x - 1$ and $y > 4 - 2x$.

Exam Questions

Q1 Find the set of values for x that satisfy the inequalities below.
a) $3x + 2 \leq x + 6$ [1 mark]
b) $20 - x - x^2 > 0$ [2 marks]
c) both $3x + 2 \leq x + 6$ and $20 - x - x^2 > 0$ [1 mark]

Q2 Solve the inequalities:
a) $3 \leq 2p + 5 \leq 15$ [2 marks]
b) $q^2 - 9 > 0$ [2 marks]

Q3 Draw and label the region that satisfies the following: $y > 2x^2 - x - 3$ and $y \geq 1 - \frac{1}{2}x$ [4 marks]

Inequalities $\geq$ vectors > biology...

For inequality questions you could be given any linear and/or quadratic inequalities to sketch (or find intersection points). Don't forget to use a solid line for inequalities with $\leq$ or $\geq$ and a dotted line for $<$ or $>$ — this could cost you marks in the exam. There are plenty of inequality questions to get stuck into here, so get cracking.

Cubics

*Remember how much you enjoyed factorising quadratics? Well factorising cubics is a little bit similar —
only harder, better, faster, stronger. Okay maybe just harder, but at least you still get to do a bit of sketching.*

Factorising *a cubic given* One Factor

A **cubic** function has an x^3 term as the highest power. When you factorising a cubic, you put it into (up to) three
brackets. If the examiners are feeling nice they'll give you **one** of the factors, which makes it a bit **easier** to factorise.

Example: Given that $(x+2)$ is a factor of $f(x) = 2x^3 + x^2 - 8x - 4$,
express $f(x)$ as the product of three linear factors.

The first step is to find a quadratic factor. So write down
the factor you know, along with another set of brackets:

$(x + 2)($ $) = 2x^3 + x^2 - 8x - 4$

Put the x^2 bit in this new set of brackets.
These have to multiply together to give you this:

$(x + 2)(2x^2$ $) = 2x^3 + x^2 - 8x - 4$

Find the number for the second set of brackets.
These have to multiply together to give you this:

$(x + 2)(2x^2$ $- 2) = 2x^3 + x^2 - 8x - 4$

These multiply to give you $-2x$, but there's
$-8x$ in $f(x)$ — so you need an 'extra' $-6x$.
And that's what this $-3x$ is for:

$(x + 2)(2x^2 - 3x - 2) = 2x^3 + x^2 - 8x - 4$

Before you go any further, check that there
are the same number of x^2's on both sides:

4x^2 from here...

$(x + 2)(2x^2 - 3x - 2) = 2x^3 + x^2 - 8x - 4$

...and $-3x^2$ from here add together to give this x^2.

If this is okay, factorise the quadratic into two linear factors.

$2x^2 - 3x - 2 = (2x + 1)(x - 2)$

And so... $2x^3 + x^2 - 8x - 4 = (x + 2)(2x + 1)(x - 2)$

Factorising Cubics

1) Write down the **factor** $(x - k)$.

2) Put in the x^2 **term**.

3) Put in the **constant**.

4) Put in the x term by **comparing** the
number of x's on both sides.

5) **Check** there are the same **number of x^2's**
(or x's) on both sides.

6) **Factorise** the quadratic you've found
— if that's possible.

*If every term in the cubic
contains an 'x' (i.e. $ax^3 + bx^2 + cx$)
then just take out x as your first
factor before factorising the
remaining quadratic as usual.*

*You only need $-3x$ because it's
going to be multiplied by 2
which makes $-6x$.*

*If you wanted to solve a cubic, you'd do it
exactly the same way — put it in the form
$ax^3 + bx^2 + cx + d = 0$ and factorise.*

Use the **Factor Theorem** to factorise a cubic given **No Factors**

If the nasty examiner has given you **no factors**, you can find one using the Factor Theorem (see p.11) and
then use the **method** above to factorise the rest. As if by magic, here's a reminder of the **Factor Theorem**:

> If **f(x)** is a polynomial, and **f(k) = 0**, then **(x − k)** is a **factor** of f(x).

Example: Factorise $f(x) = 2x^3 + x^2 - 8x - 4$ fully.

Try small numbers until f(something) = 0:

For example, calculate f(1), f(−1), f(2), f(−2), etc.

$f(1) = 2(1^3) + 1^2 - 8(1) - 4 = -9$

$f(-1) = 2(-1)^3 + (-1)^2 - 8(-1) - 4 = 3$

$f(2) = 2(2^3) + 2^2 - 8(2) - 4 = 0$

Using the Factor Theorem:

$f(2) = 0$, so $(x - 2)$ is a factor.

Write down another set of brackets:

$(x - 2)($ $) = 2x^3 + x^2 - 8x - 4$

Use the method described above to get:

$2x^3 + x^2 - 8x - 4 = (x - 2)(2x + 1)(x + 2)$

*This is actually the same example
as above but the working will be
slightly different because you're
starting with the factor $(x - 2)$.*

Cubics

If you know the *Factors* of a cubic — the graph's easy to *Sketch*

All cubics have a similar shape: '**bottom-left to top-right**' if the coefficient of x^3 is **positive** or
'**top-left to bottom-right**' if the coefficient of x^3 is **negative**.

Once you know the **factors** of a cubic, the graph is easy to sketch — just find where the function is **zero**.

Example: Sketch the graphs of the following cubic functions:

a) $f(x) = x(x - 1)(2x + 1)$ b) $g(x) = (1 - x)(x^2 - 2x + 2)$ c) $m(x) = (x - 3)^2(x + 1)$ d) $n(x) = (2 - x)^3$

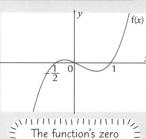
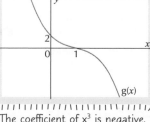
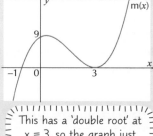
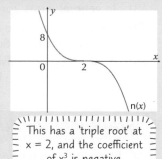

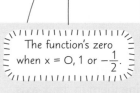
The function's zero when $x = 0$, 1 or $-\frac{1}{2}$.

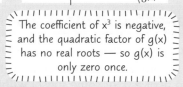
The coefficient of x^3 is negative, and the quadratic factor of $g(x)$ has no real roots — so $g(x)$ is only zero once.

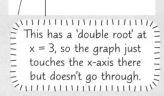
This has a 'double root' at $x = 3$, so the graph just touches the x-axis there but doesn't go through.

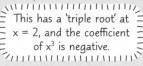
This has a 'triple root' at $x = 2$, and the coefficient of x^3 is negative.

Peter spent too much time sketching his cubic graph in the exam.

> The **power** of a factor $(x - a)^n$ affects what happens at **x = a**:
> **even** power $\Rightarrow$ the curve **touches** the x-axis but doesn't cross it
>   (e.g. the 'double root' in $m(x)$ above)
> **odd** power $\Rightarrow$ the curve **crosses** the x-axis
>   (e.g. the 'triple root' in $n(x)$ above).

This is also true for other polynomials — e.g. quartics (p.30).

Practice Questions

Q1 Sketch these cubic graphs. Go on, this is the fun part.

   a) $y = (x - 4)^3$ b) $y = (3 - x)(x + 2)^2$ c) $y = (1 - x)(x^2 - 6x + 8)$ d) $y = (x - 1)(x - 2)(x - 3)$

Q2 Show that the expressions below are factors of the given functions. Hence factorise the functions fully.

   a) $(x - 1)$ is a factor of $f(x) = x^3 - x^2 - 2x + 2$ b) $(x + 4)$ is a factor of $g(x) = x^3 + 3x^2 - 10x - 24$
   c) $(2x - 1)$ is a factor of $h(x) = 2x^3 + 3x^2 - 8x + 3$ d) $(3x - 2)$ is a factor of $k(x) = 3x^3 + 10x^2 + 10x - 12$

Q3 Given that $(x + 5)$ is a factor of $f(x) = x^3 - 3x^2 - 33x + 35$, factorise $f(x)$ fully.

Exam Questions

Q1   The curve C has the equation $y = (2x + 1)(x - 2)^2$
     Sketch C, clearly showing the points at which the curve meets the x- and y-axes   [3 marks]

Q2   a) Show that $(2x + 1)$ is a factor of $f(x) = 6x^3 + 37x^2 + 5x - 6$ [2 marks]
     b) Hence, or otherwise, factorise $f(x)$ fully.   [2 marks]
     c) Sketch $y = f(x)$, clearly showing the points at which the curve meets the x- and y-axes.   [3 marks]

Q3   If $f(x) = 7x^3 - 26x^2 + 13x + 6$, solve $f(x) = 0$.   [4 marks]

Does your cubic have the x factor? Only if x is in every term...

Factorising cubics might seem daunting but once you're used to the method it gets easier. For sketches, always find where the cubic crosses the x- and y-axis — even if you're not sure what shape the curve will be. This goes for most other kinds of graph too, not just cubics. You'll be seeing some of these other curves very soon — happy sketching.

Modulus

*The modulus of a number is really useful if you don't care whether something's positive or negative —
like if you were more interested in the size than the sign. It pops up in a few different places in A-level maths.*

Modulus is the Size of a number

1) The **modulus** of a number is its **size** — it doesn't matter if it's **positive** or **negative**. So for a **positive** number, the modulus is just the **same** as the number itself, but for a **negative** number, the modulus is its **positive value**. For example, the modulus of 8 is 8, and the modulus of −8 is also 8.

2) The modulus of a number, x, is written $|x|$. So the example above would be written $|8| = |-8| = 8$.

3) In **general** terms, for $x \geq 0$, $|x| = x$ and for $x < 0$, $|x| = -x$.

4) **Functions** can have a modulus too — the modulus of a function $f(x)$ is its **positive value**. Suppose $f(x) = -6$, then $|f(x)| = 6$. In general terms:

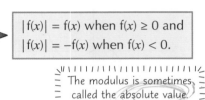

$$|f(x)| = f(x) \text{ when } f(x) \geq 0 \text{ and}$$
$$|f(x)| = -f(x) \text{ when } f(x) < 0.$$

5) If the modulus is **inside** the brackets in the form $f(|x|)$, then you make the x-value positive **before** applying the function. So $f(|-2|) = f(2)$.

The modulus is sometimes called the absolute value.

Graphs of Modulus functions are Reflected in the Axes

It's likely that you'll have to draw the **graph** of a modulus function — and there are **three different types**.

1) For the graph of $y = |f(x)|$, any **negative** values of $f(x)$ are made **positive** by **reflecting** them in the **x-axis**. This **restricts** the **range** of the modulus function to $|f(x)| \geq 0$ (or some subset **within** $|f(x)| \geq 0$, e.g. $|f(x)| \geq 1$).

2) For the graph of $y = f(|x|)$, the **negative** x-values produce the **same result** as the corresponding **positive** x-values. So the graph of $f(x)$ for $x \geq 0$ is **reflected** in the **y-axis** for the negative x-values.

3) For the graph of $y = |f(-x)|$, the x-values change from **positive to negative** (or **negative to positive**), so the graph is **reflected** in the **y-axis**. Then any **negative** values of $f(x)$ are made **positive** by **reflecting** them in the **x-axis**. As with the graph of $y = |f(x)|$, the **range** is **restricted**.

4) The easiest way to draw these graphs is to draw $f(x)$ (**ignoring** the modulus for now), then **reflect** it in the **appropriate axis** (or **axes**). This will probably make more sense when you've had a look at an **example**:

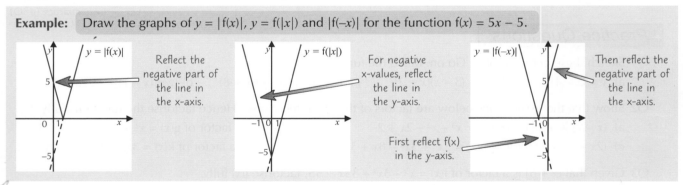

Example: Draw the graphs of $y = |f(x)|$, $y = f(|x|)$ and $|f(-x)|$ for the function $f(x) = 5x - 5$.

Reflect the negative part of the line in the x-axis.

For negative x-values, reflect the line in the y-axis.

First reflect f(x) in the y-axis.

Then reflect the negative part of the line in the x-axis.

Solving modulus functions usually produces More Than One solution

Here comes the method for solving '$|f(x)| = n$'. Solving '$|f(x)| = g(x)$' is **exactly the same** — just replace n with g(x).

Solving Modulus Equations of the form $|f(x)| = n$

1) First, **sketch** the functions $y = |f(x)|$ and $y = n$, on the **same** axes.

2) From the graph, work out the **ranges of x** for which $f(x) \geq 0$ and $f(x) < 0$:
   E.g. $f(x) \geq 0$ for $x \leq a$ or $x \geq b$ and $f(x) < 0$ for $a < x < b$.

3) Use this to write two **new equations**, one true for each range of x:
   (1) $f(x) = n$ for $x \leq a$ or $x \geq b$ (2) $-f(x) = n$ for $a < x < b$

4) Finally, just **solve** each equation and check that any solutions are valid — get rid of any solutions outside the range of x you've got for that equation. You can also look back at the graph to **check** that your solutions look right.

The solutions you're trying to find are where the functions intersect.

These ranges should 'fit' together to cover all possible values of x.

Modulus

Sketch the Graph to see How Many Solutions there are

Okay, so that method probably sounds complicated, but it really makes a lot more sense when you see it in action.

Example: Solve $|2x - 4| = 5 - x$.

This is an example of $|f(x)| = g(x)$, where $f(x) = 2x - 4$ and $g(x) = 5 - x$.

First off, sketch the graphs of $y = |2x - 4|$ and $y = 5 - x$.
They cross at 2 different points, so there should be 2 solutions.

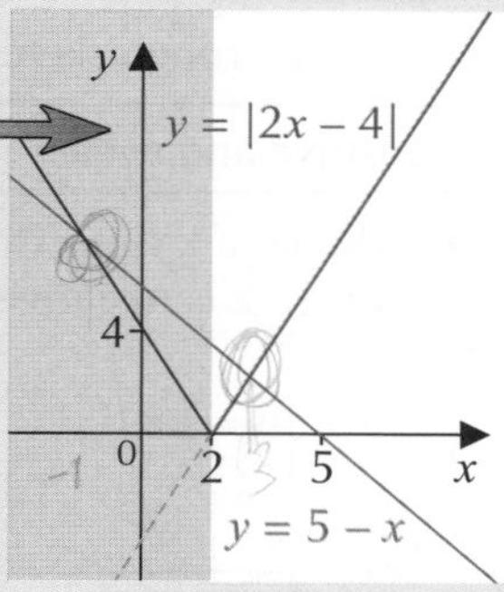

Now find out where $f(x) \geq 0$ and $f(x) < 0$:
$2x - 4 \geq 0$ for $x \geq 2$, and $2x - 4 < 0$ for $x < 2$ (shaded).

Form two equations for the different ranges of x:
(1) $2x - 4 = 5 - x$ for $x \geq 2$ (2) $-(2x - 4) = 5 - x$ for $x < 2$

Solving (1) gives: $3x = 9 \Rightarrow$ $\mathbf{x = 3}$ ← valid because $3 \geq 2$

Solving (2) gives: $-x = 1 \Rightarrow$ $\mathbf{x = -1}$ ← valid because $-1 < 2$

Check back against the graphs — we've found two solutions and they're in the right places. Nice.

*You can also **Solve** modulus equations **Algebraically***

Using the graphical method isn't too bad for equations of the form $|f(x)| = g(x)$, but when you're faced with something like $|f(x)| = |g(x)|$, it can get pretty complicated (you've got to think about where $f(x)$ is positive and negative, **and** where $g(x)$ is positive and negative — total hassle).
Fortunately there's also an **algebraic** method you can use:

If $|a| = |b|$ then $a^2 = b^2$.
So if $|f(x)| = |g(x)|$ then $[f(x)]^2 = [g(x)]^2$.

Example: Solve $|x - 2| = |3x + 4|$.

Start by squaring both sides:
$$|x - 2| = |3x + 4|$$
$$(x - 2)^2 = (3x + 4)^2$$
Now expand and simplify:
$$x^2 - 4x + 4 = 9x^2 + 24x + 16$$
$$8x^2 + 28x + 12 = 0$$
$$2x^2 + 7x + 3 = 0$$
$$(2x + 1)(x + 3) = 0$$
So the solutions are: $\mathbf{x = -\frac{1}{2}}$ and $\mathbf{x = -3}$

You can also use these methods to solve **modulus inequalities**. Since you often end up **solving a quadratic** in this kind of question, the **graphical method** from p.24 is pretty darn useful.
Another useful rule is that:
$|x - a| < b \Leftrightarrow a - b < x < a + b$

discriminant:
$b^2 - 4ac > 0$ 2 solutions
$b^2 - 4ac < 0$ no solutions
$b^2 - 4ac = 0$ 1 solution.

Practice Questions

Q1 a) For the function $f(x) = 2x - 1$, $x \in \mathbb{R}$, sketch the graphs of:
(i) $y = |f(x)|$ (ii) $y = f(|x|)$
b) Hence, or otherwise, solve the equation $|2x - 1| = 5$.

Q2 Find the range of values of x that satisfy:
a) $|x| < 4$ b) $|2x| > 12$ c) $|x + 3| \leq 3$

Exam Questions

Q1 Solve the equation $3|-x - 6| = x + 12$. [3 marks]

Q2 a) Show that the equation $|2x + 1| = |x - k|$ can be transformed into the quadratic equation $3x^2 + (4 + 2k)x + (1 - k^2) = 0$. [3 marks]
b) Hence find the value(s) of k for which $|2x + 1| = |x - k|$ has exactly one solution. [4 marks]

My name is Modulus Functionas Meridius...

So if the effect of the modulus is to make a negative positive, I guess that means that |exam followed by detention followed by getting splashed by a car| = sleep-in followed by picnic followed by date with Hugh Jackman. I wish.

Graphs of Functions

A picture speaks a thousand words... and graphs are as close as you're going to get in maths. They're dead useful for getting your head round tricky questions, and time spent learning how to sketch graphs is time well spent.

The graph of $y = kx^n$ is a different **Shape** for different **k** and **n**

Usually, you only need a **rough** sketch of a graph — so just knowing the basic shapes of these graphs will do.

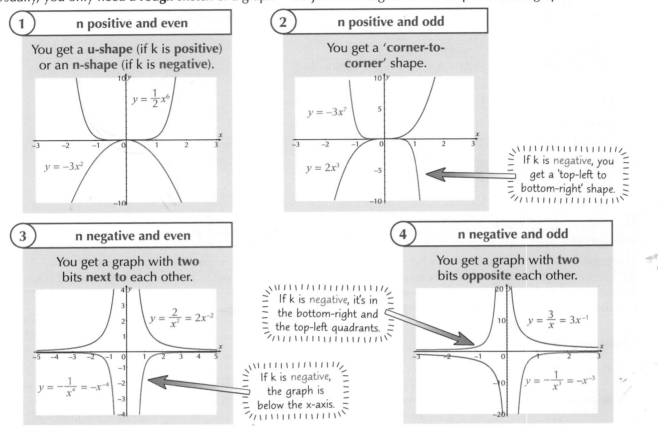

① n positive and even

You get a **u-shape** (if k is **positive**) or an **n-shape** (if k is **negative**).

$y = \frac{1}{2}x^6$

$y = -3x^2$

② n positive and odd

You get a **'corner-to-corner'** shape.

$y = -3x^7$

$y = 2x^3$

If k is negative, you get a 'top-left to bottom-right' shape.

③ n negative and even

You get a graph with **two** bits **next to** each other.

$y = \frac{2}{x^2} = 2x^{-2}$

$y = -\frac{1}{x^4} = -x^{-4}$

If k is negative, the graph is below the x-axis.

④ n negative and odd

You get a graph with **two** bits **opposite** each other.

If k is negative, it's in the bottom-right and the top-left quadrants.

$y = \frac{3}{x} = 3x^{-1}$

$y = -\frac{1}{x^3} = -x^{-3}$

An **asymptote** of a curve is a **line** which the curve gets **infinitely close** to, but **never touches**. So graphs 3 and 4 both have asymptotes at $x = 0$ and $y = 0$.

Find where the curve **Crosses** the **x-axis** to sketch **Quartics**

A **quartic** has an x^4 term as the highest power. If you're asked to sketch one of these it's likely to be **factorised**, so you can easily work out where it **crosses** or **touches** the x-axis. Then you can figure out what the curve looks like.

Quartics with **positive coefficients** of x^4 are always positive for **very** positive and negative values of x. For **negative coefficients** of x^4 the curve is negative for **very** positive and negative x-values — this is similar to quadratics.

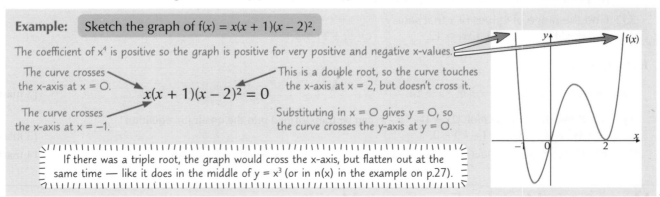

Example: Sketch the graph of $f(x) = x(x + 1)(x - 2)^2$.

The coefficient of x^4 is positive so the graph is positive for very positive and negative x-values.

The curve crosses the x-axis at $x = 0$.

$x(x + 1)(x - 2)^2 = 0$

This is a double root, so the curve touches the x-axis at $x = 2$, but doesn't cross it.

The curve crosses the x-axis at $x = -1$.

Substituting in $x = 0$ gives $y = 0$, so the curve crosses the y-axis at $y = 0$.

If there was a triple root, the graph would cross the x-axis, but flatten out at the same time — like it does in the middle of $y = x^3$ (or in n(x) in the example on p.27).

Graphs of Functions

There are **Four** main **Graph Transformations**

You'll have come across graph transformations before — **translations** (adding things to **shift** the graph vertically or horizontally) and **reflections** in the x- or y- axis. You also need to know **stretches** (either vertical or horizontal). Each transformation has the same effect on any function — here they're applied to $f(x) = \sin x$:

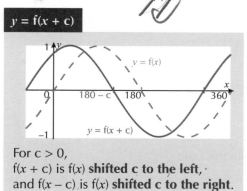

$y = f(x + c)$

For $c > 0$,
$f(x + c)$ is $f(x)$ **shifted c to the left**,
and $f(x - c)$ is $f(x)$ **shifted c to the right**.

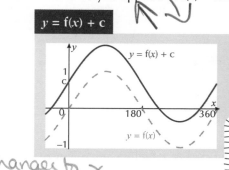

$y = f(x) + c$

For $c > 0$, $f(x) + c$ is
$f(x)$ **shifted c upwards**,
and $f(x) - c$ is
$f(x)$ **shifted c downwards**.

Don't forget to shift any asymptotes as well — e.g. the graph of $y = \dfrac{1}{x + a} + b$ has asymptotes at $y = b$ and $x = -a$.

changes to x.

Reflections in the x-axis flip f(x) vertically and reflections in the y-axis flip f(x) horizontally.

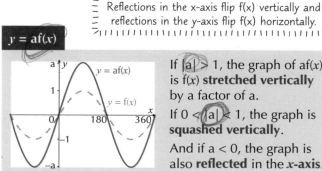

$y = af(x)$

If $|a| > 1$, the graph of $af(x)$
is $f(x)$ **stretched vertically**
by a factor of a.
If $0 < |a| < 1$, the graph is
squashed vertically.
And if $a < 0$, the graph is
also **reflected** in the x-axis.

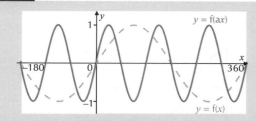

$y = f(ax)$

If $|a| > 1$, the graph of $f(ax)$ is $f(x)$
squashed horizontally by a factor of a.
If $0 < |a| < 1$, the graph is **stretched horizontally**.
And if $a < 0$, the graph is also **reflected** in the y-axis.

A squash by a factor of a is really a stretch by a factor of $\dfrac{1}{a}$.

$\dfrac{1}{2}f(2 \times \text{orange}) =$

Do **Combinations** of transformations **One at a Time**

Combinations of transformations can look a bit tricky, but if you take them **one step** at a time they're not too bad. Don't do **all** the transformations at once — break it up into **separate bits** (as above) and draw a **graph** for **each stage**.

Example: The graph below shows the function $y = f(x)$. Draw the graph of $y = 3f(x + 2)$, showing the coordinates of the turning points.

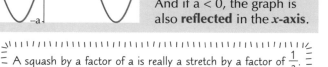

Don't try to do everything at once. First draw the graph of $y = f(x + 2)$ and work out the coordinates of the turning points.

Now use your graph of $y = f(x + 2)$ to draw the graph of $y = 3f(x + 2)$.

Make sure you do the transformations the right way round — you should do the bit in the brackets first.

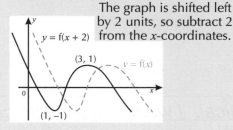

The graph is shifted left by 2 units, so subtract 2 from the x-coordinates.

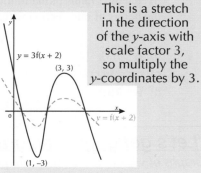

This is a stretch in the direction of the y-axis with scale factor 3, so multiply the y-coordinates by 3.

Section 2 — Algebra and Functions

Graphs of Functions

Practice Questions

Q1 Four graphs, A, B, C and D, are shown below. Match each of the following functions to one of the graphs.

a) $y = \dfrac{4}{x^4}$ b) $y = -3x^6$ c) $y = -1.5x^3$ d) $y = \dfrac{2}{3x}$

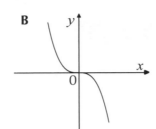 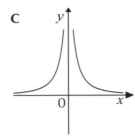 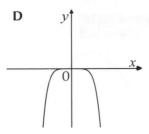

Q2 Sketch the following curves, labelling any points of intersection with the axes:

a) $y = -2x^4$ b) $y = \dfrac{7}{x^2}$ c) $y = -5x^3$ d) $y = -\dfrac{2}{x^5}$

Q3 Sketch the graph of $y = f(x)$, where $f(x) = x^2(x + 3)^2$.

Q4 The function $y = f(x)$ is shown on the graph below.

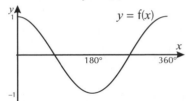

Sketch the graphs of the following:

a) $y = \dfrac{1}{4}f(x)$ b) $y = 2f(x) + 1$ c) $y = f(3(x + 180))$

Exam Questions

Q1 $f(x) = (1 - x)(x + 4)^3$

Sketch the graph of $y = f(x)$, labelling the points where the curve intersects the x- and y-axes.   [4 marks]

Q2 The graph below shows the curve $y = f(x)$, and the intercepts of the curve with the x- and y-axes.

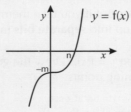

Sketch the graphs of the following transformations on separate axes, clearly labelling the points of intersection with the x- and y-axes in terms of m and n.

a) $y = f(3x)$ [2 marks]

b) $y = |f(x)|$ [2 marks]

c) $y = -3f(x)$ [2 marks]

d) $y = f(|x|)$ [2 marks]

"Let's get graphical, graphical. I want to get graphical"...

Graphs of $y = kx^n$ and quartics are probably less likely to come up than quadratics or cubics. But if you're struggling to remember the right shape of any graph, test different x-values (e.g. positive values, negative values, values either side of any roots). For graph transformations you might find it useful to remember that stuff outside the brackets affects $f(x)$ vertically and stuff inside affects $f(x)$ horizontally. Now get out there and get sketching (graphs).

Proportion

Variables that are in proportion are closely related. Think of this page as like a daytime TV DNA test for variables.

Direct Proportion graphs are Straight Lines through the Origin

If two variables are in **direct proportion**, it means that changing one variable will change the other by the same scale factor. So multiplying or dividing by **any** constant will have the same effect on both variables.
To say that "y is directly proportional to x", you can write:

$$y \propto x$$ which is equivalent to writing $$y = kx$$

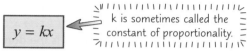
k is sometimes called the constant of proportionality.

Example: The circumference of a circle, C, is directly proportional to its radius, r.
 a) Find the constant of proportionality and sketch the graph of C against r.
 b) A circle with a radius of p cm has a circumference of 13 cm.
    Find the circumference of a circle with a radius of $2.5p$ cm.

$y = kx$ is a straight line with gradient k that passes through the origin (O, O).

a) The circumference of a circle is given by $2\pi r$:
   $C \propto r$ means $C = kr$. So $kr = 2\pi r \Rightarrow k = 2\pi$

The graph is a straight line through the origin with gradient 2π:

b) You can do this without using the circumference formula. The radius of the second circle is 2.5 times the size of the first so the circumference will be 2.5 times the first as well:
   $C = 2.5 \times 13 = \mathbf{32.5}$ **cm**

Inverse Proportion graphs are of the form y = k / x

If two variables are in **inverse proportion**, it means that changing one variable will change the other by the **reciprocal** of the scale factor. So **multiplying** one variable by **any** constant is the same as **dividing** the other by the same constant.
Saying that "y is inversely proportional to x" is the same as saying "y is directly proportional to $\frac{1}{x}$", so you can write:

$$y \propto \frac{1}{x}$$ which is equivalent to writing $$y = \frac{k}{x}$$

k is still the constant of proportionality.

Example: The pressure of a gas, P N/m², is modelled as being inversely proportional to the volume of its container, v m³.
 a) A container with volume 12 m³ contains a gas with pressure 0.125 N/m². Find the constant of proportionality.
 b) Sketch the graph of P against v.

a) $P \propto \frac{1}{v}$ is the same as saying $P = \frac{k}{v}$.

   Use the values from the question:
   When $v = 12$, $P = 0.125$, so $0.125 = \frac{k}{12}$
   $\Rightarrow k = 0.125 \times 12 = \mathbf{1.5}$

b) $P = \frac{1.5}{v}$ is of the form $P = kv^n$
   with $k = 1.5$ and $n = -1$ (see p.30).
   But volume cannot be negative so you only need positive values of v.

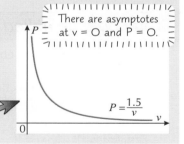

There are asymptotes at v = O and P = O.

Practice Questions

Q1 If m is directly proportional to n and $m = 12$ when $n = 3$, find the constant of proportionality, k.

Q2 If p is inversely proportional to q and $p = 3$ when $q = 5$, find the constant of proportionality, k.

Exam Question

Q1 After a storm, the area of a small island was reduced by erosion in the following years. The area, A km², of the island is modelled as being inversely proportional to t, the time in years since the storm, for $t \geq 1$.
 a) 5.5 years after the storm, the area of the island was 2.6 km². Find the constant of proportionality, k. [1 mark]
 b) Sketch the graph of t against A, stating the equations of any asymptotes. [2 marks]
 c) Suggest one reason why this model has the restriction $t \geq 1$. [1 mark]

Time spent checking your phone is inversely proportional to exam marks...

Watch out for other proportion relationships — e.g. you might come across relations such as $y \propto x^2$ or $y \propto 1/\sqrt{x}$.

Composite and Inverse Functions

A mapping takes one number and transforms it into another — e.g. 'multiply by 5', 'square root' and 'divide by 7' are all mappings. Sadly they have more to do with functions than drawing a map with rivers, mountains and secret tunnels.

A **Function** is a type of **Mapping**

1) A **function** is an operation that takes numbers and **maps** each one to only one number — e.g. x^2 is written $f(x) = x^2$ or $f : x \to x^2$.

2) The set of starting numbers is the **domain** and the numbers they become is the **range** (or **image**).

3) The domain and/or range is often the set of **real numbers**, $\mathbb{R}$ (any number, fraction, surd etc.). If x can take **any real value** it's usually written $x \in \mathbb{R}$.

4) A **one-to-one** function maps **one** element in the **domain** to **one** element in the **range**.

5) A **many-to-one** function maps **more than one** element in the **domain** to **one** element in the **range**.

6) **One-to-many** mappings can take an element in the domain to **more than one** element in the range (e.g. 'take the square root' could map 1 to +1 or –1) — so by definition, they're **not functions**.

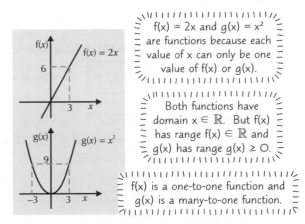

$f(x) = 2x$ and $g(x) = x^2$ are functions because each value of x can only be one value of $f(x)$ or $g(x)$.

Both functions have domain $x \in \mathbb{R}$. But $f(x)$ has range $f(x) \in \mathbb{R}$ and $g(x)$ has range $g(x) \geq 0$.

$f(x)$ is a one-to-one function and $g(x)$ is a many-to-one function.

Functions can be **Combined** to make a **Composite Function**

1) If you have two functions f and g, you can **combine** them (do one followed by the other) to make a new function. This is called a **composite function**.

2) Composite functions are written $fg(x)$ — this means do g first, then f. **Brackets** can be handy here, so $fg(x) = f(g(x))$. The **order** is really important — usually $fg(x) \neq gf(x)$.

3) If you get a composite function that's written $f^2(x)$, it means $ff(x)$ — you do f **twice**.

Composite functions made up of more than two functions work in the same way.

> **Example:** For the functions $f : x \to 2x^3 \ \{x \in \mathbb{R}\}$ and $g: x \to x - 3 \ \{x \in \mathbb{R}\}$, find:
> a) $fg(4)$ b) $gf(4)$ c) $fg(x)$ d) $f^2(x)$.

From parts a) and b) you can see that $fg(4) \neq gf(4)$.

a) $fg(4) = f(g(4)) = f(4 - 3) = f(1) = 2 \times 1^3 = \mathbf{2}$

b) $gf(4) = g(f(4)) = g(2 \times 4^3) = g(128) = 128 - 3 = \mathbf{125}$

c) $fg(x) = f(g(x)) = f(x - 3) = \mathbf{2(x - 3)^3}$

d) $f^2(x) = f(f(x)) = f(2x^3) = 2(2x^3)^3 = \mathbf{16x^9}$

You could be asked to **Solve** a **Composite Function Equation**

If you're asked to **solve** an equation involving a composite function, such as $fg(x) = 8$, start by finding $fg(x)$.

> **Example:** For the functions $f : x \to \sqrt{x}$, domain $\{x \geq 0\}$ and $g : x \to \dfrac{1}{x - 1}$, domain $\{x > 1\}$, solve $fg(x) = \dfrac{1}{2}$ and state the range of $fg(x)$, giving your answer in set notation.

$\sqrt{x}$ means the positive root, so f is a function.

First, find $fg(x)$: $\quad fg(x) = f\left(\dfrac{1}{x - 1}\right) = \sqrt{\dfrac{1}{x - 1}} = \dfrac{1}{\sqrt{x - 1}}$

$\qquad\qquad\qquad$ So $\dfrac{1}{\sqrt{x - 1}} = \dfrac{1}{2}$

Rearrange this equation to find x:

$$\dfrac{1}{\sqrt{x - 1}} = \dfrac{1}{2} \Rightarrow \sqrt{x - 1} = 2 \Rightarrow x - 1 = 4 \Rightarrow x = 5$$

You can see the range of $fg(x)$ from the graph.

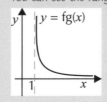
$y = fg(x)$

The range is $fg(x) > 0$. In set notation, that's $\{fg(x) : fg(x) > 0\}$

The domain of $fg(x)$ is $x > 1$ or $\{x : x > 1\}$.

Only **One-to-One Functions** have **Inverses**

1) An **inverse function** does the **opposite** to the function. For a function $f(x)$, the inverse is written $\mathbf{f^{-1}(x)}$.

2) An inverse function **maps** an element in the **range** to an element in the **domain** — the opposite of a function. This means that only **one-to-one functions** have inverses, otherwise it wouldn't be a function by definition.

3) For **any** inverse $f^{-1}(x)$, doing the function and then the inverse is the same as doing the inverse then doing the function — both just give you x.

$\boxed{f^{-1}f(x) = x = ff^{-1}(x)}$

4) The **domain** of the **inverse** is the **range** of the **function**, and the **range** of the **inverse** is the **domain** of the **function**.

Composite and Inverse Functions

Work out the *Inverse Function* using *Algebra*

For **simple** functions it's easy to work out what the inverse is just by **looking** at it — e.g. $f(x) = x + 1$ has the inverse $f^{-1}(x) = x - 1$. But for more **complex** functions, you need to **rearrange** the original function to **change** the **subject**.

Example: Find the inverse of the function $f(x) = 3x^2 + 2$ with domain $x \geq 0$, and state its domain and range.

1) First, replace $f(x)$ with y — its easier to work with than $f(x)$:
$$y = 3x^2 + 2$$

2) Rearrange the equation to make x the subject:
$$y - 2 = 3x^2 \Rightarrow \frac{y-2}{3} = x^2 \Rightarrow \sqrt{\frac{y-2}{3}} = x$$
$x \geq 0$ so you don't need the negative square root.

3) Replace x with $f^{-1}(x)$ and y with x:
$$f^{-1}(x) = \sqrt{\frac{x-2}{3}}$$

4) Swap the domain and range:
The range of $f(x)$ is $f(x) \geq 2$,
so $f^{-1}(x)$ has domain $x \geq 2$ and range $f^{-1}(x) \geq 0$.

You might have to *Draw the Graph* of the *Inverse*

The inverse of a function is its **reflection** in the line $y = x$.

Example: Sketch the graph of the inverse of the function $f(x) = x^2 - 8$ with domain $x \geq 0$.

It's easy to see what the domains and ranges are from the graph — $f(x)$ has domain $x \geq 0$ and range $f(x) \geq -8$, and $f^{-1}(x)$ has domain $x \geq -8$ and range $f^{-1}(x) \geq 0$.

1. Draw $f(x)$

2. Then draw $y = x$

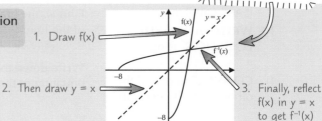

The inverse function is $f^{-1}(x) = \sqrt{x + 8}$.

3. Finally, reflect $f(x)$ in $y = x$ to get $f^{-1}(x)$

Practice Questions

Q1 For each pair of functions f and g, find fg(2), gf(1) and fg(x).
   a) $f(x) = \frac{3}{x}$, $x > 0$ and $g(x) = 2x + 3$, $x \in \mathbb{R}$
   b) $f(x) = 3x^2$, $x \geq 0$ and $g(x) = x + 4$, $x \in \mathbb{R}$

Q2 A one-to-one function f has domain $x \in \mathbb{R}$ and range $f(x) \geq 3$.
   Does this function have an inverse? If so, state its domain and range.

Q3 Using algebra, find the inverse of the function $f(x) = \sqrt{2x - 4}$, $x \geq 2$.
   State the domain and range of the inverse in set notation.

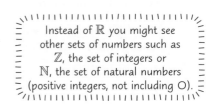

Instead of $\mathbb{R}$ you might see other sets of numbers such as $\mathbb{Z}$, the set of integers or $\mathbb{N}$, the set of natural numbers (positive integers, not including O).

Exam Questions

Q1 The functions f and g are given by: $f(x) = x^2 - 3$, $x \in \mathbb{R}$ and $g(x) = \frac{1}{x}$, $x \in \mathbb{R}$, $x \neq 0$.
   a) Find an expression for gf(x). [2 marks]
   b) Solve $gf(x) = \frac{1}{6}$ [1 mark]

Q2 The function $f(x)$ is defined as follows: $f : x \rightarrow \frac{1}{x + 5}$, domain $x > -5$.
   a) State the range of $f(x)$. [1 mark]
   b) (i) Find the inverse function, $f^{-1}(x)$. [3 marks]
      (ii) State the domain and range of $f^{-1}(x)$. [2 marks]
   c) On the same axes, sketch the graphs of $y = f(x)$ and $y = f^{-1}(x)$. [2 marks]

Inverses — putting the 'nuf' in functions since 1877...

Sorry for making functions more confusing than what you're used to — it's the exam board's fault, honestly. Just make sure you know how to find the domain and range and understand what the notation means. The rest of it isn't so bad, but have a good practice anyway — functions definitely fall into the 'completely forgot what that means' category.

Geometry of Lines and Circles

You need to know about a billion things about lines, midpoints, circles, equations — all manner of geometrical goodies.
Okay, maybe not quite a billion, but enough to fill four whole pages, and that's more than enough for me.

Finding the **Equation of a Line**

You need to know three different ways of writing the equation of a straight line:

$$y - y_1 = m(x - x_1)$$ $$y = mx + c$$ $$ax + by + c = 0$$ where *a*, *b* and *c* are **integers**

You might be asked to write the equation of a line in **any** of these forms — but they're all similar.
Basically, if you find an equation in one form, you can easily **convert** it into either of the others.

The Easiest to find is **y − y₁ = m(x − x₁)**...

Equations of Lines

1) **LABEL** the points (x_1, y_1) and (x_2, y_2).
2) **GRADIENT** — find it and call it *m*.
3) **WRITE DOWN THE EQUATION** using $y - y_1 = m(x - x_1)$.
4) **CONVERT** to one of the other forms, if necessary.

Example: Find the equation of the line that passes through the points (–3, 10) and (1, 4), in the form $y - y_1 = m(x - x_1)$.

Label the points: $(x_1, y_1) = (-3, 10)$ and $(x_2, y_2) = (1, 4)$
It doesn't matter which way round you label them.

Find *m*, the gradient of the line: $m = \dfrac{y_2 - y_1}{x_2 - x_1} = \dfrac{4 - 10}{1 - (-3)} = \dfrac{-6}{4} = -\dfrac{3}{2}$
Be careful here — y goes on the top, x on the bottom.

Write down the equation of the line:
$$y - y_1 = m(x - x_1)$$
$$y - 10 = -\frac{3}{2}(x - (-3))$$ $x_1 = -3$ and $y_1 = 10$
$$y - 10 = -\frac{3}{2}(x + 3)$$

You might recognise this method for finding m from GCSE.

...and then you can **Rearrange**

Once you've got the equation in the form $y - y_1 = m(x - x_1)$, it's pretty easy to **convert** it to either of the other forms. Here's how you'd do it for the example above:

For the form $y = mx + c$, take **everything except the *y*** over to the right.
$$y - 10 = -\frac{3}{2}(x + 3)$$
$$\Rightarrow y = -\frac{3}{2}x - \frac{9}{2} + 10$$
$$\Rightarrow y = -\frac{3}{2}x + \frac{11}{2}$$

To find the form $ax + by + c = 0$, take **everything** over to one side — and then get rid of any fractions.
$$y = -\frac{3}{2}x + \frac{11}{2}$$
$$\Rightarrow \frac{3}{2}x + y - \frac{11}{2} = 0$$
$$\Rightarrow 3x + 2y - 11 = 0$$
a, b and c have to be integers, so multiply the whole equation by 2 to get rid of the 2s on the bottom of the fractions.

If you end up with an equation like $\frac{3}{2}x - \frac{4}{3}y + 6 = 0$, where you've got a 2 and a 3 on the bottom of the fractions, multiply everything by the lowest common multiple of 2 and 3, i.e. 6.

You can find the **Midpoint** of a **Line Segment**

A **line segment** is just a straight line that goes between two points. Since it has a beginning and an end, it also has a middle (like all good books), and you can work out the coordinates of the **midpoint** using the formula:

$$\text{Midpoint (AB)} = \left(\frac{x_A + x_B}{2}, \frac{y_A + y_B}{2} \right)$$

You could think of this formula as the mean of the x-coordinates and the mean of the y-coordinates.

Example: Find the midpoint of the line segment between (4, 3) and (–2, 5).

Use the midpoint formula: $\text{Midpoint} = \left(\dfrac{4 + (-2)}{2}, \dfrac{3 + 5}{2} \right) = \left(\dfrac{2}{2}, \dfrac{8}{2} \right) = (1, 4)$

Geometry of Lines and Circles

Use Pythagoras' Theorem to find the Length of a line segment

To find the **length** of a line segment (or the **distance between two points**), you can imagine a right-angled triangle, like in the diagram on the right. Then it's just a matter of using Pythagoras' theorem:

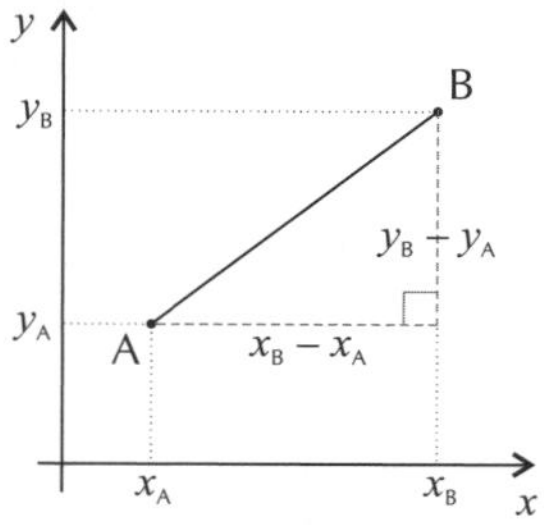

$$\text{Length (AB)} = \sqrt{(x_B - x_A)^2 + (y_B - y_A)^2}$$

Example: Find the exact length of the segment of the line with equation $y = 5x - 2$ between $x = 3$ and $x = 4$.

First, find the y-coordinates at $x = 3$ and $x = 4$:

When $x = 3$, $y = 5(3) - 2 \Rightarrow y = 15 - 2 = 13$

When $x = 4$, $y = 5(4) - 2 \Rightarrow y = 20 - 2 = 18$

So: $(x_A, y_A) = (3, 13)$ and $(x_B, y_B) = (4, 18)$

Now substitute these values into the formula:

Length $= \sqrt{(4-3)^2 + (18-13)^2} = \sqrt{1+25} = \sqrt{\mathbf{26}}$

The question says "exact", so leave it as a surd.

Pythagoras had to go to great lengths to discover his theorem.

Parallel Lines have equal Gradient

That's what makes them parallel — the fact that the gradients are the same.

Example: The equation of the line l_1 can be written as $y = \frac{3}{4}x - \frac{7}{4}$ or $3x - 4y - 7 = 0$. Find the line parallel to l_1 that passes through the point (3, –1).

Parallel lines have the same gradient.

The original equation is: $y = \frac{3}{4}x - \frac{7}{4}$

So the new equation will be: $y = \frac{3}{4}x + c$ ← We just need to find c.

We know that the line passes through (3, –1), so stick x = 3, y = –1 into the equation to find c.

At (3, –1), $-1 = \frac{3}{4} \times 3 + c \Rightarrow c = -1 - \frac{9}{4} = -\frac{13}{4}$

So the equation of the line is: $\mathbf{y = \frac{3}{4}x - \frac{13}{4}}$

Or with the ax + by + c = 0 form it's even easier:

The original line is: $3x - 4y - 7 = 0$

So the new line is: $3x - 4y + k = 0$

Then use the values of x and y at (3, –1) to find k.

$3 \times 3 - 4 \times (-1) + k = 0$

$\Rightarrow 9 + 4 + k = 0$

$\Rightarrow k = -13$

So the equation is: $\mathbf{3x - 4y - 13 = 0}$

The gradient of a Perpendicular line is –1 ÷ the Other Gradient

Finding **perpendicular** lines (or **'normals'**) is just as easy as finding parallel lines — as long as you remember the gradient of the perpendicular line is **–1 ÷ the gradient of the other one**.

Example: The equation of the line l_2 can be written as $y = \frac{1}{3}x - 1$ or $x - 3y - 3 = 0$. Find the line perpendicular to l_2 that passes through the point (–2, 4).

l_2 has equation: $y = \frac{1}{3}x - 1$

So if the equation of the new line is $y = mx + c$, then

$m = -1 \div \frac{1}{3}$

$\Rightarrow m = -3$

Since the gradient of a perpendicular line is –1 ÷ the other one.

At $x = -2$, $y = 4$: $4 = (-3) \times (-2) + c$

$\Rightarrow c = 4 - 6 = -2$

So the equation of the perpendicular line is $\mathbf{y = -3x - 2}$

Or if you start with: l_2 $x - 3y - 3 = 0$

To find a perpendicular line, swap these two numbers around, and change the sign of **one of them**. So here, 1 and –3 become 3 and 1.

So the new line has equation $3x + y + k = 0$

Or you could have used –3x – y + k = 0.

So at $x = -2$, $y = 4$: $3 \times (-2) + 4 + k = 0$

$\Rightarrow k = 2$

And so the equation of the perpendicular line is $\mathbf{3x + y + 2 = 0}$

Geometry of Lines and Circles

Equation of a circle: $(x - a)^2 + (y - b)^2 = r^2$

The equation of a circle looks complicated, but it's all based on Pythagoras' theorem.
Take a look at the circle below, with centre (6, 4) and radius 3.

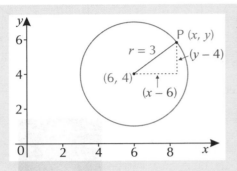

Joining a point P (x, y) on the circumference of the circle to its centre (6, 4), we can create a **right-angled triangle**.

Now let's see what happens if we use **Pythagoras' theorem**:

$$(x - 6)^2 + (y - 4)^2 = 3^2$$
$$\text{or: } (x - 6)^2 + (y - 4)^2 = 9$$

This is the equation for the circle. It's as easy as that.

In general, a circle with radius r and centre (a, b) has the equation:

$$(x - a)^2 + (y - b)^2 = r^2$$

Example: Find the centre and radius of the circle with equation $(x - 2)^2 + (y + 3)^2 = 16$.

Compare the equation... $(x - 2)^2 + (y + 3)^2 = 16$
...with the general form: $(x - a)^2 + (y - b)^2 = r^2$

So $a = 2$, $b = -3$ and $r = 4$.

So the centre (a, b) is **(2, −3)** and the radius r is **4**.

Example: Write down the equation of the circle with centre (−4, 2) and radius 6.

The question says, 'Write down...', so you know you don't need to do any working.

The centre of the circle is (−4, 2), so $a = -4$ and $b = 2$.
The radius is 6, so $r = 6$.

Using the general equation $(x - a)^2 + (y - b)^2 = r^2$
you can write: $(x + 4)^2 + (y - 2)^2 = 36$

Complete the Square to get into the Familiar Form

Not all circle equations look like $(x - a)^2 + (y - b)^2 = r^2$. If they don't, it can be a bit of a pain, because you can't immediately tell what the **radius** is or where the **centre** is. But all it takes is a bit of **rearranging**.

Example: Write the equation $x^2 + y^2 - 6x + 4y + 4 = 0$ in the form $(x - a)^2 + (y - b)^2 = r^2$.

Complete the square on the x and y terms.

Have a look at page 16 for more on completing the square.

$$x^2 + y^2 - 6x + 4y + 4 = 0$$
$$x^2 - 6x + y^2 + 4y + 4 = 0$$
$$(x - 3)^2 - 9 + (y + 2)^2 - 4 + 4 = 0$$
$$(x - 3)^2 + (y + 2)^2 = 9$$

Collect the x and y terms together...

...then find squares that give the terms you need, and add constants to balance things up.

This is the recognisable form, so the centre is **(3, −2)** and the radius is $\sqrt{9}$ = 3.

Don't forget the Properties of Circles

You will have seen the circle properties at GCSE. You'll sometimes need to dredge them up from the darkest depths of your memory for these circle questions. Here's a reminder of the ones you need to know for this course.

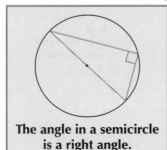

The angle in a semicircle is a right angle.

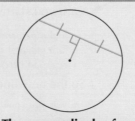

The perpendicular from the centre to a chord bisects the chord.

A radius and tangent to the same point will meet at right angles.

Bob thinks the Magic Circle rules. Bunnykin isn't so sure.

Geometry of Lines and Circles

Use the **Gradient Rule** for **Perpendicular Lines**

Remember that the tangent at a given point will be perpendicular to the radius at that same point.

Example: Point A (6, 4) lies on a circle with the equation $(x - 2)^2 + (y - 1)^2 = 25$.
Find the equation of the tangent to the circle at A.

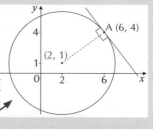

The equation of the circle tells you the centre is (2, 1).
The tangent you're interested in is at right angles to the radius at (6, 4).

The gradient of the **radius** at (6, 4) $= \dfrac{4-1}{6-2} = \dfrac{3}{4}$,

so the gradient of the **tangent** at (6, 4) $= \dfrac{-1}{\frac{3}{4}} = -\dfrac{4}{3}$.

It often helps with questions like this to use what you know at the start to sketch the graph.

So using $y - y_1 = m(x - x_1)$, the tangent at (6, 4) is: $y - 4 = -\dfrac{4}{3}(x - 6) \Rightarrow 3y - 12 = -4x + 24 \Rightarrow \mathbf{3y + 4x - 36 = 0}$

Practice Questions

Q1 Find the equations of the lines that pass through the points: a) (2, –1) and (–4, –19), b) $\left(0, -\dfrac{1}{3}\right)$ and $\left(5, \dfrac{2}{3}\right)$.
Write each answer in the forms:
(i) $y - y_1 = m(x - x_1)$, (ii) $y = mx + c$, (iii) $ax + by + c = 0$, where a, b and c are integers.

Q2 The line l has equation $y = \dfrac{3}{2}x - \dfrac{2}{3}$. Find the equation of the line parallel to l, going through the point (4, 2).

Q3 The line k passes through the point (6, 1) and is perpendicular to $2x - y - 7 = 0$. What is the equation of k?

Q4 The coordinates of points R and S are (–8, 15) and (10, 3) respectively. Find, in the form $y = mx + c$, the equation of the line perpendicular to RS, passing through the midpoint of RS.

Q5 Write the equation of the circle with centre (3, –1) and radius 7.

Q6 Give the radius and the coordinates of the centre of the circles with the following equations:
a) $x^2 + y^2 = 9$ b) $(x - 2)^2 + (y + 4)^2 = 4$ c) $x(x + 6) = y(8 - y)$

Exam Questions

Q1 The line segment PQ has equation $4x + 3y = 15$, where P has coordinates $(0, p)$ and Q has coordinates $(q, -3)$.
a) Find: (i) the gradient of PQ, (ii) the length of PQ. [3 marks]
b) The point R is the midpoint of PQ. Find the equation of the line which passes through the point R and is perpendicular to PQ, giving your answer in the form $y = mx + c$. [3 marks]

Q2 The line l passes through the point S $(7, -3)$ and has gradient -2.
a) Find an equation of l, giving your answer in the form $y = mx + c$. [2 marks]
b) The point T has coordinates (5, 1). Show that T lies on l. [1 mark]

Q3 The points J and K have coordinates (–1, 4) and (5, 8) respectively. The line l_1 passes through the midpoint, L, of the line segment JK, and is perpendicular to JK, as shown.
a) Find an equation for l_1 in the form $ax + by + c = 0$, where a, b, and c are integers. [5 marks]
The line l_1 intersects the y-axis at the point M and the x-axis at the point N.
b) Find the coordinates of M. [2 marks]
c) Find the coordinates of N. [2 marks]

Q4 C is a circle with the equation: $x^2 + y^2 - 2x - 10y + 21 = 0$.
a) Find the centre and radius of C. [5 marks]
b) The line joining P $(3, 6)$ and Q $(q, 4)$ is a diameter of C. Show that $q = -1$. [3 marks]
c) Find the equation of the tangent to C at Q, giving your answer in the form $ax + by + c = 0$, where a, b and c are integers. [3 marks]

A Geometry of Lines and Circles, Book 1 — A Game of Maths...

Well, that sure was a lot of geometry to deal with. Just make sure you've got all of these formulas and properties committed to memory for the exam. After all, when you play the Game of Maths, you win or you get no marks.

Parametric Equations

Parametric equations seem a bit weird to start with, but they're actually pretty clever. You can use them to replace one horrifically complicated equation with two fairly normal-looking ones. I bet that's just what you always wanted...

Parametric Equations split up x and y into Separate Equations

Normally, graphs in the (x, y) plane are described using a **Cartesian equation** — a single equation linking x and y.

Sometimes, particularly for more **complicated** graphs, it's easier to have two linked equations, called **parametric equations**.

In parametric equations, x and y are each **defined separately** in terms of a **third variable**, called a **parameter**. The parameter is usually either t or θ.

Example: Sketch the graph given by the parametric equations $x = t + 1$ and $y = t^2 - 1$.

Start by making a **table of coordinates**.
Choose some values for t and calculate x and y at these values.

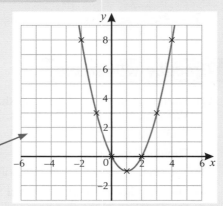

t	-3	-2	-1	0	1	2	3
x	-2	-1	0	1	2	3	4
y	8	3	0	-1	0	3	8

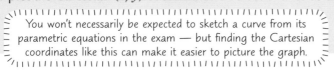

$x = -2 + 1 = -1$, and $y = (-2)^2 - 1 = 3$

$x = 1 + 1 = 2$, and $y = 1^2 - 1 = 0$

Now plot the **Cartesian** (x, y) **coordinates** on a set of axes as usual.

You won't necessarily be expected to sketch a curve from its parametric equations in the exam — but finding the Cartesian coordinates like this can make it easier to picture the graph.

You can use the parametric equations of a graph to find **coordinates** of points on the graph, and to find the value of the **parameter** for given **x- or y-coordinates**.

Example: A curve is defined by the parametric equations $x = 2t - 3$ and $y = \frac{1}{3t}$, $t \neq 0$.

a) Find the x- and y- values of the point the curve passes through when $t = 4$.

b) What value of t corresponds to the point where $y = 9$?

c) What is the value of y when $x = -15$?

Nothing to this question — just sub the right values into the right equations and you're away:

Use the equation for x to find t first, then use that value of t in the other equation to find y.

a) When $t = 4$, $x = 8 - 3 = 5$, and $y = \frac{1}{12}$

b) $9 = \frac{1}{3t} \Rightarrow t = \frac{1}{27}$

c) $-15 = 2t - 3 \Rightarrow t = -6 \Rightarrow y = -\frac{1}{18}$

Circles can be given by Parametric Equations too

You saw the **Cartesian equations** of circles on page 38, but now you get to use their **parametric equations**.

A circle with **centre (0, 0)** and **radius** r is defined by the parametric equations $x = r \cos \theta$ and $y = r \sin \theta$ and a circle with **centre (a, b)** and **radius** r is defined by the parametric equations $x = r \cos \theta + a$ and $y = r \sin \theta + b$.

Examples: Sketch the graph given by the equations $x = 4 \cos \theta$ and $y = 4 \sin \theta$.

This is a circle with radius 4 and centre (0, 0).

Sketch the graph given by the equations $x = 3 \cos \theta + 1$ and $y = 3 \sin \theta + 2$.

This is a circle with radius 3 and centre (1, 2).

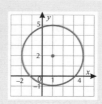

If the values of r are **different** in each equation, you'll get an **ellipse** instead of a circle.
For example, the ellipse given by $x = 2 \cos \theta$ and $y = 3 \sin \theta$ will be 4 units wide and 6 units tall.

Parametric Equations

Use *Parametric Equations* to find where graphs *Intersect*

You might have to find points where a parametric equation **intersects** another line.

Example: The curve shown in the sketch on the right has the parametric equations $x = 4t^2 - 1$ and $y = t^3 - t$.
Find the coordinates of the points where the graph crosses:
a) the x-axis,   b) the line $8y = 3x + 3$.

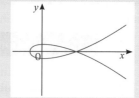

Part a) is pretty straightforward. You've got the y-coordinates already:

a) On the x-axis, $y = 0$.

Use the parametric equation for y to find the values of t where the graph crosses the x-axis:

So: $0 = t^3 - t$ $\Rightarrow$ $t(t^2 - 1) = 0$
$\Rightarrow$ $t(t + 1)(t - 1) = 0$
$\Rightarrow$ $t = 0, t = -1, t = 1$

Now use those values to find the x-coordinates:

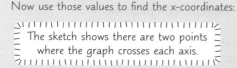
The sketch shows there are two points where the graph crosses each axis.

$t = 0$ $\Rightarrow$ $x = 4(0)^2 - 1 = -1$
$t = -1$ $\Rightarrow$ $x = 4(-1)^2 - 1 = 3$
$t = 1$ $\Rightarrow$ $x = 4(1)^2 - 1 = 3$

$t = -1$ and $t = 1$ give the same coordinates — that's where the curve crosses over itself.

So the graph crosses the x-axis at the points **(–1, 0)** and **(3, 0)**.

Part b) is just a little trickier. First, sub the parametric equations into $8y = 3x + 3$:

b) $8y = 3x + 3$ $\Rightarrow$ $8(t^3 - t) = 3(4t^2 - 1) + 3$

Rearrange and factorise to find the values of t you need:

$\Rightarrow$ $8t^3 - 8t = 12t^2$ $\Rightarrow$ $8t^3 - 12t^2 - 8t = 0$

$\Rightarrow$ $4t(2t + 1)(t - 2) = 0$ $\Rightarrow$ $t = 0, t = -\frac{1}{2}, t = 2$

Go back to the parametric equations to find the x- and y-coordinates:

$t = 0$ $\Rightarrow$ $x = -1, y = 0$
$t = -\frac{1}{2}$ $\Rightarrow$ $x = 4\left(-\frac{1}{2}\right)^2 - 1 = 0, y = \left(-\frac{1}{2}\right)^3 + \frac{1}{2} = \frac{3}{8}$
$t = 2$ $\Rightarrow$ $x = 4(2)^2 - 1 = 15, y = 2^3 - 2 = 6$

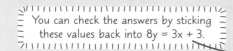
You can check the answers by sticking these values back into $8y = 3x + 3$.

So the graph crosses the line $8y = 3x + 3$
at the points **(–1, 0)**, $\left(\mathbf{0, \frac{3}{8}}\right)$, **(15, 6)**.

To find the points where the graph crosses the y-axis, you'd find the values of t where x = 0, then use them find the corresponding y-values.

Practice Questions

Q1 A curve is defined by the parametric equations $x = \frac{6-t}{2}$ and $y = 2t^2 + t + 4$.
a) Find the values of x and y when $t = 0, 1, 2$ and 3.
b) What are the values of t when: (i) $x = -7$,   (ii) $y = 19$?

Q2 For the following circles, write down the radius and the coordinates of the centre:
a) The circle given by the parametric equations $x = 7 \cos \theta$ and $y = 7 \sin \theta$.
b) The circle given by the parametric equations $x = 5 \cos \theta + 2$ and $y = 5 \sin \theta - 1$.

Q3 A curve has parametric equations $x = t^2 - 1$ and $y = 4 + \frac{3}{t}$, $t \neq 0$.
What are the coordinates of the points where this curve crosses: a) the y-axis, b) the line $x + 2y = 14$?

Exam Question

Q1 Curve C has parametric equations $x = t^3 + t$, $y = t^2 - 2t + 2$.
a) K is a point on C, and has the coordinates $(a, 1)$. Find the value of a.   [2 marks]
b) The line $8y = x + 6$ passes through C at points K, L and M.
Find the coordinates of L and M, given that the x-coordinate of M is greater than the x-coordinate of L.   [6 marks]

Time to make like x and y in a set of parametric equations, and split...

You quite often get given a sketch of the curve that the parametric equations define. Don't forget that the sketch can be useful for checking your answers — if the curve crosses the x-axis twice, and you've only found one x-coordinate for when y = 0, you know something's gone a bit pear-shaped and you should go back and sort it out, sunshine.

More on Parametric Equations

Now that you've learnt a bit about parametric equations and how great they are...
...here's a page about how to get rid of them.

Rearrange *Parametric Equations to get the* Cartesian Equation

Some parametric equations can be converted into **Cartesian equations**. There are **two main ways** to do this:

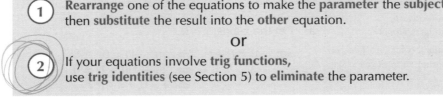

> **To Convert Parametric Equations to a Cartesian Equation:**
>
> (1) **Rearrange** one of the equations to make the **parameter** the **subject,** then **substitute** the result into the **other** equation.
>
> or
>
> (2) If your equations involve **trig functions,** use **trig identities** (see Section 5) to **eliminate** the parameter.

You can use the first method to combine the parametrics used in the examples on page 40:

Example: Give the Cartesian equations, in the form $y = f(x)$, of the curves represented by the following pairs of parametric equations:

 a) $x = t + 1$ and $y = t^2 - 1$, b) $x = 2t - 3$ and $y = \dfrac{1}{3t}$, $t \neq 0$.

a) You want the answer in the form $y = f(x)$, so leave y alone for now, and **rearrange** the equation for x to make t the subject: ⟶ $x = t + 1 \Rightarrow t = x - 1$

Now you can **eliminate** t from the equation for y: ⟶ $y = t^2 - 1 \Rightarrow y = (x-1)^2 - 1 = x^2 - 2x + 1 - 1$
$$\Rightarrow y = x^2 - 2x$$

b) **Rearrange** the equation for x to make t the subject: ⟶ $x = 2t - 3 \Rightarrow t = \dfrac{x+3}{2}$

Eliminate t from the equation for y: ⟶ $y = \dfrac{1}{3t} \Rightarrow y = \dfrac{1}{3\left(\dfrac{x+3}{2}\right)}$

$$\Rightarrow y = \dfrac{1}{\dfrac{3(x+3)}{2}} \Rightarrow y = \dfrac{2}{3x+9}$$

If there are Trig Functions... use Trig Identities

Things get a little trickier when the likes of sin and cos decide to put in an appearance:

Example: A curve has parametric equations
$$x = 1 + \sin\theta, \quad y = 1 - \cos 2\theta$$
Give the Cartesian equation of the curve in the form $y = f(x)$.

Trigmund, Trigby, Trigor, Triguel and Trigourney tried to conceal their identities.

If you try to make θ the subject of these equations, things will just get **messy**. The trick is to find a way to get both x and y in terms of the same **trig function**. You can get $\sin\theta$ into the equation for y using the **identity** $\cos 2\theta \equiv 1 - 2\sin^2\theta$:
$$y = 1 - \cos 2\theta$$
$$= 1 - (1 - 2\sin^2\theta) = 2\sin^2\theta$$

Rearranging the equation for x gives:

$\sin\theta = x - 1$, so $y = 2\sin^2\theta$

> If one of the parametric equations includes $\cos 2\theta$ or $\sin 2\theta$, that's probably the one you need to substitute — so make sure you know the **double angle formulas** (see p.71).

$$\Rightarrow y = 2(x-1)^2$$
$$\Rightarrow y = 2x^2 - 4x + 2$$

The equation is only valid for $0 \leq x \leq 2$, due to the range of $\sin\theta$ (i.e. $-1 \leq \sin\theta \leq 1$).

More on Parametric Equations

Parametric Equations are used in **Modelling**

Sometimes it makes sense to use parametric equations to model a real-life situation. For example, if you're modelling the movement of an object, you can use the parameter t to show how its x- and y-coordinates change with time.

Example: A flying disc is thrown from the point $(0, 0)$. After t seconds, it has travelled x m horizontally and y m vertically, modelled by the parametric equations $x = t^2 + 2t$ and $y = 6t - t^2$ $(0 \leq t \leq 6)$.
 a) Find the x- and y- values of the position of the disc after 2.5 seconds.
 b) After how many seconds does the disc reach a height of 5 metres?
 c) How far above its starting point is the disc when it reaches the point $x = 24$ m?

a) **Substitute** $t = 2.5$ into the equations for x and y: $t = 2.5 \Rightarrow x = 2.5^2 + 2 \times 2.5 = 6.25 + 5 = $ **11.25**
$\Rightarrow y = 6 \times 2.5 - 2.5^2 = 15 - 6.25 = $ **8.75**

b) Now you want the value of t when $y = 5$: $5 = 6t - t^2 \Rightarrow t^2 - 6t + 5 = 0$
$\Rightarrow (t-1)(t-5) = 0$
$\Rightarrow t = $ **1 s** and $t = $ **5 s**

c) Use the equation for x to find t first: $24 = t^2 + 2t \Rightarrow t^2 + 2t - 24 = 0$
$\Rightarrow (t+6)(t-4) = 0$
$\Rightarrow t = -6$ or $t = 4$, but $0 \leq t \leq 6$, so $t = $ 4 s
Then use it in the other equation to find y: $t = 4 \Rightarrow y = 6 \times 4 - 4^2 = 24 - 16 = $ **8 m**

In the example above, the parametric equations are only **valid** for certain values of t.
The **domain** of the parameter is sometimes **restricted**, for example:

1) If the equations are modelling a situation where only certain values of the parameter make sense — e.g. to avoid negative values for time or height.

2) To avoid repeating values of x and y — e.g. if the parametric equations involve $\cos \theta$ or $\sin \theta$, the value of θ might be restricted to $-\pi \leq \theta \leq \pi$ or $0 \leq \theta \leq 2\pi$.

3) To avoid dividing by zero — e.g. in the examples on pages 40 and 42, where $y = \frac{1}{3t}$, t is restricted to $t \neq 0$ so you don't end up with zero on the bottom of the fraction.

Restrictions on the value of the parameter will, in turn, usually restrict the values of x and y. The range of a function can also restrict x and y — e.g. $-1 \leq \sin \theta \leq 1$.

Practice Questions

Q1 Find the Cartesian equation of the curve defined by the parametric equations $x = \frac{t+2}{3}$ and $y = 2t^2 - 3$.

Q2 The parametric equations of a curve are $x = 2 \sin \theta$ and $y = \cos^2 \theta + 4$, $-\frac{\pi}{2} \leq \theta \leq \frac{\pi}{2}$.
 a) What is the Cartesian equation of the curve?
 b) What restrictions are there on the values of x for this curve?

Q3 Curve C is defined by the parametric equations $x = \frac{\sin \theta}{3}$ and $y = 3 + 2 \cos 2\theta$. Find the Cartesian equation of C.

Exam Questions

Q1 A football is kicked from the point $(0, 0)$ on the surface of a flat field. After t seconds, it is modelled as having travelled x m horizontally and y m vertically from its starting point, where $x = 15t$ and $y = 20t - 5t^2$.
 a) Find the Cartesian equation for the movement of the ball. [2 marks]
 b) How far is the ball from its starting point after 2 seconds? [2 marks]
 c) The model is valid for $0 \leq t \leq 4$. Suggest why it is not valid for values of t outside this range. [2 marks]

Q2 The parametric equations of curve C are $x = 3 + 4 \sin \theta$, $y = \frac{1 + \cos 2\theta}{3}$, $-\frac{\pi}{2} \leq \theta \leq \frac{\pi}{2}$.
 a) Show that the Cartesian equation of C can be written $y = \frac{-x^2 + 6x + 7}{24}$. [4 marks]
 b) State the domain of values of x for the curve C. [1 mark]

Cartesy peasy, lemon squeezy...
To get a Cartesian equation, you don't always need to get the parameter on its own. If you can rearrange both equations to have the same function of the parameter on one side (e.g. t^3 or $\sin \theta$), then the other sides are equal. Remember, a Cartesian equation just has to link x and y — it doesn't always have to be in the form $y = f(x)$.

Sequences

A sequence is a list of numbers that follow a certain pattern. Sequences can be finite or infinite (infinity — oooh), and there are a couple of types you need to know about. And guess what? You have to know everything about them.

A **Sequence** can be defined by its **n^{th} Term**

You almost definitely covered this stuff at GCSE, so **no excuses** for mucking it up.
The point of all this is to show how you can work out any **value** (**the nth term**) from its **position** in the sequence (**n**).

> **Example:**   Find the nth term of the sequence 5, 8, 11, 14, 17, ...
>
>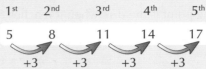
>
> Each term is **3 more** than the one before it. That means that you need to start by **multiplying n by 3**.
> Take the first term (where $n = 1$). If you multiply n by 3, you still have to **add 2** to get 5.
> The same goes for $n = 2$. To get 8 you need to multiply n by 3, then add 2.
> Every term in the sequence is worked out exactly the same way. So the nth term is **$3n + 2$**.

You can define a sequence by a **Recurrence Relation** too

Don't be put off by the fancy name — recurrence relations are pretty **easy** really.

$u_n = n^{th}$ term

> The main thing to remember is:
> u_n **just means the nth term of the sequence**

The **next term** in the sequence is u_{n+1}. You need to describe how to **work out** u_{n+1} if you're given u_n.

> **Example:**   Find the recurrence relation of the sequence 5, 8, 11, 14, 17, ...
>
> From the example above, you know that each term equals the one before it, plus 3.
> This is written like this: $u_{n+1} = u_n + 3$
> So, if $n = 5$, $u_n = u_5$ which stands for the 5th term, and $u_{n+1} = u_6$ which stands for the 6th term.
> In everyday language, $u_{n+1} = u_n + 3$ means that the sixth term equals the fifth term plus 3.
> **BUT** $u_{n+1} = u_n + 3$ on its own **isn't enough** to describe 5, 8, 11, 14, 17, ...
> For example, the sequence 87, 90, 93, 96, 99, ... **also** has each term being 3 more than the one before.
> The description needs to be more **specific**, so you've got to **give one term** in the sequence,
> as well as the recurrence relation. You almost always give the **first value**, u_1.
> Putting all of this together gives 5, 8, 11, 14, 17, ... as $u_{n+1} = u_n + 3$, $u_1 = 5$.

Arithmetic Progressions Add a Fixed Amount each time

The **first term** of an arithmetic progression is given the symbol **a**. The **amount you add** each time is called the common difference, or **d**. The **position of any term** in the sequence is called **n**.

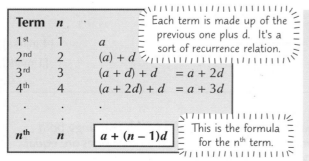

Term	n	
1st	1	a
2nd	2	$(a) + d$
3rd	3	$(a + d) + d \quad = a + 2d$
4th	4	$(a + 2d) + d \quad = a + 3d$
.	.	.
.	.	.
.	.	.
n^{th}	n	$a + (n - 1)d$

Each term is made up of the previous one plus d. It's a sort of recurrence relation.

This is the formula for the nth term.

> **Example:**   Find the 20th term of the arithmetic progression
> 2, 5, 8, 11, ... and find the formula for the nth term.
>
> Here $a = 2$ and $d = 3$. ◄——— To get d, just find the difference between two terms next to each other — e.g. $11 - 8 = 3$.
> So 20th term $= a + (20 - 1)d$
> $= 2 + 19 \times 3 = \mathbf{59}$
>
> The **general term** is the nth **term**, i.e. $a + (n - 1)d$
> $= 2 + (n - 1)3$
> $= \mathbf{3n - 1}$

Sequences

Geometric Progressions Multiply by a Constant each time

Geometric progressions work like this: the next term in the sequence is obtained by **multiplying the previous** one by a **constant value**. Couldn't be easier.

$$u_1 = a \qquad\qquad = a$$
$$u_2 = a \times r \qquad\quad = ar$$
$$u_3 = a \times r \times r \qquad = ar^2$$
$$u_4 = a \times r \times r \times r = ar^3$$

The first term (u_1) is called 'a'.

The number you multiply by each time is called 'the common ratio', symbolised by 'r'.

Ah, the classic chessboard example...

Here's the formula describing any term in the geometric progression: $\boxed{u_n = ar^{n-1}}$

Example: There is a 64-square chessboard with a 1p piece on the first square, 2p on the second square, 4p on the third, 8p on the fourth and so on. Calculate how much money is on the board.

This is a **geometric progression**, where you get the next term in the sequence by multiplying the previous one by 2.

So $a = 1$ (because you start with 1p on the first square) and $r = 2$.

So $u_1 = 1$, $u_2 = 2$, $u_3 = 4$, $u_4 = 8$ ...

To be continued... (once we've gone over how to sum the terms of a geometric progression on p.48)

Sequences can be Increasing, Decreasing or Periodic (or none of these)

In an **increasing sequence**, each term is larger than the previous term, so $u_{k+1} > u_k$ for all terms. The sequence of square numbers (1, 4, 9, 16, ...) is an increasing sequence.

In a **decreasing sequence**, each term is smaller than the previous term, so $u_{k+1} < u_k$ for all terms. The sequence 10 000, 1000, 100, 10, ... is a decreasing sequence.

In a **periodic sequence**, the terms **repeat** in a cycle. The number of terms in one cycle is known as the **order**. The sequence 1, 0, 1, 0, ... is a periodic sequence with order 2.

Some sequences are neither increasing, decreasing nor periodic — for example 1, –2, 3, –4, 5, ...

Example: A sequence has n^{th} term $7n - 16$. Show that the sequence is increasing.

Use the nth term formula to find u_k and u_{k+1}: $\quad u_k = 7k - 16$, $u_{k+1} = 7(k + 1) - 16 = 7k - 9$

Show that $u_{k+1} > u_k$ for all k: $\quad 7k - 9 > 7k - 16 \Rightarrow -9 > -16$

This is true so it is an **increasing sequence**.

Here, $u_{k+1} > u_k$ for any value of k, but you only need to show it's true for integer values of k.

Practice Questions

Q1 Describe the arithmetic sequence 32, 37, 42, 47, ... using a recurrence relation.

Q2 Find the common difference in an arithmetic sequence that starts with –2, ends with 19 and has 29 terms.

Q3 For the geometric progression 2, –6, 18, ... find: a) the common ratio,   b) the 10th term.

Q4 Show that the sequence with n^{th} term $55 - 3n$ is decreasing.

Exam Questions

Q1 Ned has 15 cuboid pots that need filling with soil. Each pot is taller than the one before it. The different capacities of his 15 pots form an arithmetic sequence with first term (representing the smallest pot) a ml and the common difference d ml. The 7th pot has a capacity of 580 ml and largest pot has a capacity of 1020 ml. Find the value of a and the value of d. [5 marks]

Q2 A geometric sequence has first term 12 and common ratio 1.3. Find the value of the tenth term in the sequence. [2 marks]

Triangle, square, pentagon — that's my idea of a geometric progression...

Make sure you understand the difference between arithmetic and geometric progressions — you need to be really happy with them for the next couple of pages, so it's worth spending a bit of time getting your head around them now.

Arithmetic Series

OK, now you know what a sequence is, it's time to move on to series. A series is very like a sequence, but there is one very important difference — in a series, you add the terms together.

A *Series* is when you *Add the Terms* to *Find the Total*

S_n is the total of the first n terms of the arithmetic progression:

$$S_n = a + (a + d) + (a + 2d) + (a + 3d) + \dots + (a + (n-1)d)$$

or: $S_n = a + (a + d) + (a + 2d) + \dots + (l - 2d) + (l - d) + l$

The l stands for the last value in the progression. You work it out as l = a + (n − 1)d

There's a really neat formula you can use to find S_n: $\boxed{S_n = n \times \dfrac{(a + l)}{2}}$

Write S_n in terms of a and l.

Here's the proof of the formula:

$$S_n = a + (a + d) + (a + 2d) + \dots + (l - 2d) + (l - d) + l$$
$$S_n = l + (l - d) + (l - 2d) + \dots + (a + 2d) + (a + d) + a$$
$$2S_n = (a + l) + (a + l) + (a + l) + \dots + (a + l) + (a + l) + (a + l)$$
$$2S_n = n(a + l)$$

Then write the same thing with the terms in reverse order.

Now, add these together, term by term. All the ds cancel and you're left with (a + l), n times.

Now just divide by 2 to get the formula.

If you don't like formulas, just think of it as the **average** of the **first and last** terms multiplied by the **number of terms**.

Example: Find the sum of the arithmetic series with first term 3, last term 87 and common difference 4.

Use the information about the last value, l: $\quad a + (n-1)d = 87$
Then **plug in** the other values: $\quad 3 + 4(n - 1) = 87$
$$4n - 4 = 84$$
$$4n = 88 \implies n = 22$$

Here you know a, d and l, but you don't know n yet.

n = 22 means that there are 22 terms in the progression.

So $S_{22} = 22 \times \dfrac{(3 + 87)}{2} = \mathbf{990}$

The S_n formula is in the formula booklet as $S_n = \frac{1}{2}n(a + l)$, which is equivalent to the formula above.

They *Won't* always give you the *Last Term*

Don't panic though — there's a formula to use when the **last term is unknown**.

You know $l = a + (n - 1)d$ and $S_n = n \times \dfrac{(a + l)}{2}$.

Plug l into S_n and rearrange to get this formula, which is also in the formula booklet:

$$\boxed{S_n = \frac{n}{2}[2a + (n - 1)d]}$$

Example: For the arithmetic sequence −5, −2, 1, 4, 7, … find the sum of the first 20 terms.

So $a = -5$ and $d = 3$. The question says $n = 20$ too.
$$S_{20} = \frac{20}{2}[2 \times (-5) + (20 - 1) \times 3]$$
$$= 10[-10 + 19 \times 3]$$
$$S_{20} = \mathbf{470}$$

There's *Another* way of *Writing Series*, too

So far, the letter S has been used for the sum. The Greeks did a lot of work on this — their capital letter for S is Σ or **sigma**. This is used today, together with the general term, to mean the **sum** of the series.

Example: Find $\displaystyle\sum_{n=1}^{15} (2n + 3)$

…and ending with n = 15
Starting with n = 1…

A useful result is $\displaystyle\sum_{1}^{n} 1 = n$.

This means you have to find the sum of the **first 15 terms** of the series with n^{th} term $2n + 3$.
The first term ($n = 1$) is **5**, the second term ($n = 2$) is **7**, the third is **9**, … and the last term ($n = 15$) is **33**.
In other words, you need to find $5 + 7 + 9 + \dots + 33$. This gives $a = 5$, $d = 2$, $n = 15$ and $l = 33$.
You know all of a, d, n and l, so you can use either formula:

It doesn't matter which method you use.

$$S_n = n \times \frac{(a + l)}{2}$$
$$S_{15} = 15 \times \frac{(5 + 33)}{2} = 15 \times 19$$
$$S_{15} = \mathbf{285}$$

$$S_n = \frac{n}{2}[2a + (n - 1)d]$$
$$S_{15} = \frac{15}{2}[2 \times 5 + 14 \times 2] = \frac{15}{2}[10 + 28]$$
$$S_{15} = \mathbf{285}$$

Arithmetic Series

Use **Arithmetic Progressions** to add up the **Natural Numbers**

Natural numbers are just positive whole numbers.

The **sum of the first n natural numbers** looks like this:

$$S_n = 1 + 2 + 3 + \dots + (n-2) + (n-1) + n$$

So $a = 1$, $l = n$ and also $n = n$.
Now just plug those values into the formula:

$$S_n = n \times \frac{(a+l)}{2} \longrightarrow S_n = \frac{1}{2}n(n+1)$$

It's pretty easy to **prove** this:

1) Say, $S_n = 1 + 2 + 3 + \dots + (n-2) + (n-1) + n$ ①

2) ① is just addition, so it's also true that:
$S_n = n + (n-1) + (n-2) + \dots + 3 + 2 + 1$ ②

3) Add ① and ② together to get:
$2S_n = (n+1) + (n+1) + (n+1) + \dots + (n+1)$
$+ (n+1) + (n+1)$
$\Rightarrow 2S_n = n(n+1) \Rightarrow S_n = \frac{1}{2}n(n+1)$. Voilà.

Example: On Day 1, Erica puts £1 in her piggy bank. On Day 2, she puts in £2, on Day 3 she puts in £3, etc. How much money will she have after 100 days?

This sounds pretty hard, but it's just asking for the sum of the whole numbers from 1 to 100 — so all you have to do is stick it into the formula:

$$S_{100} = \frac{1}{2} \times 100 \times 101 = \textbf{£5050}$$

Example: The sum of the first k natural numbers is 861. Find the value of k.

Form an equation in k:
$$\frac{1}{2}k(k+1) = 861$$
$$k^2 + k = 1722$$
$$k^2 + k - 1722 = 0$$

Now factorise:
$$(k+42)(k-41) = 0$$
$$k = -42 \text{ or } k = 41$$

k can't be negative so $k = \textbf{41}$

Practice Questions

Q1 Find the sum of the arithmetic series that starts with 7, ends with 35 and has 8 terms.

Q2 Find the sum of the arithmetic series that begins with 5, 8, … and ends with 65.

Q3 An arithmetic series has first term 7 and fifth term 23.
Find: a) the common difference, b) the 15th term, c) the sum of the first 10 terms.

Q4 An arithmetic series has 7th term 36 and 10th term 30. Find the nth term and the sum of the first five terms.

Q5 Find: a) $\sum_{n=1}^{20}(3n-1)$ b) $\sum_{n=1}^{10}(48-5n)$

Exam Questions

Q1 An arithmetic sequence $a_1, a_2, a_3, \dots$ is defined by $a_1 = k$, $a_{n+1} = 3a_n + 11$, $n \geq 1$, where k is a constant.
a) Show that $a_4 = 27k + 143$. [3 marks]
b) Find the value of k, given that $\sum_{r=1}^{4} a_r = 278$. [3 marks]

Q2 Ed's personal trainer has given him a timetable to improve his upper-body strength, which gradually increases the amount of push-ups Ed does by the same amount each day.

The timetable for the first four days is shown:

Day:	Mon	Tue	Wed	Thur
Number of push-ups:	6	14	22	30

a) Find an expression, in terms of n, for the number of push-ups he will have to do on day n. [2 marks]

b) Calculate how many push-ups Ed will have done in total if he follows his routine for 10 days. [1 mark]

The trainer recommends that Ed takes a break when he has done a cumulative total of 2450 push-ups.

c) Given that Ed completes his exercises on day k, but reaches the recommended limit part-way through day $(k+1)$, show that k satisfies $(2k-49)(k+25) < 0$ and find the value of k. [5 marks]

This sigma notation is all Greek to me...

A sequence is just a list of numbers (with commas between them) and a series is when you add all the terms together. It doesn't sound like a big difference, but mathematicians get all hot under the collar when you get the two mixed up. Remember that BlackADDer was a great TV series, not a TV sequence. (Sounds daft, but I bet you remember it now.)

Geometric Series

Remember that a geometric sequence is one where you multiply by a common ratio to get from one term to the next.
If you add the terms in a geometric sequence, you get a geometric series.

There's a **Formula** for the **Sum** of a **Geometric Series**

To work out the formula for the sum of a geometric progression,
you use **two series** and **subtract**:

For a geometric progression: $S_n = a + ar + ar^2 + ar^3 + \dots + ar^{n-1}$

Multiplying by r gives: $rS_n = ar + ar^2 + ar^3 + \dots + ar^{n-2}\ ar^{n-1} + ar^n$

Subtracting gives: $S_n - rS_n = a - ar^n$

Factorising: $(1 - r)S_n = a(1 - r^n) \implies$ $\boxed{S_n = \dfrac{a(1 - r^n)}{1 - r}}$

If the series were subtracted the other way around you'd get $S_n = \dfrac{a(r^n - 1)}{r - 1}$. Both versions are correct, but the $(1 - r)$ version is the one that appears in the formula booklet.

Example: Calculate how much money is on the chessboard on p.45.

Here, you have to work out S_{64} (because there are 64 squares on a chessboard).
$a = 1$, $r = 2$ and $n = 64$. Putting these values into the formula gives:

$$S_{64} = \frac{1(1 - 2^{64})}{1 - 2} = 1.84 \times 10^{19} \text{ pence or £}1.84 \times 10^{17}$$

$\approx$ 16 million times the number of 1p coins in circulation

The chessboard had suddenly turned a bit sinister.

Geometric progressions can either **Grow** or **Shrink**

In the chessboard example, each term was **bigger** than the previous one: 1, 2, 4, 8, 16, …
You can create a series where each term is **smaller** than the previous one by using a **small value of r**.

Example: If $a = 20$ and $r = \frac{1}{5}$, find the first five terms of the geometric sequence and the 20th term.

$u_1 = 20$, $u_2 = 20 \times \frac{1}{5} = 4$, $u_3 = 4 \times \frac{1}{5} = 0.8$, $u_4 = 0.8 \times \frac{1}{5} = 0.16$, $u_5 = 0.16 \times \frac{1}{5} = 0.032$

$u_{20} = 20 \times \left(\frac{1}{5}\right)^{19} = 1.048576 \times 10^{-12}$

*The sequence is **tending towards zero**, but won't ever get there.*

Each term is the previous one multiplied by r.

In general, for each term to be **smaller** than the one before, you need $|r| < 1$.
A sequence with $|r| < 1$ is called **convergent**, since the terms converge to a limit.
Any other sequence (like the chessboard example above) is called **divergent**.

$|r|$ means the modulus (or size) of r, ignoring the sign of the number (see p.28). So $|r| < 1$ means that $-1 < r < 1$.

A **Convergent Series** has a **Sum** to **Infinity**

S_∞ just means 'sum to infinity'.

In other words, if you just **kept** adding terms to a **convergent series**, you'd get
closer and closer to a certain number, but you'd never actually reach it.

If $|r| < 1$ and n is very, very **big**, then r^n will be very, very
small — or to put it technically, $r^n \to 0$ (try working out
$(\frac{1}{2})^{100}$ on your calculator if you don't believe me).

This means $(1 - r^n)$ is really, really close to 1.

So, for $|r| < 1$, as $n \to \infty$, $S_n \to \dfrac{a}{1 - r}$

This is given in the formula booklet as $\boxed{S_\infty = \dfrac{a}{1 - r}}$

Example: If $a = 2$ and $r = \frac{1}{2}$, find the sum to infinity of the geometric series.

Using the **sum to infinity formula**: $S_\infty = \dfrac{a}{1 - r} = \dfrac{2}{1 - \frac{1}{2}} = 4$

You can show this **graphically**:
The curve is getting **closer
and closer** to 4, but it'll never
actually get there.

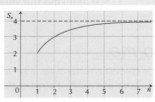

You can see it getting closer and closer to 4
if you work out the individual sums:

$S_1 = 2$ $S_4 = 3\frac{3}{4}$ $S_7 = 3\frac{31}{32}$

$S_2 = 3$ $S_5 = 3\frac{7}{8}$ …and so on…

$S_3 = 3\frac{1}{2}$ $S_6 = 3\frac{15}{16}$ …and so forth…

Geometric Series

A *Divergent* series *Doesn't* have a sum to infinity

Example: If $a = 2$ and $r = 2$, find the sum to infinity of the geometric series.

$u_1 = 2$ so $S_1 = 2$
$u_2 = 2 \times 2 = 4$ so $S_2 = 2 + 4 = 6$
$u_3 = 4 \times 2 = 8$ so $S_3 = 2 + 4 + 8 = 14$
$u_4 = 8 \times 2 = 16$ so $S_4 = 2 + 4 + 8 + 16 = 30$
$u_5 = 16 \times 2 = 32$ so $S_5 = 2 + 4 + 8 + 16 + 32 = 62$

This is an exponential graph — see p.77.

As $n \to \infty$, $S_n \to \infty$ in a big way. So big, in fact, that eventually you **can't work it out** — so don't bother. There is **no sum to infinity** for a **divergent** series.

Example: On a child's 1st birthday, £3000 is invested in an account with a fixed compound interest rate of 4% per year. The interest is paid in every year, on the child's birthday.
a) What will the account be worth on the child's 7th birthday?
b) When will the account have doubled in value?

It's compound interest, so multiply by 1.04 each year.

a) $u_1 = a = 3000$

This is the interest.

$u_2 = 3000 + (4\% \text{ of } 3000)$
$= 3000 + (0.04 \times 3000) = 3000(1 + 0.04)$
$= 3000 \times 1.04$ ← So $r = 1.04$

$u_3 = u_2 \times 1.04 \times 2 = (3000 \times 1.04) \times 1.04$
$= 3000 \times (1.04)^2$
$u_4 = 3000 \times (1.04)^3$
⋮   ⋮   ⋮
$u_7 = 3000 \times (1.04)^6$
$= £3795.96$ (to the nearest penny)

b) You need to know when $u_n > 6000$ (double the original value).
From part a) you know that $u_n = 3000 \times (1.04)^{n-1}$
So $3000 \times (1.04)^{n-1} > 6000$
$(1.04)^{n-1} > 2$

To complete this you need to use **logs** (see p.76):

$\log(1.04)^{n-1} > \log 2$
$(n - 1) \log(1.04) > \log 2$
$n - 1 > \dfrac{\log 2}{\log 1.04}$
$n - 1 > 17.67$
$n > 18.67$ (2 d.p.)

So u_{19} (the amount at the start of the 19th year) will be more than double the original amount.

So the account will have doubled in value when the interest is paid in on the child's **19th** birthday.

Practice Questions

Q1 Find the sum of the first 12 terms of the following geometric series:
   a) $2 + 8 + 32 + ...$ b) $30 + 15 + 7.5 + ...$

Q2 Find the common ratio for the following geometric series. State which ones are convergent and which are divergent.
   a) $1 + 2 + 4 + ...$ b) $81 + 27 + 9 + ...$ c) $1 + \dfrac{1}{3} + \dfrac{1}{9} + ...$

Q3 For the geometric progression 24, 12, 6, ..., find:
   a) the common ratio,   b) the seventh term,
   c) the sum of the first 10 terms,   d) the sum to infinity.

Exam Question

Q1 A geometric series has second term $u_2 = 5$ and sum to infinity $S_\infty = 36$.
   a) Show that $36r^2 - 36r + 5 = 0$, where r represents the two possible values of the common ratio.   **[3 marks]**
   b) Hence find the possible values of r, and the two corresponding first terms.   **[4 marks]**

To infinity and beyond (unless it's a convergent series, in which case, to 4)...

I find it odd that I can keep adding things to a sum forever, but the sum never gets really really big. If this is really blowing your mind, draw a quick sketch of the graph (like in the example above) so you can see what's happening.

Binomial Expansions

If you're feeling a bit stressed, just take a couple of minutes to relax before trying to get your head round this page — it's a bit of a stinker in places. Have a cup of tea and think about something else for a couple of minutes. Ready...

Writing **Binomial Expansions** is all about **Spotting Patterns**

Doing binomial expansions just involves **multiplying out** brackets. It would get nasty when you raise the brackets to **higher powers** — but once again I've got a **cunning plan**...

$$(1 + x)^0 = 1$$
$$(1 + x)^1 = 1 + x$$
$$(1 + x)^2 = 1 + 2x + x^2$$
$$(1 + x)^3 = 1 + 3x + 3x^2 + x^3$$
$$(1 + x)^4 = 1 + 4x + 6x^2 + 4x^3 + x^4$$

Anything to the power of O is 1.

$$(1 + x)^3 = (1 + x)(1 + x)^2$$
$$= (1 + x)(1 + 2x + x^2)$$
$$= 1 + 2x + x^2 + x + 2x^2 + x^3$$
$$= 1 + 3x + 3x^2 + x^3$$

A Frenchman named Pascal spotted the pattern in the coefficients and wrote them down in a **triangle**.
So it was called '**Pascal's Triangle**' (imaginative, eh?).
The pattern's easy — each number is the **sum** of the two above it.

So, the next line will be: **1 5 10 10 5 1**
giving $(1 + x)^5 = 1 + 5x + 10x^2 + 10x^3 + 5x^4 + x^5$.

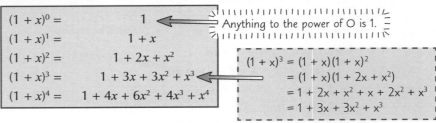

You **Don't** need to write out Pascal's Triangle for **Higher Powers**

There's a **formula** that gives you the numbers from the triangle. It looks **horrible** (take a glance at the next page — blegh...) but fortunately some kind soul has included it in the formula booklet. Make sure to say thank you.

Example: Expand $(1 + x)^{20}$, giving the first four terms in ascending powers of x.

This includes the x^0 term (i.e. the constant term).

Here's the basic expansion for $(1 + x)^n$. In this example $n = 20$.

$$(1+x)^n = 1 + \frac{n}{1}x + \frac{n(n-1)}{1 \times 2}x^2 + \boxed{\frac{n(n-1)(n-2)}{1 \times 2 \times 3}x^3} + \dots + x^n$$

This binomial expansion stuff will be really important in some of the stats chapters — see p.161.

Here's a closer look at the term in the blue box:

<u>Start here</u>. The power of x is 3 and everything else here is based on 3.

There are <u>three things</u> multiplied together on the top row. If n = 20, this would be 20 × 19 × 18.

$$\frac{n(n-1)(n-2)}{1 \times 2 \times 3}x^3$$

There are <u>three integers</u> here multiplied together. 1 × 2 × 3 is written as 3! and called 3 <u>factorial</u>.

This means, if $n = 20$ and you were asked for '**the term in x^7**' you should write $\frac{20 \times 19 \times 18 \times 17 \times 16 \times 15 \times 14}{1 \times 2 \times 3 \times 4 \times 5 \times 6 \times 7}x^7$.

This can be **simplified** to $\frac{20!}{7!13!}x^7$. $\quad 20 \times 19 \times 18 \times 17 \times 16 \times 15 \times 14 = \frac{20!}{13!}$ because it's the numbers from 20 to 1 multiplied together, divided by the numbers from 13 to 1 multiplied together.

Believe it or not, there's an even **shorter** form: $\quad \frac{20!}{7!13!}$ is written as $^{20}C_7$ or $\binom{20}{7}$

$$^nC_r = \binom{n}{r} = \frac{n!}{r!(n-r)!}$$
$$\binom{n}{0} = \binom{n}{n} = 1$$

Your calculator should have an nCr function for working this out.

So, to finish the example, $(1 + x)^{20} = 1 + \frac{20}{1}x + \frac{20 \times 19}{1 \times 2}x^2 + \frac{20 \times 19 \times 18}{1 \times 2 \times 3}x^3 + \dots$

$$= 1 + \binom{20}{1}x + \binom{20}{2}x^2 + \binom{20}{3}x^3 + \dots$$

$$= 1 + 20x + 190x^2 + 1140x^3 + \dots$$

This is the way you'll normally see it written, since you'd usually just get your calculator to do all the hard work multiplying and dividing for you.

Binomial Expansions

There's a *General Formula* for *Expanding* $(a + b)^n$

So far, you've seen the expansion for $(1 + x)^n$. The **general formula** works on anything that looks like $(a + b)^n$, as long as n is a **positive integer**. This is the one that's given in your formula booklet, and it looks like this:

$$(a + b)^n = a^n + \binom{n}{1}a^{n-1}b + \binom{n}{2}a^{n-2}b^2 + \ldots + \binom{n}{r}a^{n-r}b^r + \ldots + b^n \quad n \in \mathbb{N}$$

This bit just means that n has to be a 'natural number' — basically, a positive integer.

If you set a = 1 and b = x, then you'd get your original binomial expansion formula. Go on — give it a go if you don't believe me.

These are those ^nC_r fellas that you met at the bottom of the last page.

Example: a) Find the first four terms in the expansion of $(2 - 3x)^6$, in ascending powers of x.

Here, $a = 2$, $b = (-3x)$ and $n = 6$. Using the formula:

$$(2 - 3x)^6 = 2^6 + \binom{6}{1}2^5(-3x) + \binom{6}{2}2^4(-3x)^2 + \binom{6}{3}2^3(-3x)^3 + \ldots$$

$$= 64 + (6 \times 32 \times -3x) + (15 \times 16 \times 9x^2) + (20 \times 8 \times -27x^3) + \ldots$$

$$= \mathbf{64 - 576x + 2160x^2 - 4320x^3 + \ldots}$$

b) Use your answer to give an estimate for the value of 1.7^6.

$(2 - 3x)^6 = 1.7^6$ when $x = 0.1$. Substitute this into your expansion:

$$1.7^6 \approx 64 - 576(0.1) + 2160(0.1)^2 - 4320(0.1)^3$$

$$= 64 - 57.6 + 21.6 - 4.32$$

$$= \mathbf{23.68}$$

The actual value of 1.7^6 is 24.137... so this is a pretty good estimate.

Estimates like this one work best when x is small, so that x^n gets tiny as n gets bigger — that way, the terms that you miss out won't affect the answer as much.

Example: Find the coefficient of x^9 in the expansion of $(4 - 2x)^{11}$.

You could work out the whole expansion up to x^9, but it's much quicker to just use one bit of the formula: $(a + b)^n = \ldots + \binom{n}{r}a^{n-r}b^r + \ldots$

$$(4 - 2x)^{11} = \ldots + \binom{11}{9}4^{11-9}(-2x)^9 + \ldots = \ldots + (55 \times 16 \times -512x^9) + \ldots = \ldots - 450\,560x^9 + \ldots$$

So the coefficient of x^9 is **−450 560**.

Watch out — the **term** is "−450 560x⁹", but the **coefficient** is just "−450 560". Make sure you've checked what the question's asking for.

Practice Questions

Q1 Write down the sixth row of Pascal's triangle (hint: it starts with a '1').

Q2 Give the first four terms in the expansion of $(1 + x)^{12}$, in ascending powers of x.

Q3 What are the first four terms in the expansion of $(1 - 2x)^{16}$, in ascending powers of x?

Q4 Find the first four terms in the expansion of $(2 + 3x)^5$, in ascending powers of x.

Exam Questions

Q1 Find the first five terms in the binomial expansion of $(4 + 3x)^6$, in ascending powers of x. [5 marks]

Q2 The coefficient of the x^3 term in the binomial expansion of $(1 + px)^7$ is 280.
Find the value of p. [3 marks]

Pascal was great at maths but bad at music — he only played the triangle...

That nCr function is pretty bloomin' useful (remember that it could be called something else on your calculator) — it saves a lot of button pressing and errors. Just make sure you put your numbers in the right way round.

Binomial Expansions as Infinite Sums

Unfortunately, you only get a nice, neat, finite expansion when you've got a positive integer n.
But that pesky n sometimes likes to be a negative number or a fraction. n for nuisance, n for naughty.

If **n** is **Negative** or a **Fraction** the expansion is an **Infinite Sum**

You'll be happy to know (possibly?) that you can expand $(1 + x)^n$ even when n **isn't** a positive integer.
The formula is very similar to the one on p.50:

$$(1 + x)^n = 1 + nx + \frac{n(n-1)}{1 \times 2}x^2 + \dots + \frac{n(n-1)\dots(n-r+1)}{1 \times 2 \times \dots \times r}x^r + \dots \qquad (|x| < 1, \, n \in \mathbb{R})$$

This bit is just like the expansion in the example on p.50.

This means that n is a 'real number', which basically means any number — negative, fraction, irrational etc.

If n isn't a positive integer, this expansion is an **infinite sum** (if n is a positive integer, all the terms with $r > n$ are zero, and you get the formula from p.50). It's only valid for $|x| < 1$ — otherwise you get a **divergent series** (see p.48).

Because the expansion is infinite, a question will usually tell you **how many terms** to work out.

Example: Find the binomial expansion of $\dfrac{1}{(1+x)^2}$ up to and including the term in x^3.

First, **rewrite the expression:** $\dfrac{1}{(1+x)^2} = (1+x)^{-2}$.

Now use the **general formula.** Here, $n = -2$:

n = -2   *n(n − 1)*

$$(1+x)^{-2} = 1 + (-2)x + \frac{(-2) \times (-2-1)}{1 \times 2}x^2 + \frac{(-2) \times (-2-1) \times (-2-2)}{1 \times 2 \times 3}x^3 + \dots$$

$$= 1 + (-2)x + \frac{(-2) \times (-3)}{1 \times 2}x^2 + \frac{(-2) \times (-3) \times (-4)}{1 \times 2 \times 3}x^3 + \dots$$

$$= 1 + (-2)x + \frac{3}{1}x^2 + \frac{-4}{1}x^3 + \dots$$

$$= 1 - 2x + 3x^2 - 4x^3 + \dots$$

> *With a negative n, you'll never get zero as a coefficient. If the question hadn't told you to stop, the expansion could go on forever.*

You can cancel down before you multiply — but be careful with those minus signs.

We've left out all the terms after $-4x^3$, so the cubic equation you've ended up with is an **approximation** to the original expression. You could also write the answer like this: $\dfrac{1}{(1+x)^2} \approx 1 - 2x + 3x^2 - 4x^3$.

Because the formula is in the form $(1 + x)^n$, you might need to do a bit of factorising first...

Example: Find the binomial expansion of $\sqrt{4+3x}$ up to and including the term in x^3.

This time we've got a **fractional power:** $\sqrt{4+3x} = (4+3x)^{\frac{1}{2}}$

You need the first term to be 1, so take out a factor of 2:

$$(4+3x)^{\frac{1}{2}} = \left(4\left(1+\tfrac{3}{4}x\right)\right)^{\frac{1}{2}} = 4^{\frac{1}{2}}\left(1+\tfrac{3}{4}x\right)^{\frac{1}{2}} = 2\left(1+\tfrac{3}{4}x\right)^{\frac{1}{2}}$$

So this time $n = \frac{1}{2}$, and you also need to replace x with $\frac{3}{4}x$:

n = ½   *n(n − 1)*

$$\left(1+\tfrac{3}{4}x\right)^{\frac{1}{2}} = 1 + \tfrac{1}{2}\left(\tfrac{3}{4}x\right) + \frac{\tfrac{1}{2} \times \left(\tfrac{1}{2}-1\right)}{1 \times 2}\left(\tfrac{3}{4}x\right)^2 + \frac{\tfrac{1}{2} \times \left(\tfrac{1}{2}-1\right) \times \left(\tfrac{1}{2}-2\right)}{1 \times 2 \times 3}\left(\tfrac{3}{4}x\right)^3 + \dots$$

$$= 1 + \tfrac{3}{8}x + \frac{\tfrac{1}{2} \times \left(-\tfrac{1}{2}\right)}{2}\tfrac{9}{16}x^2 + \frac{\tfrac{1}{2} \times \left(-\tfrac{1}{2}\right) \times \left(-\tfrac{3}{2}\right)}{6}\tfrac{27}{64}x^3 + \dots$$

$$= 1 + \tfrac{3}{8}x + \left(-\tfrac{1}{8} \times \tfrac{9}{16}\right)x^2 + \left(\tfrac{3}{48} \times \tfrac{27}{64}\right)x^3 + \dots$$

$$= 1 + \tfrac{3}{8}x - \tfrac{9}{128}x^2 + \tfrac{27}{1024}x^3 + \dots$$

So $(4+3x)^{\frac{1}{2}} = 2\left(1+\tfrac{3}{4}x\right)^{\frac{1}{2}}$

$$= 2\left(1 + \tfrac{3}{8}x - \tfrac{9}{128}x^2 + \tfrac{27}{1024}x^3 + \dots\right) = 2 + \tfrac{3}{4}x - \tfrac{9}{64}x^2 + \tfrac{27}{512}x^3 + \dots$$

Gus didn't have any friends, so he didn't even qualify for the standard 'bi-gnome-ial' joke.

> *Cancelling down is much trickier with this type of expansion — it's usually safer to multiply everything out fully.*

Binomial Expansions as Infinite Sums

Some **Binomial Expansions** are only **Valid** for **Certain Values** of **x**

When you find a binomial expansion, you usually have to state which values of x the expansion is valid for.

If n is a **positive integer**, the binomial expansion of $(p + qx)^n$ is valid for **all values of** x.

If n is a **negative integer** or a **fraction**, the binomial expansion of $(p + qx)^n$ is valid when $\left|\dfrac{qx}{p}\right| < 1$ (or $|x| < \left|\dfrac{p}{q}\right|$).

So, in the examples on the previous page:

$(1 + x)^{-2} = 1 - 2x + 3x^2 - 4x^3 + \dots$
This expansion is valid for $|x| < 1$.

$(1 + 2x)^{\frac{1}{3}} = 1 + \dfrac{2}{3}x - \dfrac{4}{9}x^2 + \dfrac{40}{81}x^3 + \dots$
This expansion is valid if $|2x| < 1 \Rightarrow 2|x| < 1 \Rightarrow |x| < \dfrac{1}{2}$.

You can use the formula on a **Combination** of expansions

Some nasty expressions can be expanded by doing two or more simple expansions and multiplying them together.

Example: Find the first three terms in the expansion of $\dfrac{(1 + 2x)^3}{(1 - x)^2}$, stating the range of x for which it is valid.

First re-write the expression as a **product** of two expansions: $\dfrac{(1 + 2x)^3}{(1 - x)^2} = (1 + 2x)^3(1 - x)^{-2}$

Expand each of these separately using the **formula**:

$(1 + 2x)^3 = 1 + 3(2x) + \dfrac{3 \times 2}{1 \times 2}(2x)^2 + \dfrac{3 \times 2 \times 1}{1 \times 2 \times 3}(2x)^3 = 1 + 6x + 3(4x^2) + 8x^3 = \mathbf{1 + 6x + 12x^2 + 8x^3}$

$(1 - x)^{-2} = 1 + (-2)(-x) + \dfrac{(-2) \times (-3)}{1 \times 2}(-x)^2 + \dfrac{(-2) \times (-3) \times (-4)}{1 \times 2 \times 3}(-x)^3 + \dots = \mathbf{1 + 2x + 3x^2 + 4x^3 + \dots}$

Multiply the two expansions together. Since you're only asked for the **first three terms**, ignore any terms with **higher powers** of x than x^2.

$(1 + 2x)^3(1 - x)^{-2} = (1 + 6x + 12x^2 + 8x^3)(1 + 2x + 3x^2 + 4x^3 + \dots)$

$= 1(1 + 2x + 3x^2) + 6x(1 + 2x) + 12x^2(1) + \dots$

$= 1 + 2x + 3x^2 + 6x + 12x^2 + 12x^2 + \dots = \mathbf{1 + 8x + 27x^2 + \dots}$

Now find the **validity** of each expansion: $(1 + 2x)^3$ is valid for **all values** of x, since n is a **positive integer**.

$(1 - x)^{-2}$ is valid if $|-x| < 1 \Rightarrow |x| < 1$.

So the expansion of $\dfrac{(1 + 2x)^3}{(1 - x)^2}$ is only valid if $|x| < 1$.
For the **combined** expansion to be **valid**, x must be in the valid range for **both** expansions, i.e. the **narrowest** of the valid ranges.

Practice Questions

Q1 Find the binomial expansion of each of the following, up to and including the term in x^3:

a) $\dfrac{1}{(1 + x)^4}$ b) $\dfrac{1}{(1 - 3x)^3}$ c) $\sqrt{1 - 5x}$

Q2 If the binomial expansion of $(4 - 2x)^n$ is an infinite series, what values of x is the expansion valid for?

Q3 Give the binomial expansions of the following, up to and including the term in x^2.
State which values of x each expansion is valid for.   a) $\dfrac{1}{(3 + 2x)^2}$ b) $\sqrt[3]{8 - x}$

Exam Question

Q1 a) Find the binomial expansion of $\dfrac{1}{\sqrt{9 - 4x}}$, up to and including the term in x^3.   [5 marks]

b) Hence find the first three terms in the expansion of $\dfrac{2 - x}{\sqrt{9 - 4x}}$.   [4 marks]

This is by-no-means the last page on binomials...

I'm afraid that the formula from p.51 won't help with these expansions — if it's not a 1 in the brackets, you'll have to factorise before using the formula (and make sure to raise the factor to the negative or fractional power as well).

Further Binomial Expansions

Binomial expansions on their own are pretty nifty, but when you combine them with partial fractions (see p.14-15) they become all-powerful. I'm sure there's some sort of message about friendship or something in there...

Split functions into **Partial Fractions**, then add the **Expansions**

You can find the binomial expansion of even more complicated functions by splitting them into partial fractions first.

Example: $f(x) = \dfrac{x-1}{(3+x)(1-5x)}$

a) f(x) can be expressed in the form $\dfrac{A}{(3+x)} + \dfrac{B}{(1-5x)}$. Find the values of A and B.

b) Use your answer to part a) to find the binomial expansion of f(x) up to and including the term in x^2.

c) Find the range of values of x for which your answer to part b) is valid.

a) Convert f(x) into **partial fractions**:

$$\frac{x-1}{(3+x)(1-5x)} \equiv \frac{A}{(3+x)} + \frac{B}{(1-5x)} \Rightarrow x-1 \equiv A(1-5x) + B(3+x)$$

Let $x = -3$, then $-3-1 = A(1-(-15)) \Rightarrow -4 = 16A \Rightarrow A = -\dfrac{1}{4}$

Let $x = \dfrac{1}{5}$, then $\dfrac{1}{5} - 1 = B\left(3 + \dfrac{1}{5}\right) \Rightarrow -\dfrac{4}{5} = \dfrac{16}{5}B \Rightarrow B = -\dfrac{1}{4}$

See p.14-15 if you need a reminder about how to do partial fractions.

b) Start by **rewriting** the partial fractions in $(a + bx)^n$ form:

$$f(x) = -\frac{1}{4}(3+x)^{-1} - \frac{1}{4}(1-5x)^{-1}$$

Now do the two **binomial expansions**:

$$(3+x)^{-1} = \left(3\left(1 + \frac{1}{3}x\right)\right)^{-1}$$
$$= \frac{1}{3}\left(1 + \frac{1}{3}x\right)^{-1}$$
$$= \frac{1}{3}\left(1 + (-1)\left(\frac{1}{3}x\right) + \frac{(-1)(-2)}{2}\left(\frac{1}{3}x\right)^2 + ...\right)$$
$$= \frac{1}{3}\left(1 - \frac{1}{3}x + \frac{1}{9}x^2 + ...\right)$$
$$= \frac{1}{3} - \frac{1}{9}x + \frac{1}{27}x^2 + ...$$

$$(1-5x)^{-1} = 1 + (-1)(-5x) + \frac{(-1)(-2)}{2}(-5x)^2 + ...$$
$$= 1 + 5x + 25x^2 + ...$$

And put **everything together**: $f(x) = -\dfrac{1}{4}(3+x)^{-1} - \dfrac{1}{4}(1-5x)^{-1}$

$$\approx -\frac{1}{4}\left(\frac{1}{3} - \frac{1}{9}x + \frac{1}{27}x^2\right) - \frac{1}{4}(1 + 5x + 25x^2)$$
$$= -\frac{1}{12} + \frac{1}{36}x - \frac{1}{108}x^2 - \frac{1}{4} - \frac{5}{4}x - \frac{25}{4}x^2$$
$$= -\frac{1}{3} - \frac{11}{9}x - \frac{169}{27}x^2$$

c) Each of the two expansions from part b) is valid for different values of x. The combined expansion of f(x) is valid where these two ranges **overlap**, i.e. over the **narrower of the two ranges**.

Remember — the expansion of $(p + qx)^n$ is valid when $\left|\dfrac{qx}{p}\right| < 1$.

The expansion of $(3+x)^{-1}$ is valid when $\left|\dfrac{x}{3}\right| < 1 \Rightarrow \dfrac{|x|}{|3|} < 1 \Rightarrow |x| < 3$.

The expansion of $(1-5x)^{-1}$ is valid when $|-5x| < 1 \Rightarrow |-5||x| < 1 \Rightarrow |x| < \dfrac{1}{5}$.

The expansion of f(x) is valid for values of x in both ranges,

so the expansion of f(x) is valid for $|x| < \dfrac{1}{5}$.

You might already know the rules $|ab| = |a||b|$ and $\left|\dfrac{a}{b}\right| = \dfrac{|a|}{|b|}$. If you don't, then get to know them — they're handy for rearranging these limits.

Further Binomial Expansions

To find **Approximations**, substitute the right value of **x**

When you've done an **expansion**, you can use it to **estimate** the value of the original expression for given values of x.

Example: The binomial expansion of $(1 + 3x)^{\frac{1}{3}}$ up to the term in x^3 is $(1 + 3x)^{\frac{1}{3}} \approx 1 + x - x^2 + \frac{5}{3}x^3$.
The expansion is valid for $|x| < \frac{1}{3}$.
Use this expansion to approximate $\sqrt[3]{1.3}$. Give your answer to 4 d.p.

For this type of question, you need to find **the right value of** x to make the expression you're expanding equal to the thing you're looking for.

In this case it's pretty straightforward: $\sqrt[3]{1.3} = (1 + 3x)^{\frac{1}{3}}$ when $x = 0.1$ ⟵ 0.1 < $\frac{1}{3}$, so the expansion is valid for this approximation.

$$\sqrt[3]{1.3} = (1 + 3(0.1))^{\frac{1}{3}}$$

Don't forget to use a "≈" here — the answer's an approximation because you're only using the expansion up to the x^3 term.

$$\approx 1 + 0.1 - (0.1)^2 + \frac{5}{3}(0.1)^3$$

This is the expansion given in the question, with x = 0.1.

$$= 1 + 0.1 - 0.01 + \frac{0.005}{3}$$

$$= \mathbf{1.0917} \text{ (4 d.p.)}$$

In **trickier cases** you have to do a spot of **rearranging** to get to the answer.

Example: The binomial expansion of $(1 - 5x)^{\frac{1}{2}}$ up to the term in x^2 is $(1 - 5x)^{\frac{1}{2}} \approx 1 - \frac{5x}{2} - \frac{25}{8}x^2$ for $|x| < \frac{1}{5}$.
Use $x = \frac{1}{50}$ in this expansion to find an approximate value for $\sqrt{10}$, and find the percentage error in your approximation, giving your answer to 2 significant figures.

First, sub $x = \frac{1}{50}$ into **both sides** of the expansion:

$$\sqrt{\left(1 - 5\left(\frac{1}{50}\right)\right)} \approx 1 - \frac{5}{2}\left(\frac{1}{50}\right) - \frac{25}{8}\left(\frac{1}{50}\right)^2$$

$$\sqrt{\left(1 - \frac{1}{10}\right)} \approx 1 - \frac{1}{20} - \frac{1}{800}$$

$$\sqrt{\frac{9}{10}} \approx \frac{759}{800}$$

Now **simplify** the square root and **rearrange** to find an estimate for $\sqrt{10}$:

$$\sqrt{\frac{9}{10}} = \frac{\sqrt{9}}{\sqrt{10}} = \frac{3}{\sqrt{10}} \approx \frac{759}{800} \Rightarrow \sqrt{10} \approx 3 \div \frac{759}{800} = \frac{800}{253}$$

So this is a pretty darn good estimate.

The **percentage error** is $\left|\dfrac{\text{real value} - \text{estimate}}{\text{real value}}\right| \times 100 = \left|\dfrac{\sqrt{10} - \frac{800}{253}}{\sqrt{10}}\right| \times 100 = \mathbf{0.0070\%}$ (2 s.f.)

Practice Questions

Q1 Given that $f(x) = \dfrac{2x - 7}{(x + 1)(x - 2)} \equiv \dfrac{3}{x + 1} - \dfrac{1}{x - 2}$, find the binomial expansion of $f(x)$ up to and including the x^2 term.

Q2 Use the approximation $\sqrt{\dfrac{1 + 2x}{1 - 3x}} \approx 1 + \frac{5}{2}x + \frac{35}{8}x^2$ with $x = \frac{2}{15}$ to show that $\sqrt{19} \approx \frac{127}{30}$.

Exam Questions

Q1 a) Find the binomial expansion of $(16 + 3x)^{\frac{1}{4}}$, for $|x| < \frac{16}{3}$, up to and including the term in x^2. [5 marks]

   b) (i) Estimate $\sqrt[4]{12.4}$ by substituting a suitable value of x into your expansion from part (a). Give your answer to 6 decimal places. [2 marks]

       (ii) What is the percentage error in this estimate? Give your answer to 3 significant figures. [2 marks]

Q2 Find the binomial expansion, up to the term in x^2, of $f(x) = \dfrac{13x - 17}{(5 - 3x)(2x - 1)}$ for $|x| < \frac{5}{3}$. [9 marks]

Don't mess with me — I'm a partial arts expert...

You can also use the binomial expansion to estimate the values of fractions — for example, the binomial expansion of $(1 + 3x)^{-1}$ can be used to estimate $\frac{100}{103}$. Just write $\frac{100}{103}$ as $\frac{1}{1 + 0.03}$, then substitute $x = 0.01$ into the expansion.

Angles, Arc Length and Sector Area

You should be familiar with angles measured in degrees. For A Level Maths, you also need to measure them in radians.

Radians are another way of Measuring Angles

You need to know how radians relate to **degrees**.
In short, **180 degrees = π radians**. The table below shows you how to convert between the two units:

Converting angles	
Radians to degrees: Divide by π, multiply by 180.	Degrees to radians: Divide by 180, multiply by π.

Here's a table of some of the **common angles** you're going to need — in degrees and radians:

Degrees	0	30	45	60	90	120	180	270	360
Radians	0	$\frac{\pi}{6}$	$\frac{\pi}{4}$	$\frac{\pi}{3}$	$\frac{\pi}{2}$	$\frac{2\pi}{3}$	π	$\frac{3\pi}{2}$	2π

"...and bake in an oven preheated to π radians for around 40 minutes."

Draw Triangles to remember sin, cos and tan of the Important Angles

You should know the values of **sin**, **cos** and **tan** at 30°, 60° and 45°. But to help you remember, you can draw these two triangles. It may seem a complicated way to learn a few numbers, but it does make it easier. Honest. The idea is you draw the triangles below, putting in their angles and side lengths. Then you can use them to work out trig values like **sin 45°** or **cos 60°** more accurately than a calculator (which only gives a few decimal places).

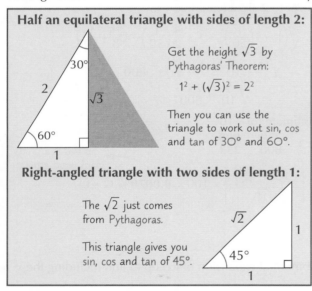

Half an equilateral triangle with sides of length 2:

Get the height $\sqrt{3}$ by Pythagoras' Theorem:

$$1^2 + (\sqrt{3})^2 = 2^2$$

Then you can use the triangle to work out sin, cos and tan of 30° and 60°.

Right-angled triangle with two sides of length 1:

The $\sqrt{2}$ just comes from Pythagoras.

This triangle gives you sin, cos and tan of 45°.

Remember: SOH CAH TOA...

$$\sin = \frac{opp}{hyp} \qquad \cos = \frac{adj}{hyp} \qquad \tan = \frac{opp}{adj}$$

Trig Values from Triangles		
$\sin 30° = \frac{1}{2}$	$\sin 60° = \frac{\sqrt{3}}{2}$	$\sin 45° = \frac{1}{\sqrt{2}}$
$\cos 30° = \frac{\sqrt{3}}{2}$	$\cos 60° = \frac{1}{2}$	$\cos 45° = \frac{1}{\sqrt{2}}$
$\tan 30° = \frac{1}{\sqrt{3}}$	$\tan 60° = \sqrt{3}$	$\tan 45° = 1$

You need to know these values for x given in radians too.

Find angles from the Unit Circle

The **unit circle** is a circle with **radius 1**, centred on the **origin**. For any point on the unit circle, the coordinates are **(cos θ, sin θ)**, where θ is the angle measured from the **positive** x-axis in an **anticlockwise** direction. The points on the **axes** of the unit circle give you the values of sin and cos of 0° and 90°. So at the point (1, 0): **cos 0° = 1, sin 0° = 0**. And at the point (0, 1): **cos 90° = 0, sin 90° = 1**.

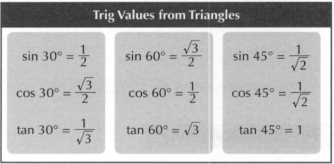

Example: The coordinates of a point on the unit circle, given to 3 s.f., are (0.788, 0.616). Find θ to the nearest degree.

The point is on the unit circle, so you know that the coordinates are (cos θ, sin θ). So cos θ = 0.788 and sin θ = 0.616.

You only need one of these to find the value of θ.
cos θ = 0.788 ⇒ θ = cos⁻¹ (0.788) = **38°** (to the nearest degree).

The hypotenuse is always the radius — so it's always 1.

Angles, Arc Length and Sector Area

Find the **Length of an Arc** and the **Area of a Sector** of a circle

If you have a **sector of a circle** (like a section of pie chart), you can work out the **length** of the **curved side** (the **arc**) and its **area** — as long as you know the **angle** at the centre (θ, in **radians**) and the length of the **radius** (r).

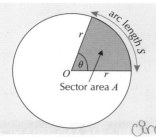

For a circle with a **radius of r**, where the angle θ is measured in **radians**, you can work out S, the **length of the arc**, using:

$$S = r\theta$$

To find A, the **area of the sector**, use:

$$A = \frac{1}{2}r^2\theta$$

$\pi = 180^\circ \quad \pi = 360$ ·

If you put $\theta = 2\pi$ into either formula (and so make the sector equal to the whole circle), you get the normal circumference and area formulas.

circumference = $r2\pi = 2\pi r = \pi D$ ·
area = $\frac{1}{2}r^2 2\pi = \pi r^2$

arc length = radius × θ (in radians)
area of sector = $\frac{1}{2}$ radius² × θ (in radians)

Use **Radians** with **Both Formulas**

Example: Find the exact length L and area A in the diagram.

Right, first things first... it's an **arc length** and **sector area**, so you need the angle in **radians**.

$$45^\circ = \frac{45 \times \pi}{180} = \frac{\pi}{4} \text{ radians}$$

Or you could just quote this if you've learnt the stuff on the previous page.

Now bung everything in your formulas:

$$L = r\theta = 20 \times \frac{\pi}{4} = 5\pi \text{ cm} \qquad A = \frac{1}{2}r^2\theta = \frac{1}{2} \times 20^2 \times \frac{\pi}{4} = 50\pi \text{ cm}^2$$

You could also use the total angle of all the shaded sectors (π) to go straight to the answer. Or you could notice that exactly half of the area of the circle is shaded.

Example: Find the area of the shaded part of the symbol.

You need the area of the 'leaves' and so use the formula $\frac{1}{2}r^2\theta$.

Each leaf has area $\frac{1}{2} \times 10^2 \times \frac{\pi}{4} = \frac{25\pi}{2} \text{ cm}^2$

So the area of the whole symbol $= 4 \times \frac{25\pi}{2} = 50\pi \text{ cm}^2$

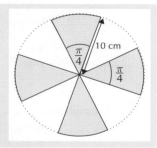

Practice Questions

Q1 Write down the exact value of: a) $\frac{3\pi}{2}$ radians in degrees, b) 120° in radians.

Q2 Calculate the value of the angle 50° in radians, to 3 decimal places.

Q3 Write down the exact value of: a) $\cos 30^\circ$, b) $\sin 45^\circ$, c) $\tan 60^\circ$, d) $\sin \frac{\pi}{6}$.

Q4 A sector of a circle with radius 5 cm has an arc length of 15 cm. Find the centre angle, in degrees to 1 d.p.

Exam Question

Q1 The diagram shows the dimensions of a child's wooden toy.
The toy has a constant cross-section and a height of 10 cm.
Its cross-section is a sector of a circle with radius 20 cm and angle $\frac{\pi}{4}$ radians.

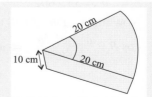

a) Show that the volume of the toy, $V = 500\pi \text{ cm}^3$. [3 marks]

b) Show that the surface area of the toy, $S = (150\pi + 400) \text{ cm}^2$. [4 marks]

$\pi = 3.14159265358979323846264338327950288419716939\text{9...}$ *(make sure you know it)*
It's worth repeating, just to make sure — the formulas for arc length and sector area only work with angles in radians.

Trig Formulas and Identities

There are some more trig formulas you need to know for the exam.
So here they are — learn them or you're seriously stuffed. Worse than an aubergine.

The **Sine Rule** and **Cosine Rule** work for **Any** triangle

Remember, these three formulas work for **ANY** triangle, not just right-angled ones.

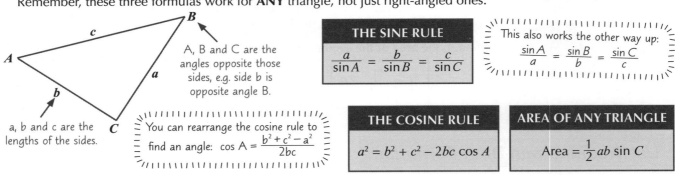

A, B and C are the angles opposite those sides, e.g. side b is opposite angle B.

a, b and c are the lengths of the sides.

THE SINE RULE

$$\frac{a}{\sin A} = \frac{b}{\sin B} = \frac{c}{\sin C}$$

This also works the other way up:
$$\frac{\sin A}{a} = \frac{\sin B}{b} = \frac{\sin C}{c}$$

You can rearrange the cosine rule to find an angle: $\cos A = \frac{b^2 + c^2 - a^2}{2bc}$

THE COSINE RULE

$$a^2 = b^2 + c^2 - 2bc \cos A$$

AREA OF ANY TRIANGLE

$$\text{Area} = \frac{1}{2} ab \sin C$$

Sine Rule or **Cosine Rule** — which one is it...

To decide which of these two rules you need to use, look at what you **already** know about the triangle.

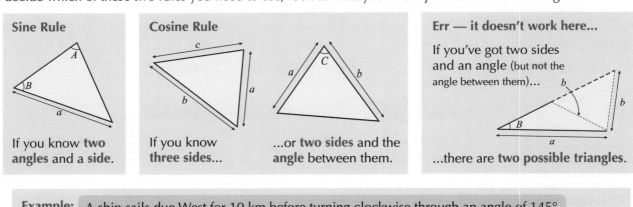

Sine Rule

If you know **two angles** and a **side**.

Cosine Rule

If you know **three sides**...

...or **two sides** and the **angle** between them.

Err — it doesn't work here...

If you've got two sides and an angle (but **not** the angle between them)...

...there are **two possible triangles**.

Example: A ship sails due West for 10 km before turning clockwise through an angle of 145° and sailing in a straight line for another 6.5 km. Find the shortest distance back to its starting point, and the angle it would need to turn through to get there.

1) First draw a sketch of the problem, labelling all the lengths and angles you know.

2) You know 2 sides and the angle between them, so you're going to need the **cosine rule** to find side *a*, the distance back to the start:

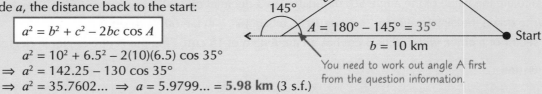

X is the angle the ship needs to turn through to get back.

$A = 180° - 145° = 35°$

You need to work out angle A first from the question information.

$$a^2 = b^2 + c^2 - 2bc \cos A$$

$a^2 = 10^2 + 6.5^2 - 2(10)(6.5) \cos 35°$
$\Rightarrow a^2 = 142.25 - 130 \cos 35°$
$\Rightarrow a^2 = 35.7602... \Rightarrow a = 5.9799... = \textbf{5.98 km}$ (3 s.f.)

3) Now that you've got all the sides, you can use the **cosine rule** again to find angle *B*:

$\cos B = \frac{a^2 + c^2 - b^2}{2ac} \Rightarrow \cos B = \frac{35.7602... + 42.25 - 100}{2 \times 5.9799... \times 6.5}$

$\Rightarrow \cos B = \frac{-21.979...}{77.739...} = -0.2828...$

$\Rightarrow B = \cos^{-1} -0.2828... = \textbf{106.43...°}$

4) So the angle, *X*, that the ship needs to turn through is $180° - 106.43...° = \textbf{73.6°}$ (1 d.p.)

You could use the sine rule to find angle *B*, but watch out if you do — any value of $\sin \theta$ in the range $0 < \sin \theta < 1$ corresponds to two values of θ between 0° and 180°. Your calculator will give you the acute angle for *B*, but in this case you actually want the obtuse angle instead.

Trig Formulas and Identities

The *Formulas* work with *Radians* as well as *Degrees*

Example: In the triangle ABC, $A = \frac{2\pi}{9}$ radians, $a = 27$ m and $B = \frac{4\pi}{9}$ radians. Find the missing angles and sides, and calculate the area of the triangle.

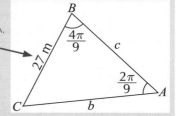

1) Draw a quick sketch first — don't worry if it's not deadly accurate, though.

2) You're given 2 angles and a side, so you need the **sine rule**.

   Make sure you put side a opposite angle A.
   The angles in a triangle add up to π radians.

   First of all, get the other angle: $\angle C = \pi - \frac{2\pi}{9} - \frac{4\pi}{9} = \frac{\pi}{3}$ **radians**

3) Then find the other sides, one at a time:

   $$\frac{a}{\sin A} = \frac{b}{\sin B} \Rightarrow \frac{27}{\sin \frac{2\pi}{9}} = \frac{b}{\sin \frac{4\pi}{9}}$$

   $$\Rightarrow b = \frac{\sin \frac{4\pi}{9}}{\sin \frac{2\pi}{9}} \times 27 = 41.366... = \textbf{41.4 m} \text{ (1 d.p.)}$$

   $$\frac{c}{\sin C} = \frac{a}{\sin A} \Rightarrow \frac{c}{\sin \frac{\pi}{3}} = \frac{27}{\sin \frac{2\pi}{9}}$$

   $$\Rightarrow c = \frac{\sin \frac{\pi}{3}}{\sin \frac{2\pi}{9}} \times 27 = \textbf{36.4 m} \text{ (1 d.p.)}$$

4) Now just use the formula to find its area:

   Area $\triangle ABC = \frac{1}{2} ab \sin C$

   $= \frac{1}{2} \times 27 \times 41.366... \times \sin \frac{\pi}{3}$

   Use a more accurate value for b here, rather than the rounded value 41.4.

   $= \textbf{483.6 m}^2$ (1 d.p.)

The *Best* has been saved till last...

These two identities are really important. You'll need them **loads**.

$$\tan x \equiv \frac{\sin x}{\cos x} \qquad \sin^2 x + \cos^2 x \equiv 1$$

$$\Rightarrow \sin^2 x \equiv 1 - \cos^2 x$$
$$\cos^2 x \equiv 1 - \sin^2 x$$

Essential kit for maintaining two identities.

These two come up in exam questions **all the time**. Learn them.
Learnthemlearnthemlearnthemlearnthemlearnthemlear... okay, I'll stop now.

Work out these two using $\sin^2 x + \cos^2 x \equiv 1$.

Practice Questions

Q1 Find the missing sides and angles in: a) $\triangle ABC$, in which $A = 30°$, $C = 25°$, $b = 6$ m, and find its area.

b) $\triangle PQR$, in which $p = 3$ km, $q = 23$ km, $R = 10°$. (answers to 2 d.p.)

Q2 My pet triangle Freda has sides of length 10, 20 and 25. Find her angles (in radians to 3 s.f.).

Exam Questions

Q1 For an angle x, $3 \cos x = 2 \sin x$. Find $\tan x$. [2 marks]

Q2 Two walkers, X and Y, walked in different directions from the same start position. X walked due south for 150 m. Y walked 250 m on a bearing of 100°.

a) Calculate the final distance between the two walkers, in m to the nearest m. [2 marks]

b) θ is the final bearing of Y from X. Show that $\frac{\sin \theta}{\sin 80°} = 0.93$ to 2 decimal places. [3 marks]

Tri angles — go on... you might like them.

Formulas and trigonometry go together even better than Ant and Dec. I can count 7 formulas on these pages. That's not many, so please, make sure you know them. If you haven't learnt them I will cry for you. I will sob.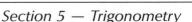

Trig Graphs

Before you leave this page, you should be able to close your eyes and picture these three graphs in your head, properly labelled and everything. If you can't, you need to learn them more. I'm not kidding.

sin x and cos x are always in the range –1 to 1

sin x and **cos x** are similar — they just bob up and down between –1 and 1.

They bounce up and down from –1 to 1 — they can <u>never</u> have a value outside this range.

sin x and cos x are both **periodic** (repeat themselves) with **period 360°**

$\cos(x + 360°) = \cos x$ $\sin(x + 360°) = \sin x$

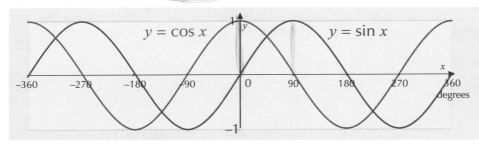

$y = \cos x$ $y = \sin x$

sin x goes through the **origin** — that means **sin 0 = 0**.

cos x crosses the *y*-axis at *y* = 1 — that means **cos 0 = 1**.

Symmetry in the **vertical** axis: $\cos(-x) = \cos x$ $\sin(-x) = -\sin x$

...but not beyond?

tan x can be Any Value at all

tan x is **different** from sin x or cos x.
It doesn't go gently up and down between –1 and 1 — it goes **between –∞ and +∞**.

tan x is also periodic — but with **period 180°**

tan x is **undefined** at ±90°, ±270°, ±450°,...

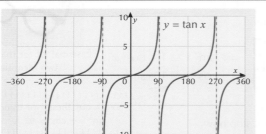

$y = \tan x$

As you approach one of these undefined points from the left, tan x just shoots up to **infinity**.

As you approach from the right, it drops to **minus infinity**.

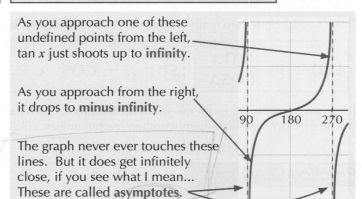

tan x goes from –∞ to +∞ **every 180°**

So it's got period 180°, and takes **every possible value** in each 180° interval.

$\tan(x + 180°) = \tan x$

The graph never ever touches these lines. But it does get infinitely close, if you see what I mean...
These are called **asymptotes**.

The easiest way to sketch any of these graphs is to plot the **important points** which happen **every 90°** (i.e. **–180°, –90°, 0°, 90°, 180°, 270°, 360°**...) and then just join the dots up.

You have to know the graphs in Radians too

The graphs of sin *x*, cos *x* and tan *x* are exactly the **same shape** whether *x* is in **radians** or **degrees** — you just need to remember the **key points** of the graphs in both units.

x°	–360	–270	–180	–90	0	90	180	270	360
x radians	-2π	$-\frac{3\pi}{2}$	$-\pi$	$-\frac{\pi}{2}$	0	$\frac{\pi}{2}$	π	$\frac{3\pi}{2}$	2π
sin *x*	0	1	0	–1	0	1	0	–1	0
cos *x*	1	0	–1	0	1	0	–1	0	1
tan *x*	0	—	0	—	0	—	0	—	0

The '—' here means tan x is undefined, so draw an asymptote.

Trig Graphs

There are 3 basic types of Transformed Trig Graph

Transformed trigonometric graphs look much the same as the bog-standard ones, just a little **different**. There are three main types of transformation.

$y = n \sin x$ — a VERTICAL STRETCH or SQUASH

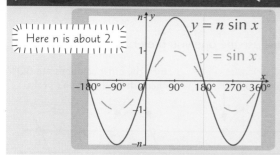

Here n is about 2.

If $n > 1$, the graph of $y = \sin x$ is **stretched vertically** by a factor of n.

If $0 < n < 1$, the graph is **squashed**.

And if $n < 0$, the graph is also **reflected** in the x-axis.

Change in y coordinate

$y = \sin nx$ — a HORIZONTAL SQUASH or STRETCH

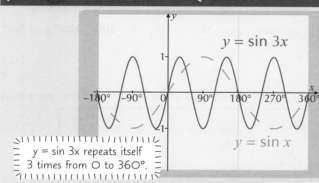

$y = \sin 3x$

$y = \sin x$

$y = \sin 3x$ repeats itself 3 times from O to 360°.

If $n > 1$, the graph of $y = \sin x$ is **squashed horizontally** by a factor of n.

If $0 < n < 1$, the graph is **stretched**.

And if $n < 0$, the graph is also **reflected** in the y-axis.

Change in x coordinate

$y = \sin (x + c)$ — a TRANSLATION along the x-axis

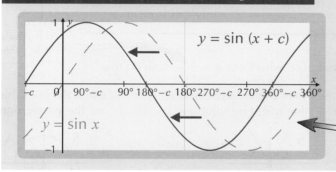

$y = \sin (x + c)$

$y = \sin x$

For $c > 0$, $\sin (x + c)$ is just $\sin x$ **translated c to the left**.

Similarly, $\sin (x - c)$ is just $\sin x$ **translated c to the right**.

For $y = \sin(x + c)$, the 'interesting' points are when $x + c = $ O, 90°, 180°, 270°, etc., i.e. when $x = -c$, 90 - c, 180 - c, 270 - c, ...

Practice Questions

Q1 Sketch the graphs for $\sin x$, $\cos x$ and $\tan x$ where x is in radians. Label all the max/min/zero/undefined points.

Q2 Sketch: a) $y = \frac{1}{2} \cos x$ (for $0° \leq x \leq 360°$), b) $y = \sin \left(x + \frac{\pi}{6}\right)$ (for $0 \leq x \leq 2\pi$), c) $y = \tan 3x$ (for $0° \leq x \leq 180°$).

Exam Questions

Q1 a) Sketch, for $0 \leq x \leq 360°$, the graph of $y = \cos (x + 60°)$. [2 marks]

b) Write down all the values of x, for $0 \leq x \leq 360°$, where $\cos (x + 60°) = 0$. [2 marks]

Q2 Sketch, for $0 \leq x \leq \pi$, the graph of $y = \sin 4x$. [2 marks]

Curling up on the sofa with 2 cos x — that's my idea of cosiness...

It's really really really really really important that you can draw and transform the trig graphs on these pages. Trust me.

Solving Trig Equations

I used to really hate trig stuff like this. But once I'd got the hang of it, I just couldn't get enough. I stopped going out, lost interest in romance — the CAST method became my life. Learn it, but be careful. It's addictive.

There are **Two Ways** to find **Solutions** in an **Interval**

Example: Solve $\cos x = \frac{1}{2}$ for $-360° \le x \le 720°$.

Like I said — there are **two ways** to solve this kind of question. Just use the one you prefer...

You can draw a **graph**...

1) Draw the **graph** of $y = \cos x$ for the range you're interested in...
2) Get the first solution from your **calculator** and mark this on the graph,
3) Use the **symmetry of the graph** to work out what the other solutions are:

Your calculator gives you a solution of 60°... then the other solutions are 60° either side of the graph's peaks.

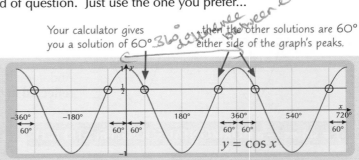

So the solutions are: **−300°, −60°, 60°, 300°, 420° and 660°**.

...or you can use the **CAST** diagram

CAST stands for **COS, ALL, SIN, TAN** — and the CAST diagram shows you where these functions are **positive**:

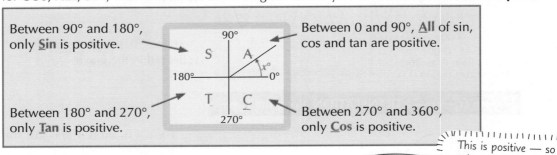

Between 90° and 180°, only **S**in is positive.

Between 0 and 90°, **A**ll of sin, cos and tan are positive.

Between 180° and 270°, only **T**an is positive.

Between 270° and 360°, only **C**os is positive.

This is positive — so you're only interested in where cos is positive.

First, to find all the values of x between 0° and 360° where $\cos x = \frac{1}{2}$ — you do this:

Put the first solution onto the CAST diagram.

The angle from your calculator goes anticlockwise from the x-axis (unless it's negative — then it would go clockwise into the 4th quadrant).

Find the other angles between 0° and 360° that might be solutions.

The other possible solutions come from making the same angle from the horizontal axis in the other 3 quadrants.

Ditch the ones that are the wrong sign.

cos x = ½, which is positive. The CAST diagram tells you cos is positive in the 4th quadrant — but not the 2nd or 3rd — so ditch those two angles.

So you've got solutions 60° and 300° in the range 0° to 360°. But you need **all the solutions** in the range **−360° to 720°**. Get these by repeatedly **adding or subtracting 360°** onto each until you go out of range:

$x = 60° \Rightarrow$ (adding 360°) $x = 420°$, 780° (too big)

and (subtracting 360°) $x = -300°$, −660° (too small)

$x = 300° \Rightarrow$ (adding 360°) $x = 660°$, 1020° (too big)

and (subtracting 360°) $x = -60°$, −420° (too small)

So the solutions are: $x = $ **−300°, −60°, 60°, 300°, 420° and 660°**.

Solving Trig Equations

Sometimes you end up with *sin kx = number*...

For these, it's definitely easier to draw the **graph** rather than use the CAST method —
that's one reason why being able to sketch trig graphs properly is so important.

Example: Solve: $\sin 3x = -\dfrac{1}{\sqrt{2}}$ for $0 \leq x \leq 2\pi$.

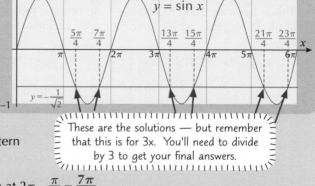

1) You've got $3x$ instead of x, which means the interval
   you need to find solutions in is $0 \leq 3x \leq 6\pi$.
   So draw the graph of $y = \sin x$ between 0 and 6π.

2) You should recall that $\dfrac{1}{\sqrt{2}}$ is $\sin \dfrac{\pi}{4}$ (see p.56),

   and so $-\dfrac{1}{\sqrt{2}}$ is $\sin\left(-\dfrac{\pi}{4}\right)$, which gives $3x = -\dfrac{\pi}{4}$

   — but this is **outside the interval** for $3x$, so use the pattern
   of the graph to find a solution in the interval.

   These are the solutions — but remember that this is for 3x. You'll need to divide by 3 to get your final answers.

   As the sin curve repeats every 2π, there'll be a solution at $2\pi - \dfrac{\pi}{4} = \dfrac{7\pi}{4}$.

3) Now use your graph to find the other 5 solutions. You can see that there's another solution at $\pi + \dfrac{\pi}{4} = \dfrac{5\pi}{4}$.

4) Then add on 2π and 4π to both $\dfrac{5\pi}{4}$ and $\dfrac{7\pi}{4}$ to get: $3x = \dfrac{5\pi}{4}, \dfrac{7\pi}{4}, \dfrac{13\pi}{4}, \dfrac{15\pi}{4}, \dfrac{21\pi}{4}$ and $\dfrac{23\pi}{4}$

5) **Divide by 3** to get the solutions for x: $x = \dfrac{5\pi}{12}, \dfrac{7\pi}{12}, \dfrac{13\pi}{12}, \dfrac{15\pi}{12}, \dfrac{21\pi}{12}$ and $\dfrac{23\pi}{12}$

6) **Check** your answers by putting these values into your calculator.

It really is mega-important that you check these answers — it's dead easy to make a silly mistake. They should all be in the range $0 \leq x \leq 2\pi$.

...or *Something More Complicated*...

All the steps in this example are basically the same as in the one above, although at first sight it looks nightmarish.
Just take it step by step and enjoy the modellinginess* of it all...

Example: A simplified model of the phases of the moon is given by $P = 50 \sin\left(\left(\dfrac{90t}{7}\right)^{\circ} + 90^{\circ}\right) + 50$,
where P is the percentage of the moon visible at night, and t is the number of days after a full
(100%) moon was recorded. On which days, over 12 weeks, will there be a half moon?

1) Start by figuring out the interval for the solutions. 12 weeks = 84 days, so $0 \leq t \leq 84$.
   But you've got $\left(\left(\dfrac{90t}{7}\right)^{\circ} + 90^{\circ}\right)$, so the interval is:

   $$\left(\dfrac{90 \times 0}{7}\right)^{\circ} + 90^{\circ} \leq \left(\left(\dfrac{90t}{7}\right)^{\circ} + 90^{\circ}\right) \leq \left(\dfrac{90 \times 84}{7}\right)^{\circ} + 90^{\circ} \Rightarrow 90^{\circ} \leq \left(\left(\dfrac{90t}{7}\right)^{\circ} + 90^{\circ}\right) \leq 1170^{\circ}$$

2) The question is asking you to find the values of t when $P = 50$, so put this into the model:

   $$50 = 50 \sin\left(\left(\dfrac{90t}{7}\right)^{\circ} + 90^{\circ}\right) + 50$$

   $$\Rightarrow \qquad 0 = \sin\left(\left(\dfrac{90t}{7}\right)^{\circ} + 90^{\circ}\right)$$

   $$\Rightarrow \left(\dfrac{90t}{7}\right)^{\circ} + 90^{\circ} = \sin^{-1} 0 = 0^{\circ}$$

   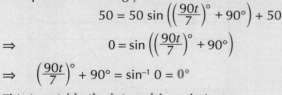

   This is **outside the interval** for solutions,
   so consult the graph of $y = \sin x$ again.

3) You should know the x-intercepts of this graph
   off by heart by now — they're every 180° from zero.
   So $\left(\dfrac{90t}{7}\right)^{\circ} + 90^{\circ} = 180^{\circ}, 360^{\circ}, 540^{\circ}, 720^{\circ}, 900^{\circ}, 1080^{\circ}, 1260^{\circ}...$ ← *This is above 1170° so it's not in the interval.*

4) To solve for t, subtract 90° from each answer and divide by $\dfrac{90}{7}$: $t = 7, 21, 35, 49, 63$ and 77.
   So there will be a half moon **7, 21, 35, 49, 63** and **77** days after the first recorded full moon.

*Almost certainly a proper word somewhere.

Section 5 — Trigonometry

Solving Trig Equations

For equations with **tan x** in, it often helps to use this...

$$\tan x \equiv \frac{\sin x}{\cos x}$$

⎧ You'll also have to use this identity A LOT when you're
doing trig proofs — coming up on pages 74-75. ⎫

This is a handy thing to know — and one the examiners love testing. Basically, if you've got a trig equation with a tan in it, together with a sin or a cos — chances are you'll be better off if you rewrite the tan using this formula.

Example: Solve: $3 \sin x - \tan x = 0$, for $0 \leq x \leq 2\pi$.

1) It's got **sin** and **tan** in it — so writing $\tan x$ as $\frac{\sin x}{\cos x}$ is probably a good move:

$$3 \sin x - \tan x = 0$$
$$\Rightarrow 3 \sin x - \frac{\sin x}{\cos x} = 0$$

2) Get rid of the **cos x** on the bottom by multiplying the whole equation by $\cos x$.

$$\Rightarrow 3 \sin x \cos x - \sin x = 0$$

3) Now — there's a **common factor** of $\sin x$. Take that outside a bracket.

$$\Rightarrow \sin x (3 \cos x - 1) = 0$$

4) And now you're almost there. You've got two things multiplying together to make zero. That means either **one or both** of them is **equal to zero**.

$$\Rightarrow \sin x = 0 \ \text{ or } \ 3 \cos x - 1 = 0$$

⎧ CAST gives any solutions
in the interval $0 \leq x \leq 2\pi$. ⎫

sin x = 0

The first solution is:
$$\sin 0 = 0$$
Now find the other points where $\sin x$ is zero in the interval $0 \leq x \leq 2\pi$.

Remember the sin graph is zero every π radians.
$$\Rightarrow x = 0, \pi, 2\pi \text{ radians}$$

Having memorised the roots of sin x, smug young Sherlock had ample time to entertain his classmates as they caught up.

3 cos x − 1 = 0

Rearrange:
$$\cos x = \frac{1}{3}$$
So the first solution is:
$$\cos^{-1}\left(\frac{1}{3}\right) = 1.23095...$$
$$= 1.231 \text{ (3 d.p.)}$$

CAST (or the graph of cos x) gives another positive solution in the 4th quadrant, where $x = 2\pi - 1.23095... = 5.052$ (3 d.p.)

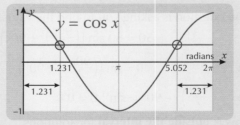

So altogether you've got **five** possible solutions:
$$\Rightarrow x = \textbf{0, 1.231}, \pi, \textbf{5.052}, 2\pi \textbf{ radians}$$

And the two solutions from this part are:
$$\Rightarrow x = 1.231, 5.052 \text{ radians}$$

Be warned — you might be tempted to simplify an equation by **dividing** by a trig function. But you can **only** do this if the trig function you're dividing by is **never zero** in the range the equation is valid for. Dividing by zero is not big or clever, or even possible.

Solving Trig Equations

And if you have **sin² x** or **cos² x**, think of this straight away...

$$\sin^2 x + \cos^2 x \equiv 1 \implies \begin{array}{l} \sin^2 x \equiv 1 - \cos^2 x \\ \cos^2 x \equiv 1 - \sin^2 x \end{array}$$

Use this identity to get rid of a sin² or a cos² that's making things awkward...

Example: Solve: $2 \sin^2 x + 5 \cos x = 4$, for $0° \leq x \leq 360°$.

1) You can't do much while the equation's got both sin's and cos's in it.
So replace the **sin² x** bit with **1 − cos² x**:
$$2(1 - \cos^2 x) + 5 \cos x = 4 \quad \longleftarrow \text{ Now the only trig function is cos.}$$

2) Multiply out the bracket and rearrange it so that you've got zero on one side
— and you get a **quadratic** in cos x:
$$\implies 2 - 2\cos^2 x + 5\cos x = 4$$
$$\implies 2\cos^2 x - 5\cos x + 2 = 0$$

3) This is a quadratic in cos x. It's easier to factorise this if you make the substitution $y = \cos x$.
$$2y^2 - 5y + 2 = 0 \quad \longleftarrow \quad 2y^2 - 5y + 2 = (2y\ ?)(y\ ?)$$
$$\implies (2y - 1)(y - 2) = 0 \qquad = (2y - 1)(y - 2)$$
$$\implies (2\cos x - 1)(\cos x - 2) = 0$$

4) Now one of the brackets must be **0**. So you get 2 equations as usual:

You did this example on page 62. $\quad 2\cos x - 1 = 0$ or $\cos x - 2 = 0$

$\cos x = \frac{1}{2} \implies x = 60°$ and $x = 300°$ and $\cos x = 2$ — This is a bit weird. cos x is always between −1 and 1, so you don't get any solutions from this bracket.

So at the end of all that, the only solutions you get are $x = 60°$ and $x = 300°$. How boring.

Practice Questions

Q1 a) Solve each of these equations for $0 \leq \theta \leq 2\pi$: (i) $\sin \theta = -\frac{\sqrt{3}}{2}$, (ii) $\tan \theta = -1$, (iii) $\cos \theta = -\frac{1}{\sqrt{2}}$

b) Solve each of these equations for $-180° \leq \theta \leq 180°$ (giving your answer to 1 d.p.):
(i) $\cos 4\theta = -\frac{2}{3}$ (ii) $\sin(\theta + 35°) = 0.3$ (iii) $\tan\left(\frac{1}{2}\theta\right) = 500$

Q2 Find all the solutions to $6\sin^2 x = \cos x + 5$ in the range $0 \leq x \leq 2\pi$ (answers to 3 s.f. where appropriate).

Q3 Solve $3\tan x + 2\cos x = 0$ for $-90° \leq x \leq 90°$.

Q4 Simplify: $(\sin y + \cos y)^2 + (\cos y - \sin y)^2$.

Exam Questions

Q1 a) Solve $2\cos\left(x - \frac{\pi}{4}\right) = \sqrt{3}$, for $0 \leq x \leq 2\pi$. [3 marks]

b) Solve $\sin 2x = -\frac{1}{2}$, for $0° \leq x \leq 360°$. [3 marks]

Q2 a) Show that the equation $2(1 - \cos x) = 3\sin^2 x$ can be written as $3\cos^2 x - 2\cos x - 1 = 0$. [2 marks]

b) Use this to solve the equation $2(1 - \cos x) = 3\sin^2 x$ for $0 \leq x \leq 360°$, giving your answers to 1 d.p. [6 marks]

Q3 Solve the equation $3\cos^2 x = \sin^2 x$, for $-\pi \leq x \leq \pi$. [6 marks]

Trig equations are sinful (and cosful and tanful)...

...but they are a definite source of marks — you can bet your last penny they'll be in the exam. That substitution trick to get rid of a sin² or a cos² and end up with a quadratic in sin x or cos x is a real examiners' favourite. Remember to use CAST or graphs to find all the possible solutions in the given interval, not just the one on your calculator display.

Further Trig

*Just when you thought you'd seen all the functions that trigonometry could throw at you, here come six more.
The ones at the bottom of the page are particularly handy when you're solving trig equations.*

Arcsin, Arccos and Arctan are the Inverses of Sin, Cos and Tan

In Section 2 you saw that some functions have **inverses**, which reverse the effect of the function.
The **trig functions** have inverses too.

> **ARCSINE** is the **inverse of sine**. You might see it written as **arcsin** or **sin⁻¹**.
> **ARCCOSINE** is the **inverse of cosine**. You might see it written as **arccos** or **cos⁻¹**.
> **ARCTANGENT** is the **inverse of tangent**. You might see it written as **arctan** or **tan⁻¹**.

You should have buttons for doing arcsin, arccos and arctan on your calculator — they'll probably be labelled $\sin^{-1}$, $\cos^{-1}$ and $\tan^{-1}$.

The inverse trig functions **reverse** the effect of sin, cos and tan. For example, if sin 30° = 0.5, then arcsin 0.5 = 30°.

To Graph the Inverse Functions you need to Restrict their Domains

1) The functions sine, cosine and tangent are NOT **one-to-one mappings** (see p.34) — lots of values of x give the same value for sin x, cos x or tan x. For example: $\cos 0 = \cos 2\pi = \cos 4\pi = 1$, and $\tan 0 = \tan \pi = \tan 2\pi = 0$.

2) Only **one-to-one functions** have inverses, so for the inverse to be a function you have to **restrict the domain** of the trig function to make it one-to-one (see graphs below). This means that you only plot the graphs between certain x values, so that for **each x value**, you end up with **one y value**.

3) As the graphs are inverse functions, they're also **reflections** of the sin, cos and tan functions in the line $y = x$.

Arcsine	Arccosine	Arctangent
For arcsin, limit the domain of sin x to $-\frac{\pi}{2} \le x \le \frac{\pi}{2}$ (the range of sin x is still $-1 \le \sin x \le 1$). This means the domain of arcsin x is $-1 \le x \le 1$ and its range is $-\frac{\pi}{2} \le \arcsin x \le \frac{\pi}{2}$.	For arccos, limit the domain of cos x to $0 \le x \le \pi$ (the range of cos x is still $-1 \le \cos x \le 1$). This means the domain of arccos x is $-1 \le x \le 1$ and its range is $0 \le \arccos x \le \pi$.	For arctan, limit the domain of tan x to $-\frac{\pi}{2} < x < \frac{\pi}{2}$ (this doesn't limit the range of tan x). This means that the domain of arctan x isn't limited, but its range is limited to $-\frac{\pi}{2} < \arctan x < \frac{\pi}{2}$.
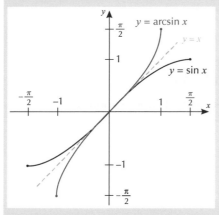	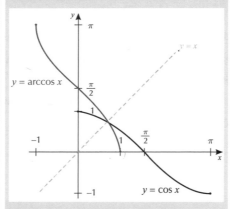	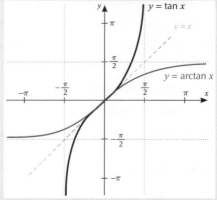
This graph goes through the origin. The coordinates of its endpoints are $\left(1, \frac{\pi}{2}\right)$ and $\left(-1, -\frac{\pi}{2}\right)$.	This graph crosses the y-axis at $\left(0, \frac{\pi}{2}\right)$. The coordinates of its endpoints are $(-1, \pi)$ and $(1, 0)$.	This graph goes through the origin. It has asymptotes at $y = \frac{\pi}{2}$ and $y = -\frac{\pi}{2}$.

Cosec, Sec and Cot are the Reciprocals of Sin, Cos and Tan

When you take the **reciprocal** of the three main trig functions, sin, cos and tan, you get
three new trig functions — **cosecant** (or **cosec**), **secant** (or **sec**) and **cotangent** (or **cot**).

$$\operatorname{cosec} \theta \equiv \frac{1}{\sin \theta} \qquad \sec \theta \equiv \frac{1}{\cos \theta} \qquad \cot \theta \equiv \frac{1}{\tan \theta}$$

The trick for remembering which is which is to look at the third letter — co$\underline{s}$ec (1/$\underline{s}$in), se$\underline{c}$ (1/$\underline{c}$os) and co$\underline{t}$ (1/$\underline{t}$an).

Since $\tan \theta = \frac{\sin \theta}{\cos \theta}$, you can also think of **cot θ** as being $\frac{\cos \theta}{\sin \theta}$.

Further Trig

Graphing Cosec, Sec and Cot

Cosec This is the graph of $y = \text{cosec } x$.

1) Since $\text{cosec } x = \frac{1}{\sin x}$, $y = \text{cosec } x$ is **undefined** at any point where $\sin x = 0$. So $\text{cosec } x$ has **asymptotes** at $x = n\pi$ (where n is any integer).

2) The graph of $\text{cosec } x$ has **minimum** points at $y = 1$ (wherever the graph of $\sin x$ has a maximum).

3) It has **maximum** points at $y = -1$ (wherever $\sin x$ has a minimum).

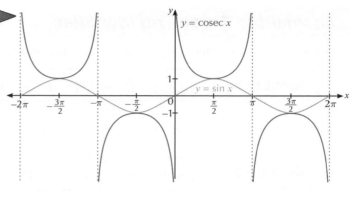

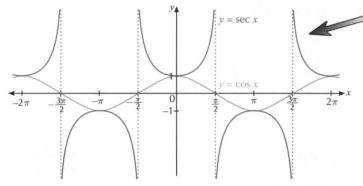

Sec This is the graph of $y = \sec x$.

1) As $\sec x = \frac{1}{\cos x}$, $y = \sec x$ is **undefined** at any point where $\cos x = 0$. So $\sec x$ has **asymptotes** at $x = \left(n\pi + \frac{\pi}{2}\right)$ (where n is any integer).

2) The graph of $\sec x$ has **minimum** points at $y = 1$ (wherever the graph of $\cos x$ has a maximum).

3) It has **maximum** points at $y = -1$ (wherever $\cos x$ has a minimum).

Cot This is the graph of $y = \cot x$.

1) Since $\cot x = \frac{1}{\tan x}$, $y = \cot x$ is **undefined** at any point where $\tan x = 0$. So $\cot x$ has **asymptotes** at $x = n\pi$ (where n is any integer).

2) $y = \cot x$ **crosses the x-axis** at every place where the graph of $\tan x$ has an **asymptote** — this is any point with the coordinates $\left(\left(n\pi + \frac{\pi}{2}\right), 0\right)$.

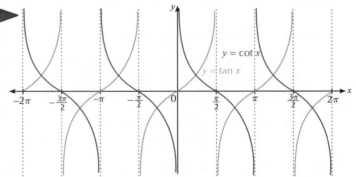

Practice Questions

Q1 Giving your answers in radians, find the exact values of: a) $\arcsin 1$, b) $\arccos \frac{1}{\sqrt{2}}$, c) $\arctan \sqrt{3}$.

Q2 For $\theta = 30°$, find the exact values of: a) $\text{cosec } \theta$, b) $\sec \theta$, c) $\cot \theta$.

Q3 Solve $\text{cosec } x = \sqrt{2}$, where $0° \leq x \leq 360°$.

Exam Questions

Q1 Solve, to 3 significant figures, the equation $\arccos x = 2$ radians for the interval $0 \leq \arccos x \leq \pi$. [2 marks]

Q2 a) Sketch the graph of $y = \text{cosec } x$ for $-\pi \leq x \leq \pi$. [3 marks]

b) Solve the equation $\text{cosec } x = \frac{5}{4}$ for $-\pi \leq x \leq \pi$. Give your answers correct to 3 significant figures. [3 marks]

c) Solve $\text{cosec } x = 3 \sec x$ for $-\pi \leq x \leq \pi$. Give your answers correct to 3 significant figures. [3 marks]

Why did I multiply cot x by sin x? Just 'cos...

If I were you, I'd get the shapes of all these graphs memorised — you can find the range and domain of the functions just by looking at them (and they're pretty, too). You might also have to transform a trig graph — use the same method as you would for other graphs (see p.31). And remember that tip about looking at the third letter — it's a belter.

Further Trig Identities and Approximations

Ahh, more trig identities. More useful than a monkey wrench, and more fun than a pair of skateboarding rabbits. Or have I got that the wrong way round...

Learn these **Three Trig Identities**

Hopefully you're familiar with this handy little **trig identity** by now:

Identity 1: $\cos^2 \theta + \sin^2 \theta \equiv 1$

> Remember, the $\equiv$ sign tells you that this is true for all values of θ, rather than just certain values.

You can use this one to produce a couple of other identities that you need to know about...

Remember that $\cos^2 \theta = (\cos \theta)^2$.

Identity 2: $\sec^2 \theta \equiv 1 + \tan^2 \theta$

To get this, you just take everything in Identity 1, and **divide** it by $\cos^2 \theta$:

$$\frac{\cos^2 \theta}{\cos^2 \theta} + \frac{\sin^2 \theta}{\cos^2 \theta} \equiv \frac{1}{\cos^2 \theta}$$
$$1 + \tan^2 \theta \equiv \sec^2 \theta$$

Identity 3: $\operatorname{cosec}^2 \theta \equiv 1 + \cot^2 \theta$

You get this one by **dividing** everything in Identity 1 by $\sin^2 \theta$:

$$\frac{\cos^2 \theta}{\sin^2 \theta} + \frac{\sin^2 \theta}{\sin^2 \theta} \equiv \frac{1}{\sin^2 \theta}$$
$$\cot^2 \theta + 1 \equiv \operatorname{cosec}^2 \theta$$

Use the **Trig Identities** to **Simplify Equations**

You can use any of the identities you've learnt to get rid of any trig functions that are making an equation difficult to solve.

More fun.

Example: Solve the equation $\cot^2 x + 5 = 4 \operatorname{cosec} x$ in the interval $0° \leq x \leq 360°$.

1) You can't solve this while it has **both** cot and cosec in it, so use **Identity 3** to swap $\cot^2 x$ for $\operatorname{cosec}^2 x - 1$:

   $\operatorname{cosec}^2 x - 1 + 5 = 4 \operatorname{cosec} x$

2) Now rearranging the equation gives:

   $\operatorname{cosec}^2 x + 4 = 4 \operatorname{cosec} x \implies \operatorname{cosec}^2 x - 4 \operatorname{cosec} x + 4 = 0$

3) So you've got a **quadratic** in cosec x — factorise it like you would any other quadratic equation.

   $\operatorname{cosec}^2 x - 4 \operatorname{cosec} x + 4 = 0$ If it helps, think of this as $y^2 - 4y + 4 = 0$.
   $(\operatorname{cosec} x - 2)(\operatorname{cosec} x - 2) = 0$ Factorise it, and then replace the y with cosec x.

4) One of the brackets must be **equal to zero** — here they're both the same, so you only get **one equation**:

   $(\operatorname{cosec} x - 2) = 0 \implies \operatorname{cosec} x = 2$ To find the other values of x, draw a quick sketch of the sin curve:

5) Now you can convert this into sin x, and solve it easily:
   $\operatorname{cosec} x = 2 \implies \sin x = \frac{1}{2}$
   $x = 30°$ **and** $x = 150°$

   From the graph, you can see that sin x takes the value of $\frac{1}{2}$ twice in the given interval, once at x = 30° and once at x = 180 − 30 = 150°.

   > You could also use the CAST diagram (see p.62) — sin is positive in the 1st and 2nd quadrants, where x = 30° and 180° − 30° = 150°.

You'll also have to use these identities for trigonometric proofs, or to 'show that' one expression is the same as another.
Look at pages 74-75 for some examples.

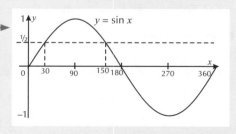

$\cos^2\theta + \sin^2\theta = 1$
$\sec^2\theta = 1 + \tan^2\theta$
$\operatorname{cosec}^2\theta = 1 + \cot^2\theta$

More useful.

Further Trig Identities and Approximations

The **Small Angle Approximations** simplify equations too

When an angle θ (measured in **radians**) is **very small** (< 1), you can approximate the value of $\sin \theta$, $\cos \theta$ and $\tan \theta$ using the **small angle approximations**:

$$\sin \theta \approx \theta \qquad \tan \theta \approx \theta \qquad \cos \theta \approx 1 - \frac{1}{2}\theta^2$$

Example: Approximate $\cos 10°$ to 6 d.p, and find the percentage error.

1) First convert the angle to **radians**, and check it's **small enough**:

$10° = \frac{10 \times \pi}{180} = 0.1746329...$ radians θ is a lot smaller than 1, so you can use the approximations.

2) The small angle approximation for cos is $\cos \theta \approx 1 - \frac{1}{2}\theta^2$, so:

$$\cos 0.1746329... \approx 1 - \frac{1}{2}(0.1746329...)^2 = \mathbf{0.984769}\ (6\ \text{d.p.})$$

3) The **actual value** of $\cos 10° = 0.984808$ (6 d.p.),

so the **percentage error** in the approximation $= \dfrac{\text{actual value} - \text{approximation}}{\text{actual value}} \times 100\%$

$$= \frac{0.984808 - 0.984769}{0.984808} \times 100\% = \mathbf{0.004}\%\ (3\ \text{d.p.})$$

So the small angle approximation is pretty accurate.

You can use them to approximate more **complicated functions**, involving sin, cos and tan of **multiples** of θ (i.e. $n\theta$ when $n\theta < 1$).

Make sure that you apply the approximation to **everything** inside the trig function, e.g. $\sin \frac{1}{2}\theta \approx \frac{1}{2}\theta$, $\cos 3\theta \approx 1 - \frac{1}{2}(3\theta)^2$.

Example: Find an approximation for $f(x) = 4 \cos 2x \tan 3x$ when x is small.

Replace cos and tan with the small angle approximations:

$\cos \theta \approx 1 - \frac{1}{2}\theta^2$ $f(x) \approx 4 \times (1 - \frac{1}{2}(2x)^2) \times (3x)$ $\tan \theta \approx \theta$

$$= (4 - 8x^2) \times 3x$$
$$= 12x - 24x^3 \ \text{or}\ 12x(1 - 2x^2)$$

As with the identities, you'll be expected to use the small angle approximations in **proofs** and '**show that**' questions — see pages 74-75.

Practice Questions

Q1 Use the identity $\cos^2 \theta + \sin^2 \theta \equiv 1$ to produce the identity $\sec^2 \theta \equiv 1 + \tan^2 \theta$.

Q2 Use the identity $\operatorname{cosec}^2 \theta \equiv 1 + \cot^2 \theta$ to simplify and solve $\operatorname{cosec}^2 \theta = -2\cot \theta$, for $0 \le \theta \le \pi$.

Q3 Use the small angle approximations for: a) $\sin 0.256$, b) $\cos 0.02$, c) $2 \tan 0.1 \sin 0.1$.

Exam Questions

Q1 a) (i) Show that $3 \tan^2 \theta - 2 \sec \theta = 5$ can be written as $3 \sec^2 \theta - 2 \sec \theta - 8 = 0$. [2 marks]

   (ii) Hence or otherwise show that $\cos \theta = -\frac{3}{4}$ or $\cos \theta = \frac{1}{2}$. [3 marks]

 b) Use your results from part a) to solve the equation $3 \tan^2 2x - 2 \sec 2x = 5$ for $0 \le x \le 180°$, to 2 d.p. [3 marks]

Q2 a) Find an approximation for $\theta \sin\left(\frac{\theta}{2}\right) - \cos \theta$, when θ is small. [2 marks]

 b) Hence give an approximate value of $\theta \sin\left(\frac{\theta}{2}\right) - \cos \theta$ when $\theta = 0.1$. [1 mark]

This section has more identities than Clark Kent...

I was devastated when my secret identity was revealed — I'd been masquerading as a mysterious caped criminal mastermind with an army of minions and a hidden underground lair. It was great fun, but I had to give it all up and write about trig. And lucky for you I did — who else would distract you from solving equations with cute bunny pics?

Addition and Double Angle Formulas

You might have noticed that there are quite a lot of formulas lurking in this here trigonometry jungle.
There are some more coming up on these pages too I'm afraid, so brace yourself.

You can use the **Addition Formulas** to find **Sums of Angles**

You can use the **addition formulas** to find the sin, cos or tan of the **sum** or **difference** of two angles.

When you have an expression like sin $(x + 60°)$ or cos $\left(n - \frac{\pi}{2}\right)$, you can use these formulas to **expand the brackets**.

Fran activated the 'hard trig' setting on her new-fangled adding machine.

$$\sin (A \pm B) \equiv \sin A \cos B \pm \cos A \sin B$$

$$\cos (A \pm B) \equiv \cos A \cos B \mp \sin A \sin B$$

$$\tan (A \pm B) \equiv \frac{\tan A \pm \tan B}{1 \mp \tan A \tan B}$$

These formulas are given to you in the formula booklet.

Watch out for the ± and ∓ signs in the formulas — especially for cos and tan. If you use the sign on the top on the RHS, you have to use the sign on the top on the left-hand side too — so cos(A + B) = cos A cos B − sin A sin B.

Use the **Formulas** to find the **Exact Value** of trig expressions

You should know the value of sin, cos and tan for **common angles** (in **degrees** and **radians**). These values come from using **Pythagoras** on **right-angled triangles** — see p.56.

In the exam you might be asked to calculate the **exact value** of sin, cos or tan for **another angle** using your knowledge of those angles and the **addition formulas**.

Find a **pair of angles** from the table which **add or subtract** to give the angle you're after. Then plug them into the **addition formula**, and work it through.

	0°	30°	45°	60°	90°
	0	$\frac{\pi}{6}$	$\frac{\pi}{4}$	$\frac{\pi}{3}$	$\frac{\pi}{2}$
sin	0	$\frac{1}{2}$	$\frac{1}{\sqrt{2}}$	$\frac{\sqrt{3}}{2}$	1
cos	1	$\frac{\sqrt{3}}{2}$	$\frac{1}{\sqrt{2}}$	$\frac{1}{2}$	0
tan	0	$\frac{1}{\sqrt{3}}$	1	$\sqrt{3}$	n/a

Example: Using the addition formula for tan, show that tan 15° = $2 - \sqrt{3}$.

1) Pick two angles that **add or subtract to give 15°**, and put them into the tan addition formula. It's easiest to use **tan 60°** and **tan 45°** here, since neither of them are fractions.

$$\tan 15° = \tan (60° - 45°) = \frac{\tan 60° - \tan 45°}{1 + \tan 60° \tan 45°}$$

Using tan$(A - B) = \frac{\tan A - \tan B}{1 + \tan A \tan B}$

2) **Substitute** the values for tan 60° and tan 45° into the equation: $= \frac{\sqrt{3} - 1}{1 + (\sqrt{3} \times 1)} = \frac{\sqrt{3} - 1}{\sqrt{3} + 1}$

3) Now rationalise the denominator of the fraction to get rid of the $\sqrt{3}$:

$$= \frac{\sqrt{3} - 1}{\sqrt{3} + 1} \times \frac{\sqrt{3} - 1}{\sqrt{3} - 1} = \frac{3 - 2\sqrt{3} + 1}{3 - \sqrt{3} + \sqrt{3} - 1}$$

If you can't remember how to rationalise the denominator have a peek at page 7.

4) Simplify the expression... $= \frac{4 - 2\sqrt{3}}{2} = 2 - \sqrt{3}$ ...and there's the **right-hand side**.

Example: Using the addition formula for sin, find sin $(A + B)$, where sin $A = \frac{4}{5}$ and sin $B = \frac{7}{25}$.

1) Look at the **addition formula** for sin: sin $(A + B) \equiv \sin A \cos B + \cos A \sin B$

2) You're given sin A and sin B, but you need cos A and cos B too. The numbers in the fractions should make you think of **right-angled triangles**: The triangles which have sin $A = \frac{4}{5}$ and sin $B = \frac{7}{25}$ have cos $A = \frac{3}{5}$ and cos $B = \frac{24}{25}$.

Because sin $= \frac{\text{opp}}{\text{hyp}}$ and cos $= \frac{\text{adj}}{\text{hyp}}$.

5, Angle A, 4, $\sqrt{5^2 - 4^2} = 3$

25, Angle B, 7, $\sqrt{25^2 - 7^2} = 24$

3) Putting these values into the formula gives:

$$\sin (A + B) = \left(\frac{4}{5} \times \frac{24}{25}\right) + \left(\frac{3}{5} \times \frac{7}{25}\right) = \frac{117}{125}$$

Addition and Double Angle Formulas

There's a Double Angle Formula for Each Trig Function

Whenever you see a trig expression with an **even multiple of** x in it, like $\sin 2x$, you can use one of the **double angle formulas** to prune it back to an expression just in terms of a **single** x. They are just a slightly different kind of **identity**. You need to know the double angle formulas for **sin**, **cos** and **tan**:

$$\sin 2A \equiv 2 \sin A \cos A$$

$$\begin{aligned} \cos 2A &\equiv \cos^2 A - \sin^2 A \\ \text{or} \quad &\equiv 2 \cos^2 A - 1 \\ \text{or} \quad &\equiv 1 - 2 \sin^2 A \end{aligned}$$

$$\tan 2A \equiv \frac{2 \tan A}{1 - \tan^2 A}$$

You get these formulas by writing 2A as A + A and using the addition formulas from the previous page.

You can use the identity $\cos^2 A + \sin^2 A \equiv 1$ to get the other versions of the cos 2A formula.

Use the Double Angle Formulas to Simplify and Solve Equations

If an equation has a **mixture** of **sin x** and **sin $2x$** terms in it, there's not much that you can do with it. So that you can **simplify** it, and then **solve** it, you have to use one of the **double angle formulas**.

Example: Solve the equation $\cos 2x - 5 \cos x = 2$ in the interval $0 \le x \le 2\pi$.

1) First use the double angle formula $\cos 2A \equiv 2 \cos^2 A - 1$ to get rid of cos $2x$: $2 \cos^2 x - 1 - 5 \cos x = 2$
   Use this version so that you don't end up with a mix of sin and cos terms.

2) Simplify so you have zero on one side...
   ...then factorise and solve the quadratic that you've made:

   $2 \cos^2 x - 5 \cos x - 3 = 0$
   $(2 \cos x + 1)(\cos x - 3) = 0$
   So $(2 \cos x + 1) = 0$ or $(\cos x - 3) = 0$

3) The second bracket gives you $\cos x = 3$, which has no solutions since $-1 \le \cos x \le 1$.

4) So all that's left is to solve the first bracket to find x:

   $2 \cos x + 1 = 0$
   $\cos x = -\frac{1}{2} \Rightarrow x = \frac{2}{3}\pi$ or $x = \frac{4}{3}\pi$

   Sketch the graph of cos x to find all values of x in the given interval: $\cos x = -\frac{1}{2}$ twice, once at $\frac{2}{3}\pi$ and once at $2\pi - \frac{2}{3}\pi = \frac{4}{3}\pi$.

   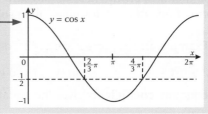

   (Or you can use the CAST method if you prefer — see p.62.)

Practice Questions

Q1 Using the addition formula for cos, find the exact value of $\cos \frac{\pi}{12}$.

Q2 Use the double angle formula to solve the equation: $\sin 2\theta = -\sqrt{3} \sin \theta$, $0° \le \theta \le 360°$.

Q3 Use the double angle formulas to write: a) $\sin \frac{x}{2} \cos \frac{x}{2}$ in terms of sin x,   b) tan $6x$ in terms of tan $3x$.

Exam Questions

Q1   Using double angle and addition identities, find an expression for sin $3x$ in terms of sin x only.   [4 marks]

Q2   Using the cos addition formula, show that if $\sin \theta = \cos\left(\frac{\pi}{4} - \theta\right)$ for $-\frac{\pi}{2} < \theta < \frac{\pi}{2}$, then $\theta = 1.18$ to 2 d.p.   [4 marks]

Q3   Solve the equation $2 \tan 4x = \tan 2x$ for $-90° \le x \le 90°$.   [6 marks]

Double the angles, double the fun...

You need to know the double angle formulas off by heart — unlike the addition ones, they WON'T be in the formula booklet. Watch out for questions where you need to use a double angle formula to turn a '4x' into a '2x', four x-ample.

The R Addition Formulas

Now for a different kind of addition formula, that lets you go from an expanded expression to one with brackets...

Use the **R Formulas** when you've got a **Mix** of **Sin** and **Cos**

If you're solving an equation that contains **both** $\sin \theta$ and $\cos \theta$ terms, e.g. $3 \sin \theta + 4 \cos \theta = 1$, you need to **rewrite** it so that it only contains **one** trig function.
The formulas that you use to do that are known as the **R formulas**:

One set for **sine**: $\boxed{a \sin \theta \pm b \cos \theta \equiv R \sin (\theta \pm \alpha)}$

And one set for **cosine**: $\boxed{a \cos \theta \pm b \sin \theta \equiv R \cos (\theta \mp \alpha)}$

... where a and b are **positive**. Again, you need to be careful with the + and − signs here — see p.70.

Using the R Formulas

1) You'll start with an **identity** like $2 \sin x + 5 \cos x \equiv R \sin (x + \alpha)$, where R and α need to be found.

2) First, **expand the RHS** using the **addition** formulas (see p.70):
$2 \sin x + 5 \cos x \equiv R \sin x \cos \alpha + R \cos x \sin \alpha$.

This is because $\dfrac{R \sin \alpha}{R \cos \alpha} = \tan \alpha$.

3) **Equate the coefficients** of $\sin x$ and $\cos x$. You'll get two equations:
① $R \cos \alpha = 2$ and ② $R \sin \alpha = 5$.

$(R \sin \alpha)^2 + (R \cos \alpha)^2$ $\equiv R^2(\sin^2 \alpha + \cos^2 \alpha)$ $\equiv R^2$ (using the identity $\sin^2 \alpha + \cos^2 \alpha \equiv 1$).

4) To find α, **divide** equation ② by equation ①, then take **tan⁻¹** of the result.

5) To find R, **square** equations ① and ② and **add** them together, then take the **square root** of the answer.

This method looks a bit scary, but follow the example below through and it should make more sense.

Solve the equation in Stages

You'll almost always be asked to solve equations like this in **different stages** — first **writing out** the equation in the form of one of the R formulas, then **solving** it. You might also have to find the **maximum** or **minimum** value.

Example a): Express $2 \sin x - 3 \cos x$ in the form $R \sin (x - \alpha)$, given that $R > 0$ and $0 \leq \alpha \leq 90°$.

$2 \sin x - 3 \cos x \equiv R \sin (x - \alpha)$, so **expand the RHS** to get $2 \sin x - 3 \cos x \equiv R (\sin x \cos \alpha - \cos x \sin \alpha)$.

Equating coefficients gives the equations $R \cos \alpha = 2$ and $R \sin \alpha = 3$.

Solving for α:
$\dfrac{R \sin \alpha}{R \cos \alpha} = \dfrac{3}{2} = \tan \alpha$

This value fits into the correct range so you can leave it as it is.

$\alpha = \tan^{-1} 1.5 = \mathbf{56.3°}$ (1 d.p.)

Look at the coefficients of sin x on each side of the equation — on the LHS it's 2 and on the RHS it's R cos α, so 2 = R cos α. You find the coefficient of cos x in the same way.

Solving for R: $(R \cos \alpha)^2 + (R \sin \alpha)^2 = 2^2 + 3^2 = R^2$
$R = \sqrt{2^2 + 3^2} = \sqrt{13}$

So $2 \sin x - 3 \cos x = \sqrt{13} \sin (x - 56.3°)$

Example b): Hence solve $2 \sin x - 3 \cos x = 1$ in the interval $0 \leq x \leq 360°$, giving your answers to 1 d.p.

If $2 \sin x - 3 \cos x = 1$, that means $\sqrt{13} \sin (x - 56.3°) = 1$,
so $\sin (x - 56.3°) = \dfrac{1}{\sqrt{13}}$.

Careful — you're looking for solutions between −56.3° and 303.7° here.

$0 \leq x \leq 360°$, so $-56.3° \leq x - 56.3° \leq 303.7°$.

Solve the equation using arcsin:

$x - 56.3° = \sin^{-1} \left(\dfrac{1}{\sqrt{13}} \right) = \mathbf{16.1°}$ or $180 - 16.1 = \mathbf{163.9°}$

So $x = 16.1 + 56.3 = \mathbf{72.4°}$ (1 d.p.)
or $x = 163.9 + 56.3 = \mathbf{220.2°}$ (1 d.p.)

Example c): What are the max and min values of $2 \sin x - 3 \cos x$?

The maximum and minimum values of sin (and cos) are ±1, so the maximum and minimum values of $R \sin (x - \alpha)$ are $\pm R$.

As $2 \sin x - 3 \cos x = \sqrt{13} \sin (x - 56.3°)$, $R = \sqrt{13}$, so the maximum and minimum values are $\pm\sqrt{13}$.

The R Addition Formulas

The **Factor Formulas** come from the **Addition Formulas**

As if there weren't enough **trig formulas** already, here come a few more.

$$\sin A + \sin B \equiv 2 \sin\left(\frac{A+B}{2}\right)\cos\left(\frac{A-B}{2}\right)$$

$$\sin A - \sin B \equiv 2 \cos\left(\frac{A+B}{2}\right)\sin\left(\frac{A-B}{2}\right)$$

$$\cos A + \cos B \equiv 2 \cos\left(\frac{A+B}{2}\right)\cos\left(\frac{A-B}{2}\right)$$

$$\cos A - \cos B \equiv 2 \sin\left(\frac{A+B}{2}\right)\sin\left(\frac{A-B}{2}\right)$$

Learning trig is tiring.
Take regular naps.

These are the **factor formulas**, and they come from the **addition formulas** (see below). They come in handy for some **integrations** — it's a bit tricky to integrate $2\cos 3\theta \cos \theta$, but integrating $\cos 4\theta + \cos 2\theta$ is much easier.

Example: Use the addition formulas to show that $\cos A + \cos B \equiv 2 \cos\left(\frac{A+B}{2}\right)\cos\left(\frac{A-B}{2}\right)$.

Use the **cos addition formulas:** $\cos(x+y) \equiv \cos x \cos y - \sin x \sin y$
and: $\cos(x-y) \equiv \cos x \cos y + \sin x \sin y$.

Add them together to get: $\cos(x+y) + \cos(x-y) \equiv \cos x \cos y - \sin x \sin y + \cos x \cos y + \sin x \sin y$

$$\cos(x+y) + \cos(x-y) \equiv 2 \cos x \cos y$$

Now **substitute** in $A = x+y$ and $B = x-y$.

Subtracting these gives: $A - B = x+y-(x-y) = 2y$, so $y = \frac{A-B}{2}$

Adding gives: $A + B = x+y+(x-y) = 2x$, so $x = \frac{A+B}{2}$

Substitute for $(x+y)$, $(x-y)$, x and y.

You can derive the other formulas using the same method.

So $\cos A + \cos B \equiv 2 \cos\left(\frac{A+B}{2}\right)\cos\left(\frac{A-B}{2}\right)$.

Practice Questions

Q1 Which two R formulas could you use to write $a\cos\theta + b\sin\theta$ (a, $b > 0$) in terms of just sin or just cos?

Q2 Write $5\sin\theta - 6\cos\theta$ in the form $R\sin(\theta - \alpha)$, where $R > 0$ and $0 \le \alpha \le 90°$.

Q3 Use the addition formulas to show that $\sin A - \sin B \equiv 2\cos\left(\frac{A+B}{2}\right)\sin\left(\frac{A-B}{2}\right)$.

Exam Questions

Q1 a) Write $9\sin\theta + 12\cos\theta$ in the form $R\sin(\theta + \alpha)$, where $R > 0$ and $0 \le \alpha \le \frac{\pi}{2}$. [3 marks]

b) Using the result from part a), solve $9\sin\theta + 12\cos\theta = 3$, giving all solutions for θ in the range $0 \le \theta \le 2\pi$. [5 marks]

c) $f(x) = 10 - 9\sin\theta - 12\cos\theta$. Find the maximum and minimum values of $f(x)$. [3 marks]

Q2 a) Write $5\cos\theta + 12\sin\theta$ in the form $R\cos(\theta - \alpha)$, where $R > 0$ and $0 \le \alpha \le 90°$. [3 marks]

b) Hence solve $5\cos\theta + 12\sin\theta = 2$ for $0 \le \theta \le 360°$, giving your answers to 2 decimal places. [5 marks]

c) Use your results from part a) above to find the minimum value of $(5\cos\theta + 12\sin\theta)^3$. [2 marks]

Q3 Use the factor formulas to write $4\sin\left(\frac{\pi}{2}\right)\cos\left(\frac{\pi}{12}\right)$ in the form $k(\sin A + \sin B)$. [3 marks]

A pirate's favourite trigonometry formula...

The R formulas might look a bit scary, but they're OK really — just do lots of examples until you're happy with the method. Careful with adjusting the interval for solutions though — it's pretty fiddly and easy to get muddled over.

Trigonometric Proofs

They say the proof of the pudding is in the eating, but trigonometry ain't no pudding, treacle.

Use the **Trig Identities** to prove something is the **Same** as something else

As well as simplifying and solving nasty trig equations, you can also use **identities** to **prove** or 'show that' two **trig expressions** are **the same**. A bit like this, in fact:

Example: Show that $\dfrac{\cos^2\theta}{1+\sin\theta} \equiv 1 - \sin\theta$.

1) Prove things like this by playing about with one side of the equation until you get the other side.
   Left-hand side: $\dfrac{\cos^2\theta}{1+\sin\theta}$ See page 59.

2) The only thing I can think of doing here is replacing $\cos^2\theta$ with $1 - \sin^2\theta$.
   (Which is good because it works.)

   $\equiv \dfrac{1-\sin^2\theta}{1+\sin\theta}$ The next trick is the hardest to spot. Look at the top — does that remind you of anything?

3) The top line is a **difference of two squares:** $1 - a^2 = (1+a)(1-a)$
   $\Rightarrow 1 - \sin^2\theta = (1+\sin\theta)(1-\sin\theta)$

   $\equiv \dfrac{(1+\sin\theta)(1-\sin\theta)}{1+\sin\theta}$

   $\equiv 1 - \sin\theta$, **the right-hand side.**

Example: Show that $\dfrac{\tan^2 x}{\sec x} \equiv \sec x - \cos x$.

Again, take one side of the identity and play about with it until you get the other side:
Left-hand side: $\dfrac{\tan^2 x}{\sec x}$

Try replacing $\tan^2 x$ with $\sec^2 x - 1$: $\equiv \dfrac{\sec^2 x - 1}{\sec x} \equiv \dfrac{\sec^2 x}{\sec x} - \dfrac{1}{\sec x} \equiv \sec x - \cos x$ ...which is the **right-hand side.**

This example uses an identity from page 68.

You might have to use **Addition** or **Double Angle Identities**

You might be asked to use the **addition formulas** to prove an identity (see p.70). Just put the **numbers** and **variables** from the **left-hand side** into the addition formulas and **simplify** until you get the expression you're after.

Example: Prove that $\cos(a + 60°) + \sin(a + 30°) \equiv \cos a$.   Be careful with the + and − signs here.

Put the numbers from the question into the **addition formulas:**

$\cos(a + 60°) + \sin(a + 30°) \equiv (\cos a \cos 60° - \sin a \sin 60°) + (\sin a \cos 30° + \cos a \sin 30°)$

Now **substitute** in any sin and cos values that you know... $= \dfrac{1}{2}\cos a - \dfrac{\sqrt{3}}{2}\sin a + \dfrac{\sqrt{3}}{2}\sin a + \dfrac{1}{2}\cos a$

See p.56.   ...and **simplify:** $= \dfrac{1}{2}\cos a + \dfrac{1}{2}\cos a = \cos a$

Maths criminals: innocent until proven sin y.

Whenever you have an expression that contains any angle that's **twice the size** of another, you can use the **double angle formulas** (see p.71)— whether it's $\sin x$ and $\sin 2x$, $\cos 2x$ and $\cos 4x$ or $\tan x$ and $\tan\frac{x}{2}$.

Example: Prove that $2\left(\cot\frac{x}{2}\right)\left(1 - \cos^2\frac{x}{2}\right) \equiv \sin x$.

This hellish example uses loads of different identities — there are more like this on the next page too. Woohoo.

First, use the identity $\sin^2\theta + \cos^2\theta \equiv 1$ to replace $1 - \cos^2\frac{x}{2}$ on the left-hand side: **Left-hand side:** $2\cot\frac{x}{2}\sin^2\frac{x}{2}$

Now write $\cot\theta$ as $\dfrac{\cos\theta}{\sin\theta}$: $2\dfrac{\cos\frac{x}{2}}{\sin\frac{x}{2}}\sin^2\frac{x}{2} \equiv 2\cos\frac{x}{2}\sin\frac{x}{2}$ ← Now you can use the sin 2A double angle formula to write $\sin x \equiv 2\sin\frac{x}{2}\cos\frac{x}{2}$ (using $A = \frac{x}{2}$).

So using the **sin double angle** formula... $\equiv \sin x$ ...you get the **right-hand side.**

Trigonometric Proofs

Small Angle Approximations *can pop up too*

Remember those lovely **small angle approximations** from p.69? No?
Well you'd better flick back a few pages for a recap before this example.

Example: Show that $\dfrac{2x\sin 2x}{1-\cos 5x} \approx \dfrac{8}{25}$ when x is (small).

> This is a whopping clue (pun intended) as to how you're going to tackle this question. If an exam question mentions an angle being 'small', think 'small angle approximations'.

Use the **small angle approximations** for each trig function, then **simplify**:

$$\sin\theta \approx \theta \qquad \cos\theta \approx 1 - \tfrac{1}{2}\theta^2$$

$$\frac{2x\sin 2x}{1-\cos 5x} \approx \frac{2x(2x)}{1-\left(1-\tfrac{1}{2}(5x)^2\right)} = \frac{4x^2}{\tfrac{25}{2}x^2} = \frac{8}{25}$$

You might have to use Different Bits *of* Trig *in the* Same Question

Some exam questions might try to catch you out by making you use **more than one** identity...

Example: Show that $\cos 3\theta \equiv 4\cos^3\theta - 3\cos\theta$.

> You have to use both the addition formula and the double angle formulas in this question.

First, write **cos 3θ** as **cos(2θ + θ)**, then you can use the **cos addition formula**:

$$\cos(3\theta) \equiv \cos(2\theta + \theta) \equiv \cos 2\theta\cos\theta - \sin 2\theta\sin\theta$$

Now you can use the cos and sin **double angle formulas** to get rid of the 2θ:

$$\cos 2\theta\cos\theta - \sin 2\theta\sin\theta \equiv (2\cos^2\theta - 1)\cos\theta - (2\sin\theta\cos\theta)\sin\theta$$

> This uses the identity $\sin^2\theta + \cos^2\theta \equiv 1$ in the form $\sin^2\theta \equiv 1 - \cos^2\theta$.

$$\equiv 2\cos^3\theta - \cos\theta - 2\sin^2\theta\cos\theta \equiv 2\cos^3\theta - \cos\theta - 2(1 - \cos^2\theta)\cos\theta$$

$$\equiv 2\cos^3\theta - \cos\theta - 2\cos\theta + 2\cos^3\theta \equiv 4\cos^3\theta - 3\cos\theta$$

This next question looks short and sweet, but it's actually pretty nasty
— you need to know a sneaky **conversion** between **sin** and **cos**.

Example: If $y = \arcsin x$ for $-1 \le x \le 1$ and $-\tfrac{\pi}{2} \le y \le \tfrac{\pi}{2}$, show that $\arccos x = \tfrac{\pi}{2} - y$.

$y = \arcsin x$, so $x = \sin y$ (as arcsin is the inverse of sin — see p.66).

Now the next bit isn't obvious — you need to use an identity
to **switch from sin to cos**. This gives: $x = \cos\left(\tfrac{\pi}{2} - y\right)$

Now, **taking inverses** gives: $\arccos x = \arccos\left[\cos\left(\tfrac{\pi}{2} - y\right)\right]$

$$\Rightarrow \arccos x = \frac{\pi}{2} - y$$

> Converting sin to cos (and back):
> $$\sin t \equiv \cos\left(\tfrac{\pi}{2} - t\right)$$
> and $\cos t \equiv \sin\left(\tfrac{\pi}{2} - t\right)$.
> Remember sin is just cos shifted by $\tfrac{\pi}{2}$ and vice versa.

Practice Questions

Q1 Show that $\dfrac{\sin^4 x + \sin^2 x\cos^2 x}{\cos^2 x - 1} \equiv -1$.

Q2 Use trig identities to show that: a) $\cot^2\theta + \sin^2\theta \equiv \operatorname{cosec}^2\theta - \cos^2\theta$, b) $\dfrac{\cos\theta}{\sin\theta} + \dfrac{\sin\theta}{\cos\theta} \equiv 2\operatorname{cosec} 2\theta$.

Exam Questions

Q1 a) Show that $\dfrac{2\sin x}{1-\cos x} - \dfrac{2\cos x}{\sin x} \equiv 2\operatorname{cosec} x$. [4 marks]

   b) Use this result to find all the solutions for which $\dfrac{2\sin x}{1-\cos x} - \dfrac{2\cos x}{\sin x} = 4$, $0 < x < 2\pi$. [3 marks]

Q2 Find an approximation for $(4x)^{-1}\operatorname{cosec} 3x\,(2\cos 7x - 2)$, for sufficiently small values of x. [4 marks]

Q3 Prove the identity $\cos\theta\cos 2\theta + \sin\theta\sin 2\theta \equiv \cos\theta$. [4 marks]

Did someone mention treacle pudding...?

And that's your lot for this section. There is nothing left to prove. Except for your well-honed trig skills in the exam...

Exponentials and Logs

Don't be put off by your parents or grandparents telling you that logs are hard. Logarithm (log for short) is just a fancy word for power, and once you know how to use them you can solve all sorts of equations.

You need to be able to **Switch** between **Different Notations**

Exponentials and **logs** can describe the same thing because they are **inverses** of each other.

$\log_a b = c$ means the same as $a^c = b$

That means that $\log_a a = 1$ and $\log_a 1 = 0$

> The little number 'a' after 'log' is called the **base**. Logs can be to any base, but **base 10** is the most common — this is usually left out, i.e. '$\log_{10}$' is just 'log'.

Example: Index notation: $10^2 = 100$ log notation: $\log_{10} 100 = 2$

So the **logarithm** of 100 to the **base 10** is 2, because 10 raised to the **power** of 2 is 100.

> Your calculator might have a 'log ▪□' button and a 'log' button.

Examples: Write down the values of the following:
a) $\log_2 8$ b) $\log_5 5$

a) 8 is 2 raised to the power of 3,
   so $2^3 = 8$ and $\log_2 8 = 3$

b) Anything to the power of 1 is itself,
   so $\log_5 5 = 1$

Write the following using log notation:
a) $5^3 = 125$ b) $3^0 = 1$

a) 3 is the power or **logarithm** that 5 (the **base**) is raised to to get 125,
   so $\log_5 125 = 3$

b) You'll need to remember this one:
   $\log_3 1 = 0$

The **Laws of Logarithms** are **Unbelievably Useful**

Whenever you have to deal with **logs**, you'll probably end up using the **laws** below. That means it's not a bad idea to **learn them** by heart right now.

Laws of Logarithms

$\log_a x + \log_a y = \log_a (xy)$ $\log_a x - \log_a y = \log_a \left(\dfrac{x}{y}\right)$ $\log_a x^k = k \log_a x$

> So $\log_a \dfrac{1}{x} = -\log_a x$

Use the **Laws** to **Manipulate Logs**

Example: Write each expression in the form $\log_a n$, where n is a number.
a) $\log_a 5 + \log_a 4$ b) $2\log_a 6 - \log_a 9$

a) $\log_a x + \log_a y = \log_a (xy)$ $\log_a 5 + \log_a 4 = \log_a (5 \times 4)$
                                                            $= \log_a 20$

b) $\log_a x^k = k \log_a x$ $2\log_a 6 = \log_a 6^2 = \log_a 36$
   $\log_a 36 - \log_a 9 = \log_a (36 \div 9)$
                                      $= \log_a 4$

You can use **Logs** to **Solve Equations**

Example: Solve $2^{4x} = 3$ to 3 significant figures.

You want x on its own, so take logs of both sides
(by writing 'log' in front of both sides): $\log 2^{4x} = \log 3$

Use $\log x^k = k \log x$: $4x \log 2 = \log 3$

Divide both sides by '4 log 2' to get x on its own: $x = \dfrac{\log 3}{4 \log 2}$

But $\dfrac{\log 3}{4 \log 2}$ is just a number you can find using a calculator: $x = \mathbf{0.396}$ **(to 3 s.f.)**

> Alternatively, you could do:
> $2^{4x} = 3 \Rightarrow \log_2 3 = 4x$
> $\Rightarrow x = \frac{1}{4}\log_2 3 = 0.396$ (to 3 s.f.)

Exponentials and Logs

Graphs of a^x never reach Zero

All the graphs of $y = a^x$ (**exponential graphs**) where $a > 1$ have the **same basic shape**. The graphs for $a = 2$, $a = 3$ and $a = 4$ are shown on the right.

- a is greater than 1 — so **y increases as x increases**.
- The **bigger** a is, the **quicker** the graphs increase.
- As x **decreases**, y **decreases** at a **smaller and smaller rate** — y will approach zero, but never actually get there.

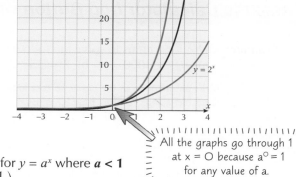

All the graphs go through 1 at $x = 0$ because $a^0 = 1$ for any value of a.

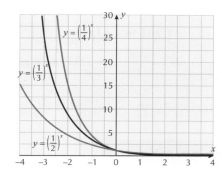

The graphs on the left are for $y = a^x$ where **$a < 1$** $\left(\text{they're for } a = \frac{1}{2}, \frac{1}{3} \text{ and } \frac{1}{4}\right)$.

- a is less than 1 — so **y decreases as x increases**.
- As x **increases**, y **decreases** at a **smaller and smaller rate** — again, y will approach zero, but never actually get there.

You can also use Exponentials and Logs to Solve Equations

Example: Solve $7 \log_{10} x = 5$ to 3 significant figures.

You want x on its own, so begin by dividing both sides by 7:
$$\log_{10} x = \frac{5}{7}$$

You now need to take exponentials of both sides by doing '10 to the power of both sides' (since the log is to base 10):
$$10^{\log_{10} x} = 10^{\frac{5}{7}}$$

Logs and exponentials are inverse functions, so they cancel out:
$$x = 10^{\frac{5}{7}}$$

But $10^{\frac{5}{7}}$ is just a number you can find using a calculator:
$$x = 5.18 \text{ (to 3 s.f.)}$$

John's new shoes didn't improve his logarithm.

Practice Questions

Q1 Write down the values of the following: a) $\log_3 27$ b) $\log_3 \left(\frac{1}{27}\right)$ c) $\log_3 18 - \log_3 2$

Q2 Simplify the following: a) $\log 3 + 2 \log 5$ b) $\frac{1}{2} \log 36 - \log 3$ c) $\log 2 - \frac{1}{4} \log 16$

Q3 Simplify $\log_b (x^2 - 1) - \log_b (x - 1)$

Q4 Solve these jokers to 4 significant figures: a) $10^x = 240$ b) $\log_{10} x = 5.3$ c) $10^{2x+1} = 1500$

Exam Questions

Q1 Solve the equation $\log_7 (y + 3) + \log_7 (2y + 1) = 1$, where $y > 0$. [4 marks]

Q2 a) Solve the equation $3^x = 5$, giving your answer to 2 decimal places. [3 marks]

b) Hence, or otherwise, solve the equation $3^{2x} - 14(3^x) = -45$ [4 marks]

It's sometimes hard to see the wood for the trees — especially with logs...

Tricky... I think of $\log_a b$ as 'the power I have to raise a to if I want to end up with b' — that's all it is. And the log laws make a bit more sense if you think of 'log' as meaning 'power'. For example, you know that $2^a \times 2^b = 2^{a+b}$ — this just says that if you multiply the two numbers, you add the powers. Well, the first law of logs is saying the same thing. Any road, even if you don't quite understand why they work, make sure you know the log laws like the back of your hand.

Using Exponentials and Logs

Now that you're familiar with the log laws, it's time to reveal their true power. Okay, maybe that's a slight exaggeration, but they are pretty useful in a variety of situations. Read on to find out more.

Use the *Calculator Log Button* whenever you can

Example: Use logarithms to solve the following for x, giving your answers to 4 s.f.
a) $10^{3x} = 4000$ b) $7^x = 55$ c) $\log_2 x = 5$

There's an unknown in the power, so take logs of both sides (if your calculator has a '$\log_{10}$' button, base 10 is usually a good idea):

a) $\log 10^{3x} = \log 4000$

You can choose any base, but use the same one for both sides.

Use one of the log laws: $\log x^k = k \log x$

$3x \log 10 = \log 4000$

Since $\log_{10} 10 = 1$, solve the equation to find x:

$3x = \log 4000$, so $x = \textbf{1.201 to 4 s.f.}$

Again, take logs of both sides, and use the log rules:

b) $x \log_{10} 7 = \log_{10} 55$, so $x = \dfrac{\log_{10} 55}{\log_{10} 7} = \textbf{2.059 to 4 s.f.}$

To get rid of a log, you 'take exponentials', meaning you do '2 (the base) to the power of each side'.

c) $2^{\log_2 x} = 2^5$,
so $x = 2^5 = \textbf{32}$

Or using base 7 for b):
$x = \log_7 55 = 2.059$ (4 s.f.)

You might have to *Combine* the *Laws of Logs* to *Solve* equations

If the examiners are feeling particularly mean, they might make you use **more than one** law to solve an equation.

Example: Solve the equation $\log_3(2 - 3x) - 2\log_3 x = 2$.

First, combine the log terms into one term (you can do this because they both have the same base):

$\log_3 \dfrac{2 - 3x}{x^2} = 2$

Remember that $a \log x = \log x^a$.

Then take exponentials of both sides:

$3^{\log_3 \frac{2-3x}{x^2}} = 3^2 \Rightarrow \dfrac{2 - 3x}{x^2} = 9$

Finally, rearrange the equation and solve for x:

$2 - 3x = 9x^2 \Rightarrow 0 = 9x^2 + 3x - 2$
$\Rightarrow 0 = (3x - 1)(3x + 2) \Rightarrow x = \dfrac{1}{3}$

Ignore the negative solution because you can't take logs of a negative number.

Exponential Growth and *Decay* applies to *Real-life* problems

Logs can even be used to model **real-life** situations — see pages 82-83 to see more of this.

Example: The radioactivity of a substance decays by 20 percent over a year. The initial level of radioactivity is 400. Find the time taken for the radioactivity to fall to 200 (the half-life).

$R = 400 \times 0.8^T$ where R is the **level of radioactivity** at time T years.
We need $R = 200$, so solve $200 = 400 \times 0.8^T$

The 0.8 comes from 100% − 20% decay.

$0.8^T = \dfrac{200}{400} = 0.5 \Rightarrow T \log 0.8 = \log 0.5 \Rightarrow T = \dfrac{\log 0.5}{\log 0.8} = \textbf{3.106 years}$ (4 s.f.)

Exponential **models** often have a **time restriction** — for larger times the numbers get too big or small.

Exponential equations can be *Reduced to Linear Form*

Equations like $y = ax^n$ and $y = ab^x$ can be a bit awkward to use. Fortunately, using the **laws of logs**, they can be rewritten to look like a form you've seen before — good old $y = mx + c$. Just take **logs** of both sides and rearrange:

$$y = ax^n \Rightarrow \log y = n \log x + \log a$$

$$y = ab^x \Rightarrow \log y = x \log b + \log a$$

The equations look pretty horrendous now, I'll admit. But look at them carefully — they're just a nasty-looking version of $y = mx + c$.

Once the equations are in this form you can draw their **straight line graphs** — you just need to **label** the axes **log x** (top) or **x** (bottom) against **log y**. Now your graph is **easier** to work with than the exponential graph.

Using Exponentials and Logs

Example: The number of employees, p, working for a company t years after it was founded can be modelled by the equation $p = at^b$. The table below shows the number of employees the company has:

Age of company (t years)	2	5	8	13	25
Number of employees (p)	3	7	10	16	29

a) Show that $p = at^b$ can be written in the form $\log p = b \log t + \log a$.

b) Plot a graph of $\log t$ against $\log p$ and draw a line of best fit for your graph.

c) Use your graph to estimate the values of a and b in the equation $p = at^b$.

Starting with $p = at^b$, take logs of both sides:

Now use the laws of logs to rearrange into required form:

Make a table of the values of $\log t$ and $\log p$ using p and t as given in the question:

Now plot a graph of $\log t$ against $\log p$ and draw a line of best fit:

a) $\log p = \log at^b$

$\log p = \log a + \log t^b = b \log t + \log a$

b)
$\log t$	0.301	0.699	0.903	1.114	1.398
$\log p$	0.477	0.845	1.000	1.204	1.462

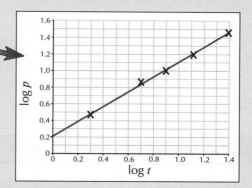

c) From part a), the graph has equation $\log p = b \log t + \log a$. Compare this to $y = mx + c$:

b is the gradient of the line and
$\log a$ is the vertical intercept of the line.

Use the coordinates of two points on the line to find the gradient:
E.g. use coordinates $(1.0, 1.1)$ and $(0, 0.2)$:

$b = \dfrac{y_2 - y_1}{x_2 - x_1} = \dfrac{1.1 - 0.2}{1.0 - 0} = \mathbf{0.9}$

You can also read the vertical intercept off the graph — 0.2.
BUT this value is equal to $\log a$, so take exponentials of both sides:
$a = 10^{0.2} = \mathbf{1.585}$ **to 3 d.p.**

So $b = 0.9$ and $a = 1.585$, and the original equation $p = at^b$ is $p = 1.585t^{0.9}$.

Be careful when using models like this to predict values outside the range of the given data — this is extrapolation (see p.183).

Practice Questions

Q1 If $6^{(3x+2)} = 9$, find x to 3 significant figures.

Q2 If $3^{(y^2-4)} = 7^{(y+2)}$, find y to 3 significant figures.

Q3 The value of a painting is modelled as increasing by 5% each year. If the initial price of the painting is £1000, find the time taken in years for the price to reach £2000. Give your answer to 1 d.p.

Exam Question

Q1 The yearly income from book sales of a particular author has tended to increase with time.
The table below shows his income from book sales over the first five years after his book was published.

Number of years after book published (t)	1	2	3	4	5
Income (£p thousand)	10	13	17	24	35

The relationship is modelled by the equation $p = ab^t$, where a and b are constants to be found.

a) Plot a graph of t against $\log_{10} p$. Draw, by eye, a line of best fit for your graph. [2 marks]

b) State, in terms of a and b, the gradient and vertical-axis intercept of your graph. Hence use your graph to find the values of a and b. [4 marks]

c) Predict the author's income 10 years after his book was published. [1 mark]

d) Suggest one reason why the prediction in part c) might not be accurate. [1 mark]

Reducing to linear form is hard work — you'll sleep like a log tonight...

The results you get with the method shown in the example will depend on your line of best fit, so make sure you draw it carefully. It doesn't hurt to check your final answer using the values in the original table to see how well it fits the data. And don't forget that the vertical intercept is a log — you'll need to take exponentials to get the value you want.

eˣ and ln x

Of all the exponential functions in the world (and there are infinite exponential functions), only one can be called <u>the</u> exponential function. The most powerful, most incredible — eˣ. Wait, what do you mean, "anticlimactic"?

The **Gradient** of the **Exponential Function** $y = e^x$ is e^x

There is a value of 'a' for which the **gradient** of $y = a^x$ is **exactly the same as a^x**. That value is known as **e**, an **irrational number** around **2.7183** (it's stored in your calculator, just like π). Because e is just a number, the graph of $y = e^x$ has all the properties of $y = a^x$...

1) $y = e^x$ crosses the y-axis at **(0, 1)**.
2) As $x \to \infty$, $e^x \to \infty$ and as $x \to -\infty$, $e^x \to 0$.
3) $y = e^x$ **does not exist** for $y \le 0$ (i.e. e^x **can't be zero or negative**).

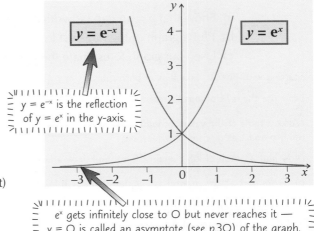

$y = e^{-x}$

$y = e^{-x}$ is the reflection of $y = e^x$ in the y-axis.

$y = e^x$

e^x gets infinitely close to O but never reaches it — $y = O$ is called an asymptote (see p.3O) of the graph.

The fact that the **gradient** of e^x is e^x (i.e. e^x is its own gradient) is used lots in the differentiation section — see page 96.

$y = e^{ax + b} + c$ is a transformation (see p.31) of $y = e^x$. The value of **a** stretches the graph horizontally, **b** shifts it horizontally and **c** shifts it vertically.

ln x is the **Inverse Function** of e^x

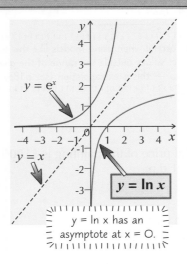

$y = e^x$

$y = x$

$y = \ln x$

$y = \ln x$ has an asymptote at $x = O$.

ln x (also known as $\log_e x$, or 'natural log'*) is the **inverse function** of e^x (see p.34):

1) $y = \ln x$ is the **reflection** of $y = e^x$ in the line $y = x$.
2) It crosses the x-axis at **(1, 0)** (so **ln 1 = 0**).
3) As $x \to \infty$, $\ln x \to \infty$ (but slowly), and as $x \to 0$, $\ln x \to -\infty$.
4) **ln x does not exist** for $x \le 0$ (i.e. x can't be zero or negative).

Because $\ln x$ is a logarithmic function and the inverse of e^x, we get these juicy **formulas** and **log laws**...

$$e^{\ln x} = x$$
$$\ln (e^x) = x$$

i.e. doing one function then the other to x takes you back to x.

These formulas are **extremely useful** for dealing with **equations** containing 'e^x's or '$\ln x$'s.

'Log laws' for ln x

$$\ln x + \ln y = \ln xy$$
$$\ln x - \ln y = \ln \left(\frac{x}{y}\right)$$
$$\ln x^k = k \ln x$$

These are the same old log laws from p.76, applied to ln x.

Use **Inverses** and **Log Laws** to **Solve Equations**

Just as with other logs and exponentials (p.76), you can use e^x and $\ln x$ to cancel each other out.

Example: If $e^{2x} = 9$, find the exact value of x.

Take ln of both sides: $\ln e^{2x} = \ln 9$

Using $\ln x^k = k \ln x$: $2x \ln e = \ln 9 \Rightarrow 2x = \ln 9$

$\Rightarrow x = \frac{1}{2} \ln 9 = \ln 9^{\frac{1}{2}} = \mathbf{\ln 3}$

The 'exact value of x' means 'leave x in terms of e and/or ln.'

Example: If $\ln (x - 5) = 3$, find the exact value of x.

Take exponentials of both sides: $e^{\ln (x - 5)} = e^3$

$x - 5 = e^3$

$\Rightarrow x = 5 + e^3$

All logs and no play makes Jill a dull girl.

*Certified organic

e^x and $\ln x$

You might have to solve a **Quadratic Equation** with **e** or **In**

Example: a) Solve the equation $2 \ln x - \ln 2x = 6$, giving your answer as an exact value of x.

Use the log laws to simplify: $\qquad 2 \ln x - \ln 2x = 6$
$$\Rightarrow \ln x^2 - \ln 2x = 6 \Rightarrow \ln (x^2 \div 2x) = 6 \Rightarrow \ln \left(\frac{x}{2}\right) = 6$$

Now apply the inverse function e^x to both sides
— this will remove the $\ln \left(\frac{x}{2}\right)$: $\qquad e^{\ln\left(\frac{x}{2}\right)} = e^6 \Rightarrow \frac{x}{2} = e^6 \Rightarrow x = 2e^6$

Using $e^{\ln x} = x$ from the last page.

b) Find the exact solutions of the equation $e^x + 5e^{-x} = 6$.

When you're asked for more than one solution think quadratics. $\qquad e^x + 5e^{-x} = 6$
Multiply each part of the equation by e^x to get rid of that e^{-x}: $\qquad \Rightarrow e^{2x} + 5 = 6e^x \Rightarrow e^{2x} - 6e^x + 5 = 0$

Basic power laws — $(e^x)^2 = e^{2x}$ and $e^{-x} \times e^x = e^0 = 1$.

It starts to look a bit nicer if you substitute y for e^x: $\qquad y^2 - 6y + 5 = 0$

Factorise to find solutions: $\qquad (y - 1)(y - 5) = 0 \Rightarrow y = 1$ and $y = 5$

Put e^x back in: $\qquad e^x = 1$ and $e^x = 5$

Using $\ln e^x = x$.

Take 'ln' of both sides to solve: $\qquad \ln e^x = \ln 1 \Rightarrow x = \ln 1 = \mathbf{0}$ and $\ln e^x = \ln 5 \Rightarrow x = \mathbf{\ln 5}$

Practice Questions

Q1 Four graphs, A, B, C and D, are shown below. Match the graphs to each of the following equations:
a) $y = 4e^x$ 　　　　 b) $y = 4e^{-x}$ 　　　　 c) $y = 4 \ln x$ 　　　　 d) $y = \ln 4x$

A 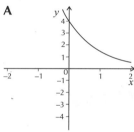 　　　 **B** 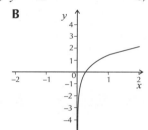 　　　 **C** 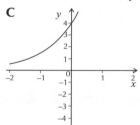 　　　 **D**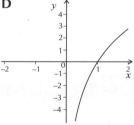

Q2 Find the value of x, to 4 decimal places, when:
a) $e^{2x} = 6$ 　　　 b) $\ln (x + 3) = 0.75$ 　　　 c) $3e^{-4x+1} = 5$ 　　　 d) $\ln x + \ln 5 = \ln 4$

Q3 Solve the following equations, giving your solutions as exact values:
a) $\ln (2x - 7) + \ln 4 = -3$ 　　　　　　 b) $2e^{2x} + e^x = 3$

Exam Questions

Q1 　a) Given that $6e^x = 3$, find the exact value of x. 　　　　　　　　　　　　　[2 marks]

　　b) Find the exact solutions to the equation $e^{2x} - 8e^x + 7 = 0$. 　　　　　　　[4 marks]

　　c) Given that $4 \ln x = 3$, find the exact value of x. 　　　　　　　　　　　[2 marks]

　　d) Solve the equation $\ln x + \dfrac{24}{\ln x} = 10$, giving your answers as exact values of x. 　　[4 marks]

Q2 Solve the following equations, giving your answers as exact values of x.
　　a) $2e^x + 18e^{-x} = 20$ 　　　　　　　　　　　　　　　　　　　　　[4 marks]

　　b) $2 \ln x - \ln 3 = \ln 12$ 　　　　　　　　　　　　　　　　　　　　[3 marks]

No problems — only solutions...
All the individual steps to solving these equations are easy — the hard bit is spotting what combination of things to try. A good thing to look for is hidden quadratics, so try and substitute for e^x or $\ln x$ to make things look a bit nicer. There's more about sketches on the next page, so don't worry too much if they're a bit confusing at the minute.

Modelling with eˣ and ln x

This page is all about models. Except they're modelling exponential growth and decay in real-world applications rather than the Chanel Autumn/Winter collection. Unless Chanel's lineup is growing exponentially, I suppose.

You can **Sketch** $y = e^{ax + b} + c$ and $y = \ln (ax + b)$

You should be familiar with the shape of the bog-standard exponential graphs, but most exponential functions will be **transformed** in some way. You need to know how the **key features** of the graph change depending on the function.

> **Example:** Sketch the following functions, labelling any key points and giving the equations of any asymptotes.
> a) $y = e^{-7x + 1} - 5$ $(x \in \mathbb{R})$ and b) $y = \ln (2x + 4)$ $(x \in \mathbb{R})$.

a) $y = e^{-7x + 1} - 5$

- 'Key points' usually means where the graph crosses the axes, i.e. where x and y are 0:
  When $x = 0$, $y = e^1 - 5 = \mathbf{-2.28}$ (3 s.f.)
  When $y = 0$, $e^{-7x + 1} = 5 \Rightarrow -7x + 1 = \ln 5 \Rightarrow x = \mathbf{-0.0871}$ (3 s.f.)

- Next see what happens as x tends to $\pm\infty$ to find any **asymptotes**:
  As $x \to \infty$, $e^{-7x + 1} \to 0$, so $y \to -5$.
  As $x \to -\infty$, $e^{-7x + 1} \to \infty$, so $y \to \infty$.
  y can't go below -5, so there's a horizontal asymptote at $y = \mathbf{-5}$.

- Now use all the information to sketch out a graph.

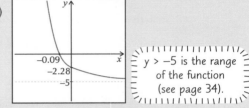

$y > -5$ is the range of the function (see page 34).

b) $y = \ln (2x + 4)$

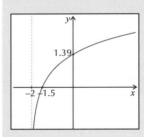

- First, the intercepts: When $x = 0$, $y = \ln 4 = \mathbf{1.39}$ (3 s.f.)
  When $y = 0$, $2x + 4 = e^0 = 1 \Rightarrow x = \mathbf{-1.5}$ (3 s.f.)

- As $x \to \infty$, $y \to \infty$ (gradually). As $x \to -\infty$, y decreases until $2x + 4 = 0$, at which point it can no longer exist (since $\ln x$ can only exist for $x > 0$). This gives an **asymptote** at $2x + 4 = 0$, i.e. $x = \mathbf{-2}$.

- Sketch the graph using all of the information.

$x > -2$ is the domain (see p.34).

Use **Exponential Functions** to **Model** real-life **Growth and Decay**

In the **exam** you might be given a background story to an exponential equation.
They may then ask you to **find some values**, work out a **missing part** of the equation, or even **sketch a graph**.
There's nothing here you haven't seen before — you just need to know how to deal with all the **wordy** bits.

> **Example:** The exponential growth of a colony of bacteria can be modelled by the equation $B = 60e^{0.03t}$, where B is the number of bacteria, and t is the time in hours from the point at which the colony is first monitored $(t \geq 0)$. Use the model to predict:

a) the number of bacteria after 4 hours,

You need to find B when $t = 4$, so put the numbers into the equation:
$B = 60 \times e^{(0.03 \times 4)}$
$= 60 \times 1.1274...$
$= 67.6498...$
So $B = \mathbf{67}$ **bacteria**

You shouldn't round up here — there are only 67 whole bacteria, not 68.

b) the time taken for the colony to grow to 1000.

- You need to find t when $B = 1000$, so put the numbers into the equation:
  $1000 = 60e^{0.03t}$
  $\Rightarrow e^{0.03t} = 1000 \div 60 = 16.6666...$

- Now take 'ln' of both sides as usual:
  $\ln e^{0.03t} = \ln (16.6666...)$
  $\Rightarrow 0.03t = 2.8134...$
  $\Rightarrow t = 2.8134... \div 0.03 = \mathbf{93.8}$ **hours** (3 s.f.)

You might need to think about whether the model is suitable for large values of t — populations can't go on forever. A sketch of the function can help here.

Modelling with eˣ and ln x

Example: The concentration (C) of a drug in the bloodstream, t hours after taking an initial dose, decreases exponentially according to $C = Ae^{-kt}$, where k is a constant. If the initial concentration is 0.72, and this halves after 5 hours, find the values of A and k and sketch the graph of C against t.

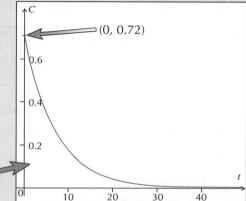
(0, 0.72)

- The 'initial concentration' is 0.72 when $t = 0$, so put this information into the equation to find A:
  $0.72 = A \times e^0 \Rightarrow 0.72 = A \times 1 \Rightarrow A = 0.72$

- The question also says that when $t = 5$ hours, C is half of 0.72. So using the value for A found above:
  $C = 0.72e^{-kt}$
  $0.72 \div 2 = 0.72 \times e^{(-k \times 5)}$
  $\Rightarrow 0.36 = 0.72 \times e^{-5k} \Rightarrow 0.36 = \dfrac{0.72}{e^{5k}} \Rightarrow e^{5k} = \dfrac{0.72}{0.36} = 2$

- Now take 'ln' of both sides to solve:
  $\ln e^{5k} = \ln 2 \Rightarrow 5k = \ln 2$
  $\Rightarrow k = \ln 2 \div 5 = 0.139$ (3 s.f.)

- So the equation is $C = 0.72e^{-0.139t}$.
  You still need to do a **sketch** though, so find the intercepts and asymptotes as you did on the last page:
  When $t = 0$, $C = 0.72$. As $t \to \infty$, $e^{-0.139t} \to 0$, so $C \to 0$.

The sketch should make sense for the situation in the question — here t can only be positive as it is the time after an event, so only sketch the graph for t ≥ O.

Practice Questions

Q1 Sketch graphs of the following, labelling key points and asymptotes:
  a) $y = 2 - e^{x+1}$ b) $y = 5e^{0.5x} + 5$ c) $y = \ln(2x) + 1$ d) $y = \ln(x + 5)$

Q2 The value of a motorbike (£V) varies with age (in t years from new) according to $V = 7500e^{-0.2t}$.
  a) How much did it originally cost?
  b) What will its value be after 10 years (to the nearest £)?
  c) After how many years will the motorbike's value have fallen to £500? Give your answer to 1 d.p.
  d) Sketch a graph showing how the value of the motorbike varies with age, labelling all key points.

Exam Questions

Q1 A breed of mink is introduced to a new habitat.
  The number of mink, M, after t years in the habitat, is modelled by: $M = 74e^{0.6t}$ ($t \geq 0$)
  a) State the number of mink that were introduced to the new habitat originally. [1 mark]
  b) Predict the number of mink after 3 years in the habitat. [2 marks]
  c) Predict the number of complete years it would take for the population of mink to exceed 10 000. [2 marks]
  d) Sketch a graph to show how the mink population varies with time in the new habitat. [2 marks]

Q2 A radioactive substance decays exponentially so that its activity, A, can be modelled by $A = Be^{-kt}$, where t is the time in days, and $t \geq 0$. Some experimental data is shown in the table.

t	0	5	10
A	50	42	

  a) State the value of B. [1 mark]
  b) Find the value of k, to 3 significant figures. [2 marks]
  c) Estimate the missing value from the table, to the nearest whole number. [2 marks]
  d) The half-life of a substance is the time it takes for the activity to halve. Find the half-life of this substance, in days. Give your answer to the nearest day. [3 marks]

Learn this and watch your knowledge grow exponentially...

For these wordy problems, the key is just to extract the relevant information and solve like you did on the previous pages. The more you practise, the more familiar they'll become — soon you'll be able to do them with your eyes shut.

Differentiation

Differentiation is a great way to work out gradients of graphs. You take a function, differentiate it, and you can quickly tell how steep a graph is. It's magic. No, wait, the other thing — it's <u>calculus</u>.

Use this **Formula** to **Differentiate Powers of x**

'Derivative' just means 'the thing you get when you differentiate something'.

For a function $f(x) = x^n$, the **derivative** $f'(x)$ can be found using this formula:

$\frac{d}{dx}$ just means 'the derivative of the thing in the brackets with respect to x'.

$$f'(x) = \frac{d}{dx}(x^n) = nx^{n-1}$$

If you have y = (some function of x), its derivative is written $\frac{dy}{dx}$, which means 'the rate of change of y with respect to x'.

Functions are much easier to **differentiate** when they're written as **powers of x** — like writing $\sqrt{x}$ as $x^{\frac{1}{2}}$ (see p.6). When you've done this, you can use the formula in the box above to differentiate the function.

Use the differentiation formula:

For 'normal' powers:

E.g. $f(x) = x^2$ *n is just the power of x.*

Here, $n = 2$, so:

$f'(x) = nx^{n-1} = 2x^1 = 2x$

For **negative** powers:

E.g. $f(x) = \frac{1}{x^2} = x^{-2}$ *Always rewrite the function as a power of x.*

Here $n = -2$, so:

$f'(x) = nx^{n-1} = -2x^{-3} = -\frac{2}{x^3}$

For **fractional** powers:

E.g. $f(x) = \sqrt{x} = x^{\frac{1}{2}}$.   *Write the square root as a power of x.*

Here, $n = \frac{1}{2}$, so:

$f'(x) = \frac{1}{2}x^{-\frac{1}{2}} = \frac{1}{2\sqrt{x}}$

Differentiate each term **Separately**

Even if there are loads of terms in the function, it doesn't matter.
Differentiate each bit **separately** and you'll be fine. Here are a couple of examples:

Example: Differentiate $y = 3\sqrt{x} = 3x^{\frac{1}{2}}$

If the function is being multiplied by a constant (3 in this case)...

$\frac{dy}{dx} = 3\left(\frac{1}{2}x^{-\frac{1}{2}}\right)$ *...multiply the derivative by the same number.*

$\frac{dy}{dx} = \frac{3}{2} \times x^{-\frac{1}{2}} = \frac{3}{2\sqrt{x}}$

Example: Differentiate $y = 6x^2 + \frac{4}{\sqrt[3]{x}} - \frac{2}{x^2} + 1$

Write each term as a power of x, including the constants: $1 = x^0$

Differentiate each bit separately and add or subtract the results.

$y = 6x^2 + 4x^{-\frac{1}{3}} - 2x^{-2} + x^0$

$\frac{dy}{dx} = 6(2x) + 4\left(-\frac{1}{3}x^{-\frac{4}{3}}\right) - 2(-2x^{-3}) + 0x^{-1}$

$\frac{dy}{dx} = 12x - \frac{4}{3\sqrt[3]{x^4}} + \frac{4}{x^3}$

A constant always differentiates to 0.

You can **Differentiate** to find **Gradients**

Differentiating tells you the **gradient** of a curve at any given point, which is the same as the gradient of the **tangent** to the curve at that point. Tangents will become a lot more important on the next page, so stay tuned...

Example: Find the gradient of the graph $y = x^2$ at $x = 1$ and $x = -2$.

You need the **gradient** of the graph of: $y = x^2$

So **differentiate** this function to get: $\frac{dy}{dx} = 2x$

When $x = 1$, $\frac{dy}{dx} = 2(1) = 2$, so the gradient at $x = 1$ is **2**.

When $x = -2$, $\frac{dy}{dx} = 2(-2) = -4$, so the gradient at $x = -2$ is **-4**.

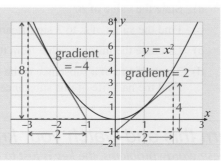

Differentiation

You can find the **Equation** of a **Tangent** or a **Normal** to a curve

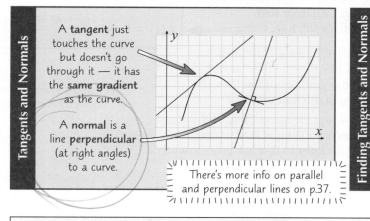

Tangents and Normals

A **tangent** just touches the curve but doesn't go through it — it has the **same gradient** as the curve.

A **normal** is a line **perpendicular** (at right angles) to a curve.

There's more info on parallel and perpendicular lines on p.37.

Finding Tangents and Normals

1) Differentiate the function.

2) Find the gradient of the tangent or normal.
   For a **tangent**, this is the gradient of the curve.
   For a **normal**, this is $\dfrac{-1}{\text{gradient of the curve}}$.
   perpendicular.

3) Write the equation of the tangent or normal in the form $y - y_1 = m(x - x_1)$ or $y = mx + c$.

4) Use the coordinates of a point on the line to complete the equation of the line .

Tangents have the **Same Gradient** as the curve

Example: Find the tangent to the curve $y = (4 - x)(x + 2)$ at the point $(2, 8)$.

To find the **gradient** of the curve (and the tangent), first write the equation in a **form** you can differentiate:

$$y = (4 - x)(x + 2) = 8 + 2x - x^2$$

Then **differentiate** it: $\dfrac{dy}{dx} = 2 - 2x$

The **gradient** of the tangent at $(2, 8)$ will be the gradient of the curve at $x = 2$.

$$\text{At } x = 2, \frac{dy}{dx} = -2$$

So the tangent has equation $y - y_1 = -2(x - x_1)$, *(You could also use $y = mx + c$ here.)*

and since it passes through the point $(2, 8)$, this becomes:

$$y - 8 = -2(x - 2) \quad \text{or} \quad y = 12 - 2x$$

You can give your answer in any of the forms from p.36.

"Sir, I'm picking up something abnormal in the system..."

Normals are **Perpendicular** to the curve

Example: Find the normal to the curve $y = \dfrac{(x + 2)(x + 4)}{6\sqrt{x}}$ at the point $(4, 4)$.

Write the equation of the curve in a **form** you can differentiate:

$$y = \frac{x^2 + 6x + 8}{6x^{\frac{1}{2}}} = \frac{1}{6}x^{\frac{3}{2}} + x^{\frac{1}{2}} + \frac{4}{3}x^{-\frac{1}{2}}$$

Divide everything on the top line by everything on the bottom line.

Then **differentiate** it:
$$\frac{dy}{dx} = \frac{1}{6}\left(\frac{3}{2}x^{\frac{1}{2}}\right) + \frac{1}{2}x^{-\frac{1}{2}} + \frac{4}{3}\left(-\frac{1}{2}x^{-\frac{3}{2}}\right)$$
$$= \frac{1}{4}\sqrt{x} + \frac{1}{2\sqrt{x}} - \frac{2}{3\sqrt{x^3}}$$

Find the **gradient** at $(4, 4)$: At $x = 4$, $\dfrac{dy}{dx} = \dfrac{1}{4} \times 2 + \dfrac{1}{2 \times 2} - \dfrac{2}{3 \times 8} = \dfrac{2}{3}$

So the **gradient** of the **normal** is $-1 \div \dfrac{2}{3} = -\dfrac{3}{2}$ — *Because the gradients of perpendicular lines multiply to give −1.*

And the **equation** of the normal is $y - y_1 = -\dfrac{3}{2}(x - x_1)$,

and since it passes through the point $(4, 4)$, this becomes:

$$y - 4 = -\frac{3}{2}(x - 4) \quad \text{or} \quad 3x + 2y - 20 = 0$$

Differentiation

You can also **Differentiate** from **First Principles**

You can use this **formula** to find the derivative of a function from **first principles**. I know it looks nasty, but don't worry — it doesn't bite. ⟹

$$f'(x) = \lim_{h \to 0} \left(\frac{f(x + h) - f(x)}{h} \right)$$

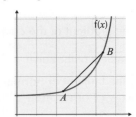

- To see where this comes from, imagine the graph of f(x), and a line joining two points on the graph, A and B.
- As B moves closer to A, the gradient of the line AB gets closer to the gradient of the function at A.
- The formula is basically doing the same thing, but instead of the points A and B, you're looking at (x, f(x)) and ($x + h$, f($x + h$)) — as h gets closer to 0, $x + h$ gets closer to x.

You might see 'δx' instead of h in the formula, but it means the same thing

because x/A+0 = x/A.

Here's one of our classic step-by-step guides on how to tackle a question like this:

1) Find $\dfrac{f(x + h) - f(x)}{h}$ and **simplify** (you need to **remove** h from the **denominator** when you're simplifying).

2) Find the **limit** of the expression as h tends to zero (written $\lim_{h \to 0}$) by setting $h = 0$ and simplifying.

3) If needed, put the **x-value** for your given point into the expression to find the **gradient** of f(x) at that point.

Example: Differentiate f(x) = x^2 from first principles.

Substitute f(x) = x^2 into the formula:

$$f'(x) = \lim_{h \to 0} \left(\frac{(x + h)^2 - x^2}{h} \right)$$

The x^2s cancel on the top, and then you can cancel h from the bottom too.

$$= \lim_{h \to 0} \left(\frac{x^2 + 2hx + h^2 - x^2}{h} \right)$$

$$= \lim_{h \to 0} \left(\frac{2hx + h^2}{h} \right)$$

Now you can set $h = 0$ (without dividing by 0) to find the derivative:

$$= \lim_{h \to 0} (2x + h)$$

$$= 2x \qquad \text{what a shocker...}$$

Practice Questions

Q1 Differentiate these functions with respect to x: a) $y = x^2 + 2$ b) $y = x^4 + \sqrt{x}$ c) $y = \dfrac{7}{x^2} - \dfrac{3}{\sqrt{x}} + 12x^3$

Q2 Find the gradient of the graph of $y = x^3 - 7x^2 - 1$ at $x = 2$.

Q3 Find the equations of the tangent and the normal to the curve $y = \sqrt{x^3} - 3x - 10$ at $x = 16$.

Q4 Use differentiation from first principles to find the derivative of f(x) = 5x.

Exam Questions

Q1 Find the gradient of the curve $y = \dfrac{1}{\sqrt{x}} + \dfrac{1}{x}$ at the point $\left(4, \dfrac{3}{4}\right)$. [2 marks]

Q2 The curve C is given by the equation $y = mx^3 - x^2 + 8x + 2$, for a constant m.

   a) Find $\dfrac{dy}{dx}$. [1 mark]

   The point P lies on C, and has an x-coordinate of 5.
   The normal to C at P is parallel to the line given by the equation $y + 4x - 3 = 0$.

   b) Find the gradient of curve C at P. [2 marks]

   c) Hence or otherwise, find: (i) the value of m, [3 marks]
                         (ii) the y-coordinate of P. [2 marks]

Q3 Show that the lines $y = \dfrac{x^3}{3} - 2x^2 - 4x + \dfrac{86}{3}$ and $y = \sqrt{x}$ both go through the point (4, 2), and are perpendicular at that point. [6 marks]

Q4 Use a binomial expansion to differentiate f(x) = x^4 from first principles. [5 marks]

---

f(x) and g(x) are like identical twins — it can be hard to differentiate them...

This is where A-level maths really kicks off, but don't get carried away and forget the basics. Always write out your working really clearly, particularly when differentiating from first principles. I mean, I know the answer's obvious, and I know you know the answer's obvious, but if they've asked you to use the formula then you'd better do it properly.

Stationary Points

Let me tell you about a special place — it's a magical point called a stationary point, where the gradient of the graph is zero, and there's a pot of g- oh no, wait, it's actually just the gradient thing. Turns out they're pretty ordinary, really.

Stationary Points are when the gradient is Zero

Stationary points are points on a graph where the curve **flattens out** — i.e. the **gradient is zero**.
A stationary point could be...

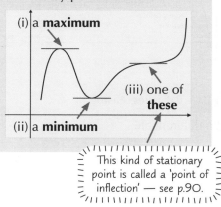

(i) a **maximum**

(iii) one of **these**

(ii) a **minimum**

This kind of stationary point is called a 'point of inflection' — see p.90.

Example: Find the coordinates of the stationary points of the curve $y = 2x^3 - 3x^2 - 12x + 5$, and determine the nature of each.

You need to find where $\frac{dy}{dx} = 0$. So first, **differentiate** the function.

$$y = 2x^3 - 3x^2 - 12x + 5 \Rightarrow \frac{dy}{dx} = 6x^2 - 6x - 12$$

Then set this derivative equal to **zero** and solve for x:

$$6x^2 - 6x - 12 = 0 \Rightarrow x^2 - x - 2 = 0$$
$$\Rightarrow (x + 1)(x - 2) = 0 \Rightarrow x = -1 \text{ or } x = 2$$

So the graph has **two stationary points**, at $x = -1$ and $x = 2$.

When $x = -1$, $y = 2(-1)^3 - 3(-1)^2 - 12(-1) + 5$
$$= -2 - 3 + 12 + 5 = 12$$

When $x = 2$, $y = 2(2)^3 - 3(2)^2 - 12(2) + 5$
$$= 16 - 12 - 24 + 5 = -15$$

So the stationary points are at **(-1, 12)** and **(2, -15)**. To be continued...

Decide if it's a Maximum or a Minimum by differentiating Again

Once you've found where the stationary points are, you have to decide whether each one is a **maximum** or a **minimum** — that's all a question means when it says, '...determine the nature of the turning points' (a '**turning point**' is either a maximum or minimum — points of inflection don't count).

To decide whether a stationary point is a **maximum** or a **minimum**, differentiate again to find $\frac{d^2y}{dx^2}$, or $f''(x)$. $f''(x)$ is called the **second order derivative**, and is the **rate of change** of the gradient.

$\frac{d^2y}{dx^2}$ is read 'd 2 y by dx squared'.

If $f''(x) > 0$, it's a **minimum**.

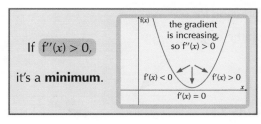
the gradient is increasing, so $f''(x) > 0$
$f'(x) < 0$ $f'(x) > 0$
$f'(x) = 0$

If $f''(x) < 0$, it's a **maximum**.

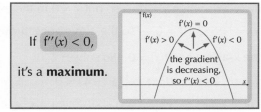
$f'(x) = 0$
$f'(x) > 0$ $f'(x) < 0$
the gradient is decreasing, so $f''(x) < 0$

If $\frac{d^2y}{dx^2} = 0$, then it could be any type of stationary point — see p.90.

Last time, on 'Strictly Come Differentiating'...

...you found that the stationary points were at **(-1, 12)** and **(2, -15)**.

$\frac{dy}{dx} = 6x^2 - 6x - 12$, so differentiate again: $\frac{d^2y}{dx^2} = 12x - 6$

Now find the value of $\frac{d^2y}{dx^2}$ at the stationary points:

At $x = -1$, $\frac{d^2y}{dx^2} = 12(-1) - 6 = -18$

This is **negative**, so **(-1, 12)** is a **maximum**.

At $x = 2$, $\frac{d^2y}{dx^2} = 12(2) - 6 = 18$

This is **positive**, so **(2, -15)** is a **minimum**.

Finding the maximum and minimum points of a function makes it a lot easier to sketch the graph — check out the stuff on the next two pages.

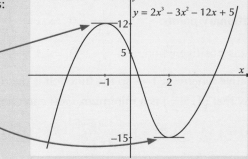
$y = 2x^3 - 3x^2 - 12x + 5$

Stationary Points

Find out if a function is Increasing or Decreasing

You can use differentiation to work out exactly where a function is **increasing** or **decreasing** — and how quickly.

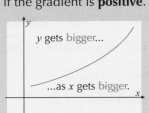

A function is **increasing** if the gradient is **positive**.

y gets bigger... ...as *x* gets bigger.

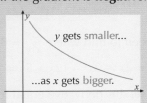

A function is **decreasing** if the gradient is **negative**.

y gets smaller... ...as *x* gets bigger.

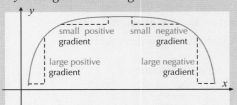

The **bigger** the gradient, the **quicker** *y* changes as *x* changes.

small positive gradient   small negative gradient

large positive gradient   large negative gradient

Example: Find the range of *x*-values for which the graph of $f(x) = 4 + 3x - 2x^2$ is increasing.

You want to find where the gradient is positive, i.e. where $f'(x) > 0$. So differentiate:

$$f(x) = 4 + 3x - 2x^2 \Rightarrow f'(x) = 3 - 4x$$

Now find where $f'(x) > 0$: $\quad 3 - 4x > 0 \Rightarrow 4x < 3 \Rightarrow x < \frac{3}{4}$

Use differentiation to make Curve Sketching easier

Now, you might be wondering where I'm going with all of this stuff about increasing functions and stationary points and gradients... Well, as it happens, it's all really helpful for sketching graphs of complicated functions. So sit tight — here comes one mega-example that you won't soon forget:

1) Find where the curve crosses the Axes

Example: Sketch the graph of $f(x) = \frac{x^2}{2} - 2\sqrt{x}$ for $x \geq 0$.

The curve crosses the *y*-**axis** when $x = 0$ — so put $x = 0$ in the expression for *y*.

When $x = 0$, $f(x) = \frac{0^2}{2} - 2\sqrt{0} = 0$ — so the curve goes through the **origin**.

The curve crosses the *x*-**axis** when $f(x) = 0$. So solve:

$$\frac{x^2}{2} - 2\sqrt{x} = 0 \Rightarrow x^2 - 4x^{\frac{1}{2}} = 0 \Rightarrow x^{\frac{1}{2}}\left(x^{\frac{3}{2}} - 4\right) = 0$$

$$x^{\frac{1}{2}} = 0 \Rightarrow x = 0 \quad \text{and} \quad x^{\frac{3}{2}} - 4 = 0 \Rightarrow x^{\frac{3}{2}} = 4 \Rightarrow x = 4^{\frac{2}{3}} \ (\approx 2.5)$$

So the curve crosses the *x*-axis when $x = 0$ and when $x \approx 2.5$.

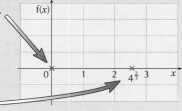

2) Differentiate to find information about the Gradient and Stationary Points

Differentiating the function gives: $f'(x) = \frac{1}{2}(2x) - 2\left(\frac{1}{2}x^{-\frac{1}{2}}\right) = x - x^{-\frac{1}{2}} = x - \frac{1}{\sqrt{x}}$

Find any **stationary points**: $\quad x - \frac{1}{\sqrt{x}} = 0 \Rightarrow x = \frac{1}{\sqrt{x}} \Rightarrow x^{\frac{3}{2}} = 1 \Rightarrow x = 1 \longrightarrow$ At $x = 1$, $f(x) = \frac{1}{2} - 2 = -\frac{3}{2}$

The gradient is **positive** when: $\quad x - \frac{1}{\sqrt{x}} > 0 \Rightarrow x > \frac{1}{\sqrt{x}} \Rightarrow x^{\frac{3}{2}} > 1 \Rightarrow x > 1$

and it's **negative** when $x < 1$ — so the function is decreasing for $0 < x < 1$, then increasing for $x > 1$.

So you know that $\left(1, -\frac{3}{2}\right)$ **is a minimum**. You can check this by differentiating again:

$$f''(x) = 1 - \left(-\frac{1}{2}x^{-\frac{3}{2}}\right) = 1 + \frac{1}{2\sqrt{x^3}} \qquad f''(1) = 1 + \frac{1}{2\sqrt{1^3}} = 1 + \frac{1}{2} > 0 \text{ so } x = 1 \text{ is a minimum.}$$

Stationary Points

3) Find out what happens when x gets **Big**

You can also try and decide what happens as x gets very **big** — in both the positive and negative directions. There's a handy trick you can use to help with this when your function is made up of **powers of** x — **factorise** to take out the **highest power of** x from every term.

> If the highest power of x is negative, then the graph will flatten out as x gets larger — see p.30 for more.

Factorise f(x) by taking the **biggest** power outside the brackets...

$$\frac{x^2}{2} - 2\sqrt{x} = x^2\left(\frac{1}{2} - 2x^{-\frac{3}{2}}\right) = x^2\left(\frac{1}{2} - \frac{2}{x^{\frac{3}{2}}}\right)$$

As x gets large, the $\frac{2}{x^{\frac{3}{2}}}$ gets smaller and smaller — so the bit in brackets gets closer to $\frac{1}{2}$.

So as x gets larger, f(x) gets closer and closer to $\frac{1}{2}x^2$ — and this just keeps growing and growing.

So the final graph looks like this:

It passes through **(0, 0)** and **$(4\frac{2}{3}, 0)$**,

has a minimum point at $\left(1, -\frac{3}{2}\right)$,

and gets larger and larger as x increases.

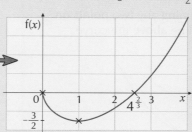

You should normally also think about what happens when x is big and negative, but you don't have to here as the graph is for x ≥ 0.

Practice Questions

Q1 Find the stationary points of the graph of $y = x^3 - 6x^2 - 63x + 21$.

Q2 Find the stationary points of the function $y = x^3 + \frac{3}{x}$.
Decide whether each stationary point is a minimum or a maximum.

Q3 Find when these functions are increasing and decreasing:
   a) $y = 6(x + 2)(x - 3)$ b) $y = \frac{1}{x^2}$

Q4 Sketch the graph of $y = x^3 - 4x$, clearly showing the coordinates of any turning points.

Exam Questions

Q1 a) Find $\frac{dy}{dx}$ for the curve $y = 6 + \frac{4x^3 - 15x^2 + 12x}{6}$.   [2 marks]

   b) Hence find the coordinates of the stationary points of the curve.   [3 marks]

   c) Determine the nature of each stationary point.   [3 marks]

Q2 a) Find the coordinates of the stationary points for the curve $y = (x - 1)(3x^2 - 5x - 2)$.   [4 marks]

   b) Determine whether each of these points is a maximum or minimum.   [3 marks]

   c) Sketch the graph of $y = (x - 1)(3x^2 - 5x - 2)$.   [3 marks]

Q3 The function $f(x) = \frac{1}{2}x^4 - 3x$ has a single stationary point.

   a) Find the coordinates of the stationary point.   [3 marks]

   b) Determine the nature of the stationary point.   [2 marks]

   c) State the range of values of x for which f(x) is:
      (i) increasing   [1 mark]
      (ii) decreasing   [1 mark]

   d) Sketch the graph of $y = $ f(x).   [2 marks]

Curve sketching's important — but don't take my word for it...

Curve sketching — an underrated skill, in my opinion. As Shakespeare once wrote, 'Those who can do fab sketches of graphs and stuff are likely to get pretty good grades in maths exams, no word of a lie'. Well, he probably would've written something like that if he was into maths. And he would've written it because graphs are helpful when you're trying to work out what a question's all about — and once you know that, you can decide the best way forward. And if you don't believe me, remember the saying of the ancient Roman Emperor Julius Caesar, 'If in doubt, draw a graph'.

Convex and Concave Curves

On p.87, we briefly mentioned the third type of stationary point — the mythical "point of inflection". But before we can get to those, I should introduce you to my good friends Convex and Concave Curves (they're siblings, by the way).

Curves can be **Convex** or **Concave**

Convex and concave are some handy words that you can use to describe the **shape** of a graph. They can be used for the **whole graph**, or just **parts** of it. It can be easy to forget which is which, so I'd pay close attention here.

Convex	Concave
Convex curves are ones that curve **downwards**. A straight line joining any two points on the curve will be **above** the curve.	**Concave curves** are ones that curve **upwards**. A straight line joining any two points on the curve will be **below** the curve.
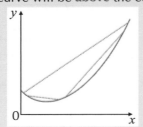	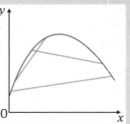
A curve is **convex** when $f''(x) > 0$ i.e. when its **gradient** is **increasing**.	A curve is **concave** when $f''(x) < 0$ i.e. when its **gradient** is **decreasing**.

Example: Find the range of x-values for which the graph of $y = 2x^3 - x^2 + 5$ is concave.

Start by finding the **second derivative**:
$$y = 2x^3 - x^2 + 5$$
$$\frac{dy}{dx} = 6x^2 - 2x$$
$$\frac{d^2y}{dx^2} = 12x - 2$$

The graph is concave when the second derivative is **negative**:
$$\frac{d^2y}{dx^2} < 0 \Rightarrow 12x - 2 < 0 \Rightarrow 12x < 2 \Rightarrow x < \frac{1}{6}$$

If you're having trouble remembering which is which, here's a handy tip: concave is the one that looks like the entrance to a cave.

Points of Inflection occur when the curve **Changes** from one to the other

A point where the curve **changes** between concave and convex (i.e. where $f''(x)$ changes between positive and negative) is called a **point of inflection**. At a point of inflection, $f''(x) = 0$ — but not all points where $f''(x) = 0$ are points of inflection. You need to look what's happening on **either side** of the point to see if the **sign** of $f''(x)$ is changing.

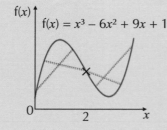

$f''(x) = 6x - 12$, so $f''(x) = 0$ when $x = 2$
$f''(x) < 0$ for $x < 2$ and $f''(x) > 0$ for $x > 2$

The curve changes from **concave** to **convex** at this point, so there is a **point of inflection** at $x = 2$.

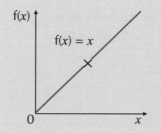

$f''(x) = 0$ for all x

The curve is **never** concave or convex, so there are **no** points of inflection.

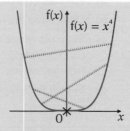

$f''(x) = 12x^2$, so $f''(x) = 0$ when $x = 0$ but $f''(x) \geq 0$ for all x

The whole curve is **convex**, so $(0, 0)$ is **not** a point of inflection.

Convex and Concave Curves

Points of Inflection can also be Stationary Points

If you have a point of inflection that also happens to be a stationary point (i.e. f'(x) = 0 as well), then you've got yourself what's called a **stationary point of inflection**. And the award for 'Least Imaginative Name' goes to...

Example: Show that the graph of $y = x^3 - 9x^2 + 27x - 26$ has a stationary point of inflection at $x = 3$.

To show that $x = 3$ is a stationary point of inflection, you need to show **three** things:
1) the first derivative is **zero** at $x = 3$,   2) the second derivative is **zero** at $x = 3$,
3) the second derivative **changes sign** either side of $x = 3$. ◀

i.e. the curve changes between convex and concave at this point.

So start by **differentiating** the function **twice**: $\dfrac{dy}{dx} = 3x^2 - 18x + 27$ and $\dfrac{d^2y}{dx^2} = 6x - 18$

1) When $x = 3$, $\dfrac{dy}{dx} = 3(3)^2 - 18(3) + 27 = 27 - 54 + 27 = 0$ — so there is a **stationary point** at $x = 3$.

2) When $x = 3$, $\dfrac{d^2y}{dx^2} = 6(3) - 18 = 18 - 18 = 0$.

3) When $x > 3$, $\dfrac{d^2y}{dx^2} > 0$, and when $x < 3$, $\dfrac{d^2y}{dx^2} < 0$ — so there is a **point of inflection** at $x = 3$.

So the graph has a **stationary point of inflection at $x = 3$**, as required.

Example: Find all of the stationary points of $f(x) = 3x^5 - 5x^3$, and determine their nature.

Start by finding the stationary points:
$f'(x) = 15x^4 - 15x^2 = 15x^2(x^2 - 1)$, so $f'(x) = 0$ when $x^2 = 0$ or when $(x^2 - 1) = 0$, i.e. when $x = 0$ or $x = \pm1$
$f(0) = 0$, $f(1) = -2$ and $f(-1) = 2$, so the stationary points are at $(0, 0)$, $(1, -2)$ and $(-1, 2)$.
Find the value of $f''(x)$ to determine their nature:
$f''(x) = 60x^3 - 30x = 30x(2x^2 - 1)$ When $x = -1$, $f''(x) = -30 < 0$, so $(-1, 2)$ **is a maximum**
When $x = 1$, $f''(x) = 30 > 0$, so $(1, -2)$ **is a minimum**
When $x = 0$, $f''(x) = 0$, so check $f''(x)$ on either side of 0.

When x is small and positive, $30x$ is positive and $(2x^2 - 1)$ is negative, so $f''(x)$ is **negative**.
When x is small and negative, $30x$ is negative and $(2x^2 - 1)$ is negative, so $f''(x)$ is **positive**.

So $f''(x)$ changes sign either side of 0, i.e. $f(x)$ changes from convex to concave, meaning that $(0, 0)$ **is a stationary point of inflection**.

Practice Questions

Q1 For each of the following intervals, determine whether $y = x^5 - 2x^4 - 3x + 2$ is concave over the whole interval, convex over the whole interval, or has a point of inflection in the interval:
a) $-1 < x < 0$,   b) $0 < x < 1$,   c) $1 < x < 2$,   d) $2 < x < 3$.

Q2 The graph of $y = 2x^3 - x^4$ has two points of inflection, one of which is a stationary point of inflection. Find the coordinates of both and determine which one is the stationary point of inflection.

Exam Questions

Q1 Show that $f(x) = 2x^6 - 6x^5 + 5x^4$ has no points of inflection. [5 marks]

Q2 For $f(x) = x^4 + \dfrac{5}{3}x^3 + x^2 - 2x$, find the ranges of x for which $f(x)$ is concave and convex. [5 marks]

Q3 Find any stationary points of the curve $y = 4 - 2x^2 + \dfrac{4}{3}x^3 - \dfrac{1}{4}x^4$, and determine their nature. [9 marks]

Cases of convex/concave confusion cause crying in classrooms...

I hope you enjoyed that, because that's the last mention of graphs for a while now. Be extra careful with those 'stationary point of inflection' questions — it's not enough to show that f'(x) and f''(x) are zero, you also need to show that f''(x) changes sign at the point. I always forgot that bit, and it got me into a whole world of trouble — turns out polishing derivatives is really dull. What I'm trying to say is: don't repeat my mistakes — check for a change of sign.

Using Differentiation

Differentiation isn't just mathematical daydreaming. It can be applied to real-life problems. For instance, you can use differentiation to find out the maximum possible volume of a box, given a limited amount of cardboard. Thrilling.

Differentiation is used to find **Rates of Change** in **Mechanics...**

Rates of change are particularly important in **mechanics** (you'll see more of this in Section 16) — and that means **differentiation** is important. You should know that **speed** is the rate of change of **distance travelled**, and **acceleration** is the rate of change of **speed** (see p.190 for more).

> **Example:** The distance travelled by a car, s (in m), t seconds after it moves off, is given by: $s = \frac{9}{4}t^2 - \frac{1}{3}t^3$ for $0 \le t \le 4$. Find: a) the car's speed after 3 seconds, b) when the car is decelerating.

a) The **speed** of the car is the **rate of change** of the **distance travelled**, i.e. $\frac{ds}{dt}$:

$$\frac{ds}{dt} = \frac{9}{2}t - t^2 \quad \text{When } t = 3, \quad \frac{ds}{dt} = \frac{9}{2}(3) - (3)^2 = 13.5 - 9 = \textbf{4.5 ms}^{-1}$$

The units of $\frac{ds}{dt}$ are $\frac{\text{units of } s}{\text{units of } t}$, which are $\frac{m}{s}$, or ms^{-1}.

b) If the car is **decelerating**, then its acceleration is **negative**.

Acceleration is the **rate of change** of speed, i.e. $\frac{d}{dt}\left(\frac{ds}{dt}\right)$ or $\frac{d^2s}{dt^2}$:

$$\frac{d^2s}{dt^2} = \frac{9}{2} - 2t \qquad \frac{d^2s}{dt^2} < 0 \Rightarrow \frac{9}{2} - 2t < 0 \Rightarrow 4t > 9 \Rightarrow t > 2.25 \text{ s}$$

So the car is decelerating for **2.25 < t ≤ 4.**

Remember that the equation given is only valid up to t = 4.

...and for finding **Maximum** or **Minimum Values** for **Volume** and **Area**

To find the maximum for a shape's volume, all you need is an equation for the volume **in terms of only one variable** — then just **differentiate as normal**. But examiners don't hand it to you on a plate — there's usually one too many variables chucked in. So you need to know how to manipulate the information to get rid of that unwanted variable.

> **Example:** A jewellery box with a lid and dimensions $3x$ cm by x cm by y cm is made using a total of 450 cm² of wood.
> a) Show that the volume of the box can be expressed as: $V = \frac{675x - 9x^3}{4}$.
> b) Use calculus to find the maximum possible volume.

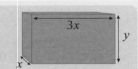

a) You know the basic equation for **volume**: $V = \text{width} \times \text{depth} \times \text{height} = 3x \times x \times y = 3x^2y$

But the question asks for volume in terms of x only — you don't want that pesky y in there. So you need to find y **in terms of** x and substitute that in.

Write an expression for the **surface area**:

$$A = 2[(3x \times x) + (3x \times y) + (x \times y)] = 450 \Rightarrow 3x^2 + 4xy = 225$$

Be careful when finding the surface area — here there's a lid so there are two of each side, but sometimes you'll get an open-topped shape.

Then rearrange to find an expression for y:

$$4xy = 225 - 3x^2 \Rightarrow y = \frac{225 - 3x^2}{4x}$$

Finally, **substitute** this into the equation for the volume: $V = 3x^2y = 3x^2 \times \frac{225 - 3x^2}{4x} = \frac{3x(225 - 3x^2)}{4}$

$$\Rightarrow V = \frac{675x - 9x^3}{4} \text{ as required}$$

b) You want to find the **maximum** value of V, so **differentiate** and set $\frac{dV}{dx} = 0$:

$$\frac{dV}{dx} = \frac{675 - 27x^2}{4}, \quad \frac{dV}{dx} = 0 \Rightarrow \frac{675 - 27x^2}{4} = 0 \Rightarrow 675 = 27x^2 \Rightarrow x^2 = 25 \Rightarrow x = 5$$

Ignore the other solution, $x = -5$, since you can't have a negative length.

(You could check that this is a maximum by finding $\frac{d^2V}{dx^2}$ when $x = 5$: $\frac{d^2V}{dx^2} = -\frac{27}{2}x = -\frac{135}{2} < 0$)

$\frac{d^2V}{dx^2}$ is negative — so it's a maximum.

So the maximum volume is: $V = \frac{(675 \times 5) - (9 \times 5^3)}{4} = \textbf{562.5 cm}^3$

Using Differentiation

Another example? Coming right up. You want pie in this one? No probl- oh hang on — do you mean pie, or pi? I'll use both, just to make sure — I wouldn't want you to be disappointed. I really spoil you, don't I...

Example: Ned uses a circular tin to bake his pies in. The tin is t cm high with a d cm diameter. The volume of the pie tin is 1000 cm³.
a) Prove that the surface area of the tin, $A = \frac{\pi}{4}d^2 + \frac{4000}{d}$.
b) Find the minimum surface area.

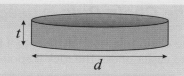

a) A = area of tin's base + area of tin's curved face = $\pi\left(\frac{d}{2}\right)^2 + (\pi d \times t) = \frac{\pi}{4}d^2 + \pi dt$

This shape is open-topped, so only count the area of the circle once.

You want to get rid of the t, so use the given value of volume to find an expression for t in terms of d:
$$V = \pi\left(\frac{d}{2}\right)^2 t = 1000 \Rightarrow \pi d^2 t = 4000 \Rightarrow t = \frac{4000}{\pi d^2}$$

Substitute your expression for t into the equation for surface area:
$$A = \frac{\pi}{4}d^2 + \left(\pi d \times \frac{4000}{\pi d^2}\right) \Rightarrow A = \frac{\pi}{4}d^2 + \frac{4000}{d} \text{ as required.}$$

b) Differentiate and find the stationary point:
$$\frac{dA}{dd} = \frac{\pi}{2}d - \frac{4000}{d^2} \Rightarrow \frac{\pi}{2}d - \frac{4000}{d^2} = 0 \Rightarrow d^3 = \frac{8000}{\pi} \Rightarrow d = \frac{20}{\sqrt[3]{\pi}}$$

Check it's a minimum: $\frac{d^2A}{dd^2} = \frac{\pi}{2} + \frac{8000}{d^3} = \frac{\pi}{2} + \frac{8000}{\left(\frac{8000}{\pi}\right)} = \frac{3\pi}{2}$

$\frac{d^2A}{dd^2}$ is positive — so it's a minimum.

Calculate the area for this value of d: $A = \frac{\pi}{4}\left(\frac{20}{\sqrt[3]{\pi}}\right)^2 + \left(\frac{4000}{\left(\frac{20}{\sqrt[3]{\pi}}\right)}\right) = \textbf{439 cm}^2$ (3 s.f.)

Practice Questions

Q1 1 litre of water is poured into a bowl. The volume (v) of water in the bowl (in ml) is modelled by the function: $v = 17t^2 + 10t$. Find the rate at which water is poured into the bowl when $t = 4$ seconds.

Q2 The height (h m) a firework can reach is related to the mass (m g) of fuel it carries by: $h = \frac{m^2}{10} - \frac{m^3}{800}$
Find the mass of fuel required to achieve the maximum height and state what the maximum height is.

Exam Questions

Q1 A steam train travels between Haverthwaite and Eskdale at a speed of x miles per hour and burns y units of coal, where y is modelled by: $2\sqrt{x} + \frac{27}{x}$, for $x > 2$.
a) Find the speed that gives the minimum coal consumption. [4 marks]
b) Find $\frac{d^2y}{dx^2}$, and hence show that this speed gives the minimum coal consumption. [2 marks]
c) Calculate the minimum coal consumption. [1 mark]

Q2 Ayesha is building a closed-back bookcase. She uses a total of 72 m² of wood (not including shelving) to make a bookcase that is x metres high, $\frac{x}{2}$ metres wide and d metres deep, as shown.
a) Show that the full capacity of the bookcase is given by: $V = 12x - \frac{x^3}{12}$. [4 marks]
b) Find the value of x for which V is stationary. Leave your answer in surd form. [3 marks]
c) Show that this is a maximum point and hence calculate the maximum V. [4 marks]

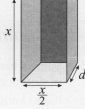

All this page has done is maximise my hunger for pie...

I hope I've managed to convince you that differentiation can pop up pretty much anywhere — those cheeky examiners can make a whole question about it without so much as a single 'd'. Don't fall for their evil schemes.

Chain Rule

Now it's time to upgrade your differentiation with some new exciting features. And about time too — I bet you were starting to get bored of doing the same old 'multiply by the power, reduce it by one' rigmarole every time.

The **Chain Rule** is used for **Functions of Functions**

The **chain rule** is a nifty little tool that allows you to differentiate complicated functions by **splitting them up** into easier ones. The trick is spotting **how** to split them up, and choosing the right bit to **substitute**.

Chain Rule Method

- Pick a suitable function of x for 'u' and rewrite y in terms of u.
- Differentiate u (with respect to x) to get $\dfrac{du}{dx}$, and differentiate y (with respect to u) to get $\dfrac{dy}{du}$.
- Stick it all in the formula.

If $y = f(u)$ and $u = g(x)$ then:
$$\frac{dy}{dx} = \frac{dy}{du} \times \frac{du}{dx}$$

Example: Find the exact value of $\dfrac{dy}{dx}$ when $x = 1$ for $y = \dfrac{1}{\sqrt{x^2 + 4x}}$.

First, write y in terms of **powers** to make it easier to differentiate: $y = (x^2 + 4x)^{-\frac{1}{2}}$.

Pick a chunk of the equation to call 'u', and rewrite y **in terms of** u — in this case let $u = x^2 + 4x$, so $y = u^{-\frac{1}{2}}$.

Now differentiate both bits **separately**: $\quad u = x^2 + 4x \Rightarrow \dfrac{du}{dx} = 2x + 4 \quad$ and $\quad y = u^{-\frac{1}{2}} \Rightarrow \dfrac{dy}{du} = -\dfrac{1}{2}u^{-\frac{3}{2}}$

Use the **chain rule** to find $\dfrac{dy}{dx}$: $\qquad \dfrac{dy}{dx} = \dfrac{dy}{du} \times \dfrac{du}{dx} = -\dfrac{1}{2}u^{-\frac{3}{2}} \times (2x + 4)$

Substitute in $u = x^2 + 4x$ and **rearrange**: $\quad \dfrac{dy}{dx} = -\dfrac{1}{2}(x^2 + 4x)^{-\frac{3}{2}} \times (2x + 4) = -\dfrac{x + 2}{(\sqrt{x^2 + 4x})^3}$

Finally, put in $x = 1$ to get the answer: $\qquad \dfrac{dy}{dx} = -\dfrac{1 + 2}{(\sqrt{1^2 + 4})^3} = -\dfrac{3}{5\sqrt{5}} = -\dfrac{3\sqrt{5}}{25}$ ◄── 'Exact' means leave in surd form where necessary.

Use **dy/dx = 1 ÷ dx/dy** for **x = f(y)**

The **principle** of the chain rule can also be used where x **is given in terms of** y (i.e. $x = f(y)$). $\dfrac{dy}{dx} \times \dfrac{dx}{dy} = \dfrac{dy}{dy} = 1$, so rearranging gives this formula.

For $x = f(y)$, use
$$\frac{dy}{dx} = \frac{1}{\left(\dfrac{dx}{dy}\right)}$$

Example: A curve has the equation $x = y^3 + 2y - 7$. Find $\dfrac{dy}{dx}$ at the point $(-4, 1)$.

Forget that the x's and y's are in the 'wrong' places and differentiate as usual: $\quad \dfrac{dx}{dy} = 3y^2 + 2$

Use $\dfrac{dy}{dx} = \dfrac{1}{\left(\dfrac{dx}{dy}\right)}$ to find $\dfrac{dy}{dx}$ at $(-4, 1)$: $\quad \dfrac{dy}{dx} = \dfrac{1}{3y^2 + 2} \Rightarrow$ when $y = 1$, $\dfrac{dy}{dx} = \dfrac{1}{3(1)^2 + 2} = \dfrac{1}{5}$

$\dfrac{dy}{dx}$ isn't a fraction, but it acts a bit like one here.

The **Chain Rule** lets you **Connect** different **Rates of Change**

1) Some situations have a number of **linked variables**, like length, surface area and volume, or distance, speed and acceleration.

2) If you know the rate of change of **one** of these linked variables, and the **equations that connect** the variables, you can use the chain rule to help you find the rate of change of the **other variables**.

3) There might be a **hidden derivative** given in words, so keep an eye out for words like '**rate**' or '**per**'. Watch out — if you're told that something is '**decreasing**' or something similar, the rate might be **negative**.

4) Make sure you know whether the question is asking for $\dfrac{dy}{dx}$ or $\dfrac{dx}{dy}$ — use the rule above if you need to.

Chain Rule

This is one of those topics where the most awkward bit is **getting your head round** the information in the question. The actual maths is **nowhere near** as bad as the questions usually make it sound. Honest.

Example: A scientist is testing how a new material expands when it is gradually heated. The diagram shows the sample being tested, which is shaped like a triangular prism. After t minutes, the triangle that forms the base of the prism has base length $7x$ cm and height $4x$ cm, and the height of the prism is also $4x$ cm. If the sample expands at a constant rate, given by $\frac{dx}{dt} = 0.05$ cm min^{-1}, find an expression in terms of x for $\frac{dV}{dt}$, where V is the volume of the prism.

The best way to start this kind of question is to write down what you know. There's enough information to write an expression for the volume of the prism: $V = \left(\frac{1}{2} \times 7x \times 4x\right) \times 4x = 56x^3$ cm^3

Differentiate this with respect to x: $\frac{dV}{dx} = 168x^2$

You know that $\frac{dx}{dt} = 0.05$. So use the **chain rule** to find $\frac{dV}{dt}$: $\frac{dV}{dt} = \frac{dV}{dx} \times \frac{dx}{dt} = 168x^2 \times 0.05 = 8.4x^2$

Example: A giant metal cube from space is cooling after entering the Earth's atmosphere. As it cools, the surface area of the cube decreases at a constant rate of 0.027 m^2 s^{-1}. If the side length of the cube after t seconds is x m, find $\frac{dx}{dt}$ at the point when $x = 15$ m.

The cube has side length x m, so the surface area of the cube is $A = 6x^2 \Rightarrow \frac{dA}{dx} = 12x$ This value is negative because A is decreasing.

A decreases at a constant rate of 0.027 m^2 s^{-1} — we can write this as $\frac{dA}{dt} = -0.027$

Now use the **chain rule** to find $\frac{dx}{dt}$: $\frac{dx}{dt} = \frac{dx}{dA} \times \frac{dA}{dt} = \frac{1}{\left(\frac{dA}{dx}\right)} \times \frac{dA}{dt} = \frac{1}{12x} \times -0.027 = -\frac{0.00225}{x}$

So when $x = 15$, $\frac{dx}{dt} = -\frac{0.00225}{x} = -\frac{0.00225}{15} = $ **−0.00015 m s^{-1}**

Practice Questions

$y = (x^3 + 2a^2)^{1/2}$
$u = x^3 + 2a^2$ $y = u^{1/2}$ $\frac{1}{2}u^{-1/2} \times 3x^2 + 4x$
$\frac{du}{dx} = 3x^2 + 4x$ $y = \frac{1}{2}u^{-1/2}$ $\frac{1}{2}(x^3 + 2a^2)^{-1/2} \times 3x^2 + 4x$

Q1 Differentiate with respect to x: a) $y = \sqrt{x^3 + 2x^2}$ b) $y = \frac{1}{\sqrt{x^3 + 2x^2}}$

Q2 A cuboid of length x cm, width $2x$ cm and height $3x$ cm is expanding, for some unexplained reason. If A is its surface area and V is its volume, find $\frac{dA}{dx}$ and $\frac{dV}{dx}$, and hence show that if $\frac{dV}{dt} = 3$, then $\frac{dA}{dt} = \frac{22}{3x}$.

Exam Questions

Q1 a)   Find $\frac{dy}{dx}$ for the curve given by the equation $x = \sqrt{y^2 + 3y}$ at the point (2, 1).   [5 marks]

  b)   Hence find the equation of the tangent to the curve at (2, 1), in the form $y = mx + c$.   [2 marks]

Q2 The triangular prism shown in the diagram is expanding. The dimensions of the prism after t seconds are given in terms of x. The prism is $4x$ m long, and its cross-section is an isosceles triangle with base $\frac{3}{2}x$ m and height x m.

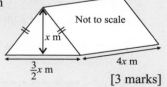

  a)   Show that, if the surface area of the prism after t seconds is A m^2, then $A = \frac{35}{2}x^2$.   [3 marks]

  The surface area of the prism is increasing at a constant rate of 0.07 m^2 s^{-1}.

  b)   Find $\frac{dx}{dt}$ when $x = 0.5$.   [3 marks]

  c)   If the volume of the prism is V m^3, find the rate of change of V when $x = 1.2$.   [4 marks]

I'm in the middle of a chain rule differentiation...

If you get stuck on a question like this, don't panic. Somewhere in the question there'll be enough information to write at least one equation linking some of the variables. If in doubt, write down any equations you can make, differentiate them, and see which of the resulting expressions you can link using the chain rule to make the thing you're looking for.

Differentiating e^x, ln x and a^x

Remember those special little functions from Section 6? Well you're about to find out just how special they are as we take a look at how to differentiate them. I can tell you're overcome by excitement so I won't keep you waiting...

The **Gradient** of $y = e^x$ is e^x

In the last section (see p.80) you saw that 'e' was just a number for which the **gradient of e^x** was e^x — which makes it pretty simple to **differentiate**. Don't worry if you have a constant in there as well — just multiply the whole thing by the constant when you differentiate.

$$\frac{d}{dx}(e^{kx}) = ke^{kx}$$

Example: If $f(x) = e^{x^2} + 2e^x$, find $f'(x)$ for $x = 0$.

Break down the function into its two bits and differentiate them **separately**:

$$y = e^{x^2} \qquad \text{and} \qquad y = 2e^x$$

This is the tricky bit.
Use the **chain rule** from p.94: $u = x^2$ and $y = e^u$
Both u and y are now easy to differentiate:
$$\frac{du}{dx} = 2x \text{ and } \frac{dy}{du} = e^u$$
$$\frac{dy}{dx} = \frac{dy}{du} \times \frac{du}{dx} = e^u \times 2x = e^{x^2} \times 2x = \mathbf{2xe^{x^2}}$$

This bit's easy.
If $y = 2e^x$ then $\frac{dy}{dx} = 2e^x$ too.

Put the bits back together and you end up with $f'(x) = 2xe^{x^2} + 2e^x$.

So when $x = 0$, $f'(x) = 0 + 2e^0 = \mathbf{2}$

There's a general rule you can use when you have a **function** in the exponent (e.g. e^{x^2}):

$$\frac{d}{dx}(e^{f(x)}) = f'(x)e^{f(x)}$$

You can prove this using the **chain rule**.

Turn $y = \ln x$ into $x = e^y$ to **Differentiate**

$$y = \ln x$$
$$\frac{dy}{dx} = \frac{1}{x}$$

You can just **learn** this result, but it comes from another bit of mathematical fiddling:
If $y = \ln x$, then $x = e^y$ (see p.80).
Differentiating gives $\frac{dx}{dy} = e^y$, and $\frac{dy}{dx} = \frac{1}{\left(\frac{dx}{dy}\right)} = \frac{1}{e^y} = \frac{1}{x}$ (since $x = e^y$). Nice eh?

Example: Find $\frac{dy}{dx}$ if $y = \ln(x^2 + 3)$.

Use the **chain rule** again for this one: $y = \ln u$ and $u = x^2 + 3$.
$\frac{dy}{du} = \frac{1}{u}$ (from above) and $\frac{du}{dx} = 2x$, so: $\frac{dy}{dx} = \frac{dy}{du} \times \frac{du}{dx} = \frac{1}{u} \times 2x = \frac{2x}{x^2 + 3}$

Just like before, there's a handy rule that you can learn for when there's a function **inside** the ln (e.g. $\ln(x^2 + 3)$):

$$y = \ln(f(x))$$
$$\frac{dy}{dx} = \frac{f'(x)}{f(x)}$$

Again, you can use the **chain rule** to prove this result.

No Arthur, that's chain mail. You're not going to differentiate anything with that.

Differentiating eˣ, ln x and aˣ

Learn the rule for Differentiating aˣ

Here's another little rule you need to **learn**:

For any constant a,
$$\frac{d}{dx}(a^x) = a^x \ln a$$

The rule $\frac{d}{dx}(e^x) = e^x$ is actually just a special case of this rule, since $\ln e = 1$.

You can prove this rule using implicit differentiation (see p.105), but for now you can just use the result it without worrying about where it comes from.

Example: Find the equation of the tangent to the curve $y = 3^{-2x}$ at the point $\left(\frac{1}{2}, \frac{1}{3}\right)$.

Use the **chain rule** to find $\frac{dy}{dx}$: $u = -2x$ and $y = 3^u \Rightarrow \frac{du}{dx} = -2$ and $\frac{dy}{du} = 3^u \ln 3$ (using the rule above)

$$\Rightarrow \frac{dy}{dx} = \frac{dy}{du} \times \frac{du}{dx} = 3^u \ln 3 \times -2 = -2(3^{-2x} \ln 3)$$

Now you can find the equation of the **tangent**: At $\left(\frac{1}{2}, \frac{1}{3}\right)$, $\frac{dy}{dx} = -2(3^{-2x} \ln 3) = -\frac{2}{3} \ln 3$

Using the equation $y - y_1 = m(x - x_1)$:

$$y - \frac{1}{3} = \left(-\frac{2}{3}\ln 3\right)\left(x - \frac{1}{2}\right) \Rightarrow 3y - 1 = \ln 3 - (2\ln 3)x$$

$$\Rightarrow (2 \ln 3)x + 3y - (1 + \ln 3) = 0$$

This is in the form $ax + by + c = 0$, but any of the forms from p.36 would be fine.

Practice Questions

Q1 Find $\frac{dy}{dx}$ when
a) $y = e^{5x^2}$
b) $y = \ln(6 - x^2)$
c) $x = 2e^y$
d) $x = \ln(2y + 3)$
e) $y = 10^x$
f) $x = 5^y$

Q2 a) Find the derivative, with respect to x, of $f(x) = 3^x + 4x$.
b) Hence find the derivative, with respect to x, of $g(x) = \ln(3^x + 4x)$.

Q3 a) Differentiate $y = 2^{-2x}$ with respect to x.
b) Find the gradient of this curve when $x = 1$.
c) Hence find the equation of the normal to the curve at $x = 1$.

Exam Questions

Q1 Differentiate the following with respect to x.
a) $\sqrt{e^x + e^{2x}}$ [3 marks]
b) $3e^{2x+1} - \ln(1 - x^2) + 2x^3$ [3 marks]

Q2 A sketch of the function $f(x) = 4 \ln 3x$ is shown in the diagram on the right.
a) Find $f'(x)$ at the point where $x = 1$. [3 marks]
b) Find the equation of the tangent to the curve at the point $x = 1$. [3 marks]

Q3 a) Curve A has the equation $y = 4^x$.
What are the coordinates of the point on A where $\frac{dy}{dx} = \ln 4$? [2 marks]
b) Curve B has the equation $y = 4^{(x-4)^3}$.
Find the gradient of B at the point $\left(3, \frac{1}{4}\right)$. [4 marks]

This is a topic for lumberjacks — it's all about logs and aˣes...

Well, I don't know about you but my heart is still racing from all that excitement. Doesn't it feel nice to differentiate something that isn't some boring power of x? Don't worry, you can thank me later — there's plenty more to learn first.

Differentiating sin, cos and tan

So you think you know all there is to know about trigonometry. Well think again, 'cos here it comes again. (You see what I did there with the 'cos'? Pun #27 from 'Ye Olde Booke of Maths Punnes'...)

The **Rules** for differentiating **sin**, **cos** and **tan** only work in **Radians**

For **trigonometric functions**, where the angle is measured in **radians** (see p.56), the following rules apply:

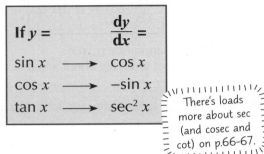

If $y =$	$\dfrac{dy}{dx} =$
$\sin x$	$\cos x$
$\cos x$	$-\sin x$
$\tan x$	$\sec^2 x$

The derivative of tan is given in the formula booklet.

There's loads more about sec (and cosec and cot) on p.66-67.

You can use the chain rule to show that, if k is a constant:

$\sin kx \longrightarrow k \cos kx$
$\cos kx \longrightarrow -k \sin kx$
$\tan kx \longrightarrow k \sec^2 kx$

It's handy to know these so you don't have to write out the chain rule every time.

Use the **Chain Rule** with **sin/cos/tan (f(x))**

Example: Differentiate $y = \cos 2x + \sin (x + 1)$ with respect to x.

It's the **chain rule** (again) for both parts of this equation:

This is the result in the box above, with k = 2.

1) Differentiate $y = \cos 2x$: $y = \cos u$, $u = 2x$,
   so $\dfrac{dy}{du} = -\sin u$ (see above) and $\dfrac{du}{dx} = 2 \Rightarrow \dfrac{dy}{dx} = -2 \sin 2x$

2) Differentiate $y = \sin (x + 1)$: $y = \sin u$, $u = x + 1$,
   so $\dfrac{dy}{du} = \cos u$ (see above) and $\dfrac{du}{dx} = 1 \Rightarrow \dfrac{dy}{dx} = \cos (x + 1)$

3) Put it all together to get: $\dfrac{dy}{dx} = -2 \sin 2x + \cos (x + 1)$

Example: Find $\dfrac{dy}{dx}$ for $x = \tan 3y$ at the point $\left(1, \frac{\pi}{12}\right)$.

You can just write this down if you know the result — you don't have to write out the chain rule.

1) First use $\dfrac{dy}{dx} = \dfrac{1}{\left(\frac{dx}{dy}\right)}$ to find $\dfrac{dy}{dx}$: $x = \tan 3y \Rightarrow \dfrac{dx}{dy} = 3 \sec^2 3y \Rightarrow \dfrac{dy}{dx} = \dfrac{1}{3 \sec^2 3y} = \dfrac{1}{3} \cos^2 3y$

2) Now **substitute** $y = \frac{\pi}{12}$: $\dfrac{dy}{dx} = \dfrac{1}{3} \cos^2 \dfrac{\pi}{4} = \dfrac{1}{3} \times \left(\dfrac{1}{\sqrt{2}}\right)^2 = \dfrac{1}{3 \times 2} = \dfrac{1}{6}$

The rule $\dfrac{dy}{dx} = \dfrac{1}{\left(\frac{dx}{dy}\right)}$ was on p.94 if you want a reminder.

Remember to use **Trig Identities** where **Necessary**

Example: For $y = 2 \cos^2 x + \sin 2x$, show that $\dfrac{dy}{dx} = 2(\cos 2x - \sin 2x)$.

1) Writing out the equation in a **slightly different way** helps with the chain rule: $y = 2(\cos x)^2 + \sin 2x$.

2) For the first bit, $y = 2u^2$, $u = \cos x$, so $\dfrac{dy}{du} = 4u$ and $\dfrac{du}{dx} = -\sin x$.

   For the second bit, $y = \sin u$, $u = 2x$, so $\dfrac{dy}{du} = \cos u$ and $\dfrac{du}{dx} = 2$.

   You could also use the identity $\cos 2x \equiv 2 \cos^2 x - 1$ before differentiating. You'll get the same answer.

3) Putting it all in the chain rule formula gives $\dfrac{dy}{dx} = -4 \sin x \cos x + 2 \cos 2x$.

4) From the target answer in the question it looks like we need a $\sin 2x$ from somewhere, so use the **double angle formula** (see p.71) $\sin 2x \equiv 2 \sin x \cos x$:
   $\dfrac{dy}{dx} = -2 \sin 2x + 2 \cos 2x$, which **rearranges** nicely to give $\dfrac{dy}{dx} = 2(\cos 2x - \sin 2x)$. Et voilà.

Differentiating sin, cos and tan

Use the **Chain Rule** for **Combinations** of functions

You should be able to use the chain rule to differentiate functions that are combinations of any of the functions from this section. So make sure you haven't forgotten the rules for differentiating exponentials and logs already.

Example: Find f'(x), where $f(x) = e^{\cos 3x}$.

Use the **chain rule:** $y = e^u$ and $u = \cos 3x$, so $\dfrac{dy}{du} = e^u$ and $\dfrac{du}{dx} = -3\sin 3x$

So $\dfrac{dy}{dx} = \dfrac{dy}{du} \times \dfrac{du}{dx} = e^u \times (-3\sin 3x) = -3e^u \sin 3x = \mathbf{-3e^{\cos 3x} \sin 3x}$

You can **Differentiate sin** and **cos** from **First Principles**

You saw how to differentiate a function from **first principles** back on p.86. You can do this for sin and cos too, but you'll need to dust off your **small angle approximations** (p.69) and your **addition formulas** (p.70).

Example: Differentiate f(x) = sin x from first principles.

Start by writing out the formula: $f'(x) = \lim\limits_{h \to 0}\left(\dfrac{f(x+h) - f(x)}{h}\right)$

Substitute f(x) = sin x: $= \lim\limits_{h \to 0}\left(\dfrac{\sin(x+h) - \sin x}{h}\right)$

Expand sin(x + h) with the **addition formula**: $= \lim\limits_{h \to 0}\left(\dfrac{(\sin x \cos h + \cos x \sin h) - \sin x}{h}\right)$

It's helpful to collect the sin x and cos x terms here: $= \lim\limits_{h \to 0}\left(\dfrac{\sin x(\cos h - 1) + \cos x(\sin h)}{h}\right)$

You're interested in when h gets really small (as $h \to 0$), so you can use the **small angle approximations** (sin h ≈ h, cos h ≈ $1 - \frac{1}{2}h^2$): $= \lim\limits_{h \to 0}\left(\dfrac{\left(-\frac{1}{2}h^2\right)\sin x + h\cos x}{h}\right)$

h appears on the top and bottom of the fraction, so cancel it: $= \lim\limits_{h \to 0}\left(-\frac{1}{2}h\sin x + \cos x\right)$

As $h \to 0$, $\frac{1}{2}h\sin x \to 0$, so it disappears: $= \cos x$

Practice Questions

Q1 Find f'(x) for the following functions:

a) $f(x) = 2\cos 3x$
b) $f(x) = \sqrt{\tan x}$
c) $f(x) = \cos(e^x) + e^{\sin x}$

Q2 Differentiate $\sin^2(x + 2)$ with respect to x.

When studying nest architecture, a solid understanding of twigonometry and differeggtiation is essential.

Exam Questions

Q1 Find the gradient of the tangent to the curve $y = \sin^2 x - 2\cos 2x$ at the point where $x = \dfrac{\pi}{12}$ radians. [4 marks]

Q2 Find the equation of the normal to the curve $x = \sin 4y$ that passes through the point $\left(0, \dfrac{\pi}{4}\right)$. Give your answer in the form $y = mx + c$, where m and c are constants to be found. [6 marks]

Q3 By differentiating from first principles, prove that the derivative of cos x is –sin x. [5 marks]

I'm having an identity crisis — I can't differentiate between sin and cos...

Don't get tied down by the chain rule (pun #28...). After a bit of practice you'll be able to do it a lot quicker in one step — just say in your working 'using the chain rule...' so the examiner can see how clever you are.

Product and Quotient Rules

In maths-speak, multiplying two things gives you a 'product' and dividing them gives you a 'quotient'. And since the world of maths is a beautiful, harmonious place full of natural symmetry, there's a rule for differentiating each.

Use the **Product Rule** to differentiate **Two Functions Multiplied Together**

This is what it looks like: ⟶

$$\text{If } y = u(x)v(x)$$
$$\frac{dy}{dx} = u\frac{dv}{dx} + v\frac{du}{dx}$$ (where u and v are functions of x)

And here's how to use it:

Examples: Differentiate the following with respect to x:

a) $x^3 \tan x$

1) The crucial thing is to write down everything in **steps**. Start with **identifying 'u' and 'v'**:
$$u = x^3 \text{ and } v = \tan x$$

2) Now differentiate these two **separately**:
$$\frac{du}{dx} = 3x^2 \text{ and } \frac{dv}{dx} = \sec^2 x$$

3) Very carefully put all the bits into the **formula**:
$$\frac{dy}{dx} = u\frac{dv}{dx} + v\frac{du}{dx} = (x^3 \times \sec^2 x) + (\tan x \times 3x^2)$$

4) Finally, **rearrange** to make it look nicer:
$$\frac{dy}{dx} = x^3 \sec^2 x + 3x^2 \tan x$$

b) $e^{2x}\sqrt{2x-3}$

1) Again, start with **identifying 'u' and 'v'**:
$$u = e^{2x} \text{ and } v = \sqrt{2x-3}$$

2) Each of these needs the **chain rule** to differentiate:
$$\frac{du}{dx} = 2e^{2x} \text{ and } \frac{dv}{dx} = \frac{1}{\sqrt{2x-3}} \text{ (do it in steps if you need to...)}$$

3) Put it all into the product rule **formula**:
$$\frac{dy}{dx} = u\frac{dv}{dx} + v\frac{du}{dx} = \left(e^{2x} \times \frac{1}{\sqrt{2x-3}}\right) + (\sqrt{2x-3} \times 2e^{2x})$$

4) **Rearrange** and **simplify**:
$$\frac{dy}{dx} = e^{2x}\left(\frac{1}{\sqrt{2x-3}} + 2\sqrt{2x-3}\right) = e^{2x}\left(\frac{1 + 2(2x-3)}{\sqrt{2x-3}}\right)$$
$$= \frac{e^{2x}(4x-5)}{\sqrt{2x-3}}$$

Use the rules **Together** to differentiate **Complicated Functions**

Example: Solve the equation $\frac{d}{dx}((x^3 + 3x^2)\ln x) = 2x^2 + 5x$, leaving your answer as an exact value of x.

1) Since $(x^3 + 3x^2)\ln x$ is a product of two functions, use the **product rule**:
$$u = x^3 + 3x^2 \Rightarrow \frac{du}{dx} = 3x^2 + 6x \quad \text{and} \quad v = \ln x \Rightarrow \frac{dv}{dx} = \frac{1}{x} \text{ (see p.96)}$$
So $\frac{d}{dx}((x^3 + 3x^2)\ln x) = \left[(x^3 + 3x^2) \times \frac{1}{x}\right] + [\ln x \times (3x^2 + 6x)] = x^2 + 3x + (3x^2 + 6x)\ln x$.

2) Now put this into the **equation** from the question in place of $\frac{d}{dx}((x^3 + 3x^2)\ln x)$:
$$x^2 + 3x + (3x^2 + 6x)\ln x = 2x^2 + 5x$$

3) **Rearrange** and **solve** as follows:
$$(3x^2 + 6x)\ln x = 2x^2 + 5x - x^2 - 3x \Rightarrow (3x^2 + 6x)\ln x = x^2 + 2x$$
$$\Rightarrow \ln x = \frac{x^2 + 2x}{3(x^2 + 2x)} = \frac{1}{3} \Rightarrow x = e^{\frac{1}{3}}$$

You're asked for an exact value so leave in terms of e.

Use the **Quotient Rule** for one function **Divided By** another

A **quotient** is one function **divided by** another one.
The **rule** for differentiating quotients looks like this: ⟶

You could, if you wanted to, just use the **product rule** on $y = uv^{-1}$
(try it — you'll get the same answer).
This way is so much **quicker** and **easier** though — and it's in the **formula booklet**.

$$\text{If } y = \frac{u(x)}{v(x)}$$
$$\frac{dy}{dx} = \frac{v\frac{du}{dx} - u\frac{dv}{dx}}{v^2}$$

Product and Quotient Rules

The quotient rule might look a little ugly, but it's lovely when you get to know it. That's why I call it Quotimodo...

Example: Find the gradient of the tangent to the curve with equation $y = \frac{(2x^2-1)}{(3x^2+1)}$, at the point (1, 0.25).

1) 'Gradient' means **differentiate**, so identify u and v for the **quotient rule**, and differentiate **separately**:

$$u = 2x^2 - 1 \Rightarrow \frac{du}{dx} = 4x \quad \text{and} \quad v = 3x^2 + 1 \Rightarrow \frac{dv}{dx} = 6x$$

2) It's very important that you get things in the **right order**, so concentrate on what's going where:

$$\frac{dy}{dx} = \frac{v\frac{du}{dx} - u\frac{dv}{dx}}{v^2} = \frac{(3x^2+1)(4x)-(2x^2-1)(6x)}{(3x^2+1)^2}$$

3) Now you can **simplify** things:

$$\frac{dy}{dx} = \frac{x[4(3x^2+1)-6(2x^2-1)]}{(3x^2+1)^2} = \frac{x[12x^2+4-12x^2+6]}{(3x^2+1)^2} = \frac{10x}{(3x^2+1)^2}$$

4) Finally, put in $x = 1$ to find the **gradient** at (1, 0.25): $\frac{dy}{dx} = \frac{10}{(3+1)^2} = \textbf{0.625}$

Find **Further Rules** using the **Quotient Rule**

Example: Use the quotient rule to differentiate $y = \frac{\cos x}{\sin x}$, and hence show that for $y = \cot x$, $\frac{dy}{dx} = -\text{cosec}^2 x$.

1) Start off by **identifying** u and v: $u = \cos x$ and $v = \sin x \Rightarrow \frac{du}{dx} = -\sin x$ and $\frac{dv}{dx} = \cos x$ (see p.98)

2) Putting everything in the quotient rule **formula** gives:

$$\frac{dy}{dx} = \frac{(\sin x \times -\sin x) - (\cos x \times \cos x)}{(\sin x)^2} = \frac{-\sin^2 x - \cos^2 x}{\sin^2 x}$$

There's more on cosec, sec and cot on the next page.

3) Use a **trig identity** to simplify this ($\sin^2 x + \cos^2 x \equiv 1$ should do the trick...):

$$\frac{dy}{dx} = \frac{-(\sin^2 x + \cos^2 x)}{\sin^2 x} = -\frac{1}{\sin^2 x}$$

4) Linking this back to the question, since $\tan x = \frac{\sin x}{\cos x}$, and $\cot x = \frac{1}{\tan x}$, then $y = \frac{\cos x}{\sin x} = \cot x$.

And since $\text{cosec } x = \frac{1}{\sin x}$, $\frac{dy}{dx} = -\frac{1}{\sin^2 x} = -\textbf{cosec}^2 x$. QED*   *Quite Exciting Differentiation

Practice Questions

Q1 Find the value of the gradient for: a) $y = e^{2x}(x^2 - 3)$ when $x = 0$,   b) $y = \ln x \sin x$ when $x = 1$.

Q2 Find the equation of the tangent to the curve $y = \frac{6x^2+3}{4x^2-1}$ at the point (1, 3).

Exam Questions

Q1 Find $\frac{dy}{dx}$ for each of the following functions. Simplify your answer where possible.

   a) $y = \ln(3x+1)\sin(3x+1)$ [4 marks]

   b) $y = \frac{\sqrt{x^2+3}}{\cos 3x}$ [4 marks]

Q2 Given that $y = \frac{e^x + x}{e^x - x}$, find $\frac{dy}{dx}$ when $x = 0$.   [3 marks]

It's not my fault that I love maths — I'm a product of my environment...

Sing along with me: "A function of a function wants the — chain rule. A function times a function wants the — product rule. A function over a function wants the — quotient rule. A rate of change is connected to the — knee bone..."

More Differentiation

Now that you're a master of the product and quotient rules, there are some more functions you can differentiate. Can you feel your power growing? Soon, no function will be able to stand against you and your mighty calculus.

d/dx of cosec, sec and cot come from the Quotient Rule

Since **cosec**, **sec** and **cot** are just the **reciprocals** of sin, cos and tan, the quotient rule can be used to differentiate them. The results are in the formula booklet, but it will help a lot if you can show **where they come from**.

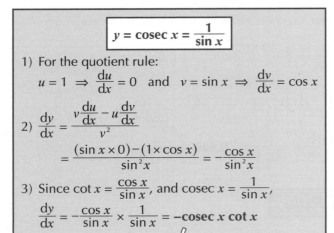

$$y = \operatorname{cosec} x = \frac{1}{\sin x}$$

1) For the quotient rule:
$$u = 1 \Rightarrow \frac{du}{dx} = 0 \quad \text{and} \quad v = \sin x \Rightarrow \frac{dv}{dx} = \cos x$$

2) $$\frac{dy}{dx} = \frac{v\frac{du}{dx} - u\frac{dv}{dx}}{v^2}$$
$$= \frac{(\sin x \times 0) - (1 \times \cos x)}{\sin^2 x} = -\frac{\cos x}{\sin^2 x}$$

3) Since $\cot x = \frac{\cos x}{\sin x}$, and $\operatorname{cosec} x = \frac{1}{\sin x}$,
$$\frac{dy}{dx} = -\frac{\cos x}{\sin x} \times \frac{1}{\sin x} = -\operatorname{cosec} x \cot x$$

$$y = \sec x = \frac{1}{\cos x}$$

1) For the quotient rule:
$$u = 1 \Rightarrow \frac{du}{dx} = 0 \quad \text{and} \quad v = \cos x \Rightarrow \frac{dv}{dx} = -\sin x$$

2) $$\frac{dy}{dx} = \frac{v\frac{du}{dx} - u\frac{dv}{dx}}{v^2}$$
$$= \frac{(\cos x \times 0) - (1 \times -\sin x)}{\cos^2 x} = \frac{\sin x}{\cos^2 x}$$

3) Since $\tan x = \frac{\sin x}{\cos x}$, and $\sec x = \frac{1}{\cos x}$,
$$\frac{dy}{dx} = \frac{\sin x}{\cos x} \times \frac{1}{\cos x} = \sec x \tan x$$

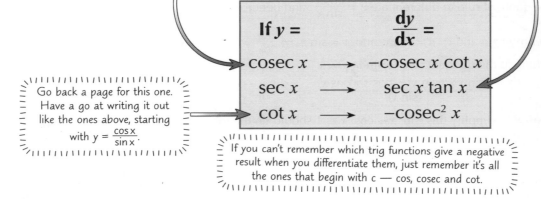

If $y =$	$\dfrac{dy}{dx} =$
$\operatorname{cosec} x$	$\longrightarrow \quad -\operatorname{cosec} x \cot x$
$\sec x$	$\longrightarrow \quad \sec x \tan x$
$\cot x$	$\longrightarrow \quad -\operatorname{cosec}^2 x$

Go back a page for this one. Have a go at writing it out like the ones above, starting with $y = \frac{\cos x}{\sin x}$.

If you can't remember which trig functions give a negative result when you differentiate them, just remember it's all the ones that begin with c — cos, cosec and cot.

I'm too sec-sy for my shirt, cosec-sy it hurts...

Use the Chain, Product and Quotient Rules with cosec, sec and cot

Once you're familiar with the three rules in the box above you can use them with the **chain**, **product** and **quotient** rules and in combination with all the **other functions** we've seen so far.

Examples: Find $\dfrac{dy}{dx}$ for the following functions:

a) $y = \sec(2x^2)$

This is a function of a function, so think 'chain rule':
$$y = \sec u \quad \text{and} \quad u = 2x^2$$

Differentiate y and u:
$$\frac{dy}{du} = \sec u \tan u \text{ (see above)}$$
$$= \sec(2x^2) \tan(2x^2)$$
$$\frac{du}{dx} = 4x$$

Then put these into the formula:
$$\frac{dy}{dx} = \frac{dy}{du} \times \frac{du}{dx} = 4x \sec(2x^2) \tan(2x^2)$$

b) $y = e^x \cot x$

This is a product of two functions, so think 'product rule':
$$u = e^x \quad \text{and} \quad v = \cot x$$

Differentiate u and v:
$$\frac{du}{dx} = e^x$$
$$\frac{dv}{dx} = -\operatorname{cosec}^2 x \text{ (see above)}$$

Then put these into the formula:
$$\frac{dy}{dx} = u\frac{dv}{dx} + v\frac{du}{dx} = (e^x \times -\operatorname{cosec}^2 x) + (\cot x \times e^x)$$
$$= e^x(\cot x - \operatorname{cosec}^2 x)$$

More Differentiation

The **Rules** might need to be used **Twice**

Some questions will really stretch your alphabet with a multitude of *u*'s and *v*'s:

Example: Differentiate $y = e^x \tan^2 3x$

1) First off, this is a **product**, so use the **product rule**: $u = e^x$ (so $\frac{du}{dx} = e^x$) and $v = \tan^2 3x$

2) To find $\frac{dv}{dx}$ for the product rule, you need the **chain rule**:

$$v = u_1^2, \text{ where } u_1 = \tan 3x$$

$$\frac{dv}{du_1} = 2u_1 = 2\tan 3x \text{ and } \frac{du_1}{dx} = 3\sec^2 3x \Rightarrow \frac{dv}{dx} = 6\tan 3x \sec^2 3x$$

3) Now you can put this result in the product rule formula to get $\frac{dy}{dx}$:

$$\frac{dy}{dx} = (e^x \times 6\tan 3x \sec^2 3x) + (\tan^2 3x \times e^x) = e^x \tan 3x\,(6\sec^2 3x + \tan 3x)$$

Differentiate **Again** for **d²y/dx²**, **Turning Points**, **Stationary Points** etc.

Example: Determine the nature of the stationary point of the curve $y = \dfrac{\ln x}{x^2}$ $(x > 0)$.

1) First use the **quotient rule** to find $\frac{dy}{dx}$: $u = \ln x \Rightarrow \frac{du}{dx} = \frac{1}{x}$, $v = x^2 \Rightarrow \frac{dv}{dx} = 2x$. So $\frac{dy}{dx} = \frac{1 - 2\ln x}{x^3}$.

2) The stationary points occur where $\frac{dy}{dx} = 0$: $\frac{1 - 2\ln x}{x^3} = 0 \Rightarrow \ln x = \frac{1}{2} \Rightarrow x = e^{\frac{1}{2}}$

3) To find out if it's a maximum or minimum, differentiate $\frac{dy}{dx}$ (using the quotient rule again) to get $\frac{d^2 y}{dx^2}$:

$$u = 1 - 2\ln x \Rightarrow \frac{du}{dx} = -\frac{2}{x}, \ v = x^3 \Rightarrow \frac{dv}{dx} = 3x^2. \quad \text{So } \frac{d^2 y}{dx^2} = \frac{6\ln x - 5}{x^4}.$$

Put all the bits into the quotient rule formula for yourself to make sure you're happy where these come from.

4) When $x = e^{\frac{1}{2}}$, $\frac{d^2 y}{dx^2} < 0$ (i.e. **negative**), which means it's a **maximum point** (see p.87).

Practice Questions

Q1 Differentiate $f(x) = \sec(4x) - \cot(x + 1)$ with respect to x.

Q2 Find $\frac{dy}{dx}$ when $x = 0$ for $y = \operatorname{cosec}(3x - 2)$.

Exam Questions

Q1 Find $\frac{dy}{dx}$ for $y = \sin^3(2x^2)$. Simplify your answer where possible. [3 marks]

Q2 A curve with equation $y = e^x \sin x$ has 2 turning points in the interval $-\pi \le x \le \pi$.
  a) Find the value of x at each of these turning points. [6 marks]
  b) Determine the nature of each of the turning points. [3 marks]

Q3 a) Show that, if $f(x) = \cot x$, then $f''(x) = \dfrac{2\cos x}{\sin^3 x}$. [5 marks]
  b) Hence show that $\left(\frac{\pi}{2}, 0\right)$ is a point of inflection of the graph of $y = \cot x$. [3 marks]

Differentiation rule #33 047 — always wear nice socks when differentiating...

Whew — they sure can pack a lot of rules into one question, can't they? Well, the good news is that the formula booklet contains lots of helpful tidbits, like the derivatives of cosec, sec and cot. It's not as helpful as this book, though.

Differentiation with Parametric Equations

Oh look — it's your old friend, parametric equations. If you've forgotten about them already, go look them up ~~on social media~~ in Section 3. Don't look up parametric equations on social media — they always post such rubbish...

Differentiating Parametric Equations is a lot Simpler than you might expect

Just suppose you've got a **curve** defined by two **parametric equations**, with the parameter t: $y = f(t)$ and $x = g(t)$.

If you can't find the **Cartesian equation**, it seems like it would be a bit tricky to find the gradient, $\frac{dy}{dx}$.

Luckily the chain rule (see p.94) is on hand to help out:

$$\frac{dy}{dx} = \frac{dy}{dt} \div \frac{dx}{dt}$$

This is the same as on p.94, except we're using t instead of u, and we've replaced '$\times \frac{dt}{dx}$' with '$\div \frac{dx}{dt}$'.

> **Example:** The curve C is defined by the parametric equations $x = t^2 - 1$ and $y = t^3 - 2t + 4$.
>
> Find: a) $\frac{dy}{dx}$ in terms of t, b) the equation of the normal to the curve C when $t = -1$.
>
> a) Start by **differentiating** the two parametric equations **with respect to** t: $\quad \frac{dy}{dt} = 3t^2 - 2, \frac{dx}{dt} = 2t$
>
> Now use the **chain rule** to combine them: $\frac{dy}{dx} = \frac{dy}{dt} \div \frac{dx}{dt} = \frac{3t^2 - 2}{2t}$
>
> *To be continued...*

Use the Gradient to find Tangents and Normals

Of course, it's rarely as straightforward as just finding $\frac{dy}{dx}$. A lot of the time, you'll have to **use** it to find the equation of a **tangent** or **normal** (see p.85) to the parametric curve.

> b) Find the coordinates of the point where $t = -1$: $\quad y = (-1)^3 - 2(-1) + 4 = 5, \quad x = (-1)^2 - 1 = 0$
>
> So the point has coordinates **(0, 5)**.
>
> Use the answer to a) to find the **gradient** when $t = -1$: $\quad \frac{dy}{dx} = \frac{3(-1)^2 - 2}{2(-1)} = \frac{3-2}{-2} = -\frac{1}{2}$
>
> So the normal to C has a gradient of: $\quad -1 \div -\frac{1}{2} = 2$
>
> *It's often easier to use the equation $y - y_1 = m(x - x_1)$, but since the point you're using is (0, 5), you know that the y-intercept (c) is 5.*
>
> The normal passes through (0, 5) and has a gradient of 2. Write this in the form $y = mx + c$: $\quad \boldsymbol{y = 2x + 5}$

Practice Question

Q1 A curve is defined by the parametric equations $x = t^2$ and $y = 3t^3 - 4t$.

    a) Find $\frac{dy}{dx}$ for this curve.

    b) Find the coordinates of the stationary points of the curve.

Exam Questions

Q1 The curve C is defined by the parametric equations $x = 3\theta - \cos 3\theta$, $y = 2 \sin \theta$, $-\pi \leq \theta \leq \pi$.

    a) Show that the gradient of C at the point $(\pi + 1, \sqrt{3})$ is $\frac{1}{3}$. [6 marks]

    b) Find the equation of the normal to C when $\theta = \frac{\pi}{6}$. [4 marks]

Q2 A curve, C, has parametric equations $x = t^2 + 2t - 3$, $y = 2 - t^3$.

    a) The line L is the tangent to C at $y = -6$. Show that the equation of L is $y = -2x + 4$. [4 marks]

    b) L also meets C at point P. Find the equation of the normal to the curve C at P. [7 marks]

You can figure out when it's going to rain using barometric differentiation...

If you ask me, having a 'find the tangent/normal' part in one of these questions is like having chocolate on a digestive biscuit — it makes it at least 4 times better (and in case you were wondering, tangent = milk and normal = dark).

Implicit Differentiation

This really isn't as complicated as it looks... in fact, I think you'll find that if something's implicit between x and y, it can be ximplicity itself. No, that's not a typo, it's a hilarious joke... 'implicit' between 'x' and 'y'... do you see?...

You need *Implicit Differentiation* if you *Can't* write the equation as *y = f(x)*

1) An '**implicit relation**' is the maths name for any equation in x and y that's written in the form $f(x, y) = g(x, y)$ instead of $y = f(x)$.

> $f(x, y)$ and $g(x, y)$ don't actually both have to include x and y — one of them could even be a constant.

2) Some implicit relations are either awkward or impossible to rewrite in the form **y = f(x)**. This can happen, for example, if the equation contains a number of **different powers of y**, or terms where **x is multiplied by y**.

3) This can make implicit relations tricky to **differentiate** — the solution is **implicit differentiation**:

Implicit Differentiation

To find $\dfrac{dy}{dx}$ for an implicit relation between x and y:

1) Differentiate terms in x **only** (and constant terms) with respect to x, as normal.

2) Use the **chain rule** to differentiate terms in y **only**:

$$\frac{d}{dx}f(y) = \frac{d}{dy}f(y)\frac{dy}{dx}$$

> In other words, 'differentiate with respect to y, and stick a $\frac{dy}{dx}$ on the end'.

3) Use the **product rule** to differentiate terms in **both x and y**:

$$\frac{d}{dx}u(x)v(y) = u(x)\frac{d}{dx}v(y) + v(y)\frac{d}{dx}u(x)$$

4) **Rearrange** the resulting equation in x, y and $\dfrac{dy}{dx}$ to make $\dfrac{dy}{dx}$ the subject.

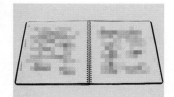

This is explicit differentiation, but... well... you'll learn about that when you're older.

> This version of the product rule is slightly different from the one on p.100 — here, v is a function of y, not x.

This might sound complicated, but don't worry — all it means really is 'differentiate like normal, but multiply by $\dfrac{dy}{dx}$ every time you differentiate a y-term'. Watch out for terms in x and y where you have to use the product rule — but if you're happy with everything from p.100, you should be able to handle it.

Example: Use implicit differentiation to find $\dfrac{dy}{dx}$ if $2x^2y + y^3 = 6x^2 + 5$.

You need to **differentiate each term** of the equation with respect to x.

Start by sticking '$\frac{d}{dx}$' in front of each term:

$$\frac{d}{dx}2x^2y + \frac{d}{dx}y^3 = \frac{d}{dx}6x^2 + \frac{d}{dx}5$$

First, deal with the **terms in x** and **constant terms** — in this case that's the two terms on the RHS:

$$\frac{d}{dx}2x^2y + \frac{d}{dx}y^3 = 12x + \cancel{0}$$

Now use the **chain rule** on the **term in y**:

$$\frac{d}{dx}2x^2y + 3y^2\frac{dy}{dx} = 12x$$

Using the chain rule from the box above, $f(y) = y^3$. — Leave this $\frac{dy}{dx}$ here for now.

Use the **product rule** on the term in x and y:

$$2x^2\frac{d}{dx}(y) + y\frac{d}{dx}(2x^2) + 3y^2\frac{dy}{dx} = 12x$$

So in terms of the box above, $u(x) = 2x^2$ and $v(y) = y$.

$$2x^2\frac{dy}{dx} + y4x + 3y^2\frac{dy}{dx} = 12x$$

You get a $\frac{dy}{dx}$ term here too (from the '$\frac{d}{dx}v(y)$' bit).

Finally, **rearrange** to make $\dfrac{dy}{dx}$ the subject:

$$\frac{dy}{dx}(2x^2 + 3y^2) = 12x - 4xy$$

$$\frac{dy}{dx} = \frac{12x - 4xy}{2x^2 + 3y^2}$$

Implicit Differentiation

Implicit Differentiation still gives you an expression for the Gradient

Most **implicit differentiation** questions aren't really that different at heart to any other **differentiation question**. Once you've got an expression for the **gradient**, you'll have to **use it** to do the sort of stuff you'd normally expect.

Example: Curve A has the equation $x^2 + 2xy - y^2 = 10x + 4y - 21$

    a)   Find $\dfrac{dy}{dx}$ and show that when $\dfrac{dy}{dx} = 0$, $y = 5 - x$.

    b)   Hence find the coordinates of the stationary points of A.

a)   For starters, you're going to need to find $\dfrac{dy}{dx}$ by **implicit differentiation**:

$$\frac{d}{dx}x^2 + \frac{d}{dx}2xy - \frac{d}{dx}y^2 = \frac{d}{dx}10x + \frac{d}{dx}4y - \frac{d}{dx}21$$

Differentiate x^2, $10x$ and 21 with respect to x.

$$2x + \frac{d}{dx}2xy - \frac{d}{dx}y^2 = 10 + \frac{d}{dx}4y - 0$$

Use the chain rule to differentiate y^2 and $4y$.

$$2x + \frac{d}{dx}2xy - 2y\frac{dy}{dx} = 10 + 4\frac{dy}{dx}$$

$$2x + 2x\frac{dy}{dx} + y\frac{d}{dx}2x - 2y\frac{dy}{dx} = 10 + 4\frac{dy}{dx}$$

Use the product rule to differentiate $2xy$.

$$2x + 2x\frac{dy}{dx} + 2y - 2y\frac{dy}{dx} = 10 + 4\frac{dy}{dx}$$

$$2x\frac{dy}{dx} - 2y\frac{dy}{dx} - 4\frac{dy}{dx} = 10 - 2x - 2y$$

Collect '$\frac{dy}{dx}$' terms on one side, and everything else on the other side.

$$\frac{dy}{dx} = \frac{10 - 2x - 2y}{2x - 2y - 4} = \frac{5 - x - y}{x - y - 2}$$

So when $\dfrac{dy}{dx} = 0$, $\dfrac{5 - x - y}{x - y - 2} = 0 \Rightarrow 5 - x - y = 0 \Rightarrow y = 5 - x$

This is one mammoth example, isn't it?
Let's just take a break with this llama for a minute.

Ahh, so peaceful...

Right then — back to work.

b)   You can **use** the answer to part a) in the equation of the **curve** to find the points where $\dfrac{dy}{dx} = 0$.

When $\dfrac{dy}{dx} = 0$, $y = 5 - x$. So at the stationary points,

$$x^2 + 2xy - y^2 = 10x + 4y - 21$$

$$x^2 + 2x(5 - x) - (5 - x)^2 = 10x + 4(5 - x) - 21$$

Substitute $y = 5 - x$ into the original equation to find the values of x at the stationary points.

$$x^2 + 10x - 2x^2 - 25 + 10x - x^2 = 10x + 20 - 4x - 21$$

$$-2x^2 + 20x - 25 = 6x - 1$$

$$-2x^2 + 14x - 24 = 0$$

Simplify until you're left with a quadratic that you can solve.

$$x^2 - 7x + 12 = 0$$

$$(x - 3)(x - 4) = 0$$

$$x = 3 \quad \text{or} \quad x = 4$$

Don't forget to find the y-values, since the question asks you for the coordinates.

$$x = 3 \Rightarrow y = 5 - 3 = 2 \quad \text{and} \quad x = 4 \Rightarrow y = 5 - 4 = 1$$

So the stationary points of A are **(3, 2)** and **(4, 1)**.

Implicit Differentiation

You can differentiate *Inverse Trig Functions* implicitly

Once upon a time, you met the inverse trig functions **arcsin**, **arccos** and **arctan** (well, actually it was on p.66). You can use implicit differentiation to differentiate these little blighters — the method goes a little bit like this:

Example: Use implicit differentiation to show that, if $y = \arcsin x$, then $\frac{dy}{dx} = \frac{1}{\sqrt{1-x^2}}$.

Take sin of both sides to get rid of the arcsin: $\sin y = x$

Now use **implicit differentiation**: $\frac{d}{dx}(\sin y) = \frac{d}{dx}(x)$

Use the **chain rule** to deal with $\frac{d}{dx}(\sin y)$: $\frac{d}{dy}(\sin y)\frac{dy}{dx} = 1$

$\cos y \frac{dy}{dx} = 1$

Rearrange to make $\frac{dy}{dx}$ the subject: $\frac{dy}{dx} = \frac{1}{\cos y}$

Use $\cos^2 \theta + \sin^2 \theta \equiv 1$ to get this in terms of $\sin y$: $\frac{dy}{dx} = \frac{1}{\sqrt{\cos^2 y}} = \frac{1}{\sqrt{1-\sin^2 y}}$

Now use the equation $\sin y = x$ to get rid of y: $\frac{dy}{dx} = \frac{1}{\sqrt{1-x^2}}$ as required.

See p.68 for a reminder of your go-to trig identities.

You can also differentiate arccos and arctan the same way — here are the answers you should get: ⟹

$f(x) =$	$\arcsin x$	$\arccos x$	$\arctan x$
$f'(x) =$	$\frac{1}{\sqrt{1-x^2}}$	$-\frac{1}{\sqrt{1-x^2}}$	$\frac{1}{1+x^2}$

Practice Questions

Q1 Use implicit differentiation to find $\frac{dy}{dx}$ for each of the following equations:

a) $4x^2 - 2y^2 = 7x^2y$ b) $3x^4 - 2xy^2 = y$ c) $(\cos x)(\sin y) = xy$

Q2 Using your answers to question 1, find:

a) the gradient of the tangent to the graph of $4x^2 - 2y^2 = 7x^2y$ at $(1, -4)$,

b) the gradient of the normal to the graph of $3x^4 - 2xy^2 = y$ at $(1, 1)$.

Exam Questions

Q1 The equation of curve C is $6x^2y - 7 = 5x - 4y^2 - x^2$.

a) The line T has the equation $y = c$ and passes through a point on C where $x = 2$. Find c, given that $c > 0$. [2 marks]

b) T also crosses C at point Q.

(i) Find the coordinates of Q. [2 marks]

(ii) Find the gradient of C at Q. [6 marks]

Q2 The curve C has the equation $3e^x + 6y = 2x^2y$.

a) Use implicit differentiation to find an expression for $\frac{dy}{dx}$. [3 marks]

b) Show that at the stationary points of C, $y = \frac{3e^x}{4x}$. [2 marks]

c) Hence find the exact coordinates of the two stationary points of C. [4 marks]

Q3 Use implicit differentiation to differentiate the function $f(x) = \arctan x$. [5 marks]

If an imp asks to try your ice lolly, don't let the imp lick it...

Wowzers — implicit differentiation really is a bit more involved than regular old differentiation... Well, I'm happy to inform you that this is the end of differentiation as we know it (well, as you need to know it for the exams anyway). There was a lot to get to grips with in this section, so make sure it's all sunk in before moving on to the next bit.

Integrating f(x) = xⁿ

Integration is the 'opposite' of differentiation — and so if you can differentiate, you can be pretty confident you'll be able to integrate too. There's just one extra thing you have to remember — the constant of integration...

The Fundamental Theorem of Calculus

When you differentiate y, you get $\frac{dy}{dx}$.

And when you integrate $\frac{dy}{dx}$, you get y plus a **constant of integration**.

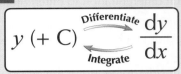

$$y\ (+\ C)\ \xrightarrow{\text{Differentiate}}\ \frac{dy}{dx}$$
$$y\ (+\ C)\ \xleftarrow{\text{Integrate}}\ \frac{dy}{dx}$$

You need the constant because there's **More Than One** right answer

When you **integrate** something, you're trying to find a function that differentiates to give what you started with. You add the **constant of integration** to allow for the fact that there's **more than one** possible function that does this...

This means the **integral** of 2x **with respect to x**.

$$\int 2x\ dx =$$

$$\begin{aligned} &x^2 - 207.253 \\ &x^2 - 1 \\ &x^2 \\ &x^2 + \pi \end{aligned}$$

If you differentiate any of these functions, you get the thing on the left — they're **all** possible answers.

So the answer to this integral is actually...

$$\int 2x\ dx = x^2 + C$$

The 'C' just means 'any number'. This is the **constant of integration**.

You only need to add a constant of integration to **indefinite integrals** like these ones. Definite integrals are just integrals with **limits** (or little numbers) next to the integral sign (see p.110).

Up the power by **One** — then **Divide** by it

The formula below tells you how to integrate **any** power of x (except x^{-1}).

This is an indefinite integral — it doesn't have any limits (numbers) next to the integral sign.

$$\int x^n\ dx = \frac{x^{n+1}}{n+1} + C$$

You can't do this to $\frac{1}{x} = x^{-1}$. When you increase the power by 1 (to get **zero**) you end up dividing by zero — and that's a big problem.

See p.114 if you just can't wait to find out how to integrate x^{-1}.

In a nutshell, this says:

To integrate a power of x: (i) increase the power by one — then divide by it,

and (ii) stick a constant on the end.

Examples: Use the integration formula...

1 For 'normal' powers

$$\int x^3\ dx = \frac{x^4}{4} + C$$

Increase the power to 4... ...and then divide by 4.

2 For negative powers

$$\int \frac{1}{x^3}\ dx = \int x^{-3}\ dx$$
$$= \frac{x^{-2}}{-2} + C$$
$$= -\frac{1}{2x^2} + C$$

Increase the power by 1 to −2... ...and then divide by −2.

3 For fractional powers

$$\int \sqrt[3]{x^4}\ dx = \int x^{\frac{4}{3}}\ dx$$
$$= \frac{x^{\frac{7}{3}}}{(7/3)} + C$$
$$= \frac{3\sqrt[3]{x^7}}{7} + C$$

Add 1 to the power... ...then divide by this new power.

4 And for complicated looking stuff...

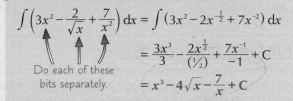

$$\int \left(3x^2 - \frac{2}{\sqrt{x}} + \frac{7}{x^2}\right) dx = \int \left(3x^2 - 2x^{-\frac{1}{2}} + 7x^{-2}\right) dx$$
$$= \frac{3x^3}{3} - \frac{2x^{\frac{1}{2}}}{(1/2)} + \frac{7x^{-1}}{-1} + C$$
$$= x^3 - 4\sqrt{x} - \frac{7}{x} + C$$

Do each of these bits separately.

CHECK YOUR ANSWERS:
You can check you've integrated properly by **differentiating** the **answer** — you should end up with the thing you started with.

Integrating f(x) = xⁿ

You sometimes need to find the Value of the Constant of Integration

When they tell you something else about the curve in addition to its derivative, you can work out the value of that **constant of integration**. Usually the something is the **coordinates** of one of the points the curve goes through.

> **Example:** The curve $y = f(x)$ goes through the point (2, 8) and $f'(x) = 6x(x - 1)$. Find f(x).

You know the derivative $f'(x)$ and need to find the function f(x) — so **integrate**.

$$f'(x) = 6x(x - 1) = 6x^2 - 6x$$

So integrating both sides gives...

$$f(x) = \int (6x^2 - 6x)\,dx$$

$$\Rightarrow f(x) = 6\int (x^2 - x)\,dx$$

6 is a constant factor of both terms, so you can take it outside the integral.

$$\Rightarrow f(x) = 6\left(\frac{x^3}{3} - \frac{x^2}{2} + C\right)$$

You don't need to write 6C here, as C is just 'some unknown number'.

$$\Rightarrow f(x) = 2x^3 - 3x^2 + C$$

f'(x) is just another way of saying $\frac{dy}{dx}$. So when you integrate f'(x) you get f(x).

> Check this is correct by **differentiating** it and making sure you get what you started with.
>
> $$f(x) = 2x^3 - 3x^2 + C = 2x^3 - 3x^2 + C$$
> $$f'(x) = 2(3x^2) - 3(2x^1) + 0$$
> $$f'(x) = 6x^2 - 6x$$

A constant always differentiates to zero.

Remember: Even if you don't have any extra information about the curve — you still have to add a constant when you work out an integral without limits.

So this function's got the **correct derivative** — but you now need to **find C**.

You do this using the fact that the curve goes through (2, 8). Putting $x = 2$ and $f(x) = 8$ into the equation above gives:

$$8 = (2 \times 2^3) - (3 \times 2^2) + C$$
$$\Rightarrow 8 = 16 - 12 + C$$
$$\Rightarrow C = 4$$

So the answer you need is this one:

$$f(x) = 2x^3 - 3x^2 + 4$$

It's a cubic equation — and the graph looks like this...

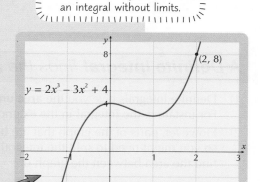

$$y = 2x^3 - 3x^2 + 4$$

Practice Questions

Q1 Integrate: a) $\int 10x^4\,dx$, b) $\int (3x + 5x^2)\,dx$, c) $\int x^2(3x + 2)\,dx$

Q2 Find the equation of the curve that has derivative $\frac{dy}{dx} = 6x - 7$ and goes through the point (1, 0).

Q3 f(x) passes through (1, 0) and $f'(x) = 3x^3 + 2$. Work out the equation of f(x).

Exam Questions

Q1 a) Show that $(5 + 2\sqrt{x})^2$ can be written in the form $a + b\sqrt{x} + cx$, stating the values of the constants a, b and c. [3 marks]

b) Hence find $\int (5 + 2\sqrt{x})^2\,dx$. [3 marks]

Q2 Curve C has equation $y = f(x)$, $x \neq 0$, where the derivative is given by $f'(x) = x^3 - \frac{2}{x^2}$. The point P (1, 2) lies on C.

a) Find an equation for the tangent to C at the point P, giving your answer in the form $y = mx + c$, where m and c are integers. [4 marks]

b) Find f(x). [4 marks]

Indefinite integrals — joy without limits...

This integration lark isn't so bad then — there are only a couple of things to remember and then you can do it no problem. But that constant of integration catches loads of people out — it's so easy to forget — and you'll definitely lose marks if you do forget it. You have been warned. Other than that, there's not much to it. Hurray.

Definite Integrals

Some integrals have limits (i.e. little numbers) next to the integral sign. You integrate them in exactly the same way — but you don't need a constant of integration. Much easier. And scrummier and yummier too.

Definite Integrals are like regular integrals, but with Limits

Definite integrals are ones that have little numbers on the top and bottom called **limits**. These are the values of x that you're 'integrating between'.

Finding a definite integral isn't really any harder than an indefinite one — there's just an **extra** stage you have to do. After you've integrated the function, you have to work out the value of this new function by **sticking in** the limits, and **subtracting** what the **bottom** limit gave you from what the **top** limit gave you.

Example: Evaluate $\int_1^3 (x^2 + 2)\, dx$.

> This is the integral of $x^2 + 2$ "from 1 to 3".

Find the integral in the normal way, then use the limits:

$$\int_1^3 (x^2 + 2)\, dx = \left[\frac{x^3}{3} + 2x\right]_1^3$$

> Put the integrated function in **square brackets** and rewrite the limits on the right-hand side.

$2 = 2x^0$ — so increase the power (to 1) and divide by 1 to get 2x.

$$= \left(\frac{(3)^3}{3} + 2\,(3)\right) - \left(\frac{(1)^3}{3} + 2\,(1)\right)$$

> Do '**top limit** minus **bottom limit**'.

$$= 15 - \frac{7}{3} = \frac{38}{3}$$

> You don't need a constant of integration with a **definite** integral.

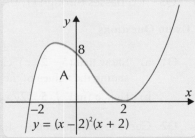

"I'm looking for a loan to start my business — Integrals, Ltd."

A Definite Integral finds the Area Under a Curve

1) Definite integrals give you the **area under the graph** of the function you're integrating. For instance, the integral in the example above gives this area:

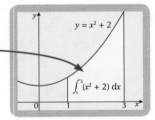

2) However, parts of the graph that are **below the x-axis** will give a **negative answer**, so you might need to split the integral up into bits. For example, if you wanted to find the area between the graph of $y = x^3$ and the x-axis between $x = -2$ and $x = 2$:

This is the right-hand side of the area you're finding...

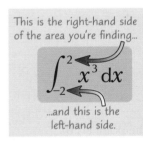

$$\int_{-2}^2 x^3\, dx$$

...and this is the left-hand side.

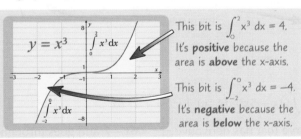

This bit is $\int_0^2 x^3\, dx = 4$.
It's **positive** because the area is **above** the x-axis.

This bit is $\int_{-2}^0 x^3\, dx = -4$.
It's **negative** because the area is **below** the x-axis.

The **value** of the integral $\int_{-2}^2 x^3\, dx$ is **zero**, because the area below the x-axis 'cancels out' the area above. To find the **area**, you need to work out the two parts **separately** and **add** them together. In this example, the **area = 4 + 4 = 8**.

Example: The curve $y = (x - 2)^2(x + 2)$ is shown on the diagram. Find the area bounded by the curve and the x-axis.

To find the area, you want to integrate $y = (x - 2)^2(x + 2)$ between −2 and 2.

Expand the brackets: $\quad y = (x^2 - 4x + 4)(x + 2) = x^3 - 2x^2 - 4x + 8$

$$A = \int_{-2}^2 y\, dx = \int_{-2}^2 x^3 - 2x^2 - 4x + 8\, dx$$

> Integrate each term separately.

$$= \left[\frac{x^4}{4} - \frac{2x^3}{3} - 2x^2 + 8x\right]_{-2}^2$$

$$= \left(\frac{2^4}{4} - \frac{2\,(2)^3}{3} - 2\,(2)^2 + 8\,(2)\right) - \left(\frac{(-2)^4}{4} - \frac{2\,(-2)^3}{3} - 2\,(-2)^2 + 8\,(-2)\right)$$

> Stick the limits in.

$$= \frac{20}{3} - -\frac{44}{3}$$

$$= \frac{64}{3}$$

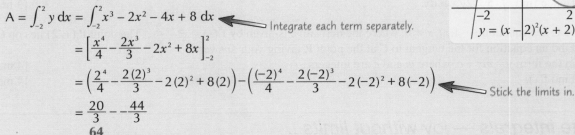

Definite Integrals

Sometimes you have to **Add Two Integrals** together

You could be asked to find "the area enclosed by [a couple of boring old curves] and the *x*-axis".
This might sound pretty hard — until you draw a picture and see what it's all about.
Then it's just a matter of choosing your limits wisely...

Example: Find the area enclosed by the curve $y = x^2$, the line $y = 2 - x$ and the *x*-axis.

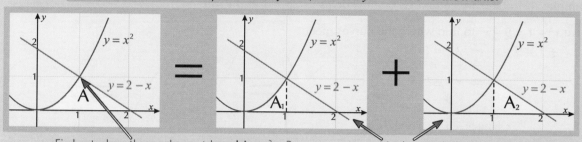

Find out where the graphs meet by **solving** $x^2 = 2 - x$
— they meet at $x = 1$ (they also meet at $x = -2$, but this isn't in A).

You have to find area A — but you'll
need to **split** it into two smaller pieces.

It's pretty clear from the picture that you'll have to find the area in two lumps, A_1 and A_2:

The first area you
need to find is A_1:

$$A_1 = \int_0^1 x^2 \, dx$$
$$= \left[\frac{x^3}{3}\right]_0^1 = \left(\frac{1}{3} - 0\right) = \frac{1}{3}$$

The other area you need is A_2.
A_2 is just a triangle, with base
length $2 - 1 = 1$ and height $= 1$.
So the area of the triangle is:

$$\frac{1}{2} \times b \times h = \frac{1}{2} \times 1 \times 1 = \frac{1}{2}$$

And the area the question
actually asks for is:

$$A = A_1 + A_2$$
$$= \frac{1}{3} + \frac{1}{2} = \frac{5}{6}$$

Practice Questions

Q1 Evaluate the following definite integrals:

a) $\int_0^1 (4x^3 + 3x^2 + 2x + 1) \, dx$ b) $\int_1^2 \left(\frac{8}{x^5} + \frac{3}{\sqrt{x}}\right) dx$ c) $\int_1^6 \frac{3}{x^2} \, dx$.

Q2 a) Evaluate $\int_{-3}^3 (9 - x^2) \, dx$

b) Sketch the area represented by this integral.

Exam Questions

Q1 Find the exact value of $\int_1^4 \left(2x - 6x^2 + \sqrt{x}\right) dx$.   [5 marks]

Q2 The diagram on the right shows a sketch of the curve C, $y = (x - 3)^2(x + 1)$.
Calculate the shaded area between point A, where C intersects
the *x*-axis, and point B, where C touches the *x*-axis.   [7 marks]

Q3 The curve $y = -(x - 2)^2$ and line $y = \frac{1}{2}x - 6$ are shown on the diagram on the right.
a) Show that the curve and line intersect at the point P (4, –4).   [3 marks]
b) Find the shaded area A, bounded by the curve $y = -(x - 2)^2$,
the line $y = \frac{1}{2}x - 6$ and the *x*-axis.   [6 marks]

My hobbies? Well, I'm really inte grating. Especially carrots.

*It's still integration — but this time you're putting two numbers into an expression afterwards. So once you've got
the hang of indefinite integration, this definite stuff should easily fall into place. Maths is like that. Though, I admit
it's probably not as much fun as, say, a big banoffee cake. But Maths and cake together? Now we're talking...*

Further Definite Integrals

What's that? You want some more tasty examples of definite integrals, with parametric equations thrown in to spice things up a bit? It's your lucky day, my friend — read on.

Sometimes you have to **Subtract** integrals

As on page 111, it's best to draw a **sketch** to work out exactly what you need to do.

Example: Find the area enclosed by the curves $y = x^2 + 1$ and $y = 9 - x^2$.

Solve $x^2 + 1 = 9 - x^2$ to find where the curves meet:

$$x^2 + 1 = 9 - x^2 \Rightarrow 2x^2 = 8$$
$$\Rightarrow x^2 = 4$$
$$\Rightarrow x = \pm 2$$

So you'll have to integrate between −2 and 2.

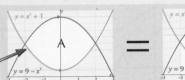

The area under the purple curve is:

$$A_1 = \int_{-2}^{2} (9 - x^2)\, dx$$
$$= \left[9x - \frac{x^3}{3} \right]_{-2}^{2}$$
$$= \left(18 - \frac{2^3}{3} \right) - \left(-18 - \frac{(-2)^3}{3} \right)$$
$$= \left(18 - \frac{8}{3} \right) - \left(-18 - \frac{-8}{3} \right)$$
$$= \frac{46}{3} - \left(-\frac{46}{3} \right) = \frac{92}{3}$$

The area under the green curve is:

$$A_2 = \int_{-2}^{2} (x^2 + 1)\, dx$$
$$= \left[\frac{x^3}{3} + x \right]_{-2}^{2}$$
$$= \left(\frac{2^3}{3} + 2 \right) - \left(\frac{(-2)^3}{3} + (-2) \right)$$
$$= \left(\frac{8}{3} + 2 \right) - \left(\frac{-8}{3} - 2 \right)$$
$$= \frac{14}{3} - \left(-\frac{14}{3} \right) = \frac{28}{3}$$

And the area you need is the difference between these:

$$A = A_1 - A_2$$
$$= \frac{92}{3} - \frac{28}{3} = \frac{64}{3}$$

Instead of integrating before subtracting — you could try 'subtracting the curves', and then integrating. This overall area is also:

$$A = \int_{-2}^{2} [(9 - x^2) - (x^2 + 1)]\, dx$$

Use the **Chain Rule** to **Integrate Parametrics**

1) Normally, to find the area under a graph, you can do a simple integration. But if you've got **parametric equations** (see page 40), things are more difficult — you can't find $\int y\, dx$ if y isn't written in terms of x.

2) There's a sneaky way to get around this. Suppose your parameter's t, then

$$\int y\, dx = \int y\, \frac{dx}{dt}\, dt$$

3) Both y and $\frac{dx}{dt}$ are written in terms of t, so you can **multiply** them together to get an expression you can **integrate** with respect to t.

This comes from the chain rule (see p.94) — if you think of dx as $\frac{dx}{1}$, then $\frac{dx}{1} = \frac{dx}{dt} \times \frac{dt}{1}$.

Example: a) A curve is defined by the parametric equations $x = t^3 + 3$ and $y = t^2 + 2t + 3$. Show that $\int y\, dx = \int (3t^4 + 6t^3 + 9t^2)\, dt$.

$\frac{dx}{dt} = 3t^2$, so using the formula above:

$$\int y\, dx = \int y\, \frac{dx}{dt}\, dt = \int (t^2 + 2t + 3)(3t^2)\, dt = \int (3t^4 + 6t^3 + 9t^2)\, dt.$$

b) Hence, find $\int y\, dx$ between $t = 0$ and $t = 1$.

You know that $\int y\, dx = \int (3t^4 + 6t^3 + 9t^2)\, dt$, so integrate between the given limits:

$$\int_{0}^{1} 3t^4 + 6t^3 + 9t^2\, dt = \left[\frac{3t^5}{5} + \frac{3t^4}{2} + 3t^3 \right]_{0}^{1}$$

These terms have been simplified from $\frac{6t^4}{4}$ and $\frac{9t^3}{3}$ respectively.

$$= \left[\frac{3(1^5)}{5} + \frac{3(1^4)}{2} + 3(1^3) \right] - [0 + 0 + 0]$$
$$= 0.6 + 1.5 + 3 = 5.1$$

Asparametric equations are integral to any summer dish.

Further Definite Integrals

With a **definite integral** involving parametric equations, you need to **alter the limits** as well. You can do this by **substituting** the x-limits into the parametric equation for x to find the corresponding values of t.

Example: The shaded region marked A on this sketch is bounded by the lines $y = 0$ and $x = 2$, and by the curve with parametric equations $x = t^2 - 2$ and $y = t^2 - 9t + 20$, $t \geq 0$, which crosses the x-axis at $x = 14$. Find the area of A.

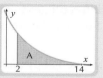

You need to use $\int y \, dx = \int y \frac{dx}{dt} \, dt$, so find: $\frac{dx}{dt} = \frac{d}{dt}(t^2 - 2) = 2t$

> You can ignore the negative solutions here as you're told $t \geq 0$ in the question.

Now you need to convert the **limits**.
2 and 14 are the limits **with respect to** x,
so find the **corresponding values of** t:

$x = 2 \Rightarrow t^2 - 2 = 2 \Rightarrow t^2 = 4 \Rightarrow t = 2$
$x = 14 \Rightarrow t^2 - 2 = 14 \Rightarrow t^2 = 16 \Rightarrow t = 4$

Now **integrate** to find the area of A:

$A = \int_2^{14} y \, dx = \int_2^4 y \frac{dx}{dt} \, dt = \int_2^4 (t^2 - 9t + 20)(2t) \, dt = \int_2^4 (2t^3 - 18t^2 + 40t) \, dt$

$= \left[\frac{1}{2}t^4 - 6t^3 + 20t^2 \right]_2^4 = \left(\frac{1}{2}(4)^4 - 6(4)^3 + 20(4)^2 \right) - \left(\frac{1}{2}(2)^4 - 6(2)^3 + 20(2)^2 \right) = 64 - 40 = \mathbf{24}$

Practice Questions

Q1 Find the area bounded by the curve $y = 1 - x^2$ and the line $y = 1 - x$.

Q2 A curve has parametric equations $y = 4 + \frac{3}{t}$ and $x = t^2 - 1$. Write the integral $\int y \, dx$ in the form $\int f(t) \, dt$.

Exam Questions

Q1 The diagram on the right shows the curve $y = (x + 1)(x - 5)$.
Points J $(-1, 0)$ and K $(4, -5)$ lie on the curve.

a) Find the equation of the straight line joining J and K in the form $y = mx + c$. [2 marks]

b) Calculate $\int_{-1}^{4} (x + 1)(x - 5) \, dx$. [5 marks]

c) Find the area of the shaded region. [3 marks]

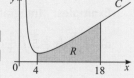

Q2 The curve C has parametric equations $x = t^2 + 3t$ and $y = t^2 + \frac{1}{t^3}$, $t > 0$.
The shaded region marked R is enclosed by C, the x-axis and the lines $x = 4$ and $x = 18$.

a) Show that the area of R is given by $\int_1^3 \frac{(t^5 + 1)(2t + 3)}{t^3} \, dt$. [4 marks]

b) Hence, find the area of R. [4 marks]

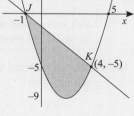

Q3 The parametric equations of curve C are $x = 3 + 4\sin\theta$, $y = \frac{1 + \cos 2\theta}{3}$, $-\frac{\pi}{2} \leq \theta \leq \frac{\pi}{2}$.
Point H on C has coordinates $\left(5, \frac{1}{2}\right)$.

a) Find the value of θ at point H. [2 marks]

The region R is enclosed by C, the line $x = 5$, and the x-axis, as shown.

b) Show that the area of R is given by the integral $\frac{8}{3} \int_{-\frac{\pi}{2}}^{\frac{\pi}{6}} \cos^3\theta \, d\theta$. [5 marks]

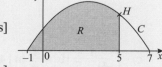

Sick of regular integration? Call the parametrics...

If you're asked to find an area, it's really useful to draw a sketch (or annotate, if given in the question). To integrate a curve defined by parametric equations, you'll need to remember the formula on page 112 — or know the trick to derive it using the chain rule. The limits will need converting to the corresponding values of t (or whatever) as well.

Integrating eˣ and 1/x

Sometimes you get integrals that look really nasty — like exponentials and fractions.
However, once you learn the clever tricks for dealing with them, they're quite easy to integrate really.

eˣ integrates to give eˣ (+ C)

As e^x **differentiates** to give e^x
(see p.96), it makes sense that

$$\int e^x \, dx = e^x + C$$

Don't forget the constant of integration.

Once you're happy with that, you can use it to solve lots of integrations that have an e^x term in them.
If the **coefficient** of x isn't 1, you need to **divide** by that coefficient when you **integrate** — so $\int e^{kx} dx = \frac{1}{k}e^{kx} + C$

Examples: Integrate the following: a) e^{7x} b) $2e^{4-3x}$ c) $e^{\frac{x}{2}}$

a) $\int e^{7x} dx = \frac{1}{7}e^{7x} + C$

If you differentiated e^{7x} using the chain rule, you'd get $7e^{7x}$.
So when you integrate, you need to **divide by 7** (the coefficient of x).
This is so that if you differentiated your answer you'd get back to e^{7x}.

b) $\int 2e^{4-3x} dx = -\frac{2}{3}e^{4-3x} + C$

This one isn't as bad as it looks — if you differentiated $2e^{4-3x}$, you'd get $-6e^{4-3x}$,
so you need to **divide by –3** (the coefficient of x) when you integrate.
Differentiating your answer gives you $2e^{4-3x}$.

c) $\int e^{\frac{x}{2}} dx = \int e^{\frac{1}{2}x} dx = 2e^{\frac{x}{2}} + C$ If you differentiated $e^{\frac{x}{2}}$ using the chain rule, you'd get $\frac{1}{2}e^{\frac{x}{2}}$,
so you need to **multiply by 2** when you integrate.

You can always differentiate your answer to check that it works.

1/x integrates to ln |x| (+ C)

When you started integration on page 108, you couldn't integrate $\frac{1}{x}$ ($= x^{-1}$) by **increasing**
the **power** by 1 and **dividing** by it, as you ended up **dividing by 0** (which is baaaaad).

However, on p.96, you saw that $\ln x$ **differentiates** to give $\frac{1}{x}$, so:

Don't worry about where the modulus sign (see p.28) comes from — using |x| just means that there isn't a problem when x is negative.

$$\int \frac{1}{x} \, dx = \ln|x| + C$$

There's also a general version of this rule:

rules of ln are the same as log

$$\int \frac{1}{ax+b} \, dx = \frac{1}{a}\ln|ax+b| + C$$

Examples: Integrate the following: a) $\frac{5}{x}$ b) $\frac{1}{3x}$ c) $\frac{1}{4x+5}$

a) $\int \frac{5}{x} dx = 5\int \frac{1}{x} dx = 5 \ln|x| + C$ 5 is a constant coefficient — you can
take it outside the integral if you want.

You could also write 5 ln |x| as ln |x⁵|.

b) $\int \frac{1}{3x} dx = \frac{1}{3}\int \frac{1}{x} dx = \frac{1}{3} \ln|x| + C$ Don't make the mistake of putting just $\ln|3x| + C$, as this would differentiate to
give $\frac{1}{x}$ ($\ln|3x| = \ln|x| + \ln 3$, so ln 3 disappears when you differentiate).

If you use the general rule here, you get $\frac{1}{3} \ln|3x| + C$. The two answers are the
same because $\frac{1}{3}\ln|3x| = \frac{1}{3}\ln|x| + \frac{1}{3}\ln 3$, so it's just the value of C that's different.

c) $\int \frac{1}{4x+5} dx = \frac{1}{4} \ln|4x+5| + C$ Use the general rule for this one — don't forget to divide by a (in this case, 4).

If you have a fraction that has a **function of x** in the **numerator** and a **different function of x**
in the **denominator** (e.g. $\frac{x-2}{x^3+1}$), you won't be able to use this formula to integrate it.

However, if you can **differentiate** the **denominator** to get the **numerator** (e.g. $\frac{3x^2}{x^3+1}$,

since the derivative of $x^3 + 1$ is $3x^2$), then there's a useful trick that you can use instead...

Integrating eˣ and 1/x

Some *Fractions* integrate to *ln*

In general terms, if you're trying to integrate a fraction where the **numerator** is the **derivative** of the **denominator**, you can use this formula:

$$\int \frac{f'(x)}{f(x)}\, dx = \ln|f(x)| + C$$

This is another one that comes from the chain rule (p.94) — if you differentiated ln |f(x)|, you'd end up with the fraction on the left.

The hardest bit about questions like this is **recognising** that the denominator **differentiates** to give the numerator. Once you've spotted that, it's dead easy.

*The numerator might be a **multiple** of the derivative of the denominator, just to confuse things, so watch out for that.*

Examples: Find: a) $\int \frac{8x^3 - 4}{x^4 - 2x}\, dx$, b) $\int \frac{3\sin 3x}{\cos 3x + 2}\, dx$.

a) $\frac{d}{dx}(x^4 - 2x) = 4x^3 - 2$
and $8x^3 - 4 = 2(4x^3 - 2)$
The numerator is 2 × the derivative of the denominator, so:
$$\int \frac{8x^3 - 4}{x^4 - 2x}\, dx = 2\int \frac{4x^3 - 2}{x^4 - 2x}\, dx$$
$$= 2\ln|x^4 - 2x| + C$$

b) $\frac{d}{dx}(\cos 3x + 2) = -3\sin 3x$
The numerator is −1 × the derivative of the denominator, so:
$$\int \frac{3\sin 3x}{\cos 3x + 2}\, dx = -\int \frac{-3\sin 3x}{\cos 3x + 2}\, dx$$
$$= -\ln|\cos 3x + 2| + C$$

Using C = −ln k, you could combine all the terms into one using the laws of logs:
−ln |cos 3x + 2| − ln k
= −ln |k(cos 3x + 2)|

You can use *Partial Fractions* to integrate

In Section 2 (pages 14-15), you saw how to **break down** a scary-looking **algebraic fraction** into **partial fractions**. This comes in pretty handy when you're **integrating** — you could try other methods, but it would get **messy** and probably **end in tears**. Fortunately, once you've split it up into **partial fractions**, it's much **easier** to integrate.

Example: Find $\int \frac{12x + 6}{4x^2 - 9}\, dx$.

This is the example from p.14,
and it can be written as partial fractions like this: $\frac{2}{2x + 3} + \frac{4}{2x - 3}$

Be careful with the coefficients here. Try differentiating them to see where they come from if you're not sure.

Integrating the partial fractions is much easier: $\int \left(\frac{2}{2x + 3} + \frac{4}{2x - 3} \right) dx = \ln|2x + 3| + 2\ln|2x - 3| + C$
$$= \ln|(2x + 3)(2x - 3)^2| + C$$

This answer's been simplified using the log laws (see p.76).

Practice Questions

Q1 Find: a) $\int 4e^{2x}\, dx$, b) $\int e^{3x - 5}\, dx$, c) $\int \frac{2}{3x}\, dx$, d) $\int \frac{2}{2x + 1}\, dx$.

Q2 Integrate $\int \frac{20x^4 + 12x^2 - 12}{x^5 + x^3 - 3x}\, dx$.

Q3 $\frac{3x + 10}{(2x + 3)(x - 4)} \equiv \frac{A}{2x + 3} + \frac{B}{x - 4}$. Find the value of A and B, and hence find $\int \frac{3x + 10}{(2x + 3)(x - 4)}\, dx$.

Exam Questions

Q1 Find $\int 3e^{(5 - 6x)}\, dx$. [2 marks]

Q2 Given that $x = 1$ is a root of $x^3 - 6x^2 + 11x - 6$, completely factorise $x^3 - 6x^2 + 11x - 6$, and hence find $\int \frac{4x - 10}{x^3 - 6x^2 + 11x - 6}\, dx$. [8 marks]

Don't cheat in your exams — copying's derivative, so revising's integral...

There's quite a lot of different techniques to take in on these pages. Don't forget to try differentiating your answer at the end, so you know if it's gone wrong somewhere — checking my answers has saved my skin more times than I can tell you (28). Make sure you're a master of partial fractions before you even think about integrating them.

Integrating Trig Functions

You thought you'd killed off the dragon that is trigonometry back in Section 5, but it rears its ugly head again now — you need to know how to integrate trig functions. Equip your most trusty dragon-slaying sword and read on...

Sin and Cos are Easy to integrate

On page 98, you saw that **sin x** differentiates to give **cos x**, **cos x** differentiates to give **–sin x** and **tan x** differentiates to give **sec²x** (where the angle *x* is in **radians**). So it's pretty obvious that:

$$\int \sin x \, dx = -\cos x + C$$
$$\int \cos x \, dx = \sin x + C$$
$$\int \sec^2 x \, dx = \tan x + C$$

Integrating tan x is a bit different — see the next page.

The derivative of tan x is in the formula booklet, so you can work backwards to this result.

If *x* has a **coefficient** that **isn't 1** (e.g. sin 3*x*), you just **divide** by the **coefficient** when you integrate — just like on page 114.

Example: Find $\int \left(\cos 4x - 2 \sin 2x + \sec^2 \frac{1}{2}x\right) dx$.

Integrate each term separately using the results from above:

$$\int \cos 4x \, dx = \frac{1}{4} \sin 4x \qquad \int -2 \sin 2x \, dx = -2\left(-\frac{1}{2} \cos 2x\right) = \cos 2x \qquad \int \sec^2 \frac{1}{2}x \, dx = \frac{1}{\frac{1}{2}} \tan \frac{1}{2}x = 2 \tan \frac{1}{2}x$$

Putting these terms together and adding the constant gives:

$$\int \left(\cos 4x - 2 \sin 2x + \sec^2 \frac{1}{2}x\right) dx = \frac{1}{4} \sin 4x + \cos 2x + 2 \tan \frac{1}{2}x + C$$

There are some Results you can just Learn

There's a list of **trig integrals** that you can just **learn** — you don't need to know where they came from, you can just **use** them. You've met these ones before — they're the **results** of differentiating **cosec x**, **sec x** and **cot x**.

$$\int \operatorname{cosec} x \cot x \, dx = -\operatorname{cosec} x + C$$
$$\int \sec x \tan x \, dx = \sec x + C$$
$$\int \operatorname{cosec}^2 x \, dx = -\cot x + C$$

You saw how to differentiate cosec, sec and cot on p.102.

The coefficients of x have to be the same in each term — e.g. you couldn't integrate sec x tan 3x using this method.

As usual, you need to **divide** by the **coefficient of** *x* when you integrate.

Example: Find $\int \left(10 \sec 5x \tan 5x + \frac{1}{2} \operatorname{cosec} 3x \cot 3x - \operatorname{cosec}^2(6x + 1)\right) dx$.

This one looks a bit scary, but take it one step at a time. Integrate each bit in turn to get:

$$\int 10 \sec 5x \tan 5x \, dx = 10\left(\frac{1}{5} \sec 5x\right) = 2 \sec 5x$$

$$\int \frac{1}{2} \operatorname{cosec} 3x \cot 3x \, dx = \frac{1}{2}\left(-\frac{1}{3} \operatorname{cosec} 3x\right) = -\frac{1}{6} \operatorname{cosec} 3x$$

$$\int -\operatorname{cosec}^2(6x + 1) \, dx = -\left(-\frac{1}{6} \cot(6x + 1)\right) = \frac{1}{6} \cot(6x + 1)$$

The + 1 inside the brackets has no effect on the integration — differentiate to see why.

Putting these terms together and adding the constant gives:

$$\int \left(10 \sec 5x \tan 5x + \frac{1}{2} \operatorname{cosec} 3x \cot 3x - \operatorname{cosec}^2(6x + 1)\right) dx = 2 \sec 5x - \frac{1}{6} \operatorname{cosec} 3x + \frac{1}{6} \cot(6x + 1) + C$$

Integrating Trig Functions

On page 115 you saw that there was a **formula** for integrating a **fraction** where the **numerator** was the **derivative** of the **denominator** (or a **multiple** of it anyway). You may also have noticed that we've very suspiciously not integrated tan x yet. Well, we can use our fraction trick to finally work out the integral of tan:

$\tan x = \dfrac{\sin x}{\cos x}$ and $\dfrac{d}{dx}(\cos x) = -\sin x$, so you can write $\int \tan x\, dx$ in the form $\int -\dfrac{f'(x)}{f(x)}\, dx$:

$$\int \tan x\, dx = \int \frac{\sin x}{\cos x}\, dx = -\ln|\cos x| + C$$

$-\ln|\cos x|$ is the same as $\ln|\sec x|$ — this comes from the laws of logs (see p.76).

You can integrate some other **trig functions** in a similar way:

Example: Show that $\int \cot x\, dx = \ln|\sin x| + C$.

Use a similar method to the box above:

- Write cot x as a fraction: $\cot x = \dfrac{\cos x}{\sin x}$
- Differentiate the denominator: $\dfrac{d}{dx}(\sin x) = \cos x$
- Use the formula: $\int \cot x\, dx = \int \dfrac{f'(x)}{f(x)}\, dx$, where $f(x) = \sin x$

So $\int \cot x\, dx = \ln|f(x)| + C$
$= \ln|\sin x| + C$ as required

The **Double Angle Formulas** are useful for **Integration**

If you're given a tricky **trig function** to integrate, see if you can **simplify** it using one of the **double angle formulas**. They're especially useful for things like **cos²x**, **sin²x** and **sin x cos x**. Here are the double angle formulas (see p.71):

$$\sin 2x \equiv 2\sin x \cos x \qquad \cos 2x \equiv \cos^2 x - \sin^2 x$$
$$\tan 2x \equiv \frac{2\tan x}{1-\tan^2 x} \qquad \cos 2x \equiv 2\cos^2 x - 1$$
$$\cos 2x \equiv 1 - 2\sin^2 x$$

You can rearrange the second two cos 2x formulas to get expressions for cos² x and sin² x:
$\cos^2 x = \frac{1}{2}(\cos 2x + 1)$
$\sin^2 x = \frac{1}{2}(1 - \cos 2x)$

Once you've **replaced** the **original function** with one of the **double angle formulas**, you can just **integrate** as normal.

Examples: Find: a) $\int \sin^2 x\, dx$, b) $\int \cos^2 5x\, dx$, c) $\int \sin x \cos x\, dx$.

a) Using the double angle formula above, write sin²x as $\frac{1}{2}(1 - \cos 2x)$, then integrate.

$$\int \sin^2 x\, dx = \int \frac{1}{2}(1 - \cos 2x) = \frac{1}{2}\left(x - \frac{1}{2}\sin 2x\right) + C = \frac{1}{2}x - \frac{1}{4}\sin 2x + C$$

b) Using the double angle formula above, write cos² 5x as $\frac{1}{2}(\cos 10x + 1)$, then integrate.

$$\int \cos^2 5x\, dx = \int \frac{1}{2}(\cos 10x + 1) = \frac{1}{2}\left(\frac{1}{10}\sin 10x + x\right) + C = \frac{1}{20}\sin 10x + \frac{1}{2}x + C$$

Don't forget to double the coefficient of x here. You'll also need to divide by 10 when you integrate.

c) Using the double angle formula above, write sin x cos x as $\frac{1}{2}\sin 2x$, then integrate.

$$\int \sin x \cos x\, dx = \int \frac{1}{2}\sin 2x\, dx = \frac{1}{2}\left(-\frac{1}{2}\cos 2x\right) + C = -\frac{1}{4}\cos 2x + C$$

Integrating Trig Functions

Use the *Identities* to get a function you *Know* how to *Integrate*

There are a couple of other **identities** you can use to **simplify trig functions** (see p.68):

$$\sec^2 \theta \equiv 1 + \tan^2 \theta$$

$$\operatorname{cosec}^2 \theta \equiv 1 + \cot^2 \theta$$

These two identities are really useful if you have to integrate **tan²x** or **cot²x**, as you already know how to integrate **sec²x** and **cosec²x** (see p.116). Don't forget the stray **1s** flying around — they'll just integrate to **x**.

Examples: Find: a) $\int (\tan^2 x - 1)\,dx$, b) $\int (\cot^2 3x)\,dx$.

a) Rewrite the function in terms of sec²x:
$\tan^2 x - 1 \equiv \sec^2 x - 1 - 1 \equiv \sec^2 x - 2$.
Now integrate:
$\int (\sec^2 x - 2)\,dx = \tan x - 2x + C$

b) Get the function in terms of cosec²:
$\cot^2 3x \equiv \operatorname{cosec}^2 3x - 1$.
Now integrate:
$\int (\operatorname{cosec}^2 3x - 1)\,dx = -\dfrac{1}{3}\cot 3x - x + C$

Remember to divide by 3, the coefficient of x, when you integrate.

Example: Evaluate $\int_0^{\frac{\pi}{3}} \left(6\sin 3x \cos 3x + \tan^2 \frac{1}{2}x + 1\right) dx$.

Using the identities, $6\sin 3x \cos 3x \equiv 3\sin 6x$
and $\tan^2 \frac{1}{2}x + 1 \equiv \sec^2 \frac{1}{2}x$ gives:

$$\int_0^{\frac{\pi}{3}} \left(3\sin 6x + \sec^2 \tfrac{1}{2}x\right) dx = \left[-\frac{3}{6}\cos 6x + 2\tan \tfrac{1}{2}x\right]_0^{\frac{\pi}{3}}$$

$$= \left[-\frac{1}{2}\cos 6\left(\frac{\pi}{3}\right) + 2\tan \frac{1}{2}\left(\frac{\pi}{3}\right)\right] - \left[-\frac{1}{2}\cos 6(0) + 2\tan \frac{1}{2}(0)\right]$$

$$= \left[-\frac{1}{2}\cos(2\pi) + 2\tan\left(\frac{\pi}{6}\right)\right] - \left[-\frac{1}{2}\cos(0) + 2\tan(0)\right]$$

$$= \left[-\frac{1}{2}(1) + 2\left(\frac{1}{\sqrt{3}}\right)\right] - \left[-\frac{1}{2}(1) + 2(0)\right] = -\frac{1}{2} + \frac{2}{\sqrt{3}} + \frac{1}{2} = \frac{2}{\sqrt{3}}$$

Use the table of common trig angles on p.56 to help you here.

Sadly, Boris' identity wasn't making it any easier to integrate at all.

Practice Questions

Q1 Find $\int (\cos 4x - \sec^2 7x)\,dx$.

Q2 Evaluate $\int \left(6\sec 3x \tan 3x - \operatorname{cosec}^2 \frac{x}{5}\right) dx$.

Q3 Integrate $\int -\frac{\cos x}{3\sin x}\,dx$.

Q4 Use an appropriate trig identity to find $\int \frac{2\tan 3x}{1 - \tan^2 3x}\,dx$.

Q5 Use the trig identity $\sec^2 x \equiv 1 + \tan^2 x$ to find $\int (2\tan^2 3x + 2)\,dx$.

Exam Questions

Q1 Find $\int \frac{\operatorname{cosec}^2 x - 2}{\cot x + 2x}\,dx$. [3 marks]

Q2 Use an appropriate identity to find $\int 2\cot^2 x \,dx$. [3 marks]

This is startin' to grate on me now...

Some of these integrals are in the formula booklet. The ones from the bottom of p.116 are on the list of differentiation formulas, so if you can work backwards (i.e. from f'(x) to f(x)), you can sneakily use these results without having to remember them at all. Don't tell the examiners though — I don't think they've noticed yet... (disclaimer: they definitely have)

Integrating Using the Chain Rule Backwards

Most integrations aren't as bad as they look — a few pages ago, you saw how to integrate special fractions, and now it's time for certain products. There are some things you can look out for when you're integrating...

You can use the **Chain Rule** in **Reverse**

You came across the **chain rule** back on p.94 — it's where you write the thing you're differentiating in terms of *u* (and *u* is a **function** of *x*). You end up with the **product** of **two derivatives** ($\frac{dy}{du}$ and $\frac{du}{dx}$).

When it comes to integrating, if you spot that your integral is a **product** where one bit is the **derivative** of another bit, you can use this rule:

$$\int \frac{du}{dx} f'(u)\, dx = f(u) + C$$ where *u* is a function of *x*.

Examples: Find: a) $\int 6x^5 e^{x^6}\, dx$, b) $\int e^{\sin x} \cos x\, dx$.

a) $\int 6x^5 e^{x^6}\, dx = e^{x^6} + C$ If you differentiated $y = e^{x^6}$ using the chain rule, you'd get $6x^5 e^{x^6}$, which is the function you had to integrate. In the formula, $u = x^6$ and $f(u) = e^u$.

b) $\int e^{\sin x} \cos x\, dx = e^{\sin x} + C$ If you differentiated $y = e^{\sin x}$ using the chain rule, you'd get $e^{\sin x}\cos x$, which is the function you had to integrate. Again, $f(u) = e^u$ and $u = \sin x$.

Some **Products** are made up of a **Function** and its **Derivative**

Similarly, if you spot that part of a **product** is the **derivative** of the other part of it (which is raised to a **power**), you can integrate it using this **rule**:

$$\int (n+1) f'(x) [f(x)]^n\, dx = [f(x)]^{n+1} + C$$

Remember that the **derivative** will be a **multiple** of *n + 1* (not *n*) — watch out for any other multiples too. This will probably make more sense if you have a look at an **example**:

Examples: Find: a) $\int 12x^3(2x^4 - 5)^2\, dx$, b) $\int 8 \operatorname{cosec}^2 x \cot^3 x\, dx$. ← This one looks pretty horrific, but it isn't too bad once you spot that $-\operatorname{cosec}^2 x$ is the derivative of cot x.

a) Here, $f(x) = 2x^4 - 5$, so differentiating gives $f'(x) = 8x^3$. $n = 2$, so $n + 1 = 3$.

Putting all this into the rule above gives: $\int 3(8x^3)(2x^4 - 5)^2\, dx = \int 24x^3(2x^4 - 5)^2\, dx = (2x^4 - 5)^3 + C$

Divide everything by 2 to match the original integral: $\int 12x^3(2x^4 - 5)^2\, dx = \frac{1}{2}(2x^4 - 5)^3 + C$

b) For this one, $f(x) = \cot x$, so differentiating gives $f'(x) = -\operatorname{cosec}^2 x$. $n = 3$, so $n + 1 = 4$.

Putting all this into the rule gives: $\int -4 \operatorname{cosec}^2 x \cot^3 x\, dx = \cot^4 x + C$

Multiply everything by –2 to match the original integral: $\int 8 \operatorname{cosec}^2 x \cot^3 x\, dx = -2 \cot^4 x + C$

Practice Questions

Q1 Integrate a) $\int 3x^2 e^{x^3}\, dx$ b) $\int 8x \cos (x^2)\, dx$.

Q2 Find $\int 36x^2(3x^3 + 4)^3\, dx$.

Exam Questions

Q1 Integrate the function $f(x) = -\sin x\, (3 \cos^2 x)$ with respect to *x*. [3 marks]

Q2 Find the indefinite integral $\int 6x(\operatorname{cosec}^2 x^2 - \sec x^2 \tan x^2)\, dx$. [6 marks]

To get rid of hiccups, drink a glass of water backwards...

It seems to me that most of this section is about reversing the things you learnt in Section 7. I don't know why they ask you to differentiate stuff if you're just going to have to integrate it right back again. Well, at least it keeps you busy...

Integration by Substitution

So, I know we said that the stuff on the last page was the chain rule backwards, but (and bear with me here) integration by substitution is also the reverse of the chain rule. Just a different reverse. You know what, just read on...

Use **Integration by Substitution** on **Products** of **Two Functions**

On the previous page, you saw how to **integrate** certain **products of functions** using the **chain rule backwards**. **Integration by substitution** lets you integrate **functions of functions** by **simplifying** the **integral**. Like the chain rule, you have to write part of the function in terms of u, where u is some **function** of x.

Integration by Substitution

1) You'll be given an integral that's made up of two functions of x (one is often just x) — e.g. $x(3x + 2)^3$.

$3x + 2 = u$
$x = \dfrac{u - 2}{3}$

2) Substitute u for one of the functions of x (to give a function that's easier to integrate) — e.g. $u = 3x + 2$. $\quad u^3$

> You won't always be told what substitution to use, but bits inside brackets or square roots are a good place to start.

3) Next, find $\dfrac{du}{dx}$, and rewrite it so that dx is on its own — e.g. $\dfrac{du}{dx} = 3$, so d$x = \dfrac{1}{3}$ du.

> $\dfrac{du}{dx}$ isn't really a fraction, but you can treat it as one for this bit.

4) Rewrite the original integral in terms of u and du — e.g. $\int x(3x + 2)^3 \, dx$ becomes $\int \left(\dfrac{u-2}{3}\right) u^3 \dfrac{1}{3} du = \int \dfrac{u^4 - 2u^3}{9} \, du$.

5) You should now be left with something that's easier to integrate — just integrate as normal, then at the last step replace u with the original substitution (so for this one, replace u with $3x + 2$).

Example: Use the substitution $u = x^2 - 2$ to find $\int 4x(x^2 - 2)^4 \, dx$.

As $u = x^2 - 2$, $\dfrac{du}{dx} = 2x$, so d$x = \dfrac{1}{2x} du$.

Substituting gives $\quad \int 4x(x^2 - 2)^4 \, dx = \int 4xu^4 \dfrac{1}{2x} du = \int 2u^4 \, du$.

Integrate... $\qquad\qquad \int 2u^4 \, du = \dfrac{2}{5}u^5 + C$

...and substitute x back in: $\qquad = \dfrac{2}{5}(x^2 - 2)^5 + C$

> The x's cancel, making it a lot easier to integrate — this often happens.

"Come — substitute your boring old shoes for one of my beautiful products."

For **Definite Integrals**, you have to **Change** the **Limits**

If you're given a **definite integral**, it's really important that you remember to **change the limits** to u. Doing it this way means you **don't** have to **put x back in** at the last step — just put the numbers into the integration for u.

Example: Use the substitution $u = \cos x$ to find $\int_{\frac{\pi}{2}}^{2\pi} -12 \sin x \cos^3 x \, dx$.

As $u = \cos x$, $\dfrac{du}{dx} = -\sin x$, so d$x = -\dfrac{1}{\sin x} du$.

Find the limits of u: $\quad$ When $x = \dfrac{\pi}{2}$, $u = \cos \dfrac{\pi}{2} = 0$, when $x = 2\pi$, $u = \cos 2\pi = 1$. So the limits of u are 0 and 1.

> Make sure you keep the top limit on the top and the bottom limit on the bottom — even if the bottom limit ends up as the bigger one.

Substituting all this gives: $\qquad \int_{\frac{\pi}{2}}^{2\pi} -12 \sin x \cos^3 x \, dx = \int_0^1 -12 \sin x \, u^3 \dfrac{-1}{\sin x} du = \int_0^1 12u^3 \, du$

Integrating and putting in the values of the limits gives: $\qquad \int_0^1 12u^3 \, du = [3u^4]_0^1 = [3(1)^4] - [3(0)^4] = \mathbf{3}$

> You could also have solved this one using the method on the previous page.

Integration by Substitution

You can use *Integration by Substitution* on *Fractions*

When faced with an **algebraic fraction** to integrate, you might be able to use the methods on pages 114-115. However, sometimes it's a lot easier to use a **substitution** (usually with u = the **denominator** or something in the denominator) to simplify the fraction into something you can integrate with ease.

Example: Find $\int \dfrac{3x^2}{(2x^3-1)^{\frac{1}{3}}}\, dx$, using a suitable substitution.

You're not given a substitution to use here, so pick something that looks like it might help. The $(2x^3 - 1)$ in the denominator is a sensible choice.

Let $u = (2x^3 - 1)$, then $\dfrac{du}{dx} = 6x^2$, so $dx = \dfrac{1}{6x^2}\, du$

Substituting gives: $\int \dfrac{3x^2}{(2x^3-1)^{\frac{1}{3}}}\, dx = \int \dfrac{3x^2}{u^{\frac{1}{3}}} \times \dfrac{1}{6x^2}\, du = \int \dfrac{1}{2} u^{-\frac{1}{3}}\, du$

Now you can integrate: $\int \dfrac{1}{2} u^{-\frac{1}{3}}\, du = \dfrac{1}{2}\left(\dfrac{3}{2} u^{\frac{2}{3}}\right) + C = \dfrac{3}{4}(2x^3 - 1)^{\frac{2}{3}} + C$

You could also use the method from p.119 here, using n = $-\dfrac{1}{3}$

Some *Trig Integrals* can be really *Nasty*

Unfortunately, the vast range of **trig identities** and **formulas** you've seen can all show up in one of these questions, meaning that there's no end to the **evil integration questions**. Here's a particularly nasty example:

Example: Use the substitution $u = \tan x$ to find $\int \dfrac{\sec^4 x}{\sqrt{\tan x}}\, dx$.

First, work out what all the substitutions will be: If $u = \tan x$, then $\dfrac{du}{dx} = \sec^2 x$, so $dx = \dfrac{1}{\sec^2 x}\, du$.

This will leave $\sec^2 x$ on the numerator — you need to find this in terms of u: From the identity $\sec^2 x \equiv 1 + \tan^2 x$, you get $\sec^2 x \equiv 1 + u^2$.

Then substitute all these bits into the integral:

$$\int \dfrac{\sec^4 x}{\sqrt{\tan x}}\, dx = \int \left(\dfrac{\sec^4 x}{\sqrt{\tan x}} \times \dfrac{1}{\sec^2 x}\right) du = \int \dfrac{1 + u^2}{\sqrt{u}}\, du$$

$$= \int \left(\dfrac{1}{\sqrt{u}} + \dfrac{u^2}{\sqrt{u}}\right) du = \int \left(u^{-\frac{1}{2}} + u^{\frac{3}{2}}\right) du$$

Remember to stick u = tan x back into the equation.

$$= 2u^{\frac{1}{2}} + \dfrac{2}{5} u^{\frac{5}{2}} + C = 2\sqrt{\tan x} + \dfrac{2}{5}\sqrt{\tan^5 x} + C$$

Practice Questions

Q1 Use the substitution $u = e^x - 1$ to find $\int e^x (e^x + 1)(e^x - 1)^2\, dx$.

Q2 Find the exact value of $\int_{\frac{\pi}{4}}^{\frac{\pi}{3}} \sec^4 x \tan x\, dx$, using the substitution $u = \sec x$.

Q3 Use a suitable substitution to find the value of $\int_0^{\frac{\pi}{2}} \dfrac{\sin x}{(\cos x + 2)^3}\, dx$.

Exam Questions

Q1 Find the value of $\int_1^2 \dfrac{8}{x}(\ln x + 2)^3\, dx$ using the substitution $u = \ln x$. Give your answer to 4 s.f. [6 marks]

Q2 a) Use a suitable substitution to show that $\int \dfrac{1}{\sqrt{u}(\sqrt{u}-1)^2}\, du = -\dfrac{2}{(\sqrt{u}-1)} + C$ [4 marks]

b) Hence use the substitution $u = x^3$ to find $\int \dfrac{3\sqrt{x}}{(x^{\frac{3}{2}}-1)^2}\, dx$ in terms of x. [4 marks]

Maths Pick-Up Line #7 — I wanna substitute my x for u...
Life is full of limits — time limits, height limits, limits of how many times I can gaze at my Hugh Jackman poster while still getting my work done... But at least limits of integration will get you exam marks, so it's worth practising them.

Integration by Parts

Just like you can differentiate products using the product rule (see p.100), you can integrate products using... er... integration by parts. Not quite as catchy I know, but just as thrilling.

Integration by Parts is the Reverse of the Product Rule

If you have to integrate a **product** but can't use integration by substitution (see the previous pages), you might be able to use **integration by parts**. The **formula** for integrating by parts is:

This is in the formula booklet — and rightly so.

$$\int u\frac{dv}{dx}\,dx = uv - \int v\frac{du}{dx}\,dx$$
where u and v are both functions of x.

...or for definite integrals,
$$\int_a^b u\frac{dv}{dx}\,dx = [uv]_a^b - \int_a^b v\frac{du}{dx}\,dx$$

The hardest thing about integration by parts is **deciding** which bit of your product should be u and which bit should be $\frac{dv}{dx}$. There's no set rule for this — you just have to look at both parts and see which one **differentiates** to give something **nice**, then set that one as u. For example, if you have a product that has a **single x** as one part of it, choose this to be u. It differentiates to **1**, which makes **integrating** $v\frac{du}{dx}$ dead easy.

If you have a product that has ln x as one of its factors, let u = ln x, as ln x is easy to differentiate but quite tricky to integrate (see below).

Examples: Find: a) $\int 2xe^x\,dx$, b) $\int_{\frac{\pi}{2}}^{\pi} x\sin x\,dx$.

a) Let $u = 2x$ and let $\frac{dv}{dx} = e^x$.

Then u differentiates to give $\frac{du}{dx} = 2$ and $\frac{dv}{dx}$ integrates to give $v = e^x$.

Put these into the integration by parts formula: $\int 2xe^x\,dx = 2xe^x - \int 2e^x\,dx$
$$= 2xe^x - 2e^x + C$$

b) Let $u = x$ and let $\frac{dv}{dx} = \sin x$.

Then u differentiates to give $\frac{du}{dx} = 1$ and $\frac{dv}{dx}$ integrates to give $v = -\cos x$.

Putting these into the formula gives: $\int_{\frac{\pi}{2}}^{\pi} x\sin x\,dx = [-x\cos x]_{\frac{\pi}{2}}^{\pi} - \int_{\frac{\pi}{2}}^{\pi}(-\cos x)\,dx$
$$= [-x\cos x]_{\frac{\pi}{2}}^{\pi} + [\sin x]_{\frac{\pi}{2}}^{\pi}$$
$$= \left[(-\pi\cos\pi) - \left(-\frac{\pi}{2}\cos\frac{\pi}{2}\right)\right] + \left[\sin\pi - \sin\frac{\pi}{2}\right]$$
$$= [\pi - 0] + [0 - 1] = \pi - 1$$

You can integrate ln x using Integration by Parts

Up till now, you haven't been able to integrate **ln x**, but all that is about to change. There's a little trick you can use — write (ln x) as (1 × ln x) then **integrate by parts**.

Examples: Find: a) $\int \ln x\,dx$, b) $\int(9x^2 - 2)\ln x\,dx$.

a) To find $\int \ln x\,dx$, write $\ln x = 1 \times \ln x$.

Let $u = \ln x$ and let $\frac{dv}{dx} = 1$.

Then u differentiates to give $\frac{du}{dx} = \frac{1}{x}$ and $\frac{dv}{dx}$ integrates to give $v = x$.

Putting these into the formula gives: $\int \ln x\,dx = x\ln x - \int x\frac{1}{x}\,dx$
$$= x\ln x - \int 1\,dx = x\ln x - x + C$$

b) Let $u = \ln x$ and let $\frac{dv}{dx} = 9x^2 - 2$.

Then u differentiates to give $\frac{du}{dx} = \frac{1}{x}$ and $\frac{dv}{dx}$ integrates to give $v = 3x^3 - 2x$.

Putting these into the formula gives: $\int(9x^2 - 2)\ln x\,dx = (3x^3 - 2x)\ln x - \int(3x^3 - 2x)\frac{1}{x}\,dx$
$$= (3x^3 - 2x)\ln x - \int(3x^2 - 2)\,dx$$
$$= (3x^3 - 2x)\ln x - (x^3 - 2x) + C$$
$$= (3x^3 - 2x)\ln x - x^3 + 2x + C$$

Integration by Parts

You might have to integrate by parts More Than Once

If you have an integral that **doesn't** produce a nice, easy-to-integrate function for $v\frac{du}{dx}$, you might have to carry out integration by parts **more than once**.

Examples: Find: a) $\int 3x^2 e^x \, dx$, b) $\int x^2 \sin x$.

a) Let $u = 3x^2$ and let $\frac{dv}{dx} = e^x$.

Then u differentiates to give $\frac{du}{dx} = 6x$ and $\frac{dv}{dx}$ integrates to give $v = e^x$.

Putting these into the formula gives: $\int 3x^2 e^x \, dx = 3x^2 e^x - \int 6x e^x \, dx$

To work out $\int 6x e^x \, dx$, use integration by parts again:

> Let $u = 6x$ and let $\frac{dv}{dx} = e^x$. Then $\frac{du}{dx} = 6$ and $v = e^x$.
>
> Putting these into the formula gives: $\int 6x e^x \, dx = 6x e^x - \int 6 e^x \, dx = \mathbf{6x e^x - 6e^x}$

So $\int 3x^2 e^x \, dx = 3x^2 e^x - (6x e^x - 6e^x) + C = \mathbf{3x^2 e^x - 6x e^x + 6e^x + C}$

b) Let $u = x^2$ and let $\frac{dv}{dx} = \sin x$.

Then u differentiates to give $\frac{du}{dx} = 2x$ and $\frac{dv}{dx}$ integrates to give $v = -\cos x$.

Putting these into the formula gives: $\int x^2 \sin x \, dx = -x^2 \cos x - \int -2x \cos x \, dx$
$$= -x^2 \cos x + \int 2x \cos x \, dx$$

$2x \cos x$ isn't very easy to integrate, so integrate by parts again:

> Let $u = 2x$ and let $\frac{dv}{dx} = \cos x$. Then $\frac{du}{dx} = 2$ and $v = \sin x$.
>
> Putting these into the formula gives: $\int 2x \cos x \, dx = 2x \sin x - \int 2 \sin x \, dx$
> $$= \mathbf{2x \sin x + 2 \cos x}$$

So $\int x^2 \sin x \, dx = \mathbf{-x^2 \cos x + 2x \sin x + 2 \cos x + C}$

Practice Question

Q1 Use integration by parts to find: a) $\int 3x^2 \ln x \, dx$, b) $\int 4x \cos 4x \, dx$, c) $\int 8x e^{2x} \, dx$.

Exam Question

Q1 A park occupies the area between a straight road modelled by the function $y = 0$, and another road which follows a path modelled by the function $y = e^x \sin x$, as shown in the diagram as area A.

a) Use integration by parts twice to show that the area of the park satisfies the equation:
$A = [e^x \sin x]_0^2 - [e^x \cos x]_0^2 - A$ [5 marks]

b) Hence find the area of the park between the boundaries at $x = 0$ and $x = 2$, correct to 3 s.f. [2 marks]

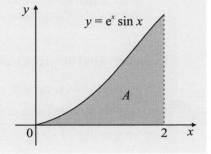

Not those 'parts', sunshine — put 'em away...

After you've had a go at some examples, you'll probably realise that integrals with e^x, $\sin x$ or $\cos x$ in them are actually quite easy, as all three are really easy to integrate and differentiate. Fingers crossed you get one of them in the exam.

Differential Equations

Differential equations are tricky little devils that have a lot to do with differentiation as well as integration.
They're often about rates of change, so the variable t pops up quite a lot.

Differential Equations have a dy/dx Term $\quad$ (or $\frac{dP}{dt}, \frac{ds}{dt}, \frac{dV}{dr}$, etc. — depending on the variables)

1) A **differential equation** is one that has a **derivative term** (such as $\frac{dy}{dx}$), as well as **other terms** (like x and y).

2) Before you even think about **solving** them, you have to be able to **set up** ('**formulate**') differential equations.

3) Differential equations tend to involve a **rate of change** (giving a derivative term) and a **proportion relation**.
Remember — if $a \propto b$, then $a = kb$ for some **constant** k (see p.33).

> **Example:** The number of bacteria in a petri dish is increasing over time, t, at a rate directly proportional to the number of bacteria at the time, b. Formulate a differential equation to show this information.
>
> The rate of change, $\frac{db}{dt}$, is proportional to b, so $\frac{db}{dt} \propto b$. This means that $\frac{db}{dt} = kb$ for some constant k, $k > 0$.

> **Example:** The volume of interdimensional space jelly, V, in a container is decreasing over time, t, at a rate directly proportional to the square of its volume. Show this as a differential equation.
>
> The rate of change, $\frac{dV}{dt}$, is proportional to V^2, so $\frac{dV}{dt} \propto V^2$. $\frac{dV}{dt} = -kV^2$ for some constant k, $k > 0$.

V is decreasing, so don't forget the −.

Solve differential equations by Integrating

Now comes the really juicy bit — **solving** differential equations. It's not as bad as it looks (honest).

Solving Differential Equations

1) You can only solve differential equations if they have separable variables — where x and y can be separated into functions $f(x)$ and $g(y)$.

Remember — it might not be in terms of x and y.

2) Write the differential equation in the form $\frac{dy}{dx} = f(x)g(y)$.

3) Then rearrange the equation to get all the terms with y on the left-hand side and all the terms with x on the right-hand side.

It'll look something like this: $\frac{1}{g(y)} \, dy = f(x) \, dx$.

Like in integration by substitution, you can treat dy/dx as a fraction here.

4) Now integrate both sides: $\int \frac{1}{g(y)} \, dy = \int f(x) \, dx$.

5) Rearrange your answer to get it in a nice form — you might be asked to find it in the form $y = h(x)$. Don't forget the constant of integration (you only need one — not one on each side). It might be useful to write the constant as ln k rather than C (see p.115).

6) If you're asked for a general solution, leave C (or k) in your answer. If they want a particular solution, they'll give you x and y values for a certain point. All you do is put these values into your equation and use them to find C (or k).

> **Example:** Find the particular solution of $\frac{dy}{dx} = 2y(1 + x)^2$ when $x = -1$ and $y = 4$.
>
> This equation has separable variables: $f(x) = 2(1 + x)^2$ and $g(y) = y$.
>
> Rearranging this equation gives: $\frac{1}{y} \, dy = 2(1 + x)^2 \, dx$
>
> And integrating: $\int \frac{1}{y} \, dy = \int 2(1 + x)^2 \, dx \implies \ln|y| = \frac{2}{3}(1 + x)^3 + C$
>
> Now put in the values of x and y to find the value of C:
>
> $\ln|4| = \frac{2}{3}(1 + (-1))^3 + C \implies \ln 4 = C$
>
> So the particular solution is $\ln|y| = \frac{2}{3}(1 + x)^3 + \ln 4$

If you were asked for a general solution, you could just leave it in this form.

You could be asked to sketch members of the family of solutions of a differential equation — this just means the graph of the general solution, for a few different values of C (or k). Graph transformations (see p.31) are very handy for figuring out what they look like.

Differential Equations

You might be given **Extra Information**

1) In the exam, you might be given a question that uses differential equations to **model** a **real-life problem**.

2) **Population** questions are an example of this — the population might be **increasing** or **decreasing**, and you have to find and solve differential equations to show it. In cases like this, one of the variables will usually be t, **time**.

3) You might be given a **starting condition** — e.g. the **initial population**. The important thing to remember is that:

> The starting condition occurs when $t = 0$.   *This is pretty obvious, but it's really important.*

4) You might also be given **extra information** — e.g. a **specific population** (where you have to figure out what t is when the population reaches this number), or a **specific time** (where you have to work out what the population will be at this time). Make sure you always **link** the numbers you get back to the **situation**.

> **Example:** The population of rabbits in a park is decreasing as winter approaches. The decrease in the population, P, after t days, is modelled by the differential equation $\dfrac{dP}{dt} = -0.1P$.
> Find the time at which the population of rabbits will have halved, to the nearest day.

First, solve the differential equation to find the general solution: $\dfrac{dP}{dt} = -0.1P \Rightarrow \dfrac{1}{P}\,dP = -0.1\,dt$

Integrating this gives: $\displaystyle\int \dfrac{1}{P}\,dP = \int -0.1\,dt \Rightarrow \ln P = -0.1t + C$ *You don't need modulus signs for ln P as $P \geq 0$ — you can't have a negative population.*

At $t = 0$, $P = P_0$. Putting these values into the equation gives: $\ln P_0 = -0.1(0) + C \Rightarrow \ln P_0 = C$

So the differential equation becomes: $\ln P = -0.1t + \ln P_0 \Rightarrow P = e^{(-0.1t + \ln P_0)} = e^{-0.1t}e^{\ln P_0} \Rightarrow P = P_0 e^{-0.1t}$ *Remember that $e^{\ln x} = x = \ln e^x$.*

When the population of rabbits has halved, $P = \dfrac{1}{2}P_0$:

$\dfrac{1}{2}P_0 = P_0 e^{-0.1t} \Rightarrow \dfrac{1}{2} = e^{-0.1t} \Rightarrow \ln \dfrac{1}{2} = -0.1t \Rightarrow -0.6931... = -0.1t \Rightarrow t = 6.931...$

So, to the nearest day, it will take **7 days** for the population of rabbits to halve.

You could also be asked to talk about **limitations** of a model, and suggest possible **changes** that would **improve** it. Think about things like:

- **missing information** (e.g. **above**, you weren't told P_0),
- what happens for really **big/small** values of the variables (e.g. as t gets large, P gets small but **never** reaches 0),
- how **appropriate** the model is (e.g. $P_0 e^{-0.1t}$ is a **continuous** function, but population is a **discrete** variable),
- **any other factors** that haven't been included (e.g. what happens to the poor rabbits when **winter** arrives).

Practice Question

Q1 Find the general solution to the following differential equations, giving your answers in the form $y = f(x)$:

a) $\dfrac{dy}{dx} = \dfrac{1}{y} \cos x \ \ (y > 0)$ b) $\dfrac{dy}{dx} = 2y^2 - 3(xy)^2$ c) $\dfrac{dy}{dx} = e^{x-y}$

Exam Questions

Q1 a) Find the general solution to the differential equation $\dfrac{dy}{dx} = \dfrac{\cos x \cos^2 y}{\sin x}$, $0 < x < \pi$, $-\dfrac{\pi}{2} < y < \dfrac{\pi}{2}$.   [4 marks]

    b) Given that $y = 0$ when $x = \dfrac{\pi}{6}$, solve the differential equation above.   [2 marks]

Q2 A company sets up an advertising campaign to increase sales of margarine. After the campaign, the number of tubs of margarine sold each week, m, increases over time, t (in weeks), at a rate that is directly proportional to the square root of the number of tubs sold.

    a) Formulate a differential equation in terms of t, m and a constant k.   [2 marks]

    b) At the start of the campaign, the company was selling 900 tubs of margarine a week. Use this information to solve the differential equation, giving m in terms of k and t.   [5 marks]

    c) Hence calculate the number of tubs sold in the fifth week after the campaign, given that $k = 2$.   [2 marks]

    d) Explain why the model is not likely to be accurate for large values of t.   [2 marks]

At t = 10, we kill all the bunnies...

These questions can get a bit morbid — just how I like them. They might look a bit scary, as they throw a lot of information at you in one go, but once you know how to solve them, they're a walk in the park. Rabbit traps optional.

Location of Roots

Time to go back to your roots — and by 'roots' I mean, 'values of x for which f(x) = 0'. When all those lovely algebraic methods you've learnt just won't do the trick, these numerical methods should get you close enough.

A **Change of Sign** from **f(a) to f(b)** means a **Root Between a and b**

You may be asked to '**solve**' or '**find the roots of**' an equation (where **f(x) = 0**). This is **exactly the same** as finding the **value of x** where the graph **crosses** (or just **touches**) the **x-axis**. The **graph** of the function gives you a rough idea **how many** roots there are (**if any**) and **where**.

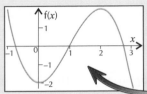

E.g. the function $f(x) = 3x^2 - x^3 - 2$ (shown here) has **3 roots** in the interval $-1 \leq x \leq 3$, since it crosses the x-axis **three times** (i.e. there are 3 solutions to the equation $3x^2 - x^3 - 2 = 0$).

You can also see from the graph that $x = 1$ is a root, and the other roots are **close to** $x = -1$ and $x = 3$.

Look at the graph above at the root $x = 1$. For x-values **just before** the root, f(x) is **negative**, and **just after** the root, f(x) is **positive**. It's the other way around for the other two roots, but either way:

> if f(x) **changes sign**, then you know it has passed through a root.

This is only true for functions that are **continuous** over the interval you're looking at — ones that are **joined up** all the way along with no 'jumps' or gaps. If not, the sign change might be because of something other than the root.

f(x) = tan x is an example of a non-continuous function — it has gaps where f(x) changes sign even though there's no root (see p.60).

> **To show that a root lies in the interval between two values 'a' and 'b':**
>
> 1) Find **f(a)** and **f(b)**.
> 2) If the two answers have **different signs**, and the function is **continuous** over that interval, there's a root somewhere between 'em.

You can have roots where f(x) doesn't change sign. This happens if the graph of f(x) just touches the x-axis, rather than passing through it.

"You're going to show me what in the interval?!"

Example: Show that $x^4 + 3x - 5 = 0$ has a root in the interval $1.1 \leq x \leq 1.2$.

1) Put both 1.1 and 1.2 into the expression: $f(1.1) = (1.1)^4 + (3 \times 1.1) - 5 = -0.2359$
$$f(1.2) = (1.2)^4 + (3 \times 1.2) - 5 = 0.6736$$

2) f(1.1) and f(1.2) have **different signs**, and f(x) is **continuous**, so there's a root in the interval [1.1, 1.2].

Make sure you're familiar with the different notation for closed and open intervals:
[1.1, 1.2] means 1.1 ≤ x ≤ 1.2, (1.1, 1.2) means 1.1 < x < 1.2, and (1.1, 1.2] means 1.1 < x ≤ 1.2.

A **Large Interval** may **Hide Roots**

You need to be careful that the interval you're looking at is not **too large**. If it's too big, there could be an **even number of roots** within the interval — so the sign would **not** appear to change and you'd miss those roots.

- For the function shown here, f(0.5) and f(1.5) are both **positive**, so you might **incorrectly** assume that there are **no roots** in the interval $0.5 \leq x \leq 1.5$.

- But the graph shows that there are actually **two roots** — one in the interval [0.5, 1.0] and another in the interval [1.0, 1.5]. So f(x) changes from positive to negative then **back to positive again**.

- You can also see here that although f(x) **changes sign** before and after $x = 0$, this is **not caused by a root** — the function is **not continuous** over this interval as there is an **asymptote** at $x = 0$.

Similarly, if there were **3** roots in an interval, the sign might change from positive to negative to positive to negative — you might make the mistake of thinking there was only one root in the interval, when in fact there were 3.

Location of Roots

Use **Upper and Lower Bounds** to 'Show that' a root is correct

You might be given an approximation to a root and be asked to **show** that it's correct to a certain **accuracy**. This is like showing that the root lies in a certain interval — the trick is to work out the **right interval**.

Example: Show that $x = 2.472$ is a root of the equation $x^3 - x^2 - 9 = 0$ to 3 d.p.

1) If $x = 2.472$ is a root rounded to 3 decimal places, the exact root must lie between the **upper and lower bounds** of this value — **2.4715** and **2.4725**. Any value in this interval would be rounded to 2.472 to 3 d.p.

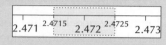

2) The function $f(x) = x^3 - x^2 - 9$ is **continuous**, so you know the root lies in the interval $2.4715 \leq x \leq 2.4725$ if $f(2.4715)$ and $f(2.4725)$ have **different signs**.

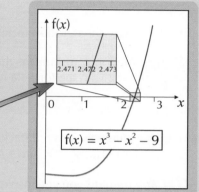

3) $f(2.4715) = 2.4715^3 - 2.4715^2 - 9 = \mathbf{-0.0116...}$
   and $f(2.4725) = 2.4725^3 - 2.4725^2 - 9 = \mathbf{0.0017...}$

4) $f(2.4715)$ and $f(2.4725)$ have different signs, so there must be a root in between them. Since any value between would be rounded to 2.472 to 3 d.p. this answer **must be correct**.

$$f(x) = x^3 - x^2 - 9$$

Practice Questions

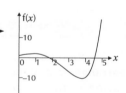

Q1 The graph shows the function $f(x) = e^x - x^3$ for $0 \leq x \leq 5$.
    How many roots does the equation $e^x - x^3 = 0$ have in the interval $0 \leq x \leq 5$?

Q2 Show that there is a root in the interval:
    a) (3, 4) for $\sin(2x) = 0$ (x in radians),
    b) (2.1, 2.2) for $\ln(x - 2) + 2 = 0$,
    c) [4.3, 4.5] for $x^3 - 4x^2 = 7$.

Q3 By selecting an appropriate interval, show that $x = 1.2$ is a root of the equation $x^3 + x - 3 = 0$ to 1 d.p.

Exam Questions

Q1 The graph of the function $f(x) = 2xe^x - 3$ crosses the x-axis at the point $P(p, 0)$.
    a) Show that $0.7 < p < 0.8$.   [2 marks]
    b) Show that $p = 0.726$ to 3 d.p.   [3 marks]

Q2 The function $g(x) = \operatorname{cosec} x - 2$.
    a) Give two reasons why using a change of sign method to check for a root of $g(x)$ over the interval $[0, \pi]$ will fail.   [2 marks]
    b) Show that $x = 0.5$ is an approximation to one root of $g(x) = 0$ to 1 decimal place.   [3 marks]
    c) Solve $g(x) = 0$ to find an exact value for the first root in the interval $[0, \pi]$.   [2 marks]
    d) Show that $g(x)$ has a second root in the interval (2.6, 2.7).   [2 marks]

The signs they are a-changin'...

You could come across these 'show that' questions nestled inside bigger ones on numerical methods. They might start by asking you to 'show that' a root is in an interval, then find it using iteration (coming up next), then 'show that' the answer you found was correct to a given accuracy. Just remember that the sign changes when the function passes through a root (as long as the function is continuous and the interval is small enough to capture a single root). Job done.

Iterative Methods

Without further ado, let's have a look at how to home in on those roots of functions using iteration formulas.
Iteration is like turbo-charged trial and improvement, so grab your calculator and prepare to write down a lot of digits.

Use an **Iteration Formula** to find **Approximations** of **Roots**

Some equations are just too darn tricky to **solve properly**. For these, you need to find **approximations** to the roots, to a certain level of **accuracy**. You'll usually be told the value of x that a root is close to, or the interval that it lies in (as on the previous pages), and then **iteration** does the rest.

Iteration works like this: you put an approximate value of a root x into an **iteration formula**, and out pops a slightly more accurate value. Then you **repeat** as necessary until you have an **accurate enough** answer.

Example: Use the **iteration formula** $x_{n+1} = \sqrt[3]{x_n + 4}$ to solve $x^3 - 4 - x = 0$ to 2 d.p. Start with $x_0 = 2$.

1) The notation x_n just means the **approximation of x at the nth iteration**.
   So putting x_0 in the formula for x_n gives you x_{n+1}, which is x_1, the first iteration.

2) $x_0 = 2$, so $x_1 = \sqrt[3]{x_0 + 4} = \sqrt[3]{2 + 4} = \mathbf{1.8171...}$ ◄——————— Leave this in your calculator for accuracy.

3) This value now gets put back into the formula to find x_2:
   $x_1 = 1.8171...$, so $x_2 = \sqrt[3]{x_1 + 4} = \sqrt[3]{1.8171... + 4} = \mathbf{1.7984...}$ ◄—— You should now just be able to type '$\sqrt[3]{(ANS + 4)}$' in your calculator and keep pressing enter for each iteration.

4) Carry on until you get answers that are the **same** when **rounded to 2 d.p**:
   $x_2 = 1.7984...$, so $x_3 = \sqrt[3]{x_2 + 4} = \sqrt[3]{1.7984... + 4} = \mathbf{1.7965...}$

5) x_2, x_3, and all further iterations are the same when rounded to 2 d.p., so the root is $x = \mathbf{1.80}$ **to 2 d.p.**

Rearrange the Equation to get the Iteration Formula

The iteration formula is just a **rearrangement** of the equation, leaving a **single 'x'** on one side.

There are often lots of **different ways** to rearrange the equation, so in the exam you'll probably be asked to '**show that**' it can be rearranged in a certain way, rather than starting from scratch.

\\\\\\|||||||||||||||||||||||||||||||||//,
You can also rearrange $x^3 - x^2 - 9 = 0$
into the iteration formula $x_{n+1} = \sqrt{x_n^3 - 9}$,
which behaves differently, as shown below.
//||||||||||||||||||||||||||||||||||||\\\

Example: Show that $x^3 - x^2 - 9 = 0$ can be rearranged into $x = \sqrt{\dfrac{9}{x - 1}}$.

The '9' is on its own in the fraction so try: ——————► $x^3 - x^2 - 9 = 0$
$\Rightarrow x^3 - x^2 = 9$

The LHS can be factorised now: ——————► $x^2(x - 1) = 9$

Get the x^2 on its own by dividing by $x - 1$: ——————► $x^2 = \dfrac{9}{x - 1}$

Finally take the square root of both sides: ——————► $x = \sqrt{\dfrac{9}{x - 1}}$

You can now use the **iteration formula** $x_{n+1} = \sqrt{\dfrac{9}{x_n - 1}}$ to find approximations of the roots.

Sometimes an iteration formula just will not find a root. In these cases, no matter how close to the root you have x_0, the iteration sequence **diverges** — the numbers get further and further apart. The iteration might also **stop working** — e.g. if you have to take the **square root** of a **negative number**.

Example: The equation $x^3 - x^2 - 9 = 0$ has a root close to $x = 2.5$.
What is the result of using $x_{n+1} = \sqrt{x_n^3 - 9}$ with $x_0 = 2.5$ to find this root?

Start with $x_1 = \sqrt{2.5^3 - 9} = \mathbf{2.5739...}$ (seems okay so far...)

Subsequent iterations give: $x_2 = \mathbf{2.8376...}$, $x_3 = \mathbf{3.7214...}$, $x_4 = \mathbf{6.5221...}$ — so the sequence **diverges**.

An iteration formula $x_{n+1} = f(x_n)$ will converge to a root a if the following two conditions are satisfied:
1) The starting value x_0 is **sufficiently close** to a
2) The **derivative** of $f(x)$ is **small** at a, i.e. $|f'(a)| < 1$. ◄———

\\|||||||||||||||||||||||//,
See p.130 for more about
what this looks like.
//|||||||||||||||||||||||\\\

Iterative Methods

The **Newton-Raphson Method** uses **Differentiation**

There's another method you can use to find a root — it's called the **Newton-Raphson method**.
To find **roots** of an equation in the form **f(x) = 0**, find **f'(x)** then use this formula:

It works by finding the **x-intercept** of the **tangent** to the graph of f(x) at x_n, and using this value as x_{n+1}. As you can see from the diagram below, this will (usually) get you closer and closer to the root:

$$x_{n+1} = x_n - \frac{f(x_n)}{f'(x_n)}$$

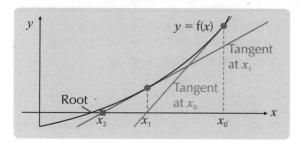

Beware: there are a few things that can cause the Newton-Raphson method to fail to find a root — see p.132 for more on this.

Example: Find a root of the equation $x^2 \ln x = 5$ to 5 s.f., using $x_0 = 2$.

1) First, **rearrange** the equation so it's in the form f(x) = 0: $x^2 \ln x - 5 = 0$.

2) Next, **find f'(x)**:
   Using the product rule (see p.100), let $u = x^2$, so $\frac{du}{dx} = 2x$. Let $v = \ln x$, so $\frac{dv}{dx} = \frac{1}{x}$.
   Putting this into the product rule formula gives: $\frac{dy}{dx} = x(1 + 2\ln x)$.

3) The **formula** for the **Newton-Raphson** method is $x_{n+1} = x_n - \frac{x_n^2 \ln x_n - 5}{x_n(1 + 2\ln x_n)}$.

4) Starting with $x_0 = 2$, this gives $x_1 = 2 - \frac{2^2 \ln 2 - 5}{2(1 + 2\ln 2)} = 2.466709...$

5) Further iterations give:
   $x_2 = 2.395369...$, $x_3 = 2.393518...$, $x_4 = 2.393517...$, $x_5 = 2.393517...$

6) So a root of $x^2 \ln x = 5$ is **2.3935** (5 s.f.).

Unfortunately, Newton and Raphson were less proficient at finding routes.

Practice Questions

Q1 Use the formula $x_{n+1} = \sqrt{\ln x_n + 4}$, with $x_0 = 2$, to find a root of $x^2 - \ln x - 4 = 0$ to 3 d.p.

Q2 a) Show that the equation $2x^2 - x^3 + 1 = 0$ can be written in the form:
   (i) $x = \sqrt{\frac{-1}{2-x}}$,   (ii) $x = \sqrt[3]{2x^2 + 1}$,   (iii) $x = \sqrt{\frac{x^3 - 1}{2}}$.
   b) Use iteration formulas based on each of the above rearrangements with $x_0 = 2.3$ to find a root of $2x^2 - x^3 + 1 = 0$ to 2 d.p. Which of the three formulas converge to a root?

Q3 Use the Newton-Raphson method to find a root of $x^4 - 2x^3 = 5$ to 5 s.f., starting with $x_0 = 2.5$.

Exam Question

Q1 a) Show that the equation $\sin 3x + 3x = 1$ can be written as $x = \frac{1}{3}(1 - \sin 3x)$.   [1 mark]

b) Starting with $x_0 = 0.2$, use the iteration $x_{n+1} = \frac{1}{3}(1 - \sin 3x_n)$ to find x_4 in radians to 3 d.p.   [2 marks]

c) Use the Newton-Raphson method to find the same root to 3 d.p., starting with $x_0 = 0.2$ again.
   Comment on which method was more effective.   [5 marks]

The hat — an approximate solution to root problems...

Just to re-iterate (ho ho) — you can often find a decent approximation to a root by using an iteration formula.
Either rearrange the equation to get a single x on one side, or differentiate it and use the Newton-Raphson formula.

More on Iterative Methods

Whilst iterations are relatively thrilling on their own, put them into a diagram and the world is your lobster.
Well, that might be a bit of an exaggeration, but you can show convergence or divergence easily on a pretty diagram.

You can show **Iterations** on a **Diagram**

Once you've calculated a **sequence of iterations** using $x_{n+1} = f(x_n)$, you can plot the points on a **diagram** and use it to show whether your sequence **converges** or **diverges**.

Sketching Iterations
1) First, sketch the graphs of $y = x$ and $y = f(x)$ (where f(x) is the iterative formula). The point where the **two graphs meet** is the root you're aiming for.
2) Draw a **vertical line** from the x-value of your starting point (x_0) until it meets the curve $y = f(x)$.
3) Now draw a **horizontal line** from this point to the line $y = x$. At this point, the x-value is x_1, the value of your first iteration. This is **one step**.
4) Draw **another step** — a vertical line from this point to the curve, and a horizontal line joining it to the line $y = x$.
5) **Repeat step 4)** for each of your iterations.
6) If your steps are getting **closer and closer to the root**, the sequence of iterations is **converging**. If the steps are moving **further and further away** from the root, the sequence is **diverging**.

This method produces two different types of diagrams — cobweb diagrams and staircase diagrams.

Convergent iterations **Home In** on the **Root**

It's probably easiest to follow the method by looking at a few **examples**:

1
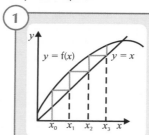
This is an example of a **convergent staircase diagram**. Starting at x_0, the next iterations x_1, x_2 and x_3 are getting **closer** to the point where the two graphs intersect (the root).

In each case, the diagram will look different depending on where your starting point is.

In general, these diagrams will converge if your starting value x_0 is close enough to the root, and if the graph of f(x) isn't too steep at the root (the gradient f'(x) needs to be between −1 and 1) — these conditions were on p.128.

2
This is an example of a **convergent cobweb diagram**. In this case, the iterations **alternate** between being **below** the root and **above** the root, but are still getting **closer** each time.
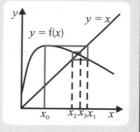

3
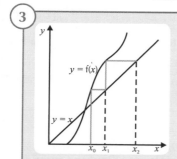
This is an example of a **divergent staircase diagram**. Starting at x_0, the iterations x_1 and x_2 are getting **further away** from the root.

After hours of futile iteration, Todd realised his staircase was divergent.

More on Iterative Methods

Exam Questions combine all the Different Methods

In exam questions, you might have to use **different methods** to find roots — like in this giant worked example.

Example: The graph below shows both roots of the continuous function $f(x) = 6x - x^2 + 13$.
   a) Show that the positive root, α, of $f(x) = 0$ lies in the interval $7 < x < 8$.
   b) Show that $6x - x^2 + 13 = 0$ can be rearranged into the formula $x = \sqrt{6x + 13}$.
   c) Use the iteration formula $x_{n+1} = \sqrt{6x_n + 13}$ and $x_0 = 7$ to find α to 1 d.p.
   d) Sketch a diagram to show the convergence of the sequence for x_1, x_2 and x_3.
   e) Use the Newton-Raphson method to find the negative root, β, to 5 s.f.
      Start with $x_0 = -1$. Use bounds to check your root.

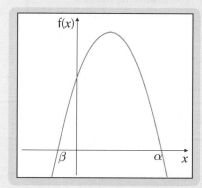

a) $f(x)$ is a **continuous function**, so if $f(7)$ and $f(8)$ have
    different signs then there is a root in the interval $7 < x < 8$:
    $$f(7) = (6 \times 7) - 7^2 + 13 = 6.$$
    $$f(8) = (6 \times 8) - 8^2 + 13 = -3.$$
    There is a **change of sign** so $7 < \alpha < 8$.

b) Get the x^2 on its own to make: $6x + 13 = x^2$
    Now take the (positive) square root to leave: $x = \sqrt{6x + 13}$

c) Using $x_{n+1} = \sqrt{6x_n + 13}$ with $x_0 = 7$, gives $x_1 = \sqrt{6 \times 7 + 13} = 7.4161...$

> The list of results from each iteration x_1, x_2, x_3... is called the iteration sequence.

Continuing the iterations:
$x_2 = \sqrt{6 \times 7.4161... + 13} = 7.5826...$ $x_3 = \sqrt{6 \times 7.5826... + 13} = 7.6482...$
$x_4 = \sqrt{6 \times 7.6482... + 13} = 7.6739...$ $x_5 = \sqrt{6 \times 7.6739... + 13} = 7.6839...$
$x_6 = \sqrt{6 \times 7.6839... + 13} = 7.6879...$ $x_7 = \sqrt{6 \times 7.6879... + 13} = 7.6894...$

x_4 to x_7 all round to **7.7 to 1 d.p.**, so to 1 d.p. $\alpha = 7.7$

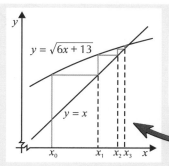

d) Sketch $y = \sqrt{6x + 13}$ and $y = x$ on the same axes, and mark on the
    position of x_0. All you have to do is draw on the **lines** and label the
    values of x_1, x_2 and x_3. You can see from the diagram that the sequence
    is a **convergent staircase**.

e) Find $f'(x)$: $f'(x) = 6 - 2x$.

Putting this into the **Newton-Raphson formula** gives: $x_{n+1} = x_n - \dfrac{6x_n - x_n^2 + 13}{6 - 2x_n}$

Starting with $x_0 = -1$, this gives $x_1 = -1 - \dfrac{6(-1) - (-1)^2 + 13}{6 - 2(-1)} = -1.75$
Further iterations give $x_2 = -1.690789...$
$x_3 = -1.690415...$
$x_4 = -1.690415...$ So $\beta = -1.6904$ to 5 s.f.

The **upper and lower bounds** for this are -1.69035 and -1.69045,
and $f(-1.69035) = 0.0006$, $f(-1.69045) = -0.0003$.

There is a **sign change** so the root is accurate to 5 s.f.

You might have to **compare** the different iteration methods — to do this, all you have to do is use each
method to find the same root, then think about which one was the **easiest to use**, which was the **quickest**
(i.e. took the fewest iterations), etc.

More on Iterative Methods

The **Newton-Raphson** formula can **Stop Working**

Like with any iteration formula, if x_0 is **too far away** from the root, the **Newton-Raphson** method might give you a **divergent** iteration sequence.

But the Newton-Raphson formula also runs into problems when the **gradient of the tangent** at x_n is close to, or equal to, **zero**.

> Another drawback of the Newton-Raphson method is that you can only use it if you can differentiate the function — which won't always be easy, or even possible.

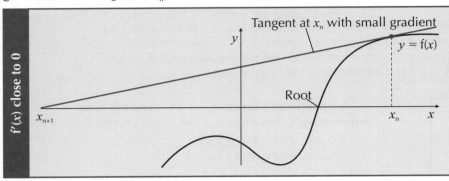

f'(x) close to 0

Tangent at x_n with small gradient

$y = \text{f}(x)$

Root

x_{n+1} x_n x

If you hit a point in the iteration sequence where the **tangent** to f(x) has a very **shallow gradient**, the tangent meets the x-axis a **really long way away** from the root, which could make the sequence **diverge**.

f'(x) = 0

If the tangent to f(x) is **horizontal** at the point x_n (so x_n is a **stationary point**) then the method will **fail**. The tangent **never meets** the x-axis, so there's no x_{n+1} value for the next iteration.

The tangent is horizontal when **f'(x) = 0**, so the iteration formula would **stop working** at this point because you'd be **dividing by zero**:

You won't get an answer if you divide by O here.

$$x_{n+1} = x_n - \frac{\text{f}(x_n)}{\text{f}'(x_n)}$$

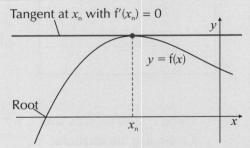

Tangent at x_n with f'(x_n) = 0

$y = \text{f}(x)$

Root x_n x

Practice Questions

Q1 Using the position of x_0 as given on the graph, draw a staircase or cobweb diagram showing how the sequence converges. Label x_1 and x_2 on the diagram.

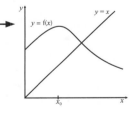

Q2 a) Show that the equation $x^4 - x^5 + 3 = 0$ has a root in the interval $(1, 2)$, then find this root to 1 d.p. from a starting value of $x_0 = 1$, using:
  (i)   the iteration formula $x_{n+1} = \sqrt[5]{x_n^4 + 3}$,
  (ii) the Newton-Raphson method.

  b) Use bounds to check that your answer is a root to 1 d.p.

  c) Compare the effectiveness of the two methods.

Exam Question

Q1 A graph plotted from experimental data is modelled as a function f(x), where $\text{f}(x) = \ln(x + 3) - x + 2$, $x > -3$. f(x) has a root at $x = m$.

  a) Show that m lies between 3 and 4.   [2 marks]

  b) Find, using iteration, the value of m correct to 2 decimal places.
     Use the iteration formula $x_{n+1} = \ln(x_n + 3) + 2$, with $x_0 = 3$.   [2 marks]

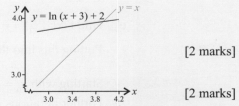

  c) Show the convergence of the first 2 iterations found in b) on the diagram above.   [2 marks]

  d) Apply the Newton-Raphson method with $x_0 = 3$ to find m correct to 5 decimal places.   [4 marks]

  e) Explain why the Newton-Raphson method fails with $x_0 = -2$.   [1 mark]

I feel like stopping working sometimes...

Just like the other iteration methods, the Newton-Raphson method might fail if you start too far away from the root. In the exam, you might have to show off your mad iteration skillz using all the different methods — so be prepared.

Numerical Integration

Let's leave roots behind for now and have a look at numerical methods for integration. Sometimes the algebraic methods you saw in Section 8 just won't get the job done. That's when the trapezium rule comes in handy...

The **Trapezium Rule** is used to find the **Approximate Area** under a curve

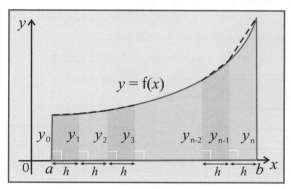

Instead of using **integration** to find the **exact area** under a curve (see p.110), you can find an **approximation** by summing the areas of **trapeziums** drawn between the limits a and b. This is known as the **trapezium rule**.

The area of each trapezium is $A = \dfrac{h}{2}(y_n + y_{n+1})$.

The area represented by $\int_a^b y\,dx$ is approximately:

$$\int_a^b y\,dx \approx \frac{h}{2}[y_0 + 2(y_1 + y_2 + \ldots + y_{n-1}) + y_n]$$

where n is the number of strips or intervals and h is the width of each strip.

This will be in the formula booklet in the exam — but you'll need to remember how to use it.

You can find the width of each strip using $h = \dfrac{(b-a)}{n}$.

$y_0, y_1, \ldots, y_n$ are the heights of the sides of the trapeziums — you get these by putting the x-values into the equation of the curve.

Example: Find an approximate value for $\int_0^2 \sqrt{4-x^2}\,dx$ using 4 strips. Give your answer to 4 s.f.

1) Start by working out the width of each strip: $h = \dfrac{(b-a)}{n} = \dfrac{(2-0)}{4} = 0.5$ *The question specifies 4 strips, so n = 4.*

2) This means the x-values are $x_0 = 0$, $x_1 = 0.5$, $x_2 = 1$, $x_3 = 1.5$ and $x_4 = 2$.

3) Set up a **table** and work out the y-values (or heights) using the equation in the integral:

x	$y = \sqrt{4-x^2}$
$x_0 = 0$	$y_0 = \sqrt{4-0^2} = 2$
$x_1 = 0.5$	$y_1 = \sqrt{4-0.5^2} = \sqrt{3.75}$
$x_2 = 1.0$	$y_2 = \sqrt{4-1^2} = \sqrt{3}$
$x_3 = 1.5$	$y_3 = \sqrt{4-1.5^2} = \sqrt{1.75}$
$x_4 = 2.0$	$y_4 = \sqrt{4-2^2} = 0$

4) Now put all the y-values into the **formula** with h and n:

$$\int_0^2 \sqrt{4-x^2}\,dx$$

$$\approx \frac{0.5}{2}[2 + 2(\sqrt{3.75} + \sqrt{3} + \sqrt{1.75}) + 0]$$

$$= 0.25[2 + 2 \times 4.9914\ldots] = 2.9957\ldots$$

$$= \mathbf{2.996} \text{ (4 s.f.)}$$

Watch out — if they ask you to work out a question with 5 y-values (or '**ordinates**') then this is the **same** as 4 strips. The x-values usually go up in **nice jumps** — if they don't then **check** your calculations carefully.

The **Approximation** might be an **Overestimate** or an **Underestimate**

Whether the approximation is **too big** or **too small** depends on the **shape** of the curve — a sketch can show whether the tops of the trapeziums lie **above** the curve or stay **below** it.

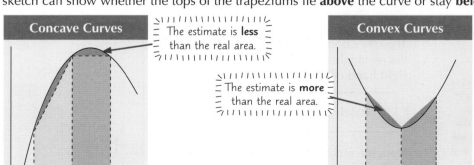

Concave Curves — *The estimate is less than the real area.*

Convex Curves — *The estimate is more than the real area.*

Underestimate Mabel at your peril...

(See p.90 for the definitions of **concave** and **convex**.)

Numerical Integration

Use **More Strips** to get a **More Accurate** answer

Using **more strips** (i.e. increasing n) gives you a more **accurate approximation**.

Example: Use the trapezium rule to approximate the area of $\int_0^4 \dfrac{6x^2}{x^3+2}\, dx$, to 3 d.p., using a) $n = 2$ and b) $n = 4$.

a) For 2 strips, the width of each strip is
$h = \dfrac{4-0}{2} = 2$, so the x-values are 0, 2 and 4.

x	$y = \dfrac{6x^2}{x^3+2}$
$x_0 = 0$	$y_0 = 0$
$x_1 = 2$	$y_1 = 2.4$
$x_2 = 4$	$y_2 = 1.454...$

Putting these y-values into the formula gives:
$$\int_0^4 \frac{6x^2}{x^3+2}\, dx$$
$$\approx \frac{2}{2}[0 + 2(2.4) + 1.454...]$$
$$= [4.8 + 1.454...]$$
$$= 6.2545...$$
$$= \mathbf{6.255} \ (3\ \text{d.p.})$$

b) For 4 strips, the width of each strip is
$h = \dfrac{4-0}{4} = 1$, so the x-values are 0, 1, 2, 3 and 4.

x	$y = \dfrac{6x^2}{x^3+2}$
$x_0 = 0$	$y_0 = 0$
$x_1 = 1$	$y_1 = 2$
$x_2 = 2$	$y_2 = 2.4$
$x_3 = 3$	$y_3 = 1.862...$
$x_4 = 4$	$y_4 = 1.454...$

Putting these y-values into the formula gives:
$$\int_0^4 \frac{6x^2}{x^3+2}\, dx$$
$$\approx \frac{1}{2}[0 + 2(2 + 2.4 + 1.862...) + 1.454...]$$
$$= \frac{1}{2}[12.524... + 1.454...]$$
$$= 6.9893... = \mathbf{6.989} \ (3\ \text{d.p.})$$

If you know the exact answer, you can check how **accurate** your estimate is by working out the **percentage error**.

Example: Calculate the percentage error for a) and b) above to 2 d.p.

This was calculated using the method on p.115.

First, work out the exact value of the integral: $\int_0^4 \dfrac{6x^2}{x^3+2}\, dx = [2\ln|x^3+2|]_0^4 = [2\ln 66] - [2\ln 2] = 6.99301...$

For part a), the percentage error is $\dfrac{6.993... - 6.254...}{6.993...} \times 100 = \mathbf{10.56\%}$ (2 d.p.)

For part b) it's $\dfrac{6.993... - 6.989...}{6.993...} \times 100 = \mathbf{0.05\%}$ (2 d.p.)

Percentage error $= \dfrac{\text{actual answer} - \text{estimate}}{\text{actual answer}} \times 100$

The approximation with **more strips** has a **smaller percentage error** — so it's a **more accurate** approximation.

Find **Upper** and **Lower Bounds** using **Rectangles**

When you approximate the area under a curve using the trapezium rule, the approximate value will lie between **two bounds**. These bounds can be found by considering **rectangular strips** that lie **above** and **below** the curve.

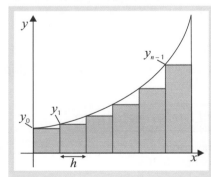

One bound can be found by summing the areas of the rectangles which meet f(x) with their **left hand corner**, using this formula:

$$\int_a^b f(x)\, dx \approx h[y_0 + y_1 + y_2 + ... + y_{n-1}]$$

In this example, the rectangles are **below the curve**, so they give a **lower bound**.

*For an **increasing function** like the one shown here, using the 'left hand corner' will give the lower bound, and using the 'right hand corner' will give the upper bound. But for a **decreasing** function, it's the other way around.*

To calculate a bound of a curve with a turning point, do a separate calculation either side of the turning point — one will use the right hand corners, and the other will use the left.

The other bound is the sum of the areas of the rectangles which meet f(x) with their **right hand corner**, using this formula:

$$\int_a^b f(x)\, dx \approx h[y_1 + y_2 + y_3 + ... + y_n]$$

Here the rectangles are **above the curve**, so they give an **upper bound**.

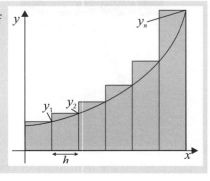

Numerical Integration

Integration is the Limit of the Sum of Rectangles

'Differentiating from first principles' involves finding the **gradient** of a **straight line** between two points on a curve over a **tiny interval**, δx. As the interval **approaches zero** ($\delta x \to 0$), the gradient of the line matches that of the curve. You'll be pleased to know* that you can do a similar thing for the **integral** of a curve **between two points**, *a* and *b*, using those rectangles on the previous page:

The **area** of each rectangle under the curve is its **height**, f(x) × **width**, δx.

So the approximate area under the curve is the **sum** of the areas of the rectangles, from [f($a + \delta x$) × δx] to [f(b) × δx].

This is written as:

$$\sum_{x=a+\delta x}^{b} f(x)\delta x$$

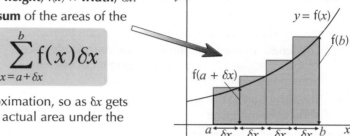

Using more, narrower strips gives a better approximation, so as δx gets smaller and **approaches 0**, the sum matches the actual area under the curve. This is how we define an **integral** — as the **limit of a sum** of areas.

So as $\delta x \to 0$, $a + \delta x \to a$, and the lower value of the sum can be replaced with *a*:

$$\lim_{\delta x \to 0} \sum_{a+\delta x}^{b} f(x)dx = \int_{a}^{b} f(x)dx$$

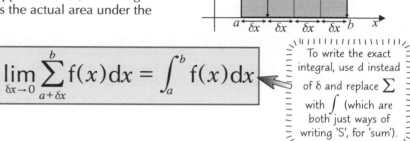

To write the exact integral, use d instead of δ and replace $\sum$ with $\int$ (which are both just ways of writing 'S', for 'sum').

Practice Questions

Q1 Use the trapezium rule to estimate the value of $\int_{0}^{6}(6x - 12)(x^2 - 4x + 3)^2 \, dx$, first using 4 strips and then again with 6 strips. Calculate the percentage error for each answer.

Q2 Would the trapezium rule underestimate or overestimate the area under the curve $y = e^x$? Explain why.

Q3 Find the exact upper and lower bounds of a trapezium rule approximation to $\int_{0}^{2\pi} \sin\left(\frac{x}{2}\right) dx$ using 5 ordinates.

Exam Questions

Q1 The following experimental data is being modelled as an unknown function, $r = f(t)$, as sketched on the graph:

Time (t s)	0	5	10	15	20	25	30	35	40
Flow rate (r gs^{-1})	0	0.6	1.7	3.5	6.4	11.2	19.1	32.1	53.6

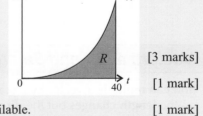

a) Use the trapezium rule with 4 strips to estimate the area under the curve, R. [3 marks]

b) Explain whether this estimate is higher or lower than the actual value of R. [1 mark]

c) Explain how a more accurate estimate could be obtained using the data available. [1 mark]

Q2 Use the trapezium rule with 5 ordinates to find an estimate of $\int_{0}^{\pi} x \sin x \, dx$ to 3 decimal places. [4 marks]

Q3 a) Show that $\int_{0}^{10} \ln(x + 1) \, dx$ is approximately equal to $\ln(11 \times 945^2)$, using the trapezium rule with 5 strips. [4 marks]

b) The trapezium rule with 10 strips is used to find another estimate to the integral in part a). Show that a lower bound for this estimate is $\ln(10!)$. [4 marks]

Numerical integration is the limit of my concentration span...

It can seem like a bit of a faff to work out all those y-values to stick in the trapezium rule formula — but it's often much simpler than integrating a messy function, and reasonably accurate too if you use enough strips. Unfortunately, you might have to do both in an exam question, and compare the answers. Don't say I didn't warn you...

*Assuming that, by this point in the book, you have lowered your expectations.

Vectors

You might have seen vectors before at GCSE. If you haven't, no worries, you're in for a treat.
We're going to start with the basics — like what vectors are and how to add them together.

Vectors have Magnitude and Direction — Scalars Don't

1) Vectors have both **size and direction** — e.g. a velocity of 2 m/s on a bearing of 050°, or a displacement of 3 m north. **Scalars** are just quantities **without a direction**, e.g. a speed of 2 m/s, a distance of 3 m.

2) Vectors are drawn as lines with arrowheads on them.
   - The **length** of the line represents the **magnitude** (size) of the vector (e.g. the speed component of velocity). Sometimes vectors are drawn **to scale**.
   - The **direction** of the arrowhead shows the **direction** of the vector.

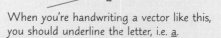

There are two ways of writing vectors:
1) Using a lower case, bold letter.

When you're handwriting a vector like this, you should underline the letter, i.e. <u>a</u>.

2) Putting an arrow over the endpoints.

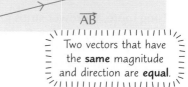

*Two vectors that have the **same** magnitude and direction are **equal**.*

Find the Resultant by Drawing Vectors Nose to Tail

You can add vectors together by drawing the arrows **nose to tail**.
The single vector that goes from the start to the end of the vectors is called the **resultant** vector.

a + b

Resultant: **r = a + b**

a + b = b + a

Resultant: **r = a + b + c**

Subtracting a Vector is the Same as Adding a Negative Vector

1) The vector **–a** is in the **opposite direction** to the vector **a**. They're both the **same size**.

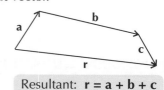

2) So **subtracting a vector** is the same as **adding the negative vector**:

$$b - a = b + (-a)$$

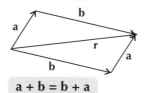

3) You can use the adding and subtracting rules to find a vector **in terms of other vectors**.

Example: Find $\overrightarrow{WZ}$ and $\overrightarrow{ZX}$ in terms of **p, q** and **r**.
$$\overrightarrow{WZ} = -p + q - r \qquad \overrightarrow{ZX} = r - q$$

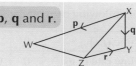

Vectors a, 2a and 3a are all Parallel

You can **multiply** a vector by a **scalar** (just a number, remember) — the **length changes** but the **direction stays the same**.

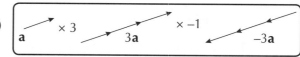

Multiplying a vector by a non-zero scalar always produces a **parallel vector**.

All these vectors are **parallel**: $9a + 15b$ $-18a - 30b$ $6a + 10b$

This is $\frac{2}{3}(9a + 15b)$.

This is $-2(9a + 15b)$.

To show that two vectors are **parallel**, you just need to show they are **scalar multiples** of each other.

Example: $\overrightarrow{CA} = \mathbf{v}$, $\overrightarrow{CB} = \mathbf{u}$. P divides $\overrightarrow{CA}$ in the ratio 1:2, Q divides $\overrightarrow{CB}$ in the ratio 1:2. Show that $\overrightarrow{PQ}$ is parallel to $\overrightarrow{AB}$.

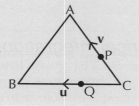

$\overrightarrow{AB} = -\mathbf{v} + \mathbf{u}$. P divides $\overrightarrow{CA}$ in the ratio 1:2 so P is one third of the way along $\overrightarrow{CA}$.
This means $\overrightarrow{CP} = \frac{1}{3}\mathbf{v}$, so $\overrightarrow{PC} = -\frac{1}{3}\mathbf{v}$. Similarly, $\overrightarrow{CQ} = \frac{1}{3}\mathbf{u}$.
So, $\overrightarrow{PQ} = -\frac{1}{3}\mathbf{v} + \frac{1}{3}\mathbf{u} = \frac{1}{3}(-\mathbf{v} + \mathbf{u}) = \frac{1}{3}\overrightarrow{AB}$. This shows that $\overrightarrow{PQ}$ is parallel to $\overrightarrow{AB}$.

Vectors

Position Vectors Describe Where a Point Lies

You can use a vector to describe the **position of a point**, in relation to the **origin, O**.

> The position vector of point A is $\overrightarrow{OA}$. It's usually called vector **a**.
> The position vector of point B is $\overrightarrow{OB}$. It's usually called vector **b**.

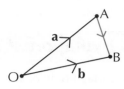

You can write other vectors in terms of position vectors: $\overrightarrow{AB} = -\overrightarrow{OA} + \overrightarrow{OB} = \overrightarrow{OB} - \overrightarrow{OA} = -\mathbf{a} + \mathbf{b} = \mathbf{b} - \mathbf{a}$

Vectors can be described using i and j Units or Column Vectors

1) A **unit vector** is any vector with a **magnitude of 1 unit**.

2) The vectors **i** and **j** are **standard unit vectors**. **i** is in the direction of the *x*-axis, and **j** is in the direction of the *y*-axis. They each have a magnitude of **1 unit**.

3) You use them to say how far **horizontally** and **vertically** you have to go to get from the start of the vector to the end.

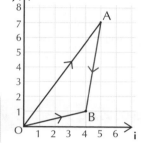

> The position vector of point A = **a** = 5**i** + 7**j**
> The position vector of point B = **b** = 4**i** + **j**

This tells you that point B lies 4 units to the right and 1 unit above the origin — it's just like coordinates.

> Vector $\overrightarrow{AB}$ = **b** − **a**
> = (4**i** + **j**) − (5**i** + 7**j**)
> = −**i** − 6**j**

*Add/subtract the **i** and **j** components separately.*

To go from A to B, you go 1 unit left and 6 units down. It's just like a translation.

4) Column vectors are a really easy way of writing out vectors.

$$x\mathbf{i} + y\mathbf{j} = \begin{pmatrix} x \\ y \end{pmatrix}$$

5) **Calculating** with them is a breeze. Just add or subtract the **top row**, then add or subtract the **bottom row** separately.

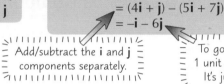

$$\mathbf{a} = 5\mathbf{i} + 7\mathbf{j} = \begin{pmatrix} 5 \\ 7 \end{pmatrix} \qquad \mathbf{b} = 4\mathbf{i} + \mathbf{j} = \begin{pmatrix} 4 \\ 1 \end{pmatrix}$$
$$\overrightarrow{AB} = \mathbf{b} - \mathbf{a} = \begin{pmatrix} 4 \\ 1 \end{pmatrix} - \begin{pmatrix} 5 \\ 7 \end{pmatrix} = \begin{pmatrix} -1 \\ -6 \end{pmatrix}$$

6) When you're **multiplying** a column vector by a **scalar**, you multiply **each number** in the column vector by the scalar.

$$2\mathbf{b} - 3\mathbf{a} = 2\begin{pmatrix} 4 \\ 1 \end{pmatrix} - 3\begin{pmatrix} 5 \\ 7 \end{pmatrix} = \begin{pmatrix} 8 \\ 2 \end{pmatrix} - \begin{pmatrix} 15 \\ 21 \end{pmatrix} = \begin{pmatrix} -7 \\ -19 \end{pmatrix}$$

Practice Questions

Q1 Using the diagram on the right, find these vectors in terms of vectors **a**, **b** and **c**:
  a) $\overrightarrow{AB}$ b) $\overrightarrow{BA}$ c) $\overrightarrow{CB}$ d) $\overrightarrow{AC}$

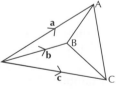

Q2 Give the position vector of point P, which has the coordinates (2, −4). Give your answer in unit vector form.

Q3 Given that vectors **a** and **b** have position vectors $\begin{pmatrix} 3 \\ -4 \end{pmatrix}$ and $\begin{pmatrix} -2 \\ -1 \end{pmatrix}$ respectively, what is 3**a** − 2**b**?

Exam Questions

Q1 The points W, X and Y have position vectors $\begin{pmatrix} 1 \\ 3 \end{pmatrix}$, $\begin{pmatrix} -2 \\ 1 \end{pmatrix}$ and $\begin{pmatrix} 5 \\ 4 \end{pmatrix}$ respectively.
  Find the position vector of Z such that $\overrightarrow{WX} = \overrightarrow{YZ}$. [3 marks]

Q2 The points A and B have position vectors −2**i** + 4**j** and 5**i** + **j** respectively.
  Point P is on the line AB such that AP : PB = 1 : 3. Determine the position vector of P. [4 marks]

I've got B and Q units in my kitchen...

If you're asked to show that two vectors are parallel, remember that this is the same as showing they are scalar multiples of each other. So, just show that you can write one as the other multiplied by a scalar and you're laughing.

More Vectors

The magnitude of a vector is its length. The direction of a vector is the angle that the vector makes with the horizontal axis. I know that you're oh so eager to know how to calculate these, so without further ado...

Use **Pythagoras' Theorem** to Find Vector **Magnitudes**

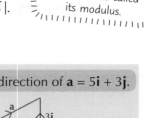

A vector's magnitude is sometimes called its modulus.

1) The **magnitude** of vector **a** is written as $|\mathbf{a}|$, and the magnitude of $\overrightarrow{AB}$ is written as $|\overrightarrow{AB}|$.

2) The **i** and **j** components of a vector form a **right-angled triangle**, so you can use the **Pythagoras formula** to find a vector's magnitude.

3) You might be asked to find a **unit vector** in the direction of a particular vector.

> A unit vector in the direction of vector $\mathbf{a} = \dfrac{\mathbf{a}}{|\mathbf{a}|}$

Remember — a unit vector has a magnitude of 1 (see the previous page).

Example: Find the unit vector in the direction of $\mathbf{a} = 5\mathbf{i} + 3\mathbf{j}$.

First find the magnitude of **a**:
$$|\mathbf{a}| = \sqrt{5^2 + 3^2} = \sqrt{34} = 5.83\ldots$$
So, the unit vector is:
$$\frac{\mathbf{a}}{|\mathbf{a}|} = \frac{\mathbf{a}}{\sqrt{34}} = \frac{1}{\sqrt{34}}(5\mathbf{i} + 3\mathbf{j})$$

Resolving Means Writing a Vector as **Component Vectors**

1) Splitting a vector up into **i** and **j** vectors means you can work things out with **one component at a time**. When **adding** vectors to get a **resultant vector**, it's easier to **add** the **horizontal** and **vertical** components **separately**.

2) So you **split** the vector into components first — this is called **resolving the vector**.

3) You use a combination of **trig** and **Pythagoras' theorem** to **resolve** a vector into its **component form**.

Example: A ball is travelling at 5 ms⁻¹ at an angle of 30° to the horizontal. Find the horizontal and vertical components of the ball's velocity, **v**.

First, draw a diagram and make a right-angled triangle:
Use trigonometry to find x and y:
$$\cos 30° = \frac{x}{5} \Rightarrow x = 5 \cos 30°$$
$$\sin 30° = \frac{y}{5} \Rightarrow y = 5 \sin 30°$$
So $\mathbf{v} = (5 \cos 30°\mathbf{i} + 5 \sin 30°\mathbf{j})\ \text{ms}^{-1} = \left(\dfrac{5\sqrt{3}}{2}\mathbf{i} + \dfrac{5}{2}\mathbf{j}\right)\ \text{ms}^{-1}$

Victor and Hector decided to resolve this the old-fashioned way...

4) The **direction** of a vector is usually measured going **anticlockwise** from the **positive x-axis**. Give the direction in this form unless the question implies otherwise (e.g. if the direction is a bearing).

Example: The acceleration of a body is given by the vector $\mathbf{a} = 6\mathbf{i} - 2\mathbf{j}\ \text{ms}^{-2}$. Find the magnitude and direction of the acceleration.

Start with a diagram again. Remember, the y-component "–2" means "down 2".
Using Pythagoras' theorem, you can work out the magnitude of **a**:
$$|\mathbf{a}|^2 = 6^2 + (-2)^2 = 40 \Rightarrow |\mathbf{a}| = \sqrt{40} = 6.32\ \text{ms}^{-2}\ (\text{3 s.f.})$$
Use trigonometry to work out the angle:
$$\tan \theta = \frac{2}{6} \Rightarrow \theta = \tan^{-1}\left(\frac{2}{6}\right) = 18.4°\ (\text{1 d.p.})$$
So the direction of **a** is $360° - 18.4° = 341.6°\ (\text{1 d.p.})$

So vector **a** has magnitude $6.32\ \text{ms}^{-2}$ (3 s.f.) and direction $341.6°$ (1 d.p.).

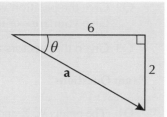

The angle $\theta = \tan^{-1}\frac{y}{x}$ and the direction are often different — drawing a diagram can help you figure out what's what.

> In general, a vector with magnitude r and direction θ can be written as $r \cos \theta\,\mathbf{i} + r \sin \theta\,\mathbf{j}$.
>
> The vector $x\mathbf{i} + y\mathbf{j}$ has magnitude $r = \sqrt{x^2 + y^2}$ and makes an angle of $\theta = \tan^{-1}\left(\frac{y}{x}\right)$ with the horizontal.

More Vectors

Use a **Vector's Magnitude** to Find the **Distance Between Two Points**

You can calculate the **distance between two points** by finding the **vector**
between them, and then using **Pythagoras' Theorem** to calculate its **magnitude**.

Example: The position vectors of points A and B are $4\mathbf{i} - 2\mathbf{j}$ and $2\mathbf{i} + 5\mathbf{j}$ respectively. Calculate the distance between points A and B to 2 decimal places.

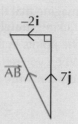

Find the vector $\overrightarrow{AB}$ between the points.

$\overrightarrow{AB} = 2\mathbf{i} + 5\mathbf{j} - (4\mathbf{i} - 2\mathbf{j}) = (2 - 4)\mathbf{i} + (5 - (-2))\mathbf{j} = -2\mathbf{i} + 7\mathbf{j}$.

Draw a diagram, and then calculate the magnitude of $\overrightarrow{AB}$ using Pythagoras' theorem.

$|\overrightarrow{AB}| = \sqrt{(-2)^2 + 7^2} = \sqrt{53}$ so the distance between points A and B is **7.28** (2 d.p.).

Use the **Cosine Rule** to Find the **Angle Between Two Vectors**

The angle between two vectors **a** and **b** can be calculated by constructing a triangle with **a** and **b** as two of its sides.
First, calculate the **magnitude** of these vectors, then use the **cosine rule** (see p.58) to find the angle between them.

Example: Find the angle θ between the vectors $\overrightarrow{PQ} = 3\mathbf{i} - \mathbf{j}$ and $\overrightarrow{PR} = -\mathbf{i} + 4\mathbf{j}$.

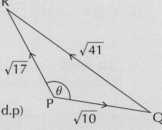

The side lengths of the triangle PQR are: $\overrightarrow{QR} = \overrightarrow{PR} - \overrightarrow{PQ} = -\mathbf{i} + 4\mathbf{j} - (3\mathbf{i} - \mathbf{j}) = -4\mathbf{i} + 5\mathbf{j}$

$|\overrightarrow{PQ}| = \sqrt{3^2 + (-1)^2} = \sqrt{10}$, $|\overrightarrow{PR}| = \sqrt{(-1)^2 + 4^2} = \sqrt{17}$ and $|\overrightarrow{QR}| = \sqrt{(-4)^2 + 5^2} = \sqrt{41}$

Use the cosine rule to find angle θ:

$\cos\theta = \dfrac{(\sqrt{10})^2 + (\sqrt{17})^2 - (\sqrt{41})^2}{2 \times \sqrt{17} \times \sqrt{10}} = \dfrac{-14}{2\sqrt{170}} = \dfrac{-7}{\sqrt{170}}$, so: $\theta = \cos^{-1}\left(\dfrac{-7}{\sqrt{170}}\right) = $ **122.5°** (1 d.p)

Practice Questions

Q1 Find the unit vector in the direction of $\mathbf{q} = -2\mathbf{i} + 5\mathbf{j}$.

Q2 If A = (1, 2) and B = (3, −1), find: a) $|\overrightarrow{OA}|$ b) $|\overrightarrow{OB}|$ c) $|\overrightarrow{AB}|$

Q3 A vector **s** has a magnitude of 7 and direction 20° above the horizontal. Write **s** in the form $a\mathbf{i} + b\mathbf{j}$.

Q4 The velocity of a ball is modelled with the vector $\mathbf{v} = -\mathbf{i} + 3\mathbf{j}$. Calculate the direction of the vector **v**.

Q5 The position vector of point X is $\begin{pmatrix} 7 \\ -1 \end{pmatrix}$, the position vector of point Y is $\begin{pmatrix} 3 \\ 2 \end{pmatrix}$. Calculate the distance between points X and Y. Hence find the angle between vectors $\overrightarrow{OX}$ and $\overrightarrow{OY}$.

Exam Questions

Q1 The following sketch shows a triangle ABC.
M is the midpoint of line BC.
Given that $\overrightarrow{AB} = -5\mathbf{i} + 2\mathbf{j}$ and $\overrightarrow{AC} = -2\mathbf{i} + 4\mathbf{j}$, find $|\overrightarrow{AM}|$. [3 marks]

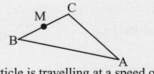

Q2 a) The movement of a particle is modelled by vector **p**. The particle is travelling at a speed of 7 m/s with direction of 15° above the horizontal. Write **p** in component form. [2 marks]

  b) The particle strikes another particle. Its movement is now modelled by vector $\mathbf{q} = 2\sqrt{2}(\mathbf{i} + \mathbf{j})$. Find the amount by which the particle's speed has decreased and state the particle's new direction. [3 marks]

Q3 Points S, T, U and V make a parallelogram, STUV. The position vectors of S, T and V are $\mathbf{i} + \mathbf{j}$, $8\mathbf{i} + \mathbf{j}$ and $-\mathbf{i} + 5\mathbf{j}$ respectively. Find the distance between S and U. Leave your answer in exact surd form. [4 marks]

I don't think you've quite grasped the magnitude of the situation...

The magnitude is just a scalar, which means it doesn't have a direction — i.e. $|\overrightarrow{AB}| = |\overrightarrow{BA}|$. Squaring the numbers gets rid of any minus signs, so it doesn't make any difference which way round you subtract the coordinates. Superb.

3D Vectors

Vectors in 3D work the same as vectors in 2D, but the calculations and the diagrams can be a little trickier.
Now, if you put on your (uncomfortable and overpriced) special glasses, this page is available in 3D...

In **Three Dimensions** you use **Unit Vectors i, j and k**

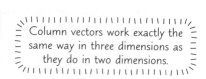

Column vectors work exactly the same way in three dimensions as they do in two dimensions.

1) Imagine that the x- and y-axes lie **flat** on the page. Then imagine a **third axis** sticking **straight through** the page at right angles to it — this is the **z-axis**.

2) The points in three dimensions are given (x, y, z) **coordinates**.

3) When you're talking vectors, **k** is the **unit vector** in the direction of the **z-axis**.

4) You can write three-dimensional vectors as **column vectors** like this: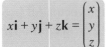

$$x\mathbf{i} + y\mathbf{j} + z\mathbf{k} = \begin{pmatrix} x \\ y \\ z \end{pmatrix}$$

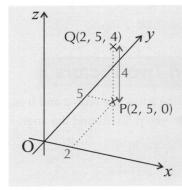

Example: The point Q has coordinates (2, 5, 4). Write down $\overrightarrow{OQ}$ as a column vector.

The position vector of Q is given by its coordinates. It's two in the x-direction, 5 in the y-direction and 4 in the z-direction.

So, $\overrightarrow{OQ} = \begin{pmatrix} 2 \\ 5 \\ 4 \end{pmatrix}$.

Drawing diagrams for 3D vectors can be a little tricky — make sure you take your time and label everything carefully.

5) **3D vectors** work just like **2D vectors**, so all the things you saw on p.136 — vector addition and subtraction, multiplying by scalars, and showing if two vectors are parallel — apply to 3D vectors as well.

You Can Use **Pythagoras** in **Three Dimensions** Too

1) You can use a variation of **Pythagoras' theorem** to find the distance of any point in 3 dimensions from the origin, O.

The distance of point (x, y, z) from the origin is $\sqrt{x^2 + y^2 + z^2}$.

2) This means that you can use Pythagoras' theorem to find the magnitude of a 3D vector the same way you used it in two dimensions.

Example (continued): Find $|\overrightarrow{OQ}|$.

$$|\overrightarrow{OQ}| = \sqrt{x^2 + y^2 + z^2}$$
$$= \sqrt{2^2 + 5^2 + 4^2}$$
$$= \sqrt{45}$$
$$= \mathbf{6.7\ units}\ (1\ d.p.)$$

Example: Find the magnitude of the vector $\mathbf{r} = 5\mathbf{i} + 7\mathbf{j} + 3\mathbf{k}$ to 1 d.p.

$|\mathbf{r}| = \sqrt{5^2 + 7^2 + 3^2} = \sqrt{83} = \mathbf{9.1\ units}$ (1 d.p.)

3) There's also a Pythagoras-based formula for finding **the distance between any two points**.

The distance between points (x_1, y_1, z_1) and (x_2, y_2, z_2) is $\sqrt{(x_1 - x_2)^2 + (y_1 - y_2)^2 + (z_1 - z_2)^2}$.

Example: The position vector of point A is $3\mathbf{i} + 2\mathbf{j} + 4\mathbf{k}$, and the position vector of point B is $2\mathbf{i} + 6\mathbf{j} - 5\mathbf{k}$. Find $|\overrightarrow{AB}|$.

A has the coordinates (3, 2, 4), B has the coordinates (2, 6, –5).
$|\overrightarrow{AB}| = \sqrt{(x_1 - x_2)^2 + (y_1 - y_2)^2 + (z_1 - z_2)^2} = \sqrt{(3-2)^2 + (2-6)^2 + (4-(-5))^2} = \sqrt{1 + 16 + 81} = \mathbf{9.9\ units}$ (1 d.p.)

3D Vectors

Break up **3D Vector** Problems into **Smaller Chunks**

Visualising 3D vector problems can be quite hard. So, if you're given a **difficult** 3D vector problem with **multiple steps**, it helps to break it down into **chunks** and draw them with simple **2D diagrams**.

> **Example:** Points P and Q have position vectors $\mathbf{i} - 2\mathbf{j} + 3\mathbf{k}$ and $-\mathbf{i} + 3\mathbf{j} + 2\mathbf{k}$ respectively. Point R divides the line PQ in the ratio 3:1. Find the position vector of R.
>
> First you need to find the vector $\overrightarrow{PQ}$:
>
>
>
> $\overrightarrow{PQ} = \overrightarrow{OQ} - \overrightarrow{OP}$
> $= (-1 - 1)\mathbf{i} + (3 - (-2))\mathbf{j} + (2 - 3)\mathbf{k}$
> $= -2\mathbf{i} + 5\mathbf{j} - \mathbf{k}$
>
>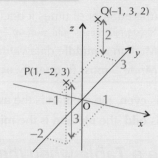
>
> R divides $\overrightarrow{PQ}$ in the ratio 3:1, so R is $\frac{3}{4}$ of the way along $\overrightarrow{PQ}$.
>
> This means $\overrightarrow{PR} = \frac{3}{4}\overrightarrow{PQ} = \frac{3}{4}(-2\mathbf{i} + 5\mathbf{j} - \mathbf{k}) = -\frac{3}{2}\mathbf{i} + \frac{15}{4}\mathbf{j} - \frac{3}{4}\mathbf{k}.$
>
> So $\overrightarrow{OR} = \overrightarrow{OP} + \overrightarrow{PR} = (\mathbf{i} - 2\mathbf{j} + 3\mathbf{k}) + -\frac{3}{2}\mathbf{i} + \frac{15}{4}\mathbf{j} - \frac{3}{4}\mathbf{k}$
> $= \left(1 - \frac{3}{2}\right)\mathbf{i} + \left((-2) + \frac{15}{4}\right)\mathbf{j} + \left(3 - \frac{3}{4}\right)\mathbf{k} = -\frac{1}{2}\mathbf{i} + \frac{7}{4}\mathbf{j} + \frac{9}{4}\mathbf{k}$
>
> You could also do $\overrightarrow{OR} = \overrightarrow{OQ} + \overrightarrow{QR}$.

Practice Questions

Q1 Point P has the coordinates $(7, -3, -2)$. Find the position vector of P. Give your answer in **unit vector** form.

Q2 Find the **magnitudes** of these vectors: a) $3\mathbf{i} + 4\mathbf{j} - 2\mathbf{k}$ b) $\begin{pmatrix} 1 \\ 2 \\ -1 \end{pmatrix}$

Q3 Show that the vectors $\mathbf{v} = \begin{pmatrix} 3 \\ -3 \\ 6 \end{pmatrix}$ and $\mathbf{u} = \begin{pmatrix} -2 \\ 2 \\ -4 \end{pmatrix}$ are parallel.

Q4 Find $\mathbf{a} + 2\mathbf{b} - 3\mathbf{c}$ where $\mathbf{a} = 3\mathbf{i} + 7\mathbf{j} + \mathbf{k}$, $\mathbf{b} = -2\mathbf{i} + 2\mathbf{j} - 3\mathbf{k}$ and $\mathbf{c} = \mathbf{i} - 3\mathbf{j} + 2\mathbf{k}$.

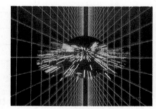

If vectors could dream, it would look something like this (probably)...

Q5 The position vectors of point S and T are $2\mathbf{i} - 3\mathbf{j} + \mathbf{k}$ and $-\mathbf{i} + 2\mathbf{j} - 2\mathbf{k}$ respectively. Calculate the length of the line ST.

Exam Questions

Q1 Points P, Q and R have position vectors $\begin{pmatrix} 2 \\ 4 \\ -2 \end{pmatrix}$, $\begin{pmatrix} -2 \\ -1 \\ -1 \end{pmatrix}$ and $\begin{pmatrix} 2 \\ 7 \\ -5 \end{pmatrix}$ respectively.
Show that $\overrightarrow{OP}$ is parallel to $\overrightarrow{QR}$. [2 marks]

Q2 A skateboard ramp has vertices modelled with position vectors $O = (0\mathbf{i} + 0\mathbf{j} + 0\mathbf{k})$ m, $X = (3\mathbf{i} - \mathbf{j})$ m, $Y = 5\mathbf{j}$ m and $Z = 4\mathbf{k}$ m. Calculate the distance from the midpoint of OZ to the midpoint of XY to 3 s.f. [3 marks]

Q3 a) The points A and B have position vectors $2\mathbf{i} + 3\mathbf{j} + 4\mathbf{k}$ and $-3\mathbf{i} + \mathbf{j} - 3\mathbf{k}$ respectively.
Show that $\overrightarrow{AB} = -5\mathbf{i} - 2\mathbf{j} - 7\mathbf{k}$. [1 mark]

b) The point M divides the line AB in the ratio 2:1. Calculate the distance of M from the origin. [5 marks]

Vectors let you flit between dimensions like your favourite sci-fi hero...

What do you mean you don't have a favourite sci-fi hero? Urgh, you haven't lived. Three dimensions doesn't really make things much more difficult — it just gives you an extra number to calculate with. You add, subtract and multiply 3D column vectors in the same way as 2D ones — you just have three rows to deal with.

Central Tendency and Variation

The mean, median and mode are measures of central tendency or location (roughly speaking, where the centre of the data lies). Then there's the variance and standard deviation, which measure variation and- hey, don't fall asleep...

The **Definitions** are really GCSE stuff

You probably already know these measures of **central tendency**, so learn them now — you'll be needing them loads.

> Mean $= \bar{x} = \dfrac{\Sigma x}{n}$ or $\dfrac{\Sigma fx}{\Sigma f}$ where each x is a **data value**, f is the **frequency** of each x (the number of times it occurs), and n is the **total number** of data values.
> Σ (sigma) means 'add stuff up' — so Σx means 'add up all the values of x'.
> Median = **middle** data value when all the data values are placed **in order of size**.
> Mode = **most frequently occurring** data value.

If n is **even**, the **median** is the **average of the middle two values** (the $\frac{n}{2}$th and the $\left(\frac{n}{2}+1\right)$th values).

If n is **odd**, the **median** is the **middle value** (round up $\frac{n}{2}$ to find its position).

Use a **Table** when there are a lot of **Numbers**

Example: The number of letters received one day in 100 houses was recorded. Find the mean, median and mode of the number of letters.

No. of letters	No. of houses
0	11
1	25
2	27
3	21
4	9
5	7

The first thing to do is make a **table** like this one:

No. of letters (x)	No. of houses (f)	fx
0	11 (11)	0
1	25 (36)	25
2	27 (63)	54
3	21	63
4	9	36
5	7	35
Totals	100	213

Multiply x by f to get this column.

Put the running total in brackets — it's handy when you're finding the median (but you can stop when you get past halfway).

$\Sigma f = 100$

$\Sigma fx = 213$

The number of letters received by each house is a discrete quantity (e.g. 3 letters). There isn't a continuous set of possible values between getting 3 and 4 letters (e.g. 3.45 letters).

1. Use the totals of the columns to find the mean: **mean** $= \dfrac{\Sigma fx}{\Sigma f} = \dfrac{213}{100} = $ **2.13 letters**

2. $\dfrac{n}{2} = \dfrac{100}{2} = 50$, so the median is **halfway between** the 50th and 51st data values.
   The **running total** of f shows that the data values in positions 37 to 63 are all 2s. This includes positions 50 and 51, so the **median = 2 letters**

3. The **highest frequency** is for 2 letters — so the **mode = 2 letters**

The mean number of letters received increased after this couple moved into the street.

The **Standard Deviation Formulas** look pretty **Tricky**

Standard deviation and **variance** both measure **variation** — i.e. how **spread out** the data is from the mean. The bigger the variance, the more spread out your readings are.

> Variance $= \dfrac{\Sigma(x - \bar{x})^2}{n}$ or $\dfrac{\Sigma x^2}{n} - \bar{x}^2$ or $\dfrac{\Sigma fx^2}{\Sigma f} - \bar{x}^2$
>
> Standard deviation $= \sqrt{\text{variance}}$

The x-values are the data, $\bar{x}$ is the mean, f is the frequency of each x, and n is the number of data values.

You might see S_{xx} used instead of $\Sigma(x - \bar{x})^2$.

Example: Find the mean and standard deviation of the following numbers: 2, 3, 4, 4, 6, 11, 12

Find the total of the numbers first: $\Sigma x = 2 + 3 + 4 + 4 + 6 + 11 + 12 = 42$

Then the mean is easy: mean $= \bar{x} = \dfrac{\Sigma x}{n} = \dfrac{42}{7} = 6$

Next find the sum of the squares: $\Sigma x^2 = 4 + 9 + 16 + 16 + 36 + 121 + 144 = 346$

Use this to find the variance: Variance $= \dfrac{\Sigma x^2}{n} - \bar{x}^2 = \dfrac{346}{7} - 6^2 = 49.428... - 36 = 13.428...$

Take the square root to find the standard deviation: Standard deviation $= \sqrt{13.428...} = $ **3.66** (3 s.f.)

Central Tendency and Variation

Questions about Standard Deviation can look a bit Weird

They can ask questions about standard deviation in different ways. But you just need to use the same old formulas.

Example: The mean of 10 boys' heights is 180 cm, and the standard deviation is 10 cm.
The mean for 9 girls is 165 cm, and the standard deviation is 8 cm.
Find the mean and standard deviation of the whole group of 19 girls and boys.

Let the boys' heights be x and the girls' heights be y.

Write down the formula for the mean and put the numbers in for the boys: $\bar{x} = \frac{\Sigma x}{n} \Rightarrow 180 = \frac{\Sigma x}{10} \Rightarrow \Sigma x = 1800$

Do the same for the girls: $165 = \frac{\Sigma y}{9} \Rightarrow \Sigma y = 1485$

So the sum of the heights for the boys and the girls = $\Sigma x + \Sigma y = 1800 + 1485 = 3285$

And the **mean height** of the boys and the girls is: $\frac{3285}{19} = \mathbf{172.9}$ **cm** (1 d.p.)

Round the fraction to give your answer. But if you need to use the mean in more calculations, use the fraction (or your calculator's memory) so you don't lose accuracy.

Now for the **variance**.

Write down the formula for the boys first:

$10^2 = \frac{\Sigma x^2}{n} - \bar{x}^2 \Rightarrow 10^2 = \frac{\Sigma x^2}{10} - 180^2 \Rightarrow \Sigma x^2 = 10 \times (100 + 32\,400) = 325\,000$

Do the same for the girls:

$8^2 = \frac{\Sigma y^2}{n} - \bar{y}^2 \Rightarrow 8^2 = \frac{\Sigma y^2}{9} - 165^2 \Rightarrow \Sigma y^2 = 9 \times (64 + 27\,225) = 245\,601$

So the sum of the squares of the heights of the boys and the girls is: $\Sigma x^2 + \Sigma y^2 = 325\,000 + 245\,601$
$= 570\,601$

Don't use the rounded mean (172.9) — you'll lose accuracy.

The **variance** of all the heights is: $\frac{570\,601}{19} - \left(\frac{3285}{19}\right)^2 = 139.041... \text{ cm}^2$

The **standard deviation** of all the heights is: $\sqrt{139.041...} = \mathbf{11.8}$ **cm** (3 s.f.)

The standard deviation uses the same units as the mean, so the units for the variance must be squared.

Practice Questions

Q1 Calculate the mean, median and mode of the data in the table on the right.

x	0	1	2	3	4
f	5	4	4	2	1

Q2 Find the mean and standard deviation of the following numbers:
11, 12, 14, 17, 21, 23, 27

Q3 The scores from 50 reviews of a product are recorded in the table below.

Score	1	2	3	4	5
Frequency	6	11	22	9	2

For Q3, add rows for fx and fx². Then use the third variance formula given on the previous page.

Calculate the mean and variance of the data.

Q4 a) The mean, $\bar{x}$, of a set of six numbers is 85.5. Find the value of Σx.
   b) One more data value is added to the set. The new mean is 84.9. Find the data value that was added.

Exam Question

Q1 In a supermarket, two types of chocolate drops were compared.
The weights, a grams, of 20 chocolate drops of brand A are summarised by: $\Sigma a = 60.3$ g, $\Sigma a^2 = 219$ g²
The mean weight of 30 chocolate drops of brand B was 2.95 g, and the standard deviation was 1 g.

a) Find the mean weight of a brand A chocolate drop. [1 mark]
b) Find the standard deviation of the weight of the brand A chocolate drops. [2 marks]
c) Compare the weights of chocolate drops from brands A and B. [2 marks]
d) Find the standard deviation of the weight of all 50 chocolate drops. [4 marks]

People who enjoy this stuff are standard deviants...

You don't always need to find values like Σx^2 or Σfx — sometimes they're given in exam questions. Your calculator can probably find the mean and standard deviation of a data set too. But you also need to understand the formulas, so make sure you can do these calculations by hand — you could easily get asked to show your working.

Displaying Data

Data can be shown on lots of different charts and graphs. The ones you need to know for this course are shown on the next few pages. You've probably seen a fair few of them before, so they should be bread and butter by now.

Data can be represented Graphically

Bar charts, dot plots and vertical line charts are all simple ways to show how data is distributed.

15 people were given a blind taste test of four drinks, labelled A, B, C and D, then asked which was their favourite. The number of people who voted for each drink is shown on the diagrams below.

Dot plot:

Each dot represents 1 vote, so 4 people voted for D.

For a large amount of data, drawing dots would be inconvenient, so a bar chart might be more appropriate.

Bar chart:

Vertical line charts are like bar charts, but using lines instead of bars (as you might expect).

Stem and Leaf Diagrams show all the data

Stem and leaf diagrams are another way to represent data — the diagrams show the data values themselves. Each data value is split into a 'stem' and a 'leaf'. A complete stem and leaf diagram looks something like this:

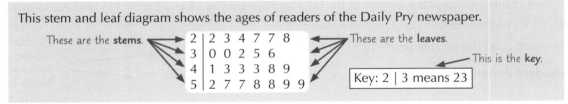

This stem and leaf diagram shows the ages of readers of the Daily Pry newspaper.

These are the stems.

These are the leaves.

This is the key.

```
2 | 2 3 4 7 7 8
3 | 0 0 2 5 6
4 | 1 3 3 3 8 9
5 | 2 7 7 8 8 9 9
```

Key: 2 | 3 means 23

A stem and leaf diagram always needs a key to tell you how to read it. So, in the stem and leaf diagram above, the first row represents the values 22, 23, 24, 27, 27, and 28, while the second row represents the values 30, 30, 32, 35 and 36. You can read the other two rows in a similar way.

You can show Two Data Sets on a Back-To-Back stem and leaf diagram

Two stem and leaf diagrams can be drawn either side of the same stem — i.e. back-to-back. The data on the left hand side of the stem is read 'backwards' — because the stems are on the right of the leaves.

Example:
a) Draw a back-to-back stem and leaf diagram to represent the following data:
Boys' test marks: 50, 20, 18, 38, 34, 19, 8, 44, 15, 32, 9, 19, 41, 26, 22
Girls' test marks: 36, 24, 42, 46, 35, 12, 38, 45, 31, 38, 21, 43, 37, 29, 46

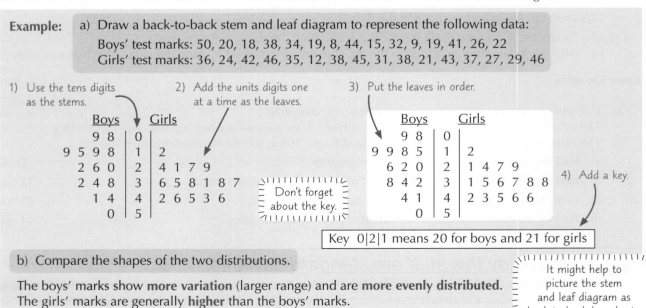

1) Use the tens digits as the stems.
2) Add the units digits one at a time as the leaves.
3) Put the leaves in order.

Don't forget about the key.

4) Add a key.

Key 0|2|1 means 20 for boys and 21 for girls

It might help to picture the stem and leaf diagram as back-to-back bar charts.

b) Compare the shapes of the two distributions.

The boys' marks show more variation (larger range) and are more evenly distributed. The girls' marks are generally higher than the boys' marks.

Displaying Data

From a stem and leaf diagram you could be asked to find measures of central tendency (e.g. mean, median, mode).

> **Example:** For the test marks data on the previous page, find:
> a) the mode of the boys' marks,
> b) the median of the boys' marks and the median of the girls' marks. Compare your answers.

a) All the data values for the boys' data appear once except 19, which appears twice — so **mode = 19**.

b) boys' data: there are 15 values, so the median is the 8th value — so **median = 22**.

girls' data: there are 16 values, so the median is halfway between the 8th and 9th values
— so **median** = (36 + 37) ÷ 2 = **36.5**

The median of the girls' data is **higher** than the median of the boys' data,
which suggests that girls scored higher in the test than boys.

Histograms *show* Frequency Density

Histograms are glorified bar charts. The main difference is that you plot the **frequency density** rather than the frequency.
Frequency density = **frequency ÷ class width**.

The **area** of a bar (**not** its height) represents the **frequency**.

To get histograms right, you have to use the right **upper and lower boundaries** to find each class width (see p.146).

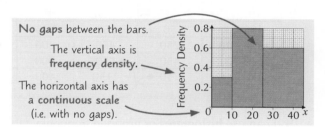

No gaps between the bars.

The vertical axis is frequency density.

The horizontal axis has a continuous scale (i.e. with no gaps).

Practice Questions

Q1 a) Draw a vertical line chart for the data below:

Rating (1-5)	1	2	3	4	5
Frequency	2	4	9	5	1

b) Find the mode of the data.

c) Comment on the distribution of the data.

Vinnie was a talented stem and leaf drawer.

Q2 Draw a stem and leaf diagram to represent the data below:
Class attendance (%): 89, 92, 90, 95, 100, 85, 77, 87, 95, 98

Q3 Find the frequency density in the following cases:
a) frequency = 25, class width = 10,   b) frequency = 33, class width = 15.

Exam Questions

Q1 The number of runs scored by two cricketers, in 10 matches, are shown below.

Cricketer A: 50, 32, 17, 45, 0, 26, 3, 50, 15, 12
Cricketer B: 27, 22, 33, 34, 38, 44, 41, 17, 20, 31

a) Draw a back-to-back stem and leaf diagram to represent the data.   [2 marks]
b) Find the median number of runs scored by both cricketers.   [2 marks]

Q2 The stem and leaf diagram shows the ages at which 30 men and 16 women became grandparents.

	Men		Women
	8, 3, 3	4	
	8, 7, 7, 7, 5, 3, 2	5	5, 6, 7
	9, 7, 6, 6, 5, 5, 2, 2, 1, 1, 0	6	1, 2, 3, 3, 4, 5, 6, 7, 9
	9, 9, 8, 5, 4, 3, 1, 0, 0	7	2, 4, 8, 9

Key: 5 | 6 | 2 means a man who became a grandfather at 65 and a woman who became a grandmother at 62.

a) Find the median age for the men.   [1 mark]
b) Compare the distribution of the two data sets.   [2 marks]

Time to make like a stem and leaf diagram and leave...

...but read these last few notices first. You can tell a lot about central tendency and variation from the shape of a distribution. And don't worry if you're a bit unsure on histograms, they're covered in more detail on the next page.

Grouped Data

Sometimes, some helpful person will put a set of data into groups for you. Which isn't always actually very helpful...

To draw a **Histogram** find the **Frequency Density**

Histograms can be drawn for **continuous** data that is **grouped** into 'classes'. As you saw on page 145, you need to plot the **frequency density**, which is found using: frequency density = **frequency ÷ class width**.

Example: Draw a histogram to represent the data in this table, showing the masses of parcels.

Mass (to nearest 100 g)	100-200	300-400	500-700	800-1100
Number of parcels	100	250	600	50

First draw a table showing the **upper and lower class boundaries**, plus the **frequency density**:

Now you can draw the histogram:

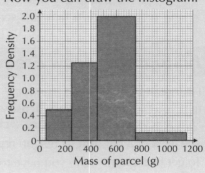

Smallest mass of parcel that will go **in that class**.

Biggest mass that will go **in that class**.

Mass of parcel (to nearest 100 g)	Lower class boundary (lcb)	Upper class boundary (ucb)	Class width = ucb − lcb	Frequency	Freq. density = frequency ÷ class width
100-200	50	250	200	100	0.5
300-400	250	450	200	250	1.25
500-700	450	750	300	600	2
800-1100	750	1150	400	50	0.125

Look — no gaps between each ucb and the next lcb.

You can use **histograms** or grouped frequency tables to **estimate** the number of readings in a **given range**.

Example: Estimate the number of readings above $x = 20$ on the histogram on the right.

The **area of the bar** is the **total frequency** for that class. You're interested in the **last third** of the class 10–25, and the whole of the class 25–45, so add those two areas:

$$(15 \times 0.8) \div 3 + 20 \times 0.6 = \mathbf{16}$$

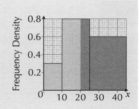

You can also show grouped data on a **frequency polygon**. For each class, plot the **class midpoint** against the **frequency**, then join the points with **straight lines**.

This is a frequency polygon for the parcels data above:

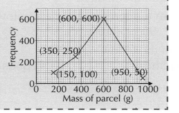

For some people, studying histograms is always a classy affair.

If the data's **Grouped** you can **Estimate** the **Mean**

For **grouped data**, you can't find the mean, median or mode **exactly**. You have to estimate them instead.

Example: The data in this table represents the heights of a number of trees. Estimate the mean of these heights.

Height (to nearest m)	0-5	6-10	11-15	16-20
Number of trees	26	17	11	6

Here, you assume that every reading in a class takes the **class midpoint** (which you find by adding the **lower class boundary** to the **upper class boundary** and **dividing by 2**). It's best to make another table...

Height (to nearest m)	Class midpoint (x)	Number of trees (f)	fx
0-5	2.75	26 (26)	71.5
6-10	8	17 (43)	136
11-15	13	11	143
16-20	18	6	108
Totals		60 (= Σf)	458.5 (= Σfx)

Lower class boundary = 0
Upper class boundary = 5.5
So the mid-class value
= (0 + 5.5) ÷ 2 = 2.75

Estimated mean = $\dfrac{458.5}{60}$

= **7.64 m** (3 s.f.)

I've added running totals here — you don't need them for this question, but trust me, they'll come in handy over the next couple of pages...

With grouped data you can't find the mode — only the **modal class**. If all the classes are the **same width**, this is the class with the **highest frequency**. If the classes have different widths, it's the class with the **highest frequency density**. In this example, the modal class is **0-5 m**.

Interquartile Range and Outliers

Outliers fall Outside Fences

An **outlier** is a **freak** piece of data that lies a long way from the rest of the readings. There are various ways to decide if a reading is an outlier — the method to use will depend on what information you're given in the question.

Example: A data value is said to be an outlier if it is more than 1.5 times the IQR above the upper quartile or more than 1.5 times the IQR below the lower quartile. The lower and upper quartiles of a data set are 70 and 100. Decide whether the data values 30 and 210 are outliers.

This is one of two methods for finding outliers that you should be familiar with. The other one is 'more than 2 standard deviations away from the mean'.

First you need the IQR: $Q_3 - Q_1 = 100 - 70 = 30$
Then it's a piece of cake to find where your **fences** are.

*25 and 145 are called **fences**. Any reading lying outside the fences is considered an **outlier**.*

Lower fence: $Q_1 - (1.5 \times IQR) = 70 - (1.5 \times 30) = 25$ Upper fence: $Q_3 + (1.5 \times IQR) = 100 + (1.5 \times 30) = 145$

30 is **inside** the lower fence, so it is **not** an outlier. 210 is **outside** the upper fence, so it **is** an outlier.

Outliers Affect what Measure of Variation is Best to Use

- Outliers affect whether the **variance** and **standard deviation** are good measures of **variation**.
- Outliers can make the variance (and standard deviation) **much** larger than it would be otherwise — which means these **freak** pieces of data are having more influence than they deserve.
- If a data set contains outliers, then a better measure of variation is the **interquartile range**.

Use Central Tendency and Variation to Compare Distributions

Example: The table below summarises the marks obtained in Maths 'calculator' and 'non-calculator' papers. Comment on the location and variation of the distributions.

	Lower quartile, Q_1	Median, Q_2	Upper quartile, Q_3	Mean	Standard deviation
Calculator Paper	40	58	70	55	21.2
Non-calculator Paper	35	42	56	46.1	17.8

Location: The **mean**, the **median** and the **quartiles** are all higher for the calculator paper. This means that scores were **generally higher** on the calculator paper.

Variation: The **interquartile range** (IQR) for the calculator paper is $Q_3 - Q_1 = 70 - 40 = 30$.
The **interquartile range** (IQR) for the non-calculator paper is $Q_3 - Q_1 = 56 - 35 = 21$.
So the **IQR** and the **standard deviation** are both **higher** for the calculator paper.
So the scores on the calculator paper are **more spread out** than for the non-calculator paper.

Practice Question

Q1 A data value is considered to be an outlier if it's more than 2 times the standard deviation above or below the mean. If the mean and standard deviation of a data set are 72 and 6.7 respectively, decide which of the following data values are outliers: a) 85   b) 95   c) 0

Exam Question

Q1 The table shows the number of hits received by people at a paintball party.

No. of hits	12	13	14	15	16	17	18	19	20	21	22	23	24	25
Frequency	2	4	6	7	6	4	4	2	1	1	0	0	0	1

a) Find the median and mode number of hits.   [3 marks]

b) An outlier is a data value which is more than $1.5 \times (Q_3 - Q_1)$ above Q_3 or below Q_1. Is 25 an outlier? Show your working.   [2 marks]

c) Explain why the median might be considered a more reliable measure of central tendency than the mean for a data set that is thought to contain an outlier.   [1 mark]

I like my data how I like next door's dog — on the right side of the fence...

Measures of location and variation are supposed to capture the essential characteristics of a data set in just one or two numbers. Don't choose an average that's heavily affected by freaky, far-flung outliers — it won't be much good.

Cumulative Frequency Graphs and Boxplots

Cumulative frequency means 'running total'. Cumulative frequency graphs make medians and quartiles easy to find.

Use **Cumulative Frequency Graphs** to estimate the **Median** and **Quartiles**

Example: The ages of 200 students are shown in the table.

Age in completed years	11-12	13-14	15-16	17-18
Number of students	50	65	58	27

Draw a cumulative frequency graph and use it to estimate the median age, the interquartile range of ages, and how many students have already had their 18th birthday.

1) First draw a table showing the **upper class boundaries** and the **cumulative frequency** (CF):

Age in completed years	Upper class boundary (ucb)	Number of students, f	Cumulative frequency (CF)
Under 11	11	0	0
11-12	13	50	50
13-14	15	65	115
15-16	17	58	173
17-18	19	27	200

The **first** reading in a **cumulative frequency** table **must** be zero — so add this **extra row** to show the number of students with age **less than 11** is 0.

The CF is the number of students with an age **up to** the ucb — it's basically a **running total**.

The **last** number in the CF column should always be the **total number** of readings.

People say they're '18' right up until their 19th birthday — so the **ucb** of class 17-18 is **19**.

Always plot the upper class boundary of each class.

Next draw the **axes** — cumulative frequency **always** goes on the **vertical axis**. Here, age goes on the other axis.

Then plot the **upper class boundaries** against the **cumulative frequencies**, and join the points.

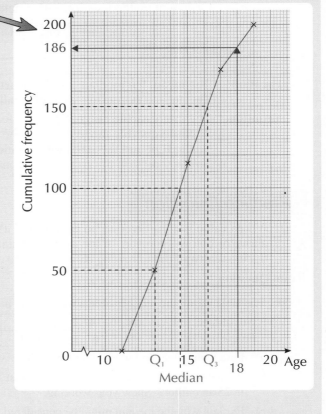

2) To estimate the **median** from a cumulative frequency graph, go to the **median position** on the vertical scale and read off the value from the horizontal axis.

median position $= \frac{1}{2} \times 200 = 100$,

so median ≈ **14.5 years**

> You can only **estimate** the median, since your data values are in **groups**. This is similar to linear interpolation — see page 147.

Then you can estimate the **quartiles** in the same way. Find their positions first:

Q_1 position $= \frac{1}{4} \times 200 = 50$,
so lower quartile, Q_1 ≈ **13 years**

Q_3 position $= \frac{3}{4} \times 200 = 150$,
so upper quartile, Q_3 ≈ **16.2 years**

$IQR = Q_3 - Q_1 = 16.2 - 13 =$ **3.2 years**

> Because the question says estimate, a **range** of answers would be **correct** for the median and IQR —
> e.g. anything between 14.25 and 14.75 for the median and anything between 3 and 3.5 for the IQR.

3) To estimate how many students have **not** yet had their 18th birthday, go up from 18 on the **horizontal axis**, and read off the number of students **'younger'** than 18 (= 186).

Then the number of students who are **'older'** than 18 is approximately 200 − 186 = **14**.

Cumulative Frequency Graphs and Boxplots

Box Plots are a **Visual Summary** of a Distribution

Box plots show the median and quartiles in an easy-to-look-at kind of way.
They look like this:

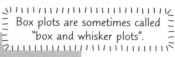
Box plots are sometimes called "box and whisker plots".

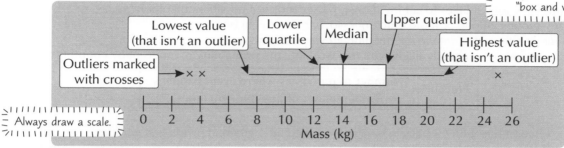

Outliers marked with crosses → × ×

Lowest value (that isn't an outlier)

Lower quartile

Median

Upper quartile

Highest value (that isn't an outlier)

×

Always draw a scale.

0 2 4 6 8 10 12 14 16 18 20 22 24 26
Mass (kg)

Use **Box Plots** to **Compare** two **Distributions**

Example: Compare the distributions represented by these two box plots:

Distribution 1:

Distribution 2:

0   20   40   60   80   100
Percentage (%)

Tian Tian was plotting something fiendish. It was a box plot...

Location: The **median** is higher for Distribution 1, showing that the data values are **generally higher** than for Distribution 2.

Variation: The **interquartile range** (IQR) and the **range** for Distribution 1 are higher, showing that the values are **more varied** for Distribution 1 than for Distribution 2.

Practice Questions

Q1 Draw a cumulative frequency diagram of the data given in this table.

Length of tadpole (cm)	0-2	2-4	4-6	6-8
Number of tadpoles	22	12	4	2

Use your diagram to estimate the median and interquartile range.

Q2 Draw a box and whisker diagram for the data below, using the fences $1.5 \times$ IQR above Q_3 or below Q_1 to identify any outliers. Amount of pocket money (in £) received per week by twenty 15-year-olds:
10, 5, 20, 50, 5, 1, 6, 5, 15, 20, 5, 7, 5, 10, 12, 4, 8, 6, 7, 30.

Exam Question

Q1 Two workers iron clothes. Each irons 10 items, and records the time it takes for each, to the nearest minute:

Worker A: 3, 5, 2, 7, 10, 4, 5, 5, 4, 12
Worker B: 3, 4, 8, 6, 7, 8, 9, 10, 11, 9

a) Find the median, the lower quartile and the upper quartile for worker A's times. [2 marks]

b) On graph paper, draw two box plots to show this data, one for each worker.
Use the same scale for both plots and assume there are no outliers. [4 marks]

c) Worker A claims he deserves a pay rise because he works faster than Worker B.
State, giving a reason, whether the data given above supports Worker A's claim. [2 marks]

"It's a cumulative frequency table," she said. It was all starting to add up...

'Cumulative frequency' sounds a bit scarier than 'running total' — but just remember, they're the same thing. And remember to plot the points at the upper class boundary — this makes sense if you remember that a cumulative frequency graph shows how many data values are less than the figure on the x-axis. The rest is more or less easyish.

Random Events and Venn Diagrams

Random events happen by chance. Probability is a measure of how likely they are. It can be a chancy business.

A **Random Event** has **Various Outcomes**

1) In a **trial** (or experiment) the things that can happen are called **outcomes**
   (so if I time how long it takes to eat my dinner, 63 seconds is a possible outcome).
2) **Events** are 'groups' of one or more outcomes (so an event might be
   'it takes me less than a minute to eat my dinner every day one week').
3) When all outcomes are **equally likely**, you can work out the **probability** of an event by **counting** the outcomes:

$$P(\text{event}) = \frac{\text{Number of outcomes where event happens}}{\text{Total number of possible outcomes}}$$

Example: I have a bag with 15 balls in — 5 red, 6 blue and 4 green. I pick a ball without looking.
What is the probability the ball is: a) red, b) blue, c) green, d) either red or green?

Any ball is **equally likely** to be picked — there are **15 possible outcomes**.
Of these 15 outcomes, 5 are red, 6 are blue and 4 are green.

And so: a) $P(\text{red ball}) = \frac{5}{15} = \frac{1}{3}$ b) $P(\text{blue ball}) = \frac{6}{15} = \frac{2}{5}$ c) $P(\text{green ball}) = \frac{4}{15}$

You can find the probability of **either** red **or** green in a similar way: d) $P(\text{red or green}) = \frac{5+4}{15} = \frac{9}{15} = \frac{3}{5}$

Venn Diagrams show which **Outcomes** correspond to which **Events**

Say you've got 2 events, **A** and **B**. A **Venn diagram** can show which outcomes satisfy event A,
which satisfy B, which satisfy both, and which satisfy neither.

(i)   All outcomes satisfying event A go in one part of the diagram,
      and all outcomes satisfying event B go in another bit.
(ii) If they satisfy '**both A and B**', they go in the dark green middle bit,
      written **A ∩ B** (and called the **intersection** of A and B).
(iii) The whole of the green area is written **A ∪ B** — it means 'either A or B' (and is called the **union** of A and B).

Again, you can work out probabilities of events by counting outcomes and using the formula above.
You can also get a nice formula linking P(A ∩ B) and P(A ∪ B).

$$P(A \cup B) = P(A) + P(B) - P(A \cap B)$$

If you just add up the outcomes in A and B, you end up counting A ∩ B twice — that's why you have to subtract it.

Example: If I roll a dice, event A could be 'I get an even number', and
B 'I get a number bigger than 4'. The Venn diagram would be:

$P(A) = \frac{3}{6} = \frac{1}{2}$ $P(B) = \frac{2}{6} = \frac{1}{3}$

$P(A \cap B) = \frac{1}{6}$ $P(A \cup B) = \frac{4}{6} = \frac{2}{3}$

Here, I've just counted outcomes — but I could have used the formula.

Example: A survey was carried out to find what pets people like.

The probability they like dogs is 0.6. The probability they like cats is 0.5.
The probability they like gerbils is 0.4. The probability they like dogs and cats is 0.4.
The probability they like cats and gerbils is 0.1, and the probability they like gerbils and dogs is 0.2.
Finally, the probability they like all three kinds of animal is 0.1.

Draw a Venn diagram to show this information, using C for the event 'likes cats',
D for 'likes dogs' and G for 'likes gerbils'.

① Stick in the middle one first
  — 'likes all 3 animals' (i.e. C ∩ D ∩ G).

② Then do the 'likes 2 animals' probabilities by taking 0.1
  from each given 'likes 2 animals' probability. (If they like
  3 animals, they'll also be in the 'likes 2 animals' bits.)

③ Then do the 'likes 1 kind of animal' probabilities,
  by making sure the total probability in each
  circle adds up to the probability in the question.

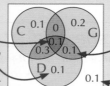

④ Finally, subtract all the probabilities so far from
  1 to find 'likes none of these animals'.

Random Events and Venn Diagrams

Example (cont.): Find: a) the probability that someone likes either dogs or cats,
b) the probability that someone likes gerbils but not dogs,
c) the probability that someone who likes dogs **also** likes cats.

a) From the Venn diagram, the probability that someone
likes either dogs or cats is: $0.1 + 0 + 0.1 + 0.3 + 0.1 + 0.1 = \mathbf{0.7}$

b) The probability that someone likes gerbils but not dogs is: $0 + 0.2 = \mathbf{0.2}$

c) For the probability that a dog-lover **also** likes cats,
ignore everything outside the 'dogs' circle.

$$P(\text{dog-lover also like cats}) = \frac{0.3 + 0.1}{0.3 + 0.1 + 0.1 + 0.1} = \frac{2}{3}$$

The **Complement** of 'Event A' is '**Not Event A**'

An event A will either happen or not happen. The event 'A doesn't happen'
is called the **complement** of A (or **A'**). On a Venn diagram, it looks like this: ⟶

At least one of A and A' has to happen, so... $\boxed{P(A) + P(A') = 1 \quad \text{or} \quad P(A') = 1 - P(A)}$

Example: Nic keeps his socks loose in a box. He picks out a sock. He calculates that the probability of then
picking out a matching sock is 0.56. What is the probability of him not picking a matching sock?

Call event A 'picks a matching sock'. Then A' is 'doesn't pick a matching sock'.
Now A and A' are **complementary events** (and P(A) = 0.56), so $P(A') = 1 - 0.56 = \mathbf{0.44}$

Example: For two events, A and B: P(A') = 0.42, P(A ∩ B') = 0.15, P(B) = 0.55
Use a two-way table to find: a) P(A ∩ B), b) P(A ∪ B').

Start by filling in P(A') = **0.42**, P(A ∩ B') = **0.15** and P(B) = **0.55** in the table,
then use the fact that the probabilities should add up to **1** to find the rest:

a) P(A ∩ B) is the entry in the A column and the B row — this is **0.43**.

b) P(A ∪ B') is the sum of all of the entries in either the A column OR the B'
row – so P(A ∪ B') = 0.43 + 0.15 + 0.3 = **0.88**.
Make sure you don't just add the totals P(A) + P(B') — you'd be counting the 0.15
twice. I've shaded in the bits of the table you want so that you can see what I mean.

	A	A'	Total
B	0.43	0.12	**0.55**
B'	**0.15**	0.3	0.45
Total	0.58	**0.42**	1

You can also have two-way tables showing numbers of outcomes instead of probabilities. You probably saw these at GCSE.

Practice Questions

Q1 Arabella rolls two standard dice and adds the two results together. What is the probability that she scores:
a) a prime number, b) a square number, c) a number that is either a prime number or a square number?

Q2 Half the students in a sixth-form college eat sausages for dinner and 20% eat chips. 10% of those who eat chips
also eat sausages. Show this information in a two-way table, and use it to find the percentage of students who:
a) eat both chips and sausages, b) eat chips but not sausages, c) eat either chips or sausages but not both.

Exam Question

Q1 A soap company asked 120 people about the types of soap (from Brands A, B and C) they bought. Brand A was
bought by 40 people, Brand B by 30 people and Brand C by 25. Both Brands A and B were bought by 8 people,
B and C were bought by 10 people, and A and C by 7 people. All three brands were bought by 3 people.

a) Represent this information in a Venn diagram. [5 marks]

b) (i) If a person is selected at random, find the probability that they buy at least one of the soaps. [2 marks]
(ii) If a person is selected at random, find the probability that they buy at least two of the soaps. [2 marks]

I took some scales with me to the furniture shop — I like to weigh tables...

*I must admit — I kind of like these pages. This stuff isn't too hard, and it's really useful for answering loads of
questions. And one other good thing is that Venn diagrams look, well, nice somehow. But more importantly,
the thing to remember when you're filling one in is that you usually need to 'start from the inside and work out'.*

Tree Diagrams and Conditional Probability

Tree diagrams — they blossom from a tiny question-acorn into a beautiful tree of possibility. Inspiring and useful.

Tree Diagrams Show Probabilities for Two or More Events

Each 'chunk' of a tree diagram is a **trial**, and each branch of that chunk is a possible **outcome**.
Multiplying probabilities along the branches gives you the probability of a **series** of outcomes.

Example: If Susan plays tennis one day, the probability that she'll play the next day is 0.2. If she doesn't play tennis, the probability that she'll play the next day is 0.6. She plays tennis on Monday. What is the probability she plays tennis on the Wednesday of the same week?

Let T mean 'plays tennis', so
T' means 'doesn't play tennis'.
You're interested in **either** P(T and T) **or** P(T' and T).

$$P(\text{plays on Wednesday}) = P(T \text{ and } T) + P(T' \text{ and } T)$$
$$= 0.04 + 0.48$$
$$= \mathbf{0.52}$$

*To find the probability of one event **or** another happening, you have to **add** the probabilities.*

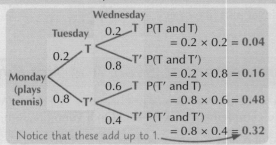

Wednesday
Tuesday
0.2 — T P(T and T) = 0.2 × 0.2 = **0.04**
0.2 — T
0.8 — T' P(T and T') = 0.2 × 0.8 = **0.16**
Monday (plays tennis)
0.6 — T P(T' and T) = 0.8 × 0.6 = **0.48**
0.8 — T'
0.4 — T' P(T' and T') = 0.8 × 0.4 = **0.32**

Notice that these add up to 1.

Susan was ready for some unlikely outcomes on the tennis court.

Example: A box of biscuits contains 5 chocolate biscuits and 1 lemon biscuit. George takes out 2 biscuits at random, one at a time, and eats them. Find the probability that the second biscuit is chocolate.

Let C mean 'picks a chocolate biscuit' and let L mean 'picks the lemon biscuit'.
The second biscuit being chocolate is shown by 2 'paths' along the branches
— so you can add up the probabilities:

$$P(\text{second biscuit is chocolate}) = \left(\frac{5}{6} \times \frac{4}{5}\right) + \left(\frac{1}{6} \times 1\right) = \frac{2}{3} + \frac{1}{6} = \frac{5}{6}$$

1st pick 2nd pick

$\frac{4}{5}$ C $\frac{5}{6} \times \frac{4}{5} = \frac{2}{3}$
$\frac{5}{6}$ C
$\frac{1}{5}$ L $\frac{5}{6} \times \frac{1}{5} = \frac{1}{6}$
$\frac{1}{6}$ L
1 C $\frac{1}{6} \times 1 = \frac{1}{6}$

There's a quicker way to do this, as there's only one outcome where the chocolate **isn't** picked last:
$P(\text{second biscuit is } \textbf{not} \text{ chocolate}) = \frac{5}{6} \times \frac{1}{5} = \frac{1}{6}$, so $P(\text{second biscuit is chocolate}) = 1 - \frac{1}{6} = \frac{5}{6}$

It's sometimes easier to find the probability of the **complement** of the event you're interested in.

Here there are no lemon biscuits left, so the tree diagram doesn't branch.

If an object is chosen **with replacement**, the probability of choosing a particular item is **the same** for each pick. In the example above, if George puts his first biscuit back instead of eating it, the probability of picking 2 chocolate biscuits becomes:

$$P(C \text{ and } C) = \frac{5}{6} \times \frac{5}{6} = \frac{25}{36} > \frac{2}{3}$$

P(C and C) is slightly greater with replacement. This makes sense — there are more chocolate biscuits available for his 2nd pick, so he is more likely to choose one.

P(B | A) means Probability of B, given that A has Already Happened

Conditional probability means the probability of something, **given that** something else has **already happened**. For example, **P(B | A)** means the probability of B, given that A has already happened. Back to tree diagrams...

If you multiply probabilities along the branches, you get:

$$P(A \text{ and } B) = P(A \cap B) = P(A) \times P(B \mid A)$$

You can rewrite this as: $\boxed{P(B \mid A) = \dfrac{P(A \cap B)}{P(A)}}$

These are conditional probabilities, since something (A or A') has already happened.

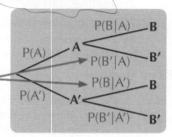

P(A) — A — P(B|A) — B
       — P(B'|A) — B'
P(A') — A' — P(B|A') — B
        — P(B'|A') — B'

Example: Horace either walks (W) or runs (R) to the bus stop. The probability that he walks to the bus stop is 0.4. If he walks, the probability that he catches the bus (C) is 0.3. If he runs, the probability that he catches the bus is 0.7. Find the probability that Horace catches the bus.

$$P(C) = P(C \cap W) + P(C \cap R)$$
$$= P(W)\,P(C \mid W) + P(R)\,P(C \mid R)$$
$$= (0.4 \times 0.3) + (0.6 \times 0.7) = 0.12 + 0.42 = \mathbf{0.54}$$

This is easier to follow if you match each part of this working to the probabilities in the tree diagram.

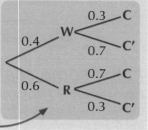

0.4 — W
       0.3 — C
       0.7 — C'
0.6 — R
       0.7 — C
       0.3 — C'

Tree Diagrams and Conditional Probability

If **B is Conditional** on A then **A is Conditional** on B

If B depends on A then A depends on B — regardless of which event happens first.

Example: Horace turns up at school either late (L) or on time (L'). He is then either shouted at (S) or not (S'). The probability that he turns up late is 0.4. If he turns up late the probability he is shouted at is 0.7. If he turns up on time the probability that he is shouted at is 0.2.
If you hear Horace being shouted at, what is the probability that he turned up late?

1) The probability you want is P(L|S). *Get this the right way round — he's **already** being shouted at.*

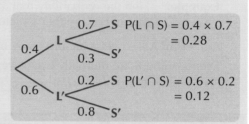

2) Use the conditional probability formula: $P(L \mid S) = \dfrac{P(L \cap S)}{P(S)}$

3) The best way to find P(L ∩ S) and P(S) is with a tree diagram.

$$P(L \cap S) = 0.4 \times 0.7 = 0.28$$
$$P(S) = P(L \cap S) + P(L' \cap S) = 0.28 + 0.12 = 0.40$$

Be careful with questions like this — the information in the question tells you what you need to know to draw the tree diagram with L (or L') considered first. But you need P(L|S) — where S is considered first. So don't just rush in.

4) Put these in your conditional probability formula to get: $P(L \mid S) = \dfrac{0.28}{0.4} = \mathbf{0.7}$

Practice Questions

Q1 In a school orchestra (made up of pupils in either the upper or lower school), 40% of the musicians are boys. Of the boys, 30% are in the upper school. Of the girls in the orchestra, 50% are in the upper school.
   a) Represent this information on a tree diagram.
   b) Find the probability that a musician chosen at random is in the upper school.

Q2 For lunch, I eat either chicken or beef for my main course, and either chocolate cake or ice cream for dessert. The probability that I eat chicken is $\frac{1}{3}$, the probability that I eat ice cream given that I have chicken is $\frac{2}{5}$, and the probability that I have ice cream given that I have beef is $\frac{3}{4}$. Find the probability that:
   a) I have either chicken or ice cream — but not both,   b) I eat ice cream,
   c) I had chicken, given that you see me eating ice cream.

Exam Questions

Q1 For a particular biased dice, the event 'throw a 6' is called event B. P(B) = 0.2.
This biased dice and a fair dice are rolled together. Find the probability that:
   a) the biased dice doesn't show a 6,   [1 mark]
   b) at least one of the dice shows a 6,   [2 marks]
   c) exactly one of the dice shows a 6, given that at least one of them shows a 6.   [3 marks]

Q2 A jar contains 3 red counters and 6 green counters. Three random counters are removed from the jar one at a time. The counters are not replaced after they are drawn.
   a) Draw a tree diagram to show the probabilities of the various outcomes.   [3 marks]
   b) Find the probability that the third counter is green.   [2 marks]
   c) Find the probability that all of the counters are the same colour.   [2 marks]
   d) Find the probability that at least one counter is red.   [2 marks]

Are you oak-ay, or pine-ing fir tree diagrams? (I willow-nly ash-k this once...)
Conditional probability questions can be a bit brain-twisting, but there's a fair chance that any probability question in the exam will have a conditional part to it — so it's worth doing a bit of practice to help get your head around them.

Mutually Exclusive and Independent Events

There's so much on these pages, it wouldn't all fit in the title — over on the right there's a bonus bit about modelling.

Mutually Exclusive Events have No Overlap

If two events **can't both happen** at the same time (i.e. $P(A \cap B) = 0$) they're called **mutually exclusive** (or just 'exclusive'). If A and B are exclusive, then the probability of A **or** B is: $P(A \cup B) = P(A) + P(B)$.

More generally, | For n **exclusive** events (i.e. only one of them can happen at a time): $$P(A_1 \cup A_2 \cup ... \cup A_n) = P(A_1) + P(A_2) + ... + P(A_n)$$ |

This is the formula from p.152, with $P(A \cap B) = 0$.

Example: Find the probability that a card pulled at random from a standard pack of cards (no jokers) is either a picture card (a Jack, Queen or King) or the 7, 8 or 9 of clubs.

Call **event A** — 'I get a picture card', and **event B** — 'I get the 7, 8 or 9 of clubs'. Then $P(A) = \frac{12}{52}$ and $P(B) = \frac{3}{52}$.
Events A and B are **mutually exclusive** — they can't both happen.
So the probability of either A or B is: $P(A \cup B) = P(A) + P(B) = \frac{12}{52} + \frac{3}{52} = \frac{15}{52}$

Independent Events have No Effect on each other

If the probability of B happening doesn't depend on whether or not A has happened, then A and B are **independent**.
1) If A and B are independent, $P(A \mid B) = P(A)$. *the probability of A given that B has already happened*
2) If you put this in the conditional probability formula, you get: $P(A \mid B) = P(A) = \dfrac{P(A \cap B)}{P(B)}$

Or, to put that another way: | For independent events: $P(A \cap B) = P(A)P(B)$ |

Example: V and W are independent events, where $P(V) = 0.2$ and $P(W) = 0.6$. Find: a) $P(V \cap W)$, b) $P(V \cup W)$.

a) Just put the numbers into the formula for independent events: $P(V \cap W) = P(V)P(W) = 0.2 \times 0.6 = \mathbf{0.12}$
b) Using the formula on page 152: $P(V \cup W) = P(V) + P(W) - P(V \cap W) = 0.2 + 0.6 - 0.12 = \mathbf{0.68}$

Sometimes you'll be asked if two events are independent or not. Here's how you work it out...

Example: You are exposed to two infectious diseases — one after the other. The probability you catch the first (A) is 0.25, the probability you catch the second (B) is 0.5, and the probability you catch both of them is 0.2. Are catching the two diseases independent events?

Compare $P(A \mid B)$ and $P(A)$ — if they're different, the events **aren't independent**.

$P(A \mid B) = \dfrac{P(A \cap B)}{P(B)} = \dfrac{0.2}{0.5} = 0.4$ $P(A) = 0.25$ $P(A \mid B)$ and $P(A)$ are different, so they're **not independent**.

Take Your Time with Tough Probability Questions

Example: A and B are two events, with $P(A) = 0.4$, $P(B \mid A) = 0.25$, and $P(A' \cap B) = 0.2$.
a) Find: (i) $P(A \cap B)$, (ii) $P(A')$, (iii) $P(B' \mid A)$, (iv) $P(B \mid A')$, (v) $P(B)$, (vi) $P(A \mid B)$.
b) Say whether or not A and B are independent.

a) (i) $P(B \mid A) = \dfrac{P(A \cap B)}{P(A)} = 0.25$, so $P(A \cap B) = 0.25 \times P(A) = 0.25 \times 0.4 = \mathbf{0.1}$

(ii) $P(A') = 1 - P(A) = 1 - 0.4 = \mathbf{0.6}$

(iii) $P(B' \mid A) = 1 - P(B \mid A) = 1 - 0.25 = \mathbf{0.75}$

(iv) $P(B \mid A') = \dfrac{P(B \cap A')}{P(A')} = \dfrac{0.2}{0.6} = \dfrac{1}{3}$ $P(B \cap A') = P(A' \cap B)$

(v) $P(B) = P(B \mid A)P(A) + P(B \mid A')P(A') = (0.25 \times 0.4) + \left(\dfrac{1}{3} \times 0.6\right) = \mathbf{0.3}$

(vi) $P(A \mid B) = \dfrac{P(A \cap B)}{P(B)} = \dfrac{0.1}{0.3} = \dfrac{1}{3}$

b) If $P(B \mid A) = P(B)$, then A and B are independent.
But $P(B \mid A) = 0.25$, while $P(B) = 0.3$, so A and B are **not** independent.

A Venn diagram can make it easier to see what's going on. Fill in the numbers as you work them out.

$P(A) = 0.4$ and from (i) $P(A \cap B) = 0.1$, so this must be 0.3.

$P(A' \cap B)$

Or use the Venn diagram.

Or you could say $P(A \cap B) = 0.1$ and $P(A)P(B) = 0.4 \times 0.3 = 0.12$ — they're different, so A and B are not independent.

Section 12 — Probability

Mutually Exclusive and Independent Events

Modelling with Probabilities Involves Assumptions

In most models, the probability of an event is based on some **assumptions**.

For example, when tossing a coin, you assume that each side is **equally likely** to come up, so the probability is 0.5 for each. But it's possible that the coin is **biased**, giving the two outcomes **different probabilities**.

Evaluating and **criticising** the assumptions being made is an important part of the modelling process.

Some common issues to think about are:

- Have you assumed that two (or more) events are **equally likely**? Is this true? Could the probabilities be **biased** in some way?

- Is the probability based on **past data**? Is the data **appropriate**? How **reliable** is the data? How was the data **sampled**?

- Is the experiment itself **truly random**? Is there anything about the way that the experiment is being **carried out** that could affect the outcome?

You'll see on page 170 that choosing a probability distribution also involves making assumptions.

Me, back in my modelling days.

> **Example:** Sanaa wants to know the probability that it will rain tomorrow. She looks up the weather data for the previous 30 days, and finds that it has rained on 12 of them. She concludes that the probability that it will rain is $\frac{12}{30} = 0.4$. Give a reason why this model might be inaccurate.

Sanaa has used the relative frequency of the event to estimate the probability — you might have seen this at GCSE.

There are lots of answers you could give. For example:

- She has only taken data from the past 30 days, which might not be a **large enough sample** to give an accurate estimate, or might not take **seasonal variations** into account.

- She has assumed that the probability that it rains on one day is **not affected** by whether or not it rained the day before (i.e. that they are **independent events**) but this might not be true.

Practice Questions

Q1 Zofia has 20 cards numbered 1-20. She picks two cards at random, one at a time, without replacement.
    a) Are the events 'both numbers are prime numbers' and 'the sum of the numbers is less than 10' mutually exclusive? Explain your answer.
    b) Are the events 'the first number is even' and 'the second number is odd' independent? Explain your answer.

Q2 Two candidates, A and B, are standing in an election. Two weeks before the vote, a polling company surveys a random sample of people who say they voted in the previous election to ask who they will vote for. Based on the responses, the company predicts that candidate A has a 75% probability of winning. Suggest two assumptions that have been made which may mean this model is inaccurate.

Exam Questions

Q1 Event J and Event K are independent events, where $P(J) = 0.7$ and $P(K) = 0.1$.
    a) Find: (i) $P(J \cap K)$ [1 mark]
         (ii) $P(J \cup K)$ [2 marks]
    b) If L is the event that neither J or K occurs, find $P(L \mid K')$.   [4 marks]

Q2 Erwin drives a delivery van for a company that sells fragile glass sculptures of cats. Erwin often has to drive quickly to deliver the sculptures on time. Sometimes, when the customer opens the box, the sculpture is broken. The probability that a sculpture is delivered on time is 0.8. The probability that a sculpture is broken, given that it is delivered on time is 0.56.
    a) Erwin claims that the probability of a sculpture being broken is not affected by whether or not he delivers it on time. If Erwin is correct, what is the probability that a sculpture is broken when it is delivered?   [2 marks]
    b) Erwin is in fact incorrect, and the probability that any sculpture is broken when it is delivered is 0.5. Find the probability that a sculpture was delivered late, given it wasn't broken when it was delivered.   [6 marks]

EXCLUSIVE — assumptions made about model at independent event...

Probability questions can be tough. For tricky questions, try drawing a Venn diagram or a tree diagram, even if the question doesn't tell you to — they're really useful for understanding what on earth is going on in a question. And don't forget the definitions of mutually exclusive and independent events — they're key terms you need to know.

Probability Distributions

You need to know about a couple of specific statistical distributions for A-Level Maths.
But first of all, you need to know what statistical distributions are...

Random Variables *have* Probability Distributions

This first bit isn't particularly interesting. But understanding the difference between X and x (bear with me)
might make the later stuff a bit less confusing.

1) X (upper case) is just the name of a **random variable**. So X could be 'score on a fair, six-sided dice'.

2) A **random variable** doesn't have a **fixed** value. Like with the dice score — the value on any 'roll'
is all down to **chance**.

3) x (lower case) is a **particular value that X can take**. So for one roll of the dice, x could be 1, 2, 3, 4, 5 or 6.

4) **Discrete** random variables only have a **certain number** of possible values. Often these values
are whole numbers, but they don't have to be. Usually there are only a few possible values
(e.g. the possible scores with one roll of a dice).

5) A **probability distribution** is a table showing the **possible values** of x, and the **probability** for each one.

6) A **probability function** is a formula that generates the probabilities for different values of x.

All the probabilities *Add Up To 1*

For a discrete random variable X:

$$\sum_{\text{all } x} P(X = x) = 1$$

This says that if you add up the probabilities of all the possible values of X, you get 1.

Example: The random variable X, where X can only take values 1, 2, 3, has
probability function $P(X = x) = kx$ for $x = 1, 2, 3$. Find the value of k.

X has three possible values ($x = 1, 2$ and 3), and the
probability of each is kx (where you need to find k).

It's easier to understand with a table:

x	1	2	3
$P(X = x)$	$k \times 1 = k$	$k \times 2 = 2k$	$k \times 3 = 3k$

For a discrete random variable where every value of X is equally likely, you get a discrete uniform distribution — e.g. rolling a normal unbiased dice.

Now just use the formula: $\sum_{\text{all } x} P(X = x) = 1$

Here, this means: $k + 2k + 3k = 6k = 1$, so $k = \dfrac{1}{6}$

The **mode** is the **most likely** value — so it's the value with the **biggest probability**.

Example: The discrete random variable X, where X can only take values 0, 1, 2, 3, 4,
has the probability distribution shown below.

x	0	1	2	3	4
$P(X = x)$	0.1	0.2	0.3	0.2	a

Find: a) the value of a, 　b) $P(2 \leq X < 4)$, 　c) the mode.

a) Use the formula $\sum_{\text{all } x} P(X = x) = 1$ again.

From the table: $0.1 + 0.2 + 0.3 + 0.2 + a = 1$
$0.8 + a = 1$
$\mathbf{a = 0.2}$

Careful with the inequality signs — you need to include x = 2 but not x = 4.

b) This is asking for the probability that 'X is greater than or equal to 2, but less than 4'.
Easy — just add up the probabilities.
$P(2 \leq X < 4) = P(X = 2) + P(X = 3) = 0.3 + 0.2 = \mathbf{0.5}$

c) The mode is the value of x with the biggest probability — so **mode = 2**.

Probability Distributions

Draw a Diagram showing All Possible Outcomes

Example: An unbiased six-sided dice has faces marked 1, 1, 1, 2, 2, 3.
The dice is rolled twice. Let X be the random variable "sum of the two scores on the dice".
a) Show that $P(X = 4) = \frac{5}{18}$.   b) Find the probability distribution of X.

a) Make a table showing the 36 possible outcomes.

Score on roll 1

+	1	1	1	2	2	3
1	2	2	2	3	3	4
1	2	2	2	3	3	4
1	2	2	2	3	3	4
2	3	3	3	4	4	5
2	3	3	3	4	4	5
3	4	4	4	5	5	6

(Score on roll 2)

You can see from the table that
10 of these have the outcome $X = 4$,
so $P(X = 4) = \frac{10}{36} = \frac{5}{18}$

b) Use the table to work out the probabilities for the other outcomes and then fill in a table summarising the probability distribution:

$\frac{9}{36}$ of the outcomes are a score of 2

$\frac{12}{36}$ of the outcomes are a score of 3

$\frac{4}{36}$ of the outcomes are a score of 5

$\frac{1}{36}$ of the outcomes are a score of 6

x	2	3	4	5	6
$P(X = x)$	$\frac{1}{4}$	$\frac{1}{3}$	$\frac{5}{18}$	$\frac{1}{9}$	$\frac{1}{36}$

Do complicated questions Bit By Bit

Example: A game involves rolling two fair, six-sided dice. If the sum of the scores is greater than 10 then the player wins 50p. If the sum is between 8 and 10 (inclusive) then they win 20p. Otherwise they get nothing. If X is the random variable "amount player wins in pence", find the probability distribution of X.

There are **3 possible values** for X (0, 20 and 50) and you need the **probability** of each.
To work these out, you need the probability of getting various totals on the dice.

1) You need to know $P(8 \leq \text{score} \leq 10)$ — the probability that the score is between 8 and 10 **inclusive** (i.e. including 8 and 10) and $P(11 \leq \text{score} \leq 12)$ — the probability that the score is **greater than** 10. Use a table:

Score on dice 1

+	1	2	3	4	5	6
1	2	3	4	5	6	7
2	3	4	5	6	7	8
3	4	5	6	7	8	9
4	5	6	7	8	9	10
5	6	7	8	9	10	11
6	7	8	9	10	11	12

(Score on dice 2)

The table: making things easier to understand since 3000 BC (DISCLAIMER: CGP takes no responsibility for the historical accuracy of this 'fact').

2) There are **36 possible outcomes**:

12 of these have a total of **8, 9 or 10** so $P(8 \leq \text{score} \leq 10) = \frac{12}{36} = \frac{1}{3}$

3 of these have a total of **11 or 12** so $P(11 \leq \text{score} \leq 12) = \frac{3}{36} = \frac{1}{12}$

3) Use these to find the probabilities you need:

$P(X = 20p) = P(8 \leq \text{score} \leq 10) = \frac{1}{3}$

$P(X = 50p) = P(11 \leq \text{score} \leq 12) = \frac{1}{12}$

To find $P(X = 0)$ take the total of the two probabilities above from 1 (since $X = 0$ is the only other possibility).

$P(X = 0) = 1 - \left[\frac{12}{36} + \frac{3}{36}\right] = 1 - \frac{15}{36} = \frac{21}{36} = \frac{7}{12}$

4) Now just stick all this info in a table (and check that the probabilities all add up to 1):

x	0	20	50
$P(X = x)$	$\frac{7}{12}$	$\frac{1}{3}$	$\frac{1}{12}$

Check: $\frac{7}{12} + \frac{1}{3} + \frac{1}{12} = \frac{7}{12} + \frac{4}{12} + \frac{1}{12} = 1$ ✓

Probability Distributions

The **Cumulative Distribution Function** is a **Running Total** of probabilities

The **cumulative distribution function** F(x) gives the probability that X will be **less than or equal to** a particular value.

$$F(x_0) = P(X \leq x_0) = \sum_{x \leq x_0} p(x)$$

p(x) = P(X = x)

Example: The probability distribution of the discrete random variable H, where H can only take values 0.1, 0.2, 0.3, 0.4, is shown in the table. Draw up a table to show the cumulative distribution of H.

h	0.1	0.2	0.3	0.4
P(H = h)	$\frac{1}{4}$	$\frac{1}{4}$	$\frac{1}{3}$	$\frac{1}{6}$

There are 4 values of h, so you have to find the probability that H is **less than or equal to** each of them in turn. It sounds trickier than it actually is — you only have to add up a few probabilities...

F(0.1) = P(H ≤ 0.1) — this is the same as P(H = 0.1), since H can't be less than 0.1. So **F(0.1)** = $\frac{1}{4}$

F(0.2) = P(H ≤ 0.2) — this is the probability that H = 0.1 or H = 0.2.

F(0.2) = P(H = 0.1) + P(H = 0.2) = $\frac{1}{4} + \frac{1}{4} = \frac{1}{2}$

F(0.3) = P(H ≤ 0.3) = P(H ≤ 0.2) + P(H = 0.3) = $\frac{1}{2} + \frac{1}{3} = \frac{5}{6}$ ◄ Here you're just adding one more probability to the previous cumulative probability.

F(0.4) = P(H ≤ 0.4) = P(H ≤ 0.3) + P(H = 0.4) = $\frac{5}{6} + \frac{1}{6} = 1$

Finally, put these values in a table, and you're done:

h	0.1	0.2	0.3	0.4
F(h) = P(H ≤ h)	$\frac{1}{4}$	$\frac{1}{2}$	$\frac{5}{6}$	1

P(X ≤ largest value of x) is always 1.

Example: For a discrete random variable X, where X can only take values 1, 2, 3, 4, the cumulative distribution function F(x) = kx, for x = 1, 2, 3 and 4. Find k, and the probability function.

1) First find k. You know that X has to be 4 or less — so **P(X ≤ 4) = 1**.
   Put x = 4 into the cumulative distribution function: F(4) = P(X ≤ 4) = 4k = 1, so k = $\frac{1}{4}$.

2) Now you can work out the probabilities of X being less than or equal to 1, 2, 3 and 4.
   F(1) = P(X ≤ 1) = 1 × k = $\frac{1}{4}$, **F(2)** = P(X ≤ 2) = 2 × k = $\frac{1}{2}$, **F(3)** = P(X ≤ 3) = 3 × k = $\frac{3}{4}$, **F(4)** = P(X ≤ 4) = 1

3) Then **P(X = 4)** = P(X ≤ 4) − P(X ≤ 3) = 1 − $\frac{3}{4}$ = $\frac{1}{4}$, **P(X = 3)** = P(X ≤ 3) − P(X ≤ 2) = $\frac{3}{4} - \frac{1}{2} = \frac{1}{4}$,
   Think about it — if it's less than or equal to 4, but it's **not** less than or equal to 3, then it has to be 4.
   P(X = 2) = P(X ≤ 2) − P(X ≤ 1) = $\frac{1}{2} - \frac{1}{4} = \frac{1}{4}$ and **P(X = 1)** = P(X ≤ 1) = $\frac{1}{4}$ ◄ Because x doesn't take any values less than 1.

4) Finish it all off by making a table. The probability distribution of X is:
   So the probability function is: **P(X = x)** = $\frac{1}{4}$ for x = 1, 2, 3, 4

x	1	2	3	4
P(X = x)	$\frac{1}{4}$	$\frac{1}{4}$	$\frac{1}{4}$	$\frac{1}{4}$

This is a uniform distribution (see p.158).

Practice Question

Q1 The random variable X, where X takes values 1, 2, 3, 4, has probability function P(X = x) = kx for x = 1, 2, 3, 4.
   a) Find the value of k.
   b) Find P(X > 2)
   c) Find P(1 ≤ X ≤ 3)
   d) Draw a table to show: (i) the probability distribution, (ii) the cumulative distribution.

Exam Question

Q1 The probability function for the discrete random variable X is given by P(X = x) = $\frac{1}{k}x^2$ for x = 1, 2, 3, 4.
   Find the value of k and P(X ≤ 2). [4 marks]

Fact: the probability of this coming up in the exam is less than or equal to one...

If you've got a probability distribution, you can work out the table for the cumulative distribution function and vice versa. Don't forget, all the stuff so far is for discrete variables — these can only take a certain number of values.

The Binomial Distribution

Welcome to the Binomial Distribution. It's quite a gentle introduction, because this page is basically about counting. If you're thinking some of this looks familiar, you're dead right — you met the binomial expansion back in Section 4.

n different objects can be arranged in n! different ways...

There are $n!$ ("n **factorial**") ways of arranging n **different** objects,
where $n! = n \times (n-1) \times (n-2) \times ... \times 3 \times 2 \times 1$.

Of course, not all ornaments deserve to go on the shelf.

> **Example:** a) In how many ways can 4 different ornaments be arranged on a shelf?
> b) In how many ways can 8 different objects be arranged?

a) You have **4 choices** for the first ornament, **3 choices** for the second ornament, **2 choices** for the third ornament, and **1 choice** for the last ornament.
So there are $4 \times 3 \times 2 \times 1 = 4! = 24$ arrangements.

b) There are $8! = \mathbf{40\ 320}$ arrangements.

Calculators have a factorial button so you don't need to type all the numbers out.

...but Divide by r! if r of these objects are the Same

If r of your n objects are **identical**, then the total number of possible arrangements is $(n! \div r!)$.

> **Example:** a) In how many different ways can 5 objects be arranged if 2 of those objects are identical?
> b) In how many different ways can 7 objects be arranged if 4 of those objects are identical?

a) Imagine those 2 identical objects were **different**. Then there would be $5! = 120$ possible arrangements. But because those 2 objects are actually **identical**, you can always **swap them round** without making a different arrangement. So there are really only $120 \div 2 = \mathbf{60}$ different ways to arrange the objects.

b) There are $\frac{n!}{r!} = \frac{7!}{4!} = \frac{5040}{24} = \mathbf{210}$ different ways to arrange the objects.

Use Binomial Coefficients if there are Only Two Types of object

See p.50 for more about binomial coefficients.

Binomial Coefficients

$$\binom{n}{r} = {}^nC_r = \frac{n!}{r!(n-r)!}$$

${}^nC_r$ and $\binom{n}{r}$ both mean $\frac{n!}{r!\,(n-r)!}$

> **Example:** a) In how many different ways can n objects of two types be arranged if r are of the first type?
> b) How many ways are there to select 11 players from a squad of 16?
> c) How many ways are there to pick 6 lottery numbers from 59?

a) If the objects were all **different**, there would be $n!$ ways to arrange them.
But r of the objects are of the same type and could be **swapped around**, so divide by $r!$.
Since there are only **two types**, the other $(n-r)$ could also be **swapped around**,
so divide by $(n-r)!$. This means there are $\dfrac{n!}{r!(n-r)!}$ arrangements.

b) This is basically a 'number of different **arrangements**' problem. Imagine the 16 players are lined up — then you could '**pick**' or '**not pick**' players by giving each of them a sign marked with a tick or a cross. So just find the number of ways to arrange 11 ticks and 5 crosses — this is $\binom{16}{11} = \frac{16!}{11!5!} = \mathbf{4368}$.

c) Again, numbers are either '**picked**' or '**unpicked**',
so there are $\binom{59}{6} = \frac{59!}{6!53!} = \mathbf{45\ 057\ 474}$ possibilities.

The Binomial Distribution

Use *Binomial Coefficients* to count arrangements of 'successes' and 'failures'

For this bit, you need to use the fact that if p = **P(something happens)**, then $1 - p$ = **P(that thing doesn't happen)**.

Example: I toss a fair coin 5 times. Find the probability of: a) 0 heads, b) 1 head, c) 2 heads.

First, note that each coin toss is **independent** of the others. That means you can **multiply** individual probabilities together.

$P(\text{tails}) = P(\text{heads}) = 0.5$

These are the $\binom{5}{1}$ = 5 ways to arrange 1 head and 4 tails.

a) $P(0 \text{ heads}) = P(\text{tails}) \times P(\text{tails}) \times P(\text{tails}) \times P(\text{tails}) \times P(\text{tails}) = 0.5^5 = \mathbf{0.03125}$

b) $P(1 \text{ head}) = [P(\text{heads}) \times P(\text{tails}) \times P(\text{tails}) \times P(\text{tails}) \times P(\text{tails})] + [P(\text{tails}) \times P(\text{heads}) \times P(\text{tails}) \times P(\text{tails}) \times P(\text{tails})]$
$+ [P(\text{tails}) \times P(\text{tails}) \times P(\text{heads}) \times P(\text{tails}) \times P(\text{tails})] + [P(\text{tails}) \times P(\text{tails}) \times P(\text{tails}) \times P(\text{heads}) \times P(\text{tails})]$
$+ [P(\text{tails}) \times P(\text{tails}) \times P(\text{tails}) \times P(\text{tails}) \times P(\text{heads})]$

So $P(1 \text{ head}) = 0.5 \times (0.5)^4 \times \binom{5}{1} = 0.03125 \times \frac{5!}{1!4!} = \mathbf{0.15625}$

$= P(\text{heads}) \times [P(\text{tails})]^4$
$\times$ ways to arrange 1 head and 4 tails

c) $P(2 \text{ heads}) = [P(\text{heads})]^2 \times [P(\text{tails})]^3 \times \text{ways to arrange 2 heads and 3 tails} = (0.5)^2 \times (0.5)^3 \times \binom{5}{2} = \mathbf{0.3125}$

The *Binomial Probability Function* gives P(r successes out of n trials)

The previous example really just shows why this thing-in-a-box must be true.

Binomial Probability Function

$$P(r \text{ successes in } n \text{ trials}) = \binom{n}{r} \times [P(\text{success})]^r \times [P(\text{failure})]^{n-r}$$

This is the probability function for a binomial distribution — see below for more info.

Example: I roll a fair six-sided dice 5 times. Find the probability of rolling:
a) 2 sixes, b) 3 sixes, c) 4 numbers less than 3.

Again, note that each roll of a dice is **independent** of the other rolls.

a) For this part, call "roll a 6" a success, and "roll anything other than a 6" a failure.

Then $P(\text{roll 2 sixes}) = \binom{5}{2} \times \left(\frac{1}{6}\right)^2 \times \left(\frac{5}{6}\right)^3 = \frac{5!}{2!3!} \times \frac{1}{36} \times \frac{125}{216} = \mathbf{0.161}$ (3 d.p.)

b) Again, call "roll a 6" a success, and "roll anything other than a 6" a failure.

Then $P(\text{roll 3 sixes}) = \binom{5}{3} \times \left(\frac{1}{6}\right)^3 \times \left(\frac{5}{6}\right)^2 = \frac{5!}{3!2!} \times \frac{1}{216} \times \frac{25}{36} = \mathbf{0.032}$ (3 d.p.)

Notice how $\binom{5}{2} = \binom{5}{3}$.
In fact, $\binom{n}{r} = \binom{n}{n-r}$.

c) This time, success means "roll a 1 or a 2", while failure is now "roll a 3, 4, 5 or 6".

Then $P(\text{roll 4 numbers less than 3}) = \binom{5}{4} \times \left(\frac{1}{3}\right)^4 \times \frac{2}{3} = \frac{5!}{4!1!} \times \frac{1}{81} \times \frac{2}{3} = \mathbf{0.041}$ (3 d.p.)

There are *5 Conditions* for a *Binomial Distribution*

Binomial Distribution: B(n, p)

A random variable X follows a binomial distribution if these **5 conditions** are satisfied:

1) There is a **fixed number** (n) of trials.
2) Each trial results in either **"success"** or **"failure"**.
3) All the trials are **independent**.
4) The probability of "success" (p) is the **same** in each trial.
5) The variable is the **total number of successes** in the n trials.

Binomial variables are discrete — they only take values 0, 1, 2... n.

n and p are the **parameters** of the binomial distribution.

Then, $P(X = x) = \binom{n}{x} \times p^x \times (1-p)^{n-x}$ for $x = 0, 1, 2, ..., n$, and you can write $X \sim \mathbf{B}(n, p)$.

If you're asked to comment on the **appropriateness** of a binomial model, you should check whether the variable satisfies **all** of these conditions.

The **expected** number of successes is given by (n × p).

The Binomial Distribution

Use your **Calculator** to find **Binomial Probabilities**

Example: I have an unfair coin. When I toss this coin, the probability of getting heads is 0.35.
Find the probability that it will land on heads fewer than 3 times when I toss it 12 times in total.

If the random variable X represents the number of heads I get in 12 tosses, then $X \sim B(12, 0.35)$.
You need to find $P(X \leq 2)$. You **could** work this out 'manually'...

$$P(0 \text{ heads}) + P(1 \text{ head}) + P(2 \text{ heads}) = \left[\binom{12}{0} \times 0.35^0 \times 0.65^{12}\right] + \left[\binom{12}{1} \times 0.35^1 \times 0.65^{11}\right] + \left[\binom{12}{2} \times 0.35^2 \times 0.65^{10}\right]$$

$$= 0.00568... + 0.03675... + 0.10884... = 0.15128... = \mathbf{0.151} \text{ (3 s.f.)}$$

However, it's much quicker to use the **binomial cumulative distribution function** (cdf) on your calculator.
This calculates $P(X \leq x)$, for $X \sim B(n, p)$ — just enter the **correct values of n, p and x**.
For example, here, $n = 12$ and $p = 0.35$, and you need $P(X \leq 2)$ (i.e. $x = 2$).
The calculator tells you that this is **0.15128...**, which is what you worked out above.

Be careful though:

- Some calculators have both a binomial **probability distribution function** (pdf) and a binomial **cumulative distribution function** (cdf). You use the **pdf** to find e.g. **P(X = 2)** (as on the previous page) and the **cdf** to find e.g. **P(X ≤ 2)** (as above).
- The cdf gives you $P(X \leq x)$ — if you want $P(X \geq x)$ (or $P(X < x)$ etc.) you'll have to do some fancy probability-wrangling. E.g. $P(X < 7) = P(X \leq 6)$, or $P(X > 4) = 1 - P(X \leq 4)$.

Countless secrets contained within...

Example: I have a different unfair coin. When I toss this coin, the probability of getting tails is 0.6.
The random variable X represents the number of tails in 12 tosses, so $X \sim B(12, 0.6)$.
If I toss this coin 12 times, find the probability that:
a) it will land on tails more than 8 times,   b) it will land on heads exactly 9 times,
c) it will land on tails more than 3 but fewer than 6 times.

a) You're looking for $P(X > 8)$, which is $1 - P(X \leq 8)$ (since '$X > 8$' and '$X \leq 8$' are complementary events — see p.153). So, from your calculator: $P(X > 8) = 1 - 0.77466... = \mathbf{0.225}$ (3 s.f.)

b) If the coin lands on **heads** 9 times, then it lands on **tails** 3 times. You could use the binomial pdf to go straight to the answer, or if your calculator doesn't have one, you can use the cdf instead:
$P(\text{heads 9 times}) = P(X = 3) = P(X \leq 3) - P(X \leq 2) = 0.01526... - 0.00281... = \mathbf{0.0125}$ (3 s.f.)

c) $P(3 < X < 6) = P(X < 6) - P(X \leq 3) = P(X \leq 5) - P(X \leq 3) = 0.15821... - 0.01526... = \mathbf{0.143}$ (3 s.f.)

Practice Questions

Q1 Find the probability of: a) getting exactly 9 heads when you toss a fair coin 10 times,
b) getting at least 9 heads when you toss a fair coin 10 times.

Q2 Find, to 4 decimal places: a) $P(X = 4)$ if $X \sim B(14, 0.27)$ b) $P(Y \leq 15)$ if $Y \sim B(20, 0.4)$

Exam Questions

Q1 The random variable X follows the binomial distribution $X \sim B(12, 0.6)$. Find:
a) $P(X < 8)$ [2 marks]   b) $P(X = 5)$ [1 mark]   c) $P(3 < X \leq 7)$ [2 marks]

Q2 Apples are stored in crates of 40. The probability of any apple containing a maggot is 0.15, and is independent of any other apple containing a maggot. In a random sample of 40 apples, find the probability that:
a) fewer than 6 apples contain maggots,   [2 marks]   b) more than 2 apples contain maggots.   [2 marks]
c) Jin has 3 crates. Find the probability that more than 1 crate contains more than 2 apples with maggots.   [3 marks]
d) Give one criticism of the assumption that apples contain maggots independently of each other.   [1 mark]

I used up all my binomial jokes in Section 4...

Here's a handy trick that might save some time on certain questions: if the number of successes is X~B(n, p), then the number of failures is Y~B(n, 1 – p). For example, the number of heads in the blue example is Y~B(12, 0.4).

The Normal Distribution

The normal distribution is everywhere in statistics. Everywhere, I tell you. So learn this well...

The **Normal Distribution** is '**Bell-Shaped**'

1) Loads of things in real life are most likely to fall '**somewhere in the middle**', and are much less likely to take **extremely high** or **extremely low** values. In this kind of situation, you often get a **normal distribution**.

2) If you were to draw a graph showing how likely different values are, you'd end up with a graph that looks a bit like a **bell**. There's a peak in the middle at the **mean** (or **expected value**). And the graph is **symmetrical** — so values the same distance **above** and **below** the mean are **equally likely**.

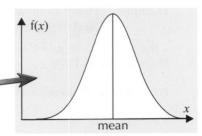

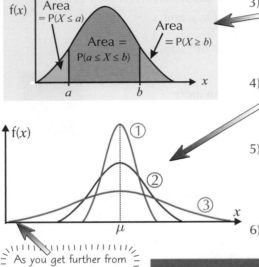

3) With a graph of a normal distribution, the probability of the random variable taking a value **between two limits** is the **area under the graph** between those limits. The **total probability** is 1, so the **total area** under the graph must also be **1**. And since the mean, μ, is in the middle, $P(X \leq \mu) = P(X \geq \mu) = 0.5$.

4) These three graphs all show normal distributions with the **same mean** (μ), but **different variances** (σ^2) — see page 142. Graph 1 has a **small** variance, and graph 3 has a **larger** variance — but the total area under all three curves is the **same** (= 1).

5) There are **points of inflection** (see p.90) at $x = \mu + \sigma$ and $x = \mu - \sigma$. **68%** of the total area lies within **1 standard deviation** of the mean (i.e. $\mu \pm \sigma$), **95%** of the total area lies within **2 standard deviations** of the mean ($\mu \pm 2\sigma$) and **99.7%** of the total area lies within 3 standard deviations of the mean ($\mu \pm 3\sigma$).

6) A very useful normal distribution is the **standard normal distribution**, or Z — this has a **mean of zero** and a **variance of 1**.

As you get further from the mean, the normal distribution tends to O, but never touches it.

Normal Distribution: $N(\mu, \sigma^2)$

- If X is normally distributed with **mean** μ and **variance** σ^2, it's written $X \sim N(\mu, \sigma^2)$.
- The **standard normal distribution** Z has **mean 0** and **variance 1**, i.e. $Z \sim N(0, 1)$.

Use your **Calculator** to work out **Probabilities**

When working out probabilities, it's usually a good idea to draw a **sketch** showing the area you're trying to find. Then you can use the **normal cumulative distribution function** on your calculator — you'll have to enter the values of the **mean** (μ), the **standard deviation** (σ) and the **x-values** you're interested in.

Example: $X \sim N(12, 16)$. Find: a) $P(X \leq 17)$, b) $P(X > 10)$, c) $P(8 \leq X \leq 15)$

a) Draw a sketch, then enter $\mu = 12$, $\sigma = \sqrt{16} = 4$, the upper bound $x = 17$ and a lower bound $x = -9999$. Then $P(X \leq 17) = \textbf{0.894}$ (3 s.f.)

If you're looking for $P(X \leq x)$ or $P(X \geq x)$, you might need to choose your own lower or upper bound — just pick a large negative or positive number (for parts a) and b) I've used −9999 and 9999 respectively).

b) As for part a), draw a sketch, then enter $\mu = 12$, $\sigma = 4$, the lower bound $x = 10$ and an upper bound $x = 9999$. Then $P(X > 10) = \textbf{0.691}$ (3 s.f.)

From the fact that the area under the graph is 1, $P(X > x) = 1 - P(X \leq x)$. For continuous random variables, $P(X > x) = P(X \geq x)$ (and $P(X < x) = P(X \leq x)$).

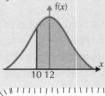

c) Here, draw a sketch then enter $\mu = 12$, $\sigma = 4$, the lower bound $x = 8$ and the upper bound $x = 15$. Then $P(8 \leq X \leq 15) = \textbf{0.615}$ (3 s.f.)

You can work out this area by splitting it up and subtracting: $P(8 \leq X \leq 15) = P(X \leq 15) - P(X \leq 8)$.

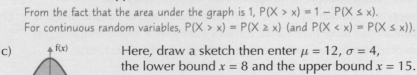

If your calculator can only do the standard normal distribution, Z, you'll have to convert your distribution to Z first — see p.166.

The Normal Distribution

The **Normal Distribution** can be used in **Real-Life** situations

Example: The times taken by a group of people to complete an assault course are normally distributed with a mean of 600 seconds and a variance of 105 seconds. Find the probability that a randomly selected person took: a) fewer than 575 seconds,   b) more than 620 seconds.

If X represents the time taken in seconds, then $X \sim N(600, 105)$.

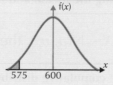

a)   You need to find $P(X < 575)$. So sketch the graph, then enter $\mu = 600$, $\sigma = \sqrt{105}$, the upper bound $x = 575$ and a lower bound $x = -9999$.
Then $P(X < 575) = \textbf{0.00735}$ (3 s.f.)

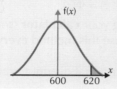

b)   This time, you're looking for $P(X > 620)$. So sketch the graph, then enter $\mu = 600$, $\sigma = \sqrt{105}$, the lower bound $x = 620$ and an upper bound $x = 9999$.
Then $P(X > 620) = \textbf{0.0255}$ (3 s.f.)

Use the **Inverse Normal Function** to find values of **x**

You might be given a **probability**, p, and asked to find the **range** of x-values where the probability of X falling in this range is p (i.e. you're told $P(X \leq a) = p$ for some value a that you have to find). For < or ≤ questions, you can do this directly on your calculator using the **inverse normal function** — just input p, μ and σ. For > or ≥ questions, subtract p from 1 to turn $P(X > a) = p$ into $P(X \leq a) = 1 - p$, then use your calculator as before.

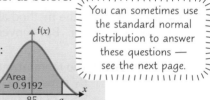

You can sometimes use the standard normal distribution to answer these questions — see the next page.

Example: $X \sim N(85, 25)$. If $P(X < a) = 0.9192$, find the value of a to 2 s.f.

Draw a sketch (the probability is > 0.5, so a will be to the **right** of the mean):
Then input probability = 0.9192, $\mu = 85$ and $\sigma = \sqrt{25} = 5$ into the **inverse normal function** on your calculator.
So $P(X < a) = 0.9192$ for $a = \textbf{92}$ (2 s.f.).

Practice Questions

Q1 If $X \sim N(50, 16)$, find the following to 4 decimal places:
   a) $P(X \leq 55)$,   b) $P(X < 42)$,   c) $P(X > 56)$,   d) $P(47 < X < 57)$.

Q2 If $X \sim N(5, 7^2)$ find the following to 4 decimal places:
   a) $P(X < 0)$,   b) $P(X \leq 1)$,   c) $P(X \geq 7)$,   d) $P(2 < X < 4)$.

Q3 If $X \sim N(28, 36)$, find the value of a such that:
   a) $P(X < a) = 0.8546$ b) $P(X \geq a) = 0.2418$ c) $P(a < X < 30) = 0.5842$

Exam Questions

Q1 The random variable X has a normal distribution with mean 120 and standard deviation 25.
   a) Find $P(X > 145)$.   [1 mark]
   b) Find the value of j such that $P(120 < X < j) = 0.4641$ [2 marks]

Q2 A garden centre sells bags of compost. The volume of compost in the bags is normally distributed with a mean of 50 litres.
   a) If the standard deviation of the volume is 0.4 litres, find the probability that a randomly selected bag will contain less than 49 litres of compost.   [1 mark]
   b) If 1000 of these bags of compost are bought, how many bags would you expect to contain more than 50.5 litres of compost?   [3 marks]

The number of ghost sightings follows a paranormal distribution...

Make sure you know how to use the normal functions on your own calculator — you'll probably use the normal cdf and inverse function a lot in these questions. It's also worth drawing a quick sketch of the graph for each question.

The Standard Normal Distribution

On p.164 I mentioned the standard normal distribution — a normal distribution with mean of 0 and a standard deviation of 1. The standard normal distribution is represented by the letter Z, so Z ~ N(0, 1).

Transform to Z by **Subtracting** μ, then **Dividing by** σ

1) You can convert **any** normally-distributed variable to Z by:
   (i) **subtracting the mean**, and then   (ii) **dividing by the standard deviation**.

   > If $X \sim N(\mu, \sigma^2)$, then $\dfrac{X - \mu}{\sigma} = Z$, where $Z \sim N(0, 1)$

   This is the Greek letter 'phi'.

2) Values of the **cumulative distribution function** of Z can be written **Φ(z)** — so $P(Z \leq z) = \Phi(z)$.

3) Once you've transformed a variable, you can work out the probabilities for Z using your **calculator** (some calculators can **only** work out probabilities for Z — in which case, you'll have to use this method **every time**).

> **Example:** If $X \sim N(5, 16)$, find $P(5 < X < 11)$ by first converting to the standard normal distribution, Z.
>
> To convert to Z, subtract μ (= 5) from any numbers and **divide by** σ (= $\sqrt{16}$ = 4).
>
> So $P(5 < X < 11) = P\left(\dfrac{5-5}{4} < Z < \dfrac{11-5}{4}\right) = P(0 < Z < 1.5)$
>
> Now use a **calculator** to find the probability. There are two ways you can do this — for each, enter $\mu = 0$ and $\sigma = 1$, then either use the limits 0 and 1.5, or do the calculation $P(Z < 1.5) - P(Z < 0) = 0.9331... - 0.5 = \textbf{0.433}$ (3 s.f.)
>
> From the symmetry of the curve, $\Phi(0) = 0.5$.

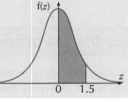

f(z)

0   1.5   z

I know, I know — the method above seems like a bit of a faff if you can just plug the numbers straight into your calculator. But converting to Z comes in handy in a couple of different places...

> **Example:** The random variable X follows a normal distribution, $X \sim N(\mu, \sigma^2)$.
> By converting to the standard normal distribution, Z, show that roughly 95% of the distribution falls within two standard deviations of the mean.
>
> Remember that to convert to Z, you need to subtract μ, and divide by σ.
> You want to know how much of the distribution is within 2σ of μ,
> i.e. the probability of X being more than $\mu - 2\sigma$ and less than $\mu + 2\sigma$:
>
> $P(\mu - 2\sigma < X < \mu + 2\sigma) = P(-2\sigma < X - \mu < 2\sigma)$ Subtract μ...
>
> $= P\left(-2 < \dfrac{X - \mu}{\sigma} < 2\right)$ ...and divide by σ...
>
> $= P(-2 < Z < 2)$ ...to get Z.
>
> Now you can use your calculator to find $P(-2 < Z < 2)$ — either directly, or by doing:
> $P(-2 < Z < 2) = P(Z < 2) - P(Z < -2) = 0.97724... - 0.02275... = \textbf{0.95449...}$
>
> So the probability of X being within two standard deviations of the mean is 95.449...% $\approx$ **95%** as required.

Pumpkinocchio was eagerly looking forward to the day that he could be transformed into a standard normal boy.

Transform to Z if μ is **Unknown**...

Converting to Z is **vital** if you need to find the value of μ.

> **Example:** $X \sim N(\mu, 2^2)$ and $P(X < 23) = 0.9015$. Find μ.
>
> Start by transforming the probability for X into a probability for Z: $P(X < 23) = P\left(Z < \dfrac{23 - \mu}{2}\right) = 0.9015$
>
> Use your calculator to find the value of z for which $\Phi(z) = 0.9015$ — this gives z = **1.29** (2 d.p.)
>
> Now form and solve an equation in μ: $\dfrac{23 - \mu}{2} = 1.29 \Rightarrow 23 - \mu = 2.58 \Rightarrow \mu = \textbf{20.42}$

The Standard Normal Distribution

...or if σ is **Unknown**

You can use a similar method if you need to find the value of σ.

> **Example:** $X \sim N(53, \sigma^2)$ and $P(X < 50) = 0.1$. Find σ.
>
> Again, transform the probability for X into a probability for Z:
>
> $P(X < 50) = P\left(Z < \dfrac{50 - 53}{\sigma}\right) = P\left(Z < -\dfrac{3}{\sigma}\right) = 0.1$
>
> Using your calculator, $-\dfrac{3}{\sigma} = -1.2815... \Rightarrow \dfrac{3}{\sigma} = 1.282 \Rightarrow \sigma = \mathbf{2.34}$ (3 s.f.)

Standard deviation has to be positive, so if you end up with a negative value for σ, you know you've gone wrong somewhere.

If you have to find μ **and** σ, you'll need to solve **Simultaneous Equations**

> **Example:** The random variable $X \sim N(\mu, \sigma^2)$. If $P(X < 9) = 0.5596$ and $P(X > 14) = 0.0322$, find μ and σ.
>
> $P(X < 9) = P\left(Z < \dfrac{9 - \mu}{\sigma}\right) = 0.5596.$
>
> Using your calculator, this tells you that $\dfrac{9 - \mu}{\sigma} = 0.15$, or $9 - \mu = \mathbf{0.15}\sigma$ ①
>
> $P(X > 14) = P\left(Z > \dfrac{14 - \mu}{\sigma}\right) = 0.0322$, which means that $P\left(Z < \dfrac{14 - \mu}{\sigma}\right) = 1 - 0.0322 = 0.9678.$
>
> Using your calculator, this tells you that $\dfrac{14 - \mu}{\sigma} = 1.85$, or $14 - \mu = \mathbf{1.85}\sigma$ ②
>
> ② − ① gives: $(14 - \mu) - (9 - \mu) = 1.85\sigma - 0.15\sigma$, or $5 = 1.7\sigma$. This gives $\sigma = 5 \div 1.7 = \mathbf{2.94}$ (3 s.f.)
>
> Now use either one of the equations to find μ: $\mu = 9 - (0.15 \times 2.94...) = \mathbf{8.56}$ (3 s.f.) ◄— So X ~ N(8.56, 2.94²).

Practice Questions

Q1 Find the value of z if: a) $P(Z < z) = 0.99$,   b) $P(Z \leq z) = 0.0005$.

Q2 Find the value of μ if: a) $X \sim N(\mu, 10)$ and $P(X < 8) = 0.8925$,
                           b) $X \sim N(\mu, 8^2)$ and $P(X < 213) = 0.3085$.

Q3 Find the value of σ if: a) $X \sim N(11, \sigma^2)$ and $P(X < 13) = 0.6$,
                           b) $X \sim N(108, \sigma^2)$ and $P(X \geq 106) = 0.9678$.

Q4 The random variable $X \sim N(\mu, \sigma^2)$.
     If $P(X < 15.2) = 0.9783$ and $P(X > 14.8) = 0.1056$, then find μ and σ.

Exam Questions

> Q1 A sweet shop sells giant marshmallows. The mass of a marshmallow, in grams, is described by the random variable Y, where $Y \sim N(75, \sigma^2)$. It is found that 10% of the marshmallows weigh less than 74 grams.
> Find σ.   [3 marks]
>
> Q2 The lifetimes of a particular type of battery are normally distributed with mean μ hours and standard deviation σ hours. A student using these batteries finds that 40% last less than 20 hours and 80% last less than 30 hours.
> Find μ and σ.   [7 marks]

The Norman Distribution came to England in 1066...

It's always the same — to transform to Z, subtract the mean and divide by the standard deviation. Just make sure you don't use the variance by mistake — remember, in N(μ, σ²), the second number always shows the variance.

Normal Approximation to B(n, p)

If n is big, a binomial distribution (B(n, p)) can be tricky to work with. However, in this situation, you can often approximate a binomial distribution with a normal distribution. Another great Maths life hack (sort of).

You can **Approximate** a **Binomial Distribution** with a **Normal Distribution**

Certain binomial distributions can be approximated by a normal distribution. For the normal approximation to a binomial distribution to work well, you need the following conditions to be true:

Normal Approximation to the Binomial

Suppose the random variable X follows a binomial distribution, i.e. $X \sim \mathbf{B(n, p)}$.

If   (i) $p \approx 0.5$,
and   (ii) n is large,

then X can be approximated by the normal distribution $Y \sim \mathbf{N(np, npq)}$ (where $q = 1 - p$).

Sometimes, using the **continuous** normal distribution to approximate a **discrete** distribution is slightly awkward.
- A **binomially distributed** variable X is **discrete**, so you can work out $P(X = 0)$, $P(X = 1)$, etc.
- A **normally distributed** variable Y is **continuous** (see p.164), and so $\mathbf{P(Y = 0) = P(Y = 1) = 0}$, etc.

To allow for this, you can use a **continuity correction**. Like a lot of this stuff, it sounds more complicated than it is.

What you do is model the discrete value $X = 1$ as being **spread out** over the continuous interval $0.5 < Y < 1.5$.
Then to approximate the **binomial $P(X = 1)$**, you find the **normal $P(0.5 < Y < 1.5)$**.
Similarly, $X = 2$ is spread out over the interval $1.5 < Y < 2.5$, and so on.

$$0 \quad \xleftarrow{} 1 \xrightarrow{} \xleftarrow{} 2 \xrightarrow{} \xleftarrow{} 3 \xrightarrow{} \xleftarrow{} 4 \xrightarrow{}$$
$$\quad\quad 0.5 \quad 1.5 \quad 2.5 \quad 3.5 \quad 4.5$$

However, when n is **large**, the approximation is **accurate enough** without needing to apply a continuity correction. In the exam, you **won't** need to make a continuity correction in order to use a normal approximation. Whew.

Example: If $X \sim B(800, 0.4)$, use a suitable approximation to find:
    a) $P(X < 350)$,   b) $P(X \geq 300)$,   c) $P(320 < X \leq 350)$.

You need to make sure first that the normal approximation is **suitable**:

n is **large**, and p is **not far** from 0.5, so the normal approximation is valid.
Next, work out np and npq: $np = 800 \times 0.4 = \mathbf{320}$ and
                           $npq = 800 \times 0.4 \times (1 - 0.4) = \mathbf{192}$

So the approximation you need is: $Y \sim \mathbf{N(320, 192)}$. ◀— The standard deviation is $\sqrt{192}$.
Now use your **calculator** to find the probabilities.

a) $P(X < 350) \approx P(Y < 350) = \mathbf{0.985}$ (3 s.f.)

b) $P(X \geq 300) \approx P(Y \geq 300) = \mathbf{0.926}$ (3 s.f.)

c) $P(320 < X \leq 350) \approx P(320 < Y \leq 350) = \mathbf{0.485}$ (3 s.f.)

If your calculator can only work out probabilities for the standard normal distribution, you'll need to convert the values of X to values of Z first, using the method on p.166.

Example: Each piglet born on a farm is equally likely to be male or female. 250 piglets are born. Use a suitable normal approximation to estimate the probability that there will be more than 130 male piglets born.

$n = 250$, and p (the probability that the piglet is male) is 0.5.
So if X represents the number of male piglets born, then $X \sim B(250, 0.5)$.

Since n is large and p is 0.5, a normal approximation is appropriate
— X can be approximated by a normal random variable $Y \sim N(\mu, \sigma^2)$:

$\mu = np = 250 \times 0.5 = \mathbf{125}$ and $\sigma^2 = npq = 250 \times 0.5 \times 0.5 = \mathbf{62.5}$

So the approximation you need is: $Y \sim \mathbf{N(125, 62.5)}$.
So, using your approximation, $P(X > 130) \approx P(Y > 130)$.
From your calculator, $P(Y > 130) = \mathbf{0.264}$ (3 s.f.)

The Piggins family didn't take kindly to being called "approximately normal".

Normal Approximation to B(n, p)

*The approximation also works as long as **np** and **nq** are **Bigger Than 5***

Even if p **isn't** all that close to 0.5, the normal approximation usually works fine as long as np and nq are both **bigger than 5**.

> **Example:**
> a) On average, only 23% of robin chicks survive to adulthood. If 200 robin chicks are randomly selected, use a suitable approximation to find the probability that at least 25% of them survive to adulthood.
> b) A student takes a sample of 11 robin chicks from her garden. Explain whether or not a normal approximation would still be appropriate to estimate the probability of at least 25% of them surviving to adulthood.

a) If X represents the number of survivors, then $X \sim B(200, 0.23)$.

Here, p **isn't** particularly close to 0.5, but n is **large**, so calculate np and nq:

$np = 200 \times 0.23 = 46$ and $nq = 200 \times (1 - 0.23) = 154$.

Both np and nq are greater than 5, so a **normal approximation** should be okay to use — $Y \sim N(46, 35.42)$.

Variance = npq
= 200 × 0.23 × 0.77
= 35.42

25% of 200 = 50, so you want to find $P(X \geq 50) \approx P(Y \geq 50)$.

Using your calculator, $P(Y \geq 50) = \mathbf{0.251}$ (3 s.f.).

> Using the original binomial distribution gives an answer of 0.27497... for part a), so this is a reasonable approximation.

b) This time, $X \sim B(11, 0.23)$, which means $np = 11 \times 0.23 = 2.53$, which is **less than 5**.

n is small and p isn't close to 0.5, so a normal approximation is **not appropriate**.

Practice Questions

Q1 The random variable X follows a binomial distribution: $X \sim B(100, 0.45)$. Using a normal approximation, find:
a) $P(X > 50)$, b) $P(X \leq 42)$, c) $P(40 < X \leq 47)$.

Q2 The number of people working in the post office is constantly adjusted depending on how busy it is, with the result that the probability of any person being served within 1 minute can be modelled as having a constant value of 0.7. Exactly 200 people come to the post office on a particular day. Using a normal approximation to a binomial distribution, estimate the probability that fewer than 60% of them are served within a minute.

Exam Questions

Q1 The random variable X is binomially distributed with $X \sim B(100, 0.6)$.
a) State the conditions needed for X to be well approximated by a normal distribution. [2 marks]
b) Using a suitable approximation, find:
(i) $P(X \geq 65)$ [2 marks]
(ii) $P(50 < X < 62)$ [1 mark]

Q2 On average, 55% of customers in a cafe order a cup of coffee. One day, the cafe served 150 customers. At the start of the day, the manager calculated that they had enough coffee to make 75 cups of coffee. By using a suitable approximation, find the probability that more then 75 customers try to order coffee. [3 marks]

Q3 The random variable X follows a binomial distribution: $X \sim B(n, p)$. X is approximated by the normally distributed random variable Y. Using this normal approximation, $P(X \leq 153) = 0.9332$ and $P(X > 127) = 0.9977$ (4 d.p.).
a) Find the mean and standard deviation of the normal approximation. [6 marks]
b) Hence, estimate n and p. [4 marks]

Admit it — the normal distribution is the most amazing thing ever...

So the normal approximation can work pretty well, even when p isn't really all that close to 0.5. But even so, you should always show that your approximation is 'suitable'. In fact, the question might even ask you to show it.

Choosing a Distribution

By now, you should be familiar with both the binomial and normal distributions. If you're not, it's worth having another read through this section until it's all clear in your head. Then come back to this page — I'll wait for you.

Learn the **Conditions** for **Binomial** and **Normal Distributions**

You might be given a situation and asked to choose which distribution would be suitable.

Conditions for a Binomial Distribution

1) The data is **discrete**.
2) The data represents the number of '**successes**' in a **fixed number of trials** (n), where each trial results in **either** 'success' or 'failure'.
3) All the trials are **independent**, and the probability of success, p, is **constant**.

If these conditions are met, the data can be modelled by a **binomial distribution**: $B(n, p)$.

You saw these conditions on p.162.

Conditions for a Normal Distribution

1) The data is **continuous**.
2) The data is roughly **symmetrically distributed**, with a **peak in the middle** (at the **mean, μ**).
3) The data '**tails off**' either side of the mean — i.e. data values become **less frequent** as you move further from the mean. Virtually **all of the data** is within **3 standard deviations** (σ) of the mean.

If these conditions are met, the data can be modelled by a **normal distribution**: $N(\mu, \sigma^2)$.

Example: For each random variable below, decide if it can be modelled by a binomial distribution, a normal distribution or neither.

a) The number of faulty items (T) produced in a factory per day, if items are faulty independently with probability 0.01 and there are 10 000 items produced every day.

Binomial — there's a **fixed number** of **independent** trials (10 000) with **two possible results** ('faulty' or 'not faulty'), a **constant probability of 'success'**, and T **is the total number** of 'faulty' items. So $T \sim B(10\ 000, 0.01)$.

b) The number of red cards (R) drawn from a standard 52-card deck in 10 picks, not replacing the cards each time.

Neither — the data is **discrete** so it can't be modelled by the normal distribution, but the **probability of 'success' changes** each time (as the cards aren't replaced) so it can't be modelled by the binomial distribution.

c) The heights (H) of all the girls in a Sixth Form college.

Normal — the data is **continuous**, and you would expect heights to be distributed **symmetrically**, with most girls' heights close to the mean and a few further away. So $H \sim N(\mu, \sigma^2)$ (where μ and σ are to be calculated).

Use **Facts** about the distribution to **Estimate Parameters**

Example: The times taken by runners to finish a 10 km race, x minutes, are normally distributed. Data from the race is shown on the diagram below. Estimate the mean and standard deviation of the times.

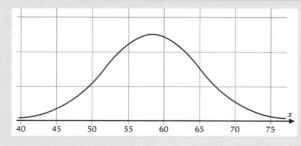

The mean is in the middle, so $\mu \approx 58$ **minutes**.

For a normal distribution there is a **point of inflection** at $x = \mu + \sigma$ (see p.164). Use the diagram to estimate the point of inflection. This is where the line changes from **concave** to **convex** (see p.90) — it looks like this at about $x \approx 65$.

Use your values for x and μ to estimate σ.

$65 = 58 + \sigma \Rightarrow \sigma \approx 7$ **minutes**

You could also use the point of inflection at $x = \mu - \sigma$.

Choosing a Distribution

Once you've *Chosen* a distribution, use it to *Answer Questions*

> **Example:** A restaurant has several vegetarian meal options on its menu. The probability of any person ordering a vegetarian meal is 0.15. One lunch time, 20 people order a meal.
> a) Suggest a suitable model to describe the number of people ordering vegetarian meals.
> b) Use this model to find the probability that at least 5 people order a vegetarian meal.

a) There are a **fixed number of trials** (20 meals), with probability of success (i.e. vegetarian meal) **0.15**. If X is the number of people ordering a vegetarian meal, then $X \sim \mathbf{B(20, 0.15)}$.

b) Use your calculator, with $n = 20$ and $p = 0.15$:
$P(X \geq 5) = 1 - P(X < 5) = 1 - P(X \leq 4) = 1 - 0.8298... = \mathbf{0.170}$ (3 s.f.)

> **Example:** The heights of 1000 sunflowers from the same field are measured.
> The distribution of the sunflowers' heights is symmetrical about the mean of 9.8 ft, with the shortest sunflower measuring 5.8 ft and the tallest measuring 13.7 ft. The standard deviation of the sunflowers' heights is 1.3 ft.
> a) Explain why the distribution of the sunflowers' heights might reasonably be modelled using a normal distribution.
> b) From these 1000 sunflowers, those that measure 7.5 ft or taller are harvested. Estimate the number of sunflowers that will be harvested.
> c) Explain why you shouldn't use your answer to part b) to estimate the number of sunflowers harvested from a crop of 1000 sunflowers from a different field.

a) The data collected is **continuous**, and the distribution of the heights is **symmetrical** about the **mean**. This is also true for a normally distributed random variable X. **Almost all** of the data is within **3 standard deviations** of the mean: $9.8 - (3 \times 1.3) = 5.9$ and $9.8 + (3 \times 1.3) = 13.7$. So the random variable $X \sim \mathbf{N(9.8, 1.3^2)}$ seems like a reasonable model for the sunflowers' heights.

b) Using a calculator: $P(X \geq 7.5) = 0.961572...$
Multiply the total number of sunflowers by this probability:
$1000 \times 0.961572... = \mathbf{962}$ (to the nearest whole number).

c) The **mean** and **standard deviation** of another crop of sunflowers could be **different** (because of varying sunlight, soil quality etc.), so you shouldn't use 962 as an estimate. However, it would still be reasonable to assume that their heights were normally distributed — just with different values of μ and σ.

Practice Question

Q1 Explain whether each random variable can be modelled by a binomial or normal distribution or neither.
   a) The number of times (T) I have to roll a fair standard six-sided dice before I roll a 6.
   b) The distances (D) of a shot put thrown by a class of 30 Year 11 students in a PE lesson.
   c) The number of red cars (R) in a sample of 1000 randomly chosen cars, if the proportion of red cars in the population as a whole is 0.08.

Exam Question

Q1 A biologist tries to catch a hedgehog every night for two weeks using a humane trap. She either succeeds in catching a hedgehog, or fails to catch one.
   a) The biologist believes that this situation can be modelled by a random variable following a binomial distribution.
      (i) State two conditions needed for a binomial distribution to arise here. [2 marks]
      (ii) State which quantity would follow a binomial distribution (assuming the above conditions are satisfied). [1 mark]
   b) If the biologist successfully catches a hedgehog, she records its weight. Explain why a normal distribution might be a suitable model for the distribution of these times. [2 marks]

You can't choose your family, but you can choose your distribution...

These two pages are really just bringing together everything you've learnt in this section — there shouldn't be anything about choosing a distribution that surprises you. I've saved all the surprises for the next section — read on, read on...

Statistical Sampling

No time for any small talk, I'm afraid. It's straight on with the business of populations and how to find out about them.

A **Population** is a **Group** of people or items

For any statistical investigation, there will be a **group** of people or items that you want to **find out about**. This group is called the **population**.

This could be:

- All the students in a maths class
- All the penguins in Antarctica
- All the chocolate puddings produced by a company in a year

1) Populations are said to be **finite** if it's possible for someone to **count how many** members there are. E.g. all the students in a maths class would be a finite population.

2) If it's **impossible to know exactly how many** members there are, the population is said to be **infinite**.

To **collect information** about your population, you can carry out a **survey**. This means questioning the people or examining the items.

> A population might have a finite number of members in theory, but if it's impossible to count them all in practice, the population is infinite. E.g. all the blades of grass in a field would be an infinite population (even though you could count them all in theory).

A **Census** surveys the **Whole Population**

When you collect information from **every member of a population**, it's called a **census**.

To do this, your population needs to be **finite**. It also helps if it's fairly **small** and **easily accessible** — so that getting information from every member is a straightforward task.

You need to know the **advantages and disadvantages** of doing a census, so here they are:

Census — Advantages	Census — Disadvantages
1) You get **accurate information** about the population, because every member has been surveyed.	1) For large populations, it takes a lot of **time and effort** to carry out.
2) It's a **true representation** of the population — it's **unbiased**.	2) This makes it **expensive** to do.
	3) It can be **difficult** to make sure **all members** are surveyed. If some are missed, bias can creep in.
	4) If the tested items are **used up or damaged** in some way, a census is impractical.

See the next page for more on bias.

Watch out for anything that might make doing a census a silly idea.

A **Sample** is **Part of a Population**

1) If doing a census is impossible or impractical, you can find out about a population by questioning or examining **just a selection** of the people or items. This **selected group** is called a **sample**.

2) Before selecting your sample, you need to identify the **sampling units** — these are the **individual members** of the population. A **full list** of all the **sampling units** is called a **sampling frame**.

3) This list must give a **unique name or number** to each sampling unit, and is used to **represent** the population when selecting a random sample (see next page).

> **Example:** A company produces 100 chocolate puddings every day, and each pudding is labelled with a unique product number. Every day, a sample of 5 puddings is eaten as part of a quality control test.
>
> a) Why is it necessary for the company to take a sample rather than carry out a census?
>
> **If they ate all the puddings, there would be none left to sell.**
>
> b) Identify the sampling units. c) Suggest a sampling frame.
>
> **The individual puddings** **A list of all one hundred unique product numbers.**

A sampling frame can only be produced when you know exactly who or what makes up the population.

Statistical Sampling

A *Sample* needs to be *Representative* of its population

Data collected from a **sample** is used to draw conclusions about the **whole population**. So it's vital that the sample is **as much like** the population as possible. A **biased** sample is one which **doesn't fairly represent** the population.

To Avoid Sampling Bias:

1) Select from the **correct population** and make sure **none** of the population is **excluded** — that means drawing up an accurate sampling frame and sticking to it. E.g. if you want to find out the views of residents from a particular street, your sample should only include residents from that street and should be chosen from a full list of the residents.

2) Select your sample at **random** — see below. Non-random sampling methods include things like the sampler just asking their friends (who might all give similar answers), or asking for volunteers (meaning they only get people with strong views on a subject).

3) Make sure all your sample members **respond** — otherwise the results could be biased. E.g. if some of your sampled residents are out when you go to interview them, it's important that you go back and get their views another time.

You need to be able to *Justify Choosing a Sample* over a census

In most situations, it's **more practical** to survey a **sample** rather than carry out a census — make sure you **can explain why**. But remember, the **downside** is that your results **might not be as reliable**, either due to sampling bias, or just the natural variability between samples (see below).

Sampling — Advantages	Sampling — Disadvantages
1) **Quicker** and **cheaper** than a census, and **easier to get hold of** all the required information. 2) It's the only option when surveyed items are **used up or damaged**.	1) **Variability between samples** — each possible sample will give different results, so you could just happen to select one which doesn't accurately reflect the population. One way to reduce the likelihood of large variability is by using a **large sample size**. The more sampling units that are surveyed, the **more reliable** the information should be. 2) Samples can easily be affected by **sampling bias**.

Different *Sampling Methods* are better in *Different Situations*

If you choose to select a sample, then you need to decide which **method** to use. There are plenty to choose from, and they all have their advantages and disadvantages.

In *Random Sampling*, all members are *Equally Likely* to be selected

In a **simple random sample**, every person or item in the population has an **equal chance** of being selected, and each selection is **independent** of every other selection.

Every single possible sample is equally likely.

To choose a random sample:

- Give a **number** to each **population member**, from a full list of the **population**.

- Generate a list of **random numbers** (using a computer, calculator, dice or random number table).

- **Match** these numbers to the population members to select your sample.

Example: A zoo has 80 raccoons. Describe how the random number table opposite could be used to select a sample of three of them, for a study on tail lengths.

8330	3992	1840
0330	1290	3237
9165	4815	0766

1) First, draw up a **list of all 80 raccoons**, giving each one a two-digit number between 01 and 80.

2) Then, find the **first three numbers** between 01 and 80 from the table (**30, 39** and **18**), and select the raccoons with the matching numbers.

Here, the 4-digit numbers were split into two 2-digit numbers. Any numbers greater than 80 were rejected.

Advantage: Every member of the population has an **equal chance** of being selected, so it's **completely unbiased**.

Disadvantage: It can be **inconvenient** if the population is spread over a **large area** — it might be difficult to track down the selected members (e.g. in a nationwide sample).

Section 14 — Statistical Hypothesis Testing

Statistical Sampling

In *Systematic Sampling*, every **nth Member** is selected

> So you could choose to select every tenth member of the population, for example.

To choose a systematic sample:
- Give a **number** to each population **member**, from a **full list** of the population.
- Calculate a **regular interval** to use by dividing the population size by the sample size.
- Generate a **random** starting point that is less than or equal to the size of the interval. The corresponding member of the population is the **first member** of your sample. Keep **adding** the interval to the starting point to select your sample.

Advantages: It can be used for quality control on a production line — a **machine** can be set up to sample every *n* items. It should also give an **unbiased** sample.

Disadvantage: The regular interval could coincide with a **pattern** — e.g. if every 10th item produced by a machine is faulty and you sample every 10th item, your sample will appear to show that **every item** produced is faulty, or that **no items** are faulty. Either way, your sample will be **biased**.

Opportunity Sampling is also known as Convenience Sampling

Opportunity sampling is where the sample is chosen from a section of the population at a particular place and time — whatever is **convenient** for the sampler.

Example: Mel thinks that most people watch her favourite television programme. She asks 20 friends whether they watch the television programme. Give a reason why Mel's sample may be biased.

Mel's friends could be of a **similar age** or the **same gender**, which is **not representative** of the whole population. OR

> Any sensible comment will do here.

Because this is Mel's favourite television programme, she might have **encouraged** her friends to watch it too.

Advantage: Data can be gathered very **quickly** and **easily**.

Disadvantage: It **isn't random** and can be **very biased** — there's no attempt to obtain a **representative** sample.

In *Stratified Sampling*, the population is divided into *Categories*

If a population is divided into **categories** (e.g. age or gender), you can use a **stratified sample** — this uses the same **proportion** of each category in the sample as there is in the population.

To choose a stratified sample:
- Divide the population into **categories**.
- Calculate the **total** population.
- Calculate the number needed for each category in the sample, using:
$$\text{Size of category in sample} = \frac{\text{size of category in population}}{\text{total size of population}} \times \text{total sample size}$$
- Select the sample for each category at **random**.

Lance, Marek, Brett and Jay were selected to represent the 'Roman soldiers not wearing trousers' category.

Example: A teacher takes a sample of 20 pupils from her school, stratified by year group. The table shows the number of pupils in each year group. Calculate how many pupils from each year group should be in her sample.

Year Group	No. of pupils
7	120
8	80
9	95
10	63
11	42

The population is already split into **five categories**, based on **year group**.

Total population = 120 + 80 + 95 + 63 + 42 = **400**

Calculate the number needed for each category, rounding to the nearest whole number:

$$\text{Year 7} = \frac{120}{400} \times 20 = 6 \qquad \text{Year 8} = \frac{80}{400} \times 20 = 4 \qquad \text{Year 9} = \frac{95}{400} \times 20 = 4.75 \approx 5$$

$$\text{Year 10} = \frac{63}{400} \times 20 = 3.15 \approx 3 \qquad \text{Year 11} = \frac{42}{400} \times 20 = 2.1 \approx 2$$

> You should check that these add up to the required sample size:
> 6 + 4 + 5 + 3 + 2 = **20**

Advantages: If the population can be divided up into distinct categories (e.g. age), it's likely to give a **representative sample**. It's useful when results may **vary** depending on category.

Disadvantages: It's not useful when there aren't any **obvious** categories. It can be **expensive** because of the extra detail involved.

Statistical Sampling

Quota Sampling also divides the population into Categories

To choose a quota sample:
- Divide the population into **categories**.
- Give each category a **quota** (number of members to sample).
- Collect data until the quotas are met in **all** categories (**without** using random sampling).

The main difference between quota and stratified sampling is that no attempt is made to be random in quota sampling. It's often used in market research.

Advantages: It can be done when there **isn't** a full list of the population. **Every** sample member responds because the interviewer continues to sample until all the quotas are met.

Disadvantage: It can be **easily biased** by the interviewer — e.g. they could **exclude** some of the population.

Clusters are a bit Different to Categories

To choose a cluster sample:
- Divide the population into **clusters** covering the **whole population**, where **no member** of the population belongs to **multiple clusters**.
- **Randomly** select clusters to use in the sample, based on the required sample size.
- Either use **all** of the members of the selected clusters (a **one-stage** cluster sample), or **randomly sample** within each cluster to form the sample (a **two-stage** cluster sample).

*The difference between **clusters** and **categories** is that categories should be groups that you expect to give **different** results to each other (e.g. if you were measuring height, different year groups in a school), while clusters should give **similar** results (e.g. different classes in Year 7).*

Advantages: It can be more **practical** than other methods (e.g. quicker or cheaper) in certain situations. You can incorporate **other sampling methods** at either stage, making it quite **adaptable**.

Disadvantages: Because you only sample certain clusters, the results can be less representative of the population as a whole. It's not always possible to separate a population into clusters in a natural way.

Practice Questions

Q1 For each of the following situations, explain whether it would be more sensible to carry out a census or a sample survey:
  a) Ryan has a biased coin. He wants to find the proportion of coin tosses that will result in 'heads'.
  b) Pies are produced in batches of 200. A quality controller wants to check how full the pies are by removing the lids and measuring the depth of the filling.
  c) There are 24 students in Louisa's maths class. She wants to know the average mark for the class in the last maths test.

Q2 Obsidian is carrying out a survey on public transport in his town. He asks 10 people who live on his street for their opinions. What type of sampling is this?

Q3 Explain how you could use systematic sampling to survey people visiting a cinema one Saturday afternoon.

Exam Questions

Q1 One of the history teachers at a school wants to survey a sample of Year 7 pupils in the school.
  a) Identify: (i) the population for the survey, (ii) a suitable sampling frame that she could use. [2 marks]
  b) She uses all of the pupils in her Year 7 class as her sample and gives them a questionnaire, which has questions on a number of different topics. For each of the topics given below, state, with an explanation, whether or not her sample is likely to be biased.
  (i) Pupils' opinions on history lessons at the school. (ii) How far away from the school pupils live. [2 marks]

Q2 A film club has 250 members. 98 of them are retired, 34 are unemployed, 83 work full- or part-time and the rest are students. The secretary wants to survey a sample of 25 members. She uses stratified sampling to select her sample. How many people in each category should she ask? [4 marks]

I need to interview 5.68 people in my class...

Make sure you know the different types of sampling and the advantages and disadvantages of each one.

Hypothesis Tests

There are a lot of technical terms to learn over the next two pages. It might feel a bit hard-going, but don't despair — it's paving the way for a return to some old friends later on (and it'll come in really handy for the exam).

A **Hypothesis** is a **Statement** you want to **Test**

Hypothesis testing is about using **sample data** to **test statements** about **population parameters**.
Unfortunately, it comes with a fleet of terms you need to know.

> *A parameter is a quantity that describes a characteristic of a population (e.g. mean or variance).*

- **Null Hypothesis (H_0)** — a statement about the value of a population parameter. Your data may allow you to **reject** this hypothesis.
- **Alternative Hypothesis (H_1)** — a statement that describes the value of the population parameter if H_0 is rejected.
- **Hypothesis Test** — a statistical test that tests the claim that H_0 makes about the parameter against that made by H_1. It tests whether H_0 should be rejected or not, using evidence from sample data.
- **Test Statistic** — a statistic calculated from sample data which is used to decide whether or not to reject H_0.

1) For any hypothesis test, you need to **write two hypotheses** — a **null hypothesis** and an **alternative hypothesis**.

2) You often choose the **null hypothesis** to be something you actually **think is false**. This is because hypothesis tests can only show that **statements are false** — they **can't** prove that things are **true**. So you're aiming to find **evidence** for what you think is **true**, by **disproving** what you think is **false**.

3) H_0 needs to give a **specific value** to the parameter, since all your calculations will be based on this value. You **assume** this value holds **true** for the test, then see if your data allows you to **reject** it. H_1 is then a statement that describes how you think the **value of the parameter differs** from the value given by H_0.

4) The **test statistic** you choose **depends on the parameter** you're interested in. It should be a **'summary'** of the sample data, and should have a sampling distribution that can be calculated using the parameter value specified by H_0.

> **Example:** A 4-sided spinner has sides labelled A–D. Jemma thinks that the spinner is biased towards side A. She spins it 20 times and counts the number of times, Y, that she gets side A.
> a) Write down a suitable null hypothesis to test Jemma's theory.
> b) Write down a suitable alternative hypothesis.
> c) Describe the test statistic Jemma should use.

a) If you assume the spinner is unbiased, each side has a probability of 0.25 of being spun. Let p = the probability of spinning side A.
Then: $H_0\colon p = 0.25$ ← *By assuming the spinner is unbiased, the parameter, p, can be given the specific value 0.25. Jemma is then interested in disproving this hypothesis.*

b) If the spinner is biased towards side A, then the probability will be greater than 0.25. So: $H_1\colon p > 0.25$ ← *This is what Jemma actually thinks.*

c) The test statistic is Y, the number of times she gets side A. ← *Assuming H_0 is true, the sampling distribution of Y is B(20, 0.25) — see p.162.*

Hypothesis Tests can be **One-Tailed** or **Two-Tailed**

> *The 'tailed' business is to do with the critical region used by the test — see the next page.*

For $H_0\colon \theta = a$, where θ is a parameter and a is a number:
1) The test is **one-tailed** if H_1 **is specific** about the value of θ compared to a, i.e. $H_1\colon \theta > a$, or $H_1\colon \theta < a$.
2) The test is **two-tailed** if H_1 **specifies only that θ doesn't equal a**, i.e. $H_1\colon \theta \neq a$.

Whether you use a one-tailed or a two-tailed test depends on how you define H_1. And that depends on **what you want to find out about the parameter** and any **suspicions** you might have about it.

> E.g. in the example above, Jemma suspects that the probability of getting side A is **greater than 0.25**. This is what she wants to test, so it is sensible to define $H_1\colon p > 0.25$.
> If she wants to test for **bias**, but is **unsure** if it's towards or against side A, she could define $H_1\colon p \neq 0.25$.

A very important thing to remember is that the results of a hypothesis test are either '**reject H_0**', or '**do not reject H_0**' — which means you haven't found enough evidence to **disprove** H_0, and **not** that you've proved it.

Hypothesis Tests

If your Data is **Significant**, Reject H_0

1) You would **reject H_0** if the **observed value** of the test statistic is **unlikely** under the null hypothesis.

2) The **significance level** of a test (α) determines **how unlikely** the value needs to be before H_0 is rejected. It also determines the **strength** of the **evidence** that the test has provided — the lower the value of α, the stronger the evidence you have for saying H_0 is false. You'll usually be told what level to use — e.g. 1% ($\alpha = 0.01$), 5% ($\alpha = 0.05$), or 10% ($\alpha = 0.1$). For a **two-tailed** test, you want a level of $\frac{\alpha}{2}$ for **each tail**.

3) To decide whether your result is **significant**:
   - Define the **sampling distribution** of the **test statistic** under the **null hypothesis**. → *supposed to be based on the model of the null hypothesis*
   - Calculate the **probability** of getting a value that's **at least as extreme** as the **observed value** from this distribution — this is known as the *p*-value.
   - If the *p*-value is **less than or equal to** α (or $\frac{\alpha}{2}$ for a two-tailed test), **reject H_0** in favour of H_1.

> **Example:** Javed wants to test at the 5% level whether or not a coin is biased towards tails. He tosses the coin 10 times and records the number of tails, X. He gets 9 tails.
> a) Define suitable hypotheses for p, the probability of getting tails.
> b) State the condition under which Javed would reject H_0.
>
> *P(at least as extreme as 9) means 9 or more (this is the p-value).*
>
> a) $H_0: p = 0.5$ and $H_1: p > 0.5$.   b) Under H_0, $X \sim B(10, 0.5)$. **If $P(X \geq 9) \leq 0.05$, Javed would reject H_0.**
>
> *Significance level*

The **Critical Region** is the **Set of Significant Values**

1) The **critical region** (CR) is the **set of all values of the test statistic** that would cause you to **reject H_0**. The first value that's **inside** the CR is called the **critical value**, so results **as extreme** (or **more**) as this are **significant**.

2) **One-tailed tests** have a **single** CR, containing the highest or lowest values. For **two-tailed tests**, the region is **split into two** — half at the lower end and half at the upper end. Each half has a probability of $\frac{\alpha}{2}$.

3) To **test whether your result is significant**, find the critical region and if it **contains the observed value**, reject H_0.

> **Example (continued):**   c) Find the critical region for the test, at the 5% level.
>
> This is a **one-tailed** test with $H_1: p > 0.5$, so you're only interested in the **upper end** of the distribution.
> Use the **binomial cdf** on your calculator (see p.163) to find the value of x such that $P(X \geq x) \leq 0.05$ (the significance level). As calculators usually give probabilities for $P(X \leq x)$ you need to use $P(X \geq x) = 1 - P(X < x)$.
> $$P(X \geq 8) = 1 - P(X < 8) = 1 - P(X \leq 7) = 1 - 0.9453... = 0.0546... > 0.05$$
> $$P(X \geq 9) = 1 - P(X < 9) = 1 - P(X \leq 8) = 1 - 0.9892... = 0.0107... < 0.05$$
> So the critical region is $X \geq 9$ ← So values of 9 or 10 would cause you to reject H_0: $p = 0.5$.
>
> *The acceptance region is where you don't reject H_0 — i.e. $X \leq 8$.*

The **actual significance level** of a test is the probability of **incorrectly rejecting H_0** — i.e. the probability of getting extreme data by chance when H_0 is true. This is often **different** from the level of significance originally asked for in the question. Here, the actual significance level is $P(X \geq 9) = 0.0107$, which is much lower than 0.05.

Practice Question

Q1 In 2012, a survey found that 68% of residents in a town used the local library. In 2016, the proportion was found to be 53%. A hypothesis test was carried out, using $H_0: p = 0.68$ and $H_1: p < 0.68$, and the null hypothesis was rejected. Does this result support the claim that the percentage of local residents using the library fell by 15%?

Exam Question

Q1 One year ago, 43% of customers rated a restaurant as 'Excellent'. Since then, a new chef has been employed, and the manager believes that the approval rating will have gone up. He decides to carry out a hypothesis test to test his belief. Define the null and alternative hypotheses the manager should use.   [1 mark]

I repeat, X has entered the critical region — we have a significant situation...

Don't mix up the p-value with the binomial probability p. I know, I know, it would have been nice if they'd used a different letter, but that's life. Remember to always divide α by 2 whenever you're doing a two-tailed test.

Hypothesis Tests and Binomial Distributions

OK, it's time to pick your best 'hypothesis testing' foot and put it firmly forward. It's also a good time to reacquaint yourself with binomial distributions, which you met in Section 13. Have a look back there before you go any further.

Use a **Hypothesis Test** to **Find Out** about the **Population Parameter p**

The first step in exam questions is to work out **which distribution** to use to model the situation — you've a choice of binomial or normal. Words like '**proportion**', '**percentage**' or '**probability**' are clues that it's **binomial**.

Hypothesis tests for the binomial parameter p all follow the **same general method** — this is what you do:

1) Define the **population parameter** in **context**
   — for a binomial distribution it's always p, a **probability** of success, or **proportion** of a population.

2) Write down the **null** hypothesis (H_0) — $H_0: p = a$ for some constant a.

3) Write down the **alternative** hypothesis (H_1)
   — H_1 will either be $H_1: p < a$ or $H_1: p > a$ (one-tailed test) or $H_1: p \neq a$ (two-tailed test).

4) State the **test statistic**, X — always just the number of '**successes**' in the sample.

5) Write down the **sampling distribution** of the test statistic under H_0 — $X \sim B(n, p)$ where n is the sample size.

6) State the **significance level**, α — you'll usually be given this.

7) Test for **significance** or find the **critical region** (see previous page).

8) Write your **conclusion** — state whether or not you have **sufficient evidence** to **reject** H_0.

null hypothesis

Example: In a past census of employees, 20% were in favour of a change to working hours. After making changes to staff contracts, the manager now believes that the proportion of staff wanting a change in their working hours has decreased. The manager carries out a random sample of 30 employees, and 2 are in favour of a change in hours. Stating your hypotheses clearly, test the manager's claim at the 5% level of significance.

1) Let p = **proportion of employees in favour of change to hours**.

2) Assume there's been **no change** in the proportion: $H_0: p = 0.2$

   You assume there's been no change in the value of the parameter, so you can give it a value of 0.2. The alternative hypothesis states what the manager actually thinks.

3) The manager's interested in whether the proportion has **decreased**, so: $H_1: p < 0.2$

4) Let X = the number of employees in the sample who are in favour of change.

5) Under H_0, $X \sim B(30, 0.2)$.

   The sampling distribution of the test statistic uses the value $p = 0.2$.

6) The **significance level** is 5%, so $\alpha = 0.05$.

7) Find the p-value — the probability of a value for your **test statistic at least as extreme** as the **observed value**. This is a **one-tailed test** and you're interested in the lower end of the distribution. So you want to find the probability of X taking a value less than or equal to 2.
   Using the binomial cdf on your calculator:
   $$P(X \leq 2) = 0.0441..., \text{ and since } 0.0441... < 0.05, \text{ the result is significant.}$$

8) Now write your **conclusion**: **There is evidence at the 5% level of significance to reject H_0 and to support the manager's claim that the proportion in favour of change has decreased.**

Always say "there is evidence to reject H_0", or "there is insufficient evidence to reject H_0", never just "accept H_0" or "reject H_1".

To find a **critical region**, your test would look the same except for step 7...

7) Find the **critical region** for a test at this level of significance. This is a **one-tailed test** and you're interested in the lower end of the distribution. The critical region is the biggest possible set of 'low' values of X with a total probability of ≤ 0.05.

   Using the binomial cdf on your calculator:
   Try $X \leq 2$: $P(X \leq 2) = 0.0441... < 0.05$. Now try $X \leq 3$: $P(X \leq 3) = 0.1227... > 0.05$.
   So **CR is $X \leq 2$**. These results fall in the CR, so the result is **significant**.

Marjorie and Edwin were ready to enter the critical region.

Hypothesis Tests and Binomial Distributions

You might be asked to find a *Critical Region* or *Actual Significance Level*

Example: Records show that the proportion of trees in a wood that suffer from a particular leaf disease is 15%. Chloe thinks that recent weather conditions might have affected this proportion. She examines a random sample of 20 of the trees. $X \sim B(20, 0.15) - H_0$

a) Using a 10% level of significance, find the critical region for a two-tailed test of Chloe's theory. The probability of rejection in each tail should be less than 0.05.

b) Find the actual significance level of a test based on your critical region from part a).

Chloe finds that 8 of the sampled trees have the leaf disease.

c) Comment on this finding in relation to your answer to part a) and Chloe's theory.

a) Let p = proportion of trees with the leaf disease.

$H_0: p = 0.15$ $H_1: p \neq 0.15$

Let X = number of sampled trees with the disease. Under H_0, $X \sim B(20, 0.15)$.

$\alpha = 0.1$, and since the test is **two-tailed**, the probability of X falling in each tail should be 0.05, at most.
This is a two-tailed test, so you're interested in both ends of the sampling distribution.
The lower tail is the biggest possible set of 'low' values of X with a total probability of ≤ 0.05.
The upper tail is the biggest possible set of 'high' values of X with a total probability of ≤ 0.05.

Using a calculator: **Lower tail:**   **Upper tail:**
$P(X \leq 0) = 0.0387... < 0.05$ $P(X \geq 6) = 1 - P(X \leq 5) = 1 - 0.9326... = 0.0673... > 0.05$
$P(X \leq 1) = 0.1755... > 0.05$ $P(X \geq 7) = 1 - P(X \leq 6) = 1 - 0.9780... = 0.0219... < 0.05$

So **CR is $X = 0$ or $X \geq 7$.**

b) The **actual significance level** is: $P(X = 0) + P(X \geq 7) = 0.0387... + 0.0219... = \mathbf{0.0607}$ or **6.07%** (3 s.f.)

c) The observed value of **8** is in the critical region. **So there is evidence at the 10% level of significance to reject H_0 and to support Chloe's theory that there has been a change in the proportion of affected trees.**

Practice Questions

Q1 Carry out the following tests of the binomial parameter p.
Let X represent the number of successes in a random sample of size 20:

a) Test $H_0: p = 0.2$ against $H_1: p \neq 0.2$, at the 5% significance level, using $x = 1$.

b) Test $H_0: p = 0.4$ against $H_1: p > 0.4$, at the 1% significance level, using $x = 15$.

Q2 Find the critical region for the following test where $X \sim B(10, p)$:
Test $H_0: p = 0.3$ against $H_1: p < 0.3$, at the 5% significance level.

Exam Question

Q1 Over a long period of time, the chef at an Italian restaurant has found that there is a probability of 0.2 that a customer ordering a dessert on a weekday evening will order tiramisu. He thinks that the proportion of customers ordering desserts on Saturday evenings who order tiramisu is greater than 0.2.

a) State the name of the probability distribution that would be used in a hypothesis test for the value of p, the proportion of Saturday evening dessert eaters ordering tiramisu. [1 mark]

A random sample of 20 customers who ordered a dessert on a Saturday evening was taken.
7 of these customers ordered tiramisu.

b) (i) Stating your hypotheses clearly, test the chef's theory at the 5% level of significance. [6 marks]

(ii) Find the minimum number of tiramisu orders needed for the result to be significant. [1 mark]

My hypothesis is — this is very likely to come up in the exam...

Remember, to make sure that you're not using the binomial pdf by accident (if your calculator has one). Of course, you can use the pdf if you need to find the probability of a single value, as long as you're doing it for the right reasons.

Hypothesis Tests and Normal Distributions

If you like normal distributions and you like hypothesis testing, you're going to love this page.
If you need a reminder of the normal distribution, have a look back at Section 13.

Use a **Hypothesis Test** to **Find Out** about the **Population Mean, μ**

You can carry out hypothesis testing on the **mean** of a **normal distribution** too. Suppose $X \sim N(\mu, \sigma^2)$.
If you take a random sample of n observations from the distribution of X, and calculate the **sample mean** $\overline{X}$,
you can use your **observed value $\overline{x}$** to test theories about the **population mean μ** using the following method:

1) The **population parameter** you're testing will always be μ, the mean of the population.

2) The **null** hypothesis will be: H_0: $\mu = a$ for some constant a.

3) The **alternative** hypothesis, H_1, will either be H_1: $\mu < a$ or H_1: $\mu > a$ (one-tailed test)
   or H_1: $\mu \neq a$ (two-tailed test)

4) State the **significance level**, α — you'll usually be given this.

5) To find the value of the **test statistic**:
   — Calculate the **sample mean** $\overline{x}$.
   This is in the formula booklet.
   — If $X \sim N(\mu, \sigma^2)$, then $\overline{X} \sim N\left(\mu, \dfrac{\sigma^2}{n}\right) \Rightarrow Z = \dfrac{\overline{X} - \mu}{\sigma/\sqrt{n}} \sim N(0, 1)$.
   number of observations
   — Then the value of your **test statistic** will be $z = \dfrac{\overline{x} - \mu}{\sigma/\sqrt{n}}$.

6) Use a **calculator** to test for significance, either by:
   — finding the **probability** of your test statistic taking a value **at least as extreme** as your
   observed value (the *p*-value) and comparing it to the significance level α.
   — finding the **critical value**(s) of the test statistic and seeing if your observed value lies in
   the **critical region**.

7) Write your **conclusion** — you'll either **reject H_0** or have **insufficient evidence** to do so.

Example: The times, in minutes, taken by the athletes in a running club to complete a certain run
have been found to follow a N(12, 4) distribution. The coach increases the number of
training sessions per week, and a random sample of 20 times run since the increase gives
a mean time of 11.2 minutes. Assuming that the variance has remained unchanged, test
at the 5% significance level whether there is evidence that the mean time has decreased.

Let μ = mean time since increase in training sessions. Then H_0: $\mu = 12$, H_1: $\mu < 12$, $\alpha = 0.05$.
   *You assume that there's been **no change** in the value of*   *This is what you're looking*
   the parameter (μ), so you can give it a value of 12.   *to find evidence for.*

Under H_0, $\overline{X} \sim N\left(12, \dfrac{4}{20}\right) \Rightarrow \overline{X} \sim N(12, 0.2)$ and $Z = \dfrac{\overline{X} - 12}{\sqrt{0.2}} \sim N(0, 1)$.

$$\overline{x} = 11.2 \Rightarrow z = \frac{11.2 - 12}{\sqrt{0.2}} = -1.789 \text{ (3 d.p.)}$$

This is a **one-tailed test** and you're interested in the lower
end of the distribution. So the **critical value** is z such that
$P(Z < z) = 0.05$. Using your calculator, you find that
$P(Z < -1.6448...) = 0.05$. So the critical value is $-1.6448...$
and the **critical region is $Z < -1.645$** (3 d.p.).

If you want, you can instead do the test by working out
the p-value, P(value at least as extreme as observed
sample mean), and comparing it to α. So here you'd do:
$P(\overline{X} \leq 11.2) = P\left(Z \leq \dfrac{11.2 - 12}{\sqrt{0.2}}\right) = P(Z \leq -1.7888...)$
$= 0.03681... < 0.05$, so reject H_0.

Since $z = -1.789 < -1.645$, the **result is significant** and there is **evidence** at the
5% level of significance to **reject H_0** and to suggest that the **mean time has decreased**.

Hypothesis Tests and Normal Distributions

For a **Two-Tailed Test**, divide α by 2

Example: The volume (in ml) of a cleaning fluid dispensed in each operation by a machine is normally distributed with mean μ and standard deviation 3.
Out of a random sample of 20 measured volumes, the mean volume dispensed was 30.9 ml.
Does this data provide evidence at the 1% level of significance that the machine is dispensing a mean volume that is different from 30 ml?

Let μ = mean volume (in ml) dispensed in all possible operations of the machine (i.e. μ is the mean volume of the 'population').

Your hypotheses will be: $\mathbf{H_0}$: $\mu = 30$ and $\mathbf{H_1}$: $\mu \neq 30$

The **significance level** is 1%, so $\alpha = 0.01$.

Now find the value of your test statistic:

$\bar{x} = 30.9$, so $z = \dfrac{\bar{x} - \mu}{\sigma/\sqrt{n}} = \dfrac{30.9 - 30}{3/\sqrt{20}} = \mathbf{1.3416...}$

This is a **two-tailed** test, so you need to check whether the p-value is less than $\frac{\alpha}{2} = 0.005$.

$P(Z \geq 1.3416...) = \mathbf{0.0898...} > \frac{\alpha}{2}$

So the result is **not significant** at this level.

This data does **not** provide sufficient evidence at the 1% level to support the claim that the machine is dispensing a mean volume different from 30 ml.

Under H_0, $X \sim N(30, 3^2)$, so $\bar{X} \sim N\left(30, \frac{3^2}{20}\right)$.

So under H_0, $Z = \dfrac{\bar{X} - 30}{3/\sqrt{20}} \sim N(0, 1)$.

You could work out the critical region instead — it's a two-tailed test, so the CR is given by $P(Z > z) = \frac{\alpha}{2} = 0.005$ or $P(Z < -z) = \frac{\alpha}{2} = 0.005$.
Using your calculator, this gives a value for z of 2.575... So the critical region is $Z > 2.575...$ or $Z < -2.575...$
Since $z = 1.3416... < 2.575...$ (and $> -2.575...$), there is insufficient evidence at the 1% level to reject H_0.

Practice Questions

Q1 Carry out the following test of the mean, μ, of a normal distribution with variance $\sigma^2 = 9$.

A random sample of 16 observations from the distribution was taken and the sample mean ($\bar{x}$) calculated. Test H_0: $\mu = 45$ against H_1: $\mu < 45$, at the 5% significance level, using $\bar{x} = 42$.

Q2 A random sample of 10 observations is taken from a normal distribution with unknown mean μ and variance $\sigma^2 = 0.81$. The results are shown below.

20.1, 18.5, 19.6, 21.1, 20.7, 20.2, 19.5, 19.7, 20.2, 18.2

a) Calculate the value of the sample mean.

b) Carry out a hypothesis test, at the 5% level of significance, of the hypotheses H_0: $\mu = 20$, H_1: $\mu < 20$.

Exam Question

Q1 The heights of trees in an area of woodland are known to be normally distributed with a mean of 5.1 m and a variance of 0.2. A random sample of 100 trees from a second area of woodland is selected and the heights, X, of the trees are measured giving the following result:

$\sum x = 490$

a) Calculate the sample mean, $\bar{x}$, for the trees in this second area. [1 mark]

b) Test at the 1% level of significance whether the trees in the second area of woodland have a different mean height from the trees in the first area. [6 marks]

A statistician's party game — pin two tails on the donkey...

You can usually use either method to answer these questions (unless you're told which one to use — i.e. sometimes you might be asked to find the critical region). I personally prefer finding the p-value — it's a bit less work when you're doing a two-tailed test — but it's entirely up to you. Whatever floats your statistically significant boat, really.

Correlation

There's a fair bit of fancy stats-speak in this section. Correlation is all about how closely two quantities are linked and linear regression is just a way to find the line of best fit. Not so scary now, eh...

Draw a **Scatter Diagram** to see **Patterns** in **Data**

1) Sometimes variables are measured in **pairs** — maybe because you want to find out **how closely** they're **linked**. Data made up of pairs of values (x, y) is known as **bivariate data** and can be plotted on a **scatter diagram**.

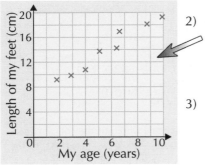

2) The variables 'my age' and 'length of my feet' seem linked — all the points lie **close** to a **line**. As I got older, my feet got bigger and bigger (though I stopped measuring when I was 10).

3) It's a lot harder to see any connection between the variables 'temperature' and 'number of accidents' — the data seems **scattered** pretty much everywhere.

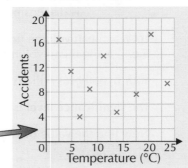

Correlation is a measure of **How Closely** variables are **Linked**

1) If, as one variable gets **bigger**, the other one also gets **bigger**, the scatter diagram might look like the age/length of feet graph above. The line of best fit would have a **positive gradient**. The two variables are **positively correlated** (or there's a positive correlation **between** them).

2) If one variable gets **smaller** as the other one gets **bigger**, then the scatter diagram might look like this one and the line of best fit would have a **negative gradient**. The two variables are **negatively correlated** (or there's a negative correlation **between** them). The circled point is an **outlier** — a point that doesn't fit the pattern of the rest of the data. Outliers can usually be **ignored** when drawing the line of best fit or describing the correlation — they can be **measurement errors** or just '**freak**' observations.

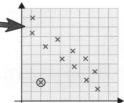

3) If the two variables **aren't** linked at all, you'd expect a **random** scattering of points (like in the temperature/accidents graph above). The variables **aren't correlated** (or there's **no correlation**).

4) Watch out for graphs that show distinct sections of the population like this one — the data will be in **separate clusters**. Here, you can describe both the **overall correlation** and the correlation in **each cluster** — so on this graph, there appears to be **negative correlation** overall, but **no correlation** within each cluster. Different clusters can also be shown on **separate graphs**, with each graph representing a different section of the population.

5) Correlation can also be described as '**strong**' or '**weak**'. The **stronger** the correlation is, the closer the points on the scatter diagram are to being in a **straight line**.

BUT you have to be **careful** when writing about two variables that are correlated — changes in one variable might **not cause** changes in the other. They could be linked by a **third factor**, or it could just be **coincidence**. The formal way of saying this is '**correlation** does not imply **causation**'.

Decide which is the **Explanatory Variable** and which is the **Response**

The variable along the **x-axis** is the **explanatory** (or **independent**) variable
— it's the variable you can **control**, or the one that is **affecting** the other.

The variable up the **y-axis** is the **response** (or **dependent**) variable — it's the variable you think is **being affected**.

Example: Tasha wants to plot a scatter diagram to show the variables 'load on a lorry' (in tonnes) and 'fuel efficiency' (in km per litre). Identify the response variable and the explanatory variable.

Changing the load on a lorry would lead to a change in the fuel efficiency (e.g. heavier loads would use more fuel). So **fuel efficiency** is the **response** variable and **load on the lorry** is the **explanatory** variable. ◄ *So Tasha should plot load on the x-axis and fuel efficiency on the y-axis.*

Correlation

The **Regression Line** (line of best fit) is in the form **y = a + bx**

The **regression line of y on x** (x is the explanatory variable and y is the response variable) is a **straight line** of the form:

$$y = a + bx, \text{ where a} = y\text{-intercept and b} = \text{gradient}$$

You need to be able to **interpret** the values of a and b.

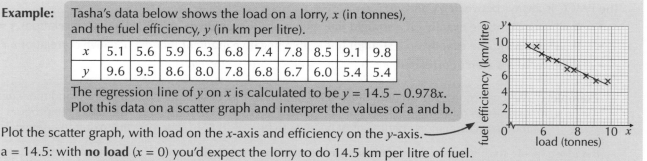

Example: Tasha's data below shows the load on a lorry, x (in tonnes), and the fuel efficiency, y (in km per litre).

x	5.1	5.6	5.9	6.3	6.8	7.4	7.8	8.5	9.1	9.8
y	9.6	9.5	8.6	8.0	7.8	6.8	6.7	6.0	5.4	5.4

The regression line of y on x is calculated to be $y = 14.5 - 0.978x$.
Plot this data on a scatter graph and interpret the values of a and b.

Plot the scatter graph, with load on the x-axis and efficiency on the y-axis.

a = 14.5: with **no load** ($x = 0$) you'd expect the lorry to do 14.5 km per litre of fuel.

b = –0.978: for every **extra** tonne carried, you'd expect the lorry's fuel efficiency to **fall** by 0.978 km per litre.

Use regression lines **With Care**

You can use your regression line to **predict** values of the **response variable**. There are two types of this.

Interpolation — use values of x **within** the data range (e.g. between 5.1 and 9.8 for the lorry example).
It's okay to do this — the predicted value should be **reliable**.

Extrapolation — use values of x **outside** the data range (e.g. outside 5.1 and 9.8 for the lorry example).
These predictions can be **unreliable**, so you need to be very cautious about them.

Example (continued): Estimate the fuel efficiency when the load is 12 tonnes. Give a reason why your estimate might be unreliable.

Use $x = 12$ in the regression line: $y = 14.5 - 0.978 \times 12 = \textbf{2.764}$

$x = 12$ is outside the data range (5.1 to 9.8) —
this is an **extrapolation** so the estimate may be unreliable.

Professor Snuffles had a fuel efficiency
of 1.5 km per doggie biscuit.

Practice Questions

Q1 Describe the correlation shown on the graphs to the right:

a)   b)   c)

Q2 Khalid wants to plot a scatter graph for the variables
'barbecue sales' (thousands) and 'amount of sunshine' (hours).
Identify the response variable and the explanatory variable.

Exam Question

Q1 The following times (in seconds) were taken by eight different runners to complete distances of 20 m and 60 m.

Runner	A	B	C	D	E	F	G	H
20-metre time (x)	3.39	3.20	3.09	3.32	3.33	3.27	3.44	3.08
60-metre time (y)	8.78	7.73	8.28	8.25	8.91	8.59	8.90	8.05

a) Plot a scatter diagram to represent the data. [2 marks]

b) Describe the correlation shown on your graph. [1 mark]

c) The equation of the regression line is calculated to be $y = 2.4x + 0.7$. Plot it on your scatter diagram. [1 mark]

d) Use the equation of the regression line to estimate the time it takes to run a distance of 60 m,
when the time taken to run 20 m is: (i) 3.15 s, (ii) 3.88 s. Comment on the reliability of your estimates. [2 marks]

What's a statistician's favourite soap — Correlation Street...

Watch out for those outliers — you might need to think about why there's an outlier. Sometimes it can only be down to some sort of error, but in others there could be a realistic reason why a data point might not fit the general trend.

The Product Moment Correlation Coefficient

Correlation coefficients measure how strongly two variables are linked. For this course you only need to know about the product moment correlation coefficient — and that's only so you can do a hypothesis test on it.

The **Product Moment Correlation Coefficient** *measures correlation*

The **Product Moment Correlation Coefficient** (**PMCC**, or *r*, for short) measures the **strength** of linear correlation between two variables — i.e. how close to a **straight line** the points on a scatter diagram lie.

The PMCC is always between +1 and –1:

- If all your points lie **exactly** on a **straight line** with a **positive gradient** (perfect positive correlation), **$r = +1$**.
- If all your points lie **exactly** on a **straight line** with a **negative gradient** (perfect negative correlation), **$r = -1$**.
- If the variables **aren't correlated**, **$r = 0$** (or more likely, pretty close to 0).

Example: Marcus records the amount of exercise (in hours) that 30 people do in a month, and the length of time (in mins) it takes them to complete a lap of a cycle route. He calculates the product moment correlation coefficient of his data to be $r = -0.866$. Interpret this result in context.

r is close to –1, so this means the data has a **strong negative correlation**.

This shows that as one variable increases, the other decreases.

This suggests that the **more** hours of exercise a person does, the **less** time it takes them to cycle the route (i.e. they can cycle quicker).

— Use the context of the question.

Always say that the data 'suggests' a conclusion like this. It's based on a sample, so you can't say for sure that it proves anything about the population.

You need to be careful with your conclusion. There isn't enough information to conclude that one variable necessarily **causes** the change — there might be **another** factor that has an effect on **both** variables, such as age.

Example: For the following sets of data, explain why the PMCC given might be misleading.

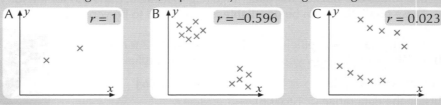

A: $r = 1$ B: $r = -0.596$ C: $r = 0.023$

In A, there are only **two data points**, so *r* would always be +1 or –1 (you can always draw a straight line between two points). This **doesn't** tell you anything about the relationship between the variables.

The scatter graph of B shows two **clusters** of data — there appears to be negative correlation overall, but none within the clusters. Similarly, C contains two data **clusters**, each with negative correlation, despite *r* suggesting virtually no correlation. Establishing what has caused the two clusters in each case and separating the data would lead to better conclusions.

PMCC Hypothesis Testing tests the value of *r*

To test whether your value of *r* is likely to mean that the two variables are **actually correlated**, you need to do a **hypothesis test**. The method used is like the hypothesis testing you did in Section 14, but with a few differences:

1) The **test statistic** is *r* (which is calculated from sample data for you).
2) The **population parameter** is the PMCC of the population, ρ (the Greek letter rho).
3) The **null hypothesis** is always that there is no correlation between the two variables — $H_0: \rho = 0$.
4) There are two kinds of **alternative hypothesis** — for a **one-tailed** test, $H_1: \rho > 0$ or $\rho < 0$
   for a **two-tailed** test, $H_1: \rho \neq 0$.

In a PMCC hypothesis testing question, you could be given a **table of critical values** and be expected to use the **sample size** and **significance level** to choose the right value. Or if the examiners are feeling kind they'll just give you the critical value instead.

The Product Moment Correlation Coefficient

Example: a) A teacher claims that test scores and hours spent revising are positively correlated. State the null and alternate hypotheses for a test of the teacher's claim.

Sample Size	Significance Level		
	0.10	0.05	0.025
4	0.8000	0.9000	0.9500
	⋮	⋮	⋮
9	0.4716	0.5822	0.6664
10	0.4428	0.5494	0.6319
11	0.4187	0.5214	0.6021

- The null hypothesis is that there is no correlation, so H_0: $\rho = 0$
- This is a **one-tailed** test, so the alternative hypothesis is H_1: $\rho > 0$

b) The teacher samples 10 students and finds that the PMCC is 0.76. Using the table of critical values provided, carry out a hypothesis test at the 5% significance level to investigate whether this result is significant.

A table or critical value will be given in the exam if needed.

- Test for significance using the significance level column $\alpha = 0.05$ and the sample size row 10:

  Using the table provided, the critical value is **0.5494**, so you would **reject H_0** if $r \geq 0.5494$. Since 0.76 > 0.5494 the result is **significant**.

- Write your conclusion — you either reject the null hypothesis H_0 or have insufficient evidence to do so:
  There is evidence at the 5% level of significance to reject H_0 and to support the alternative hypothesis that test scores and hours spent revising are positively correlated.

For more on hypothesis testing, look at pages 176-177.

Practice Questions

1 Interpret the following values of r and match each one to the most suitable set of data:
   a) $r = -0.912$ b) $r = 0.431$ c) $r = -0.041$

A

B

C

2 A shop owner records the number of pairs of sunglasses and ice creams that are sold each day in his shop, over one year. The product moment correlation coefficient is calculated to be $r = 0.786$.
   a) Interpret the value of r in context.
   b) The shop owner says 'if there's positive correlation, then that means high sunglasses sales cause high ice cream sales'. Comment on the shop owner's claim.

Exam Questions

Q1 The age of 50 adults and their time taken to do a times table test are measured. The product moment correlation coefficient is calculated to be $r = -0.24$. Stating your hypotheses clearly, carry out a hypothesis test, at the 2.5% significance level, to investigate whether the evidence suggests that age and time taken to do the test are negatively correlated, given that the critical value for such a test is -0.2787. **[2 marks]**

Q2 The diameter and the weight of 8 randomly selected biscuits are measured and the product moment correlation coefficient is calculated to be $r = 0.958$.

Sample Size	Significance Level		
	0.025	0.01	0.005
4	0.9500	0.9800	0.9900
	⋮	⋮	⋮
7	0.7545	0.8329	0.8745
8	0.7067	0.7887	0.8343
9	0.6664	0.7498	0.7977

   a) Using the table of critical values provided, find the critical region for a test at the 0.5% significance level of whether the diameter and weight of the biscuits are positively correlated. State your hypotheses clearly. **[2 marks]**
   b) Comment on the significance of r at the 0.5% significance level. **[1 mark]**

It's fun to study the P.M.C.C...

You only need to be able to interpret the value of r (not find it) — remember numbers close to +1 or −1 suggest strong positive or negative correlation (respectively) and numbers close to 0 mean no correlation. This is also a good time to check that you're comfortable with the theory behind hypothesis testing — if not, flick back to Section 14 and rejoice.

Constant Acceleration Equations

Welcome to the technicolour world of kinematics. Fashions may change, but there will always be questions that involve objects travelling in a straight line. It's just a case of picking the right equations to solve the problem.

There are **Five Constant Acceleration Equations**

These are also called "**suvat**" questions because of the five variables involved:

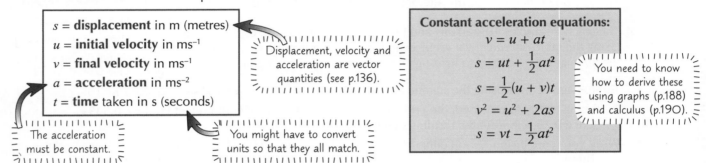

s = **displacement** in m (metres)
u = **initial velocity** in ms⁻¹
v = **final velocity** in ms⁻¹
a = **acceleration** in ms⁻²
t = **time** taken in s (seconds)

Displacement, velocity and acceleration are vector quantities (see p.136).

The acceleration must be constant.

You might have to convert units so that they all match.

Constant acceleration equations:
$$v = u + at$$
$$s = ut + \frac{1}{2}at^2$$
$$s = \frac{1}{2}(u + v)t$$
$$v^2 = u^2 + 2as$$
$$s = vt - \frac{1}{2}at^2$$

You need to know how to derive these using graphs (p.188) and calculus (p.190).

These equations are in the formula booklet, but you still need to be comfortable using them. Questions might give you **three variables** — your job is to **choose** the equation that will find you an unknown **fourth variable**.

Constant acceleration questions often have the following **modelling assumptions** (see p.218 for more on modelling):

1) **The object is a particle** — its dimensions can be ignored and no other forces (e.g. air resistance) act on it.

2) **Acceleration is constant** — so you can use the suvat equations.

Example: A jet ski travels in a straight line along a river. It passes under two bridges 200 m apart and is observed to be travelling at 5 ms⁻¹ under the first bridge and at 9 ms⁻¹ under the second bridge. Calculate its acceleration (assuming it is constant).

List the variables:

$s = 200$
$u = 5$
$v = 9$
$a = a$
$t = t$

You have to work out a.

You're not told about the time taken.

Choose the equation with s, u, v and a in it: $v^2 = u^2 + 2as$

Here the units all match — m, s, ms⁻¹ and ms⁻².

Substitute values: $9^2 = 5^2 + (2 \times a \times 200)$
Simplify: $81 = 25 + 400a$
Rearrange: $400a = 81 - 25 = 56$
Then solve: $a = \frac{56}{400} = \mathbf{0.14}$ **ms⁻²**

Motion under Gravity just means taking a = g

Assume that $g = 9.8$ ms⁻² unless the exam paper says otherwise. If you don't, you risk losing a mark for accuracy.

Don't be put off by questions involving objects **moving freely under gravity** — they're just telling you the **acceleration is g**.

If the question gives a mass or weight, then it's a **forces** question — see Section 17.

Example: A pebble is dropped into a hole 18 m deep and moves freely under gravity until it hits the bottom. Calculate the time it takes to reach the bottom. (Take $g = 9.8$ ms⁻².)

List the variables:

$s = 18$
$u = 0$
$v = v$
$a = 9.8$
$t = t$

Because the pebble was dropped, not thrown.

$a = g = 9.8$ ms⁻², because it's falling freely.

Choose the equation with s, u, a and t in it: $s = ut + \frac{1}{2}at^2$

Substitute values: $18 = (0 \times t) + \left(\frac{1}{2} \times 9.8 \times t^2\right)$
Simplify: $18 = 4.9t^2$
Rearrange to give t²: $t^2 = \frac{18}{4.9} = 3.67...$
Take the square root: $t = \sqrt{3.67...} = \mathbf{1.92}$ **s** (3 s.f.)

Time is always positive, so ignore the negative square root.

When an object is projected vertically **upwards**, it helps to choose **up** as the **positive direction**. Gravity always acts **downwards**, so you'd need to use $a = -g$.

At the object's **maximum height**, $v = 0$ — its vertical velocity is momentarily zero before it starts falling again.

Constant Acceleration Equations

Sometimes there's **More Than One Object Moving** at the **Same Time**

For these questions, t is often the same (or connected as in this example) because time ticks along at the same rate for both objects. The distance travelled might also be connected.

> **Example:** Car A travels along a straight road at a constant velocity of 30 ms⁻¹, passing point R at time $t = 0$. Exactly 2 seconds later, a second car, B, travelling at 25 ms⁻¹, moves in the same direction from point R. Car B accelerates at a constant 2 ms⁻². Show that, when the two cars are level, $t^2 - 9t - 46 = 0$.

For each car, there are different *"suvat"* variables, so write separate lists and separate equations.

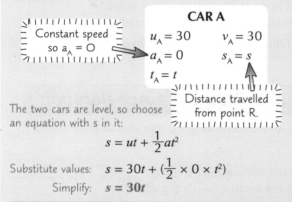

CAR A

Constant speed so $a_A = 0$

$u_A = 30$ $v_A = 30$

$a_A = 0$ $s_A = s$

$t_A = t$

Distance travelled from point R.

The two cars are level, so choose an equation with s in it:

$$s = ut + \frac{1}{2}at^2$$

Substitute values: $s = 30t + \left(\frac{1}{2} \times 0 \times t^2\right)$

Simplify: $s = 30t$

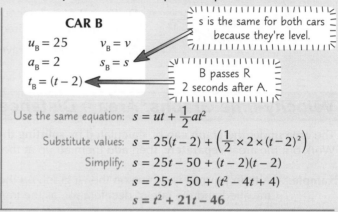

CAR B

$u_B = 25$ $v_B = v$

$a_B = 2$ $s_B = s$

$t_B = (t - 2)$

s is the same for both cars because they're level.

B passes R 2 seconds after A.

Use the same equation: $s = ut + \frac{1}{2}at^2$

Substitute values: $s = 25(t-2) + \left(\frac{1}{2} \times 2 \times (t-2)^2\right)$

Simplify: $s = 25t - 50 + (t-2)(t-2)$

$s = 25t - 50 + (t^2 - 4t + 4)$

$s = t^2 + 21t - 46$

The distance travelled by both cars is equal, so put the equations for s equal to each other and rearrange:

$30t = t^2 + 21t - 46$

$t^2 - 9t - 46 = 0$, as required

Practice Questions

Take $g = 9.8$ ms⁻² in each of these questions.

Q1 A motorcyclist accelerates uniformly from 3 ms⁻¹ to 9 ms⁻¹ in 2 seconds. What is the distance travelled by the motorcyclist during this acceleration?

Q2 A stone is projected vertically upwards at 7 ms⁻¹ from the ground. How long does it take to reach its maximum height?

Q3 A ball is projected vertically upwards at 3 ms⁻¹ from a point 1.5 m above the ground. How fast will the ball be travelling when it hits the ground?

"Model me as a falling particlllllllleeee..."

Exam Questions

Q1 A window cleaner of a block of flats accidentally drops his sandwich, which falls freely to the ground. The speed of the sandwich as it passes a high floor is u ms⁻¹. After a further 1.2 seconds the sandwich is moving at a speed of 17 ms⁻¹ past a lower floor.

a) Find the value of u.   [3 marks]

b) The vertical distance between the consecutive floors of the building is h m. It takes the sandwich another 2.1 seconds to fall the remaining 14 floors to the ground. Find h.   [4 marks]

Q2 A rocket is projected vertically upwards from a point 8 m above the ground at a speed of u ms⁻¹ and travels freely under gravity. The rocket hits the ground at 20 ms⁻¹. Find:

a) the value of u,   [3 marks]

b) how long it takes to hit the ground.   [3 marks]

Newton was one of the first people to realise that gravity sucks...

Make sure you: 1) make a list of the suvat variables EVERY time you get one of these questions,
2) look out for "hidden" values — e.g. "initially at rest..." means $u = 0$,
3) choose and solve the equation that goes with the variables you've got.

Motion Graphs

You can use displacement-time (x/t), and velocity-time (v/t) graphs to represent all sorts of motion.

Displacement-time Graphs: Height = Distance and Gradient = Velocity

The **steeper** the line, the **greater** the velocity. A **horizontal** line has a **zero gradient**, so the object **isn't moving**.

Example: A rabbit's journey is shown on this x/t graph. Describe the motion.

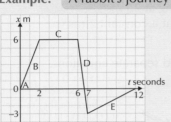

A: Starts from rest (when $t = 0$, $x = 0$).

B: Travels 6 m in 2 seconds at a velocity of $6 \div 2 = 3$ ms^{-1}.

C: Rests for 4 seconds ($v = 0$).

D: Runs 9 m in 1 second at a velocity of $-9 \div 1 = -9$ ms^{-1} in the opposite direction, passing the starting point.

Velocity is a vector quantity, so the direction needs to be included.

E: Returns to start, travelling 3 m in 5 seconds at a velocity of $3 \div 5 = 0.6$ ms^{-1}.

Velocity-time Graphs: Area = Distance and Gradient = Acceleration

The **area** under the graph can be calculated by **splitting** the area into rectangles, triangles or trapeziums. Work out the areas **separately**, then **add** them all up at the end.

Example: A train journey is shown on the v/t graph on the right. Find the distance travelled and the rate of deceleration as the train comes to a stop.

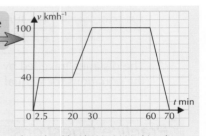

The time is given in minutes and the velocity as kilometres per hour, so divide the time in minutes by 60 to get the time in hours.

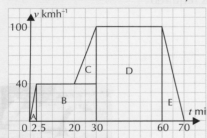

Area of A: $(2.5 \div 60 \times 40) \div 2 = 0.833...$

Area of B: $27.5 \div 60 \times 40 = 18.33...$

Area of C: $(10 \div 60 \times 60) \div 2 = 5$

Area of D: $30 \div 60 \times 100 = 50$

Area of E: $(10 \div 60 \times 100) \div 2 = 8.33...$

Total area = 82.5 so distance is **82.5 km**

You might get a speed-time graph instead of a velocity-time graph — they're pretty much the same, except speeds are always positive, whereas velocities can be negative.

Gradient at the end of the journey: -100 kmh^{-1} $\div$ $(10 \div 60)$ hours $= -600$ kmh^{-2}. So the train decelerates at **600 kmh^{-2}**.

Derive the suvat equations with a Velocity-time Graph

You met the **suvat equations** on p.186 — now it's time to see where they come from. Using a **velocity-time graph** you can derive the equations $v = u + at$ and $s = \frac{1}{2}(u + v)t$, then **use** these to derive the other equations.

Example: The graph shows a particle accelerating uniformly from initial velocity u to final velocity v in t s.

a) Use the graph to derive the equations: (i) $v = u + at$ (ii) $s = \frac{1}{2}(u + v)t$

b) Hence, show that $s = ut + \frac{1}{2}at^2$.

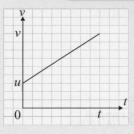

a) (i) It's a v/t graph, so the **gradient** represents the **acceleration**, a.
The graph is a **straight line**, crossing the y-axis at u,
so using '$y = mx + c$', the equation of the line is $v = u + at$.

(ii) The **area** under a v/t graph represents the **displacement**, s.
Here the area is a trapezium, so just use the formula for area of a trapezium: $s = \frac{1}{2}(u + v)t$

b) Substitute $v = u + at$ into $s = \frac{1}{2}(u + v)t$:
$s = \frac{1}{2}(u + u + at)t = \frac{1}{2}(2u + at)t \Rightarrow s = ut + \frac{1}{2}at^2$

You can derive the other suvat equations in a similar way, or by using calculus — see p.190.

Motion Graphs

Graphs can be used to **Solve Complicated Problems**

Some more complicated problems might involve working out information **not shown directly on the graph**.

> **Example:** A jogger and a cyclist set off at the same time. The jogger runs with a constant velocity. The cyclist accelerates from rest, reaching a velocity of 5 ms⁻¹ after 6 s, and then continues at this velocity. The cyclist overtakes the jogger after 15 s. Use the graph below to find the velocity, u, of the jogger.

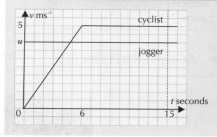

After 15 s, the distance each has travelled is the same, so you can work out the area under the two graphs to get the distances:

Jogger: distance = area = $15u$

Cyclist: distance = area = $\left(\frac{1}{2} \times 6 \times 5\right) + (9 \times 5) = 60$

So $15u = 60 \Rightarrow u = 4$ **ms⁻¹**

Practice Questions

Q1 Part of an athlete's training drill is shown on the x/t graph to the right.

   a) Describe the athlete's motion during the drill.

   b) State the velocity of the athlete at $t = 4$.

   c) Find the distance travelled by the athlete during the drill.

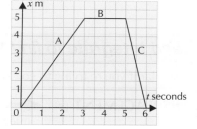

Q2 A runner starts from rest and accelerates at 0.5 ms⁻² for 5 seconds. She maintains a constant velocity for 20 seconds then decelerates to a stop at 0.25 ms⁻². Find the total distance the runner travelled.

Q3 Using $v = u + at$, and $s = \frac{1}{2}(u + v)t$, show that:

   a) $s = vt - \frac{1}{2}at^2$

   b) $v^2 = u^2 + 2as$

Exam Questions

Q1 A train journey from station A to station B is shown on the graph on the right. The total distance between stations A and B is 2.1 km.

   a) Find the value of V.   [3 marks]

   b) Calculate the distance travelled by the train while decelerating.   [2 marks]

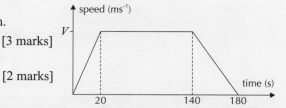

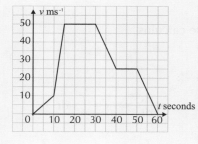

Q2 The velocity-time graph of a moving carriage on a roller coaster ride is shown on the left, where v ms⁻¹ is the velocity of the carriage.

   a) Calculate the acceleration of the carriage at $t = 12$ s.   [2 marks]

   b) Sean says that the carriage travels further in the first 30 seconds of its journey than the second 30 seconds. Is Sean's statement correct? Provide evidence to support your answer.   [4 marks]

   c) After T seconds, the carriage has travelled 700 m. Find the value of T.   [3 marks]

Random tongue-twister #1 — I wish to wash my Irish wristwatch...

If a picture is worth a thousand words then a graph is worth... um... a thousand and one. Make sure you know the features of each type of graph and know what the gradient and the area under the graph tells you.

Using Calculus for Kinematics

*The suvat equations you saw on page 186 are just grand when you've got constant acceleration.
But when the acceleration varies with time, you need a few new tricks up your sleeve...*

Differentiate to find Velocity and Acceleration from Displacement...

If you've got a particle moving in a **straight line** with acceleration that **varies with time**, you need to use **calculus** to find equations to describe the motion — look back at Sections 7 and 8 for a reminder about calculus.

1) To find an equation for **velocity**, **differentiate** the equation for **displacement** with respect to time.

2) To find an equation for **acceleration**, **differentiate** the equation for **velocity** with respect to time or differentiate the equation for displacement with respect to time **twice**.

 DISPLACEMENT (s) $\xRightarrow{\text{Differentiate}}$ VELOCITY (v) $\xRightarrow{\text{Differentiate}}$ ACCELERATION (a)

Displacement is sometimes written as x instead of s.

Example: A particle moves in a straight line. At time t seconds, the velocity of the particle is v ms^{-1}, where $v = 7t + 5t^2$. Find an expression for the acceleration of the particle at time t.

Velocity is given as a function of time, so differentiate to find the acceleration:

$$v = 7t + 5t^2$$
$$a = \frac{dv}{dt} = (7 + 10t) \text{ ms}^{-2}$$

$\frac{d}{dx}x^n = nx^{n-1}$

Tour de Kinematiques — Velo City, France.

...and Integrate to find Velocity and Displacement from Acceleration

It's similar if you're trying to go "back the other way", except you **integrate** with respect to t rather than differentiate:

DISPLACEMENT (s) $\xleftarrow{\text{Integrate}}$ VELOCITY (v) $\xleftarrow{\text{Integrate}}$ ACCELERATION (a)

Integration

Example: A particle P sets off from O and moves in a straight line. At time t seconds, its velocity is v ms^{-1}, where $v = 12 - t^2$. At $t = 0$, displacement $s = 0$. Find the time taken for P to return to O.

Velocity is given as a function of t, so integrate to find the displacement:

$$s = \int v \, dt = 12t - \frac{t^3}{3} + C$$

$\int x^n \, dx = \frac{x^{n+1}}{n+1} + C$

Use the information given in the question to find the value of the constant:

$$0 = 12(0) - \frac{0^3}{3} + C \Rightarrow C = 0 \Rightarrow s = 12t - \frac{t^3}{3}$$

P is at O when $s = O$, so solve the equation for t:

$$12t - \frac{t^3}{3} = 0 \Rightarrow t(36 - t^2) = 0 \Rightarrow t = 0, 6, \text{ or } -6$$

−6 can't be an answer, as you can't have a negative time.

Time taken for P to return to O is **6 seconds**.

Derive the suvat Equations with Calculus

You've derived the suvat equations with a v/t graph (p.188) — now it's time to use calculus.

Example: Use calculus to derive $v = u + at$ and $s = ut + \frac{1}{2}at^2$.

Acceleration is the rate of change of velocity v with time t:
$$a = \frac{dv}{dt} \Rightarrow v = \int a \, dt$$

Carry out the integration (remember that **a** is a **constant**):
$$v = \int a \, dt = at + C$$

Use the initial conditions $v = u$ when $t = O$ to find C:
$$u = a(0) + C$$
$$\Rightarrow C = u$$
$$\text{So } v = u + at$$

Velocity is the rate of change of displacement s with time t:
$$v = \frac{ds}{dt} \Rightarrow s = \int v \, dt$$

Substitute $v = u + at$ and integrate:
$$s = \int (u + at) \, dt = ut + \frac{1}{2}at^2 + C$$

Use the initial conditions $s = O$ when $t = O$ to find C:
$$0 = u(0) + \frac{1}{2}a(0)^2 + C \Rightarrow C = 0$$
$$\text{So } s = ut + \frac{1}{2}at^2$$

Using Calculus for Kinematics

Differentiate to find Maximum / Minimum values

Stationary points are when the gradient is zero (see page 87) — you need to differentiate to find them.
To decide whether a stationary point is a **maximum** or a **minimum**, differentiate again.

Example: A particle sets off from the origin at $t = 0$ and moves in a straight line.
At time t seconds, the velocity of the particle is v ms^{-1}, where $v = 9t - 2t^2$.
Find the maximum velocity of the particle.

Differentiate v and put it equal to 0
to find any stationary points:

$$v = 9t - 2t^2$$

$$\frac{dv}{dt} = 9 - 4t$$

$$\frac{dv}{dt} = 0 \text{ when } t = \frac{9}{4} = 2.25 \text{ s}$$

If $\frac{d^2y}{dx^2} < 0$, then it's a maximum.

If $\frac{d^2y}{dx^2} > 0$, then it's a minimum.

Differentiate v again to decide whether
this is a maximum or minimum:

$$\frac{d^2v}{dt^2} = -4, \text{ so } t = 2.25 \text{ s is a } \textbf{maximum}.$$

Substitute $t = 2.25$ s into the expression for v:

$$v = 9(2.25) - 2(2.25^2) = 10.125 \text{ ms}^{-1}$$

So the maximum velocity is **10.125 ms^{-1}**.

Practice Questions

Q1 A particle moves along a straight line from the origin with velocity $v = 8t^2 - 2t$.
   a) Find the acceleration of the particle at time t.
   b) Find the displacement of the particle at time t.

Q2 A particle sets off from the origin at $t = 0$ s. Its displacement, in metres, at time t is $s = 6 \sin\left(\frac{1}{3}t\right)$.
   Find an expression for the acceleration of the particle at time t.

Q3 A particle is at rest at the origin at $t = 0$ s. It moves in a straight line with acceleration a ms^{-2},
   where $a = e^{\frac{1}{4}t}$. Find the displacement of the particle at time $t = 8$ s.

Exam Questions

Q1 A model train sets off from a station at time $t = 0$ s. It travels in a straight line, then returns to the station.
   At time t seconds, the distance, in metres, of the train from the station is $s = \frac{1}{100}(10t + 9t^2 - t^3)$, where $0 \leq t \leq 10$.
   a) Sketch the graph of s against t and hence explain the restriction $0 \leq t \leq 10$ s.   [3 marks]
   b) Find the maximum distance of the train from the station.   [5 marks]

Q2 A particle sets off from the origin O at $t = 0$ s and moves in a straight line.
   At time t seconds, the velocity of the particle is v ms^{-1}, where

$$v = \begin{cases} 9t - 3t^2 & 0 \leq t \leq 2 \text{ s} \\ \dfrac{24}{t^2} & t > 2 \text{ s} \end{cases}$$

   a) Find the maximum speed of the particle in the interval $0 \leq t \leq 2$ s.   [4 marks]
   b) Find the displacement of the particle from O at
      (i) $t = 2$ s   [3 marks]
      (ii) $t = 6$ s   [4 marks]

Calculus in kinematics — it's deriving me crazy...

*This is one of those times when calculus is useful (told you so). The stuff you saw in Sections 7 and 8 can be applied
to mechanics questions, so make sure you've really got calculus nailed. Then you've just got to remember that
DISPLACEMENT differentiates to VELOCITY differentiates to ACCELERATION (and integrate to go the other way).*

Describing 2D Motion Using Vectors

*I bet you'd forgotten about vectors written with **i** and **j**. Well, they're back. You can use them to write vectors such as displacement, velocity and acceleration in terms of their separate horizontal (**i**) and vertical (**j**) components.*

For particles travelling at Constant Velocity, s = vt

If a particle is travelling at a constant velocity vector, **v**, then its displacement vector, **s**, after time, *t*, can be found using **s** = **v***t*.

Example: At *t* = 0, a particle has position vector (6**i** + 8**j**) m relative to a fixed origin *O*. The particle is travelling at constant velocity (2**i** – 6**j**) ms^{-1}. Find its position vector at *t* = 4 s.

First find its displacement using **s** = **v***t*: **s** = 4(2**i** – 6**j**) = (8**i** – 24**j**) m

Then add this to its original position vector: — Add the **i** and **j** components separately.

(6**i** + 8**j**) + (8**i** – 24**j**) = (6 + 8)**i** + (8 – 24)**j** = **(14i – 16j) m**

You might need to use the Constant Acceleration Equations

If a particle is accelerating at a constant rate, you can use the **constant acceleration equations** from page 186.

Example: A particle, *P*, has position vector $\begin{pmatrix} 3 \\ 1 \end{pmatrix}$ m and velocity $\begin{pmatrix} 2 \\ -5 \end{pmatrix}$ ms^{-1} at *t* = 0.

Given that *P* accelerates at a rate of $\begin{pmatrix} -2 \\ 1 \end{pmatrix}$ ms^{-2}, find its position vector at *t* = 6 s.

Using $\mathbf{s} = \mathbf{u}t + \frac{1}{2}\mathbf{a}t^2$: $\mathbf{s} = 6\begin{pmatrix} 2 \\ -5 \end{pmatrix} + \frac{1}{2}(6^2)\begin{pmatrix} -2 \\ 1 \end{pmatrix} = \begin{pmatrix} 12 \\ -30 \end{pmatrix} + \begin{pmatrix} -36 \\ 18 \end{pmatrix} = \begin{pmatrix} -24 \\ -12 \end{pmatrix}$ m

So new position vector = $\begin{pmatrix} 3 \\ 1 \end{pmatrix} + \begin{pmatrix} -24 \\ -12 \end{pmatrix} = \begin{pmatrix} -21 \\ -11 \end{pmatrix}$ **m**

*s, u, v, and **a** are all vectors, but t is a scalar. Since vectors can't be squared, you can't use $v^2 = u^2 + 2as$.*

Example: Find the speed and direction of motion of a particle after 3 s if its initial velocity is (6**i** + 4**j**) ms^{-1} and acceleration is (0.3**i** + 0.5**j**) ms^{-2}.

Using **v** = **u** + **a***t*: **v** = (6**i** + 4**j**) + 3(0.3**i** + 0.5**j**)
= (6**i** + 4**j**) + (0.9**i** + 1.5**j**) = **(6.9i + 5.5j) ms^{-1}**

Speed = magnitude of **v** = $\sqrt{6.9^2 + 5.5^2}$ = **8.82 ms^{-1}** (3 s.f.)

Direction = $\tan^{-1}\left(\frac{5.5}{6.9}\right)$ = **38.6°** (1 d.p.)

*The direction of a **velocity vector** gives the **direction of motion** of the object, and the direction of its **acceleration vector** is the direction of the **resultant force** (see p.200).*

See p.138 for more on the direction of a vector.

For Non-Uniform Acceleration, Differentiate or Integrate the Vectors

When you've got a particle moving in **two dimensions** you can still use the relationships between displacement, velocity and acceleration (see page 190):

DISPLACEMENT (s) ⇄ **VELOCITY (v)** ⇄ **ACCELERATION (a)**
Differentiate / Integrate

This means that you'll have to differentiate and integrate **vectors** written in **i** and **j** notation. Luckily, doing this is as easy as squeezing lemons — just differentiate/integrate **each component** of the vector **separately**:

So, if **s** = *x***i** + *y***j** is a displacement vector, then:

Velocity, $\mathbf{v} = \frac{d\mathbf{s}}{dt} = \frac{dx}{dt}\mathbf{i} + \frac{dy}{dt}\mathbf{j}$

The shorthand for $\frac{d\mathbf{s}}{dt}$ is $\dot{\mathbf{s}}$ (the single dot means differentiate s once with respect to time)...

Acceleration, $\mathbf{a} = \frac{d\mathbf{v}}{dt} = \frac{d^2\mathbf{s}}{dt^2} = \frac{d^2x}{dt^2}\mathbf{i} + \frac{d^2y}{dt^2}\mathbf{j}$.

...and the shorthand for $\frac{d^2\mathbf{s}}{dt^2}$ is $\ddot{\mathbf{s}}$ (the double dots mean differentiate s twice with respect to time).

It's a similar thing for integration:

If **v** = *w***i** + *z***j** is a velocity vector, then displacement vector, $\mathbf{s} = \int \mathbf{v}\,dt = \int (w\mathbf{i} + z\mathbf{j})\,dt = \left[\int w\,dt\right]\mathbf{i} + \left[\int z\,dt\right]\mathbf{j}$

Describing 2D Motion Using Vectors

Differentiate and Integrate the vector components Separately

Example: A particle is moving on a horizontal plane so that at time t it has velocity $\mathbf{v}$ ms^{-1}, where
$$\mathbf{v} = (8 + 2t)\mathbf{i} + (t^3 - 6t)\mathbf{j}$$
At $t = 2$, the particle has a position vector of $(10\mathbf{i} + 3\mathbf{j})$ m with respect to a fixed origin O.
a) Find the acceleration of the particle at time t.
b) Show that the position of the particle relative to O when $t = 4$ is $(38\mathbf{i} + 27\mathbf{j})$.

a) To find the acceleration vector, differentiate each component of the velocity:
$$\mathbf{a} = \dot{\mathbf{v}} = \frac{d\mathbf{v}}{dt} = \frac{d}{dt}(8 + 2t)\mathbf{i} + \frac{d}{dt}(t^3 - 6t)\mathbf{j}$$
$$= 2\mathbf{i} + (3t^2 - 6)\mathbf{j}$$

b) First find an expression for $\mathbf{s}$ in terms of t by integrating $\mathbf{v}$:
$$\mathbf{s} = \int \mathbf{v}\, dt = \left[\int (8 + 2t)\, dt\right]\mathbf{i} + \left[\int (t^3 - 6t)\, dt\right]\mathbf{j}$$

You still need a constant of integration, but it will be a vector with $\mathbf{i}$ and $\mathbf{j}$ components.

$$= (8t + t^2)\mathbf{i} + \left(\frac{t^4}{4} - 3t^2\right)\mathbf{j} + \mathbf{C}$$

When $t = 2$, $\mathbf{s} = (10\mathbf{i} + 3\mathbf{j})$, so use this info to find the vector $\mathbf{C}$:
$$10\mathbf{i} + 3\mathbf{j} = 20\mathbf{i} - 8\mathbf{j} + \mathbf{C}$$
$$\Rightarrow \mathbf{C} = (10 - 20)\mathbf{i} + (3 - -8)\mathbf{j} = -10\mathbf{i} + 11\mathbf{j}$$

Collect $\mathbf{i}$ and $\mathbf{j}$ terms and add/subtract to simplify.

So $\mathbf{s} = (8t + t^2 - 10)\mathbf{i} + \left(\frac{t^4}{4} - 3t^2 + 11\right)\mathbf{j}$

When $t = 4$, $\mathbf{s} = (32 + 16 - 10)\mathbf{i} + (64 - 48 + 11)\mathbf{j} = \mathbf{38i + 27j}$ — as required.

Practice Questions

Q1 A particle is travelling at constant velocity $\begin{pmatrix} -3 \\ 2 \end{pmatrix}$ ms^{-1}. At $t = 0$, the particle has position vector $\begin{pmatrix} 12 \\ -7 \end{pmatrix}$ m
relative to a fixed origin O. Find its position vector at $t = 7$ s.

Q2 A particle has initial velocity $(7\mathbf{i} + 3\mathbf{j})$ ms^{-1} and acceleration $(0.1\mathbf{i} + 0.3\mathbf{j})$ ms^{-2}.
Find the speed and direction of the particle after 4 seconds.

Q3 A particle moving in a plane has displacement vector $\mathbf{s}$, where $\mathbf{s} = x\mathbf{i} + y\mathbf{j}$.
What quantities are represented by the vectors $\dot{\mathbf{s}}$ and $\ddot{\mathbf{s}}$?

Q4 A particle sets off from the origin at $t = 0$ and moves in a plane with velocity $\mathbf{v} = (4t\mathbf{i} + t^2\mathbf{j})$ ms^{-1}.
Find the displacement vector $\mathbf{s}$ and the acceleration vector $\mathbf{a}$ for the particle at time t seconds.

Exam Questions

Q1 A particle P is moving in a horizontal plane with constant acceleration.
After t seconds, P has position vector:
$$[(2t^3 - 7t^2 + 12)\mathbf{i} + (3t^2 - 4t^3 - 7)\mathbf{j}]\text{ m}$$
where the unit vectors $\mathbf{i}$ and $\mathbf{j}$ are in the directions of east and north respectively. Find:
a) an expression for the velocity of P after t seconds,   [2 marks]
b) the speed of P when $t = 0.5$, and the direction of motion of P at this time.   [3 marks]

Q2 A particle is initially at position vector $(\mathbf{i} + 2\mathbf{j})$ m, travelling with constant velocity $(3\mathbf{i} + \mathbf{j})$ ms^{-1}.
After 8 s it reaches point A. A second particle has constant velocity $(-4\mathbf{i} + 2\mathbf{j})$ and
takes 5 s to travel from point A to point B. Find the position vectors of points A and B.   [4 marks]

Q3 A particle moves in a plane with acceleration $\mathbf{a} = (12t\mathbf{i} - e^{\frac{1}{3}t}\mathbf{j})$ ms^{-2}. The particle starts at the origin
with initial velocity $\mathbf{u} = (5\mathbf{i} - 4\mathbf{j})$ ms^{-1}. Find its displacement vector from the origin after 1 second.   [5 marks]

All this work in two dimensions has left me feeling a bit flat...

At least there's not much new to learn on these pages — you're just applying vectors to kinematics. You do need to be comfortable with vector notation (unit and column vectors) and calculus though. After that, it's all fine and dandy.

Projectiles and Motion Under Gravity

A 'projectile' is just any old object that's been lobbed through the air. When you're doing projectile questions you'll have to model the motion of particles in two dimensions, usually ignoring air resistance.

Split **Velocity of Projection** into **Two Components**

A particle projected with a speed u at an angle α to the horizontal has **two components** of initial velocity — one **horizontal** (parallel to the x-axis) and one **vertical** (parallel to the y-axis).
These are called **x and y components**, and they make projectile questions dead easy to deal with:

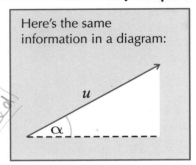

Here's the same information in a diagram:

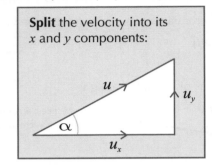

Split the velocity into its x and y components:

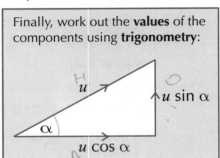

Finally, work out the **values** of the components using **trigonometry**:

Split the **Motion** into **Horizontal** and **Vertical Components** too

Split the motion into horizontal and vertical components. Then deal with them separately using the **suvat equations**. The only thing that's the same in both directions is **time** — so this connects the two directions.
For projectile questions, the only acceleration is **vertical** and due to **gravity** — horizontal acceleration is zero.

Example: a) A stone is thrown horizontally with speed 10 ms⁻¹ from a height of 2 m above the horizontal ground. Find the time taken for the stone to hit the ground and the horizontal distance travelled before impact. Use $g = 9.8$ ms⁻².

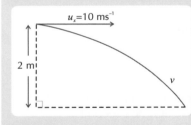

Vertical motion
(take down as +ve):

$s = 2$ $u = u_y = 0$
$a = 9.8$ $t = ?$

The stone only has velocity in the x-direction.

$s = ut + \frac{1}{2}at^2$

$2 = (0 \times t) + \left(\frac{1}{2} \times 9.8 \times t^2\right)$

$t = 0.6388... = \mathbf{0.639}$ **s** (3 s.f.)

i.e. the stone lands after 0.639 seconds.

Horizontal motion
(take right as +ve):

$s = ?$ $u = u_x = 10$
$a = 0$ $t = 0.6388...$

The same as for the vertical motion.

$s = ut + \frac{1}{2}at^2$

$= (10 \times 0.6388...) + \left(\frac{1}{2} \times 0 \times 0.6388...^2\right)$

$= \mathbf{6.39}$ **m** (3 s.f.)

i.e. the stone has travelled 6.39 m horizontally when it lands.

b) Find the speed and direction of the stone after 0.5 s.

Again, keep the vertical and horizontal bits separate:

Vertical motion $v = u + at$

$v_y = 0 + 9.8 \times 0.5$
$= 4.9$ ms⁻¹

Horizontal motion $v = u + at$

$v_x = 10 + 0 \times 0.5$
$= 10$ ms⁻¹

v_x is always equal to u_x when there's no horizontal acceleration.

Now you can find the speed and direction...

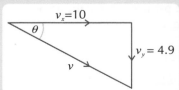

Speed $= |v| = \sqrt{4.9^2 + 10^2} = \mathbf{11.1}$ ms⁻¹ (3 s.f.)

$\tan \theta = \frac{4.9}{10} \Rightarrow \theta = \tan^{-1}\left(\frac{4.9}{10}\right) = 26.1°$ (1 d.p.)

So the direction of the stone's motion is $360° - 26.1° = \mathbf{331.9°}$ (1 d.p.)

Projectiles and Motion Under Gravity

Velocity = 0 at the Maximum Height

Example: A cricket ball is projected with a speed of 30 ms⁻¹ at an angle of 25° above the horizontal. Assume the ground is horizontal and the ball is struck from a point 1.5 m above the ground. Find:
a) the maximum height above the ground the ball reaches (h),
b) the horizontal distance travelled by the ball before it hits the ground (r),
c) the length of time the ball is at least 5 m above the ground.

a) **Vertical motion up to the maximum height** (take up as +ve):

$s = ?$ $u = 30 \sin 25°$
$v = 0$ $a = -9.8$

The ball will momentarily stop moving vertically when it reaches its maximum height.

$v^2 = u^2 + 2as$
$0 = (30 \sin 25°)^2 + 2(-9.8 \times s)$
$s = 8.20130... \text{ m}$
$h = 8.20130... + 1.5 = \mathbf{9.70 \text{ m}}$ (3 s.f.)

Don't forget to add the height from which the ball is hit.

b) **Vertical motion until ball hits ground** (take up as +ve):

$s = -1.5$
$u = 30 \sin 25°$
$a = -9.8$
$t = ?$

Using the quadratic formula you get two answers, but time can't be negative, so forget about this answer.

$s = ut + \frac{1}{2}at^2$
$-1.5 = (30 \sin 25°)t - \frac{1}{2}(9.8)t^2$
$t^2 - 2.58745...t - 0.30612... = 0$
$t = -0.11334... \text{ or } t = 2.70080...$
So $t = \mathbf{2.70 \text{ s}}$ (3 s.f.)

Horizontal motion (take right as +ve)

$s = r$ $u = 30 \cos 25°$
$a = 0$ $t = 2.70080...$

$s = ut + \frac{1}{2}at^2$
$r = 30 \cos 25°(2.70080...) + \frac{1}{2}(0)(2.70080...)^2$
$r = \mathbf{73.4 \text{ m}}$ (3 s.f.)

c) **Vertical motion whilst ball is at least 5 m above ground** (take up as +ve):

$s = 3.5$
$u = 30 \sin 25°$
$a = -9.8$
$t = ?$

The ball is hit from 1.5 m above ground, so 5 m – 1.5 m = 3.5 m

$s = ut + \frac{1}{2}at^2$
$3.5 = (30 \sin 25°)t - \frac{1}{2}(9.8)t^2$
$t^2 - (2.58745...)t + (0.71428...) = 0$
Using the quadratic formula:
$t = 0.31421... \text{ or } t = 2.27324...$

These are the two times when the ball is 5 m above the ground.

So, length of time at least 5 m above the ground:
$2.27324... - 0.311421... = \mathbf{1.96 \text{ s}}$ (3 s.f.)

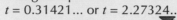

5 m   1.5 m $t = 0.31... \text{ s}$ $t = 2.27... \text{ s}$

The Components of Velocity can be described using i and j Vectors

Your old friends, **i** and **j** vectors, are pretty useful for describing projectiles.

Example: A stone is thrown from a point 1.2 metres above the horizontal ground. It travels for 4 seconds then lands on the ground. The stone is thrown with velocity $(2q\mathbf{i} + q\mathbf{j})$ ms⁻¹, where **i** and **j** are the horizontal and vertical unit vectors respectively. Find the value of q and the initial speed of the stone.

Vertical motion in j direction (take up as +ve):

$s = -1.2$ $u = q$
$a = -9.8$ $t = 4$

$s = ut + \frac{1}{2}at^2$
$-1.2 = 4q - \frac{1}{2}(9.8)4^2$
$4q = 77.2$, so $q = \mathbf{19.3}$

Now find the **initial speed** of the stone:
speed $= \sqrt{(2q)^2 + q^2}$
$= \sqrt{38.6^2 + 19.3^2} = \mathbf{43.2 \text{ ms}^{-1}}$ (3 s.f.)

The vertical component of velocity is q, and the horizontal component is $2q$.

Projectiles and Motion Under Gravity

You can Derive General Formulas for the motion of projectiles

Just one last example of projectile motion. But boy is it a beauty...

Example:

a) A golf ball is struck from a point A on a horizontal plane.
When the ball has moved a horizontal distance x, its height above the plane is y.
The ball is modelled as a particle projected with initial speed u ms^{-1} at an angle α.

Show that $y = x\tan\alpha - \dfrac{gx^2}{2u^2\cos^2\alpha}$.

← This is the general formula for the path of a projectile.

The formula includes motion in both directions (x and y), so form two equations and substitute one into the other:

Horizontal motion (taking right as +ve):

$s = x$ $u_x = u\cos\alpha$
$a = 0$ $t = t$

Using $s = ut + \frac{1}{2}at^2$:

When you're using these variables, this is the obvious equation to use.

$x = u\cos\alpha \times t$

Rearrange to make t the subject:

$t = \dfrac{x}{u\cos\alpha}$ — call this equation ①

t doesn't appear in the final formula, so by making it the subject you can eliminate it.

Vertical motion (taking up as +ve):

$s = y$ $u_y = u\sin\alpha$
$a = -g$ $t = t$

Using $s = ut + \frac{1}{2}at^2$:

$y = (u\sin\alpha \times t) - \frac{1}{2}gt^2$ — call this equation ②

It would be a massive pain to make t the subject here, so do it with the other equation.

t is the same horizontally and vertically, so you can **substitute** ① into ② and eliminate t:

$y = u\sin\alpha \times \dfrac{x}{u\cos\alpha} - \dfrac{1}{2}g\left(\dfrac{x}{u\cos\alpha}\right)^2$

$y = x\dfrac{\sin\alpha}{\cos\alpha} - \dfrac{1}{2}g\left(\dfrac{x^2}{u^2\cos^2\alpha}\right)$

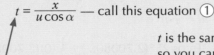 $\dfrac{\sin\theta}{\cos\theta} = \tan\theta$

$y = x\tan\alpha - \dfrac{gx^2}{2u^2\cos^2\alpha}$ — as required.

Dave took a real leap of faith with his projectile calculations...

b) The ball just passes over the top of a 10 m tall tree, which is 45 m away.
Given that $\alpha = 45°$, find the speed of the ball as it passes over the tree.

Substitute $x = 45$, $y = 10$ and $\alpha = 45°$ into the result above and rearrange to find the speed of projection u:

$10 = 45\tan 45° - \dfrac{9.8 \times 45^2}{2u^2 \times \cos^2 45°} = 45 - \dfrac{19\,845}{u^2}$

Avoid rounding if possible — your calculator's memory can be useful here.

$35u^2 = 19\,845 \Rightarrow u = 23.81176...$ ms^{-1}

Then find the components of the ball's velocity as it passes over the tree:

Horizontal motion (taking right as +ve):

$v_x = u_x = 23.81176... \cos 45° = 16.83745...$ ms^{-1}

Remember — with projectiles there's no horizontal acceleration, so v_x always equals u_x.

Vertical motion (taking up as +ve):

$s = 10$ $u_y = 23.81176... \sin 45°$
$v_y = v_y$ $a = -g$

Using $v^2 = u^2 + 2as$:

$v_y^2 = 283.5 - 2 \times 9.8 \times 10 = 87.5$

Now you can find the speed: $v = \sqrt{v_x^2 + v_y^2} = \sqrt{16.83745...^2 + 87.5}$

$v = 19.3$ ms^{-1} **(to 3 s.f.)**

Don't bother finding the square root, as you need v_y^2 in the final step. Sneaky.

Projectiles and Motion Under Gravity

Three whole pages of examples about projectiles calls for a full page of questions.
Don't worry — you'll be thanking me for all the practice come exam time.

Practice Questions

Q1 A rifle fires a bullet horizontally at 120 ms⁻¹. The target is hit at a horizontal distance of 60 m from the end of the rifle. Find how far the target is vertically below the end of the rifle. Take $g = 9.8$ ms⁻².

Q2 A golf ball takes 4 seconds to land after being hit with a golf club from a point on the horizontal ground. If it leaves the club with velocity $(2q\mathbf{i} + 3q\mathbf{j})$ ms⁻¹, find its initial horizontal velocity. Take $g = 9.8$ ms⁻².

Q3 A particle is projected with initial velocity u ms⁻¹ at an angle α above the horizontal.

    a)   Find, in terms of u and α, the horizontal and vertical components of the particle's initial velocity.

    b) (i)   Show that the particle reaches its maximum height after $\dfrac{u\sin\alpha}{g}$ seconds.

         (ii) Hence, and using a suitable trig identity, show that the horizontal range is $\dfrac{u^2\sin(2\alpha)}{g}$ metres.

    c)   Show that the maximum vertical height the particle reaches is $\dfrac{u^2\sin^2\alpha}{2g}$ metres.

Exam Questions

Q1

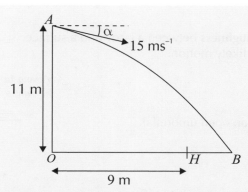

A stone is thrown from point A on the edge of a cliff, towards a point H, which is on horizontal ground. The point O is on the ground, 11 m vertically below the point of projection. The stone is thrown with speed 15 ms⁻¹ at an angle α below the horizontal, where $\tan\alpha = \dfrac{3}{4}$. The horizontal distance from O to H is 9 m. The stone misses the point H and hits the ground at point B, as shown above. Find:

    a) the time taken by the stone to reach the ground,   [5 marks]

    b) the horizontal distance the stone misses H by,   [3 marks]

    c) the speed of projection which would have ensured that the stone landed at H.   [5 marks]

Q2 A stationary football is kicked with a speed of 20 ms⁻¹, at an angle of 30° to the horizontal, towards a goal 30 m away. The crossbar is 2.5 m above the level ground. Assuming the path of the ball is not impeded, determine whether the ball passes above or below the crossbar, stating all modelling assumptions.   [6 marks]

Q3 A golf ball is hit from a tee at point O on the edge of a vertical cliff. Point O is 30 m vertically above A, the base of the cliff. The ball is hit with velocity $(14\mathbf{i} + 35\mathbf{j})$ ms⁻¹ towards a hole, H, which lies on the horizontal ground. At time t seconds, the position of the ball is $(x\mathbf{i} + y\mathbf{j})$ m, relative to O. $\mathbf{i}$ and $\mathbf{j}$ are the horizontal and vertical unit vectors respectively. Take $g = 9.8$ ms⁻².

    a) By writing down expressions for x and y in terms of t, show that $y = \dfrac{5x}{2} - \dfrac{x^2}{40}$.   [4 marks]

The ball lands on the ground at point B, 7 m beyond H, where AHB is a straight horizontal line.

    b) Find the horizontal distance AB.   [3 marks]

    c) Find the speed of the ball as it passes through a point vertically above H.   [4 marks]

Projectiles — they're all about throwing up. Or across. Or slightly down...

You've used the equations of motion before and there isn't much different here. Projectile questions can be wordy so it can help to draw a diagram of the situation before doing anything else. The main thing to remember is that horizontal acceleration is zero — great news because it makes half the calculations as easy as... something very easy.

Forces and Modelling

Force questions and modelling go hand in hand, but you need to understand all the mechanics lingo.
For starters, 'modelling' in maths doesn't have anything to do with plastic aeroplane kits... or catwalks.

Types of forces

Weight (*W*)

Due to the particle's mass, *m* and the force of gravity, *g*: $W = mg$. Weight always acts **downwards**.

The **Normal Reaction (*R* or *N*)**

The reaction from a surface. Reaction always acts **perpendicular (90°) to the surface.**

Tension (*T*)

Force in a taut rope, wire or string.

Friction (*F*)

A resistance force due to the **roughness** between a body and a surface. Always acts **against** motion, or likely motion.

Cake (*C*)
A force to be reckoned with.
Always acts towards my mouth,
and opposes likely hunger.

Thrust or **Compression**

Force in a rod (e.g. the pole of an open umbrella).

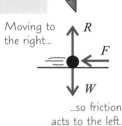

Moving to the right...

...so friction acts to the left.

Air resistance and drag forces also resist motion.

Talk the Talk

Mechanics questions use a lot of words that you already know, but here they're used to mean something very **precise**. Learn these definitions so you don't get caught out:

Particle	the body is a point so its dimensions don't matter	**Rigid**	the body does not bend
Light	the body has no mass	**Thin**	the body has no thickness
Static	not moving	**Equilibrium**	no resultant force
Rough	the surface will oppose motion with friction / drag	**Plane**	a flat surface
Beam or Rod	a long particle (e.g. a carpenter's plank)	**Inextensible**	the body can't be stretched
Uniform	the mass is evenly spread out throughout the body	**Smooth**	the surface doesn't have friction / drag opposing motion
Non-uniform	the mass is unevenly spread out		

You need to know the S.I. Units...

S.I. units are a system of units that are designed to be consistent all around the world.
The three main **base units** that you'll come across are:

Length: **metre (m)**	Time: **second (s)**	Mass: **kilogram (kg)**

Other units, such as newtons, are called **derived** S.I. units because they're **combinations** of the base units.

All quantities can be measured in units derived from the base S.I. units, which can usually be found using their formula. For example, the formula for speed is distance ÷ time. Distance is a length measured in metres, and time is measured in seconds, so the S.I. unit of speed is metres ÷ second, written m/s or ms^{-1}.

Watch out for non-S.I. units that sneak into questions here and there — you can measure length in inches and feet, but these are **imperial** units, not S.I. units. Certain units, like **miles per hour**, are **derived non-S.I.** units.

Forces and Modelling

Always start by drawing a *Simple Diagram* of the *Model*

You'll have to make lots of **assumptions** when tackling **modelling** problems.

> **Example:** Model the following situations by drawing a force diagram and listing any assumptions made.

1 The book on a table

A book is put flat on a table. One end of the table is slowly lifted and the angle to the horizontal is measured when the book starts to slide.

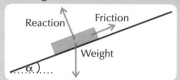

Assumptions:
The book is a **particle**, so its dimensions don't matter.
The table is **rigid**, and its surface is a **rough plane**.
There's **no** wind or other **external forces** involved.

> Modelling is a **cycle** — use the model to **solve** the problem, **compare** it to real life, **evaluate** your results, then **improve** the model and **start again**.

2 The balance

A pencil is placed on a table and a ruler is put across the pencil. A 1p coin and a 10p coin are placed on the ruler either side of the pencil, so that the ruler balances on the pencil.

Assumptions:
The coins are **particles**.
The ruler is **rigid**.
The support acts at a **single point**.

Weight ↓   ↑ Reaction   Weight ↓

3 The sledge

A sledge is being steadily pulled by a small child on horizontal snow.

Assumptions:
Friction is **too big** to be ignored (i.e. it's not ice).
The string is **horizontal** (it's a small child).
The sledge is a **particle** (so its size doesn't matter).

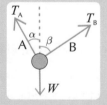

> It's easier to use just the first letter of the force in your diagram, e.g. F = friction.

4 The mass on a string

A ball is held by two strings, A and B, at angles α and β to the vertical.

Assumptions:
The ball is modelled as a **particle** (its dimensions don't matter).
The strings are **light** (their mass can be ignored).
The strings are **inextensible** (they can't stretch).

Practice Questions

Q1 The density of an object is given by its mass, divided by its volume.
Give the S.I. units of mass and volume and hence find the S.I. unit of density.

Q2 A ball is dropped onto a cushion from above. Draw a model, stating any assumptions made,
showing the ball: a) as it is released,   b) after it has landed.

Exam Question

Q1 A car is modelled as a particle travelling at a constant speed along a smooth horizontal surface.
Explain two ways in which this model could be adjusted to be more realistic.   [2 marks]

I can't get up yet — I'm modelling myself as a static particle in a rough bed...

Make sure you're completely familiar with the different forces and all the jargon that gets bandied about in mechanics. Keep your models as simple as possible — that will make answering the questions as simple as possible too.

Resolving Forces

Forces have direction and magnitude, which makes them vectors — this means that you'll need
all the stuff you learnt about vectors in Section 10. Oh come on, don't give me that look — it'll be fun, trust me.

Forces have **Components**

You've done a fair amount of **trigonometry** already, so this should be as straightforward as watching paint dry.

Example: A particle is acted on by a force of 15 N at 30° above the horizontal. Find the **horizontal** and **vertical components** of the force in both **i** and **j** form, and as a column vector.

A bit of trigonometry is all that's required:

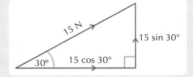

Force = 15 cos 30°**i** + 15 sin 30°**j**

$= (13.0\mathbf{i} + 7.5\mathbf{j})$ N (3 s.f.) $= \begin{pmatrix} 13.0 \\ 7.5 \end{pmatrix}$ N

(i.e. 13.0 N to the right and 7.5 N upwards)

This is also known as **resolving** a force into components.

Add the **Components** to get the **Resultant**

The **resultant force** on an object is the **resultant vector** of all of the forces acting on it. To work it out, you can either use the **'nose to tail'** method you saw back in Section 10, or **resolve** the vectors into horizontal and vertical components and add them together.

See p.136 for more about resultant vectors.

Example: A second horizontal force of 20 N to the right is also applied to the particle in the example above. Find the magnitude and direction of the resultant of these forces.

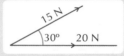

Put the arrows nose to tail:

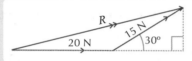 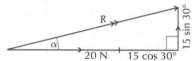

Using Pythagoras and trigonometry:

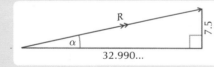

$R = \sqrt{(32.990...)^2 + 7.5^2} = \textbf{33.8 N}$ (3 s.f.)

$\alpha = \tan^{-1}\left(\dfrac{7.5}{32.99}\right) = \textbf{12.8°}$ (1 d.p.) above the horizontal

Example: Find, in **i** and **j** vector form, the resultant force acting on the particle shown below.

Resolve the forces into horizontal (**i**) and vertical (**j**) components:

The 12 N force is vertical, so it has components 0**i** + 12**j**

The components of the 20 N force are: 20 sin 60°**i** – 20 cos 60°**j** = 17.320...**i** – 10**j**

Now add the vectors together:

Resultant = (0 + 17.320...)**i** + (12 – 10)**j** = (**17.3i** + **2j**) N (3 s.f.)

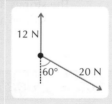

Example: Three forces of magnitudes 9 N, 12 N and 13 N act on a particle *P* in the directions shown in the diagram. Find the magnitude and direction of the resultant of the three forces, to 2 d.p.

One of the forces is already aligned with the *y*-axis, so it makes sense to start by resolving the other forces relative to this.

Along the *y*-axis: resultant = 9 sin 31° + 12 sin 50° – 13
= 4.635... + 9.192... – 13 = **0.83 N** (2 d.p.)

Along the *x*-axis: resultant = 12 cos 50° – 9 cos 31°
= 7.713... – 7.714... = **0.00 N** (2 d.p.)

Overall: **0.83 N** (2 d.p.) in the direction of the *y*-axis

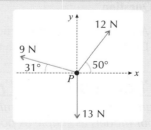

Resolving Forces

Particles in *Equilibrium* have *No Resultant Force*

When the resultant force acting on an object is **zero** (in all directions), then the object is **in equilibrium**.
A particle that's in equilibrium either stays still, or moves at a constant speed (see p.203).
More often than not, you'll be told that something's in equilibrium and have to find an **unknown force**.

Examples: a) Two perpendicular forces of magnitude 20 N act on a particle.
A third force, P, acts at 45° to the horizontal, as shown.
Given that the particle is in equilibrium, find the magnitude of P.

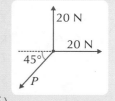

Use an arrow to show which direction you're taking as positive.

Resolving horizontally (→): $20 - P \cos 45° = 0 \Rightarrow P = 20 \div 0.707... = $ **28.3 N** (3 s.f.)

b) A force of 50 N acts on a particle at an angle of 20°
to the vertical, as shown. Find the magnitude of the two
other forces, T and S, if the particle is in equilibrium.

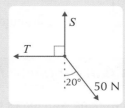

Resolving vertically (↑): $S - 50 \cos 20° = 0 \Rightarrow S = $ **47.0 N** (3 s.f.)

Resolving horizontally (←): $T - 50 \sin 20° = 0 \Rightarrow T = $ **17.1 N** (3 s.f.)

c) Three forces act upon a particle. A force of magnitude
85 N acts horizontally, the force Q acts vertically,
and the force P acts at 55° to the horizontal, as shown.
The particle is in equilibrium. Find the magnitude of P and Q.

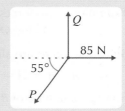

Resolving horizontally (←): $P \cos 55° - 85 = 0 \Rightarrow P = $ **148 N** (3 s.f.)

Resolving vertically (↑): $Q - P \sin 55° = 0 \Rightarrow Q = $ **121 N** (3 s.f.)

An *Inclined Plane* is a *Sloping Surface*

Things are a little trickier when you're dealing with **inclined planes**.
In fact, I'm inclined to say that they're far from plain sailing...

Now don't be silly — you know that's not what I mean.

Example: A sledge of weight 1000 N is being held on a rough inclined plane
at an angle of 35° by a force of 700 N acting parallel to the slope.
Find the normal contact force N and the frictional force F acting on the sledge.

The sledge is being held in place — that's your hint that it's in equilibrium.

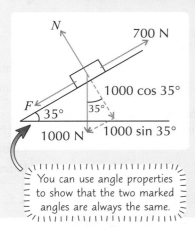

You can use angle properties to show that the two marked angles are always the same.

Apart from the weight (which always acts vertically
downwards), all the forces here act either **parallel**
or **perpendicular** to the **slope**, so it makes sense
to resolve in these directions.

Perpendicular to the slope (↖):
$N - 1000 \cos 35° = 0$
$\Rightarrow N = 1000 \cos 35° = $ **819 N** (3 s.f.)

Parallel to the slope (↗):
$700 - F - 1000 \sin 35° = 0$
$\Rightarrow F = 700 - 1000 \sin 35° = $ **126 N** (3 s.f.)

You don't have to resolve forces horizontally and vertically — for inclined planes, it's usually easier to resolve perpendicular and parallel to the plane.

Section 17 — Forces and Newton's Laws

Resolving Forces

Objects on Strings produce Tension

Example: A object of weight 117.6 N is held by two light strings, P and Q, acting at 40° and 20° to the vertical, as shown. Find the tension in each string.

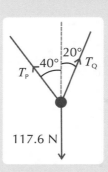

117.6 N

Resolving horizontally (←):

$T_P \sin 40° - T_Q \sin 20° = 0 \Rightarrow T_P = T_Q \dfrac{\sin 20°}{\sin 40°}$ — call this equation ①

Resolving vertically (↑):

$T_P \cos 40° + T_Q \cos 20° - 117.6 = 0$ — call this equation ②

Substituting ① into ②:

$T_Q \dfrac{\sin 20°}{\sin 40°} \cos 40° + T_Q \cos 20° - 117.6 = 0 \Rightarrow 0.407...T_Q + 0.939...T_Q = 117.6$

$\Rightarrow T_Q = 117.6 \div (1.347...) = \mathbf{87.3 \ N}$ (3 s.f.)

Substitute the value of T_Q into ① to get: $T_P = 87.28... \times 0.532... = \mathbf{46.4 \ N}$ (3 s.f.)

Forces can be given in different Vector Forms

As well as working with forces given in 'magnitude and direction' form, be prepared for **i** and **j** or **column** vectors.

Example: Two forces, $A = (2\mathbf{i} - 11\mathbf{j})$ N and $B = (7\mathbf{i} + 5\mathbf{j})$ N, act on a particle. Find the exact magnitude of the resultant force, R, on the particle.

Since the forces are already given in components, finding the resultant force is easy:

$R = A + B = (2\mathbf{i} - 11\mathbf{j}) + (7\mathbf{i} + 5\mathbf{j}) = (2 + 7)\mathbf{i} + (-11 + 5)\mathbf{j} = 9\mathbf{i} - 6\mathbf{j}$ N

So the magnitude of $R = \sqrt{9^2 + (-6)^2} = \sqrt{81 + 36} = \sqrt{117} = 3\sqrt{13}$ N

Practice Questions

Q1 Find the magnitudes and directions (measured from the horizontal) of the resultant force in each situation.

a) 3N, 4N

b) 5N, 60°, 8N

c) 6 N, 20°, 10°, 10 N, 4 N

d) $-4\mathbf{i} + \mathbf{j}$ N, $3\mathbf{i} + 6\mathbf{j}$ N, $-4\mathbf{i} - 3\mathbf{j}$ N, $5\mathbf{i} - 2\mathbf{j}$ N

Q2 A particle of weight W N is suspended in equilibrium by two light wires A and B, which make angles of 60° and 30° to the vertical respectively, as shown. The tension in A is 20 N. Find the tension in wire B and the value of W.

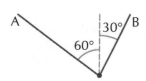

Exam Questions

Q1 A force of magnitude 7 N acts on a particle in the **i**-direction. Another force, of magnitude 4 N, acts on the particle with a direction of 30°. The resultant of these forces, R, has direction α.

Find: a) the magnitude of the force R, [3 marks]

b) the angle α. [2 marks]

Q2 A sledge is held at rest on a smooth slope angled at 25° to the horizontal. The rope holding the sledge is at an angle of 20° above the slope. The normal reaction acting on the sledge due to contact with the surface is 80 N.

Find: a) the tension, T, in the rope, [3 marks]

b) the weight of the sledge. [2 marks]

Take it from me — once you start making puns, it's a slippery slope...

Resolving forces is some pretty classic vectors stuff, but make sure those tricksy inclined planes don't catch you out.

Newton's Laws

*That clever chap Isaac Newton established 3 laws involving motion. You need to know **all** of them.*

Newton's Laws of Motion

Newton's First Law	Newton's Second Law	Newton's Third Law
A body will **stay at rest** or **maintain a constant velocity** — unless an extra force acts to **change** that motion.	$$F_{net} = ma$$ F_{net} (the **overall resultant force**) is equal to the mass multiplied by the acceleration. F_{net} and a act in the same direction.	For **two bodies** in contact with each other, the force each applies to the other is **equal in magnitude** but **opposite in direction**.

$F_{net} = ma$ is sometimes just written as $F = ma$, but it means the same thing.

Weight *is given by* Mass × Acceleration Due To Gravity

A common use of the formula $F = ma$ is calculating the **weight** of an object. An object's weight is a **force** caused by **gravity**. Gravity causes a **constant** acceleration of approximately 9.8 ms⁻², denoted *g*. Putting this into $F = ma$ gives the equation for weight (W):

$$W = mg$$

g can actually vary a little from 9.8 depending on where you are, but you can always assume it's constant.

Remember that weight is a **force** (measured in **newtons**) while mass is measured in **kg** — you might have to **convert units** before using the formula.

Example: A particle of mass 12 kg is acted on by a constant upwards force F.
The particle is accelerating vertically downwards at a rate of 7 ms⁻².
Find: a) W, the weight of the particle,   b) the magnitude of the force F.

a) Using the formula for weight:
$$W = mg$$
$$= 12 \times 9.8 = \textbf{117.6 N}$$

b) Resolving vertically (↓):
$$F_{net} = ma \Rightarrow 117.6 - F = 12 \times 7$$
$$F = 117.6 - 84 = \textbf{33.6 N}$$

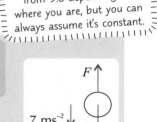

Resolve Forces *in* Perpendicular *Directions*

Example: A horizontal force of 5 N acts on a mass of 4 kg travelling along a smooth horizontal plane. Find the acceleration of the mass and the normal reaction from the plane. Take $g = 9.8$ ms⁻².

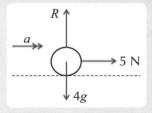

Resolve horizontally (→):
$$F_{net} = ma$$
$$5 = 4a$$
$a = \textbf{1.25 ms⁻²}$ in the direction of the horizontal force

Always write $F_{net} = ma$ first.

Resolve vertically (↑):
$$F_{net} = ma, \text{ so}$$
$$R - 4g = 4 \times 0$$
$$R = 4g = \textbf{39.2 N}$$

You might also have to use the constant acceleration equations — you know, the ones from page 186.

Example: A particle of weight 30 N is being accelerated across a smooth horizontal plane by a force of 6 N acting at an angle of 25° to the horizontal, as shown. Given that the particle starts from rest, find:
a) its speed after 4 seconds   b) the magnitude of the normal reaction with the plane.

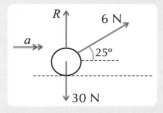

a) Resolve horizontally (→):
$$F_{net} = ma$$
$$6 \cos 25° = \frac{30}{g}a$$
$W = mg$, so the mass of the particle is $m = \frac{W}{g}$.
$$\Rightarrow a = 1.776... \text{ ms⁻²}$$
$$v = u + at$$
$$v = 0 + 1.776... \times 4 = \textbf{7.11 ms⁻¹} \text{ (3 s.f.)}$$

b) Resolve vertically (↑): There's no vertical acceleration.
$$F_{net} = ma$$
$$R + 6 \sin 25° - 30 = \frac{30}{g} \times 0$$
So $R = 30 - 6 \sin 25°$
$$= \textbf{27.5 N} \text{ (3 s.f.)}$$

Newton's Laws

You can apply F = ma to i and j Vectors too

Example: a) A particle of mass m kg is acted upon by two forces, $(6\mathbf{i} - \mathbf{j})$ N and $(2\mathbf{i} + 4\mathbf{j})$ N, resulting in an acceleration of magnitude 9 ms^{-2}. Find the value of m.

Resultant force, $F_{net} = (6\mathbf{i} - \mathbf{j}) + (2\mathbf{i} + 4\mathbf{j}) = (8\mathbf{i} + 3\mathbf{j})$ N

Magnitude of $F_{net} = |F_{net}| = \sqrt{8^2 + 3^2} = \sqrt{73} = 8.544...$ N

$F_{net} = ma$, so $8.544... = 9m$

hence $m = \mathbf{0.949}$ **kg** (3 s.f.)

b) The force of $(2\mathbf{i} + 4\mathbf{j})$ N is removed. Calculate the magnitude of the new acceleration.

Magnitude $= \sqrt{6^2 + (-1)^2} = \sqrt{37} = 6.082...$ N

$a = \dfrac{F}{m} = \dfrac{6.082...}{0.949...} = \mathbf{6.41}$ **ms**$^{-2}$ (3 s.f.)

You can put **i** and **j** or column vectors straight into $F = ma$ (or $\mathbf{F} = m\mathbf{a}$).
F and $\mathbf{a}$ will both be in vector form, but mass is always scalar.

Example: The resultant force on a particle of mass 2 kg is given by the column vector $\begin{pmatrix} 14 \\ -6 \end{pmatrix}$ N. Calculate its velocity vector, 4 seconds after it begins moving from rest.

Using $F_{net} = ma$ with vectors: $\begin{pmatrix} 14 \\ -6 \end{pmatrix} = 2a \Rightarrow a = \begin{pmatrix} 7 \\ -3 \end{pmatrix}$ ms^{-2} ← Divide each component by 2.

Now, list the variables you know: $u = \begin{pmatrix} 0 \\ 0 \end{pmatrix}$, $v = v$, $a = \begin{pmatrix} 7 \\ -3 \end{pmatrix}$, $t = 4$ It starts at rest, so each component of **u** is 0.

See p.192 for more about using vectors with the suvat equations.

Use $v = u + at$: $v = \begin{pmatrix} 0 \\ 0 \end{pmatrix} + \begin{pmatrix} 7 \\ -3 \end{pmatrix} \times 4 = \begin{pmatrix} 28 \\ -12 \end{pmatrix}$ ms^{-1}

Practice Questions

Q1 A horizontal force of 2 N acts on a 1.5 kg particle initially at rest on a smooth horizontal plane. Find the speed of the particle 3 seconds later.

Q2 A particle of mass 6 g is acted on by a constant force F. The particle reaches a velocity of $\begin{pmatrix} 200 \\ 125 \end{pmatrix}$ ms^{-1} 5 seconds after beginning to accelerate from rest. Find the magnitude and direction of F.

Q3 Two forces act on a particle of mass 8 kg which is initially at rest on a smooth horizontal plane. The two forces are $(24\mathbf{i} + 18\mathbf{j})$ N and $(6\mathbf{i} + 22\mathbf{j})$ N (with **i** and **j** being perpendicular unit vectors in the plane). Find the magnitude and direction of the particle's resulting acceleration and the magnitude of its displacement after 3 seconds.

Exam Questions

Q1 Two forces, $(x\mathbf{i} + y\mathbf{j})$ N and $(5\mathbf{i} + \mathbf{j})$ N, act on a particle P of mass 2.5 kg. The resultant of the two forces is $(8\mathbf{i} - 3\mathbf{j})$ N.

Find: a) the values of x and y, [2 marks]

b) the magnitude and direction of the acceleration of P, [5 marks]

c) the particle's velocity vector, 5 seconds after it accelerates from rest. [2 marks]

Q2 A skydiver with mass 60 kg falls vertically from rest, experiencing a constant air resistance force, R, as they fall. After 7 seconds, they have fallen 200 m.

a) Find the magnitude of the air resistance on the skydiver to 3 significant figures. [6 marks]

b) State any assumptions that you have made in part a). [2 marks]

Interesting Newton fact: Isaac Newton had a dog called Diamond...

Also, did you know that Isaac Newton and Stephen Hawking both held the same position at Cambridge University? Don't ask me how I know such things, just bask in my amazing knowledge of all things trivial.

Friction and Inclined Planes

Friction tries to prevent motion, but don't let it prevent you getting marks in the exam. It's like my gran always says — revision is the best way to keep things running smoothly and avoid chafing. Revision, and a dash of talcum powder.

Friction tries to Prevent Motion

Push hard enough and a particle will move, even though there's friction opposing the motion. A **frictional (contact) force**, *F*, has a **maximum value**. This depends on the **roughness** of the surface and the value of the **normal reaction** (or **normal contact force**) from the surface.

$$F \leq \mu R \quad \text{OR} \quad F \leq \mu N$$

(where *R* and *N* both stand for normal reaction)

μ has no units. You pronounce it 'mew'.

Try one of our refreshing smoothies — low on calories, low on μ, and one of your 5-a-day!

μ is called the "**coefficient of friction**". The **rougher** the surface, the **bigger** *μ* gets.

Example: What range of values can a frictional force take to resist a horizontal force P acting on a particle Q, of mass 12 kg, resting on a rough horizontal plane which has a coefficient of friction of 0.4? Take *g* = 9.8 ms⁻².

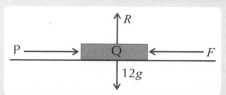

Resolving vertically: $R = 12g$
Use formula from above: $F \leq \mu R$
$F \leq 0.4(12g)$
$F \leq \mathbf{47.04 \ N}$

The **resultant** of the **frictional** contact force and the **normal** contact force is often just called the **contact force** between the object and the surface.

So friction can take any value between 0 and 47.04 N, depending on how large P is. If P < 47.04 N then Q remains in equilibrium. If P = 47.04 N then Q is **on the point of sliding** — i.e. friction is at its **limit**. If P > 47.04 then Q will start to move.

Limiting Friction is when friction is at Maximum (F = μR)

Example: A particle of mass 6 kg is placed on a rough horizontal plane which has a coefficient of friction of 0.3. A horizontal force Q is applied to the particle. Describe what happens if Q is: a)   16 N
Take *g* = 9.8 ms⁻²   b)   20 N

In **static** equilibrium, F ≤ μR, and in **limiting** equilibrium (or when **moving**), F = μR.

Resolving vertically: $R = 6g$
Using formula above: $F \leq \mu R$
$F \leq 0.3(6g)$
$F \leq \mathbf{17.64 \ N}$

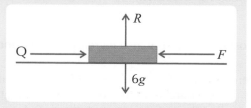

a)   Since Q < 17.64 N, it **won't move**.
b)   Since Q > 17.64 N, it'll **start moving**. No probs.

Example: A particle of mass 4 kg at rest on a rough horizontal plane is being pushed by a horizontal force of 30 N. Given that the particle is on the point of moving, find the coefficient of friction.

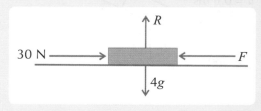

Resolving horizontally: $F = 30$
Resolving vertically: $R = 4g$
The particle's about to move, so friction is at its limit:
$$F = \mu R$$
$$30 = \mu(4g)$$
$$\mu = \frac{30}{4g} = \mathbf{0.77} \ (2 \ d.p.)$$

μ is usually given to 2 d.p.

Friction and Inclined Planes

Use F = ma in *Two Directions* for *Inclined Plane* questions

For **inclined slope** questions, it's much easier to resolve forces **parallel** and **perpendicular** to the plane's surface. Here's a nice example without friction to ease you in gently...

Example: A mass of 600 g is propelled up the line of greatest slope of a smooth plane inclined at 30° to the horizontal. If its velocity is 3 ms⁻¹ after the propelling force has stopped, find the distance it travels before v reaches 0 ms⁻¹ and the magnitude of the normal reaction. Use $g = 9.8$ ms⁻².

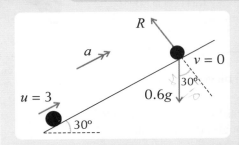

Resolve parallel to the plane ($\nearrow$):

$F_{net} = ma$

Watch the units —
m = 600 g = 0.6 kg

$-0.6g \sin 30° = 0.6a$

$\Rightarrow a = -4.9$ ms⁻²

Resolve perpendicular to plane ($\searrow$):

$v^2 = u^2 + 2as$

$0 = 3^2 + 2(-4.9)s$

So $s = \mathbf{0.918}$ **m** (3 s.f.)

$F_{net} = ma$

$R - 0.6g \cos 30° = 0.6 \times 0$

So $R = \mathbf{5.09}$ **N** (3 s.f.)

Remember that friction always acts in the **opposite** direction to the motion.

Example: A small body of weight 20 N accelerates from rest and moves a distance of 5 m down a rough plane angled at 15° to the horizontal. Draw a force diagram and find the coefficient of friction between the body and the plane given that the motion takes 6 seconds. Take $g = 9.8$ ms⁻².

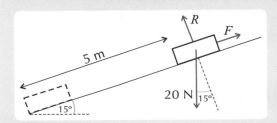

$s = 5, \quad u = 0, \quad a = a, \quad t = 6$

Use one of the equations of motion:

$s = ut + \frac{1}{2}at^2$

$5 = (0 \times 6) + \left(\frac{1}{2}a \times 6^2\right)$

so $a = \mathbf{0.2777...}$ **ms⁻²**

Resolving perpendicular ($\nwarrow$):

$F_{net} = ma$

$R - 20 \cos 15° = \frac{20}{g} \times 0$

$R = 20 \cos 15° = \mathbf{19.31...}$ **N**

Resolving parallel ($\swarrow$):

$F_{net} = ma$

$20 \sin 15° - F = \frac{20}{g} \times 0.2777...$

$F = \mathbf{4.609...}$ **N**

It's sliding, so $F = \mu R$

$4.609... = \mu \times 19.31...$

$\mu = \mathbf{0.24}$ (2 d.p.)

Friction opposes motion, so it also increases the **tension** in whatever's doing the pulling...

Example: A mass of 3 kg is being pulled up a plane inclined at 20° to the horizontal by a rope parallel to the surface. Given that the mass is accelerating at 0.6 ms⁻² and that the coefficient of friction is 0.4, find the tension in the rope. Take $g = 9.8$ ms⁻².

Resolving perpendicular ($\nwarrow$):

$F_{net} = ma$

$R - 3g \cos 20° = 3 \times 0$

$R = 3g \cos 20° = \mathbf{27.62...}$ **N**

The mass is sliding:

$F = \mu R$

$= 0.4 \times 27.62...$

$= \mathbf{11.05...}$ **N**

Resolving parallel ($\swarrow$):

$F_{net} = ma$

$T - F - 3g \sin 20° = 3 \times 0.6$

$T = 1.8 + 11.05... + 3g \sin 20° = \mathbf{22.9}$ **N** (3 s.f.)

Friction and Inclined Planes

Friction **Opposes Limiting Motion**

For a body **at rest** but on the point of moving **down** a plane, the friction force is **up** the plane. A body about to move **up** a plane is opposed by friction **down** the plane. Remember it well (it's about to come in handy).

Example: A 4 kg box is placed on a 30° plane where $\mu = 0.4$. A force Q maintains equilibrium by acting up the plane parallel to the line of greatest slope. Find Q if the box is on the point of sliding: a) up the plane, b) down the plane.

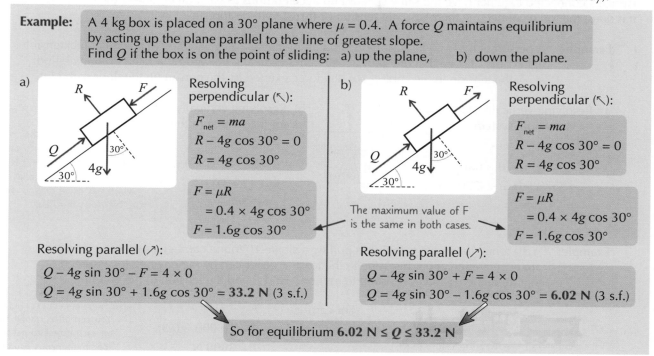

a) Resolving perpendicular (↖):

$F_{net} = ma$
$R - 4g \cos 30° = 0$
$R = 4g \cos 30°$

$F = \mu R$
$\quad = 0.4 \times 4g \cos 30°$
$F = 1.6g \cos 30°$

Resolving parallel (↗):

$Q - 4g \sin 30° - F = 4 \times 0$
$Q = 4g \sin 30° + 1.6g \cos 30° = \mathbf{33.2\ N}$ (3 s.f.)

The maximum value of F is the same in both cases.

b) Resolving perpendicular (↖):

$F_{net} = ma$
$R - 4g \cos 30° = 0$
$R = 4g \cos 30°$

$F = \mu R$
$\quad = 0.4 \times 4g \cos 30°$
$F = 1.6g \cos 30°$

Resolving parallel (↗):

$Q - 4g \sin 30° + F = 4 \times 0$
$Q = 4g \sin 30° - 1.6g \cos 30° = \mathbf{6.02\ N}$ (3 s.f.)

So for equilibrium $\mathbf{6.02\ N} \leq Q \leq \mathbf{33.2\ N}$

Practice Questions

Q1 a) Describe the motion of a mass of 12 kg pushed by a force of 50 N parallel to the rough horizontal plane on which the mass is placed. The plane has coefficient of friction $\mu = 0.5$.

b) What minimum force would be needed to move the mass in part a)?

Q2 A brick of mass 1.2 kg is sliding down a rough plane which is inclined at 25° to the horizontal. Given that its acceleration is 0.3 ms⁻², find the coefficient of friction between the brick and the plane. What assumptions have you made?

Q3 An army recruit of weight 600 N steps off a tower and accelerates down a "death slide" wire as shown. The recruit hangs from a light rope held between her hands and looped over the wire. The coefficient of friction between the rope and wire is 0.5. Given that the wire is 20 m long and makes an angle of 30° to the horizontal throughout its length, find how fast the recruit is travelling when she reaches the end of the wire.

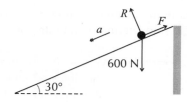

Exam Questions

Q1 A horizontal force of 8 N just stops a mass of 7 kg from sliding down a plane inclined at 15° to the horizontal, as shown.

a) Calculate the coefficient of friction between the mass and the plane to 2 d.p. [5 marks]

b) The 8 N force is now removed. Find how long the mass takes to slide a distance of 3 m down the line of greatest slope. [7 marks]

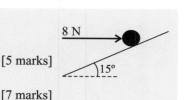

Q2 A 10 kg box is being held in equilibrium on a plane inclined at 30° to the horizontal by a force P acting parallel to the plane. Given that the coefficient of friction between the box and the plane is 0.4, find the range of possible values for the magnitude of P. [7 marks]

Sometimes friction really rubs me up the wrong way...

Friction can be a right nuisance, but without it we'd just slide all over the place, which would be worse (I imagine).

Connected Particles

Like Laurel goes with Hardy and Ben goes with Jerry, some particles are destined to be together...

Connected Particles act like One Mass

Particles connected together have the **same speeds** and **accelerations** as each other, unless the connection **fails**. If it does, the force connecting them (usually **tension** or **thrust**) will disappear.

Example: A person of mass 70 kg is standing in a lift of mass 500 kg attached to a vertical inextensible, light cable. Given that the lift is accelerating vertically upwards at a rate of 0.6 ms^{-2}, find:
a) T, the tension in the cable,   b) the force exerted by the person on the floor of the lift.

You're not given g, so take g = 9.8 ms^{-2}.

a) Resolving vertically (↑) for the **whole system**:

$F_{net} = ma$
$T - 570g = 570 \times 0.6$
$T = (570 \times 0.6) + (570 \times 9.8)$
$= 5928 \text{ N}$

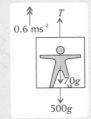

b) Resolving vertically (↑) for the **person** in the lift:

$F_{net} = ma$
$R - 70g = 70 \times 0.6$
$R = 42 + 70g$
$= 728 \text{ N}$

You could resolve all the forces on the lift, but it's easier to find the reaction force R on the person from the lift (which has equal magnitude, by Newton's third law).

Example: A 30 tonne locomotive engine is pulling a single 10 tonne carriage as shown. They are accelerating at 0.3 ms^{-2} due to the force P generated by the engine. It's assumed that there are no forces resistant to motion. Find P and the tension in the coupling.

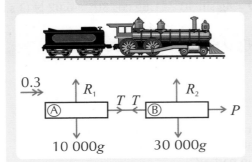

For carriage (A): $F_{net} = ma$
$T = 10\,000 \times 0.3$
$T = 3000 \text{ N}$

For engine (B): $F_{net} = ma$
$P - T = 30\,000 \times 0.3$
$P - 3000 = 9000$
$P = 12\,000 \text{ N}$

You can often resolve forces on each object to get a pair of simultaneous equations that you can solve. They're really easy here though since there's only one force on A.

Pulleys (and 'Pegs') are always Smooth

Out in the real world, things are complicated and scary. In A-level Maths, though, you can always assume that there's no **friction** on a **pulley** or a **peg**, and the **tension** in a **string** will be the **same** either side of it. What a relief.

Example: Masses of 3 kg and 5 kg are connected by an inextensible string and hang vertically either side of a smooth pulley. They are released from rest. Find their acceleration and the time it takes for each to move 40 cm. State any assumptions made in your model. Take $g = 9.8$ ms^{-2}.

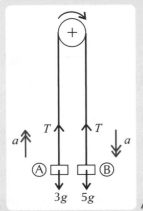

For A: $F_{net} = ma$
Resolving upwards: $T - 3g = 3a$ ①

For B: $F_{net} = ma$
Resolving downwards: $5g - T = 5a$
$T = 5g - 5a$ ②

Sub ② into ①: $(5g - 5a) - 3g = 3a$
$a = 2.45 \text{ ms}^{-2}$

List variables: $s = 0.4$ m, $u = 0$, $a = 2.45$ ms^{-2}, $t = t$

Use an equation with s, u, a and t in it: $s = ut + \frac{1}{2}at^2$

$0.4 = (0 \times t) + \left(\frac{1}{2} \times 2.45 \times t^2\right)$ So $t = \sqrt{\dfrac{0.8}{2.45}} = 0.571 \text{ s}$ (3 s.f.)

Assumptions: The 3 kg mass does not hit the pulley; there's no air resistance; the string is 'light' so the tension is the same for both A and B, and it doesn't break; the string is inextensible so the acceleration is the same for both masses.

Connected Particles

Use F = ma in the Direction Each Particle Moves

Example: A mass of 3 kg is placed on a smooth horizontal table. A light inextensible string connects it over a smooth peg to a 5 kg mass which hangs vertically as shown. Find the tension in the string if the system is released from rest. Take $g = 9.8$ ms^{-2}.

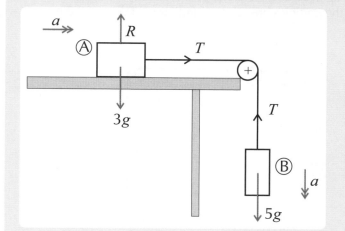

For A:
Resolve horizontally: $F_{net} = ma$
$$T = 3a$$
$$a = \frac{T}{3} \quad ①$$

For B:
Resolve vertically: $F_{net} = ma$
$$5g - T = 5a \quad ②$$

Sub ① into ②: $5g - T = 5 \times \frac{T}{3}$

So $\frac{8}{3}T = 5g$

$$T = 18.4 \text{ N (3 s.f.)}$$

Practice Questions

Q1 A person of mass 60 kg is standing in a lift of mass 600 kg connected to a light, inextensible vertical wire. The force exerted on them by the lift while it is moving is 640 N. Find the acceleration of the lift and the tension in the wire.

Q2 Two particles are connected by a light inextensible string, and hang in a vertical plane either side of a smooth pulley. When released from rest the particles accelerate at 1.2 ms^{-2}. If the heavier mass is 4 kg, find the weight of the other.

The state of these wires is certainly resulting in a **lot** of tension (don't try this at home).

Exam Questions

Q1 A car of mass 1500 kg is pulling a caravan of mass 500 kg. They experience resistance forces totalling 1000 N and 200 N respectively. The forward force generated by the car's engine is 2500 N. The coupling between the two does not break.

  a) Find the acceleration of the car and caravan.   [2 marks]

  b) Find the tension in the coupling.   [2 marks]

Q2 Two particles A and B are connected by a light inextensible string which passes over a smooth fixed pulley as shown. A has a mass of 7 kg and B has a mass of 3 kg. The particles are released from rest with the string taut, and A falls freely until it strikes the ground travelling at a speed of 5.9 ms^{-1}. A does not rebound after hitting the floor.

  a) Find the time taken for A to hit the ground.   [4 marks]

  b) How far will B have travelled when A hits the ground?   [2 marks]

  c) Find the time (in s) from when A hits the ground until the string becomes taut again.   [4 marks]

A (7 kg)

B (3 kg)

Connected particles — together forever... *isn't it beautiful?*

It makes things a lot easier when you know that connected particles act like one mass, and that you won't have to deal with rough pulleys. Those examiners occasionally do try to make your life easier, honestly (if only a little bit).

More on Connected Particles

More complicated pulley and peg questions have friction for you to enjoy too. Truly, your cup runneth over.

Remember to use F ≤ μR (or F = μR) on **Rough Planes**

Example: The model in the example on page 209 is refined to include a frictional force from the table. The coefficient of friction between the 3 kg mass and the table, μ, is assumed to be 0.5. Find the new tension in the string when the particles are released from rest. Take $g = 9.8$ ms^{-2}.

For B: Resolving vertically: $5g - T = 5a$ ①

For A: Resolving horizontally: $F_{net} = ma$
$T - F = 3a$ ②

Resolving vertically: $R - 3g = 0$
$R = 3g$

The particles are moving, so $F = \mu R = 0.5 \times 3g$
$F = \textbf{14.7 N}$

Sub this into ②: $T - 14.7 = 3a$
$a = \frac{1}{3}(T - 14.7)$

Sub this into ①: $5g - T = 5 \times \frac{1}{3}(T - 14.7)$
$8T = 147 + 73.5$
$T = \textbf{27.6 N}$ (3 s.f.)

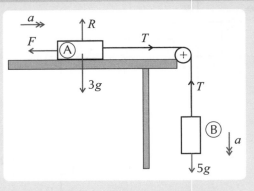

Resolve forces horizontally and vertically on each object and eventually you'll know everything there is to know about the system.

Example: Particles A and B of mass 4 kg and 10 kg respectively are connected by a light, inextensible string over a smooth pulley as shown. A force of 15 N acts on A at an angle of 25° to a rough horizontal plane where $\mu = 0.7$. When B is released from rest it takes 2 s to fall d m to the ground. Find d. Take $g = 9.8$ ms^{-2}.

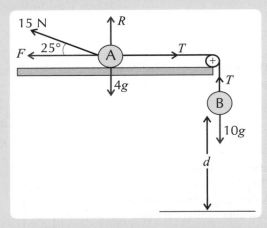

For A: Resolve vertically to find R:
$R = 4g - 15 \sin 25° = 32.86...$ N
$F = \mu R = 0.7 \times 32.86... = 23.00...$ N

Now, resolving horizontally:
$T - 23.00... - 15 \cos 25° = 4a$
so $T = 4a + 36.59...$ ①

For B: Resolve vertically:
$10g - T = 10a$
so $T = 98 - 10a$ ②

Substitute ① into ②:
$4a + 36.59... = 98 - 10a$
so $a = 4.385...$ ms^{-2}

Using $s = ut + \frac{1}{2}at^2$: $s = d$, $u = 0$, $a = 4.385...$, $t = 2$

So $d = (0 \times 2) + \frac{1}{2}(4.385... \times 2^2) = \textbf{8.77 m}$ (3 s.f.)

When B hits the ground, A carries on moving along the plane. How long does it take A to stop after B hits the ground?

Speed of A when B hits the ground:
$v = u + at$: $u = 0$, $a = 4.385...$, $t = 2$
$v = 0 + (4.385... \times 2) = 8.771...$ ms^{-1}

Resolve to find stopping force on A:
$F_{net} = 23.00... + 15 \cos 25° = 36.59...$ N

Deceleration, $a = \frac{F_{net}}{m} = \frac{36.59...}{4} = 9.149...$ ms^{-2}

Time taken to stop:
$t = \frac{(v - u)}{a}$: $v = 8.771...$, $u = 0$, $a = 9.149...$

so $t = \frac{8.771...}{9.149...} = \textbf{0.959 s}$ (3 s.f.)

More on Connected Particles

Rough Inclined Plane questions need Really Good force diagrams

You know the routine... resolve forces parallel and perpendicular to the plane... *yawn*

Example: A 3 kg mass is held in equilibrium on a rough ($\mu = 0.4$) plane inclined at 30° to the horizontal. It is attached by a light, inextensible string to a mass of M kg hanging vertically beneath a smooth pulley, as shown in the diagram. Find M if the 3 kg mass is on the point of sliding up the plane. Take $g = 9.8$ ms^{-2}.

For B: Resolving vertically: $F_{net} = ma$
$$Mg - T = M \times 0$$
$$\boldsymbol{T = Mg}$$

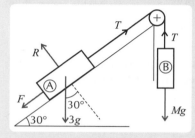

For A: Resolving perpendicular ($\nwarrow$): $F_{net} = ma$
$$R - 3g \cos 30° = 3 \times 0$$
$$\boldsymbol{R = 3g \cos 30°}$$

It's limiting friction, so: $F = \mu R = 0.4 \times 3g \cos 30°$
$$\boldsymbol{F = 1.2g \cos 30°}$$

For A: Resolving parallel ($\nearrow$):

$$T - F - 3g \sin 30° = 3 \times 0$$
$$Mg - 1.2g \cos 30° - 3g \sin 30° = 0$$
$$M - 1.039... - 1.5 = 0$$
$$\boldsymbol{M = 2.54 \text{ kg}} \text{ (3 s.f.)}$$

Practice Question

Q1 Two particles, A and B, of mass 3 kg and 4 kg respectively, are connected by a light, inextensible, string passing over a smooth pulley as shown. The 3 kg mass is on a smooth slope angled at 40° to the horizontal. Find the acceleration of the system if released from rest, and find the tension in the string. What force acting on the 3 kg mass parallel to the plane would be needed to maintain equilibrium?

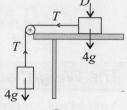

Exam Questions

Q1 Two particles P and Q of masses 1 kg and M kg respectively are linked by a light inextensible string passing over a smooth pulley as shown. Particle P is on a rough slope inclined at 20° to the horizontal, where the coefficient of friction between P and the slope is 0.1.

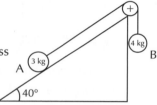

a) Given that P is about to slide down the plane, find the mass of Q to 2 s.f.   [5 marks]

b) When the mass of Q is 1 kg, it pulls P up the slope. Find the acceleration of P in this situation.   [5 marks]

Q2 A box of mass 4 kg rests on a rough table, connected to an identical box, hanging over the edge of the table, by a light, inextensible string passing over a smooth pulley. The box is held in place by a force, D, acting perpendicular to the table as shown. The coefficient of friction between the box and the table is 0.6.

a) Find the minimum magnitude of D required for the boxes to remain at rest.   [5 marks]

b) The force D is removed. Find the velocity of the boxes 2 seconds later (assuming that the boxes do not hit the floor or the pulley).   [6 marks]

Q3 Two particles of mass 5 kg and 7 kg are connected by a light inextensible string passing over a smooth pulley as shown. Given that the coefficient of friction between each particle and the rough surface is 0.15, and that neither particle strikes the pulley, find the acceleration of the 5 kg particle.   [8 marks]

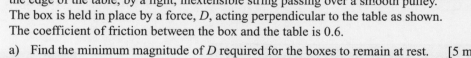

Rough, inclined planes AND connected particles? You're pulley my leg...

The key word here is rough. If a question mentions the surface is rough, then cogs should whirr and the word 'friction' should pop into your head. Take your time with force diagrams of rough inclined planes — I had a friend who rushed into drawing a diagram, and he ended up with a broken arm. But that was years later, now that I come to think of it.

Moments

In this lifetime there are moments: moments of joy and of sorrow, and those moments where you have to answer questions on moments in exams. You might also want to take a moment to brush up on resolving forces.

Moment = Force × **Perpendicular** Distance from the force's **Line of Action**

A '**moment**' is the **turning effect** a force has **around a point**. The **larger the force**, and the **greater the distance** from a point, then the **larger the moment**. In an exam question, you might be given a distance between the point and the force that's **not perpendicular** to the force's '**line of action**'. You'll need to **resolve** to find the **perpendicular distance** or the **perpendicular component** of the force.

> **Example:** Find the sum of the moments of the forces shown about the point A.
>
>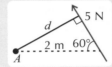
>
> Calculating the **clockwise moment** is simple as the line of action is perpendicular to A:
>
> $2 \times 1 = \mathbf{2\ Nm}$
>
> *The units of moments are newton-metres (Nm) — unimaginative, but easy to remember.*
>
> The **anticlockwise moment** is trickier as the line of action of the force **isn't perpendicular** to A. There are two ways to go about finding the moment — by finding the **perpendicular distance** or finding the **perpendicular component** of the force.
>
>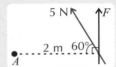
>
> Finding the **perpendicular distance**:
>
> $d = 2 \sin 60°$
>
> So, moment $= 5 \times 2 \sin 60° = 10 \sin 60° = \mathbf{5\sqrt{3}\ Nm}$
>
> Finding the **perpendicular component** of the force:
>
> $F = 5 \sin 60°$
>
> So, moment $= 5 \sin 60° \times 2 = 10 \sin 60° = \mathbf{5\sqrt{3}\ Nm}$
>
> *Both methods give the same moment. Just choose whichever you find simplest — and be sure to show your workings.*
>
> We can now find the **sum** of the moments (in this case, taking anticlockwise as negative):
>
> Clockwise + anticlockwise moments $= 2 + (-5\sqrt{3}) = -6.6602...$ Nm $= \mathbf{6.66\ Nm\ anticlockwise}$ (3 s.f.)

> If a system is in **equilibrium**, anticlockwise moments = clockwise moments about **any** point.

> **Example:** A rod, AB, of length 6 m is held in **equilibrium** by two strings, as shown. By taking moments, find the mass, m, of the rod. Take $g = 9.8$ ms^{-2}.
>
> Although you can take moments about any point, it's usually easier to take moments about a point that has an unknown force going through it. Here, the moment of T about A = O.
>
>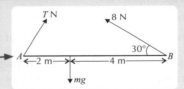
>
> By taking moments **about** A:
> clockwise moments = anticlockwise moments
> $2mg = 6 \sin 30° \times 8$
> $mg = 12$
> $m = 12 \div 9.8 = \mathbf{1.22\ kg}$ (3 s.f.)

The **Weight** acts at the **Centre** of a **Uniform** rod

A model **rod** has **negligible thickness**, so you only need to consider where along its **length** the centre of mass lies. If the rod is **uniform** then the weight acts at the **centre** of the rod.

> **Example:** A uniform rod, AB, of length l m and mass m kg is suspended horizontally in equilibrium by two inextensible wires, with tensions as shown. Find m.
>
>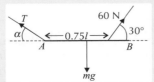
>
> Taking moments about A:
> $mg \times 0.5l = 60 \sin 30° \times 0.75l$
> $mg \times 0.5 = 30 \times 0.75$
> $4.9m = 22.5$
> $m = \mathbf{4.59\ kg}$ (3 s.f.)
>
> *Again, you can pick any point to take moments about, but it makes sense to choose A, because that eliminates the unknown force, T.*

If this chap was called Rod, this caption would've been hilarious...

Moments

You can calculate the **Centre of Mass** for **Non-Uniform** rods

If the weight acts at an **unknown** point along a rod, the point can be found in the usual way — by taking **moments**. You might also have to **resolve** the forces **horizontally** or **vertically** to find some missing information.

> **Example:** A non-uniform rod, AB, of mass 2 kg and length 1 m, is suspended in equilibrium at an angle of θ to the vertical by two vertical strings, as shown. The tensions in the strings are T N and 12 N respectively. Find the distance, x, from A to the rod's centre of mass.
>
>
>
> Taking moments about A: clockwise moments = anticlockwise moments
> $$2g \sin \theta \times x = 12 \sin \theta \times 1$$
> 2 sin θ cancels $\longrightarrow$ $gx = 6 \Rightarrow x = 0.612$ m (3 s.f.)

The '**Point of Tilting**' means **Other Reactions** are **Zero**

If a rod is **resting** on a **support**, then there will be a **normal reaction** force acting on the rod. If it's '**on the point of tilting**' or '**about to tilt**' about a particular support, then any normal reactions acting at any **other** supports along the rod will be zero. This works exactly the same way for **tension** in **strings** supporting the rod (like in the previous example). This should make sense in the context, when you think about which way the rod is about to rotate. You can usually assume that supports and strings are **fixed**, and won't move with the rod.

> **Example:** A non-uniform wooden plank of mass M kg rests horizontally on supports at A and B, as shown. When a bucket of water of mass 18 kg is placed at point C, the plank is in equilibrium, and is on the point of tilting about B. Find the value of M and the magnitude of the reaction at B.
>
> 1) Taking moments about B: The plank is on the point of tilting about B,
> $(18g \times 1.2) + 0 = Mg \times 0.8$ so $R_A = 0$ (the moment is also zero).
> $\Rightarrow M = (18 \times 9.8 \times 1.2) \div (9.8 \times 0.8) = \mathbf{27}$ **kg**
>
>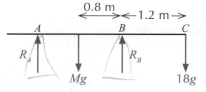
>
> 2) Resolving vertically:
> $R_A + R_B = Mg + 18g$
> $0 + R_B = 27g + 18g \Rightarrow R_B = \mathbf{441}$ **N**
>
>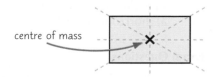

Laminas are **Two-Dimensional** objects

A **lamina** is a flat 2D object (its thickness can be ignored). The centre of mass of a **uniform rectangular** lamina is at the symmetrical centre of the rectangle.

centre of mass

> **Example:** A uniform rectangular lamina, $ABCD$, of weight 8 N, is pivoted at point A. The lamina is held in equilibrium by a vertical force F acting at point C, as shown.
> a) Find the horizontal and vertical distances of the centre of mass of the lamina from A.
> b) Find the magnitude of the force F.
>
>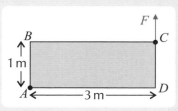
>
> a) The centre of mass is at the centre of the lamina, so the horizontal distance is $3 \div 2 = \mathbf{1.5}$ **m** and the vertical distance is $1 \div 2 = \mathbf{0.5}$ **m**
>
> You'll need to know the position of the centre of mass to figure out the perpendicular distance of the weight force from the pivot.
>
> b) Both the lamina's weight and F act vertically, so the perpendicular distance from each force to the pivot is just the horizontal distance.
> Taking moments about A: $8 \times 1.5 = F \times 3$
> $\Rightarrow F = 12 \div 3 = \mathbf{4}$ **N**
>
>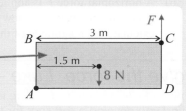

Moments

Resolve Forces relative to the Edges of the Lamina

If there are forces acting **at angles** to the sides of the lamina, it's usually easier to resolve them **perpendicular** and **parallel** to the lamina's sides. But remember that **both components** will have a turning effect on the lamina.

Example: A uniform rectangular lamina of mass 12 kg is pivoted at one corner at A. A light, inextensible string attached at the opposite corner applies a tension force T to the lamina, as shown.

Given that the string holds the lamina in equilibrium at an angle of 20° to the horizontal, find the tension in the string.

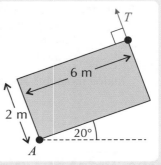

1) Here, the lamina's weight acts at 20° to its sides. Find the components of its weight parallel and perpendicular to the sides of the lamina. Drawing a diagram will be helpful:

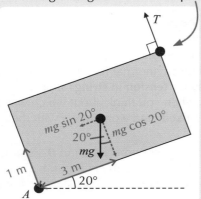

2) Now you can take moments about A, but watch out — the two components of the weight force **both** have turning effects, one clockwise and one anticlockwise. They also have **different perpendicular distances**, so don't get caught out.

3) Taking moments about A:

clockwise moments = anticlockwise moments

$$(mg \cos 20° \times 3) = (mg \sin 20° \times 1) + (T \times 6)$$
$$6T = mg(3 \cos 20° - \sin 20°)$$
$$T = 19.6(2.4770...)$$
$$= \mathbf{48.6 \text{ N}} \text{ (3 s.f.)}$$

> You could also do this without breaking the weight into components — instead, you'd find the horizontal distance from A to the COM, which is the perpendicular distance from A to the line of action of the weight.

Practice Questions

Q1 Given that the rod in the diagram is in equilibrium, calculate the value of x and the magnitude of T.

28 N
T 128.3°   120°
xy y
42 N

Q2 A painting of mass 10 kg, modelled as a uniform rectangular lamina $ABCD$, hangs from two fixed, smooth pegs at A and B, as shown. The peg at B breaks. Calculate the force required to hold the painting in equilibrium, if the force is applied:
a) horizontally at D, b) vertically at C.

Exam Questions

Q1 A uniform rod AB of mass 7 kg is suspended horizontally in equilibrium from two fixed inextensible strings. One is attached at P, 1 m from A, and the other is at Q, 2 m from B. Given that the length of the rod is 9 m, find:

a) the tension in each string, T_P and T_Q, [4 marks]

b) the maximum mass, M, that could be attached to the rod without causing it to tilt, if the mass were attached at: (i) A, (ii) B. [6 marks]

Q2 A uniform rectangular lamina, $ABCD$, of mass 20 kg, rests on two rough supports: one at C, and another at E, 8 m from C as shown.

a) Calculate the reaction forces from the supports at C and E. [4 marks]

b) A horizontal force F is applied at B, acting towards A. Given that the lamina is now on the point of tilting about E, calculate the magnitude of the force F. [3 marks]

A ←— 10 m —→ B
4 m
D   E ←— 8 m —→ C

Resolve the force, Luke — or use the perpendicular distance...

The only tricky thing here is deciding which point to take moments about. Once you've done loads of these questions, you'll find you develop a soft spot for them. Don't believe me? Search your feelings — you know it to be true.

Rigid Bodies and Friction

Where would we be without friction? Well, for one thing, using a ladder would certainly be trickier...

Reactions can have Horizontal and Vertical Components

If a rod is connected to a plane (such as a wall) by a **hinge** or **pivot**, and the forces holding it in equilibrium **aren't parallel**, the reaction at the wall **won't be perpendicular** to the wall. Resolving into components is helpful here.

Example: A non-uniform rod, AB, of length $6a$ m and mass 4 kg is held in equilibrium by a light strut at an angle of 70° to a vertical wall, as shown. The distance from A to X, the centre of mass of the rod, is xa m. The strut exerts a thrust of 16 N at the centre of the rod. A particle of weight 2 N is placed at B. Find x, and the magnitude and direction of the reaction at A.

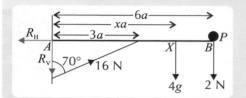

Put the unknown reaction at the wall as a horizontal and a vertical component. Don't worry about their directions — you'll just get a negative answer if you're wrong.

Taking moments about A:
$(4g \times xa) + (2 \times 6a) = 16 \cos 70° \times 3a$
$4gx = 4.416... \Rightarrow x = \textbf{0.113}$ (3 s.f.)

You're looking at the forces on the rod, so there's no reaction force upwards at B.

Resolving vertically:
$R_V + 4g + 2 = 16 \cos 70°$
so $R_V = 16 \cos 70° - 39.2 - 2$
$\Rightarrow R_V = -35.72...$ N (so R_V acts upwards)

Resolving horizontally:
$R_H = 16 \sin 70° \Rightarrow R_H = 15.03...$ N

Magnitude of reaction:
$|R| = \sqrt{R_H^2 + R_V^2} = \sqrt{15.03...^2 + 35.72...^2}$
$= \textbf{38.8 N}$ (3 s.f.)

Direction of reaction:
$\tan\theta = \dfrac{15.03...}{35.72...}$
$\Rightarrow \theta = \textbf{22.8°}$ (3 s.f.) to the wall

Friction lets you assume the Reaction is Perpendicular

A rod **attached** to a wall has a **reaction** at the wall with a **horizontal** and **vertical** component.
If the rod is held by **friction** instead, then the frictional force 'replaces' the **vertical** component.

Example: A rod, AB, rests against a rough vertical wall and is held in limiting equilibrium perpendicular to the wall by a light inextensible string attached at B at an angle of θ, as shown, where $\tan\theta = \dfrac{7}{17}$. The tension in the string is 42 N. The length AB is 5.5 m and the centre of mass is located 3.8 m from B. Find the mass of the rod, m, and the coefficient of friction, μ, between the wall and the rod.

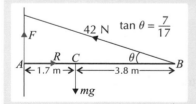

First, work out what $\sin\theta$ and $\cos\theta$ are by drawing a right-angled triangle:

$\sin\theta = \dfrac{7}{\sqrt{338}} = 0.3807...$

$\cos\theta = \dfrac{17}{\sqrt{338}} = 0.9246...$

Taking moments about A means you can find mg while ignoring the unknowns F and R. → Moments about A: $mg \times 1.7 = 42 \sin\theta \times 5.5$
$mg = 51.73...$ N
$m = \textbf{5.28 kg}$ (3 s.f.)

Now take moments about a different point to find F. I've taken them about C, but you could have used B. → Moments about C: $1.7 \times F = 3.8 \times 42 \sin\theta$
$F = 35.74...$ N

Now you know F, you only need to find R before you can find μ. → Resolving horizontally: $R = 42 \cos\theta$
$R = 38.83...$ N

Limiting equilibrium showed up on p.205 — it means that the body is on the point of moving. → Equilibrium is limiting, so: $F = \mu R$
$35.74... = 38.83...\mu$
$\mu = \textbf{0.92}$ (2 d.p.)

Rigid Bodies and Friction

Multiple Surfaces can exert a Frictional Force

When a rod rests at an angle against two surfaces, **either** or **both** of them could exert a frictional force.
'Ladder' questions are a common example of this — keep an eye out for when the floor or the wall are **rough**.

Example: A ladder, modelled as a uniform rod of mass 1.3 kg and length $5x$ m,
rests against a smooth wall at an angle of 65° to the rough ground, as shown.
A cat of mass 4.5 kg sits on the ladder at C, $4x$ m from the base.

Given that the ladder is in limiting equilibrium,
find the coefficient of friction between the ground and the ladder.

Take moments about the base of the ladder to find N:

$N \sin 65° \times 5x = (1.3g \cos 65° \times 2.5x) + (4.5g \cos 65° \times 4x)$
$4.531...xN = 13.46...x + 74.59...x$
$N = \dfrac{88.01...x}{4.531...x} = 19.42...$ N

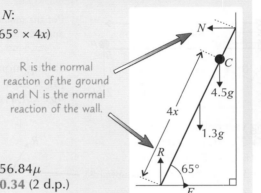

R is the normal reaction of the ground and N is the normal reaction of the wall.

Resolve vertically to find R:
$R = 1.3g + 4.5g = 56.84$ N

The ladder is in limiting equilibrium, so $F = \mu R$:
Resolving horizontally shows $F = N$, so $19.42... = 56.84\mu$
$\mu = \mathbf{0.34}$ (2 d.p.)

No ladder problems here...

Sometimes a body may be leaning against a surface that **isn't vertical** (this blows my mind).
Just remember that the **reaction force** always acts **perpendicular to the surface**.

Example: A uniform ladder of length 3 m rests against a smooth
wall slanted at 80° to the horizontal, as shown.
The ladder is at an angle of 60° to the ground.
The magnitude of the normal reaction of the
wall is 18 N. Find the mass of the ladder.

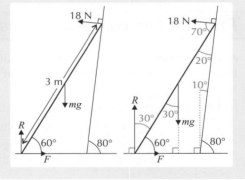

The diagram on the right shows that the angle that the
reaction force from the wall makes with the ladder is 70°.

Taking moments about the base of the ladder:
$mg \sin 30° \times 1.5 = 18 \sin 70° \times 3$
so $m = 50.74... \div 7.35 = \mathbf{6.90}$ **kg** (3 s.f.)

Bodies can be Supported Along Their Lengths

If a rod is **resting** on something along its length then the reaction is **perpendicular** to the **rod**.

Example: A uniform rod, AB, rests with end A on rough ground and upon a smooth peg at C, as shown.
A particle, P, with weight 25 N is placed at B. Given that the rod is in limiting equilibrium,
find the normal reaction, N, at the peg and the friction, F, between the rod and the ground.

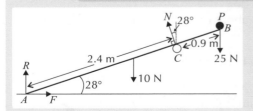

Moments about A:
$2.4N = (10 \cos 28° \times [(2.4 + 0.9) \div 2]) + (25 \cos 28° \times 3.3)$
$\Rightarrow N = \mathbf{36.4}$ **N** (3 s.f.)

It's a uniform rod, so its weight acts in the middle.

Resolving horizontally:
$F = N \sin 28° = 36.4 \sin 28°$
$\Rightarrow F = \mathbf{17.1}$ **N** (3 s.f.)

Rigid Bodies and Friction

You can work out a **Range** for μ

In limiting equilibrium, friction is at its **maximum** (i.e. $F = \mu R$). You might be asked to find μ when you **don't know** if equilibrium is limiting. Find it in the same way as if equilibrium was limiting, but replace $F = \mu R$ with $F \leq \mu R$.

Example: A rough peg supports a rod of length 1.5 m at a point B, as shown. It rests on a smooth horizontal plane at A, and its weight acts at point C. Given that the friction at the peg exerts a force of 8 N, show that $\mu \geq 0.31$ to 2 d.p.

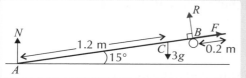

You know F, but to find μ you also need to know R.

Take moments about A to find R:

$R \times (1.5 - 0.2) = 3g \cos 15° \times 1.2$

$R = 26.2... \text{ N}$

$F \leq \mu R,$
$\mu \geq 8 \div 26.2...$
$\mu \geq \mathbf{0.31}$ (2 d.p.) as required

Practice Questions

Q1 A uniform ladder, of length l m, is placed on rough horizontal ground and rests against a smooth vertical wall at an angle of 20° to the wall. Draw a diagram modelling this system with forces labelled. State the assumptions you would make.

Q2 A non-uniform rod, AB, is freely hinged at a vertical wall. It is held horizontally in equilibrium by a strut attached to the wall at C at an angle of 55°, as shown. The thrust in the strut is 30 N. The rod is x m long, and has mass 2 kg, centred 0.4 m from A. Taking $g = 9.8$ ms^{-2}, find:

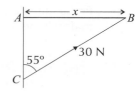

a) the length of the rod, x,

b) the magnitude and direction of the reaction at A.

Exam Questions

Whenever a numerical value of g is required in the following questions, take $g = 9.8$ ms^{-2}.

Q1 A uniform rod of mass m kg rests in equilibrium against rough horizontal ground at point A and a smooth peg at point B, making an angle of θ with the ground, where $\sin\theta = \frac{3}{5}$. The rod is l m long and B is $\frac{3}{4}l$ from A.

a) Show that the normal reaction at the peg, $N = \frac{2}{3}mg \cos\theta$. [3 marks]

b) Find the range of possible values of the coefficient of friction between the rod and the ground. [6 marks]

Q2 A uniform ladder AB rests in limiting equilibrium against a smooth vertical wall (A) and upon the rough horizontal ground (B) at an angle of θ. Clive stands on the ladder at point C a third of the way along its length from the base B. The ladder is 4.2 m long and weighs 180 N. The normal reaction at A is 490 N. Given that $\tan\theta = \frac{8}{11}$, find:

a) the mass of Clive, m, to the nearest kg, [3 marks]

b) the coefficient of friction, μ, between the ground and the ladder. [4 marks]

Q3 A uniform rod, AB, of mass 3 kg is held horizontally in limiting equilibrium against a rough wall by an inextensible string connected to the rod at point C and the wall at point D, as shown. A particle of mass m kg rests at point B. The magnitude of the normal reaction of the wall at A is 72.5 N. Find:

a) the tension, T, in the string, and the mass, m, of the particle, [5 marks]

b) the frictional force, F, between the wall and the rod. [2 marks]

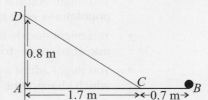

...and that's everything you need to know about anything, ever.

If you've been revising the topics in order, this is the end of A-level Maths (and the end of my quips, sadly). Of course, there's no harm in going back for another go. Have a nice cup of tea first though — you deserve it. There are also some exam tips coming up that are definitely worth checking out. You'll be a master of maths before you know it.

Modelling and Problem Solving

Modelling and problem solving are two of the three overarching themes of the A-level Maths course (the third being proof, which is covered in Section 1). This means that they could come up in exam questions on any topic.

A *Mathematical Model* simplifies a *Real-life Situation*

A **mathematical model** is a mathematical description of a real-life situation. Modelling involves **simplifying** the situation so that you can understand its behaviour and predict what is going to happen.

Modelling in maths generally boils down to using an **equation** or a **set of equations** to predict what will happen in real life. You'll meet it in **all** areas of this course including population growth in **algebra** (see pages 82-83), moving objects in **mechanics** (see Section 16) and probability distributions in **statistics** (see Section 13).

Models use Assumptions

Models are always **simplifications** of the real-life situation. When you construct a model, you have to make **assumptions**. In other words, you **ignore** or **simplify** some factors that might affect the real-life outcome, in order to keep the maths simpler. For example:

- A population growth model might ignore the fact that the population will eventually run out of **food**, because that won't happen in the **time period** you're modelling.
- A model for the speed of a moving object might ignore **air resistance**, because that would make the maths much **more complicated**, or because you might only want a **general result** for objects of all shapes and sizes.
- Probability distributions based on past data often assume the **conditions** in future trials will be the **same** as when the past data was recorded.

There are lots of special terms to describe the assumptions you might make in mechanics — there's a list of them on page 198.

Example: Leon owns a gooseberry farm. This week, he had 5 workers picking fruit, and they picked a total of 1000 punnets of gooseberries. Leon wants to hire more workers for next week. He predicts that next week, if the number of workers on his farm is w, the farm will produce p punnets of gooseberries, where $p = 200w$.
Suggest three assumptions Leon has made in his model.

This is a model because it is a prediction of how many punnets will be produced — the actual number could be higher or lower. The model predicts that the average number of punnets produced per worker each week will be the same. For example:

- There will be enough gooseberries to fill 200 punnets per worker, however many workers he employs.
- The weather is good enough to allow each worker to work the same number of hours each week.
- Any new workers he employs will work at the same speed, on average.

There are lots more possible answers here.

You might have to *Criticise* or *Refine* a model

An important part of the modelling process is **refining** a model. This usually happens after the model has been **tested** by comparing it with real-world outcomes, or if you find out some **extra information** that affects the model. Refining a model usually means changing some of the **assumptions**. For example:

- You might adjust a population growth model if you found that **larger populations** were more susceptible to **disease**, so grew more slowly.
- You might decide to refine a model for the speed of an object to take into account the **friction** from the surface the object is travelling over.
- You might adjust a probability distribution if you collect **more data** which changes the **relative frequency** of the outcomes.

You could be asked to criticise or evaluate a model — e.g. you might need to assess if any assumptions are unrealistic.

Example:
(cont.) Leon discovers that the weather forecast for next week is bad, and his workers are only likely to be able to pick gooseberries for half the number of hours they did this week. How should the model be refined?

If the workers can only pick for half the time, they'll probably pick half as many gooseberries.

The refined model would be $p = 200w \div 2 \implies \boldsymbol{p = 100w}$.

Modelling and Problem Solving

Problem Solving questions are more Challenging

Some maths questions can be straightforward to answer — you're told what maths you need to use, then you use it to get a solution. 'Problem solving' questions are those tricky ones where you have to work out for yourself exactly what maths you need to do.

Problem solving questions include:

- questions that don't have 'scaffolding' (i.e. they're not broken down into parts a), b), c) etc.),
- questions where the information is disguised (e.g. a 'wordy' context, or a diagram),
- questions that need more than one area of maths,
- questions that test if you actually understand the maths as well as being able to use it.

The Problem Solving Cycle can be Useful for maths questions

When it's not obvious what you're supposed to do with a question, you can use the problem solving cycle. This breaks the problem up into the following steps:

1. Specify the problem
The first thing to do is work out what the question is actually asking. The question might be phrased in an unusual way or it might be written in a 'wordy' context, where you need to turn the words into maths.

2. Collect information
Write down what you know. All the information you need to answer the question will either be given in the question somewhere (possibly on a diagram), or it'll require facts that you should already know.

3. Process and represent information
When you know what you're trying to find out, and what you already know, you can do the calculation to answer the question.

4. Interpret results
Don't forget to give your answer in terms of the original context. The result of your calculation won't necessarily be the final answer.

5. Repeat (if necessary)

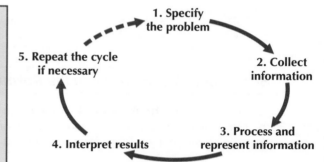

When you're doing an exam question, it's unlikely that you'll need to repeat the problem solving cycle once you've calculated the answer — just be aware that it's part of the general problem solving process.

You could also be asked to evaluate the accuracy or limitations of your solutions.

Example: Armand cuts out a semicircle from a rectangular sheet of cardboard measuring 20 cm by 40 cm and throws the rest away. The cardboard he throws away has an area of 398.08 cm². How long is the straight side of the semicircle?

1) What are you trying to find? The length of the straight side of a semicircle is the diameter of the circle, which is twice the radius.

2) What do you know? The total area of the sheet of cardboard is 20 cm × 40 cm.
398.08 cm² was thrown away, so the rest is the area of the semicircle. The area of a semicircle = $\frac{1}{2}$ × area of a circle = $\frac{1}{2}\pi r^2$.

3) Do the maths. Area of semicircle = $(20 \times 40) - 398.08 = 800 - 398.08 = 401.92$ cm²
So: $401.92 = \frac{1}{2}\pi r^2$
$\Rightarrow r^2 = 401.92 \times 2 \div \pi = 803.84 \div \pi \Rightarrow r = \sqrt{803.84 \div \pi}$ cm
$\Rightarrow d = 2r = 2 \times \sqrt{803.84 \div \pi} = 31.99... = 32.0$ cm (3 s.f.)

4) Give the answer in the context of the question. The length of the straight side of the semicircle is **32.0 cm** (3 s.f.).

99% of modelling jobs require A-level maths...

You can apply the problem solving cycle to all sorts: 1. Need to pass A-level Maths exams. 2. Buy CGP revision guide. 3. Knuckle down and get revising. 4. Do some questions and check your answers. 5. Get the kettle on and repeat.*

*cheeky plug for our fabulous Exam Practice Workbooks

Do Well in Your Exams

Exam Structure and Technique

Good exam technique can make a big difference to your mark, so make sure you read this stuff carefully.

Get familiar with the **Exam Structure**

For **A-level Mathematics**, you'll be sitting **three papers**.
Each paper has the **same** examination time, number of marks and weight.

Paper 1 won't include any topics from Sections 10-18.

Paper 1 (Pure Mathematics) 2 hours **100** marks	**33.33%** of your A-level	Covers material from **Sections 1-9** of this book.
Paper 2 (Pure Mathematics and Mechanics) 2 hours **100** marks	**33.33%** of your A-level	Covers material from **Sections 1-10 and 16-18** of this book.
Paper 3 (Pure Mathematics and Statistics) 2 hours **100** marks	**33.33%** of your A-level	Covers material from **Sections 1-9 and 11-15** of this book.

Papers 2 and 3 are split into Section A (Pure Mathematics) and Section B (Mechanics/Statistics) — worth 50 marks each. There may be some questions in Section B that need a bit of pure maths.

Some formulas are given in the **Formula Booklet**

You'll be given a **formula booklet** for the exam that lists some of
the formulas you might need. There's a copy of this on pages 256-257.
You don't need to learn these formulas but you do need to know **how to use** them.

Manage Your Time sensibly

1) The **number of marks** tells you roughly **how long** to spend on a question — you've got just over a minute per mark in the exam. If you get stuck on a question for too long, it may be best to **move on** so you don't run out of time for the others.

2) You don't have to work through the paper **in order** — you could leave questions on topics you find harder until last.

Be **Careful** with **Calculations**

You should always show your **calculations** for all questions — you may get some marks for your **method** even if you get the answer wrong. But you should bear the following in mind:

1) You should give your final answer to a sensible number of **decimal places** or **significant figures** that is **appropriate** to the context, unless the **question** specifies otherwise. In Mechanics, for example, if some of the quantities in the question are given to 3 s.f. and others are given to 2 s.f. then your final answer should be given to 2 s.f. (the **lowest degree of accuracy** in the question). Writing out the unrounded answer, then your rounded answer shows that you know your stuff.

2) Don't **round** your answer until the **very end**. A lot of calculations in A-level Maths are quite **long**, and if you round too early you could introduce errors to your final answer. When using a **calculator** you can **store** full decimals, which you can then use in further calculations.

3) For some questions, you can use your calculator to **check** your answer. Just make sure you've included **all** the working out first, so you don't lose any marks.

4) Your calculator must have an **iterative function** (usually an **ANS** key), and must be able to compute **summary statistics** and **probabilities** from **statistical distributions** (see pages 163-167 for more information).

5) **Calculators** that manipulate algebra, do symbolic differentiation tend integration or have retrievable formulas stored in them are **banned** from the exam. If you're not sure whether your calculator is allowed, **check** with your teacher or exam board.

Do Well in Your Exams

Exam Structure and Technique

Make Sure You **Read the Question**

1) It sounds obvious, but it's really important you read each question **carefully**, and give an answer that matches what you've been asked.

2) Look at **how many marks** a question is worth before answering. It'll tell you roughly **how much information** you need to include.

3) Look for **key words** in the question — often the first word in the question. These give you an idea of the **kind of answer** you should write. Some of the commonly used key words are given in the table below:

Key words	Meaning in the exam
Find / Calculate / Determine	These are general terms that could be used for pretty much **anything**. You should always **give working** to show how you found the answer.
Solve	When given an **equation**, solving means finding the **value(s)** of the **variable** (e.g. x or a).
State / Write down	No working is required — often for an **assumption**, **reason** or **example**.
Explain	You must give **reasons**, not just a description — these **can** include **calculations** as part of your explanation.
Show that	You're given a **result** that you have to show is true. Because you're given the answer, you should include **every step** of your working.
Prove	Use a **logical argument** to show the statement or equation you're asked to prove is true.
Plot	**Accurately** mark points on a graph or draw a line of best fit.
Sketch	Draw a diagram showing the **main features** of the graph. This doesn't have to be drawn to **scale**, but will need to include some of the following: correct **shape**, x- and y- **intercepts**, **asymptotes**, and **turning points**.
Verify	You're given a numerical **solution** to a problem, and you have to **show** that it really is a solution — usually by **substituting** it into an equation from earlier in the question.
Hence	Use the **previous statement** or **question** part to answer the next bit of the question. '**Hence or otherwise**' means there's another way to answer the question — so if you can't quite see what they want you to do with the 'hence' bit, you can solve it another way and still get all the marks (but be aware that the other way might take longer).
Exact	If a question asks for an **exact value**, don't round. This usually means giving an answer in terms of something like **e**, **ln**, or π, a **square** (or other) **root**, or a **fraction** you can't write as a terminating decimal.

Get **Familiar** with the **Large Data Set**

Throughout the A-level Maths course you'll be working with the **large data set**. This is a group of **tables** containing information about **purchased quantities of foods and drinks** in different regions of the UK. The large data set will only be used in Paper 3 for A-Level Maths.

Questions in this paper might:

1) assume that you're familiar with the terminology, contexts, and some of the broad trends of the data (e.g. London is generally different to the other regions),

2) use summary statistics based on the large data set (this might reduce the time needed for some calculations),

3) include statistical diagrams based on the large data set,

4) be based on a sample from the large data set.

Going through 14 years of shopping receipts was no easy task...

The last gag in the book is always a disappointment...

Revising exam technique doesn't sound the most exciting thing in the world (monkey tennis?), but it will actually make a big difference to your mark. In fact, exam technique is a skill that you can master — next time you do an exercise, try to apply the stuff you've seen on these pages to the questions. It's also worth spending some time working with the large data set — you'll be glad that you did when you're facing the large data set questions in the exam.

Answers

Section 1 — Proof

Page 3 — Proof

Practice Questions

1 a) $\{2\}$ b) $\{1, 2, 4, 7, 14, 28\}$ c) $\{-1, 1\}$

2 a) E.g. $x = 1$, $y = -2$. Any answer where $\frac{x}{y} < 1$ holds and $x > y$ is correct.

   b) E.g. $x = 0$, $y = 1$. Any x and y that satisfy $y = 1 - x$ also correct.

Exam Questions

1   Expand and simplify the brackets:

$n^2 + 12n + 36 - (n^2 + 2n + 1) = 10n + 35$ *[1 mark]*

$= 5(2n + 7)$ *[1 mark]*

If n is an integer, $(2n + 7)$ is also an integer, and any number that can be written as $5 \times$ an integer is divisible by 5.

So $(n + 6)^2 - (n + 1)^2$ is divisible by 5. *[1 mark]*

2   Prove by exhaustion. For any integer n, the difference between a number and its square is: $n^2 - n = n(n - 1)$

If n is even, $(n - 1)$ is odd and an even number times an odd number is even, so $n(n - 1)$ is even.

If n is odd, $(n - 1)$ is even and an odd number times an even number is even, so $n(n - 1)$ is even.

So, since n must either be even or odd, the difference between a number and its square is even for any integer n.

[3 marks available — 1 for considering cases where n is odd and even separately, 1 for correct working to show $n^2 - n$ is even in both cases and 1 for a correct conclusion]

3   Expand the brackets: $x^2 + x - 2 > 2x - 2 \implies x^2 - x > 0$ *[1 mark]*

When $x = 1$, $1^2 - 1 = 0$, so $x = 1$ is a counter-example. *[1 mark]*

Therefore the statement is false. *[1 mark]*

The counter-example could be any value of x in the range $0 \le x \le 1$.

Page 5 — Proof by Contradiction

Practice Questions

1   Assume the statement is not true. Then there must be an irrational number x for which $-x$ is rational.

If $-x$ is rational then $-x = \frac{a}{b}$, where a and b are non-zero integers.

Now $x = -\frac{a}{b}$, which is also rational.

But this contradicts the statement that x is irrational.

So if x is irrational, then $-x$ must also be irrational.

2   Assume that the largest multiple of 21 can be written N, where $N = 21n$ and n is an integer.

If you add 21 to this you get $N + 21 = 21n + 21 = 21(n + 1)$, which is also a multiple of 21 and is larger number than N.

This contradicts the statement that N is the largest multiple of 21. So there must be no largest multiple of 21.

3 a) Assume that the largest integer power of 10 can be written N, where $N = 10^n$ and n is an integer.

But if you multiply this by 10 you get $10N = 10^n \times 10 = 10^{n+1}$, which is a larger number than N.

This contradicts the statement that N is the largest integer power of 10. So there must be no largest integer power of 10.

  b) Assume that the smallest integer power of 10 can be written M, where $M = 10^m$ and m is an integer.

But if you divide this by 10 you get $M \div 10 = 10^m \div 10 = 10^{m-1}$, which is a smaller number than M.

This contradicts the statement that M is the smallest integer power of 10. So there must be no smallest integer power of 10.

Exam Questions

1   Assume the statement is not true. Then there exist two rational numbers p and q such that $p + q$ is irrational. *[1 mark]*

If p and q are rational, then $p = \frac{a}{b}$ and $q = \frac{c}{d}$, where a, b, c and d are integers and b and d are non-zero.

Now $p + q = \frac{a}{b} + \frac{c}{d} = \frac{ad}{bd} + \frac{bc}{bd} = \frac{ad + bc}{bd}$, which is also rational.

[1 mark]

But this contradicts the statement that $p + q$ is irrational. $p + q$ cannot be irrational if both p and q are rational. So if $p + q$ is irrational, then at least one of p or q is irrational. *[1 mark]*

2   Suppose that there exist two prime numbers p and q, $p > 2$, $q > 2$, such that pq is even. Then $pq = 2n$ for some integer n. *[1 mark]*

So 2 is a factor of pq. But p and q are prime numbers, so the only factors of pq are p, q, pq and 1. So if $pq = 2n$ then either $p = 2$ or $q = 2$. *[1 mark]*

This contradicts the statement that $p > 2$ and $q > 2$. So for any two prime numbers $p > 2$, $q > 2$, pq is always odd. *[1 mark]*

Section 2 — Algebra and Functions

Page 7 — Laws of Indices and Surds

Practice Questions

1 a) x^8 b) a^{15} c) x^6 d) a^8 e) $x^4 y^3 z$ f) $\frac{b^2 c^5}{a}$

2 a) 4 b) 2 c) 8 d) 1 e) $\frac{1}{7}$

3 a) $2\sqrt{7}$ b) $\frac{\sqrt{5}}{6}$ c) $3\sqrt{2}$ d) $\frac{3}{4}$

4   $136 + 24\sqrt{21}$

5   $3 - \sqrt{7}$

Exam Questions

1 a) $(5\sqrt{3})^2 = (5^2)(\sqrt{3})^2 = 25 \times 3 = 75$ *[1 mark]*

  b) $(5 + \sqrt{6})(2 - \sqrt{6}) = 10 - 5\sqrt{6} + 2\sqrt{6} - 6$ *[1 mark]*

$= 4 - 3\sqrt{6}$ *[1 mark]*

2   $10000\sqrt{10} = 10^4 \cdot 10^{\frac{1}{2}}$ *[1 mark]* $= 10^{4 + \frac{1}{2}}$

$= 10^{\frac{9}{2}}$, so $k = \frac{9}{2}$ *[1 mark]*

3   Multiply top and bottom by $3 + \sqrt{5}$ to rationalise the denominator:

$\frac{5 + \sqrt{5}}{3 - \sqrt{5}} = \frac{(5 + \sqrt{5})(3 + \sqrt{5})}{(3 - \sqrt{5})(3 + \sqrt{5})}$ *[1 mark]*

$= \frac{15 + 5\sqrt{5} + 3\sqrt{5} + 5}{9 - 5}$ *[1 mark]*

$= \frac{20 + 8\sqrt{5}}{4}$ *[1 mark]* $= 5 + 2\sqrt{5}$ *[1 mark]*

Page 10 — Polynomials

Practice Questions

1 a) $x^2 - y^2$ b) $x^2 + 2xy + y^2$

  c) $25y^2 + 210xy$ d) $3x^2 + 10xy + 3y^2 + 13x + 23y + 14$

2   $(\sqrt{x} + \sqrt{2})(\sqrt{x} - \sqrt{2}) = \sqrt{x}\sqrt{x} - \sqrt{2}\sqrt{x} + \sqrt{2}\sqrt{x} - \sqrt{2}\sqrt{2}$

$= \sqrt{x^2} - \sqrt{2^2} = x - \sqrt{4} = x - 2$, as required

3 a) $xy(2x + a + 2y)$ b) $a^2 x(1 + b^2 x)$

  c) $8(2y + xy + 7x)$ d) $(x - 2)(x - 3)$

4 a) $(x + 7)(x - 1)$ b) $(x + 2)(x - 6)$

  c) $(3x + 8)(3x - 8)$ d) $(4x + 5)(x - 4)$

5 a) $\frac{2x + 5}{3}$ b) $\frac{4}{x - 3}$ c) $\frac{2(x - 3)}{x + 1}$

Exam Questions

1   $\frac{2x^2 - 9x - 35}{x^2 - 49} = \frac{(2x + 5)(x - 7)}{(x + 7)(x - 7)} = \frac{2x + 5}{x + 7}$

[3 marks available — 1 for factorising numerator, 1 for factorising denominator and 1 for correct final answer]

2   $2x^4 - 32x^2 = 2x^2(x^2 - 16)$ *[1 mark]* $= 2x^2(x + 4)(x - 4)$ *[1 mark]*

3 a) The common denominator is $x^2(2x + 1)$

$\frac{x}{2x + 1} + \frac{3}{x^2} + \frac{1}{x} = \frac{x \cdot x^2}{x^2(2x + 1)} + \frac{3(2x + 1)}{x^2(2x + 1)} + \frac{x(2x + 1)}{x^2(2x + 1)}$

$= \frac{x^3 + 6x + 3 + 2x^2 + x}{x^2(2x + 1)} = \frac{x^3 + 2x^2 + 7x + 3}{x^2(2x + 1)}$

[3 marks available — 1 for method of putting all fractions over a common denominator, 1 for correct numerator and 1 for correct denominator in final answer]

Answers

b) The common denominator is $(x + 1)(x - 1)$

$$\frac{2}{x^2-1} - \frac{3x}{x-1} + \frac{x}{x+1}$$

$$= \frac{2}{(x+1)(x-1)} - \frac{3x(x+1)}{(x+1)(x-1)} + \frac{x(x-1)}{(x+1)(x-1)}$$

$$= \frac{2-3x^2-3x+x^2-x}{(x+1)(x-1)} = \frac{2-2x^2-4x}{(x+1)(x-1)} = \frac{2(1-2x-x^2)}{(x+1)(x-1)}$$

[3 marks available — 1 for method of putting all fractions over a common denominator, 1 for correct numerator and 1 for correct denominator in final answer]

Page 13 — Algebraic Division

Practice Questions

1 a) 106   b) 106   c) 41   d) 41
2 a) Factor   b) Not a factor   c) Not a factor   d) Factor
3   $(x^3 + 2x^2 - x + 19) \div (x + 4) = x^2 - 2x + 7$ remainder -9
4 a) $f(x) = (x + 2)(3x^2 - 10x + 15) - 36$
  b) $f(x) = (x + 2)(x^2 - 3) + 10$ c) $f(x) = (x + 2)(2x^2 - 4x + 14) - 31$
5   $2x^3 + 8x^2 + 7x + 8 = (2x^2 + 2x + 1)(x + 3) + 5$
  So $2x^3 + 8x^2 + 7x + 8 \div (x + 3) = 2x^2 + 2x + 1$ remainder 5

Exam Questions

1 a) (i) Remainder = $f(1) = 2(1)^3 - 5(1)^2 - 4(1) + 3 = -4$ *[1 mark]*
   (ii) Remainder = $f\left(-\frac{1}{2}\right) = 2\left(-\frac{1}{8}\right) - 5\left(\frac{1}{4}\right) - 4\left(-\frac{1}{2}\right) + 3 = \frac{7}{2}$ *[1 mark]*
  b) If $f(-1) = 0$ then $(x + 1)$ is a factor.
   $f(-1) = 2(-1)^3 - 5(-1)^2 - 4(-1) + 3$ *[1 mark]*
    $= -2 - 5 + 4 + 3 = 0$, so $(x + 1)$ is a factor of $f(x)$. *[1 mark]*
  c) $(x + 1)$ is a factor, so divide $2x^3 - 5x^2 - 4x + 3$ by $x + 1$:
   $2x^3 - 5x^2 - 4x + 3 - \underline{2x^2}(x + 1) = 2x^3 - 5x^2 - 4x + 3 - 2x^3 - 2x^2$
         $= -7x^2 - 4x + 3$
   $-7x^2 - 4x + 3 - (\underline{-7x})(x + 1) = -7x^2 - 4x + 3 + 7x^2 + 7x = 3x + 3$
   Finally $3x + 3 - \underline{3}(x + 1) = 0$
   so $2x^3 - 5x^2 - 4x + 3 = (2x^2 - 7x + 3)(x + 1)$ *[1 mark for dividing by x + 1, 1 mark for correct quadratic factor]*
   Factorising the quadratic gives:
   $2x^3 - 5x^2 - 4x + 3 = (2x - 1)(x - 3)(x + 1)$ *[1 mark]*
   You might've used a different method to divide by $(x + 1)$.
2 a) $f(p) = (4p^2 + 3p + 1)(p - p) + 5 = 0 + 5 = 5$ *[1 mark]*
  b) $f(-1) = -1$
   $f(-1) = (4(-1)^2 + 3(-1) + 1)((-1) - p) + 5 = (4 - 3 + 1)(-1 - p) + 5$
     $= 2(-1 - p) + 5 = 3 - 2p$ *[1 mark]*
   So $3 - 2p = -1 \Rightarrow p = 2$ *[1 mark]*
  c) $f(1) = (4 + 3 + 1)(1 - 2) + 5 = -3$ *[1 mark]*
3   First put $x = -6$ into both sides of the identity
   $x^3 + 15x^2 + 43x - 30 \equiv (Ax^2 + Bx + C)(x + 6) + D$:
   $(-6)^3 + 15(-6)^2 + 43(-6) - 30 = D \Rightarrow 36 = D$
   Now set $x = 0$ to get $-30 = 6C + D$, so $C = -11$
   Equating the coefficients of x^3 gives $1 = A$.
   Equating the coefficients of x^2 gives $15 = 6A + B \Rightarrow B = 9$
   So $x^3 + 15x^2 + 43x - 30 = (x^2 + 9x - 11)(x + 6) + 36$
   [3 marks available — 1 each for correct values of C and D, and 1 for correct values of A and B]
   You could also do this question by algebraic long division.

Page 15 — Partial Fractions

Practice Questions

1   $A = 1, B = 1$
2 a) $\frac{4x + 5}{(x+4)(2x-3)} \equiv \frac{1}{(x+4)} + \frac{2}{(2x-3)}$
  b) $\frac{-7x - 7}{(3x+1)(x-2)} \equiv \frac{2}{(3x+1)} - \frac{3}{(x-2)}$
  c) $\frac{x - 18}{(x+4)(3x-4)} \equiv \frac{11}{8(x+4)} - \frac{25}{8(3x-4)}$
  d) $\frac{5x}{x^2 + x - 6} \equiv \frac{3}{(x+3)} + \frac{2}{(x-2)}$

3 a) $\frac{2x + 2}{(x+3)^2} \equiv \frac{2}{(x+3)} - \frac{4}{(x+3)^2}$
  b) $\frac{-18x + 14}{(2x-1)^2(x+2)} \equiv \frac{-4}{(2x-1)} + \frac{2}{(2x-1)^2} + \frac{2}{(x+2)}$
  c) $\frac{3x}{(x-5)^2} \equiv \frac{15}{(x-5)^2} + \frac{3}{(x-5)}$
  d) $\frac{2x - 1}{(x+2)^2(x-3)} \equiv \frac{1}{(x+2)^2} - \frac{1}{5(x+2)} + \frac{1}{5(x-3)}$
4   $\frac{3x - 4}{x^3 - 16x} \equiv \frac{1}{4x} - \frac{1}{2(x+4)} + \frac{1}{4(x-4)}$

Exam Questions

1   Put over a common denominator and cancel:
   $5 + 9x \equiv A + B(1 + 3x)$
   Substitute $x = -\frac{1}{3}$: $2 = A \Rightarrow A = 2$ *[1 mark]*
   Substitute $x = 0$: $5 = 2 + B \Rightarrow B = 3$ *[1 mark]*
2   $x^2 - 1 = (x + 1)(x - 1)$, so the identity is:
   $\frac{x + 4}{(x-2)(x^2-1)} \equiv \frac{A}{(x-2)} + \frac{B}{(x+1)} + \frac{C}{(x-1)}$ *[1 mark]*
   $\Rightarrow x + 4 \equiv A(x + 1)(x - 1) + B(x - 2)(x - 1) + C(x - 2)(x + 1)$
   Substitute $x = 1$: $1 + 4 = (-1)(2)C \Rightarrow C = -\frac{5}{2}$
   Substitute $x = -1$: $-1 + 4 = (-3)(-2)B \Rightarrow B = \frac{1}{2}$
   Substitute $x = 2$: $2 + 4 = (3)(1)A \Rightarrow A = 2$
   [1 mark for a suitable method to find A, B and C]
   So $\frac{x + 4}{(x-2)(x^2-1)} = \frac{2}{x-2} + \frac{1}{2(x+1)} - \frac{5}{2(x-1)}$ *[1 mark]*
3   $(x - 6)$ is a repeated factor, so the identity is:
   $\frac{2x - 9}{x(x-6)^2} \equiv \frac{A}{x} + \frac{B}{(x-6)^2} + \frac{C}{(x-6)}$ *[1 mark]*
   $\Rightarrow 2x - 9 \equiv A(x - 6)^2 + Bx + Cx(x - 6)$
   Substitute $x = 0$: $2(0) - 9 = (-6)^2A \Rightarrow A = -\frac{1}{4}$
   Substitute $x = 6$: $2(6) - 9 = 6B \Rightarrow B = \frac{1}{2}$
   Equate coefficients of x^2: $0 = A + C \Rightarrow C = -A = \frac{1}{4}$
   [1 mark for a suitable method to find A, B and C]
   So $\frac{2x - 9}{x(x-6)^2} \equiv -\frac{1}{4x} + \frac{1}{2(x-6)^2} + \frac{1}{4(x-6)}$ *[1 mark]*
4 a) Substitute in x-values until you find x such that $f(x) = 0$:
   $f(1) = 1^3 + 5(1^2) - 1 - 5 = 0$, so $(x - 1)$ is a factor. *[1 mark]*
   Use the algebraic division formula:
   $x^3 + 5x^2 - x - 5 = (x - 1)(Ax^2 + Bx + C) + D$
   Substitute $x = 1$: $0 = D$
   Equating coefficients of x^3: $1 = A$
   Equating coefficients of x^2: $5 = -A + B = -1 + B \Rightarrow B = 6$
   Equating coefficients of x: $-1 = -B + C = C - 6 \Rightarrow C = 5$
   So $x^3 + 5x^2 - x - 5 = (x - 1)(x^2 + 6x + 5)$ *[1 mark]*
   Factorising the quadratic in the usual way gives:
   $x^3 + 5x^2 - x - 5 = (x - 1)(x + 1)(x + 5)$ *[1 mark]*
  b) Using the factorisation from part a), the identity is:
   $\frac{3x + 1}{(x-1)(x+1)(x+5)} \equiv \frac{A}{(x-1)} + \frac{B}{(x+1)} + \frac{C}{(x+5)}$
   $3x + 1 \equiv A(x + 1)(x + 5) + B(x - 1)(x + 5) + C(x + 1)(x - 1)$ *[1 mark]*
   Substitute $x = 1$: $3(1) + 1 = (2)(6)A \Rightarrow A = \frac{1}{3}$
   Substitute $x = -1$: $3(-1) + 1 = (-2)(4)B \Rightarrow B = \frac{1}{4}$
   Substitute $x = -5$: $3(-5) + 1 = (-4)(-6)C \Rightarrow C = -\frac{7}{12}$
   [1 mark for a suitable method to find A, B and C]
   So $\frac{3x + 1}{(x-1)(x+1)(x+5)} \equiv \frac{1}{3(x-1)} + \frac{1}{4(x+1)} - \frac{7}{12(x+5)}$ *[1 mark]*

Page 17 — Solving Quadratic Equations

Practice Questions

1 a) $x = 3$ or -4 b) $x = 2$ or -1 c) $x = \pm\frac{1}{2}$ d) $x = 7$ or $-\frac{2}{3}$
2   $x = 4$ or $-\frac{7}{3}$
3 a) $x = 1$ or 5   b) $x = \frac{7 + \sqrt{13}}{6}$ or $\frac{7 - \sqrt{13}}{6}$
  c) $x = \frac{3 + \sqrt{13}}{2}$ or $\frac{3 - \sqrt{13}}{2}$ d) $x = -2 + \sqrt{10}$ or $x = -2 - \sqrt{10}$
4   $x = \frac{9}{4}$ or -4

Answers

Exam Questions

1 a) $3x^2 + 2x - 2 = 3\left(x^2 + \frac{2}{3}x\right) - 2 = 3\left(x + \frac{1}{3}\right)^2 + d$ *[1 mark]*

$3\left(x + \frac{1}{3}\right)^2 + d = 3x^2 + 2x - 2 \Rightarrow 3x^2 + 2x + \frac{1}{3} + d = 3x^2 + 2x - 2$

$\Rightarrow d = -2 - \frac{1}{3} = -\frac{7}{3}$ *[1 mark]*

So $3x^2 + 2x - 2 = 3\left(x + \frac{1}{3}\right)^2 - \frac{7}{3}$ *[1 mark]*

b) $3\left(x + \frac{1}{3}\right)^2 - \frac{7}{3} = 0 \Rightarrow \left(x + \frac{1}{3}\right)^2 = \frac{7}{9} \Rightarrow x = \frac{-1 \pm \sqrt{7}}{3}$

So $x = 0.55$ or -1.22 (to 2 d.p.) *[1 mark]*

2 $6x^2 = 1 - 3x \Rightarrow 6x^2 + 3x - 1 = 0 \Rightarrow 6\left(x^2 + \frac{1}{2}x\right) - 1 = 0$ *[1 mark]*

$6\left(x^2 + \frac{1}{2}x\right) - 1 = 6\left(x + \frac{1}{4}\right)^2 + d \Rightarrow 6\left(x + \frac{1}{4}\right)^2 + d = 6x^2 + 3x - 1$

$\Rightarrow 6x^2 + 3x + \frac{3}{8} + d = 6x^2 + 3x - 1 \Rightarrow d = -1 - \frac{3}{8} = -\frac{11}{8}$ *[1 mark]*

So $6\left(x + \frac{1}{4}\right)^2 - \frac{11}{8} = 0.$ *[1 mark]* Now solve this to find x:

$6\left(x + \frac{1}{4}\right)^2 = \frac{11}{8} \Rightarrow \left(x + \frac{1}{4}\right)^2 = \frac{11}{48} \Rightarrow x = -\frac{1}{4} \pm \sqrt{\frac{11}{48}} = -\frac{1}{4} \pm \frac{\sqrt{33}}{12}$

So the exact solutions are $x = -\frac{1}{4} + \frac{\sqrt{33}}{12}$ or $-\frac{1}{4} - \frac{\sqrt{33}}{12}$ *[1 mark]*

Page 19 — Quadratic Functions and Graphs

Practice Questions

1 a)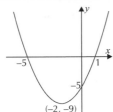

b)

c)

d)

2 Completing the square gives: $f(x) = 2(x - 3)^2 + 5$

The smallest $2(x - 3)^2$ can be is zero, so the minimum of $f(x)$ is 5.
The graph never crosses the x-axis, so $f(x) = 0$ has no real roots.

Exam Questions

1 a) E.g. If $7 + 2\sqrt{6}$ is a root of $f(x) = 0$, then $f(7 + 2\sqrt{6}) = 0$

$\Rightarrow (7 + 2\sqrt{6})^2 - 14(7 + 2\sqrt{6}) + k = 0$ *[1 mark]*

$\Rightarrow 49 + 28\sqrt{6} + 24 - 98 - 28\sqrt{6} + k = 0$ *[1 mark]*

$\Rightarrow -25 + k = 0 \Rightarrow k = 25$ *[1 mark]*

So $f(7 - 2\sqrt{6}) = (7 - 2\sqrt{6})^2 - 14(7 - 2\sqrt{6}) + 25$

$= 49 - 28\sqrt{6} + 24 - 98 + 28\sqrt{6} + 25 = 0$ *[1 mark]*

so $7 - 2\sqrt{6}$ is the other root of $f(x)$.

You'd still get the marks if you used a different method here.

b)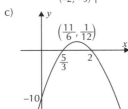

[3 marks available — 1 mark for a u-shaped curve, 1 mark for correct x- and y-intercepts and 1 mark for correct coordinates of minimum point]

2 a) The completed square is: $(x - 6)^2 + d = x^2 - 12x + 36 + d$ *[1 mark]*

Equating coefficients gives $15 = 36 + d$, so $d = -21$. *[1 mark]*

The final expression is $(x - 6)^2 - 21$.

b) The minimum occurs when the expression in brackets is equal to 0, so the minimum is -21. *[1 mark]*

The expression in brackets is equal to 0, when $x = 6$. *[1 mark]*

Page 21 — The Quadratic Formula

Practice Questions

1 a) i) discriminant = 0, 1 repeated real root   ii) $x = -\frac{7}{2}$

b) i) discriminant = -3, no real roots

c) i) discriminant = 0, 1 repeated real root   ii) $x = \frac{\sqrt{2}}{3}$

d) i) discriminant = 121, 2 real roots,   ii) $x = \frac{1}{2}$ or -5

2 $k > 4$ or $k < -4$

Exam Questions

1 For equal roots, $b^2 - 4ac = 0$. $a = 1$, $b = 2k$ and $c = 4k$, so:

$b^2 - 4ac = (2k)^2 - (4 \times 1 \times 4k)$ *[1 mark]*

$= 4k^2 - 16k = 4k(k - 4) = 0$ *[1 mark]*

so $k = 4$ (as k is non-zero) *[1 mark]*

2 a) For distinct real roots, $b^2 - 4ac > 0$ *[1 mark]*

$a = p + 1$, $b = p + 1$ and $c = 1$

so $b^2 - 4ac = (p + 1)^2 - 4(p + 1)(1) > 0$ *[1 mark]*

$\Rightarrow p^2 + 2p + 1 - 4p - 4 > 0 \Rightarrow p^2 - 2p - 3 > 0$ *[1 mark]*

b) The graph of $y = p^2 - 2p - 3$ crosses the horizontal axis when

$p^2 - 2p - 3 = (p + 1)(p - 3) = 0$ *[1 mark]*

So it crosses at $p = -1$ and $p = 3$

The quadratic is u-shaped (since the coefficient of p^2 is positive)
so $p^2 - 2p - 3 > 0$ outside of these values: *[1 mark]*

$p < -1$ or $p > 3$ *[1 mark]*

Page 23 — Simultaneous Equations

Practice Questions

1 a) $x = -3$, $y = -4$ b) $x = -\frac{1}{6}$, $y = -\frac{5}{12}$

2 a) $\left(\frac{1}{4}, -\frac{13}{4}\right)$ b) (4, 5)   c) (−5, −2)

3 a) The line and the curve meet at the points (2, −6) and (7, 4).

b) The line is a tangent to the parabola at the point (2, 26).

c) There are no solutions, so the line and the curve never meet.

Exam Questions

1 First, take the linear equation and rearrange it to get x on its own:

$x = 6 - y.$ *[1 mark]* Now substitute this into the quadratic:

$(6 - y)^2 + 2y^2 = 36$ *[1 mark]* $\Rightarrow 36 - 12y + y^2 + 2y^2 = 36$

$\Rightarrow 3y^2 - 12y = 0 \Rightarrow y^2 - 4y = 0 \Rightarrow y(y - 4) = 0$ *[1 mark]*

so $y = 0$ and $y = 4$ *[1 mark]*

Put the y-values back into the equation for x to find the x-values.

When $y = 0$, $x = 6 - y = 6 - 0 = 6$

When $y = 4$, $x = 6 - y = 6 - 4 = 2$

So the coordinates are (6, 0) and (2, 4) *[1 mark for each answer]*

2 a) *[4 marks available — 1 mark for u-shaped curve, 1 mark for correct x- and y-intercepts of curve, 1 mark for correct x- and y-intercepts of line, and 1 mark for line and curve crossing at two points]*

b) At points of intersection, $2x - 3 = (x + 2)(x - 4)$ *[1 mark]*

$2x - 3 = x^2 - 2x - 8 \Rightarrow 0 = x^2 - 4x - 5$ *[1 mark]*

c) $x^2 - 4x - 5 = 0 \Rightarrow (x - 5)(x + 1) = 0$ so $x = 5$, $x = -1$ *[1 mark]*

When $x = 5$, $y = (2 \times 5) - 3 = 7$ and when $x = -1$,

$y = (2 \times -1) - 3 = -5$, so the points of intersection are

(5, 7) and (−1, −5). *[1 mark for both points correct]*

Page 25 — Inequalities

Practice Questions

1 a) $x > \frac{5}{2}$ b) $x > -4$ c) $x \leq -3$

2 a) $x > -\frac{38}{5}$ b) $y \leq \frac{7}{8}$ c) $y \leq -\frac{3}{4}$

Answers

3 a) $-\frac{1}{3} \leq x \leq 2$ b) $x < -2$ or $x > \frac{3}{2}$ c) $x \leq -3$ or $x \geq -2$

4 a) $\{x: x \leq -3\} \cup \{x: x \geq 1\}$ b) $\{x: x < -\frac{1}{2}\} \cup \{x: x > 1\}$

    c) $\{x: -3 < x < 2\}$ or $\{x: x > -3\} \cap \{x: x < 2\}$

5

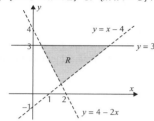

Exam Questions

1 a) $3x + 2 \leq x + 6 \Rightarrow 2x \leq 4 \Rightarrow x \leq 2$ *[1 mark]*

   b) $20 - x - x^2 > 0 \Rightarrow (4 - x)(5 + x) > 0$
     The graph crosses the x-axis at $x = 4$ and $x = -5$. *[1 mark]*.
     The coefficient of x^2 is negative so the graph is n-shaped.
     So $20 - x - x^2 > 0$ when $-5 < x < 4$. *[1 mark]*

   c) x satisfies both $x \leq 2$ and $-5 < x < 4$ when $-5 < x \leq 2$. *[1 mark]*

2 a) $3 \leq 2p + 5 \leq 15$
     Subtract 5 from each part to give: $-2 \leq 2p \leq 10$
     Now divide each part by 2 to give: $-1 \leq p \leq 5$
     [1 mark for $-1 \leq p$ and 1 mark for $p \leq 5$]
     For inequalities with three parts you add, subtract, multiply or divide
     each part by the same thing, as with regular two part inequalities.

   b) $q^2 - 9 > 0 \Rightarrow (q + 3)(q - 3) > 0$
     The function is 0 at $q = -3$ and $q = 3$. *[1 mark]*
     The coefficient of q^2 is positive so the graph is u-shaped.
     So $q^2 - 9 > 0$ when $q < -3$ or $q > 3$. *[1 mark]*

3   $y = 2x^2 - x - 3 = (2x - 3)(x + 1)$ is a u-shaped quadratic that
   crosses the x-axis at -1 and $\frac{3}{2}$.
   $y = 1 - \frac{1}{2}x$ is a straight line that crosses the x-axis at 2.
   Test the origin in the inequalities:
   $y = 2x^2 - x - 3 \Rightarrow 0 > -3$, which is true, so the region includes
   the area above the quadratic.
   $y = 1 - \frac{1}{2}x \Rightarrow 0 \geq 1$, which is false, so the region includes the
   area above the straight line.
   The region bounded by these areas is shown by R.

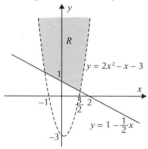

[4 marks available — 1 mark for quadratic graph drawn with correct shape and as dotted line, 1 mark for correct intercepts on quadratic, 1 mark for correct straight line drawn as solid line and 1 mark for correct region shaded]

Page 27 — Cubics
Practice Questions

1 a)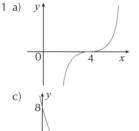

   b)

   c)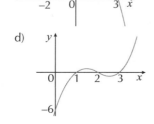

   d)

---

2 a) $f(1) = 1^3 - 1^2 - 2(1) + 2 = 0$, so $(x - 1)$ is a factor.
     $f(x) = (x - 1)(x^2 - 2)$

   b) $g(-4) = (-4)^3 + 3(-4)^2 - 10(-4) - 24 = 0$, so $(x + 4)$ is a factor.
     $g(x) = (x + 4)(x + 2)(x - 3)$

   c) $h\left(\frac{1}{2}\right) = 2\left(\frac{1}{2}\right)^3 + 3\left(\frac{1}{2}\right)^2 - 8\left(\frac{1}{2}\right) + 3 = 0$, so $(2x - 1)$ is a factor.
     $h(x) = (2x - 1)(x - 1)(x + 3)$

   d) $k\left(\frac{2}{3}\right) = 3\left(\frac{2}{3}\right)^3 + 10\left(\frac{2}{3}\right)^2 + 10\left(\frac{2}{3}\right) - 12 = 0$, so $(3x - 2)$ is a factor.
     $k(x) = (3x - 2)(x^2 + 4x + 6)$

3   $f(x) = (x + 5)(x - 1)(x - 7)$

Exam Questions

1 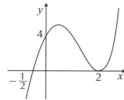

[3 marks available — 1 mark for correct shape, 1 mark for crossing x-axis at $x = -\frac{1}{2}$ and touching the x-axis at $x = 2$ and 1 mark for correct y-axis intercept at $y = 4$]

2 a) $f\left(-\frac{1}{2}\right) = 6\left(-\frac{1}{2}\right)^3 + 37\left(-\frac{1}{2}\right)^2 + 5\left(-\frac{1}{2}\right) - 6$
     $= -\frac{6}{8} + \frac{37}{4} - \frac{5}{2} - 6 = 0$ *[1 mark]*
     So, by the factor theorem, $(2x - 1)$ is a factor of $f(x)$. *[1 mark]*

   b) $f(x) = (2x + 1)(3x^2 + 17x - 6)$ *[1 mark]*
     $= (2x + 1)(3x - 1)(x + 6)$ *[1 mark]*

   c)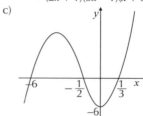

[3 marks available — 1 mark for correct shape, 1 mark for correct y-intercept and 1 mark for correct x-intercepts]

3   $f(1) = 7(1)^3 - 26(1)^2 + 13(1) + 6 = 0$, so $(x - 1)$ is a factor *[1 mark]*
   $f(x) = (x - 1)(7x^2 - 19x - 6)$ *[1 mark]*
   $f(x) = (x - 1)(7x + 2)(x - 3)$ *[1 mark]*
   So $f(x) = 0$ when $x = 1$, $x = -\frac{2}{7}$ or $x = 3$ *[1 mark]*

Page 29 — Modulus
Practice Questions

1 a) (i) 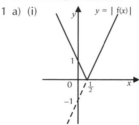   (ii)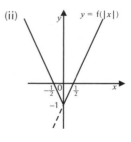

   b) $x = 3$ and $x = -2$

2 a) $-4 < x < 4$ b) $x < -6$ or $x > 6$ c) $-6 \leq x \leq 0$

Exam Questions

1   $3|-x - 6| = x + 12 \Rightarrow |-x - 6| = \frac{1}{3}x + 4$
   Sketch the graphs of $y = |-x - 6|$ and $y = \frac{1}{3}x + 4$:

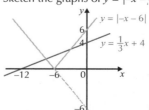

[1 mark]

Answers

From the sketch, you can see $-x - 6 \geq 0$ for $x \leq -6$ and $-x - 6 \leq 0$ for $x \geq -6$, and there's one solution in each of these ranges.

For $x \leq -6$, $-x - 6 = \frac{1}{3}x + 4 \Rightarrow -10 = \frac{4}{3}x \Rightarrow x = -7.5$ **[1 mark]**

For $x \geq -6$, $-(-x - 6) = \frac{1}{3}x + 4 \Rightarrow x + 6 = \frac{1}{3}x + 4$

$\Rightarrow \frac{2}{3}x = -2 \Rightarrow x = -3$ **[1 mark]**

2 a) Square both sides:
$|2x + 1| = |x - k| \Rightarrow (2x + 1)^2 = (x - k)^2$ **[1 mark]**
$\Rightarrow 4x^2 + 4x + 1 = x^2 - 2kx + k^2$ **[1 mark]**
$\Rightarrow 4x^2 - x^2 + 4x + 2kx + 1 - k^2 = 0$
$\Rightarrow 3x^2 + (4 + 2k)x + (1 - k^2) = 0$ as required **[1 mark]**

b) If the equation has exactly one solution,
then the discriminant of the quadratic must be 0. **[1 mark]**
$b^2 - 4ac = (4 + 2k)^2 - 4(3)(1 - k^2) = 0$ **[1 mark]**
$\Rightarrow 16 + 16k + 4k^2 - 12 + 12k^2 = 0$
$\Rightarrow 16k^2 + 16k + 4 = 0 \Rightarrow 4k^2 + 4k + 1 = 0$ **[1 mark]**
$\Rightarrow (2k + 1)^2 = 0 \Rightarrow 2k + 1 = 0 \Rightarrow k = -\frac{1}{2}$
So $k = -\frac{1}{2}$ is the only value for which
the equation has exactly one solution. **[1 mark]**

Page 32 — Graphs of Functions
Practice Questions

1 a) **C**   b) **D**   c) **B**   d) **A**

2 a) 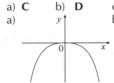   b)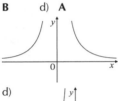

c) 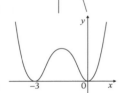   d)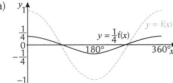

3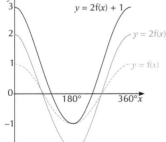

4 a)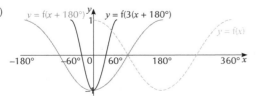

b)

c)

Exam Questions

1 For $f(x) = (1 - x)(x + 4)^3$, the coefficient of x^4 is negative, so the graph is negative for large positive and negative values of x. Putting in $x = 0$ gives the y-intercept as $(1 - 0)(0 + 4)^3 = 64$. The x-intercepts are at $x = 1$ and $x = -4$. The root at $x = -4$ is a repeated 'triple root' so the curve crosses the x-axis here.

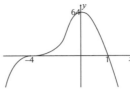

[4 marks — 1 mark for each intercept, 1 mark for correct shape]

2 a)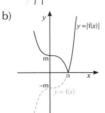

[2 marks available — 1 mark for stretching in x-axis crossing at $x = \frac{1}{3}n$, 1 mark for crossing y-axis at $y = -m$]

b)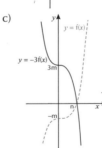

[2 marks available — 1 mark for reflecting in x-axis at $x = n$, 1 mark for crossing y-axis at $y = m$]

c)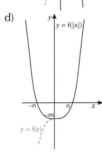

[2 marks available — 1 mark for reflecting in y-axis and 1 mark for crossing y-axis at $y = 3m$]

d)

[2 marks available — 1 mark for reflecting in y-axis and 1 mark for crossing the x-axis at $-n$]

Page 33 — Proportion
Practice Questions

1   $k = 4$
2   $k = 15$

Exam Questions

1 a) $A \propto \frac{1}{t}$, so $A = \frac{k}{t}$
So if $A = 2.6$ when $t = 5.5$: $2.6 = \frac{k}{5.5} \Rightarrow k = 14.3$ **[1 mark]**

Answers

b)

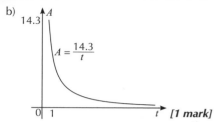

The graph has an asymptote at $A = 0$. *[1 mark]*
There's only one asymptote — the relation is only defined for t ≥ 1, so the vertical asymptote isn't needed.

c) E.g. When t is close to zero, the value of A would be very large. This would suggest that the area of the island was almost infinite immediately after the storm, which is unrealistic. *[1 mark for a valid reason why the model is inappropriate for small t]*

Page 35 — Composite and Inverse Functions

Practice Questions

1   a) $fg(2) = \frac{3}{7}$, $gf(1) = 9$, $fg(x) = \frac{3}{2x + 3}$
    b) $fg(2) = 108$, $gf(1) = 7$, $fg(x) = 3(x + 4)^2$
2   f is a one-to-one function so it has an inverse. The domain of the inverse is the range of the function and vice versa, so the domain of $f^{-1}(x)$ is $x \geq 3$ and the range is $f^{-1}(x) \in \mathbb{R}$.
3   $f^{-1}(x) = \frac{x^2}{2} + 2$
    This has domain $\{x : x \geq 0\}$ and range $\{f^{-1}(x) : f^{-1}(x) \geq 2\}$.

Exam Questions

1   a) $gf(x) = g(x^2 - 3)$ *[1 mark]* $= \frac{1}{x^2 - 3}$ *[1 mark]*
    b) $\frac{1}{x^2 - 3} = \frac{1}{6} \Rightarrow x^2 - 3 = 6 \Rightarrow x^2 = 9 \Rightarrow x = 3, x = -3$ *[1 mark]*
2   a) The range of f is $f(x) > 0$ *[1 mark]*.
    b) (i) Let $y = f(x)$. Then $y = \frac{1}{x + 5}$.
        Rearrange this to make x the subject:
        $y(x + 5) = 1 \Rightarrow x + 5 = \frac{1}{y}$ *[1 mark]* $\Rightarrow x = \frac{1}{y} - 5$ *[1 mark]*
        Write out in terms of x and $f^{-1}(x)$: $f^{-1}(x) = \frac{1}{x} - 5$ *[1 mark]*
    (ii) The domain of the inverse is the same as the range of the function, so $x > 0$ *[1 mark]*. The range of the inverse is the same as the domain of the function, so $f^{-1}(x) > -5$ *[1 mark]*.
    c)

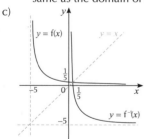

[2 marks available — 1 mark for each correct curve, each with correct intersections and asymptotes as shown]

Section 3 — Coordinate Geometry

Page 39 — Geometry of Lines and Circles

Practice Questions

1   a) i) $y + 1 = 3(x - 2)$ ii) $y = 3x - 7$ iii) $3x - y - 7 = 0$
    b) i) $y + \frac{1}{3} = \frac{1}{5}x$ ii) $y = \frac{1}{5}x - \frac{1}{3}$ iii) $3x - 15y - 5 = 0$
2   $y = \frac{3}{2}x - 4$
3   $y = -\frac{1}{2}x + 4$
4   $y = \frac{3}{2}x + \frac{15}{2}$
5   $(x - 3)^2 + (y + 1)^2 = 49$
6   a) 3, (0, 0)   b) 2, (2, –4)   c) 5, (–3, 4)

Exam Questions

1   a) i) $3y = 15 - 4x \Rightarrow y = -\frac{4}{3}x + 5$
        so the gradient of the line PQ is $m = -\frac{4}{3}$. *[1 mark]*
    ii) Find the coordinates of P and Q:
        P: $0 + 3p = 15 \Rightarrow p = 5 \Rightarrow$ P has coordinates (0, 5)
        Q: $4q + -9 = 15 \Rightarrow q = 6 \Rightarrow$ Q has coordinates (6, –3)
        [1 mark for both correct]
        Then use the formula:
        Length $= \sqrt{(6 - 0)^2 + ((-3) - 5)^2} = \sqrt{6^2 + (-8)^2} = \sqrt{36 + 64}$
        $= \sqrt{100} = 10$ *[1 mark]*
    b) Gradient of the line $= -1 \div -\frac{4}{3} = \frac{3}{4}$, *[1 mark]* so $y = \frac{3}{4}x + c$
        Use the midpoint formula to find the coordinates of R:
        Midpoint $= \left(\frac{0 + 6}{2}, \frac{5 + (-3)}{2}\right) = \left(\frac{6}{2}, \frac{2}{2}\right) = (3, 1)$ *[1 mark]*
        Now use the x- and y-values of R to find c:
        $1 = \frac{3}{4}(3) + c \Rightarrow 1 = \frac{9}{4} + c \Rightarrow c = -\frac{5}{4} \Rightarrow y = \frac{3}{4}x - \frac{5}{4}$ *[1 mark]*
2   a) Using the formula $y - y_1 = m(x - x_1)$, with the coordinates of point S for the x- and y-values and $m = -2$,
        $y - (-3) = -2(x - 7)$ *[1 mark]*
        $y + 3 = -2x + 14 \Rightarrow y = -2x + 11$ *[1 mark]*
    b) Putting $x = 5$ into $y = -2x + 11$ gives $y = 1$,
        so T does lie on the line. *[1 mark]*
3   a) Use the midpoint formula to find the coordinates of L:
        Midpoint $= \left(\frac{5 + (-1)}{2}, \frac{8 + 4}{2}\right) = \left(\frac{4}{2}, \frac{12}{2}\right) = (2, 6)$ *[1 mark]*
        Gradient of JK $= \frac{8 - 4}{5 - (-1)} = \frac{4}{6} = \frac{2}{3}$ *[1 mark]*
        so gradient of $l_1 = -1 \div \frac{2}{3} = -\frac{3}{2}$ *[1 mark]*
        Now, putting this gradient and the x- and y-coordinates of L into the formula $y - y_1 = m(x - x_1)$ gives:
        $y - 6 = -\frac{3}{2}(x - 2) \Rightarrow y = -\frac{3}{2}x + 3 + 6 \Rightarrow y = -\frac{3}{2}x + 9$ *[1 mark]*
        $\Rightarrow 3x + 2y - 18 = 0$ *[1 mark]*
    b) Putting $x = 0$ into $y = -\frac{3}{2}x + 9$ gives $y = 9$, *[1 mark]*
        so M = (0, 9). *[1 mark]*
    c) Putting $y = 0$ into $3x + 2y - 18 = 0$ gives $x = 6$, *[1 mark]*
        so N = (6, 0). *[1 mark]*
4   a) Rearrange equation and complete the square:
        $x^2 - 2x + y^2 - 10y + 21 = 0$ *[1 mark]*
        $(x - 1)^2 - 1 + (y - 5)^2 - 25 + 21 = 0$ *[1 mark]*
        $(x - 1)^2 + (y - 5)^2 = 5$ *[1 mark]*
        Compare with $(x - a)^2 + (y - b)^2 = r^2$:
        centre = (1, 5) *[1 mark]* radius $= \sqrt{5} = 2.24$ (3 s.f.) *[1 mark]*
    b) The point (3, 6) and centre (1, 5) both lie on the diameter.
        Gradient of the diameter $= \frac{6 - 5}{3 - 1} = 0.5$ *[1 mark]*
        Q (q, 4) also lies on the diameter, so $\frac{4 - 6}{q - 3} = 0.5$ *[1 mark]*
        $-2 = 0.5q - 1.5$, so $q = (-2 + 1.5) \div 0.5 = -1$ *[1 mark]*
    c) Tangent at Q is perpendicular to the diameter at Q,
        so gradient $m = -\frac{1}{0.5} = -2$
        $y - y_1 = m(x - x_1)$, and (–1, 4) is a point on the line, so:
        $y - 4 = -2(x + 1)$
        $y - 4 = -2x - 2 \Rightarrow 2x + y - 2 = 0$ is the equation of the tangent.
        [3 marks available — 1 mark for correct value for gradient, 1 mark for substituting Q in straight-line equation, 1 mark for correct equation of the tangent in the form ax + by + c = 0]

Page 41 — Parametric Equations

Practice Questions

1   a) $t = 0 \Rightarrow x = 3, y = 4$ $t = 1 \Rightarrow x = 2.5, y = 7$
        $t = 2 \Rightarrow x = 2, y = 14$ $t = 3 \Rightarrow x = 1.5, y = 25$
    b) (i) 20   (ii) –3 and 2.5
2   a) $r = 7$, centre = (0, 0)   b) $r = 5$, centre = (2, –1)
3   a) (0, 1) and (0, 7)   b) (0, 7), (3, 5.5) and (8, 3)
        If you got stuck on part b), go back and look up 'factorising cubics'.

Answers

Exam Question

1 a) Substitute $y = 1$ into the parametric equation for y:
$t^2 - 2t + 2 = 1 \Rightarrow t^2 - 2t + 1 = 0$
$\Rightarrow (t - 1)^2 = 0 \Rightarrow t = 1$ *[1 mark]*
So a is the value of x when $t = 1$. $a = t^3 + t = 1^3 + 1 = 2$ *[1 mark]*

b) Substitute the parametric equations for x and y
into the equation of the line:
$8y = x + 6 \Rightarrow 8(t^2 - 2t + 2) = (t^3 + t) + 6$ *[1 mark]*
$\Rightarrow 8t^2 - 16t + 16 = t^3 + t + 6$
$\Rightarrow t^3 - 8t^2 + 17t - 10 = 0$
We know that this line passes through K, and from a) we know
that $t = 1$ at K, so $t = 1$ is a solution of this equation,
and $(t - 1)$ is a factor:
$\Rightarrow (t - 1)(t^2 - 7t + 10) = 0$ *[1 mark]* $\Rightarrow (t - 1)(t - 2)(t - 5) = 0$
So $t = 2$ and $t = 5$ at L and M. *[1 mark]*
Substitute $t = 2$ and $t = 5$ back into the parametric equations:
[1 mark]
If $t = 2$, then $x = 2^3 + 2 = 10$ and $y = 2^2 - 2(2) + 2 = 2$
If $t = 5$, then $x = 5^3 + 5 = 130$ and $y = 5^2 - 2(5) + 2 = 17$
So L = (10, 2) *[1 mark]* and M = (130, 17) *[1 mark]*

Page 43 — More on Parametric Equations

Practice Questions

1 $y = 18x^2 - 24x + 5$

2 a) $y = 5 - \dfrac{x^2}{4}$ b) $-2 \leq x \leq 2$

3 $y = 5 - 36x^2$ (for $-\dfrac{1}{3} \leq x \leq \dfrac{1}{3}$)

Exam Questions

1 a) $x = 15t \Rightarrow t = \dfrac{x}{15}$ *[1 mark]*
Substitute this into $y = 20t - 5t^2$:
$y = 20\left(\dfrac{x}{15}\right) - 5\left(\dfrac{x}{15}\right)^2 \Rightarrow y = \dfrac{4}{3}x - \dfrac{1}{45}x^2$ *[1 mark]*

b) At $t = 2$, $x = 30$ and $y = 20(2) - 5(2)^2 = 40 - 20 = 20$ *[1 mark]*.
The distance from (0, 0) to (30, 20) $= \sqrt{30^2 + 20^2} = \sqrt{1300}$
$= 36.1$ m (to 3 s.f.) *[1 mark]*

c) When $t < 0$, the model doesn't apply because this is before the
ball is kicked. *[1 mark]* For $t > 4$, the value of y is negative.
This doesn't make sense as it represents the ball being below the
surface of the field. *[1 mark]*

2 a) Rearrange the parametric equation for x to make $\sin \theta$ the subject:
$x = 3 + 4 \sin \theta \Rightarrow \sin \theta = \dfrac{x - 3}{4}$ *[1 mark]*
Use the identity $\cos 2\theta = 1 - 2 \sin^2 \theta$ to rewrite the parametric
equation for y in terms of $\sin \theta$:
$y = \dfrac{1 + \cos 2\theta}{3} = \dfrac{1 + (1 - 2\sin^2\theta)}{3}$ *[1 mark]*
$= \dfrac{2 - 2\sin^2\theta}{3} = \dfrac{2}{3}(1 - \sin^2\theta) = \dfrac{2}{3}\left(1 - \left(\dfrac{x-3}{4}\right)^2\right)$ *[1 mark]*
$= \dfrac{2}{3}\left(1 - \dfrac{(x-3)^2}{16}\right) = \dfrac{2}{3}\left(\dfrac{16 - (x^2 - 6x + 9)}{16}\right)$
$= \dfrac{2}{3}\left(\dfrac{-x^2 + 6x + 7}{16}\right) = \dfrac{-x^2 + 6x + 7}{24}$ *[1 mark]*

b) $-\dfrac{\pi}{2} \leq \theta \leq \dfrac{\pi}{2} \Rightarrow -1 \leq \sin \theta \leq 1 \Rightarrow -4 \leq 4 \sin \theta \leq 4$
$\Rightarrow -1 \leq 3 + 4 \sin \theta \leq 7 \Rightarrow -1 \leq x \leq 7$ *[1 mark]*

Section 4 — Sequences and Series

Page 45 — Sequences

Practice Questions

1 $u_{n+1} = u_n + 5$, $u_1 = 32$

2 Common difference $(d) = 0.75$

3 a) $r = -3$ b) $u_{10} = -39366$

4 $u_k = 55 - 3k$, $u_{k+1} = 55 - 3(k + 1) = 52 - 3k$
$u_{k+1} < u_k \Rightarrow 52 - 3k < 55 - 3k \Rightarrow 52 < 55$
This is true so the sequence is decreasing.

Exam Questions

1 Using the nth term formula, $u_n = a + (n - 1)d$
$u_7 = 580 \Rightarrow a + (7 - 1)d = 580 \Rightarrow a + 6d = 580$ ①
$u_{15} = 1020 \Rightarrow a + (15 - 1)d = 1020 \Rightarrow a + 14d = 1020$ ②
② − ①: $(a + 14d) - (a + 6d) = 1020 - 580$
$8d = 440 \Rightarrow d = 55$
①: $a + 6(55) = 580 \Rightarrow a = 580 - 330 = 250$
*[5 marks available — 1 mark for forming each equation,
1 mark for attempting to solve simultaneously, 1 mark each
for correct values of a and d]*

2 $u_n = ar^{n-1} = 12 \times 1.3^{n-1}$ *[1 mark]*
$u_{10} = 12 \times 1.3^9 = 127.25$ (2 d.p.) *[1 mark]*

Page 47 — Arithmetic Series

Practice Questions

1 $S_8 = 168$ 2 $S_{21} = 735$

3 a) Common difference $(d) = 4$ b) $u_{15} = 63$ c) $S_{10} = 250$

4 $u_n = -2n + 50$, $S_5 = 220$

5 a) 610   b) 205

Exam Questions

1 a) $a_2 = 3k + 11$ *[1 mark]*
$a_3 = 3a_2 + 11 = 3(3k + 11) + 11$
$= 9k + 33 + 11 = 9k + 44$ *[1 mark]*
$a_4 = 3a_3 + 11 = 3(9k + 44) + 11$
$= 27k + 132 + 11 = 27k + 143$ *[1 mark]*

b) $\sum_{r=1}^{4} a_r = k + (3k + 11) + (9k + 44) + (27k + 143)$
$= 40k + 198$ *[1 mark]*
$40k + 198 = 278 \Rightarrow 40k = 278 - 198 = 80$ *[1 mark]*
$\Rightarrow k = 2$ *[1 mark]*

2 a) $a = 6$, $d = 8$ *[1 mark]*
$a_n = 6 + 8(n - 1)$
$= 6 + 8n - 8 = 8n - 2$ *[1 mark]*

b) $S_{10} = \dfrac{10}{2}[2 \times 6 + (10 - 1)8] = 5 \times (12 + 72) = 420$ *[1 mark]*

c) First find an expression for S_k:
$S_k = \dfrac{k}{2}[2 \times 6 + 8(k - 1)] = \dfrac{k}{2} \times (12 + 8k - 8)$
$= \dfrac{k}{2}(8k + 4)$ *[1 mark]*
$= \dfrac{8k^2 + 4k}{2} = 4k^2 + 2k$ *[1 mark]*
You know that the total sum will be less than 2450,
because he hadn't yet reached that limit by day k, so:
$4k^2 + 2k < 2450 \Rightarrow 2k^2 + k < 1225 \Rightarrow 2k^2 + k - 1225 < 0$
$\Rightarrow (2k - 49)(k + 25) < 0$ *[1 mark]*
$2k^2 + k - 1225 = 0 \Rightarrow 2k - 49 = 0$ or $k + 25 = 0$
$\Rightarrow k = 24.5$ or $k = -25$ *[1 mark]*
The coefficient of k^2 is positive so the graph is u-shaped.
You need the negative part, so $-25 < k < 24.5$.
k will be the largest whole number that satisfies
the inequality, i.e. $k = 24$. *[1 mark]*
Remember, values in a sequence can be any number (oh, the possibilities),
but the term positions are always whole numbers.

Page 49 — Geometric Series

Practice Questions

1 a) $S_{12} = 11\ 184\ 810$ b) $S_{12} = 59.985$ (3 d.p.)

2 a) $r = 2$, sequence is divergent

b) $r = \dfrac{1}{3}$, sequence is convergent

c) $r = \dfrac{1}{3}$, sequence is convergent

3 a) $r = \dfrac{1}{2}$ b) $u_7 = 0.375$ (or $\dfrac{3}{8}$)

c) $S_{10} = 47.953$ (3 d.p.)   d) $S_\infty = 48$

Answers

Exam Question

1 a) $S_\infty = \frac{a}{1-r} \Rightarrow 36 = \frac{a}{1-r} \Rightarrow 36 - 36r = a$ *[1 mark]*

$u_2 = ar \Rightarrow 5 = ar$ *[1 mark]*

Substituting for a gives: $5 = (36 - 36r)r = 36r - 36r^2$

$\Rightarrow 36r^2 - 36r + 5 = 0$ *[1 mark]*

b) Factorising gives: $(6r - 1)(6r - 5) = 0$

So $r = \frac{1}{6}$ or $r = \frac{5}{6}$ *[1 mark for each correct value]*

If $r = \frac{1}{6}$ and $ar = 5$, then $\frac{a}{6} = 5 \Rightarrow a = 30$ *[1 mark]*

If $r = \frac{5}{6}$ and $ar = 5$, then $\frac{5a}{6} = 5 \Rightarrow a = 6$ *[1 mark]*

Page 51 — Binomial Expansions

Practice Questions

1   1   5   10   10   5   1
2    $1 + 12x + 66x^2 + 220x^3$
3    $1 - 32x + 480x^2 - 4480x^3$
4    $32 + 240x + 720x^2 + 1080x^3$

Exam Questions

1   First five terms of $(4 + 3x)^6$ are:

$4^6 + \binom{6}{1}4^5(3x) + \binom{6}{2}4^4(3x)^2 + \binom{6}{3}4^3(3x)^3 + \binom{6}{4}4^2(3x)^4$

$= 4096 + (6 \times 1024 \times 3)x + (15 \times 256 \times 9)x^2 + (20 \times 64 \times 27)x^3$
$\qquad\qquad\qquad\qquad\qquad + (15 \times 16 \times 81)x^4$

$= 4096 + 18\,432x + 34\,560x^2 + 34\,560x^3 + 19\,440x^4$

[1 mark for each correct term]

2   The x^3 term in $(1 + px)^7$ is $\binom{7}{3}(px)^3$ *[1 mark]*

$35p^3x^3 = 280x^3 \Rightarrow 35p^3 = 280$ *[1 mark]*
$\Rightarrow p^3 = 8 \Rightarrow p = 2$ *[1 mark]*

Page 53 — Binomial Expansions as Infinite Sums

Practice Questions

1 a) $(1 + x)^{-4} \approx 1 - 4x + 10x^2 - 20x^3$

b) $(1 - 3x)^{-3} \approx 1 + 9x + 54x^2 + 270x^3$

c) $(1 - 5x)^{\frac{1}{2}} \approx 1 - \frac{5}{2}x - \frac{25}{8}x^2 - \frac{125}{16}x^3$

2    $\left|\frac{-2x}{4}\right| < 1 \Rightarrow |x| < 2$

3 a) $(3 + 2x)^{-2} \approx \frac{1}{9} - \frac{4}{27}x + \frac{4}{27}x^2$, valid for $|x| < \frac{3}{2}$

b) $(8 - x)^{\frac{1}{3}} \approx 2 - \frac{1}{12}x - \frac{1}{288}x^2$, valid for $|x| < 8$

Exam Question

1 a) $f(x) = (9 - 4x)^{-\frac{1}{2}} = 9^{-\frac{1}{2}}\left(1 - \frac{4}{9}x\right)^{-\frac{1}{2}} = \frac{1}{3}\left(1 - \frac{4}{9}x\right)^{-\frac{1}{2}}$

$= \frac{1}{3}\left[1 + \left(-\frac{1}{2}\right)\left(-\frac{4}{9}x\right) + \frac{\left(-\frac{1}{2}\right) \times \left(-\frac{3}{2}\right)}{1 \times 2}\left(-\frac{4}{9}x\right)^2\right.$
$\left. \qquad\qquad + \frac{\left(-\frac{1}{2}\right) \times \left(-\frac{3}{2}\right) \times \left(-\frac{5}{2}\right)}{1 \times 2 \times 3}\left(-\frac{4}{9}x\right)^3 + ...\right]$

$= \frac{1}{3}\left(1 + \left(-\frac{1}{2}\right)\left(-\frac{4}{9}x\right) + \frac{\left(\frac{3}{4}\right)}{2}\left(-\frac{4}{9}x\right)^2 + \frac{\left(-\frac{15}{8}\right)}{6}\left(-\frac{4}{9}x\right)^3 + ...\right)$

$= \frac{1}{3}\left(1 + \left(-\frac{1}{2}\right)\left(-\frac{4}{9}x\right) + \frac{3}{8}\left(-\frac{4}{9}x\right)^2 + \left(-\frac{5}{16}\right)\left(-\frac{4}{9}x\right)^3 + ...\right)$

$= \frac{1}{3}\left(1 + \frac{2}{9}x + \frac{2}{27}x^2 + \frac{20}{729}x^3 + ...\right)$

$= \frac{1}{3} + \frac{2}{27}x + \frac{2}{81}x^2 + \frac{20}{2187}x^3 + ...$

*[5 marks available — 1 mark for factorising out $9^{-\frac{1}{2}}$ or $\frac{1}{3}$,
1 mark for expansion of an expression of the form $(1 + ax)^{-\frac{1}{2}}$,
2 marks for the penultimate line of working (1 for the first two
terms in brackets correct and 1 for the 3rd and 4th terms in
brackets correct), 1 mark for the final answer correct]*

Multiplying out those coefficients can be pretty tricky. Don't try to do
things all in one go — you won't be penalised for writing an extra line of
working, but you probably will lose marks if your final answer's wrong.

b) $(2 - x)\left(\frac{1}{3} + \frac{2}{27}x + \frac{2}{81}x^2 + \frac{20}{2187}x^3 + ...\right)$

You only need the first three terms of the expansion, so just write
the terms up to x^2 when you multiply out the brackets:

$= \frac{2}{3} + \frac{4}{27}x + \frac{4}{81}x^2 + ... - \frac{1}{3}x - \frac{2}{27}x^2 + ...$

$= \frac{2}{3} - \frac{5}{27}x - \frac{2}{81}x^2 + ...$

*[4 marks available — 1 mark for multiplying your answer to
part a) by $(2 - x)$, 1 mark for multiplying out brackets to find
constant term, two x-terms and two x^2-terms, 1 mark for correct
constant and x-terms in final answer, 1 mark for correct x^2-term
in final answer]*

Page 55 — Further Binomial Expansions

Practice Questions

1    $f(x) = \frac{7}{2} - \frac{11}{4}x + \frac{25}{8}x^2 - ...$

2    $x = \frac{2}{15} \Rightarrow \sqrt{\frac{1 + \frac{4}{15}}{1 - \frac{6}{15}}} \approx 1 + \left(\frac{5}{2} \times \frac{2}{15}\right) + \left(\frac{35}{8} \times \frac{4}{225}\right)$

$\Rightarrow \sqrt{\frac{\frac{19}{15}}{\frac{9}{15}}} \approx 1 + \frac{1}{3} + \frac{7}{90} \Rightarrow \sqrt{\frac{19}{9}} \approx \frac{90}{90} + \frac{30}{90} + \frac{7}{90}$

$\Rightarrow \frac{\sqrt{19}}{\sqrt{9}} \approx \frac{90 + 30 + 7}{90} \Rightarrow \frac{\sqrt{19}}{3} \approx \frac{127}{90} \Rightarrow \sqrt{19} \approx \frac{127}{30}$ as required

Why did the binomial expansion cross the road?
Don't be silly, binomial expansions can't move independently...
...can they?

Exam Questions

1 a) $(16 + 3x)^{\frac{1}{4}} = 16^{\frac{1}{4}}\left(1 + \frac{3}{16}x\right)^{\frac{1}{4}} = 2\left(1 + \frac{3}{16}x\right)^{\frac{1}{4}}$

$\approx 2\left(1 + \left(\frac{1}{4}\right)\left(\frac{3}{16}x\right) + \frac{\frac{1}{4} \times \left(-\frac{3}{4}\right)}{1 \times 2}\left(\frac{3}{16}x\right)^2\right)$

$= 2\left(1 + \left(\frac{1}{4}\right)\left(\frac{3}{16}x\right) + \left(-\frac{3}{32}\right)\left(\frac{9}{256}x^2\right)\right)$

$= 2\left(1 + \frac{3}{64}x - \frac{27}{8192}x^2\right)$

$= 2 + \frac{3}{32}x - \frac{27}{4096}x^2$

*[5 marks available — 1 mark for factorising out $16^{-\frac{1}{2}}$ or $\frac{1}{4}$,
1 mark for expansion of an expression of the form $(1 + ax)^{-\frac{1}{2}}$,
2 marks for the penultimate line of working (1 for the first two
terms in brackets correct and 1 for the 3rd term in brackets
correct), 1 mark for the final answer correct]*

b) (i) $16 + 3x = 12.4 \Rightarrow x = -1.2$ *[1 mark]*

So $(12.4)^{\frac{1}{4}} \approx 2 + \frac{3}{32}(-1.2) - \frac{27}{4096}(-1.2)^2$

$= 2 - 0.1125 - 0.0094921875$

$= 1.878008$ (to 6 d.p.) *[1 mark]*

(ii)   Percentage error $= \left|\frac{\text{real value} - \text{estimate}}{\text{real value}}\right| \times 100$

$= \left|\frac{\sqrt[4]{12.4} - 1.878008}{\sqrt[4]{12.4}}\right| \times 100$ *[1 mark]*

$= \frac{|1.876529... - 1.878008|}{1.876529...} \times 100$

$= 0.0788\%$ (to 3 s.f.) *[1 mark]*

2   Split into partial fractions: $\frac{13x - 17}{(5 - 3x)(2x - 1)} \equiv \frac{A}{(5 - 3x)} + \frac{B}{(2x - 1)}$

$\Rightarrow 13x - 17 \equiv A(2x - 1) + B(5 - 3x)$ *[1 mark]*

Let $x = \frac{1}{2}$, then $\frac{13}{2} - 17 = B\left(5 - \frac{3}{2}\right) \Rightarrow -\frac{21}{2} = \frac{7}{2}B \Rightarrow B = -3$
[1 mark]

Let $x = \frac{5}{3}$, then $\frac{65}{3} - 17 = A\left(\frac{10}{3} - 1\right) \Rightarrow \frac{14}{3} = \frac{7}{3}A \Rightarrow A = 2$
[1 mark]

Answers

$(2x - 1)^{-1} = -(1 - 2x)^{-1}$ *[1 mark]*

$\approx -\left[1 + (-1)(-2x) + \dfrac{(-1) \times (-2)}{1 \times 2}(-2x)^2\right]$

$= -(1 + 2x + 4x^2)$

$= -1 - 2x - 4x^2$ *[1 mark]*

$(5 - 3x)^{-1} = 5^{-1}\left(1 - \dfrac{3}{5}x\right)^{-1} = \dfrac{1}{5}\left(1 - \dfrac{3}{5}x\right)^{-1}$ *[1 mark]*

$\approx \dfrac{1}{5}\left[1 + (-1)\left(-\dfrac{3}{5}x\right) + \dfrac{(-1) \times (-2)}{1 \times 2}\left(-\dfrac{3}{5}x\right)^2\right]$

$= \dfrac{1}{5}\left(1 + \dfrac{3}{5}x + \dfrac{9}{25}x^2\right)$

$= \dfrac{1}{5} + \dfrac{3}{25}x + \dfrac{9}{125}x^2$ *[1 mark]*

So $\dfrac{13x - 17}{(5 - 3x)(2x - 1)} = \dfrac{2}{(5 - 3x)} - \dfrac{3}{(2x - 1)}$

$= 2(5 - 3x)^{-1} - 3(2x - 1)^{-1}$

$\approx 2\left(\dfrac{1}{5} + \dfrac{3}{25}x + \dfrac{9}{125}x^2\right) - 3(-1 - 2x - 4x^2)$ *[1 mark]*

$= \dfrac{2}{5} + \dfrac{6}{25}x + \dfrac{18}{125}x^2 + 3 + 6x + 12x^2$

$= \dfrac{17}{5} + \dfrac{156}{25}x + \dfrac{1518}{125}x^2$ *[1 mark]*

Section 5 — Trigonometry

Page 57 — Angles, Arc Length and Sector Area
Practice Questions

1 a) $270°$ b) $\dfrac{2\pi}{3}$

2   0.873 radians (3 d.p.)

3 a) $\dfrac{\sqrt{3}}{2}$ b) $\dfrac{1}{\sqrt{2}}$ c) $\sqrt{3}$ d) $\dfrac{1}{2}$

4   $171.9°$ (1 d.p.)

Remember, the formula for the arc length will give you the angle in radians, so you'll have to convert it to degrees to get the final answer.

Exam Question

1 a) Area of cross-section $= \dfrac{1}{2}r^2\theta$ *[1 mark]*

$= \dfrac{1}{2} \times 20^2 \times \dfrac{\pi}{4} = 50\pi$ cm^2 *[1 mark]*

Volume = area of cross-section × height, so

$V = 50\pi \times 10 = 500\pi$ cm^3 *[1 mark]*

b) Surface area is made up of 2 × cross-sectional area + 2 × side rectangles + 1 curved end rectangle *[1 mark]*

Cross-sectional area = 50π (from part a))

Area of each side rectangle = $10 \times 20 = 200$ *[1 mark]*

Area of end rectangle = $10 \times$ arc length

$= 10 \times \left(20 \times \dfrac{\pi}{4}\right) = 50\pi$ *[1 mark]*

$S = (2 \times 50\pi) + (2 \times 200) + 50\pi = (150\pi + 400)$ cm^2 *[1 mark]*

Page 59 — Trig Formulas and Identities
Practice Questions

1 a) $B = 125°$, $a = 3.66$ m, $c = 3.10$ m, area $= 4.64$ m^2

b) $r = 20.05$ km, $P = 1.49°$, $Q = 168.51°$

2   1.89 rad, 0.390 rad and 0.863 rad (3 s.f.)

Exam Questions

1   $3 \cos x = 2 \sin x$, and $\tan x = \dfrac{\sin x}{\cos x}$,

Divide through by $\cos x$ to give: $3\dfrac{\cos x}{\cos x} = 2\dfrac{\sin x}{\cos x}$ *[1 mark]*

$\Rightarrow 3 = 2 \tan x \Rightarrow \tan x = \dfrac{3}{2} (= 1.5)$ *[1 mark]*

2 a) Sketch a diagram to show what's going on:

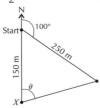

Using the cosine rule: $a^2 = b^2 + c^2 - 2bc \cos A$

If XY is a, then angle $A = 180° - 100° = 80°$.

$XY^2 = 150^2 + 250^2 - (2 \times 150 \times 250 \times \cos 80°)$ *[1 mark]*

$= 71976.386...$

$XY = \sqrt{71976.386...} = 268.284...$

$= 268$ m to the nearest m *[1 mark]*

b) Using the sine rule and the answer to part a):

$\dfrac{a}{\sin A} = \dfrac{b}{\sin B}$, so $\dfrac{250}{\sin \theta} = \dfrac{268.284...}{\sin 80°}$ *[1 mark]*

Rearranging gives:

$\dfrac{\sin \theta}{\sin 80°} = \dfrac{250}{268.284...}$ *[1 mark]* $= 0.93$ (2 d.p.) *[1 mark]*

Page 61 — Trig Graphs
Practice Questions

1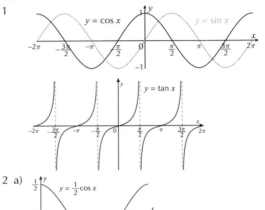

2 a)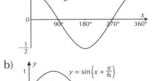

b) 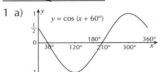   c)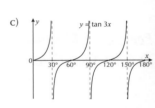

Exam Questions

1 a)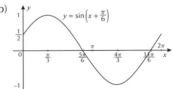

[2 marks — 1 mark for correct shape of cos x graph, 1 mark for shift of 60° to the left]

b) The graph of $y = \cos(x + 60°)$ cuts the x-axis at $30°$ and $210°$, so for $0 \leq x \leq 360°$, $\cos(x + 60°) = 0$ when $x = 30°$ *[1 mark]* and $x = 210°$. *[1 mark]*

2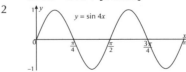

[2 marks — 1 mark for correct shape of sin x graph, 1 mark for 2 repetitions of sine wave between 0 and π]

Page 65 — Solving Trig Equations
Practice Questions

1 a) (i) $\theta = \dfrac{4\pi}{3}, \dfrac{5\pi}{3}$ (ii) $\theta = \dfrac{3\pi}{4}, \dfrac{7\pi}{4}$ (iii) $\theta = \dfrac{3\pi}{4}, \dfrac{5\pi}{4}$

b) (i) $\theta = -147.0°, -123.0°, -57.0°, -33.0°, 33.0°, 57.0°, 123.0°, 147.0°$

(ii) $\theta = -17.5°, 127.5°$ (iii) $\theta = 179.8°$

2   $x = 1.23$ (3 s.f.), $\dfrac{2\pi}{3}, \dfrac{4\pi}{3}$, 5.05 (3 s.f.)

3   $x = -30°$

4   $(\sin y + \cos y)^2 + (\cos y - \sin y)^2 \equiv 2$

Answers

Exam Questions

1 a)
Look for solutions in the range $-\frac{\pi}{4} \le x - \frac{\pi}{4} \le 2\pi - \frac{\pi}{4}$ $(= \frac{7\pi}{4})$.

$2\cos\left(x - \frac{\pi}{4}\right) = \sqrt{3} \Rightarrow \cos\left(x - \frac{\pi}{4}\right) = \frac{\sqrt{3}}{2}$ *[1 mark]*

Solving this gives $x - \frac{\pi}{4} = \frac{\pi}{6}$, which is in the range — so it's a solution. From the symmetry of the cos graph there's another solution at $2\pi - \frac{\pi}{6} = \frac{11\pi}{6}$. But this is outside the range for $x - \frac{\pi}{4}$, so you can ignore it. Using symmetry again, there's also a solution at $-\frac{\pi}{6}$ — and this one is in your range. *[1 mark]*

So solutions for $x - \frac{\pi}{4}$ are $-\frac{\pi}{6}$ and $\frac{\pi}{6}$ $\Rightarrow x = \frac{\pi}{12}$ and $x = \frac{5\pi}{12}$

[1 mark for both correct]

You might find it useful to sketch a graph — or you could use the CAST diagram if you prefer.

b)
$\sin 2x = -\frac{1}{2}$, so look for solutions in the range $0 \le 2x \le 720°$.

It's easier to see what's going on by drawing a graph for this one:

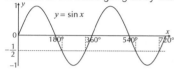

The graph shows there are 4 solutions between 0 and 720°.

Putting $\sin 2x = -\frac{1}{2}$ into your calculator gives you the solution $2x = -30°$, but this is outside the range. From the graph, you can see that the solutions within the range occur at $180° + 30°$, $360° - 30°$, $540° + 30°$ and $720° - 30°$, *[1 mark]* so $2x = 210°$, $330°$, $570°$ and $690°$. *[1 mark]*

Dividing by 2 gives: $x = 105°$, $165°$, $285°$ and $345°$

[1 mark for all 4 correct solutions]

2 a)
$\sin^2 x = 1 - \cos^2 x$, so

$2(1 - \cos x) = 3\sin^2 x \Rightarrow 2(1 - \cos x) = 3(1 - \cos^2 x)$ *[1 mark]*

$\Rightarrow 2 - 2\cos x = 3 - 3\cos^2 x$

$\Rightarrow 3\cos^2 x - 2\cos x - 1 = 0$ *[1 mark]*

b)
From (a), the equation can be written as:

$3\cos^2 x - 2\cos x - 1 = 0$

Now this looks suspiciously like a quadratic equation, so factorise:

$(3\cos x + 1)(\cos x - 1) = 0$ *[1 mark]*

$\Rightarrow \cos x = -\frac{1}{3}$ or $\cos x = 1$ *[1 mark for both]*

For $\cos x = -\frac{1}{3}$, $x = 109.5°$ (1 d.p.), *[1 mark]* and a second solution can be found from $x = (360° - 109.5°) = 250.5°$. *[1 mark]*

For $\cos x = 1$, $x = 0°$ *[1 mark]* and $x = 360°$. *[1 mark]*

3
Using $\cos^2 x + \sin^2 x = 1$:

$3\cos^2 x = \sin^2 x \Rightarrow 3\cos^2 x = 1 - \cos^2 x$ *[1 mark]*

$\Rightarrow 4\cos^2 x = 1 \Rightarrow \cos^2 x = \frac{1}{4} \Rightarrow \cos x = \pm\frac{1}{2}$ *[1 mark]*

For $\cos x = \frac{1}{2}$: $x = 60°$ *[1 mark]* and $x = -60°$ *[1 mark]*

For $\cos x = -\frac{1}{2}$: $x = 120°$ *[1 mark]* and $x = -120°$ *[1 mark]*

You shouldn't divide by $\cos^2 x$, as it can be zero in the range $-180° \le x \le 180°$ (and dividing by zero is the worst thing imaginable).

Page 67 — Further Trig

Practice Questions

1 a) $\frac{\pi}{2}$ b) $\frac{\pi}{4}$ c) $\frac{\pi}{3}$

2 a) 2 b) $\frac{2}{\sqrt{3}}$ c) $\sqrt{3}$

3     $x = 45°, 135°$

Exam Questions

1    $\arccos x = 2 \Rightarrow x = \cos 2$ *[1 mark]* $\Rightarrow x = -0.416$ (3 s.f.) *[1 mark]*

2 a)

[3 marks available — 1 mark for n-shaped curve in third quadrant and u-shaped curve in first quadrant, 1 mark for asymptotes at 0 and $\pm\pi$ and 1 mark for max/min points of the curves at −1 and 1]

b)
$\operatorname{cosec} x = \frac{5}{4} \Rightarrow \frac{1}{\sin x} = \frac{5}{4} \Rightarrow \sin x = \frac{4}{5}$ *[1 mark]*

Solving this for x gives: $x = 0.9272... = 0.927$ (3 s.f.) *[1 mark]* and $x = \pi - 0.9272... = 2.21$ (3 s.f.) *[1 mark]*

c)
$\operatorname{cosec} x = 3\sec x \Rightarrow \frac{1}{\sin x} = \frac{3}{\cos x} \Rightarrow \frac{\cos x}{\sin x} = 3$

$\Rightarrow \frac{1}{\tan x} = 3 \Rightarrow \tan x = \frac{1}{3}$ *[1 mark]*

Solving for x gives: $x = 0.3217... = 0.322$ (3 s.f.) *[1 mark]* and $x = -\pi + 0.3217... = -2.82$ (3 s.f.) *[1 mark]*

Page 69 — Further Trig Identities and Approximations

Practice Questions

1   Divide the whole identity by $\cos^2 \theta$ to get:

$\frac{\cos^2\theta}{\cos^2\theta} + \frac{\sin^2\theta}{\cos^2\theta} \equiv \frac{1}{\cos^2\theta} \Rightarrow 1 + \tan^2\theta \equiv \sec^2\theta$

(as $\sin/\cos \equiv \tan$ and $1/\cos \equiv \sec$)

2    $\operatorname{cosec}^2\theta = -2\cot\theta$

$\Rightarrow 1 + \cot^2\theta = -2\cot\theta \Rightarrow \cot^2\theta + 2\cot\theta + 1 = 0$

$\Rightarrow (\cot\theta + 1)^2 = 0 \Rightarrow \cot\theta = -1 \Rightarrow \tan\theta = -1$

Solving for θ over the given range gives $\theta = \frac{3\pi}{4}$.

3 a) 0.256   b) 0.9998   c) 0.02

Exam Questions

1 a) (i)
Rearrange the identity $\sec^2\theta \equiv 1 + \tan^2\theta$ to get $\sec^2\theta - 1 \equiv \tan^2\theta$, then replace $\tan^2\theta$ in the equation:

$3\tan^2\theta - 2\sec\theta = 5$

$3(\sec^2\theta - 1) - 2\sec\theta - 5 = 0$ *[1 mark]*

$3\sec^2\theta - 2\sec\theta - 8 = 0$ *[1 mark]*

(ii)
Factorise the equation:

$3\sec^2\theta - 2\sec\theta - 8 = 0$

$\Rightarrow (3\sec^2\theta + 4)(\sec\theta - 2) = 0$ *[1 mark]*

So $\sec\theta = -\frac{4}{3}$ or $\sec\theta = 2$. *[1 mark]*

$\sec\theta = \frac{1}{\cos\theta}$, so $\cos\theta = -\frac{3}{4}$ or $\cos\theta = \frac{1}{2}$. *[1 mark]*

b)
Let $\theta = 2x$. From above, you know that the solutions to $3\tan^2\theta - 2\sec\theta = 5$ satisfy $\cos\theta = -\frac{3}{4}$ or $\cos\theta = \frac{1}{2}$.

The range for x is $0° \le x \le 180°$, so as $\theta = 2x$, the range for θ is $0° \le \theta \le 360°$. *[1 mark]*

Solving these equations for θ gives:

$\theta = 138.59°, 221.41°$ (2 d.p.) and $\theta = 60°, 300°$. *[1 mark]*

As $\theta = 2x$, $x = \frac{\theta}{2}$, so $x = 69.30°, 110.70°, 30°, 150°$. *[1 mark]*

You don't actually need to use the double angle formulas for this one.

2 a)
For small θ, $\sin\theta \approx \theta$ and $\cos\theta \approx 1 - \frac{1}{2}\theta^2$, so:

$\theta \sin\left(\frac{\theta}{2}\right) - \cos\theta \approx \theta \times \frac{\theta}{2} - \left(1 - \frac{1}{2}\theta^2\right)$ *[1 mark]*

$= \frac{\theta^2}{2} - 1 + \frac{\theta^2}{2} = \theta^2 - 1$ *[1 mark]*

b)
$0.1 \sin\left(\frac{0.1}{2}\right) - \cos 0.1 \approx 0.1^2 - 1 = -0.99$ *[1 mark]*

Page 71 — Addition and Double Angle Formulas

Practice Questions

1    $\frac{\sqrt{2} + \sqrt{6}}{4}$

2    $\theta = 0°, 150°, 180°, 210°, 360°$

3 a) $\sin\frac{x}{2}\cos\frac{x}{2} = \frac{1}{2}\sin x$ b) $\tan 6x = \frac{2\tan 3x}{1 - \tan^2 3x}$

Answers

Exam Questions

1. $\sin 3x \equiv \sin (2x + x) \equiv \sin 2x \cos x + \cos 2x \sin x$ **[1 mark]**
   $\equiv (2\sin x \cos x)\cos x + (1 - 2\sin^2 x)\sin x$ **[1 mark]**
   $\equiv 2\sin x \cos^2 x + \sin x - 2\sin^3 x$ **[1 mark]**
   $\equiv 2\sin x(1 - \sin^2 x) + \sin x - 2\sin^3 x$ **[1 mark]**
   $\equiv 2\sin x - 2\sin^3 x + \sin x - 2\sin^3 x$
   $\equiv 3\sin x - 4\sin^3 x$ **[1 mark]**

2.   Use the cos addition formula on the right hand side:
   $\sin \theta = \cos\left(\frac{\pi}{4} - \theta\right) \Rightarrow \sin \theta = \cos \frac{\pi}{4} \cos \theta + \sin \frac{\pi}{4} \sin \theta$ **[1 mark]**
   $\Rightarrow \sin \theta = \frac{1}{\sqrt{2}}\cos \theta + \frac{1}{\sqrt{2}}\sin \theta \Rightarrow (\sqrt{2} - 1)\sin \theta = \cos \theta$ **[1 mark]**
   $\cos \theta$ is never zero in the range of values of θ, so divide by $\cos \theta$:
   $\Rightarrow \frac{\sin \theta}{\cos \theta} = \tan \theta = \frac{1}{\sqrt{2} - 1}$ **[1 mark]**
   So $\theta = \tan^{-1} \frac{1}{\sqrt{2} - 1} = 1.18$ (2 d.p.) **[1 mark]**

3. $\tan 4x = \frac{2 \tan 2x}{1 - \tan^2 2x}$, so
   $2 \tan 4x = \tan 2x \Rightarrow \frac{4 \tan 2x}{1 - \tan^2 2x} = \tan 2x$ **[1 mark]**
   $4 \tan 2x = \tan 2x(1 - \tan^2 2x)$
   I hope you resisted the temptation to divide by tan 2x here — you can't do that here, because tan 2x can be zero in the given range of x-values.
   $\tan^3 2x + 3 \tan 2x = 0$
   $\tan 2x(\tan^2 2x + 3) = 0$ **[1 mark]**
   So $\tan 2x = 0$ **[1 mark]** or $\tan^2 2x + 3 = 0 \Rightarrow \tan 2x = \sqrt{-3}$,
   which has no solutions. **[1 mark]**
   Solving $\tan 2x = 0$ over the interval $-180° \leq 2x \leq 180°$ gives the
   solutions $2x = -180°, 0°, 180°,$ **[1 mark]**
   so $x = -90°, 0°, 90°.$ **[1 mark]**

Page 73 — The R Addition Formulas

Practice Questions

1. $a \cos \theta + b \sin \theta \equiv R \cos (\theta - \alpha)$ or $b \sin \theta + a \cos \theta \equiv R \sin (\theta + \alpha)$

2. $5 \sin \theta - 6 \cos \theta \equiv \sqrt{61} \sin (\theta - 50.2°)$ (1 d.p.)

3.   Use the sin addition formulas:
   $\sin(x + y) \equiv \sin x \cos y + \cos x \sin y$
   $\sin(x - y) \equiv \sin x \cos y - \cos x \sin y$
   Take the second away from the first:
   $\sin(x + y) - \sin(x - y) \equiv 2\cos x \sin y.$
   Let $A = x + y$ and $B = x - y$, so that $x = \frac{1}{2}(A + B)$ and $y = \frac{1}{2}(A - B)$.
   Then $\sin A - \sin B \equiv 2 \cos\left(\frac{A+B}{2}\right)\sin\left(\frac{A-B}{2}\right)$.
   Hint: to get the formulas for x and y in terms of A and B, you need to treat A = x + y and B = x - y as a pair of simultaneous equations.

Exam Questions

1. a) $9 \sin \theta + 12 \cos \theta \equiv R \sin(\theta + \alpha)$. Using the sin addition formula,
   $9 \sin \theta + 12 \cos \theta \equiv R \sin \theta \cos \alpha + R \cos \theta \sin \alpha.$
   Equating coefficients of $\sin \theta$ and $\cos \theta$ gives:
   $R \cos \alpha = 9$ and $R \sin \alpha = 12$ **[1 mark]**
   $\frac{R\sin \alpha}{R\cos \alpha} = \tan \alpha$, so $\tan \alpha = \frac{12}{9} = \frac{4}{3}$
   Solving this gives $\alpha = 0.9272...$ **[1 mark]**
   $R = \sqrt{9^2 + 12^2} = \sqrt{81 + 144} = \sqrt{225} = 15$ **[1 mark]**
   So $9 \sin \theta + 12 \cos \theta = 15 \sin (\theta + 0.927)$ (3 s.f.)

   b) If $9 \sin \theta + 12 \cos \theta = 3$, then from part a),
   $15 \sin (\theta + 0.9272...) = 3$, so $\sin (\theta + 0.9272...) = 0.2.$
   The range for θ is $0 \leq \theta \leq 2\pi$, which becomes
   $0.9272... \leq \theta + 0.9272... \leq 7.2104...$
   Solving the equation gives $(\theta + 0.9272...) = 0.2013...$ **[1 mark]**

As this is outside the range, use a sketch
to find values that are in the range:

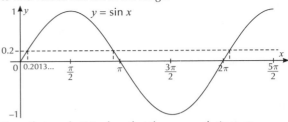

From the graph, it is clear that there are solutions at:
$\pi - 0.2013... = 2.940...$ **[1 mark]**
and $2\pi + 0.2013... = 6.484...$ **[1 mark]**
So $(\theta + 0.9272...) = 2.940...$ and $6.484...$
$\Rightarrow \theta = 2.01$ (3 s.f.) **[1 mark]** and $\theta = 5.56$ (3 s.f.) **[1 mark]**
Be careful with the range — if you hadn't extended it to $2\pi + 0.927$, you would have missed one of the solutions.

c) $9 \sin \theta + 12 \cos \theta = 15 \sin (\theta + 0.927)$, so the maximum and
   minimum values of $9 \sin \theta + 12 \cos \theta$ are $\pm 15.$ **[1 mark]**
   This means the maximum and minimum values of f(x) are
   $10 + 15 = 25$ **[1 mark]** and $10 - 15 = -5.$ **[1 mark]**

2. a) $5 \cos \theta + 12 \sin \theta \equiv R \cos(\theta - \alpha)$. Using the cos addition
   formula, $5 \cos \theta + 12 \sin \theta \equiv R \cos \theta \cos \alpha + R \sin \theta \sin \alpha.$
   Equating coefficients gives:
   $R \cos \alpha = 5$ and $R \sin \alpha = 12$ **[1 mark]**
   $\frac{R\sin \alpha}{R\cos \alpha} = \tan \alpha$, so $\tan \alpha = \frac{12}{5}$
   Solving this gives $\alpha = 67.3801...° = 67.38°$ (2 d.p.) **[1 mark]**
   $R = \sqrt{5^2 + 12^2} = \sqrt{25 + 144} = \sqrt{169} = 13$ **[1 mark]**
   So $5 \cos \theta + 12 \sin \theta = 13 \cos (\theta - 67.38°)$ (2 d.p.)

   b) From part a), if $5 \cos \theta + 12 \sin \theta = 2$, this means
   $13 \cos(\theta - 67.3801...°) = 2$, so $\cos(\theta - 67.3801...°) = \frac{2}{13}$ **[1 mark]**
   The range for θ is $0° \leq \theta \leq 360°$, which becomes
   $-67.3801...° \leq \theta - 67.3801...° \leq 292.6198...°$ **[1 mark]**
   Solving the equation gives:
   $\theta - 67.3801...° = 81.1501...°$ and $278.8598...°$ **[1 mark]**
   $\Rightarrow \theta = 148.53°$ (2 d.p.) **[1 mark]** and $346.23°$ (2 d.p.) **[1 mark]**

   c) The minimum points of the cos curve have a value of -1,
   so as $5 \cos \theta + 12 \sin \theta = 13 \cos (\theta - 67.38°)$,
   the minimum value of $5 \cos \theta + 12 \sin \theta$ is -13. **[1 mark]**
   Hence the minimum value of $(5 \cos \theta + 12 \sin \theta)^3$
   is $(-13)^3 = -2197.$ **[1 mark]**

3.   You need to find A and B such that $\frac{A+B}{2} = \frac{\pi}{2}$ and $\frac{A-B}{2} = \frac{\pi}{12}$.
   Solving these simultaneously gives $A = \frac{7\pi}{12}$ **[1 mark]**
   and $B = \frac{5\pi}{12}$. **[1 mark]**
   $\sin A + \sin B \equiv 2 \sin\left(\frac{A+B}{2}\right)\cos\left(\frac{A-B}{2}\right)$, so
   $4\sin\left(\frac{A+B}{2}\right)\cos\left(\frac{A-B}{2}\right) \equiv 2(\sin A + \sin B)$, so $k = 2.$ **[1 mark]**
   Writing this out in full gives $4 \sin \frac{\pi}{2} \cos \frac{\pi}{12} = 2\left(\sin \frac{7\pi}{12} + \sin \frac{5\pi}{12}\right)$.

Page 75 — Trigonometric Proofs

Practice Questions

1. $\frac{\sin^4 x + \sin^2 x \cos^2 x}{\cos^2 x - 1} \equiv \frac{\sin^2 x(\sin^2 x + \cos^2 x)}{(1 - \sin^2 x) - 1} \equiv \frac{\sin^2 x}{-\sin^2 x} \equiv -1$

2. a) $\cot^2 \theta + \sin^2 \theta \equiv (\csc^2 \theta - 1) + (1 - \cos^2 \theta)$
   $\equiv \csc^2 \theta - \cos^2 \theta$ as required.

   b) $\frac{\cos \theta}{\sin \theta} + \frac{\sin \theta}{\cos \theta} \equiv \frac{\cos \theta \cos \theta}{\sin \theta \cos \theta} + \frac{\sin \theta \sin \theta}{\sin \theta \cos \theta}$
   $\equiv \frac{\cos^2 \theta + \sin^2 \theta}{\sin \theta \cos \theta} \equiv \frac{1}{\sin \theta \cos \theta}$
   $\sin 2\theta \equiv 2 \sin \theta \cos \theta \Rightarrow \sin \theta \cos \theta = \frac{1}{2} \sin 2\theta$
   So $\frac{1}{\sin \theta \cos \theta} \equiv \frac{1}{\frac{1}{2}\sin 2\theta} \equiv 2 \csc 2\theta$ as required.

Answers

Exam Questions

1 a) $\dfrac{2\sin x}{1-\cos x} - \dfrac{2\cos x}{\sin x} \equiv \dfrac{2\sin^2 x - 2\cos x + 2\cos^2 x}{\sin x(1-\cos x)}$ *[1 mark]*

$\equiv \dfrac{2 - 2\cos x}{\sin x(1-\cos x)}$ *[1 mark]*

$\equiv \dfrac{2(1-\cos x)}{\sin x(1-\cos x)}$ *[1 mark]*

$\equiv \dfrac{2}{\sin x} \equiv 2\operatorname{cosec} x$ as required. *[1 mark]*

b) $2\operatorname{cosec} x = 4 \Rightarrow \operatorname{cosec} x = 2 \Rightarrow \sin x = \dfrac{1}{2}$ *[1 mark]*

The solutions in the interval $0 < x < 2\pi$ are:

$x = \dfrac{\pi}{6}$ *[1 mark]* and $x = \dfrac{5\pi}{6}$ *[1 mark]*

2 $(4x)^{-1}\operatorname{cosec} 3x\,(2\cos 7x - 2) = \dfrac{1}{4x} \times \dfrac{1}{\sin 3x} \times (2\cos 7x - 2)$

$= \dfrac{2\cos 7x - 2}{4x\sin 3x}$ *[1 mark]*

Using the small angle approximations, $\sin 3x \approx 3x$, *[1 mark]*

and $2\cos 7x \approx 2\left(1 - \dfrac{1}{2}(7x)^2\right) = 2 - 49x^2$. *[1 mark]*

So $\dfrac{2\cos 7x - 2}{4x\sin 3x} \approx \dfrac{(2 - 49x^2) - 2}{4x \times 3x} = \dfrac{-49x^2}{12x^2} = -\dfrac{49}{12}$ *[1 mark]*

3 $\cos\theta\cos 2\theta + \sin\theta\sin 2\theta$

$\equiv \cos\theta(1 - 2\sin^2\theta) + \sin\theta(2\sin\theta\cos\theta)$

[2 marks — 1 mark for each expansion]

$\equiv \cos\theta - 2\sin^2\theta\cos\theta + 2\sin^2\theta\cos\theta$ *[1 mark]*

$\equiv \cos\theta$ as required. *[1 mark]*

Section 6 — Exponentials and Logarithms

Page 77 — Exponentials and Logs

Practice Questions

1 a) 3   b) –3   c) 2
2 a) log 75   b) log 2   c) 0
3 $\log_b(x + 1)$
4 a) 2.380 (4 s.f.)   b) 199500 (4 s.f.)   c) 1.088 (4 s.f.)

Exam Questions

1 $\log_7(y + 3) + \log_7(2y + 1) = 1$

$\Rightarrow \log_7((y + 3)(2y + 1)) = 1$ *[1 mark]*

To remove the $\log_7$, do 7 to the power of each side:

$(y + 3)(2y + 1) = 7^1 = 7$ *[1 mark]*

Multiply out, rearrange, and re-factorise:

$2y^2 + 7y + 3 = 7 \Rightarrow 2y^2 + 7y - 4 = 0$

$\Rightarrow (2y - 1)(y + 4) = 0$ *[1 mark]*

$\Rightarrow y = \dfrac{1}{2}$ or $y = -4$,

but since $y > 0$, $y = \dfrac{1}{2}$ is the only solution. *[1 mark]*

2 a) $3^x = 5$, so taking logs of both sides gives $\log 3^x = \log 5$ *[1 mark]*

$\Rightarrow x\log 3 = \log 5$ *[1 mark]*

$\Rightarrow x = \dfrac{\log 5}{\log 3} = 1.46$ to 2 d.p. *[1 mark]*

b) $3^{2x} = (3^x)^2$ (from the power laws) *[1 mark]*,

so let $y = 3^x$ and $y^2 = 3^{2x}$. This gives a quadratic in y:

$y^2 - 14y = -45 \Rightarrow y^2 - 14y + 45 = 0 \Rightarrow (y - 5)(y - 9) = 0$ *[1 mark]*,

so $y = 5$ or $y = 9 \Rightarrow 3^x = 5$ or $3^x = 9$ *[1 mark for both values of 3^x]*

From a), $3^x = 5 \Rightarrow x = 1.46$ to 2 d.p.

and $3^x = 9 \Rightarrow x = 2$ (since $3^2 = 9$) *[1 mark]*

Page 79 — Using Exponentials and Logs

Practice Questions

1    $x = -0.258$ (3 s.f.)
2    $y = -2$ and $y = 3.77$ (3 s.f.)
3   14.2 years (1 d.p.)

Exam Question

1 a) Make a table of values for t and $\log_{10} p$ (round values to 3 d.p.):

t	1	2	3	4	5
$\log_{10} p$	1	1.114	1.230	1.380	1.544

[1 mark for all values correct]
Plot the graph and draw the line of best fit:

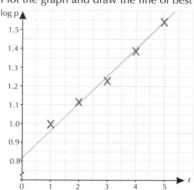

[1 mark for plotting points correctly and drawing a suitable line of best fit]

b) You are given the equation $p = ab^t$. Using the laws of logs, this rearranges to: $\log p = t\log b + \log a$

Comparing this to $y = mx + c$ shows that the gradient of the graph is equal to $\log b$ and the vertical-axis intercept is equal to $\log a$. *[1 mark for both correct]*

Use gradient $= \dfrac{y_2 - y_1}{x_2 - x_1}$ with points (x_1, y_1) and (x_2, y_2) chosen from your line of best fit to find $\log b$.

e.g. taking the points (3, 1.25) and (4, 1.4) gives

gradient $\dfrac{1.4 - 1.25}{4 - 3} = 0.15$ *[1 mark]*

So $\log b = 0.15 \Rightarrow b = 1.41$ (2 d.p.) *[1 mark for $0.9 \le b \le 1.9$]*

Now read off your vertical-axis intercept to find $\log a$:

$\log a = 0.82 \Rightarrow a = 6.61$ (2 d.p.) *[1 mark for $6.5 \le a \le 7.5$]*

Don't worry if your values aren't exactly the same as in this solution. It will depend on the line of best fit you have drawn — everybody's will be slightly different. The examiners have a range of answers which are allowed, so as long as yours are within that range then you'll be fine. Look back at page 79 if you struggled with this question — it is quite tricky.

c) $t = 10 \Rightarrow p = 6.61(1.41)^{10} = 205.30$

So the author's income will be approximately £205 000.

[1 mark for answer between £150 000 and £250 000]

d) E.g. 10 years is a large extrapolation from the data.

[1 mark for a valid reason]

Lots of things could change the author's income in this time — e.g. sales of the book slow down or the author publishes another book.

Page 81 — e^x and ln x

Practice Questions

1 a) C   b) A   c) D   d) B
2 a) $x = 0.8959$ to 4 d.p.   b) $x = -0.8830$ to 4 d.p.
   c) $x = 0.1223$ to 4 d.p.   d) $x = 0.8000$ to 4 d.p.

3 a) $x = \dfrac{e^{-3} + 28}{8}$ or $\dfrac{1}{8e^3} + \dfrac{7}{2}$ b) $x = 0$

Exam Questions

1 a) $6e^x = 3 \Rightarrow e^x = 0.5$ *[1 mark]* $\Rightarrow x = \ln 0.5$ or $-\ln 2$ *[1 mark]*

b) $e^{2x} - 8e^x + 7 = 0$. This looks like a quadratic, so use $y = e^x$.

If $y = e^x$, then $y^2 - 8y + 7 = 0$. This will factorise to give:

$(y - 7)(y - 1) = 0$ *[1 mark]* $\Rightarrow y = 7$ or $y = 1$.

So $e^x = 7$ and $e^x = 1$ *[1 mark for both]*

$\Rightarrow x = \ln 7$ and $x = \ln 1 = 0$ *[1 mark for each correct answer]*

c) $4\ln x = 3 \Rightarrow \ln x = 0.75$ *[1 mark]* $\Rightarrow x = e^{0.75}$ *[1 mark]*

Answers

d) $\ln x + \frac{24}{\ln x} = 10$

You need to get rid of that fraction, so multiply through by $\ln x$:
$(\ln x)^2 + 24 = 10 \ln x \Rightarrow (\ln x)^2 - 10 \ln x + 24 = 0$
This looks like a quadratic, so use $y = \ln x$.
$y^2 - 10y + 24 = 0 \Rightarrow (y - 6)(y - 4) = 0$ *[1 mark]*
$\Rightarrow y = 6$ or $y = 4$ *[1 mark]*
So $\ln x = 6 \Rightarrow x = e^6$ *[1 mark]*, or $\ln x = 4 \Rightarrow x = e^4$ *[1 mark]*.

2 a) $2e^x + 18e^{-x} = 20$

Multiply through by e^x to remove the e^{-x} (since $e^x \times e^{-x} = 1$).
$2e^{2x} + 18 = 20e^x \Rightarrow 2e^{2x} - 20e^x + 18 = 0 \Rightarrow e^{2x} - 10e^x + 9 = 0$
This now looks like a quadratic equation, so use $y = e^x$ to simplify.
$y^2 - 10y + 9 = 0 \Rightarrow (y - 1)(y - 9) = 0$ *[1 mark]*
$\Rightarrow y = 1$ or $y = 9$ *[1 mark]*.
So $e^x = 1 \Rightarrow x = 0$ *[1 mark]* or $e^x = 9 \Rightarrow x = \ln 9$ *[1 mark]*

b) $2 \ln x - \ln 3 = \ln 12 \Rightarrow 2 \ln x = \ln 12 + \ln 3$
Use the log laws to simplify at this point.
$\Rightarrow \ln x^2 = \ln 36$ *[1 mark]* $\Rightarrow x^2 = 36$ *[1 mark]* $\Rightarrow x = 6$ *[1 mark]*.
x must be positive as $\ln (-6)$ does not exist.

Page 83 — Modelling with e^x and $\ln x$
Practice Questions

1 a)

b)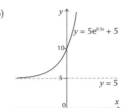

c)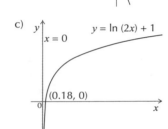

d)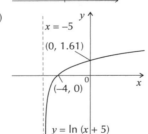

2 a) £7500
c) 13.5 years (to 1 d.p.)

b) £1015 (to the nearest £)
d)

Exam Questions

1 a) When $t = 0$ (i.e. when the mink were introduced to the habitat)
$M = 74 \times e^0 = 74$, so there were 74 mink originally. *[1 mark]*
b) After 3 years, $M = 74 \times e^{0.6 \times 3}$ *[1 mark]* $= 447$ mink. *[1 mark]*
You can't round up here as there are only 447 whole mink.
c) For $M = 10\,000$:
$10\,000 = 74e^{0.6t} \Rightarrow e^{0.6t} = 10\,000 \div 74 = 135.1351$
$\Rightarrow 0.6t = \ln 135.1351 = 4.9063$ *[1 mark]*
$\Rightarrow t = 4.9063 \div 0.6 = 8.2$ years
so it would take 9 complete years for the population
to exceed 10 000. *[1 mark]*

d)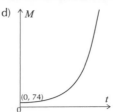

[1 mark for correct shape of graph, and 1 mark for (0, 74) as a point on the graph.]

2 a) B is the value of A when $t = 0$. From the table, $B = 50$. *[1 mark]*
b) Substitute $t = 5$ and $A = 42$ into $A = 50e^{-kt}$:
$42 = 50e^{-5k} \Rightarrow e^{-5k} = \frac{42}{50} \Rightarrow e^{5k} = \frac{50}{42}$ *[1 mark]*
$\Rightarrow 5k = \ln\left(\frac{50}{42}\right) = 0.17435$
$\Rightarrow k = 0.17435 \div 5 = 0.0349$ to 3 s.f. *[1 mark]*
c) $A = 50e^{-0.0349t}$ [using values from a) and b)],
so when $t = 10$, $A = 50 \times e^{-0.0349 \times 10}$ *[1 mark]*
$= 35$ to the nearest whole number. *[1 mark]*
d) The half-life will be the value of t when A reaches half of the
original value of 50, i.e. when $A = 25$.
$25 = 50e^{-0.0349t} \Rightarrow \frac{25}{50} = e^{-0.0349t} \Rightarrow \frac{50}{25} = e^{0.0349t}$
$\Rightarrow e^{0.0349t} = 2$ *[1 mark]*
$\Rightarrow 0.0349t = \ln 2$ *[1 mark]*
So $t = \ln 2 \div 0.0349 = 20$ days to the nearest day. *[1 mark]*

Section 7 — Differentiation

Page 86 — Differentiation
Practice Questions

1 a) $\frac{dy}{dx} = 2x$ b) $\frac{dy}{dx} = 4x^3 + \frac{1}{2\sqrt{x}}$

c) $\frac{dy}{dx} = -\frac{14}{x^3} + \frac{3}{2\sqrt{x^3}} + 36x^2$

2 $\frac{dy}{dx} = -16$

3 Tangent: $y = 3x - 42$, Normal: $x + 3y - 34 = 0$

4 $f(x) = 5x \Rightarrow f'(x) = \lim_{h \to 0} \frac{5(x+h) - 5x}{h} = \lim_{h \to 0} \frac{5x + 5h - 5x}{h}$
$= \lim_{h \to 0} \frac{5h}{h} = \lim_{h \to 0}(5) = 5$

Exam Questions

1 Rewrite the expression as $x^{\frac{1}{2}} + x^{-1}$
Then differentiate to get $\frac{dy}{dx} = -\frac{1}{2}x^{-\frac{3}{2}} - x^{-2}$ *[1 mark]*
Putting $x = 4$ into the derivative gives:
$-\frac{1}{2}4^{-\frac{3}{2}} - 4^{-2} = -\frac{1}{2}(\sqrt{4})^{-3} - \frac{1}{4^2} = -\frac{1}{16} - \frac{1}{16} = -\frac{1}{8}$ *[1 mark]*

2 a) $\frac{dy}{dx} = 3mx^2 - 2x + 8$ *[1 mark]*

b) Rearranging the equation of the line parallel to the normal
gives the equation $y = 3 - 4x$, so it has a gradient of -4. *[1 mark]*
The normal also has gradient -4 because it is parallel
to this line, so the gradient of the curve at P is
$-1 \div$ the gradient of the normal $= -1 \div -4 = \frac{1}{4}$ *[1 mark]*
c) (i) When $x = 5$, the gradient is $3mx^2 - 2x + 8 = \frac{1}{4}$ *[1 mark]*
Now find the value of m:
$m(3 \times 5^2) - (2 \times 5) + 8 = \frac{1}{4}$ *[1 mark]*
$75m - 2 = \frac{1}{4} \Rightarrow 75m = \frac{9}{4} \Rightarrow m = \frac{9}{300} = 0.03$ *[1 mark]*
(ii) When $x = 5$, $y = (0.03 \times 5^3) - (5^2) + (8 \times 5) + 2$ *[1 mark]*
$= 3.75 - 25 + 40 + 2 = 20.75$ *[1 mark]*

3 $y = \frac{x^3}{3} - 2x^2 - 4x + \frac{86}{3} \Rightarrow \frac{dy}{dx} = x^2 - 4x - 4$
When $x = 4$: $y = \frac{64}{3} - 32 - 16 + \frac{86}{3} = 2$ *[1 mark]*
$\frac{dy}{dx} = 16 - 16 - 4 = -4$ *[1 mark]*

Answers

$y = \sqrt{x} = x^{\frac{1}{2}} \Rightarrow \dfrac{dy}{dx} = \dfrac{1}{2}x^{-\frac{1}{2}} = \dfrac{1}{2\sqrt{x}}$

When $x = 4$: $y = \sqrt{4} = 2$ *[1 mark]*

$\dfrac{dy}{dx} = \dfrac{1}{2\sqrt{4}} = \dfrac{1}{4}$ *[1 mark]*

For both curves, when $x = 4$, $y = 2$,
so they both pass through the point (4, 2) *[1 mark]*.

If you multiply the two gradients at the point (4, 2) together,
you get $-4 \times \dfrac{1}{4} = -1$, so the curves are perpendicular *[1 mark]*.

4 $f(x) = x^4 \Rightarrow f'(x) = \lim\limits_{h \to 0} \dfrac{(x+h)^4 - x^4}{h}$ *[1 mark]*

Using the binomial formula:
$(x + h)^4 = x^4 + 4hx^3 + 6h^2x^2 + 4h^3x + h^4$ *[1 mark]*

So $f'(x) = \lim\limits_{h \to 0} \dfrac{x^4 + 4hx^3 + 6h^2x^2 + 4h^3x + h^4 - x^4}{h}$ *[1 mark]*

$= \lim\limits_{h \to 0} \dfrac{4hx^3 + 6h^2x^2 + 4h^3x + h^4}{h}$

$= \lim\limits_{h \to 0} (4x^3 + 6hx^2 + 4h^2x + h^3)$ *[1 mark]*

As $h \to 0$, the last three terms become 0, so $f'(x) = 4x^3$ *[1 mark]*

Page 89 — Stationary Points

Practice Questions

1 (7, −371) and (−3, 129)

2 (1, 4) is a minimum, (−1, −4) is a maximum.

3 a) Increasing when $x > 0.5$, decreasing when $x < 0.5$

   b) Increasing when $x < 0$, decreasing when $x > 0$

4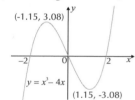

Exam Questions

1 a) $y = 6 + \dfrac{4x^3 - 15x^2 + 12x}{6} = 6 + \dfrac{2}{3}x^3 - \dfrac{5}{2}x^2 + 2x$ *[1 mark]*

   $\dfrac{dy}{dx} = 2x^2 - 5x + 2$ *[1 mark]*

   b) Stationary points occur when $2x^2 - 5x + 2 = 0$.
   Factorising the equation gives: $(2x - 1)(x - 2) = 0$
   So the stationary points are at $x = 2$ and $x = \dfrac{1}{2}$. *[1 mark]*

   When $x = 2$, $y = 6 + \dfrac{4(2^3) - 15(2^2) + (12 \times 2)}{6} = 5\dfrac{1}{3}$ *[1 mark]*

   When $x = \dfrac{1}{2}$, $y = 6 + \dfrac{4\left(\frac{1}{2}\right)^3 - 15\left(\frac{1}{2}\right)^2 + 12\left(\frac{1}{2}\right)}{6} = 6\dfrac{11}{24}$ *[1 mark]*

   So coordinates of the stationary points of the curve are $\left(2, 5\dfrac{1}{3}\right)$ and $\left(\dfrac{1}{2}, 6\dfrac{11}{24}\right)$.

   c) Differentiate again to find $\dfrac{d^2y}{dx^2} = 4x - 5$ *[1 mark]*

   When $x = 2$, $\dfrac{d^2y}{dx^2} = 4(2) - 5 = 3$, which is positive,
   so $\left(2, 5\dfrac{1}{3}\right)$ is a minimum *[1 mark]*

   When $x = \dfrac{1}{2}$, $\dfrac{d^2y}{dx^2} = 4\left(\dfrac{1}{2}\right) - 5 = -3$, which is negative,
   so $\left(\dfrac{1}{2}, 6\dfrac{11}{24}\right)$ is a maximum *[1 mark]*

2 a) First, expand the brackets to get $y = 3x^3 - 8x^2 + 3x + 2$ *[1 mark]*

   $\Rightarrow \dfrac{dy}{dx} = 9x^2 - 16x + 3$ *[1 mark]*

   $\dfrac{dy}{dx} = 0$ at the stationary point, so use the quadratic formula:
   $x = \dfrac{16 \pm \sqrt{(-16)^2 - (4 \times 9 \times 3)}}{2 \times 9} = \dfrac{16 \pm 2\sqrt{37}}{18}$
   $\Rightarrow x = 1.56$ and 0.213 (3 s.f.) *[1 mark]*

Substituting these values for x into the original equation
for y gives $y = -1.40$ and 2.31 (3 s.f.), so the stationary points
have coordinates (1.56, −1.40) and (0.213, 2.31). *[1 mark]*

   b) $\dfrac{d^2y}{dx^2} = 18x - 16$ *[1 mark]*
   At $x = 1.56$, $\dfrac{d^2y}{dx^2} = 12.16... > 0$, so it's a minimum *[1 mark]*
   At $x = 0.213$, $\dfrac{d^2y}{dx^2} = -12.16... < 0$, so it's a maximum *[1 mark]*

   c) y is a positive cubic function, with a minimum at (1.56, −1.40)
   and a maximum at (0.213, 2.31), from parts a) and b).
   The curve crosses the y-axis when $x = 0 \Rightarrow y = 2$ *[1 mark]*
   The initial equation can be factorised to find where it intersects
   the x-axis: $y = (x - 1)(3x^2 - 5x - 2) = (x - 1)(3x + 1)(x - 2)$
   So $y = 0$ when $x = 1, -\dfrac{1}{3}$ and 2. *[1 mark]*
   The sketch looks like this: *[1 mark]*

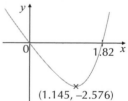

3 a) $f'(x) = 2x^3 - 3 = 0$ at the stationary point. *[1 mark]*
   $\Rightarrow 2x^3 = 3 \Rightarrow x = 1.1447... = 1.14$ (3 s.f.) *[1 mark]*
   $f(1.1447...) = \dfrac{1}{2}(1.1447...)^4 - 3(1.1447...) = -2.58$ (3 s.f.) *[1 mark]*
   So the coordinates of the stationary point are (1.14, −2.58).

   b) $f''(x) = 6x^2$ *[1 mark]*
   At the stationary point, $f''(x) = 6(1.1447...)^2 = 7.862... > 0$,
   so it is a minimum. *[1 mark]*

   c) (i) As the stationary point is a minimum, $f(x)$ is increasing on the
   right of the stationary point — i.e. when $x > 1.14$ *[1 mark]*

   (ii) Similarly, $f(x)$ is decreasing on the left of the stationary point
   — i.e. when $x < 1.14$ *[1 mark]*

   d) The graph intersects the x-axis when $f(x) = 0 \Rightarrow \dfrac{1}{2}x^4 - 3x = 0$
   $\Rightarrow x\left(\dfrac{1}{2}x^3 - 3\right) = 0 \Rightarrow x = 0$ or $x = \sqrt[3]{6} = 1.82$ (3 s.f.) *[1 mark]*
   So the graph looks like this: *[1 mark]*

Page 91 — Convex and Concave Curves

Practice Questions

1 a) Concave   b) Concave
   c) Point of inflection (at $x = 1.2$)   d) Convex

2 Point of inflection at (1, 1), stationary point of inflection at (0, 0)

Exam Questions

1 Find $f'(x)$ and $f''(x)$:
   $f'(x) = 12x^5 - 30x^4 + 20x^3$ *[1 mark]*
   $f''(x) = 60x^4 - 120x^3 + 60x^2$ *[1 mark]*
   $= 60x^2(x^2 - 2x + 1) = 60x^2(x - 1)^2$ *[1 mark]*
   Since x^2 and $(x - 1)^2$ are both ≥ 0, $f''(x) \geq 0$ for all x *[1 mark]*
   so the curve is never concave and there cannot be any
   points of inflection *[1 mark]*.

2 Differentiate twice to find $f''(x)$:
   $f'(x) = 4x^3 + 5x^2 + 2x - 2$ *[1 mark]*
   $f''(x) = 12x^2 + 10x + 2$ *[1 mark]*
   So $f''(x) > 0 \Rightarrow 12x^2 + 10x + 2 > 0 \Rightarrow 6x^2 + 5x + 1 > 0$
   $\Rightarrow (2x + 1)(3x + 1) > 0 \Rightarrow x > -\dfrac{1}{3}$ or $x < -\dfrac{1}{2}$ *[1 mark]*
   And $f''(x) < 0 \Rightarrow -\dfrac{1}{2} < x < -\dfrac{1}{3}$ *[1 mark]*
   So the curve is concave between $x = -\dfrac{1}{2}$ and $x = -\dfrac{1}{3}$,
   and convex otherwise *[1 mark]*.

Answers

3   Differentiate: $\frac{dy}{dx} = -4x + 4x^2 - x^3$ *[1 mark]*

$\frac{dy}{dx} = 0 \Rightarrow x^3 - 4x^2 + 4x = 0 \Rightarrow x(x^2 - 4x + 4) = 0$
$\Rightarrow x(x-2)^2 = 0 \Rightarrow x = 0$ or $x = 2$ *[1 mark]*

When $x = 0$, $y = 4$ and when $x = 2$, $y = 4 - 8 + \frac{32}{3} - 4 = \frac{8}{3}$
[1 mark]

To determine their nature, differentiate again:

$\frac{d^2y}{dx^2} = -4 + 8x - 3x^2$ *[1 mark]*

When $x = 0$, $\frac{d^2y}{dx^2} = -4$, so $(0, 4)$ is a maximum point *[1 mark]*

When $x = 2$, $\frac{d^2y}{dx^2} = -4 + 16 - 12 = 0$ *[1 mark]*

Check what happens to $\frac{d^2y}{dx^2}$ either side of $x = 2$:

$\frac{d^2y}{dx^2} = -(3x^2 - 8x + 4) = -(3x - 2)(x - 2)$ *[1 mark]*

When x is just larger than 2, $(3x - 2)$ is positive and $(x - 2)$ is positive, so $\frac{d^2y}{dx^2} < 0$. When x is just smaller than 2, $(3x - 2)$ is positive and $(x - 2)$ is negative, so $\frac{d^2y}{dx^2} > 0$. *[1 mark]*

So $\frac{d^2y}{dx^2}$ changes sign at $x = 2$, meaning that $\left(2, \frac{8}{3}\right)$ is a stationary point of inflection. *[1 mark]*

Page 93 — Using Differentiation

Practice Questions

1   146 ml/s

2    $m = 53.3$ g (3 s.f.), $h_{max} = 94.8$ m (3 s.f.)

Exam Questions

1 a) Find the value of x that gives the minimum value of y, i.e. the stationary point of curve y, by differentiating and solving $\frac{dy}{dx} = 0$: $\frac{dy}{dx} = \frac{1}{\sqrt{x}} - \frac{27}{x^2}$ *[1 mark]*

$\frac{dy}{dx} = 0 \Rightarrow \frac{1}{\sqrt{x}} - \frac{27}{x^2} = 0 \Rightarrow \frac{1}{\sqrt{x}} = \frac{27}{x^2} \Rightarrow x^{\frac{3}{2}} = 27$ *[1 mark]*

$\Rightarrow x = 9$ *[1 mark]*

So the minimum coal consumption is at 9 mph. *[1 mark]*

b) $\frac{d^2y}{dx^2} = \frac{54}{x^3} - \frac{1}{2\sqrt{x^3}}$ *[1 mark]*

At the stationary point, $x = 9 \Rightarrow \frac{d^2y}{dx^2} = \frac{54}{9^3} - \frac{1}{2\sqrt{9^3}} = 0.055... > 0$ so the stationary point is a minimum. *[1 mark]*

c) $y = 2\sqrt{9} + \frac{27}{9} = 9$ units of coal *[1 mark]*

2 a) Surface area $= 2(d \times x) + 2\left(d \times \frac{x}{2}\right) + \left(x \times \frac{x}{2}\right)$
$= 2dx + dx + \frac{x^2}{2} = 3dx + \frac{x^2}{2}$ *[1 mark]*

Surface area $= 72 \Rightarrow 3dx + \frac{x^2}{2} = 72 \Rightarrow x^2 + 6dx = 144$ *[1 mark]*

$\Rightarrow d = \frac{144 - x^2}{6x}$ *[1 mark]*

Volume $=$ width $\times$ height $\times$ depth $= \frac{x}{2} \times x \times d$
$V = \frac{x^2}{2} \times \frac{144 - x^2}{6x} = \frac{144x^2 - x^4}{12x} = 12x - \frac{x^3}{12}$ as required *[1 mark]*

b) Differentiate V and then solve $\frac{dV}{dx} = 0$: $\frac{dV}{dx} = 12 - \frac{x^2}{4}$ *[1 mark]*

$12 - \frac{x^2}{4} = 0 \Rightarrow \frac{x^2}{4} = 12 \Rightarrow x^2 = 48$ *[1 mark]*

$\Rightarrow x = \sqrt{48} = 4\sqrt{3}$ *[1 mark]*

c) $\frac{d^2V}{dx^2} = -\frac{x}{2}$ *[1 mark]*

so when $x = 4\sqrt{3}$, $\frac{d^2V}{dx^2} = -2\sqrt{3}$ *[1 mark]*

$\frac{d^2V}{dx^2}$ is negative, so it's a maximum point. *[1 mark]*

$x = 4\sqrt{3}$ at V_{max}, so $V_{max} = (12 \times 4\sqrt{3}) - \frac{(4\sqrt{3})^3}{12}$
$V_{max} = 55.4$ m^3 (3 s.f.) *[1 mark]*

Page 95 — Chain Rule

Practice Questions

1 a) $\frac{dy}{dx} = \frac{3x^2 + 4x}{2\sqrt{x^3 + 2x^2}}$ b) $\frac{dy}{dx} = -\frac{3x^2 + 4x}{2(\sqrt{x^3 + 2x^2})^3}$

2    $\frac{dA}{dx} = 44x$, $\frac{dV}{dx} = 18x^2$

By the chain rule: $\frac{dA}{dt} = \frac{dA}{dx} \times \frac{dx}{dt} = 44x \times \frac{dx}{dt}$

To find $\frac{dx}{dt}$, use the chain rule again:

$\frac{dx}{dt} = \frac{dx}{dV} \times \frac{dV}{dt} = \frac{1}{\left(\frac{dV}{dx}\right)} \times \frac{dV}{dt} = \frac{1}{18x^2} \times 3 = \frac{1}{6x^2}$

So $\frac{dA}{dt} = 44x \times \frac{1}{6x^2} = \frac{22}{3x}$ as required.

Exam Questions

1 a) For $x = \sqrt{y^2 + 3y}$, find $\frac{dx}{dy}$ first (using the chain rule):

$x = u^{\frac{1}{2}}$, $u = y^2 + 3y$

$\frac{dx}{du} = \frac{1}{2}u^{-\frac{1}{2}} = \frac{1}{2\sqrt{u}} = \frac{1}{2\sqrt{y^2 + 3y}}$ *[1 mark]*

$\frac{du}{dy} = 2y + 3$ *[1 mark]*

So $\frac{dx}{dy} = \frac{2y + 3}{2\sqrt{y^2 + 3y}}$ *[1 mark]* $\Rightarrow \frac{dy}{dx} = \frac{2\sqrt{y^2 + 3y}}{2y + 3}$ *[1 mark]*

At the point $(2, 1)$, $y = 1$, so: $\frac{dy}{dx} = \frac{2\sqrt{1^2 + 3}}{2 + 3} = \frac{4}{5} = 0.8$ *[1 mark]*

b) Equation of a straight line is:
$y - y_1 = m(x - x_1)$, where m is the gradient.
For the tangent at $(2, 1)$: $y_1 = 1$, $x_1 = 2$, $m = \frac{dy}{dx} = 0.8$ *[1 mark]*
So the equation is: $y - 1 = 0.8(x - 2) \Rightarrow y = 0.8x - 0.6$ *[1 mark]*

2 a) Start by finding the missing side length of the triangular faces. Call the missing length s:

$s = \sqrt{x^2 + \left(\frac{3}{4}x\right)^2} = \sqrt{x^2 + \frac{9}{16}x^2} = \sqrt{\frac{25}{16}x^2} = \frac{5}{4}x$ *[1 mark]*

Now find A by adding up the area of each of the faces:

$A = 2\left(\frac{1}{2} \times \frac{3}{4}x \times x\right) + \left(\frac{3}{2}x \times 4x\right) + 2\left(\frac{5}{4}x \times 4x\right)$ *[1 mark]*

$= \frac{3}{2}x^2 + 6x^2 + 10x^2 = \frac{35}{2}x^2$ *[1 mark]*

b) $\frac{dA}{dt} = 0.07$ *[1 mark]*

$A = \frac{35}{2}x^2 \Rightarrow \frac{dA}{dx} = 35x$ *[1 mark]*

Using chain rule, $\frac{dx}{dt} = \frac{dx}{dA} \times \frac{dA}{dt} = \frac{1}{\left(\frac{dA}{dx}\right)} \times \frac{dA}{dt}$

$\frac{dx}{dt} = \frac{1}{35x} \times 0.07 = \frac{0.07}{35 \times 0.5} = 0.004$ ms^{-1} *[1 mark]*

c) First you need to figure out what the question is asking for. 'Find the rate of change of V' means we're looking for $\frac{dV}{dt}$. Start by finding an expression for V:

$V = \left(\frac{1}{2} \times \frac{3}{2}x \times x\right) \times 4x = 3x^3$ *[1 mark]*

So $\frac{dV}{dx} = 9x^2$ *[1 mark]*

Using chain rule, $\frac{dV}{dt} = \frac{dV}{dx} \times \frac{dx}{dt} = 9x^2 \times \frac{0.07}{35x}$ *[1 mark]*

$= \frac{9(1.2)^2 \times 0.07}{35 \times 1.2} = 0.0216$ ms^{-1} *[1 mark]*

Page 97 — Differentiating e^x, $\ln x$ and a^x

Practice Questions

1 a) $\frac{dy}{dx} = 10xe^{5x^2}$ b) $\frac{dy}{dx} = -\frac{2x}{6 - x^2}$

c) $\frac{dy}{dx} = \frac{1}{2e^y}$ or $\frac{1}{x}$ d) $\frac{dy}{dx} = y + 1.5$ or $\frac{1}{2}e^x$

Answers

e) $\dfrac{dy}{dx} = 10x \ln 10$

f) $\dfrac{dy}{dx} = \dfrac{1}{5^y \ln 5}$ or $\dfrac{1}{x \ln 5}$

2 a) $f'(x) = 3^x \ln 3 + 4$

b) $g'(x) = \dfrac{3^x \ln 3 + 4}{3^x + 4x}$

3 a) $\dfrac{dy}{dx} = (-2 \ln 2)2^{-2x}$

b) $-\dfrac{\ln 2}{2}$

c) $8x - (4 \ln 2)y + (\ln 2 - 8) = 0$

Exam Questions

1 a) For $y = \sqrt{e^x + e^{2x}}$, use the chain rule:

$y = u^{\frac{1}{2}}$ where $u = e^x + e^{2x}$.

$\dfrac{dy}{du} = \dfrac{1}{2}u^{-\frac{1}{2}} = \dfrac{1}{2\sqrt{u}} = \dfrac{1}{2\sqrt{e^x + e^{2x}}}$ *[1 mark]*

$\dfrac{du}{dx} = e^x + 2e^{2x}$ *[1 mark]*

So $\dfrac{dy}{dx} = \dfrac{e^x + 2e^{2x}}{2\sqrt{e^x + e^{2x}}}$ *[1 mark]*

b) For $y = 3e^{2x+1} - \ln(1 - x^2) + 2x^3$, use the chain rule for the first 2 parts separately:

For $y = 3e^{2x+1}$, $y = 3e^u$ where $u = 2x + 1$, so $\dfrac{dy}{du} = 3e^u = 3e^{2x+1}$
and $\dfrac{du}{dx} = 2$, so $\dfrac{dy}{dx} = 6e^{2x+1}$ *[1 mark]*

For $y = \ln(1 - x^2)$, $y = \ln u$ where $u = 1 - x^2$,
so $\dfrac{dy}{du} = \dfrac{1}{u} = \dfrac{1}{(1 - x^2)}$ and $\dfrac{du}{dx} = -2x$, so $\dfrac{dy}{dx} = -\dfrac{2x}{(1 - x^2)}$ *[1 mark]*

So overall: $\dfrac{dy}{dx} = 6e^{2x+1} + \dfrac{2x}{(1 - x^2)} + 6x^2$ *[1 mark]*

2 a) For $f(x) = 4 \ln 3x$, use the chain rule:

$y = 4 \ln u$ where $u = 3x$, so $\dfrac{dy}{du} = \dfrac{4}{u} = \dfrac{4}{3x}$ and $\dfrac{du}{dx} = 3$ *[1 mark]*
so $f'(x) = \dfrac{dy}{dx} = \dfrac{12}{3x} = \dfrac{4}{x}$ *[1 mark]*
So for $x = 1$, $f'(1) = 4$ *[1 mark]*

b) Equation of a straight line is:
$y - y_1 = m(x - x_1)$, where m is the gradient.
For the tangent at $x_1 = 1$, $y_1 = 4 \ln 3$, and $m = \dfrac{dy}{dx} = 4$ *[1 mark]*
So the equation is: $y - 4 \ln 3 = 4(x - 1)$ *[1 mark]*
$\Rightarrow y = 4x - 4 + 4 \ln 3$ *[1 mark]*

3 a) $y = 4^x \Rightarrow \dfrac{dy}{dx} = 4^x \ln 4$ *[1 mark]*
So $\dfrac{dy}{dx} = \ln 4 \Rightarrow 4^x = 1 \Rightarrow x = 0 \Rightarrow y = 4^0 = 1$
$\dfrac{dy}{dx} = \ln 4$ at point $(0, 1)$ *[1 mark]*

b) Use the chain rule to find $\dfrac{dy}{dx}$: Let $u = (x - 4)^3$.
Then $\dfrac{dy}{dx} = \dfrac{dy}{du} \times \dfrac{du}{dx} = \dfrac{d}{du}(4^u) \times \dfrac{d}{dx}(x - 4)^3$ *[1 mark]*
$= (4^u \ln 4)(3(x - 4)^2 \times 1)$
$= 4^{(x-4)^3}3(x - 4)^2 \ln 4$ *[1 mark]*
So when $x = 3$, $\dfrac{dy}{dx} = 4^{(3-4)^3}3(3 - 4)^2 \ln 4$ *[1 mark]*
$\dfrac{dy}{dx} = 4^{-1} 3 \ln 4 = \dfrac{3}{4} \ln 4 = 1.04$ (3 s.f.) *[1 mark]*

Page 99 — Differentiating sin, cos and tan

Practice Questions

1 a) $f'(x) = -6 \sin 3x$

b) $f'(x) = \dfrac{\sec^2 x}{2\sqrt{\tan x}}$

c) $f'(x) = -e^x \sin e^x + \cos x \, e^{\sin x}$

2 $f'(x) = 2 \sin(x + 2) \cos(x + 2) \; [= \sin(2x + 4)]$

Exam Questions

1 For $y = \sin^2 x - 2 \cos 2x$, use the chain rule on each part:

For $y = \sin^2 x$, $y = u^2$ where $u = \sin x$, so $\dfrac{dy}{du} = 2u = 2 \sin x$
and $\dfrac{du}{dx} = \cos x$, so $\dfrac{dy}{dx} = 2 \sin x \cos x$ *[1 mark]*
For $y = 2 \cos 2x$, $y = 2 \cos u$ where $u = 2x$,
so $\dfrac{dy}{du} = -2\sin u = -2 \sin 2x$ and $\dfrac{du}{dx} = 2$,

so $\dfrac{dy}{dx} = -4 \sin 2x$ *[1 mark]*

Overall $\dfrac{dy}{dx} = 2 \sin x \cos x + 4 \sin 2x$.
$\sin 2x \equiv 2 \sin x \cos x$, so:
$\dfrac{dy}{dx} = \sin 2x + 4 \sin 2x = 5 \sin 2x$ *[1 mark]*
Gradient of the tangent when $x = \dfrac{\pi}{12}$ is $5 \times \sin \dfrac{\pi}{6} = 2.5$ *[1 mark]*

2 For $x = \sin 4y$, $\dfrac{dx}{dy} = 4 \cos 4y$ *[1 mark]*
and so $\dfrac{dy}{dx} = \dfrac{1}{4 \cos 4y}$ *[1 mark]*
At $\left(0, \dfrac{\pi}{4}\right)$, $y = \dfrac{\pi}{4}$ and so $\dfrac{dy}{dx} = \dfrac{1}{4 \cos \pi} = -\dfrac{1}{4}$ *[1 mark]*
Gradient of normal at $\left(0, \dfrac{\pi}{4}\right)$ is $-1 \div -\dfrac{1}{4} = 4$ *[1 mark]*
Equation of a straight line is:
$y - y_1 = m(x - x_1)$, where m is the gradient.
For the normal at $\left(0, \dfrac{\pi}{4}\right)$, $x_1 = 0$, $y_1 = \dfrac{\pi}{4}$, and $m = 4$ *[1 mark]*
So the equation is: $y - \dfrac{\pi}{4} = 4(x - 0) \Rightarrow y = 4x + \dfrac{\pi}{4}$ *[1 mark]*

3 $f(x) = \cos x \Rightarrow f'(x) = \lim\limits_{h \to 0} \dfrac{\cos(x + h) - \cos x}{h}$ *[1 mark]*
Using the addition formula:
$= \lim\limits_{h \to 0} \dfrac{\cos x \cos h - \sin x \sin h - \cos x}{h}$ *[1 mark]*
Use the small angle approximations on the $\sin h$ and $\cos h$ terms:
$= \lim\limits_{h \to 0} \dfrac{\cos x \left(1 - \frac{1}{2}h^2\right) - \sin x \times h - \cos x}{h}$ *[1 mark]*
$= \lim\limits_{h \to 0} \dfrac{\cos x - \frac{1}{2}h^2 \cos x - h \sin x - \cos x}{h}$
$= \lim\limits_{h \to 0} \dfrac{-\frac{1}{2}h^2 \cos x - h \sin x}{h}$
$= \lim\limits_{h \to 0}\left(-\frac{1}{2}h \cos x - \sin x\right)$ *[1 mark]*
As $h \to 0$, the first term disappears, so $f'(x) = -\sin x$. *[1 mark]*

Page 101 — Product and Quotient Rules

Practice Questions

1 a) $\dfrac{dy}{dx} = -6$

b) $\dfrac{dy}{dx} = \sin 1 = 0.841$ (3 s.f.)

2 $y = -4x + 7$

Exam Questions

1 a) For $y = \ln(3x + 1)\sin(3x + 1)$, use the product and chain rules:
Product rule: $u = \ln(3x + 1)$ and $v = \sin(3x + 1)$
Using the chain rule, $\dfrac{du}{dx} = \dfrac{3}{3x + 1}$ *[1 mark]*
and $\dfrac{dv}{dx} = 3 \cos(3x + 1)$ *[1 mark]*
So $\dfrac{dy}{dx} = u\dfrac{dv}{dx} + v\dfrac{du}{dx}$
$= [\ln(3x + 1) \times 3 \cos(3x + 1)] + \sin(3x + 1) \times \dfrac{3}{3x + 1}$ *[1 mark]*
$= 3 \ln(3x + 1)\cos(3x + 1) + \dfrac{3\sin(3x + 1)}{3x + 1}$ *[1 mark]*

b) For $y = \dfrac{\sqrt{x^2 + 3}}{\cos 3x}$, use the quotient rule and the chain rule:
Quotient rule: $u = \sqrt{x^2 + 3}$ and $v = \cos 3x$.
Using the chain rule, $\dfrac{du}{dx} = \dfrac{2x}{2\sqrt{x^2 + 3}} = \dfrac{x}{\sqrt{x^2 + 3}}$ *[1 mark]*
and $\dfrac{dv}{dx} = -3 \sin 3x$ *[1 mark]*
So $\dfrac{dy}{dx} = \dfrac{v\dfrac{du}{dx} - u\dfrac{dv}{dx}}{v^2}$
$= \dfrac{\left[\cos 3x \times \dfrac{x}{\sqrt{x^2 + 3}}\right] - \left[\sqrt{x^2 + 3} \times -3 \sin 3x\right]}{\cos^2 3x}$ *[1 mark]*
Then multiply top and bottom by $\sqrt{x^2 + 3}$ to get:
$\dfrac{dy}{dx} = \dfrac{x \cos 3x + 3(x^2 + 3)\sin 3x}{(\sqrt{x^2 + 3})\cos^2 3x} = \dfrac{x + 3(x^2 + 3)\tan 3x}{(\sqrt{x^2 + 3})\cos 3x}$ *[1 mark]*

Answers

2   For $y = \dfrac{e^x + x}{e^x - x}$, use the quotient rule:

$u = e^x + x \Rightarrow \dfrac{du}{dx} = e^x + 1$, $v = e^x - x \Rightarrow \dfrac{dv}{dx} = e^x - 1$ *[1 mark]*

$\dfrac{dy}{dx} = \dfrac{v\dfrac{du}{dx} - u\dfrac{dv}{dx}}{v^2} = \dfrac{(e^x - x)(e^x + 1) - (e^x + x)(e^x - 1)}{(e^x - x)^2}$ *[1 mark]*

When $x = 0$, $e^x = 1$, so:

$\dfrac{dy}{dx} = \dfrac{(1 - 0)(1 + 1) - (1 + 0)(1 - 1)}{(1 - 0)^2} = \dfrac{2 - 0}{1^2} = 2$ *[1 mark]*

Page 103 — More Differentiation
Practice Questions

1   $f'(x) = 4 \sec (4x) \tan (4x) + \mathrm{cosec}^2 (x + 1)$

2   $\dfrac{dy}{dx} = 1.51$ (3 s.f.)

Exam Questions

1   For $y = \sin^3 (2x^2)$, use the chain rule: $y = u^3$, $u = \sin (2x^2)$

$\dfrac{dy}{du} = 3u^2 = 3 \sin^2 (2x^2)$ *[1 mark]*

$\dfrac{du}{dx} = 4x \cos (2x^2)$ (using chain rule again) *[1 mark]*

So $\dfrac{dy}{dx} = 12x \sin^2 (2x^2) \cos (2x^2)$ *[1 mark]*

2 a) For $y = e^x \sin x$, use the product rule:

$u = e^x \Rightarrow \dfrac{du}{dx} = e^x$, $v = \sin x \Rightarrow \dfrac{dv}{dx} = \cos x$

So $\dfrac{dy}{dx} = u\dfrac{dv}{dx} + v\dfrac{du}{dx} = (e^x \times \cos x) + (\sin x \times e^x)$
$= e^x(\cos x + \sin x)$ *[1 mark]*

At the turning points, $\dfrac{dy}{dx} = 0 \Rightarrow e^x(\cos x + \sin x) = 0$ *[1 mark]*
$\Rightarrow e^x = 0$ or $\cos x + \sin x = 0$

e^x cannot be 0, so $\cos x + \sin x = 0$ *[1 mark]*

$\Rightarrow \sin x = -\cos x \Rightarrow \dfrac{\sin x}{\cos x} = -1 \Rightarrow \tan x = -1$ *[1 mark]*

In the interval $-\pi \le x \le \pi$, there are two solutions for $\tan x = -1$,
so the turning points are at $x = -\dfrac{\pi}{4}$ and $x = \dfrac{3\pi}{4}$ *[1 mark for each]*

b) To determine the nature of the turning points, find $\dfrac{d^2y}{dx^2}$:

For $\dfrac{dy}{dx} = e^x(\cos x + \sin x)$, use the product rule:

$u = e^x \Rightarrow \dfrac{du}{dx} = e^x$, $v = \cos x + \sin x \Rightarrow \dfrac{dv}{dx} = \cos x - \sin x$

$\dfrac{d^2y}{dx^2} = u\dfrac{dv}{dx} + v\dfrac{du}{dx} = [e^x \times (\cos x - \sin x)] + [(\cos x + \sin x) \times e^x]$
$= 2e^x \cos x$ *[1 mark]*

When $x = -\dfrac{\pi}{4}$, $\dfrac{d^2y}{dx^2} = 0.645$ (3 s.f.) > 0
so this is a minimum point *[1 mark]*

When $x = \dfrac{3\pi}{4}$, $\dfrac{d^2y}{dx^2} = -14.9$ (3 s.f.) < 0
so this is a maximum point *[1 mark]*

3 a) $f(x) = \cot x \Rightarrow f'(x) = -\mathrm{cosec}^2 x$ *[1 mark]*
Use the chain rule to find $f''(x)$: $y = -u^2$, $u = \mathrm{cosec}\, x$ *[1 mark]*

$\Rightarrow \dfrac{dy}{du} = -2u$, $\dfrac{du}{dx} = -\mathrm{cosec}\, x \cot x$ *[1 mark]*

So $f''(x) = (-2u)(-\mathrm{cosec}\, x \cot x) = 2\,\mathrm{cosec}^2 x \cot x$ *[1 mark]*
Write these in terms of sin and cos:

$f''(x) = 2\dfrac{1}{\sin^2 x} \times \dfrac{\cos x}{\sin x} = \dfrac{2 \cos x}{\sin^3 x}$ as required *[1 mark]*

b) At $x = \dfrac{\pi}{2}$, $f''(x) = \dfrac{2(0)}{1^3} = 0$ *[1 mark]*

Either side of $x = \dfrac{\pi}{2}$, $\sin^3 x$ is positive, and $\cos x$ changes sign
from positive to negative *[1 mark]*.
So $f''(x)$ changes sign from positive to negative which means that
$\left(\dfrac{\pi}{2}, 0\right)$ is a point of inflection *[1 mark]*.

Page 104 — Differentiation with Parametric Equations
Practice Question

1 a) $\dfrac{dy}{dx} = \dfrac{9t^2 - 4}{2t}$ b) $\left(\dfrac{4}{9}, -\dfrac{16}{9}\right)$ and $\left(\dfrac{4}{9}, \dfrac{16}{9}\right)$

Exam Questions

1 a) Start by differentiating x and y with respect to θ:

$\dfrac{dy}{d\theta} = 2 \cos \theta$ *[1 mark]*

$\dfrac{dx}{d\theta} = 3 + 3 \sin 3\theta$ *[1 mark]*

$\dfrac{dy}{dx} = \dfrac{dy}{d\theta} \div \dfrac{dx}{d\theta} = \dfrac{2 \cos \theta}{3 + 3 \sin 3\theta}$ *[1 mark]*

Find the value of θ at $(\pi + 1, \sqrt{3})$:

$y = 2 \sin \theta = \sqrt{3}$, for $-\pi \le \theta \le \pi \Rightarrow \theta = \dfrac{\pi}{3}$ or $\dfrac{2\pi}{3}$ *[1 mark]*

If $\theta = \dfrac{\pi}{3}$, then $x = 3\theta - \cos 3\theta = \pi - \cos \pi = \pi + 1$.
If $\theta = \dfrac{2\pi}{3}$, then $x = 3\theta - \cos 3\theta = 2\pi - \cos 2\pi = 2\pi - 1$.
So at $(\pi + 1, \sqrt{3})$, $\theta = \dfrac{\pi}{3}$ *[1 mark]*

$\theta = \dfrac{\pi}{3} \Rightarrow \dfrac{dy}{dx} = \dfrac{2 \cos \dfrac{\pi}{3}}{3 + 3 \sin \pi} = \dfrac{2\left(\dfrac{1}{2}\right)}{3 + 0} = \dfrac{1}{3}$ as required *[1 mark]*

b) When $\theta = \dfrac{\pi}{6}$, $x = \dfrac{\pi}{2} - \cos \dfrac{\pi}{2} = \dfrac{\pi}{2} - 0 = \dfrac{\pi}{2}$
and $y = 2 \sin \dfrac{\pi}{6} = 2 \times \dfrac{1}{2} = 1$
So $\theta = \dfrac{\pi}{6}$ at the point $\left(\dfrac{\pi}{2}, 1\right)$ *[1 mark]*

$\theta = \dfrac{\pi}{6} \Rightarrow \dfrac{dy}{dx} = \dfrac{2 \cos \dfrac{\pi}{6}}{3 + 3 \sin \dfrac{\pi}{2}} = \dfrac{2\left(\dfrac{\sqrt{3}}{2}\right)}{3 + 3(1)} = \dfrac{\sqrt{3}}{6}$ *[1 mark]*

Gradient of normal $= -1 \div \dfrac{\sqrt{3}}{6} = -\dfrac{6}{\sqrt{3}} = -\dfrac{6\sqrt{3}}{3} = -2\sqrt{3}$ *[1 mark]*
Using the equation $y - y_1 = m(x - x_1)$:

$y - 1 = -2\sqrt{3}\left(x - \dfrac{\pi}{2}\right) \Rightarrow y = -2\sqrt{3}x + 1 + \pi\sqrt{3}$ *[1 mark]*

2 a) First find the value of t when $y = -6$:
$y = 2 - t^3 = -6 \Rightarrow t^3 = 8 \Rightarrow t = 2$ *[1 mark]*
When $t = 2$, $x = (2)^2 + 2(2) - 3 = 5$
Now find the gradient of the curve:

$\dfrac{dy}{dt} = -3t^2$, $\dfrac{dx}{dt} = 2t + 2$

So $\dfrac{dy}{dx} = \dfrac{dy}{dt} \div \dfrac{dx}{dt} = \dfrac{-3t^2}{2t + 2}$ *[1 mark]*

When $t = 2$, $\dfrac{dy}{dx} = \dfrac{-3(2)^2}{2(2) + 2} = \dfrac{-12}{6} = -2$ *[1 mark]*
Using the equation $y - y_1 = m(x - x_1)$, the equation of L is:
$y + 6 = -2(x - 5) \Rightarrow y = -2x + 10 - 6 \Rightarrow y = -2x + 4$ *[1 mark]*

b) Substitute $y = 2 - t^3$ and $x = t^2 + 2t - 3$ into the equation for L:
$y = -2x + 4 \Rightarrow 2 - t^3 = -2(t^2 + 2t - 3) + 4$ *[1 mark]*
$\Rightarrow 2 - t^3 = -2t^2 - 4t + 10$
$\Rightarrow t^3 - 2t^2 - 4t + 8 = 0$
You know from part a) that $t = 2$ is a solution of this equation,
so use algebraic division, or another suitable method, to take out
a factor of $(t - 2)$:
$\Rightarrow (t - 2)(t^2 - 4) = 0$ *[1 mark]*
$\Rightarrow (t - 2)(t + 2)(t - 2) = 0$
$\Rightarrow t = 2$ or $t = -2$ *[1 mark]*
So t must be -2 at P.
When $t = -2$, $x = (-2)^2 + 2(-2) - 3 = -3$ and $y = 2 - (-2)^3 = 10$
The coordinates of P are $(-3, 10)$. *[1 mark]*

At P, $t = -2$, so $\dfrac{dy}{dx} = \dfrac{-3(-2)^2}{2(-2) + 2} = \dfrac{-12}{-2} = 6$ *[1 mark]*
So the gradient of the normal at P is: $-1 \div 6 = -\dfrac{1}{6}$ *[1 mark]*
Using the equation $y - y_1 = m(x - x_1)$, the equation
of the normal at P is: $y - 10 = -\dfrac{1}{6}(x + 3)$
$\Rightarrow y = -\dfrac{1}{6}x - \dfrac{1}{2} + 10 \Rightarrow y = -\dfrac{1}{6}x + \dfrac{19}{2}$ (or $x + 6y - 57 = 0$)
[1 mark]

Page 107 — Implicit Differentiation
Practice Questions

1 a) $\dfrac{dy}{dx} = \dfrac{8x - 14xy}{4y + 7x^2}$ b) $\dfrac{dy}{dx} = \dfrac{12x^3 - 2y^2}{1 + 4xy}$

Answers

c) $\dfrac{dy}{dx} = \dfrac{\sin x \sin y + y}{\cos x \cos y - x}$

2 a) Gradient of tangent $= -\dfrac{64}{9}$ b) Gradient of normal $= -\dfrac{1}{2}$

Exam Questions

1 a) c is the value of y when $x = 2$:

$6x^2y - 7 = 5x - 4y^2 - x^2 \Rightarrow 6(2)^2c - 7 = 5(2) - 4c^2 - (2)^2$
$\Rightarrow 24c - 7 = 6 - 4c^2$
$\Rightarrow 4c^2 + 24c - 13 = 0$
$\Rightarrow (2c + 13)(2c - 1) = 0$
$\Rightarrow c = -6.5 \text{ or } c = 0.5$ **[1 mark]**

$c > 0$, so $c = 0.5$ **[1 mark]**

b) (i) Q is another point on C where $y = 0.5$:

$6x^2y - 7 = 5x - 4y^2 - x^2 \Rightarrow 6x^2(0.5) - 7 = 5x - 4(0.5)^2 - x^2$
$\Rightarrow 3x^2 - 7 = 5x - 1 - x^2$
$\Rightarrow 4x^2 - 5x - 6 = 0$
$\Rightarrow (x - 2)(4x + 3)$
$\Rightarrow x = 2 \text{ or } x = -0.75$ **[1 mark]**

$x \neq 2$, as $x = 2$ at the other point where T crosses C.
So the coordinates of Q are $(-0.75, 0.5)$ **[1 mark]**.

(ii) To find the gradient of C, use implicit differentiation.
Differentiate each term separately with respect to x:

$\dfrac{d}{dx}(6x^2y) - \dfrac{d}{dx}(7) = \dfrac{d}{dx}(5x) - \dfrac{d}{dx}(4y^2) - \dfrac{d}{dx}(x^2)$ **[1 mark]**

Differentiate the terms in x and the constant term:

$\Rightarrow \dfrac{d}{dx}(6x^2y) - 0 = 5 - \dfrac{d}{dx}(4y^2) - 2x$ **[1 mark]**

Differentiate the terms in y using the chain rule:

$\Rightarrow \dfrac{d}{dx}(6x^2y) = 5 - \dfrac{d}{dy}(4y^2)\dfrac{dy}{dx} - 2x$

$\Rightarrow \dfrac{d}{dx}(6x^2y) = 5 - 8y\dfrac{dy}{dx} - 2x$ **[1 mark]**

Differentiate terms in both x and y using the product rule:

$\Rightarrow y\dfrac{d}{dx}(6x^2) + 6x^2\dfrac{d}{dy}(y)\dfrac{dy}{dx} = 5 - 8y\dfrac{dy}{dx} - 2x$

$\Rightarrow y(12x) + 6x^2(1)\dfrac{dy}{dx} = 5 - 8y\dfrac{dy}{dx} - 2x$

$\Rightarrow 12xy + 6x^2\dfrac{dy}{dx} = 5 - 8y\dfrac{dy}{dx} - 2x$ **[1 mark]**

Rearrange to make $\dfrac{dy}{dx}$ the subject:

$\Rightarrow 6x^2\dfrac{dy}{dx} + 8y\dfrac{dy}{dx} = 5 - 2x - 12xy$

$\Rightarrow \dfrac{dy}{dx} = \dfrac{5 - 2x - 12xy}{6x^2 + 8y}$ **[1 mark]**

At $Q = (-0.75, 0.5)$,

$\dfrac{dy}{dx} = \dfrac{5 - 2\left(-\frac{3}{4}\right) - 12\left(-\frac{3}{4}\right)\left(\frac{1}{2}\right)}{6\left(-\frac{3}{4}\right)^2 + 8\left(\frac{1}{2}\right)} = \dfrac{5 + \frac{3}{2} + \frac{9}{2}}{\frac{27}{8} + 4}$

$= \dfrac{11}{\left(\frac{59}{8}\right)} = 11 \times \dfrac{8}{59} = \dfrac{88}{59}$ **[1 mark]**

2 a) Using implicit differentiation:

$3e^x + 6y = 2x^2y \Rightarrow \dfrac{d}{dx}(3e^x) + \dfrac{d}{dx}(6y) = \dfrac{d}{dx}(2x^2y)$ **[1 mark]**

$\Rightarrow 3e^x + 6\dfrac{dy}{dx} = 2x^2\dfrac{d}{dy}(y)\dfrac{dy}{dx} + y\dfrac{d}{dx}(2x^2)$

$\Rightarrow 3e^x + 6\dfrac{dy}{dx} = 2x^2\dfrac{dy}{dx} + 4xy$ **[1 mark]**

$\Rightarrow 2x^2\dfrac{dy}{dx} - 6\dfrac{dy}{dx} = 3e^x - 4xy$

$\Rightarrow \dfrac{dy}{dx} = \dfrac{3e^x - 4xy}{2x^2 - 6}$ **[1 mark]**

b) At the stationary points of C, $\dfrac{dy}{dx} = 0 \Rightarrow \dfrac{3e^x - 4xy}{2x^2 - 6} = 0$ **[1 mark]**

$\Rightarrow 3e^x - 4xy = 0$

$\Rightarrow y = \dfrac{3e^x}{4x}$ **[1 mark]**

c) Substitute $y = \dfrac{3e^x}{4x}$ into the original equation of curve C:

$3e^x + 6y = 2x^2y \Rightarrow 3e^x + 6\dfrac{3e^x}{4x} = 2x^2\dfrac{3e^x}{4x}$ **[1 mark]**

$\Rightarrow 3e^x\left(1 + \dfrac{3}{2x} - \dfrac{x}{2}\right) = 0$

$3e^x = 0$ has no solutions, so $\left(1 + \dfrac{3}{2x} - \dfrac{x}{2}\right) = 0$ **[1 mark]**

$\left(1 + \dfrac{3}{2x} - \dfrac{x}{2}\right) = 0 \Rightarrow 2x + 3 - x^2 = 0$
$\Rightarrow x^2 - 2x - 3 = 0$
$\Rightarrow (x + 1)(x - 3) = 0$
$\Rightarrow x = -1 \text{ or } x = 3$ **[1 mark]**

$x = -1 \Rightarrow y = \dfrac{3e^{-1}}{4(-1)} = -\dfrac{3}{4e}$, $x = 3 \Rightarrow y = \dfrac{3e^3}{4(3)} = \dfrac{1}{4}e^3$

So the stationary points of C are $\left(-1, -\dfrac{3}{4e}\right)$ and $\left(3, \dfrac{1}{4}e^3\right)$ **[1 mark]**

3 $y = \arctan x \Rightarrow \tan y = x$ **[1 mark]**

Differentiating gives: $\sec^2 y\dfrac{dy}{dx} = 1$ **[1 mark]**

$\Rightarrow \dfrac{dy}{dx} = \dfrac{1}{\sec^2 y}$ **[1 mark]**

Using the identity $\sec^2\theta \equiv 1 + \tan^2\theta$: $\dfrac{dy}{dx} = \dfrac{1}{1 + \tan^2 y}$ **[1 mark]**

Now use $\tan y = x$: $\dfrac{dy}{dx} = \dfrac{1}{1 + x^2}$ as required. **[1 mark]**

Section 8 — Integration

Page 109 — Integrating f(x) = xⁿ

Practice Questions

1 a) $2x^5 + C$ b) $\dfrac{3x^2}{2} + \dfrac{5x^3}{3} + C$ c) $\dfrac{3x^4}{4} + \dfrac{2x^3}{3} + C$

2 $y = 3x^2 - 7x + 4$

3 $f(x) = \dfrac{3x^4}{4} + 2x - \dfrac{11}{4}$

Exam Questions

1 a) Multiply out the brackets and simplify the terms:
$(5 + 2\sqrt{x})^2 = (5 + 2\sqrt{x})(5 + 2\sqrt{x})$
$= 25 + 10\sqrt{x} + 10\sqrt{x} + 4x = 25 + 20\sqrt{x} + 4x$
So $a = 25$, $b = 20$ and $c = 4$
[3 marks available — 1 mark for each constant]

b) Integrate your answer from a), treating each term separately:

$\int(25 + 20\sqrt{x} + 4x)\,dx = 25x + \left(20x^{\frac{3}{2}} \div \dfrac{3}{2}\right) + \left(\dfrac{4x^2}{2}\right) + C$

$= 25x + \dfrac{40\sqrt{x^3}}{3} + 2x^2 + C$

[3 marks available — 1 mark for each term. Lose 1 mark if C missing or answers not simplified (surds not necessary)]
Don't forget to add C, don't forget to add C, don't forget to add C.
Once, twice, thrice I beg of you, because it's very important.

2 a) The tangent at $(1, 2)$ has the same gradient as the curve at that point, so use $f'(x)$ to calculate the gradient: **[1 mark]**
$f'(1) = 1^3 - 2 = -1$ **[1 mark]**
Put this into the straight-line equation $y - y_1 = m(x - x_1)$: **[1 mark]**
$y - 2 = -1(x - 1) \Rightarrow y = -x + 1 + 2 = -x + 3$ **[1 mark]**

b) $f(x) = \int\left(x^3 - \dfrac{2}{x^2}\right)dx = \int(x^3 - 2x^{-2})\,dx$ **[1 mark]**

$= \dfrac{x^4}{4} - 2\dfrac{x^{-1}}{-1} + C = \dfrac{x^4}{4} + 2x^{-1} + C = \dfrac{x^4}{4} + \dfrac{2}{x} + C$ **[1 mark]**

Now use the coordinates $(1, 2)$ to find the value of C: **[1 mark]**

$2 = \dfrac{1^4}{4} + \dfrac{2}{1} + C \Rightarrow 2 - \dfrac{1}{4} - 2 = C \Rightarrow C = -\dfrac{1}{4}$

So $f(x) = \dfrac{x^4}{4} + \dfrac{2}{x} - \dfrac{1}{4}$ **[1 mark]**

Page 111 — Definite Integrals

Practice Questions

1 a) 4 b) $-\dfrac{33}{8} + 6\sqrt{2}$ c) $\dfrac{5}{2}$

2 a) 36 b)

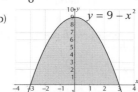

Answers

Exam Questions

1 $\int_1^4 (2x - 6x^2 + \sqrt{x})\, dx = \left[x^2 - 2x^3 + \frac{2\sqrt{x^3}}{3} \right]_1^4$

[3 marks available — 1 for each correct term]

$= \left(4^2 - (2 \times 4^3) + \frac{2\sqrt{4^3}}{3} \right) - \left(1^2 - (2 \times 1^3) + \frac{2\sqrt{1^3}}{3} \right)$ **[1 mark]**

$= -\frac{320}{3} - \left(-\frac{1}{3} \right) = -\frac{319}{3}$ **[1 mark]**

2 The limits are the x-values when $y = 0$, so first solve:

$(x - 3)^2(x + 1) = 0$ **[1 mark]**

$x = 3$ and $x = -1$ **[1 mark for both values correct]**

Hence, to find the area, calculate:

$\int_{-1}^{3} (x - 3)^2(x + 1)\, dx = \int_{-1}^{3} (x^3 - 5x^2 + 3x + 9)\, dx$ **[1 mark]**

$= \left[\frac{x^4}{4} - \frac{5}{3}x^3 + \frac{3}{2}x^2 + 9x \right]_{-1}^{3}$

[2 marks — 1 for increasing each power of x by one, 1 for correct integral]

$= \left(\frac{3^4}{4} - \frac{5}{3}3^3 + \frac{3}{2}3^2 + (9 \times 3) \right)$
$\quad - \left(\frac{(-1)^4}{4} - \left(\frac{5}{3} \times (-1)^3 \right) + \left(\frac{3}{2} \times (-1)^2 \right) + (9 \times (-1)) \right)$ **[1 mark]**

$= 15\frac{3}{4} - \left(-5\frac{7}{12} \right) = 21\frac{1}{3}$ **[1 mark]**

3 a) The curve and the line intersect when the equations are equal:

$-(x - 2)^2 = \frac{1}{2}x - 6$ **[1 mark]**

$\Rightarrow -x^2 + 4x - 4 = \frac{1}{2}x - 6 \Rightarrow 2x^2 - 7x - 4 = 0$

$\Rightarrow (2x + 1)(x - 4) = 0 \Rightarrow x = -\frac{1}{2}$ and $x = 4$

Point P has positive x coordinate, so $x = 4$. **[1 mark]**

Put this into one of the equations: $y = -(4 - 2)^2 = -4$. **[1 mark]**

So the coordinates of P are (4, –4).

b) Find where the curve and line meet the x-axis.

Curve: $0 = -(x - 2)^2 \Rightarrow x - 2 = 0 \Rightarrow x = 2$

Line: $0 = \frac{1}{2}x - 6 \Rightarrow x = 12$

Area A is the sum of the area under the curve between 2 and 4 (A_1) and the area under the line between 4 and 12 (A_2).

A_1: $\int_{2}^{4} -(x - 2)^2\, dx$ **[1 mark]** $= \int_{2}^{4} -x^2 + 4x - 4\, dx$

$= \left[-\frac{x^3}{3} + 2x^2 - 4x \right]_{2}^{4}$ **[1 mark]**

$= \left(-\frac{4^3}{3} + 2(4^2) - 4(4) \right) - \left(-\frac{2^3}{3} + 2(2^2) - 4(2) \right)$ **[1 mark]**

$= -\frac{16}{3} - -\frac{8}{3} = -\frac{8}{3}$ **[1 mark]**

So $A_1 = \frac{8}{3}$ (since area must be positive)

$A_2 = \frac{1}{2} \times (12 - 4) \times 4 = 16$ **[1 mark]**

So $A = A_1 + A_2 = \frac{8}{3} + 16 = \frac{56}{3}$ **[1 mark]**

Page 113 — Further Definite Integrals

Practice Questions

1 $\frac{1}{6}$

2 $\int (8t + 6)\, dt$

Exam Questions

1 a) $m = \frac{y_2 - y_1}{x_2 - x_1} = \frac{0 - (-5)}{(-1) - 4} = -1$ **[1 mark]**

$y - y_1 = m(x - x_1)$

$y - (-5) = -1(x - 4) \Rightarrow y + 5 = 4 - x \Rightarrow y = -x - 1$ **[1 mark]**

b) Multiply out the brackets and then integrate:

$(x + 1)(x - 5) = x^2 - 4x - 5$ **[1 mark]**

$\int_{-1}^{4} (x^2 - 4x - 5)\, dx = \left[\frac{x^3}{3} - 2x^2 - 5x \right]_{-1}^{4}$

[2 marks — 1 for increasing each power of x by one, 1 for correct integral]

$= \left(\frac{4^3}{3} - 2(4^2) - (5 \times 4) \right) - \left(\frac{(-1)^3}{3} - 2(-1)^2 - (5 \times -1) \right)$ **[1 mark]**

$= -30\frac{2}{3} - 2\frac{2}{3} = -33\frac{1}{3}$ **[1 mark]**

c) Subtract the area between the line and the x-axis from the area between the curve and the x-axis to leave the area in between. The area between the line and the x-axis is a triangle (where $b = 5$ and $h = 5$), so the area is:

$\frac{1}{2}bh = \frac{1}{2} \times 5 \times 5 = 12.5$ **[1 mark]**

$\Rightarrow A = 33\frac{1}{3} - 12\frac{1}{2}$ **[1 mark]** $= 20\frac{5}{6}$ **[1 mark]**

You could also have integrated the line $y = -x - 1$ to find the area under the line — you would get the same answer.

2 a) The area $R = \int_{4}^{18} y\, dx$ **[1 mark]**

$\frac{dx}{dt} = 2t + 3$ **[1 mark]**

Change the limits of the integral:

$x = 18 \Rightarrow t^2 + 3t - 18 = 0 \Rightarrow (t - 3)(t + 6) = 0 \Rightarrow t = 3, t = -6$

$x = 4 \Rightarrow t^2 + 3t - 4 = 0 \Rightarrow (t - 1)(t + 4) = 0 \Rightarrow t = 1, t = -4$

$t > 0$, so we can ignore the negative values of t,

so the limits are $t = 3$ and $t = 1$. **[1 mark]**

So $R = \int_{4}^{18} y\, dx = \int_{1}^{3} y \frac{dx}{dt}\, dt = \int_{1}^{3} \left(t^2 + \frac{1}{t^3} \right)(2t + 3)\, dt$

$= \int_{1}^{3} \left(\frac{t^5 + 1}{t^3} \right)(2t + 3)\, dt$

$= \int_{1}^{3} \frac{(t^5 + 1)(2t + 3)}{t^3}\, dt$ **[1 mark]**

b) $R = \int_{1}^{3} \frac{(t^5 + 1)(2t + 3)}{t^3}\, dt = \int_{1}^{3} \frac{2t^6 + 3t^5 + 2t + 3}{t^3}\, dt$

$= \int_{1}^{3} \left(\frac{2t^6}{t^3} + \frac{3t^5}{t^3} + \frac{2t}{t^3} + \frac{3}{t^3} \right)\, dt$

$= \int_{1}^{3} (2t^3 + 3t^2 + 2t^{-2} + 3t^{-3})\, dt$ **[1 mark]**

$= \left[\frac{t^4}{2} + t^3 - 2t^{-1} - \frac{3}{2}t^{-2} \right]_{1}^{3}$ **[1 mark]**

$= \left(\frac{81}{2} + 27 - \frac{2}{3} - \frac{1}{6} \right) - \left(\frac{1}{2} + 1 - 2 - \frac{3}{2} \right)$ **[1 mark]**

$= \frac{200}{3} - (-2) = \frac{206}{3}$ **[1 mark]**

3 a) Use the x- or y-coordinate of H in the relevant equation to find θ:

At H, $3 + 4 \sin \theta = 5 \Rightarrow 4 \sin \theta = 2 \Rightarrow \sin \theta = \frac{1}{2} \Rightarrow \theta = \frac{\pi}{6}$

OR at H, $\frac{1 + \cos 2\theta}{3} = \frac{1}{2} \Rightarrow 1 + \cos 2\theta = \frac{3}{2} \Rightarrow \cos 2\theta = \frac{1}{2}$

$\Rightarrow 2\theta = \frac{\pi}{3} \Rightarrow \theta = \frac{\pi}{6}$

[2 marks available — 1 mark for substituting one coordinate of H into the correct equation, 1 mark finding the correct value of θ.]

b) $R = \int_{-1}^{5} y\, dx$. To get the integral with respect to θ,

use $\int y\, dx = \int y \frac{dx}{d\theta}\, d\theta$. **[1 mark]** $\frac{dx}{d\theta} = 4 \cos \theta$ **[1 mark]**

Change the limits of the integral:

$x = 5 \Rightarrow \theta = \frac{\pi}{6}$, from part a)

$x = -1 \Rightarrow 3 + 4 \sin \theta = -1 \Rightarrow 4 \sin \theta = -4$

$\Rightarrow \sin \theta = -1 \Rightarrow \theta = -\frac{\pi}{2}$ **[1 mark]**

So $R = \int_{-1}^{5} y\, dx = \int_{-\frac{\pi}{2}}^{\frac{\pi}{6}} y \frac{dx}{d\theta}\, d\theta$

$= \int_{-\frac{\pi}{2}}^{\frac{\pi}{6}} \left(\frac{1 + \cos 2\theta}{3} \right)(4 \cos \theta)\, d\theta$ **[1 mark]**

$= \int_{-\frac{\pi}{2}}^{\frac{\pi}{6}} \frac{4}{3}(1 + \cos 2\theta)(\cos \theta)\, d\theta$

$= \int_{-\frac{\pi}{2}}^{\frac{\pi}{6}} \frac{4}{3}(2 \cos^2 \theta)(\cos \theta)\, d\theta$ ($\cos 2\theta \equiv 2 \cos^2 \theta - 1$)

$= \frac{8}{3} \int_{-\frac{\pi}{2}}^{\frac{\pi}{6}} \cos^3 \theta\, d\theta$ **[1 mark]**

Page 115 — Integrating e^x and $1/x$

Practice Questions

1 a) $2e^{2x} + C$

b) $\frac{1}{3}e^{3x - 5} + C$

c) $\frac{2}{3} \ln|x| + C$

d) $\ln|2x + 1| + C$

2 $4 \ln|x^5 + x^3 - 3x| + C$

3 $A = -1$, $B = 2$

$\int \frac{3x + 10}{(2x + 3)(x - 4)}\, dx = -\frac{1}{2} \ln|2x + 3| + 2 \ln|x - 4| + C$

Answers

Exam Questions

1 $-\frac{1}{2}e^{5-6x} + C$

[2 marks available — 1 for answer in the form $ke^{(5-6x)}$, 1 for correct value of k. Lose 1 mark if C missing]

2 Factorising, $x^3 - 6x^2 + 11x - 6 = (x-1)(x^2 - 5x + 6)$ *[1 mark]*
   $= (x-1)(x-2)(x-3)$ *[1 mark]*

So $\int \frac{4x-10}{x^3-6x^2+11x-6}\,dx = \int \frac{4x-10}{(x-1)(x-2)(x-3)}\,dx$

Now split this into partial fractions:

$\frac{4x-10}{(x-1)(x-2)(x-3)} \equiv \frac{A}{(x-1)} + \frac{B}{(x-2)} + \frac{C}{(x-3)}$ *[1 mark]*

$\Rightarrow 4x-10 = A(x-2)(x-3) + B(x-1)(x-3) + C(x-1)(x-2)$

When $x = 1$, $4 - 10 = A(-1)(-2) \Rightarrow -6 = 2A \Rightarrow A = -3$

When $x = 2$, $8 - 10 = B(1)(-1) \Rightarrow -2 = -B \Rightarrow B = 2$

When $x = 3$, $12 - 10 = C(2)(1) \Rightarrow 2 = 2C \Rightarrow C = 1$

[1 mark for a suitable method to find A, B and C]

So $\int \frac{4x-10}{(x-1)(x-2)(x-3)}\,dx = \int -\frac{3}{(x-1)} + \frac{2}{(x-2)} + \frac{1}{(x-3)}\,dx$ *[1 mark]*

$= -3\ln|x-1| + 2\ln|x-2| + \ln|x-3| + C$

[3 marks for correct final answer — 1 for each correct term. Lose 1 mark if C missing]

Page 118 — Integrating Trig Functions

Practice Questions

1 $\frac{1}{4}\sin 4x - \frac{1}{7}\tan 7x + C$

2 $2\sec 3x + 5\cot\frac{x}{5} + C$

3 $-\frac{1}{3}\ln|\sin x| + C$

4 $-\frac{1}{6}\ln|\cos 6x| + C$

The "appropriate trig identity" was the tan double angle formula.

5 $\frac{2}{3}\tan 3x + C$

Exam Questions

1 Differentiating the denominator gives $-\text{cosec}^2 x + 2$,

so this integral is of the form $k\frac{f'(x)}{f(x)}$, where $k = -1$.

Using the formula: $\int \frac{\text{cosec}^2 x - 2}{\cot x + 2x}\,dx = -\ln|\cot x + 2x| + C$

[3 marks available — 1 for attempt to use formula for integral of the form f'(x)/f(x), 1 for multiplication by −1, 1 for correct final answer. Lose 1 mark if C missing]

2 Use the identity $\text{cosec}^2 x \equiv 1 + \cot^2 x$
to write $2\cot^2 x$ as $2\text{cosec}^2 x - 2$

Then $\int 2\cot^2 x\,dx = \int 2\text{cosec}^2 x - 2\,dx = -2\cot x - 2x + C$

[3 marks available — 1 for correct use of identity, 1 for each correct term in the answer. Lose 1 mark if C missing]

Page 119 — Integrating Using the Chain Rule Backwards

Practice Questions

1 a) $e^{x^3} + C$ b) $4\sin(x^2) + C$

2 $(3x^3 + 4)^4 + C$

Exam Questions

1 If $f(x) = \cos x$, $f'(x) = -\sin x$ and $n = 2$ *[1 mark]*
So $(n+1)f'(x)[f(x)]^n = 3 \times -\sin x \times \cos^2 x = -\sin x(3\cos^2 x)$ *[1 mark]*
Then $\int -\sin x(3\cos^2 x)\,dx = \cos^3 x + C$ *[1 mark]*

2 $\int 6x(\text{cosec}^2 x^2 - \sec x^2 \tan x^2)\,dx$
$= \int 6x\,\text{cosec}^2 x^2\,dx - \int 6x\sec x^2 \tan x^2\,dx$ *[1 mark]*

Let $u = x^2$, then $\frac{du}{dx} = 2x$ *[1 mark]*

Then the first integral is in the form $3\int \frac{du}{dx}f'(u)\,dx$
where $f'(u) = \text{cosec}^2 u \Rightarrow f(u) = -\cot u = -\cot x^2$ *[1 mark]*
And the second integral is also in the form $3\int \frac{du}{dx}f'(u)\,dx$
where $f'(u) = \sec u \tan u \Rightarrow f(u) = \sec u = \sec x^2$ *[1 mark]*
So $\int 6x(\text{cosec}^2 x^2 - \sec x^2 \tan x^2)\,dx = -3\cot x^2 - 3\sec x^2 + C$

[2 marks for correct final answer — 1 for each correct term. Lose 1 mark if C missing]

There are other methods you could use to solve this (such as using the formula on the whole integral, then integrating $3(\text{cosec}^2 u - \sec u \tan u)\,du$) — any method that gives the correct final answer is fine.

Page 121 — Integration by Substitution

Practice Questions

1 $\frac{1}{4}(e^x - 1)^4 + \frac{2}{3}(e^x - 1)^3 + C$

Make sure you put $u = e^x - 1$ back into your final answer.

2 3

3 $\frac{5}{72}$

I would have gone with $u = \cos x + 2$ for this one, but if you got the right answer, it doesn't matter what substitution you used.

Exam Questions

1 If $u = \ln x$, then $\frac{du}{dx} = \frac{1}{x}$, *[1 mark]* so $x\,du = dx$.
Change the limits:
when $x = 1$, $u = \ln 1 = 0$ and when $x = 2$, $u = \ln 2$ *[1 mark]*
Substituting all this into the integral:
$\int_1^2 \frac{8}{x}(\ln x + 2)^3\,dx = \int_0^{\ln 2} \frac{8}{x}(u+2)^3 x\,du$

$= \int_0^{\ln 2} 8(u+2)^3\,du$ *[1 mark]* $= [2(u+2)^4]_0^{\ln 2}$ *[1 mark]*
$= [2(\ln 2 + 2)^4] - [2(0+2)^4]$ *[1 mark]*
$= 105.213... - 32 = 73.21$ (4 s.f.) *[1 mark]*

2 a) Let $v = \sqrt{u} - 1$, then $\frac{dv}{du} = \frac{1}{2\sqrt{u}}$, so $2\sqrt{u}\,dv = du$.

Substituting this into the integral gives:
$\int \frac{1}{\sqrt{u}\,(v)^2}2\sqrt{u}\,dv = \int 2v^{-2}\,dv$
$= -2v^{-1} + C = -\frac{2}{(\sqrt{u}-1)} + C$ as required.

[4 marks available — 1 for suitable choice of substitution, 1 for correct $\frac{dv}{du}$ (or equivalent), 1 for correct integral in terms of new variable, 1 for correct substitution back in terms of u]

b) If $u = x^3$, then $\frac{du}{dx} = 3x^2$ (so $\frac{1}{3x^2}\,du = dx$). So $x^{\frac{3}{2}} = u^{\frac{1}{2}}$.

Substituting this into the integral gives:
$\int \frac{3\sqrt{x}}{(u^{\frac{1}{2}}-1)^2}\frac{1}{3x^2}\,du = \int \frac{1}{x^{\frac{3}{2}}(\sqrt{u}-1)^2}\,du = \int \frac{1}{\sqrt{u}(\sqrt{u}-1)^2}\,du$

From part a), $\int \frac{1}{\sqrt{u}(\sqrt{u}-1)^2}\,du = -\frac{2}{(\sqrt{u}-1)} + C$

So $\int \frac{3\sqrt{x}}{(x^{\frac{3}{2}}-1)^2}\,dx = -\frac{2}{(\sqrt{u}-1)} + C = -\frac{2}{(x^{\frac{3}{2}}-1)} + C$

[4 marks available — 1 for correct $\frac{du}{dx}$, 1 for obtaining correct integral in terms of u, 1 for relating to answer from part a), 1 for correct final answer. Lose 1 mark if C missing]

Page 123 — Integration by Parts

Practice Question

1 a) $x^3\left(\ln x - \frac{1}{3}\right) + C$ b) $x\sin 4x + \frac{1}{4}\cos 4x + C$
  c) $4xe^{2x} - 2e^{2x} + C$

Answers

Answers

Exam Question

1 a) $A = \int_0^2 e^x \sin x \, dx$.

Let $u = \sin x$ and $\frac{dv}{dx} = e^x$. So $\frac{du}{dx} = \cos x$ and $v = e^x$ *[1 mark]*

Putting these into the formula gives:

$A = [\sin x \times e^x]_0^2 - \int_0^2 e^x \times \cos x \, dx$

$= [e^x \sin x]_0^2 - \int_0^2 e^x \cos x \, dx$ *[1 mark]*

Use integration by parts again to find $\int_0^2 e^x \cos x \, dx$:

Let $u = \cos x$ and $\frac{dv}{dx} = e^x$. So $\frac{du}{dx} = -\sin x$ and $v = e^x$ *[1 mark]*

Putting these into the formula gives:

$\int_0^2 e^x \cos x \, dx = [\cos x \times e^x]_0^2 - \int_0^2 e^x \times (-\sin x) \, dx$

$= [e^x \cos x]_0^2 + \int_0^2 e^x \sin x \, dx$ *[1 mark]*

So $A = [e^x \sin x]_0^2 - ([e^x \cos x]_0^2 + \int_0^2 e^x \sin x \, dx)$

$= [e^x \sin x]_0^2 - [e^x \cos x]_0^2 - A$ as required. *[1 mark]*

You could also solve this by letting $u = e^x$ and $\frac{dv}{dx} = \sin x$ — you would get the two square brackets in the other order.

b) Rearranging, $2A = [e^x \sin x]_0^2 - [e^x \cos x]_0^2$

$\Rightarrow A = \frac{1}{2}([e^x \sin x]_0^2 - [e^x \cos x]_0^2)$

$A = \frac{1}{2}([e^2 \sin 2 - e^0 \sin 0] - [e^2 \cos 2 - e^0 \cos 0])$ *[1 mark]*

$= \frac{1}{2}(e^2 \sin 2 - 0 - e^2 \cos 2 + 1)$

$= \frac{1}{2}(10.793...) = 5.40$ (3 s.f.) *[1 mark]*

Remember that any trig integration question needs to be done in radians — always check that your calculator is in the right mode before working out the answer.

Page 125 — Differential Equations

Practice Question

1 a) $y = \sqrt{2\sin x + C}$ (ignore the negative root since $y > 0$)

b) $y = \frac{1}{x^3 - 2x + C}$ c) $y = \ln(e^x + C)$

Exam Questions

1 a) $\frac{dy}{dx} = \frac{\cos x \cos^2 y}{\sin x} \Rightarrow \frac{1}{\cos^2 y} \, dy = \frac{\cos x}{\sin x} \, dx$

$\Rightarrow \int \frac{1}{\cos^2 y} \, dy = \int \frac{\cos x}{\sin x} \, dx$

$\Rightarrow \int \sec^2 y \, dy = \int \cot x \, dx \Rightarrow \tan y = \ln|\sin x| + C$

[4 marks available — 1 for separating the variables into functions of x and y, 1 for correct integration of sec² y, 1 for correct integration of cot x, 1 for general solution. Lose 1 mark if C missing]

b) If $y = 0$ when $x = \frac{\pi}{6}$, that means that:

$\tan 0 = \ln\left|\sin \frac{\pi}{6}\right| + C$

$0 = \ln\left|\frac{1}{2}\right| + C$ *[1 mark]* $= -\ln 2 + C \Rightarrow C = \ln 2$

So $\tan y = \ln|\sin x| + \ln 2$ (or $\tan y = \ln|2\sin x|$) *[1 mark]*

This is the particular solution — you found the general solution in part a).

2 a) $\frac{dm}{dt} \propto \sqrt{m}$ *[1 mark]* $\Rightarrow \frac{dm}{dt} = k\sqrt{m}, k > 0$ *[1 mark]*

b) First solve the differential equation to find m:

$\frac{dm}{dt} = k\sqrt{m} \Rightarrow \frac{1}{\sqrt{m}} \, dm = k \, dt$

$\Rightarrow \int m^{-\frac{1}{2}} \, dm = \int k \, dt$ *[1 mark]*

$\Rightarrow 2m^{\frac{1}{2}} = kt + C \Rightarrow m = \left(\frac{1}{2}(kt + C)\right)^2 = \frac{1}{4}(kt + C)^2$ *[1 mark]*

At the start of the campaign, $t = 0$.

Putting $t = 0$ and $m = 900$ into the equation gives:

$900 = \frac{1}{4}(0 + C)^2 \Rightarrow 3600 = C^2 \Rightarrow C = \pm 60$ *[1 mark]*

When $t = 0$, $\frac{dm}{dt} = \frac{1}{2}(kt + kC) = \frac{1}{2}kC$. Since $k > 0$ and $\frac{dm}{dt} > 0$

as sales are increasing, C must be positive (i.e. C = 60). *[1 mark]*

This gives the equation $m = \frac{1}{4}(kt + 60)^2$. *[1 mark]*

c) Substituting $t = 5$ and $k = 2$ into the equation gives:

$m = \frac{1}{4}((2 \times 5) + 60)^2 = 1225$ tubs sold

[2 marks available — 1 for substituting correct values of t and k, 1 for correct final answer]

d) E.g. As t grows larger, m continues to grow indefinitely. This is unrealistic, both in terms of the number of people who can buy a tub, and in terms of the number of tubs they can produce. There is likely to be a point at which m stops increasing, which is not accounted for in the model.

[2 marks available — 1 for comment about lack of limit on m, 1 for link to context to justify how this is unrealistic]

Section 9 — Numerical Methods

Page 127 — Location of Roots

Practice Questions

1   2 roots

2 a) $\sin(2 \times 3) = -0.2794...$ and $\sin(2 \times 4) = 0.9893...$

Since $\sin(2x)$ is a continuous function, the change of sign means there is a root between 3 and 4.

b) $\ln(2.1 - 2) + 2 = -0.3025...$

and $\ln(2.2 - 2) + 2 = 0.3905...$

Since the function is continuous for $x > 2$, the change of sign means there is a root between 2.1 and 2.2.

c) Rearrange first to give $x^3 - 4x^2 - 7 = 0$, then:

$4.3^3 - 4 \times (4.3^2) - 7 = -1.453$ and

$4.5^3 - 4 \times (4.5^2) - 7 = 3.125$.

The function is continuous, so the change of sign means there is a root between 4.3 and 4.5.

3   If 1.2 is a root to 1 d.p. then there should be a sign change for f(x) between the upper and lower bounds:

$f(1.15) = 1.15^3 + 1.15 - 3 = -0.3291...$

$f(1.25) = 1.25^3 + 1.25 - 3 = 0.2031...$

There is a change of sign, and the function is continuous, so there must be a root between 1.15 and 1.25, so the root is at $x = 1.2$ to 1 d.p.

Exam Questions

1 a) There will be a change of sign between f(0.7) and f(0.8) if p lies between 0.7 and 0.8.

$f(0.7) = (2 \times 0.7 \times e^{0.7}) - 3 = -0.1807...$

$f(0.8) = (2 \times 0.8 \times e^{0.8}) - 3 = 0.5608...$ *[1 mark for both]*

$f(x)$ is continuous, and there is a change of sign, so $0.7 < p < 0.8$. *[1 mark]*

b) If the root, p, is 0.726 to 3 d.p. then there must be a change of sign in f(x) between 0.7255 and 0.7265. *[1 mark]*

$f(0.7255) = (2 \times 0.7255 \times e^{0.7255}) - 3 = -0.0025...$

$f(0.7265) = (2 \times 0.7265 \times e^{0.7265}) - 3 = 0.0045...$

[1 mark for both]

$f(x)$ is continuous in the interval [0.7255, 0.7265], and there's a change of sign, so $p = 0.726$ to 3 d.p. as required. *[1 mark]*

2 a) There are asymptotes at the limits of the interval (at $x = 0$ and $x = \pi$), so f(0) and f(π) can not be evaluated. *[1 mark]*

There are two roots in this interval so there would be no apparent change of sign — the interval is too large. *[1 mark]*

b) If the root is 0.5 to 1 d.p. then there must be a change of sign in g(x) between 0.45 and 0.55. *[1 mark]*

$g(0.45) = \frac{1}{\sin 0.45} - 2 = 0.2990...$

$g(0.55) = \frac{1}{\sin 0.55} - 2 = -0.0868...$ *[1 mark for both]*

$g(x)$ is continuous in the interval [0.45, 0.55], and there's a change of sign, so $x = 0.5$ is a root to 1 d.p. *[1 mark]*

c) $\csc x - 2 = 0 \Rightarrow \frac{1}{\sin x} = 2 \Rightarrow \sin x = \frac{1}{2}$ *[1 mark]*

$\Rightarrow x = \sin^{-1}\left(\frac{1}{2}\right) = \frac{\pi}{6}$ *[1 mark]*

You're only asked for this first root in the interval $[0, \pi]$.
The other is at $\pi - \frac{\pi}{6}$.

d) $g(2.6) = \frac{1}{\sin 2.6} - 2 = -0.0601...$

$g(2.7) = \frac{1}{\sin 2.7} - 2 = 0.3398...$ *[1 mark for both]*

$g(x)$ is continuous in that interval, and there is a change of sign, so there is a root in the interval $(2.6, 2.7)$. *[1 mark]*

Page 129 — Iterative Methods
Practice Questions

1 $x = 2.187$ to 3 d.p.

2 a) i) $2x^2 - x^3 + 1 = 0 \Rightarrow 2x^2 - x^3 = -1$

$\Rightarrow x^2(2 - x) = -1 \Rightarrow x^2 = \frac{-1}{2-x} \Rightarrow x = \sqrt{\frac{-1}{2-x}}$

ii) $2x^2 - x^3 + 1 = 0 \Rightarrow x^3 = 2x^2 + 1 \Rightarrow x = \sqrt[3]{2x^2 + 1}$

iii) $2x^2 - x^3 + 1 = 0 \Rightarrow 2x^2 = x^3 - 1$

$\Rightarrow x^2 = \frac{x^3 - 1}{2} \Rightarrow x = \sqrt{\frac{x^3 - 1}{2}}$

b) Using $x_{n+1} = \sqrt[3]{2x_n^2 + 1}$ gives $x = 2.21$ to 2 d.p.
This is the only formula that converges to a root.

3 $x = 2.3738$ to 5 s.f.

Exam Question

1 a) $\sin 3x + 3x = 1 \Rightarrow 3x = 1 - \sin 3x \Rightarrow x = \frac{1}{3}(1 - \sin 3x)$ *[1 mark]*

b) $x_{n+1} = \frac{1}{3}(1 - \sin 3x_n)$ and $x_0 = 0.2$:

$x_1 = \frac{1}{3}(1 - \sin(3 \times 0.2))$ *[1 mark]* $= 0.1451...$

$x_2 = \frac{1}{3}(1 - \sin(3 \times 0.1451...)) = 0.1927...$

$x_3 = \frac{1}{3}(1 - \sin(3 \times 0.1927...)) = 0.1511...$

$x_4 = \frac{1}{3}(1 - \sin(3 \times 0.1511...)) = 0.1873...$

So $x_4 = 0.187$ to 3 d.p. *[1 mark]*

c) Putting the equation in the form $f(x) = 0$: $\sin 3x + 3x - 1 = 0$
Differentiating this gives: $f'(x) = 3\cos 3x + 3$ *[1 mark]*
So the Newton-Raphson formula is:

$x_{n+1} = x_n - \frac{\sin 3x_n + 3x_n - 1}{3\cos 3x_n + 3}$ *[1 mark]*

Starting with $x_0 = 0.2$:

$x_1 = 0.2 - \frac{\sin 3(0.2) + 3(0.2) - 1}{3\cos 3(0.2) + 3}$ *[1 mark]* $= 0.169933...$

$x_2 = 0.170324...$

$x_3 = 0.170324...$

So the root is 0.170 to 3 d.p. *[1 mark]*
This method was much better that the method used in part b), as it converged to a root much quicker (by x_3). *[1 mark]*

Page 132 — More on Iterative Methods
Practice Questions

1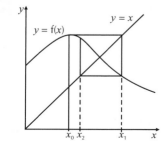

2 a) $f(1) = 1^4 - 1^5 + 3 = 3$
$f(2) = 2^4 - 2^5 + 3 = -13$
There's a change of sign and the function is continuous, so there's a root in the interval $(1, 2)$.
 i) Using e.g. $x_{n+1} = \sqrt[5]{x_n^4 + 3}$, the root is at $x = 1.5$ to 1 d.p.
 ii) Using $x_{n+1} = x_n - \frac{x_n^4 - x_n^5 + 3}{4x_n^3 - 5x_n^4}$, the root is at $x = 1.5$ to 1 d.p.

b) Lower bound: $f(1.45) = 1.0107....$
Upper bound: $f(1.55) = -0.1746...$
There's a change of sign, and the function is continuous, so 1.5 is a root to 1 d.p.

c) $x_{n+1} = \sqrt[5]{x_n^4 + 3}$ converged to a root in 4 iterations, whereas the Newton-Raphson method took 9 iterations, so the first method was more effective in this case.

Exam Question

1 a) $f(3) = \ln(3 + 3) - 3 + 2 = 0.7917...$
$f(4) = \ln(4 + 3) - 4 + 2 = -0.0540...$ *[1 mark for both]*
There is a change of sign, and the function is continuous for $x > -3$, so the root, m, must lie between 3 and 4. *[1 mark]*

b) $x_{n+1} = \ln(x_n + 3) + 2$, and $x_0 = 3$, so:
$x_1 = \ln(3 + 3) + 2$ *[1 mark]* $= 3.7917...$
$x_2 = \ln(3.7917... + 3) + 2 = 3.9157...$
$x_3 = \ln(3.9157... + 3) + 2 = 3.9337...$
$x_4 = \ln(3.9337... + 3) + 2 = 3.9364...$
$x_5 = \ln(3.9364... + 3) + 2 = 3.9367...$
So $m = 3.94$ to 2 d.p. *[1 mark]*

c)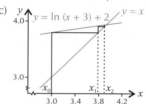

[1 mark for each of x_1 and x_2]

d) $f(x) = \ln(x + 3) - x + 2$
Differentiating this gives: $f'(x) = \frac{1}{x + 3} - 1$ *[1 mark]*
So the Newton-Raphson formula is:

$x_{n+1} = x_n - \frac{\ln(x_n + 3) - x_n + 2}{\frac{1}{x_n + 3} - 1}$ *[1 mark]*

Starting with $x_0 = 3$:

$x_1 = 3 - \frac{\ln(3 + 3) - 3 + 2}{\frac{1}{3 + 3} - 1}$ *[1 mark]* $= 3.950111...$

$x_2 = 3.936849...$

$x_3 = 3.936847...$

So the root is 3.93685 to 5 d.p. *[1 mark]*

e) $f'(-2) = \frac{1}{-2 + 3} - 1 = 0$, so the formula will involve division by zero and therefore fail to give the next iteration / the tangent at this point will be horizontal (as $x = -2$ is a stationary point) so it will not cut the x-axis to find the next iteration. *[1 mark]*

Page 135 — Numerical Integration
Practice Questions

1 Exact value of the integral = 3348
Using 4 strips, integral ≈ 4586.625, % error = 37.0% (3 s.f.)
Using 6 strips, integral ≈ 3906, % error = 16.7% (3 s.f.)
Neither of these estimates was particularly accurate — but the one with more strips had a lower % error (as you would expect).

2 Overestimate — because $y = e^x$ is convex

3 Upper bound $= \pi\left(1 + \frac{\sqrt{2}}{2}\right)$, lower bound $= \frac{\pi\sqrt{2}}{2}$
The function has a turning point at $x = \pi$, so calculate the upper and lower bounds for the first two strips and the last two strips separately.
The function is symmetrical, so lots of the numbers are the same.

Answers

Exam Questions

1 a) $n = 4$, so $h = \frac{40-0}{4} = 10$ *[1 mark]*

From the table: $t_0 = 0$, $r_0 = 0$, $t_1 = 10$, $r_1 = 1.7$, $t_2 = 20$, $r_2 = 6.4$, $t_3 = 30$, $r_3 = 19.1$, $t_4 = 40$, $r_4 = 53.6$

Using the trapezium rule:

$R \approx \frac{10}{2}[0 + 2(1.7 + 6.4 + 19.1) + 53.6]$ *[1 mark]* $= 540$ g *[1 mark]*

Since the units of t and r are s and gs^{-1} respectively, the units of the area will be s × gs^{-1} = g.

b) The curve is convex, so the trapezium rule estimate will be higher than the actual value of R. *[1 mark]*

c) By using twice as many strips, $n = 8$, $h = 5$ — this uses all the data in the table. *[1 mark]*

2 With 5 ordinates, $n = 4$, so $h = \frac{\pi-0}{4} = \frac{\pi}{4}$ *[1 mark]*

$x_0 = 0$, $y_0 = 0 \times \sin 0 = 0$

$x_1 = \frac{\pi}{4}$, $y_1 = \frac{\pi}{4} \times \sin \frac{\pi}{4} = \frac{\pi}{4\sqrt{2}}$

$x_2 = \frac{\pi}{2}$, $y_2 = \frac{\pi}{2} \times \sin \frac{\pi}{2} = \frac{\pi}{2}$

$x_3 = \frac{3\pi}{4}$, $y_3 = \frac{3\pi}{4} \times \sin \frac{3\pi}{4} = \frac{3\pi}{4\sqrt{2}}$

$x_4 = \pi$, $y_4 = \pi \times \sin \pi = 0$ *[1 mark for all correct]*

Using the trapezium rule:

$\int_0^\pi x \sin x \, dx \approx \frac{\pi}{2 \times 4}\left[0 + 2\left(\frac{\pi}{4\sqrt{2}} + \frac{\pi}{2} + \frac{3\pi}{4\sqrt{2}}\right) + 0\right]$ *[1 mark]*

$= 2.978416... = 2.978$ (3 d.p.) *[1 mark]*

3 a) $n = 5$, so $h = \frac{10-0}{5} = 2$ *[1 mark]*

$x_0 = 0$, $y_0 = \ln 1$, $x_1 = 2$, $y_1 = \ln 3$, $x_2 = 4$, $y_2 = \ln 5$, $x_3 = 6$, $y_3 = \ln 7$, $x_4 = 8$, $y_4 = \ln 9$, $x_5 = 10$, $y_5 = \ln 11$ *[1 mark for all correct]*

Using the trapezium rule:

$\int_0^{10} \ln(x+1)\, dx \approx \frac{2}{2}[\ln 1 + 2(\ln 3 + \ln 5 + \ln 7 + \ln 9) + \ln 11]$ *[1 mark]*

Simplifying using the log laws:

You'll need $\ln x + \ln y = \ln(xy)$, and $k\ln a = \ln a^k$...

$\int_0^{10} \ln(x+1)\, dx \approx 1[\ln(1 \times 11) + 2\ln(3 \times 5 \times 7 \times 9)]$

$= [\ln 11 + \ln(945)^2] = \ln(11 \times 945^2)$ *[1 mark]*

b) As $\ln(x+1)$ is an increasing function, using the left hand corner rectangle formula will give a lower bound of the trapezium rule estimate. So the lower bound will be given by:

$\int_0^{10} \ln(x+1)\, dx \approx h[y_0 + y_1 + y_2 + y_3 + y_4 + y_5 + y_6 + y_7 + y_8 + y_9]$ *[1 mark]*

$n = 10$, so $h = \frac{10-0}{10} = 1$ *[1 mark]*

$x_0 = 0$, $y_0 = \ln 1$, $x_1 = 1$, $y_1 = \ln 2$, $x_2 = 2$, $y_2 = \ln 3$, $x_3 = 3$, $y_3 = \ln 4$, $x_4 = 4$, $y_4 = \ln 5$, $x_5 = 5$, $y_5 = \ln 6$, $x_6 = 6$, $y_6 = \ln 7$, $x_7 = 7$, $y_7 = \ln 8$, $x_8 = 8$, $y_8 = \ln 9$, $x_9 = 9$, $y_9 = \ln 10$ *[1 mark for all correct]*

Using the lower bound rectangle formula:

$\int_0^{10} \ln(x+1)\, dx \approx 1[\ln 1 + \ln 2 + \ln 3 + \ln 4 + ... + \ln 10]$

$= \ln(1 \times 2 \times 3 \times 4 \times 5 \times 6 \times 7 \times 8 \times 9 \times 10)$

$= \ln(10!)$ as required. *[1 mark]*

Section 10 — Vectors

Page 137 — Vectors

Practice Questions

1 a) $\mathbf{b} - \mathbf{a}$ b) $\mathbf{a} - \mathbf{b}$ c) $\mathbf{b} - \mathbf{c}$ d) $\mathbf{c} - \mathbf{a}$

2 $2\mathbf{i} - 4\mathbf{j}$

3 $\begin{pmatrix} 13 \\ -10 \end{pmatrix}$

Exam Questions

1 $\overrightarrow{WX} = \overrightarrow{OX} - \overrightarrow{OW} = \begin{pmatrix} -2 \\ 1 \end{pmatrix} - \begin{pmatrix} 1 \\ 3 \end{pmatrix} = \begin{pmatrix} -3 \\ -2 \end{pmatrix}$ *[1 mark]*

$\overrightarrow{YZ} = \overrightarrow{OZ} - \overrightarrow{OY} = \begin{pmatrix} a \\ b \end{pmatrix} - \begin{pmatrix} 5 \\ 4 \end{pmatrix} = \begin{pmatrix} a-5 \\ b-4 \end{pmatrix}$ *[1 mark]*

$\overrightarrow{WX} = \overrightarrow{YZ} \Rightarrow \begin{pmatrix} a-5 \\ b-4 \end{pmatrix} = \begin{pmatrix} -3 \\ -2 \end{pmatrix} \Rightarrow a = 2,\ b = 2$

So $\overrightarrow{OZ} = \begin{pmatrix} 2 \\ 2 \end{pmatrix}$. *[1 mark]*

2 $\overrightarrow{AB} = (5\mathbf{i} + \mathbf{j}) - (-2\mathbf{i} + 4\mathbf{j}) = (5-(-2))\mathbf{i} + (1-4)\mathbf{j} = 7\mathbf{i} - 3\mathbf{j}$ *[1 mark]*

P is $\frac{1}{4}$ of the way along $\overrightarrow{AB}$, so $\overrightarrow{AP} = \frac{1}{4}\overrightarrow{AB} = \frac{7}{4}\mathbf{i} - \frac{3}{4}\mathbf{j}$ *[1 mark]*

$\overrightarrow{OP} = \overrightarrow{OA} + \overrightarrow{AP} = \left((-2) + \frac{7}{4}\right)\mathbf{i} + \left(4 - \frac{3}{4}\right)\mathbf{j}$ *[1 mark]*

$= -\frac{1}{4}\mathbf{i} + \frac{13}{4}\mathbf{j}$ *[1 mark]*

Page 139 — More Vectors

Practice Questions

1 $-\frac{2}{\sqrt{29}}\mathbf{i} + \frac{5}{\sqrt{29}}\mathbf{j}$

2 a) $\sqrt{5}$ b) $\sqrt{10}$ c) $\sqrt{13}$

3 $7\cos 20°\mathbf{i} + 7\sin 20°\mathbf{j}$

4 $108.4°$ (1 d.p.)

5 Distance = 5, angle = $41.8°$ (1 d.p.)

Exam Questions

1 $\overrightarrow{BC} = \overrightarrow{AC} - \overrightarrow{AB} = -2\mathbf{i} + 4\mathbf{j} - (-5\mathbf{i} + 2\mathbf{j}) = 3\mathbf{i} + 2\mathbf{j}$ *[1 mark]*

$\overrightarrow{BM} = \frac{1}{2}\overrightarrow{BC} = \frac{3}{2}\mathbf{i} + \mathbf{j}$

$\overrightarrow{AM} = \overrightarrow{AB} + \overrightarrow{BM} = -5\mathbf{i} + 2\mathbf{j} + \frac{3}{2}\mathbf{i} + \mathbf{j} = -\frac{7}{2}\mathbf{i} + 3\mathbf{j}$ *[1 mark]*

So, $|\overrightarrow{AM}| = \sqrt{\left(-\frac{7}{2}\right)^2 + 3^2} = \frac{\sqrt{85}}{2}$ *[1 mark]*

2 a) $\mathbf{p} = 7\cos 15°\,\mathbf{i} + 7\sin 15°\,\mathbf{j}$

[2 marks available — 1 for each correct component]

b) The speed is given by the magnitude of $\mathbf{q}$:

$|\mathbf{q}| = \sqrt{(2\sqrt{2})^2 + (2\sqrt{2})^2} = \sqrt{16} = 4$ m/s, *[1 mark]*

so the particle's speed has decreased by 3 m/s. *[1 mark]*

The direction of $\mathbf{q}$ is $45°$. *[1 mark]*

3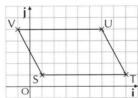

As STUV is a parallelogram, $\overrightarrow{TU}$ is parallel to $\overrightarrow{SV}$ and is the same length, so $\overrightarrow{TU} = \overrightarrow{SV}$. *[1 mark]*

$\overrightarrow{TU} = \overrightarrow{SV} = -\mathbf{i} + 5\mathbf{j} - (\mathbf{i} + \mathbf{j})$

$= -2\mathbf{i} + 4\mathbf{j}$ *[1 mark]*

$\overrightarrow{SU} = \overrightarrow{ST} + \overrightarrow{TU}$

$= (8\mathbf{i} + \mathbf{j}) - (\mathbf{i} + \mathbf{j}) + (-2\mathbf{i} + 4\mathbf{j})$

$= 5\mathbf{i} + 4\mathbf{j}$ *[1 mark]*

$|\overrightarrow{SU}| = \sqrt{5^2 + 4^2} = \sqrt{41}$ *[1 mark]*

You could also find the position vector of U ($6\mathbf{i} + 5\mathbf{j}$) — a diagram makes this pretty easy. Then $\overrightarrow{SU} = (6\mathbf{i} + 5\mathbf{j}) - (\mathbf{i} + \mathbf{j}) = 5\mathbf{i} + 4\mathbf{j}$ as before.

Page 141 — 3D Vectors

Practice Questions

1 $7\mathbf{i} - 3\mathbf{j} - 2\mathbf{k}$

2 a) $\sqrt{29}$ b) $\sqrt{6}$

3 $-\frac{2}{3}\begin{pmatrix} 3 \\ -3 \\ 6 \end{pmatrix} = \begin{pmatrix} -2 \\ 2 \\ -4 \end{pmatrix}$, so $\mathbf{v}$ and $\mathbf{u}$ are parallel.

4 $-4\mathbf{i} + 20\mathbf{j} - 11\mathbf{k}$

5 $\sqrt{43}$

Exam Questions

1 $\overrightarrow{QR} = \begin{pmatrix} 2 \\ 7 \\ -5 \end{pmatrix} - \begin{pmatrix} -2 \\ -1 \\ -1 \end{pmatrix} = \begin{pmatrix} 4 \\ 8 \\ -4 \end{pmatrix} = 2\begin{pmatrix} 2 \\ 4 \\ -2 \end{pmatrix}$ *[1 mark]*

So $\overrightarrow{QR} = 2\overrightarrow{OP}$, which means they are parallel. *[1 mark]*

Answers

2   Midpoint of OZ has position vector $\frac{1}{2}\overrightarrow{OZ} = 2\mathbf{k}$ m

Midpoint of XY has position vector $\frac{1}{2}(\overrightarrow{OX} + \overrightarrow{OY})$

$= \frac{1}{2}[5\mathbf{j} + (3\mathbf{i} - \mathbf{j})] = \frac{1}{2}(3\mathbf{i} + 4\mathbf{j}) = (1.5\mathbf{i} + 2\mathbf{j})$ m

[1 mark for both midpoints correct]

So the distance between the two midpoints is:

$|(1.5\mathbf{i} + 2\mathbf{j}) - (2\mathbf{k})| = \sqrt{1.5^2 + 2^2 + (-2)^2}$ *[1 mark]*

$= \sqrt{2.25 + 4 + 4} = \sqrt{10.25} = 3.20$ m (3 s.f.) *[1 mark]*

3 a) $\overrightarrow{AB} = \overrightarrow{OB} - \overrightarrow{OA} = -3\mathbf{i} + \mathbf{j} - 3\mathbf{k} - (2\mathbf{i} + 3\mathbf{j} + 4\mathbf{k})$

             $= -5\mathbf{i} - 2\mathbf{j} - 7\mathbf{k}$ *[1 mark]*

b) M is two thirds of the way along $\overrightarrow{AB}$, so $\overrightarrow{AM} = \frac{2}{3}\overrightarrow{AB}$. *[1 mark]*

$\overrightarrow{OM} = \overrightarrow{OA} + \overrightarrow{AM} = 2\mathbf{i} + 3\mathbf{j} + 4\mathbf{k} + \frac{2}{3}\overrightarrow{AB}$ *[1 mark]*

$= \left(2 + \left(\frac{-10}{3}\right)\right)\mathbf{i} + \left(3 + \left(\frac{-4}{3}\right)\right)\mathbf{j} + \left(4 + \left(\frac{-14}{3}\right)\right)\mathbf{k}$

$= -\frac{4}{3}\mathbf{i} + \frac{5}{3}\mathbf{j} - \frac{2}{3}\mathbf{k}$ *[1 mark]*

$|\overrightarrow{OM}| = \sqrt{\left(-\frac{4}{3}\right)^2 + \left(\frac{5}{3}\right)^2 + \left(-\frac{2}{3}\right)^2}$ *[1 mark]* $= \sqrt{5}$ *[1 mark]*

Section 11 — Data Presentation and Interpretation

Page 143 — Central Tendency and Variation

Practice Questions

1   mean = 1.375, median = 1, mode = 0
2   mean = 17.9 (3 s.f.), standard deviation = 5.57 (3 s.f.)
3   mean = 2.8, variance = 1
4 a) 513   b) 81.3

Exam Question

1 a) $\bar{a} = \frac{60.3}{20} = 3.015$ g *[1 mark]*

b) $s_A^2 = \frac{219}{20} - 3.015^2 = 1.860$ g^2 *[1 mark]*

So $s_A = 1.36$ g (3 s.f.) *[1 mark]*

c) E.g. Brand A chocolate drops are heavier on average than brand B. Brand B chocolate drops are generally much closer to their mean weight than brand A.
[1 mark for each of 2 sensible statements]
"Mmm, chocolate drops" does not count as a sensible statement...

d) Mean of A and B $= \frac{\Sigma a + \Sigma b}{50} = \frac{60.3 + (30 \times 2.95)}{50}$

                  $= 2.976$ g *[1 mark]*

$\frac{\Sigma b^2}{30} - 2.95^2 = 1$, so $\Sigma b^2 = 291.075$ *[1 mark]*

Variance of A and B $= \frac{\Sigma a^2 + \Sigma b^2}{50} - 2.976^2$

                  $= \frac{219 + 291.075}{50} - 2.976^2 = 1.3449$ *[1 mark]*

So s.d. $= \sqrt{1.3449} = 1.16$ g (3 s.f.) *[1 mark]*

Work through each step carefully so you don't make silly mistakes and lose any lovely marks.

Page 145 — Displaying Data

Practice Questions

1 a)

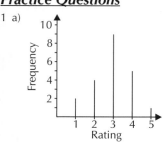

b) mode = 3
c) E.g. The distribution is fairly symmetrical about the mode.

---

2   7 | 7
      8 | 5 7 9   Key: 8 | 7 means 87% attendance
      9 | 0 2 5 5 8
   10 | 0

3 a) frequency density = 2.5   b) frequency density = 2.2

Exam Questions

1 a)

        A | | B
      3 0 | 0 |
  7 5 2 | 1 | 7
       6 | 2 | 0 2 7
       2 | 3 | 1 3 4 8
       5 | 4 | 1 4
    0 0 | 5 |

Key: 2 | 1 | 7 means 12 for A and 17 for B

[2 marks — 1 for each side correct]

b) There are 10 data values for both cricketers, so the median is halfway between the 5th and 6th values.
A: median = (17 + 26) ÷ 2 = 21.5 *[1 mark]*
B: median = (31 + 33) ÷ 2 = 32 *[1 mark]*

2 a) There are 30 data values for the men, so the median is halfway between the 15th and 16th values.
Median = (62 + 65) ÷ 2 = 63.5 years *[1 mark]*

b) E.g. The women's median is 64.5 years, which is higher than the men's median. This suggests that, in general, the women were older when they became grandparents.
[2 marks for a sensible comment and interpretation]
You could've also commented on the women's mean being higher, or the women's range being smaller, meaning the ages at which the women became grandparents were more consistent.

Page 147 — Grouped Data

Practice Questions

1

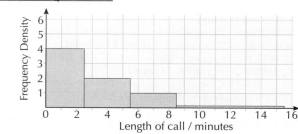

2   mean = 37.1 mph, median = 36.9 mph (3 s.f.),
   modal class = 35-39 mph

Exam Questions

1   Find the total area under the histogram: *[1 mark]*
2 + 1.5 + 2 + 2 + 1.5 + 4 + 5 + 3 + 4 = 25
So each grid square represents 2 lions. *[1 mark]*
The number of squares for lengths above 220 cm is 7, which represents 7 × 2 = 14 lions. *[1 mark]*
There are other ways you could reach this answer — any of them are fine, as long as you end up with the right number of lions in the end.

2 a)

Profit (£p million)	Class width	No. of businesses	Frequency density
$4.5 \le p < 5.0$	0.5	21	42
$5.0 \le p < 5.5$	0.5	26	52
$5.5 \le p < 6.0$	0.5	24	48
$6.0 \le p < 6.5$	0.5	19	38
$6.5 \le p < 8.0$	1.5	10	6.67

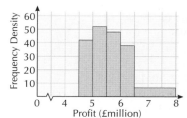

[1 mark for correct axes, plus 2 marks if all bars drawn correctly, or 1 mark for at least 3 bars correct]

Answers

b)

Profit (£p million)	Class midpoint (x)	No. of businesses (f)	fx	x^2	fx^2
$4.5 \leq p < 5.0$	4.75	21	99.75	22.5625	473.8125
$5.0 \leq p < 5.5$	5.25	26	136.5	27.5625	716.625
$5.5 \leq p < 6.0$	5.75	24	138	33.0625	793.5
$6.0 \leq p < 6.5$	6.25	19	118.75	39.0625	742.1875
$6.5 \leq p < 8.0$	7.25	10	72.5	52.5625	525.625
	Totals	100	565.5		3251.75

[1 mark for correct x and fx, 1 mark for correct x^2 and fx^2]

Estimated mean $= \frac{\Sigma fx}{\Sigma f} = \frac{565.5}{100} = £5.655$ million *[1 mark]*

Estimated variance $= \frac{\Sigma fx^2}{\Sigma f} - \overline{x}^2 = \frac{3251.75}{100} - 5.655^2$

$\qquad = 0.538475$ *[1 mark]*

So estimated s.d. $= \sqrt{0.538475} = £0.734$ million (3 s.f.) *[1 mark]*

c) $n \div 2 = 50$, $21 + 26 = 47$, so the median is in the 5.5–6.0 class *[1 mark]*.

Estimated median $= 5.5 + 0.5 \times \frac{50-47}{24}$ *[1 mark]*

$\qquad = £5.5625$ million *[1 mark]*

Page 149 — Interquartile Range and Outliers

Practice Question

1 a) 85 is not an outlier   b) 95 is an outlier   c) 0 is an outlier

Exam Question

1 a) Total number of people = 38, and $38 \div 2 = 19.2$
So the median is the average of the 19th and 20th values. *[1 mark]*
19th value = 15, 20th value = 16, so median = 15.5 hits *[1 mark]*
mode = 15 hits *[1 mark]*

b) Lower quartile = 10th value = 14,
Upper quartile = 29th value = 17 *[1 mark for both]*
So IQR = 17 − 14 = 3, and upper fence = 17 + (1.5 × 3) = 21.5
This means that 25 is outlier. *[1 mark]*

c) E.g. The value of the mean is likely to be affected more than the median by the presence of an outlier. *[1 mark]*

Page 151 — Cumulative Frequency Graphs and Boxplots

Practice Questions

1

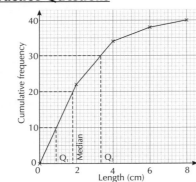

median ≈ 1.8 cm,
IQR ≈ 2.4 cm

These are estimates, so answers close to these are also correct.

2   median = £7, lower quartile = £5, upper quartile = £13.50

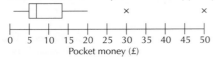

Exam Question

1 a) Times = 2, 3, 4, 4, 5, 5, 5, 7, 10, 12
$\frac{n}{2} = 5$ is a whole number, so the median is the average of the 5th and 6th terms: $Q_2 = (5 + 5) \div 2 = 5$ minutes

$\frac{n}{4} = 2.5$ is not a whole number, so the lower quartile is the 3rd term: $Q_1 = 4$ minutes
$\frac{n}{4} = 7.5$ is not a whole number, so the lower quartile is the 8th term: $Q_3 = 7$ minutes
[2 marks available — lose 1 for each incorrect answer]

b) Worker A

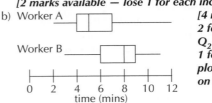

[4 marks available — 2 for correct values of Q_1, Q_2 and Q_3 for Worker B, 1 for correctly drawn box plots and 1 for putting both on a common, labelled scale]

If you used fences at 1.5 × IQR above Q_3 and below Q_1, the data value 12 for Worker A would be an outlier.

c) E.g. The data supports Worker A's claim — the median for Worker B is higher, so the times for Worker B are generally longer.
[1 mark for a correct statement comparing A and B's times, 1 mark for a sensible conclusion about A's claim]

Section 12 — Probability

Page 153 — Random Events and Venn Diagrams

Practice Questions

1 a) $\frac{5}{12}$ b) $\frac{7}{36}$ c) $\frac{11}{18}$

2

	S	S'	Total
C	2%	18%	20%
C'	48%	32%	80%
Total	50%	50%	100%

a) 2%   b) 18%   c) 66%

Exam Question

1 a) The Venn diagram would look something like this:

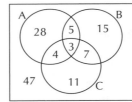

[5 marks available — 1 mark for the central figure correct, 2 marks for '5', '7' and '4' correct (or 1 mark for any 2 correct), 1 mark for '28', '15' and '11' correct, and 1 mark for a box with '47' outside the circles.]

b) (i) Add up the numbers in all the circles: 73 people out of 120 buy at least 1 type of soap. *[1 mark]*
So probability $= \frac{73}{120}$ *[1 mark]*

(ii) Add up the numbers in the intersections: 5 + 3 + 4 + 7 = 19, so 19 people buy at least two soaps, *[1 mark]* so the probability a person buys at least two types $= \frac{19}{120}$. *[1 mark]*

Page 155 — Tree Diagrams and Conditional Probability

Practice Questions

1 a)

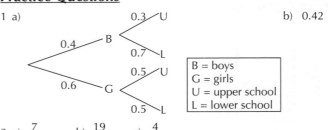

b) 0.42

B = boys
G = girls
U = upper school
L = lower school

2 a) $\frac{7}{10}$ b) $\frac{19}{30}$ c) $\frac{4}{19}$

You weren't asked to draw a tree diagram for this question, but you might find it makes it a lot easier if you do.

Answers

Exam Questions

1 Draw a tree diagram:

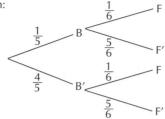

B = biased dice shows 6, F = fair dice shows 6

a) P(B') = 0.8 *[1 mark]*

b) Either at least one of the dice shows a 6 or neither of them do, so these are complementary events. Call F the event 'the fair dice shows a 6'.
Then P(F ∪ B) = 1 – P(F' ∩ B') *[1 mark]*
$= 1 - \left(\frac{4}{5} \times \frac{5}{6}\right) = 1 - \frac{2}{3} = \frac{1}{3}$ *[1 mark]*

c) P(exactly one 6 | at least one 6)
= P(exactly one 6 ∩ at least one 6) ÷ P(at least one 6).
The next step might be a bit easier to get your head round if you draw a Venn diagram:

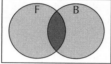

(exactly one 6) ∩ (at least one 6) = (exactly one 6)
Look at the diagram — 'exactly one 6' is the light grey area, and 'at least one 6' is the light grey area plus the dark grey bit. So the bit in common to both is just the light grey area.)
So P(exactly one 6 ∩ at least one 6) = P(B ∩ F') + P(B' ∩ F)
— this is the light grey area in the Venn diagram,
P(exactly one 6 ∩ at least one 6) $= \left(\frac{1}{5} \times \frac{5}{6}\right) + \left(\frac{4}{5} \times \frac{1}{6}\right) = \frac{9}{30} = \frac{3}{10}$
(using the fact that B and F are independent) *[1 mark]*
P(at least one 6) $= \frac{1}{3}$ (from b)).
And all of this means P(exactly one 6 | at least one 6)
$= \frac{3}{10} \div \frac{1}{3}$ *[1 mark]* $= \frac{9}{10}$ *[1 mark]*
Blauuurgh — the noise of a mind boggling. Part c) is difficult to get your head round, but it's just a matter of remembering the right formula (the one on page 154), breaking it down into separate parts and working through it step by step.

2 a)

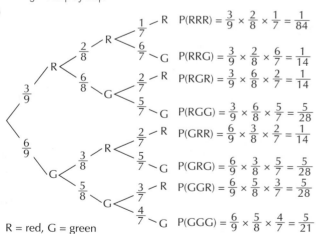

R = red, G = green

[3 marks available — 1 mark for a correctly-drawn tree diagram, 1 mark for multiplying along the branches to find combined probabilities, 1 mark for all probabilities correct.]

b) 'Third counter is green' means one of four outcomes: 'RRG', 'RGG', 'GRG' or 'GGG'. *[1 mark]*
So P(3rd is green) $= \frac{1}{14} + \frac{5}{28} + \frac{5}{28} + \frac{5}{21} = \frac{2}{3}$ *[1 mark]*

c) There are only two outcomes where all of the counters are the same colour: 'RRR' or 'GGG'. *[1 mark]*

So P(all same colour) $= \frac{1}{84} + \frac{5}{21} = \frac{1}{4}$ *[1 mark]*

d) 'At least one counter is red' is the complementary event of 'none of the counters are red', so:
P(at least one red) = 1 – P(no reds) = 1 – P(GGG) *[1 mark]*
$= 1 - \frac{5}{21} = \frac{16}{21}$ *[1 mark]*
[Alternatively, 1 mark for giving P(at least one red) as the sum of all of the outcome probabilities other than P(GGG), and 1 mark for the correct answer]

Page 157 — Mutually Exclusive and Independent Events

Practice Questions

1 a) The events are not mutually exclusive — e.g. if she picks 2 and 3, both events happen at the same time.

b) The events are not independent — the cards are not replaced, so the probability that the second number is odd will be different depending on whether or not the first number is even.

2 Any two from e.g. The sample assumes that all voters who voted in the previous election will vote in this one. / The sample assumes that voters who didn't vote in the previous election will not vote in this one. / It has been assumed that voters won't change their minds in the final two weeks before the vote. / It is assumed that voters will answer the survey honestly.

Exam Questions

1 a) (i) J and K are independent, so
P(J ∩ K) = P(J) × P(K) = 0.7 × 0.1 = 0.07 *[1 mark]*
(ii) P(J ∪ K) = P(J) + P(K) – P(J ∩ K) *[1 mark]*
= 0.7 + 0.1 – 0.07 = 0.73 *[1 mark]*

b) Drawing a quick Venn Diagram often helps:

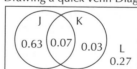

P(L|K') = P(L ∩ K') ÷ P(K')
Now L ∩ K' = L (= J' ∩ K') *[1 mark]*
All of L is contained in K', so the bits in L ∩ K' (those in both L and K') are just the bits in L.
So P(L ∩ K') = P(L) = 1 – P(K ∪ J) = 1 – 0.73 = 0.27 *[1 mark]*
P(K') = 1 – P(K) = 1 – 0.1 = 0.9 *[1 mark]*
And so P(L|K') = 0.27 ÷ 0.9 = 0.3 *[1 mark]*
You could also simplify this by thinking about what L|K' means — if you're given that K didn't happen (K'), then the probability that neither happen (L) is just the probability that J doesn't happen (J'), so P(L|K') = P(J'|K').

2 a) Let B = sculpture is broken and T = sculpture is delivered on time. Erwin is claiming B and T are independent. *[1 mark]*
If B and T are independent, then P(B) = P(B|T) = 0.56. *[1 mark]*

b) It might help to show the information in a tree diagram:

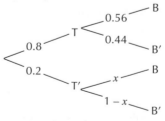

Here, x = P(B|T'), and you want to find P(T'|B').
The question says that P(B) = 0.5, so use this to form an equation:
P(B) = (0.8 × 0.56) + (0.2 × x) *[1 mark]*
⇒ 0.448 + 0.2x = 0.5 *[1 mark]* ⇒ x = 0.26 *[1 mark]*
Now you can use P(T'|B') $= \frac{P(T' \cap B')}{P(B')}$
P(B') = 1 – P(B) = 1 – 0.5 = 0.5 *[1 mark]*
P(T' ∩ B') = 0.2 × (1 – x) = 0.2 × 0.74 = 0.148 *[1 mark]*
So P(T'|B') $= \frac{0.148}{0.5} = 0.296$ *[1 mark]*
You don't have to use a tree diagram to solve this one, but it might make it a bit easier to see what to do.

Answers

Section 13 — Statistical Distributions

Page 160 — Probability Distributions

Practice Question

1 a) $k = \frac{1}{10}$ b) $P(X > 2) = \frac{7}{10}$ c) $P(1 \le X \le 3) = \frac{3}{5}$

d) i)

x	1	2	3	4
$P(X = x)$	$\frac{1}{10}$	$\frac{1}{5}$	$\frac{3}{10}$	$\frac{2}{5}$

ii)

x	1	2	3	4
$F(x) = P(X \le x)$	$\frac{1}{10}$	$\frac{3}{10}$	$\frac{3}{5}$	1

Exam Question

1   Use the fact that the probabilities add up to 1 to find k:

$\frac{1}{k}(1^2) + \frac{1}{k}(2^2) + \frac{1}{k}(3^2) + \frac{1}{k}(4^2) = 1$ **[1 mark]**

$\Rightarrow \frac{1}{k}(1 + 4 + 9 + 16) = 1 \Rightarrow \frac{30}{k} = 1 \Rightarrow k = 30$ **[1 mark]**

$P(X \le 2) = P(X = 1) + P(X = 2)$ **[1 mark]**

$= \frac{1}{30}(1^2) + \frac{1}{30}(2^2) = \frac{5}{30} = \frac{1}{6}$ **[1 mark]**

Page 163 — The Binomial Distribution

Practice Questions

1 a) 0.00977 (3 s.f.)   b) 0.0107 (3 s.f.)
2 a) $P(X = 4) = 0.2286$ (4 d.p.)   b) $P(Y \le 15) = 0.9997$ (4 d.p.)

Exam Questions

1 a) Using the binomial cdf:
   $P(X < 8) = P(X \le 7)$ **[1 mark]** $= 0.562$ (3 s.f.) **[1 mark]**
   b) Using the binomial pdf: $P(X = 5) = 0.101$ (3 s.f.) **[1 mark]**
   c) $P(3 < X \le 7) = P(X \le 7) - P(X \le 3)$ **[1 mark]**
           $= 0.56182... - 0.01526... = 0.547$ (3 s.f.) **[1 mark]**
2 a) Let X represent the number of apples that contain a maggot.
   Then $X \sim B(40, 0.15)$. So $P(X < 6) = P(X \le 5)$ **[1 mark]**
           $= 0.433$ (3 s.f.) **[1 mark]**
   b) $P(X > 2) = 1 - P(X \le 2)$ **[1 mark]**
           $= 1 - 0.04859... = 0.9514... = 0.951$ (3 s.f.) **[1 mark]**
   c) The probability that a crate contains more than 2 apples with
   maggots is 0.9514... from b). So define a random variable Y,
   where Y is the number of crates that contain more than 2 apples
   with maggots. Then $Y \sim B(3, 0.9514...)$. **[1 mark]**
   Using your calculator:
   $P(Y > 1) = 1 - P(Y \le 1)$ **[1 mark]**
           $= 1 - 0.00685... = 0.993$ (3 s.f.) **[1 mark]**
   You could also do: $P(Y > 1) = P(Y = 2) + P(Y = 3) = 3p^2(1 - p) + p^3$.
   d) E.g. maggots could spread to other nearby apples in a crate, some
   trees might have more apples with maggots than others, etc.
   [1 mark for a suitable criticism]

Page 165 — The Normal Distribution

These questions are done using a calculator with an upper bound
of 9999 or a lower bound of –9999 where needed.

Practice Questions

1 a) $P(X \le 55) = 0.8944$ (4 d.p.)   b) $P(X < 42) = 0.0228$ (4 d.p.)
   c) $P(X > 56) = 0.0668$ (4 d.p.)   d) $P(47 < X < 57) = 0.7333$ (4 d.p.)
2 a) $P(X < 0) = 0.2375$ (4 d.p.)   b) $P(X \le 1) = 0.2839$ (4 d.p.)
   c) $P(X \ge 7) = 0.3875$ (4 d.p.)   d) $P(2 < X < 4) = 0.1091$ (4 d.p.)
3 a) $a = 34.3$ (3 s.f.)   b) $a = 32.2$ (3 s.f.)   c) $a = 17.9$ (3 s.f.)

Exam Questions

1 a) Lower bound 145, upper bound 9999, $\sigma = 25$, $\mu = 120$
   Using the normal cdf function:
   $P(X > 145) = 0.159$ (3 s.f.) **[1 mark]**
   b) $P(X < j) - P(X \le 120) = 0.4641$
   $P(X < j) = 0.4641 + P(X \le 120) = 0.4641 + 0.5 = 0.9641$ **[1 mark]**
   Using the inverse normal function: $j = 165$ (3 s.f.) **[1 mark]**
2 a) Let X be the volume of compost in a bag, so $X \sim N(50, 0.4^2)$.
   Lower bound –9999, upper bound 49, $\sigma = 0.4$, $\mu = 50$
   Using the normal cdf: $P(X < 49) = 0.00621$ (3 s.f.) **[1 mark]**

b) Lower bound 50.5, upper bound 9999, $\sigma = 0.4$, $\mu = 50$
   Using the normal cdf: $P(X > 50.5) = 0.1056...$ **[1 mark]**
   So in 1000 bags, $0.1056... \times 1000$ **[1 mark]**
   ≈ 106 bags **[1 mark]** (approximately) would be expected to
   contain more than 50.5 litres of compost.

Page 167 — The Standard Normal Distribution

Practice Questions

1 a) $z = 2.326$ (3 d.p.)   b) $z = -3.291$ (3 d.p.)
2 a) $\mu = 4.08$ (3 s.f.)   b) $\mu = 217$ (3 s.f.)
3 a) $\sigma = 7.90$ (3 s.f.)   b) $\sigma = 1.08$ (3 s.f.)
4    $\sigma = 0.52$ (2 d.p.) and $\mu = 14.15$ (2 d.p.)

Exam Questions

1   Convert Y to the standard normal distribution Z:
   $P(Y < 74) = 0.10$ means $P\left(Z < \frac{74 - 75}{\sigma}\right) = P\left(Z < \frac{-1}{\sigma}\right) = 0.1$
   Use your calculator to get: $-\frac{1}{\sigma} = -1.2815...$ **[1 mark]**
   So $\sigma = \frac{1}{1.2815...} = 0.780$ grams (3 s.f.) **[1 mark]**
2   Let X be the lifetime of a battery, so $X \sim N(\mu, \sigma^2)$.
   Then $P(X < 20) = 0.4$ and $P(X < 30) = 0.8$
   Convert X to the standard normal distribution Z:
   $P\left(Z < \frac{20 - \mu}{\sigma}\right) = 0.4$ and $P\left(Z < \frac{30 - \mu}{\sigma}\right) = 0.8$ **[1 mark]**
   Use your calculator to get:
   $\frac{20 - \mu}{\sigma} = -0.2533...$ **[1 mark]** and $\frac{30 - \mu}{\sigma} = 0.8416...$ **[1 mark]**
   Now rewrite these as:
   $20 - \mu = -0.2533...\sigma$ and $30 - \mu = 0.8416...\sigma$ **[1 mark]**
   Subtract these two equations to get:
   $10 = (0.8416... + 0.2533...)\sigma$ **[1 mark]**
   $\Rightarrow \sigma = \frac{10}{0.8416... + 0.2533...} = 9.1326...$
   $= 9.13$ hours (3 s.f.) **[1 mark]**
   Now use this in one of the equations above:
   $\mu = 20 + 0.2533... \times 9.1326... = 22.3$ hours (3 s.f.) **[1 mark]**

Page 169 — Normal Approximation to B(n, p)

Practice Questions

1 a) $P(X > 50) \approx 0.157$ (3 s.f.)   b) $P(X \le 42) \approx 0.273$ (3 s.f.)
   c) $P(40 < X \le 47) = 0.499$ (3 s.f.)
2   0.00101 (3 s.f.)

Exam Questions

1 a) Need n to be large **[1 mark]** and p to be close to 0.5. **[1 mark]**
   b) i) n is large and p is fairly close to 0.5, so use the
      normal approximation $Y \sim N(60, 24)$. **[1 mark]**
      $P(X \ge 65) \approx P(Y \ge 65) = 0.154$ (3 s.f.) **[1 mark]**
      ii) $P(50 < X < 62) \approx P(50 < Y < 62) = 0.638$ (3 s.f.) **[1 mark]**
2   Let X represent the number of people who try to order coffee,
   so $X \sim B(150, 0.55)$. **[1 mark]**
   $np = 150 \times 0.55 = 82.5$ and $npq = 150 \times 0.55 \times 0.45 = 37.125$,
   so use the normal approximation $Y \sim N(82.5, 37.125)$. **[1 mark]**
   $P(X > 75) \approx P(Y > 75) = 0.891$ (3 s.f.) **[1 mark]**
3 a) The normal approximation is $Y \sim N(\mu, \sigma^2)$
   $P(X \le 153) \approx P(Y \le 153) = P\left(Z \le \frac{153 - \mu}{\sigma}\right) = 0.9332$ **[1 mark]**
   Using the inverse normal function, $\frac{153 - \mu}{\sigma} = 1.500...$
   So $\mu + 1.500...\sigma = 153$ — call this equation ① **[1 mark]**
   $P(X > 127) \approx P(Y > 127) = P\left(Z > \frac{127 - \mu}{\sigma}\right) = 0.9977$ **[1 mark]**
   Using the inverse normal function, $\frac{127 - \mu}{\sigma} = -2.833...$
   So $\mu - 2.833...\sigma = 127$ — call this equation ② **[1 mark]**
   Now subtract equation ② from equation ①:
   $4.333...\sigma = 26 \Rightarrow \sigma = 5.9992... = 6.00$ (3 s.f.) **[1 mark]**
   Putting this into one of the equations gives
   $\mu = 144.00... = 144$ (3 s.f.) **[1 mark]**

Answers

b) $\mu = np \Rightarrow np = 144.00...$ *[1 mark]*
and $\sigma^2 = npq \Rightarrow npq = (5.9992...)^2 = 35.991...$ *[1 mark]*
Dividing the second equation by the first equation gives:
$q = 35.991... \div 144.00... = 0.24993...$
$\Rightarrow p = 1 - q = 1 - 0.24993... = 0.75006... = 0.750$ (3 s.f.) *[1 mark]*
Then $n = 144 \div 0.75006... = 191.98... = 192$ (3 s.f.) *[1 mark]*

Page 171 — Choosing a Distribution
Practice Question
1 a) Neither — the data is discrete but the number of trials isn't fixed.
  b) Normal — the data is continuous and you'd expect it to be roughly symmetrical about the mean.
  c) Binomial — the data is discrete, there is a fixed number of trials (1000), there are 2 outcomes ('red' or 'not red'), there is a constant probability of success (0.08) and the trials are independent (since the sample is random).

Exam Question
1 a) i) The probability of the biologist catching a hedgehog needs to remain the same every night, *[1 mark]* and all the outcomes need to be independent (i.e. catching a hedgehog one night shouldn't affect catching one another night). *[1 mark]*
    ii) The total number of nights she catches a hedgehog (or the number of nights she doesn't catch a hedgehog). *[1 mark]*
  b)   Weight is continuous *[1 mark]* and the weights of the hedgehogs should be roughly symmetrical about the mean. *[1 mark]*

Section 14 — Statistical Hypothesis Testing
Page 175 — Statistical Sampling
Practice Questions
1 a) Sample — a census is impossible as the number of coin tosses is infinite, so he can only examine a sample of them.
  b) Sample — testing all 200 pies would take too long, and more importantly, the test will destroy the pies.
  c) Census — the population is fairly small, and the result will be more accurate if all the marks are considered.
2 Opportunity (convenience) sampling
3 First, find out how many people are at the cinema that afternoon and decide on your sample size. Divide the total population by the sample size to find your value of n. Then, generate a random starting point and ask every n^{th} person after this starting point as they leave the cinema.

Exam Questions
1 a) i) All the Year 7 pupils in the school. *[1 mark]*
    ii) A list of all Year 7 pupils, e.g. the school registers. *[1 mark]*

  b) i) E.g. Biased — as all of the students in the sample have the same history teacher, their opinions are likely to be similar, while students with a different teacher would have different opinions on history lessons. *[1 mark]*
    ii) E.g. Not biased — the distance between a pupil's home and the school is unlikely to be affected by which history class they are in, so only using pupils from one class should not introduce bias. *[1 mark]*
2 Retired people = $98 \div 250 \times 25 = 9.8 \approx 10$ people *[1 mark]*
  Unemployed people = $34 \div 250 \times 25 = 3.4 \approx 3$ people *[1 mark]*
  People who work full- or part-time = $83 \div 250 \times 25 = 8.3$ ≈ 8 people *[1 mark]*
  Students = $(250 - 98 - 34 - 83) \div 250 \times 25 = 3.5 \approx 4$ people *[1 mark]*
  Check your answer by adding up the number of people sampled:
  $10 + 3 + 8 + 4 = 25$ as required.

Page 177 — Hypothesis Tests
Practice Question
1 No — the result of the hypothesis test supports the claim that the percentage of library users has decreased, but doesn't support the claim that it has decreased by a specific amount.

Exam Question
1 Let p be the proportion of customers that rated the restaurant as 'Excellent'. Then $H_0: p = 0.43$ and $H_1: p > 0.43$.
  [1 mark for both hypotheses correct]

Page 179 — Hypothesis Tests and Binomial Distributions
Practice Questions
1 a) $H_0: p = 0.2$, $H_1: p \neq 0.2$, $\alpha = 0.05$ (so $\frac{\alpha}{2} = 0.025$) and $x = 1$:
    Under H_0, $X \sim B(20, 0.2)$. $P(X \leq 1) = 0.06917...$
    $0.06917... > 0.025$, so there is insufficient evidence at the 5% level of significance to reject H_0.
  b) $H_0: p = 0.4$, $H_1: p > 0.4$, $\alpha = 0.01$ and $x = 15$:
    Under H_0, $X \sim B(20, 0.4)$
    $P(X \geq 15) = 1 - P(X \leq 14) = 1 - 0.9983... = 0.00161...$
    $0.00161.. < 0.01$, so there is evidence at the 1% level of significance to reject H_0.
2 $H_0: p = 0.3$, $H_1: p < 0.3$, $\alpha = 0.05$
  Under H_0, $X \sim B(10, 0.3)$
  Critical region = biggest possible set of 'low' values of X with a total probability of ≤ 0.05.
  $P(X \leq 0) = 0.02824...$, $P(X \leq 1) = 0.14930...$,
  so critical region is $X = 0$.

Exam Question
1 a) Binomial *[1 mark]* 'Proportion' should set the binomial bell ringing.
  b) i) Start by stating the hypotheses:
      $H_0: p = 0.2$ and $H_1: p > 0.2$ *[1 mark for both correct]*
      $X =$ number of tiramisu orders in sample
      Under H_0, $X \sim B(20, 0.2)$ *[1 mark]*
      $\alpha = 0.05$
      Either:
      Use the binomial cdf to find the p-value (the probability of getting a value greater than or equal to 7, under H_0):
      $P(X \geq 7) = 1 - P(X \leq 6)$ *[1 mark]*
      $= 1 - 0.9133... = 0.0866...$ *[1 mark]*
      $0.0866... > 0.05$, so the result isn't significant. *[1 mark]*
      Or:
      Use the binomial cdf to find the critical region:
      $P(X \geq 7) = 1 - P(X \leq 6) = 1 - 0.9133... = 0.0866...$
      $P(X \geq 8) = 1 - P(X \leq 7) = 1 - 0.9678... = 0.0321...$
      [1 mark for attempting to find the smallest value of x such that P(X ≥ x) ≤ 0.05]
      $0.0321... < 0.05$, so the CR is $X \geq 8$. *[1 mark]*
      7 isn't in the CR, so the result isn't significant. *[1 mark]*
      So there is insufficient evidence at the 5% level of significance to support the chef's theory that the proportion of dessert eaters ordering tiramisu on a Saturday is greater than on weekdays.
      [1 mark for a suitable conclusion]
    ii) You're looking for the smallest value of x such that $P(X \geq x) \leq 0.05$.
      You know $X = 7$ isn't significant from part (i).
      Try 8: $P(X \geq 8) = 0.0321... < 0.05$,
      so the answer is 8 tiramisu orders. *[1 mark]*
      Part (ii) here is really just asking for the lower boundary of the critical region (the critical value). So if you answered part (i) by finding the critical region, you've already worked out the answer. Bonus.

Answers

Page 181 — Hypothesis Tests and Normal Distributions

Practice Questions

1   $H_0: \mu = 45$, $H_1: \mu < 45$, $\alpha = 0.05$ and $\sigma^2 = 9$.
Under H_0, $\overline{X} \sim N\left(45, \frac{9}{16}\right)$ and $Z = \dfrac{42 - 45}{\frac{3}{4}} = -4$

Critical region is $Z < -1.644...$
$-4 < -1.644...$, so there is evidence to reject H_0 at the 5% level.

2   a) $\overline{x} = \dfrac{\sum x}{n} = \dfrac{197.8}{10} = 19.78$

b) $H_0: \mu = 20$ and $H_1: \mu < 20$. $\alpha = 0.05$ and $\sigma^2 = 0.81$.
Under H_0, $\overline{X} \sim N\left(20, \frac{0.81}{10}\right)$ and $Z = \dfrac{19.78 - 20}{\frac{0.9}{\sqrt{10}}} = -0.7730...$

Critical region is $Z < -1.644...$
$-0.7730... > -1.644...$, so there is insufficient evidence to reject H_0 at the 5% significance level.

Exam Question

1   a) $\overline{x} = \dfrac{\sum x}{n} = \dfrac{490}{100} = 4.9$ m **[1 mark]**

b)   Let $\mu =$ mean height of trees in 2nd area.
$H_0: \mu = 5.1$ and $H_1: \mu \neq 5.1$ **[1 mark]**
Under H_0, $\overline{X} \sim N\left(5.1, \frac{0.2}{100}\right)$ **[1 mark]**
$Z = \dfrac{4.9 - 5.1}{\sqrt{\frac{0.2}{100}}}$ **[1 mark]** $= -4.4721...$ **[1 mark]**

This is a two-tailed test at the 1% level, so the critical values you need are z and $-z$ such that $P(Z > z) = 0.005$ (or $P(Z < z) = 0.995$). Using your calculator gives critical values of $-2.575...$ and $2.575...$ **[1 mark]**
Since $-4.4721... < -2.575...$, the result is significant.
There is evidence at the 1% level of significance to reject H_0 and to suggest that the trees in the second area have a different mean height. **[1 mark]**

You could also have answered this question by calculating the p-value (0.00000387 to 3 s.f.) — just remember to compare this to $\frac{\alpha}{2}$, not just α. It might seem weird doing a two-tailed test when you already know that the sample mean is less than the population mean, but the question says that your alternative hypothesis is that the mean height is "different", not "less". Keep an eye out for nasty tricks like this in the exam.

Section 15 — Correlation and Regression

Page 183 — Correlation

Practice Questions

1   a)   No correlation   b)   Weak negative correlation
   c)   Strong positive correlation

2   Explanatory variable = amount of sunshine
   Response variable = barbecue sales

Exam Question

1   a)

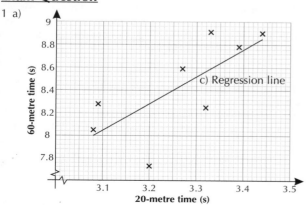

[2 marks for all points plotted correctly, otherwise 1 mark for 4-7 points plotted correctly]

b)   Weak positive correlation **[1 mark]**
c)   See graph **[1 mark for regression line plotted correctly]**
d)   (i) When $x = 3.15$, $y = (2.367 \times 3.15) + 0.709 = 8.17$ s (3 s.f.)
3.15 m is within the range you have data for (this is interpolation), so the estimate should be accurate.
[1 mark for correct y-value and sensible comment]
(ii) When $x = 3.88$, $y = (2.367 \times 3.88) + 0.709 = 9.89$ s (3 s.f.)
3.88 m is outside the range you have data for (this is extrapolation), so the estimate might not be accurate.
[1 mark for correct y-value and sensible comment]

Page 185 — The Product Moment Correlation Coefficient

Practice Questions

1   a)   strong negative correlation, **B**
   b)   fairly weak positive correlation, **A**   c)   almost no correlation, **C**

2   a) r is quite close to 1, so there is fairly strong positive correlation. This suggests that the more pairs of sunglasses are sold, the more ice creams are sold.
   b)   The claim is inaccurate — sunglasses sales and ice cream sales could be linked by a third factor that causes the change (such as temperature).
This is an example of 'correlation does not imply causation' — see p.182.

Exam Questions

1   $H_0: \rho = 0$, $H_1: \rho < 0$ **[1 mark]**
The critical value given is -0.2787.
$-0.24 > -0.2787$, so there is insufficient evidence at the 2.5% significance level to reject H_0 in favour of H_1 — the hypothesis that there is negative correlation between the age and time taken to do the times table test. **[1 mark]**

2   a) $H_0: \rho = 0$, $H_1: \rho > 0$ **[1 mark]**
The critical region for a test at a 0.5% significance level on a sample of size 8 is $r > 0.8343$ **[1 mark]**
   b) $0.958 > 0.8343$, so there is evidence at the 0.5% significance level to reject H_0 in favour of H_1 — the hypothesis that there is positive correlation between the diameter of a biscuit and its weight. **[1 mark]**

Section 16 — Kinematics

Page 187 — Constant Acceleration Equations

Practice Questions

1   12 m
2   0.714 s (3 s.f.)
3   6.20 ms^{-1} (3 s.f.)

Exam Questions

1   a)   Using $v = u + at$ **[1 mark]**
17 = $u + (9.8 \times 1.2)$ **[1 mark]** $\Rightarrow u = 5.24$ **[1 mark]**
   b)   Using $s = ut + \frac{1}{2}at^2$ **[1 mark]**
$s = (17 \times 2.1) + \frac{1}{2}(9.8 \times 2.1^2)$ **[1 mark]** $\Rightarrow s = 57.309$ **[1 mark]**
$h = \frac{s}{14} = 4.09$ m (3 s.f.) **[1 mark]**

2   a)   Using $v^2 = u^2 + 2as$ **[1 mark]**
$20^2 = u^2 + (2 \times 9.8 \times 8)$ **[1 mark]** $\Rightarrow u = \sqrt{400 - 156.8} = \sqrt{243.2}$
Ignore the negative solution as speed must be positive.
So $u = 15.59487... = 15.6$ (3 s.f.) **[1 mark]**
   b)   Using $v = u + at$ **[1 mark]**
$20 = -15.59487... + 9.8t$ **[1 mark]** $\Rightarrow 9.8t = 35.59487...$
hence $t = 3.63212... = 3.63$ s (3 s.f.) **[1 mark]**
It's best to avoid using $s = ut + \frac{1}{2}at^2$ in this question, as it gives you a second, incorrect solution. If this ever happens in a question, try using another suvat equation to figure out which is the correct solution.

Answers

Page 189 — Motion Graphs
Practice Questions

1 a) From rest, the athlete travels 5 m in 3 seconds; then rests for 2 seconds; then returns to the start, travelling 5 m in 1 second.
   b) 0 ms^{-1} c) 10 m
2 Distance = 68.75 m
3 a) $v = u + at \Rightarrow u = v - at$
   Substituting this into $s = \frac{1}{2}(u + v)t$ gives:
   $s = \frac{1}{2}(v - at + v)t = \frac{1}{2}(2v - at)t = vt - \frac{1}{2}at^2$
   b) Rearranging $v = u + at$ gives: $t = \frac{v - u}{a}$
   Substitute this into $s = \frac{1}{2}(u + v)t$:
   $s = \frac{1}{2a}(u + v)(v - u) \Rightarrow 2as = uv - u^2 + v^2 - vu \Rightarrow v^2 = u^2 + 2as$

Exam Questions

1 a) Area under graph (area of trapezium) = distance *[1 mark]*
   $\frac{120 + 180}{2} \times V = 2100$ *[1 mark]*
   $V = \frac{2100}{150} = 14$ ms^{-1} *[1 mark]*
   b) Distance = area under graph *[1 mark]*
   $= \frac{1}{2} \times 40 \times 14 = 280$ m *[1 mark]*
2 a) Acceleration is the gradient of the graph. *[1 mark]*
   acceleration $= \frac{\text{change in } y}{\text{change in } x} = \frac{50 - 10}{15 - 10} = 8$ ms^{-2} *[1 mark]*
   b)
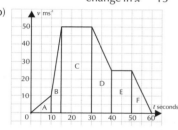
   Distance is area so:
   area of A = $(10 \times 10) \div 2 = 50$
   area of B = $\frac{10 + 50}{2} \times 5 = 150$
   area of C = $15 \times 50 = 750$
   area of D = $\frac{50 + 25}{2} \times 10 = 375$
   area of E = $10 \times 25 = 250$
   area of F = $10 \times 25 \div 2 = 125$
   [1 mark for attempting to find the area under the graph]
   First 30 s: $50 + 150 + 750 = 950$ m *[1 mark]*
   Second 30 s: $375 + 250 + 125 = 750$ m *[1 mark]*
   So Sean is correct. *[1 mark]*
   c) Using the calculations from b), $15 < T < 30$ *[1 mark]*
   (i.e. T is within C).
   Find 'how far T is through C' (as a fraction):
   $700 -$ area of A $-$ area of B $= 700 - 50 - 150 = 500$ m
   $\frac{500}{750} = \frac{2}{3}$, so T is $\frac{2}{3}$ through C. *[1 mark]*
   So $T = 15 + \left(\frac{2}{3} \times 15\right) = 25$. *[1 mark]*

Page 191 — Using Calculus for Kinematics
Practice Questions

1 a) $a = 16t - 2$ b) $s = \frac{8t^3}{3} - t^2 + C$
2 $a = -\frac{2}{3}\sin\left(\frac{1}{3}t\right)$ ms^{-2}
3 70.2 m (3 s.f.)

Exam Questions

1 a) $s = -\frac{1}{100}t(t^2 - 9t - 10) = -\frac{1}{100}t(t + 1)(t - 10)$ *[1 mark]*
   Draw a quick sketch:
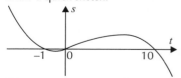
   [1 mark]
   Distance and time can't be negative so $0 \le t \le 10$ *[1 mark]*

b) s is at a maximum when $\frac{ds}{dt} = 0$, i.e. when $v = 0$ *[1 mark]*
   $v = \frac{ds}{dt} = \frac{1}{100}(-3t^2 + 18t + 10)$ *[1 mark]*
   When $v = 0$, $-3t^2 + 18t + 10 = 0$.
   Using the quadratic formula $t = 6.51188...$
   or $t = -0.511884...$ (ignore as $0 \le t \le 10$). *[1 mark]*
   When $t = 6.51188...$, $s = \frac{1}{100}[-(6.51188...)^3 + 9(6.51188...)^2$
   $+ 10(6.51188...)]$ *[1 mark]*
   $= 1.71$ m (3 s.f.) *[1 mark]*

2 a) v is at a maximum when $\frac{dv}{dt} = 0$, i.e. when $a = 0$
   So, in the interval $0 \le t \le 2$, $a = \frac{dv}{dt} = 9 - 6t$ *[1 mark]*
   When $a = 0$: $0 = 9 - 6t \Rightarrow t = 1.5$ s *[1 mark]*
   So: $v = (9 \times 1.5) - 3(1.5^2)$ *[1 mark]* $= 6.75$ ms^{-1} *[1 mark]*
   b) (i) $s = \int v\,dt = \frac{9t^2}{2} - t^3 + C$ for $0 \le t \le 2$. *[1 mark]*
   When $t = 0$, the particle is at the origin, i.e. $s = 0$
   $\Rightarrow C = 0$ *[1 mark]*
   When $t = 2$, $s = \frac{9}{2}(2^2) - 2^3 = 10$ m *[1 mark]*
   (ii) $s = \int v\,dt = \int \frac{24}{t^2}\,dt = \frac{-24}{t} + C$ for $t > 2$ *[1 mark]*
   Use the answer to part i) as initial conditions:
   when $t = 2$, $s = 10$, so $10 = \frac{-24}{2} + C$ *[1 mark]*
   $\Rightarrow C = 22$ *[1 mark]*
   When $t = 6$, $s = \frac{-24}{6} + 22 = 18$ m *[1 mark]*

Page 193 — Describing 2D Motion Using Vectors
Practice Questions

1 $\begin{pmatrix} -9 \\ 7 \end{pmatrix}$ m
2 speed $= 8.51$ ms^{-1} (3 s.f.), direction $= 29.6°$ (3 s.f.)
3 $\dot{s} = \frac{ds}{dt}$ represents the velocity of the particle, and
   $\ddot{s} = \frac{d^2s}{dt^2}$ represents the acceleration of the particle.
4 $s = 2t^2\mathbf{i} + \frac{t^3}{3}\mathbf{j}$ and $a = 4\mathbf{i} + 2t\mathbf{j}$

Exam Questions

1 a) $v = \dot{s} = [(6t^2 - 14t)\mathbf{i} + (6t - 12t^2)\mathbf{j}]$ ms^{-1} *[1 mark for attempting to differentiate the position vector, 1 mark for correct answer]*
   b) $v = \left(\frac{6}{4} - \frac{14}{2}\right)\mathbf{i} + \left(\frac{6}{2} - \frac{12}{4}\right)\mathbf{j}$ *[1 mark]* $= -5.5\mathbf{i}$
   Speed $= \sqrt{(-5.5)^2 + 0^2} = 5.5$ ms^{-1} *[1 mark]*
   The component of velocity in the direction of north is zero, and the component in the direction of east is negative, so the particle is moving due west. *[1 mark]*
2 A = original position vector + tv = $(\mathbf{i} + 2\mathbf{j}) + 8(3\mathbf{i} + \mathbf{j})$
   $= (\mathbf{i} + 2\mathbf{j}) + (24\mathbf{i} + 8\mathbf{j}) = (25\mathbf{i} + 10\mathbf{j})$ m
   [1 mark for correct working, 1 mark for correct answer]
   $B = A + tv = (25\mathbf{i} + 10\mathbf{j}) + 5(-4\mathbf{i} + 2\mathbf{j})$
   $= (25\mathbf{i} + 10\mathbf{j}) + (-20\mathbf{i} + 10\mathbf{j}) = (5\mathbf{i} + 20\mathbf{j})$ m
   [1 mark for correct working, 1 mark for correct answer]
3 Integrate $\mathbf{a}$: $v = \int \mathbf{a}\,dt = (6t^2\mathbf{i} - 3e^{\frac{1}{3}t}\mathbf{j}) + \mathbf{C}$ *[1 mark]*
   $v = 5\mathbf{i} - 4\mathbf{j}$ when $t = 0 \Rightarrow 5\mathbf{i} - 4\mathbf{j} = 0 - 3\mathbf{j} + \mathbf{C} \Rightarrow \mathbf{C} = 5\mathbf{i} - \mathbf{j}$
   So $v = (6t^2 + 5)\mathbf{i} - (3e^{\frac{1}{3}t} + 1)\mathbf{j}$ ms^{-1} *[1 mark]*
   Integrate v: $s = \int v\,dt = (2t^3 + 5t)\mathbf{i} - (9e^{\frac{1}{3}t} + t)\mathbf{j} + \mathbf{C'}$ *[1 mark]*
   $s = \mathbf{0}$ when $t = 0 \Rightarrow \mathbf{0} = 0\mathbf{i} - 9\mathbf{j} + \mathbf{C'} \Rightarrow \mathbf{C'} = 9\mathbf{j}$
   So $s = (2t^3 + 5t)\mathbf{i} + (9 - 9e^{\frac{1}{3}t} - t)\mathbf{j}$ m *[1 mark]*
   When $t = 1$, $s = [7\mathbf{i} + (8 - 9e^{\frac{1}{3}})\mathbf{j}]$ m *[1 mark]*

Answers

Page 197 — Projectiles and Motion Under Gravity

Practice Questions

1   1.23 m (3 s.f.)
2   Horizontal velocity = 13.1 ms^{-1} (3 s.f.)
3 a)   Initial horizontal velocity is $u \cos \alpha$.
     Initial vertical velocity is $u \sin \alpha$.
  b) i)   Resolving vertically upwards: $u_y = u \sin \alpha$, $v = 0$, $a = -g$, $t = t$
       $v = u + at \Rightarrow 0 = u \sin \alpha - gt \Rightarrow t = \frac{u \sin \alpha}{g}$, as required
    ii) The total time in flight is double the time taken
       to reach its maximum height, i.e. $\frac{2u \sin \alpha}{g}$.
       Consider the horizontal motion:
       Speed is constant, so $s = ut$.
       $\Rightarrow s = u\sin \alpha \times \frac{2u \sin \alpha}{g} = \frac{2u^2 (\sin \alpha)(\cos \alpha)}{g}$
       $\Rightarrow s = \frac{u^2 \sin (2\alpha)}{g}$ (using the sine double angle formula)
  c)   Resolving vertically upwards: $u_y = u \sin \alpha$, $v = 0$, $a = -g$, $s = s$
      $v^2 = u^2 + 2as \Rightarrow 0 = (u \sin \alpha)^2 - 2gs \Rightarrow s = \frac{u^2 \sin^2 \alpha}{2g}$

Exam Questions

1 a) $\tan \alpha = \frac{3}{4} \Rightarrow \sin \alpha = \frac{3}{5}$ *[1 mark]*
     Vertical motion, taking down as +ve:
     $s = 11$, $u = u_y = 15 \sin \alpha = 9$, *[1 mark]* $a = 9.8$, $t = t$
     $s = ut + \frac{1}{2}at^2$ *[1 mark]*
     $11 = 9t + 4.9t^2$ *[1 mark]*
     Using the quadratic formula: $t = 0.83898... = 0.839$ s (3 s.f.)
     [1 mark]
  b)   Horizontal motion, taking right as +ve:
     $s = s$, $u = u_x = 15 \cos \alpha = 15 \times \frac{4}{5} = 12$, *[1 mark]* $t = 0.83898...$ s
     $a = 0$, so $s = ut \Rightarrow OB = 12 \times 0.83898...$ *[1 mark]*
     $OB = 10.06785...$ m
     So it misses H by $10.06785... - 9 = 1.07$ m (3 s.f.) *[1 mark]*
  c)   Horizontal motion, taking right as +ve:
     $s = 9$, $u_x = u \cos \alpha$, $a = 0$, $t = t$
     $s = u_x t + \frac{1}{2}at^2$ *[1 mark]*
     $9 = (u \cos \alpha)t \Rightarrow t = \frac{9}{u \cos \alpha}$ *[1 mark]* — call this ①
     Vertical motion, taking down as +ve:
     $s = 11$, $u_y = u \sin \alpha$, $a = 9.8$, $t = t$
     $s = u_y t + \frac{1}{2}at^2 \Rightarrow 11 = (u \sin \alpha)t + 4.9t^2$ *[1 mark]* — call this ②
     t is the same both horizontally and vertically,
     so substitute ① in ② to eliminate t:
     $11 = 9\left(\frac{u \sin \alpha}{u \cos \alpha}\right) + 4.9\left(\frac{9}{u \cos \alpha}\right)^2$ *[1 mark]*
     $11 = 9 \tan \alpha + \frac{4.9 \times 81}{u^2 \cos^2 \alpha}$
     $\tan \alpha = \frac{3}{4}$ and $\cos \alpha = \frac{4}{5}$, so substituting and simplifying:
     $u^2 = 145.919$, so $u = 12.1$ ms^{-1} (3 s.f.) *[1 mark]*
2   Horizontal motion, taking right as +ve :
     $s = 30$, $u = 20 \cos 30°$, $a = 0$, $t = t$

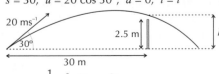

     $s = ut + \frac{1}{2}at^2$ *[1 mark]*
     $30 = (20 \cos 30° \times t) \Rightarrow t = 1.732$ s *[1 mark]*
     Vertical motion, taking up as +ve:
     $s = h$, $u = 20 \sin 30°$, $a = -9.8$, $t = 1.732$
     $s = ut + \frac{1}{2}at^2$ *[1 mark]*
     $h = (20 \sin 30° \times 1.732) + \left(\frac{1}{2} \times -9.8 \times 1.732^2\right)$
     $= 2.62$ m (to 3 s.f.) *[1 mark]*

Therefore the ball goes over the crossbar. *[1 mark]*
Assumptions: e.g. ball is a particle, crossbar has no thickness, no air or wind resistance, no spin on the ball *[1 mark]*
3 a)   Horizontal motion, taking right as +ve:
     $s = x$, $u = 14$, $a = 0$, $t = t$
     $s = ut + \frac{1}{2}at^2 \Rightarrow x = 14t$, so $t = \frac{x}{14}$ *[1 mark]* — call this ①
     Vertical motion, taking up as +ve:
     $s = y$, $u = 35$, $a = -9.8$, $t = t$
     $s = ut + \frac{1}{2}at^2 \Rightarrow y = 35t - 4.9t^2$ *[1 mark]* — call this ②
     Substitute ① into ② to eliminate t:
     $y = 35\left(\frac{x}{14}\right) - 4.9\left(\frac{x}{14}\right)^2$ *[1 mark]* $\Rightarrow y = \frac{5x}{2} - \frac{x^2}{40}$ *[1 mark]*
  b)   Use formula from part a) with $y = -30$;
     $y = -30$, because the ball lands 30 m below the point it's hit from.
     $-30 = \frac{5x}{2} - \frac{x^2}{40}$ *[1 mark]* $\Rightarrow x^2 - 100x - 1200 = 0$
     Solve quadratic using the quadratic formula: *[1 mark]*
     $x = 111$ m (3 s.f.) *[1 mark]*
  c)   Distance $AH = 110.82762... - 7 = 103.82762...$ m
     Use formula from part a) with $x = 103.82762...$ m:
     $y = \frac{5 \times 103.82762...}{2} - \frac{(103.82762...)^2}{40} = -9.93533...$ *[1 mark]*
     So, when ball is vertically above H, it is 9.93533... m
     below the level of O. Vertical motion, taking up as +ve:
     $s = -9.93533...$, $u = u_y = 35$, $v = v_y$, $a = -g$
     $v^2 = u^2 + 2as \Rightarrow v_y^2 = 1419.73249...$ *[1 mark]*
     In this case, you don't need to take the square root to find the value of v_y as you'd have to square it again to find the speed.
     No acceleration horizontally, so $v_x = u_x = 14$ ms^{-1}
     Speed $= \sqrt{v_x^2 + v_y^2}$ *[1 mark]*
     $= \sqrt{14^2 + 1419.73249...} = 40.2$ ms^{-1} (3 s.f.) *[1 mark]*
     You could also solve part c) using the suvat equations.

Section 17 — Forces and Newton's Laws

Page 199 — Forces and Modelling

Practice Questions

1   Mass: kg, volume: m^3, density: kg m^{-3} or kg/m^3
2 a)   Assumptions: The ball is a particle.
        There is no air resistance (*unless air resistance is included on diagram*).
        No other external forces act on the ball.
  b)   Assumptions: The ball is a particle.
        The ball does not bounce or roll when it hits the cushion.
        The cushion is a horizontal plane.
        No other external forces act on the ball.

Exam Question

1   Possible answers include:
     – It is unrealistic to model a car as a particle — the driver, the engine and the tyres may all have varying effects on its motion. Adjusting the model to account for these effects would make it more accurate.
     – The road is unlikely to be smooth — the model could include friction between the car and the road.
     – The car would realistically experience air resistance. Including this in the model would make it more accurate.
     – A constant speed is unrealistic — the model could account for how the speed varies with time.
     [2 marks available — 1 for each suggested improvement]

Page 202 — Resolving Forces

Practice Questions

1 a)   Magnitude = 5 N, direction = 306.9° (1 d.p.)
  b)   Magnitude = 11.4 N (3 s.f.), direction = 22.4° (1 d.p.)

Answers

c) Magnitude = 5.77 N (3 s.f.), direction = 160.9° (1 d.p.)

d) Magnitude = 2 N, direction = 90°

2   T_B = 34.6 N (3 s.f.), W = 40

Exam Questions

1 a) Resolving the 4 N force gives:
   4 cos 30°**i** + 4 sin 30°**j** N = 3.464...**i** + 2**j** N *[1 mark]*
   So R = 7**i** + 3.464...**i** + 2**j** = 10.464...**i** + 2**j** N *[1 mark]*
   Magnitude = $\sqrt{10.464...^2 + 2^2}$
   = $\sqrt{113.49...}$ = 10.7 N (3 s.f.) *[1 mark]*

   b) tan $\alpha = \frac{2}{10.464...}$ *[1 mark]* $\Rightarrow \alpha$ = 10.8° (1 d.p.) *[1 mark]*

2 a) Resolving horizontally ($\rightarrow$):
   T cos (20° + 25°) – 80 sin 25° = 0
   $\Rightarrow T = \frac{80 \sin 25°}{\cos 45°}$
   = 33.809... ÷ 0.707...
   = 47.8 N (3 s.f.)
   **[3 marks available — 1 for attempt
   to resolve forces, 1 for correct angles,
   1 for correct final answer]**
   *You could also resolve parallel and perpendicular to the slope, but then
   you'd get a pair of simultaneous equations in T and W to solve.*

   b) Resolving vertically ($\downarrow$):
   $W – T$ sin 45° – 80 cos 25° = 0 *[1 mark]*
   $\Rightarrow W$ = 33.809... + 72.504... = 106 N (3 s.f.) *[1 mark]*
   You could also resolve parallel and perpendicular to the plane.

Page 204 — Newton's Laws
Practice Questions

1   v = 4 ms⁻¹

2   Magnitude = 0.283 N (3 s.f.), direction = 32.0° (1 d.p.)
   Make sure you convert the mass into kg before using the formula.

3   Magnitude = 6.25 ms⁻², direction = 53.1° (1 d.p.),
   s = 28.1 m (3 s.f.)

Exam Questions

1 a) (8**i** – 3**j**) = (x**i** + y**j**) + (5**i** + **j**)
   So, x**i** + y**j** = (8**i** – 3**j**) – (5**i** + **j**), so x = 3 and y = –4
   [2 marks available — 1 for each correct value]

   b) Using $F_{net} = ma$: 8**i** – 3**j** = 2.5a *[1 mark]*
   $\Rightarrow a$ = 3.2**i** – 1.2**j** ms⁻² *[1 mark]*
   Magnitude of a = $\sqrt{3.2^2 + (-1.2)^2} = \sqrt{11.68}$
   = 3.42 ms⁻² (3 s.f.) *[1 mark]*
   tan $\theta = \frac{-1.2}{3.2} \Rightarrow \theta$ = –20.556...° *[1 mark]*
   F_{net} acts down-right, so direction = 360° – 20.556...°
   = 339.4° (1 d.p.) *[1 mark]*

   c) List variables: u = 0**i** + 0**j**, v = v, a = 3.2**i** – 1.2**j**, t = 5
   $v = u + at \Rightarrow v$ = 0**i** + 0**j** + 5(3.2**i** – 1.2**j**) *[1 mark]*
   = 16**i** – 6**j** ms⁻¹ *[1 mark]*

2 a) List variables: s = 200, u = 0, a = a, t = 7
   $s = ut + \frac{1}{2}at^2 \Rightarrow 200 = (0 \times 7) + \frac{1}{2} \times a \times 49$ *[1 mark]*
   $\Rightarrow a$ = 200 × 2 ÷ 49 = 8.163... ms⁻² *[1 mark]*
   $F_{net} = ma \Rightarrow F_{net}$ = 60 × 8.163... *[1 mark]*
   = 489.79... N *[1 mark]*
   Resolving forces, $F_{net} = W – R = mg – R$
   489.79... = (60 × 9.8) – R *[1 mark]*
   $\Rightarrow R$ = 588 – 489.79...
   = 98.2 N (3 s.f.) *[1 mark]*

   b) Assumptions: The skydiver is a particle, the air resistance
   force is not affected by the skydiver's speed,
   acceleration due to gravity is a constant 9.8 ms⁻²,
   no other external forces act on the skydiver.
   [2 marks available — 1 each for any valid assumption]

Page 207 — Friction and Inclined Planes
Practice Questions

1 a) 50 N isn't big enough to overcome friction, so it doesn't move.

   b) The force would have to be greater than 58.8 N.

2   μ = 0.43 (2 d.p.)
   Assumptions: The brick slides down line of greatest slope,
   acceleration is constant, no external forces (such as
   air resistance) act on the brick, the brick is a particle.

3   v = 5.12 ms⁻¹ (3 s.f.)

Exam Questions

1 a) Resolving parallel ($\nearrow$):
   $F_{net} = ma$
   8 cos 15° + F – 7g sin 15° = 7 × 0 *[1 mark]*
   F = 7g sin 15° – 8 cos 15°
   = 10.027... N *[1 mark]*
   Resolving perpendicular ($\nwarrow$):
   $F_{net} = ma$
   R – 8 sin 15° – 7g cos 15° = 7 × 0 *[1 mark]*
   R = 8 sin 15° + 7g cos 15° = 68.333... N *[1 mark]*
   Friction is limiting, so:
   $F = \mu R \Rightarrow$ 10.027... = μ × 68.333...
   $\Rightarrow \mu$ = 0.1467... = 0.15 (2 d.p.) *[1 mark]*

   b) Resolving perpendicular ($\nwarrow$):
   R – 7g cos 15° = 7 × 0 *[1 mark]*
   R = 7g cos 15° = 66.262... N *[1 mark]*
   Friction is limiting, so:
   $F = \mu R \Rightarrow F$ = 0.1467... × 66.262... = 9.723... N *[1 mark]*
   Resolving parallel ($\swarrow$):
   7g sin 15° – F = 7a *[1 mark]*
   7a = 7g sin 15° – 9.723...
   $a = \frac{8.031...}{7}$ = 1.147... ms⁻² *[1 mark]*
   List variables: s = 3, u = 0, a = 1.147..., t = t
   $s = ut + \frac{1}{2}at^2$ *[1 mark]*
   3 = (0 × t) + $\frac{1}{2}$ × 1.147... × $t^2 \Rightarrow t^2$ =5.229...
   $\Rightarrow t$ = 2.29 s (3 s.f.) *[1 mark]*

2   Friction either acts up or down the plane.
   Resolving perpendicular ($\nwarrow$):
   R – 10g cos 30° = 0 $\Rightarrow R$ = 84.87... N *[1 mark]*
   $F \leq \mu R \Rightarrow F \leq$ 0.4 × 84.87...
   $\Rightarrow F \leq$ 33.948... N *[1 mark]*
   Resolving parallel ($\nearrow$):
   If friction acts up the plane,
   $P + F$ – 10g sin 30° = 0 *[1 mark]*
   49 – P = $F \leq$ 33.948...
   $P \geq$ 49 – 33.948... $\Rightarrow P \geq$ 15.05... N *[1 mark]*
   If friction acts down the plane,
   $P – F$ – 10g sin 30° = 0 *[1 mark]*
   P – 49 = $F \leq$ 33.948...
   $P \leq$ 49 + 33.948... $\Rightarrow P \leq$ 82.94... N *[1 mark]*
   So the possible range for P is 15.05... $\leq P \leq$ 82.94... N *[1 mark]*

Page 209 — Connected Particles
Practice Questions

1   a = 0.867 ms⁻² (3 s.f.), T = 7040 N

2   W = 30.6 N (3 s.f.)

Exam Questions

1 a) Considering the car and the caravan together:
   Resolving horizontally:
   $F_{net} = ma$
   2500 – (1000 + 200) = 2000a *[1 mark]*
   a = 0.65 ms⁻² *[1 mark]*

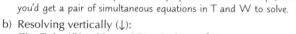

Answers

b) *Either:*
Resolving horizontally for the caravan:
$F_{net} = ma$
$T - 200 = 500 \times 0.65$
$T = 525$ N

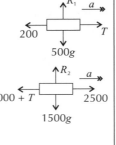

Or:
Resolving horizontally for the car:
$F_{net} = ma$
$2500 - (1000 + T) = 1500 \times 0.65$
$2500 - 1000 - T = 975$
$1500 - 975 = T$
$T = 525$ N

[2 marks available — 1 mark for resolving horizontally,
1 mark for correct final answer]

Two different methods, one correct answer. At the end of the day, it doesn't matter which you use, although it's certainly a bonus if you manage to pick the simpler way and save a bit of time in the exam.

2 a) Resolving forces acting on A: $7g - T = 7a$ ① **[1 mark]**
Resolving forces acting on B:
$T - 3g = 3a \Rightarrow T = 3a + 3g$ ② **[1 mark]**
Substituting ② into ①:
$7g - 3a - 3g = 7a \Rightarrow 4g = 10a \Rightarrow a = 3.92$ ms⁻² **[1 mark]**
List variables: $u = 0$, $v = 5.9$, $a = 3.92$, $t = t$
$v = u + at \Rightarrow 5.9 = 0 + 3.92t \Rightarrow t = 1.51$ s (3 s.f.) **[1 mark]**

b) $v^2 = u^2 + 2as \Rightarrow 5.9^2 = 0^2 + (2 \times 3.92 \times s)$ **[1 mark]**
$7.84s = 34.81 \Rightarrow s = 4.44$ m (3 s.f.) **[1 mark]**
You could have used one of the other *suvat* equations here, but using $v^2 = u^2 + 2as$ means you don't have to rely on your answer to part a) being right (I'm sure it was, of course).

c) When A hits the ground, speed of B = speed of A = 5.9 ms⁻¹.
B will then continue to rise, momentarily stop and then fall freely under gravity. The string will be taut again when the displacement of B = 0.
So, listing variables: $s = 0$, $u = 5.9$, $a = -9.8$, $t = t$ **[1 mark]**
$s = ut + \frac{1}{2}at^2 \Rightarrow 0 = 5.9t + \frac{1}{2}(-9.8)t^2 = 5.9t - 4.9t^2$ **[1 mark]**
Solve for t: $5.9t - 4.9t^2 = 0 \Rightarrow t(5.9 - 4.9t) = 0$ **[1 mark]**
$\Rightarrow t = 0$ or $t = 5.9 \div 4.9 = 1.204...$
So the string becomes taut again at $t = 1.20$ s (3 s.f.) **[1 mark]**

Page 211 — More on Connected Particles
Practice Question
1 $a = 2.90$ ms⁻² (3 s.f.), $T = 27.6$ N (3 s.f.)
A force of 20.3 N (3 s.f.) would be needed.

Exam Questions
1 a) Resolving vertically (↑) for Q:
$F_{net} = ma$
$Mg - T = 0$, so $T = Mg$ **[1 mark]**
Resolving perpendicular (↖) for P:
$F_{net} = ma$
$R - 1g \cos 20° = 0$
$R = g \cos 20°$ **[1 mark]**
Friction is limiting, so:
$F = \mu R = 0.1 \times g \cos 20°$ **[1 mark]**
Resolving parallel (↙) for P:
$F_{net} = ma$
$1g \sin 20° - F - T = 0$
$1g \sin 20° - 0.1g \cos 20° - Mg = 0$ **[1 mark]**
$\sin 20° - 0.1 \cos 20° = M$
$M = 0.25$ kg (2 s.f.) **[1 mark]**

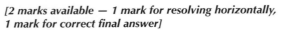

b) If $M = 1$ kg:
Resolving vertically (↓) for Q:
$F_{net} = ma$
$1g - T = 1a$
$T = g - a$ ① **[1 mark]**
Resolving perpendicular (↖) for P:
$R = g \cos 20°$
$F = \mu R = 0.1g \cos 20°$ **[1 mark]**
Resolving parallel (↗) for P:
$F_{net} = ma$
$T - 1g \sin 20° - F = 1a$
$T - g \sin 20° - 0.1g \cos 20° = a$ ② **[1 mark]**
Substituting ① into ②:
$(g - a) - g \sin 20° - 0.1g \cos 20° = a$ **[1 mark]**
$g - g \sin 20° - 0.1g \cos 20° = 2a$
$5.527... = 2a \Rightarrow a = 2.76$ ms⁻² (3 s.f.) **[1 mark]**

2 a) Resolving vertically (↑) for the hanging box:
$T - 4g = 0 \Rightarrow T = 4g$ **[1 mark]**
Resolving horizontally (←) for the box on the table:
$T - F = 0 \Rightarrow F = T = 4g$ **[1 mark]**
Resolving vertically (↑) for the box on the table:
$R - D - 4g = 0 \Rightarrow R = D + 4g$ **[1 mark]**
$F \leq \mu R$, so:
$4g \leq 0.6(D + 4g)$ **[1 mark]**
$4g \leq 0.6D + 2.4g$
$1.6g \leq 0.6D \Rightarrow D \geq 26.133...$ N
So the minimum magnitude of D is 26.1 N (3 s.f.) **[1 mark]**

b) Resolving vertically (↓) for the hanging box:
$F_{net} = ma$
$4g - T = 4a \Rightarrow T = 4g - 4a$ ① **[1 mark]**
Resolving vertically (↑) for the box on the table:
$R - 4g = 0 \Rightarrow R = 4g$ **[1 mark]**
Friction is limiting, so:
$F = \mu R \Rightarrow F = 0.6 \times 4g = 2.4g$ **[1 mark]**
Resolving horizontally (←) for the box on the table:
$F_{net} = ma$
$T - F = 4a \Rightarrow T = 2.4g + 4a$ ② **[1 mark]**
Substituting ① into ②:
$4g - 4a = 2.4g + 4a$
$1.6g = 8a \Rightarrow a = 1.96$ ms⁻² **[1 mark]**
List variables: $u = 0$, $v = v$, $a = 1.96$, $t = 2$
$v = u + at \Rightarrow v = 0 + (1.96 \times 2) = 3.92$ ms⁻¹ **[1 mark]**

3

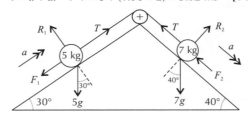

Resolving perpendicular (↖) for the 5 kg particle:
$R_1 - 5g \cos 30° = 0 \Rightarrow R_1 = 5g \cos 30°$ **[1 mark]**
Friction is limiting, so:
$F_1 = \mu R_1 \Rightarrow F_1 = 0.15 \times 5g \cos 30° = 0.75g \cos 30°$ **[1 mark]**
Resolving parallel (↗) for the 5 kg particle:
$F_{net} = ma$
$T - F_1 - 5g \sin 30° = 5a$
$T = 5a + 0.75g \cos 30° + 5g \sin 30°$ ① **[1 mark]**
Resolving perpendicular (↗) for the 7 kg particle:
$R_2 - 7g \cos 40° = 0 \Rightarrow R_2 = 7g \cos 40°$ **[1 mark]**
Friction is limiting, so:
$F_2 = \mu R_2 \Rightarrow F_2 = 0.15 \times 7g \cos 40° = 1.05g \cos 40°$ **[1 mark]**
Resolving parallel (↘) for the 7 kg particle:
$F_{net} = ma$
$7g \sin 40° - T - F_2 = 7a$
$T = 7g \sin 40° - 1.05g \cos 40° - 7a$ ② **[1 mark]**

Answers

Substitute ① into ②:

$5a + 0.75g \cos 30° + 5g \sin 30°$
$\qquad = 7g \sin 40° - 1.05g \cos 40° - 7a$ **[1 mark]**
$12a = g(7 \sin 40° - 1.05 \cos 40° - 5 \sin 30° - 0.75 \cos 30°)$
$a = 9.8(0.5456...) \div 12 = 0.4456...$
i.e. 0.446 ms^{-2} (3 s.f.) up the slope **[1 mark]**

Section 18 — Moments

Page 214 — Moments

Practice Questions

1   $x = 1.37$ (3 s.f.), $T = 22.6$ N (3 s.f.)
2   a) 55.7 N (3 s.f.)   b) 49 N

Exam Questions

1 a)

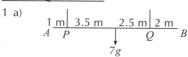

Taking moments about Q: $(T_P × 6) = (7g × 2.5)$ **[1 mark]**
$\Rightarrow T_P = 171.5 \div 6 = 28.6$ N (3 s.f.) **[1 mark]**
Taking moments about P: $(7g × 3.5) = (T_Q × 6)$ **[1 mark]**
$\Rightarrow T_Q = 240.1 \div 6 = 40.0$ N (3 s.f.) **[1 mark]**

b) i) If the maximum mass is attached at A, then the rod will be on the point of tilting about P, and T_Q will be zero. **[1 mark]**
Taking moments about P: $(7g × 3.5) = (Mg × 1)$ **[1 mark]**
$\Rightarrow M = 7 × 3.5 = 24.5$ kg **[1 mark]**

ii) If the maximum mass is attached at B, then the rod will be on the point of tilting about Q, and T_P will be zero. **[1 mark]**
Taking moments about Q: $(Mg × 2) = (7g × 2.5)$ **[1 mark]**
$\Rightarrow M = 7 × 2.5 \div 2 = 8.75$ kg **[1 mark]**

2 a) The weight of the lamina acts at a horizontal distance of 5 m from C (and a horizontal distance of 3 m from E).
Taking moments about E: $(20g × 3) = (R_C × 8)$ **[1 mark]**
$\Rightarrow R_C = 588 \div 8 = 73.5$ N **[1 mark]**
Taking moments about C: $(R_E × 8) = (20g × 5)$ **[1 mark]**
$\Rightarrow R_E = 980 \div 8 = 122.5$ N **[1 mark]**

b) The lamina is on the point of tilting about E, so $R_C = 0$.
The force F acts horizontally, so the perpendicular distance from the force to the pivot (E) is 4 m. **[1 mark]**
Taking moments about E: $(20g × 3) = (F × 4)$ **[1 mark]**
$\Rightarrow F = 588 \div 4 = 147$ N **[1 mark]**

Page 217 — Rigid Bodies and Friction

Practice Questions

1

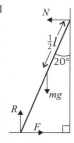

mg = weight of the ladder
F = friction between ground and ladder
R = normal reaction of the ground
N = normal reaction of the wall
As the rod is uniform the weight of the ladder acts at the centre of the rod (i.e. at half of *l*).

Assumptions: e.g. the ladder can be modelled as a rod, the ladder is rigid, friction is sufficient to keep the ladder in equilibrium, the ladder is perpendicular to the wall when viewed from above.

2 a) Taking moments about A:
$2g × 0.4 = 30 \cos 55° × x$
so $x = \dfrac{7.84}{17.20...} = 0.456$ m

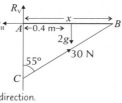

I've made an educated guess in the diagram about which directions R_V and R_H act in. If I work out their values and they turn out to be negative then I just need to reverse their direction.

b) Resolving vertically: $R_V = 2g - 30 \cos 55° = 2.392...$ N
Resolving horizontally: $R_H = 30 \sin 55° = 24.57...$ N

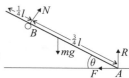

$|R| = \sqrt{2.392...^2 + 24.57...^2} = 24.7$ N (3 s.f.)
$\tan \theta = \dfrac{2.392...}{24.57...} \Rightarrow \theta = 5.56°$ (3 s.f.) to the horizontal

Exam Questions

1 a) Taking moments about A: **[1 mark]**

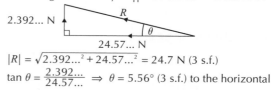

$\frac{1}{2}l × mg \cos \theta = \frac{3}{4}l × N$ **[1 mark]**
$N = \dfrac{\frac{1}{2}lmg \cos \theta}{\frac{3}{4}l} = \frac{2}{3}mg \cos \theta$ **[1 mark]**

Mechanics is harder with algebra than with numbers, but once you've mastered it, doing it with numbers will seem trivial. I know it's not nice, but at least it's useful.

b) $\sin \theta = \frac{3}{5} \Rightarrow \cos \theta = \frac{4}{5}$ **[1 mark]**
Using the result of part a) gives: $N = \frac{8}{15}mg$ **[1 mark]**
Resolving horizontally:
$F = N \sin \theta = \frac{8}{15}mg × \frac{3}{5} = \frac{8}{25}mg$ **[1 mark]**
Resolving vertically: $R + N \cos \theta = mg$
$\Rightarrow R = mg - \frac{4}{5}N = mg - \frac{32}{75}mg = \frac{43}{75}mg$ **[1 mark]**
The rod is in non-limiting equilibrium so $F \le \mu R$ **[1 mark]**
So: $\frac{8}{25}mg \le \mu \frac{43}{75}mg \Rightarrow \mu \ge \frac{24}{43} = 0.56$ (2 d.p.) **[1 mark]**

2 a) Taking moments about the base of the ladder B:
$(mg \cos \theta × 1.4) + (180 \cos \theta × 2.1)$
$\qquad\qquad\qquad = (490 \sin \theta × 4.2)$

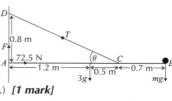

$AB = 4.2$ m
$AC = 2.8$ m
$BC = 1.4$ m

Dividing by $\cos \theta$ gives:
$1.4mg + 378 = 2058 \tan \theta = 2058 × \frac{8}{11}$
$\Rightarrow 1.4mg = 1496.72... - 378 = 1118.72...$
$\Rightarrow m = \dfrac{1118.72...}{13.72} = 81.53... = 82$ kg (nearest kg)
[3 marks available — 1 for taking moments about the base of the ladder B, 1 for correct working and 1 for correct final answer]

b) Resolving horizontally: $F = 490$ N **[1 mark]**
Resolving vertically: $R = 180 + 81.53...g = 979.09...$ N **[1 mark]**
As equilibrium is limiting, $F = \mu R$ **[1 mark]**
So: $979.09...\mu = 490 \Rightarrow \mu = 0.50$ (2 d.p.) **[1 mark]**

3 a) $\tan \theta = \dfrac{0.8}{1.7}$
$\Rightarrow \theta = 25.20...°$ **[1 mark]**
Resolve horizontally:
$T \cos \theta = 72.5$ N **[1 mark]**
$\Rightarrow T = \dfrac{72.5}{\cos 25.20...°}$
$\qquad = 80.12... = 80.1$ N (3 s.f.) **[1 mark]**

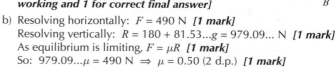

Taking moments about A:
$(1.2 × 3g) + (2.4 × mg) = 1.7 × 80.12... \sin 25.20...°$ **[1 mark]**
$\Rightarrow 23.52m = 58 - 35.28 = 22.72$
$\Rightarrow m = 0.96598... = 0.966$ kg (3 s.f) **[1 mark]**

b) Resolving vertically:
$F + 80.12... \sin 25.20...° = 3g + 0.96598...g$ **[1 mark]**
$\Rightarrow F = 38.86... - 34.11... = 4.75$ N (3 s.f) **[1 mark]**

Formula Sheet

These are the formulas you'll be given in the formula booklet.
You don't need to learn them off by heart, but make sure you know how to use them.

Sequences & Series

Arithmetic Series:

$$S_n = \frac{1}{2}n(a + l) = \frac{1}{2}n[2a + (n-1)d]$$

Geometric Series:

$$S_n = \frac{a(1 - r^n)}{1 - r}$$

$$S_\infty = \frac{a}{1 - r} \text{ for } |r| < 1$$

Binomial Series:

$$(a + b)^n = a^n + \binom{n}{1}a^{n-1}b + \binom{n}{2}a^{n-2}b^2 + \dots + \binom{n}{r}a^{n-r}b^r + \dots + b^n \quad (n \in \mathbb{N})$$

$$\text{where } \binom{n}{r} = {}^nC_r = \frac{n!}{r!(n-r)!}$$

$$(1 + x)^n = 1 + nx + \frac{n(n-1)}{1 \times 2}x^2 + \dots + \frac{n(n-1)\dots(n-r+1)}{1 \times 2 \times \dots \times r}x^r + \dots \quad (|x| < 1, n \in \mathbb{R})$$

Trigonometry

Trigonometric Identities:

$$\sin(A \pm B) = \sin A \cos B \pm \cos A \sin B$$

$$\cos(A \pm B) = \cos A \cos B \mp \sin A \sin B$$

$$\tan(A \pm B) = \frac{\tan A \pm \tan B}{1 \mp \tan A \tan B} \quad (A \pm B \neq (k + \tfrac{1}{2})\pi)$$

Small Angle Approximations:

For small angle θ,
measured in radians:

$$\sin \theta \approx \theta$$
$$\cos \theta \approx 1 - \frac{1}{2}\theta^2$$
$$\tan \theta \approx \theta$$

Differentiation

First Principles: $f'(x) = \lim\limits_{h \to 0} \dfrac{f(x + h) - f(x)}{h}$

For $y = \dfrac{f(x)}{g(x)}$, $\dfrac{dy}{dx} = \dfrac{f'(x)g(x) - f(x)g'(x)}{(g(x))^2}$

$f(x)$	$f'(x)$
$\tan x$	$\sec^2 x$
$\sec x$	$\sec x \tan x$
$\cot x$	$-\text{cosec}^2 x$
$\text{cosec } x$	$-\text{cosec } x \cot x$

Integration

$$\int u \frac{dv}{dx} dx = uv - \int v \frac{du}{dx} dx$$

$$\int \frac{f'(x)}{f(x)} dx = \ln|f(x)| + C$$

$f(x)$	$\int f(x)\, dx$
$\tan x$	$\ln|\sec x| + C$
$\cot x$	$\ln|\sin x| + C$

Formula Sheet

Numerical Methods

The Newton-Raphson iteration for solving f(x) = 0: $x_{n+1} = x_n - \dfrac{f(x_n)}{f'(x_n)}$

Trapezium rule: $\displaystyle\int_a^b y\,dx \approx \frac{1}{2}h\left[(y_0 + y_n) + 2(y_1 + y_2 + \ldots + y_{n-1})\right]$, *where* $h = \dfrac{b-a}{n}$

Probability

$P(A \cup B) = P(A) + P(B) - P(A \cap B)$

$P(A \cap B) = P(A) \times P(B|A)$

Standard Deviation

$$\sqrt{\frac{\sum(x - \overline{x})^2}{n}} = \sqrt{\frac{\sum x^2}{n} - \overline{x}^2}$$

The Binomial Distribution

If $X \sim B(n, p)$, then $P(X = x) = \dbinom{n}{x}p^x(1-p)^{n-x}$

Mean of $X = np$ Variance of $X = np(1 - p)$

Sampling Distributions

For a random sample of n observations from $N(\mu, \sigma^2)$:

$$\frac{\overline{X} - \mu}{\sigma/\sqrt{n}} \sim N(0, 1).$$

Kinematics

Motion in a straight line:

$v = u + at$

$s = ut + \dfrac{1}{2}at^2$

$s = \dfrac{1}{2}(u + v)t$

$v^2 = u^2 + 2as$

$s = vt - \dfrac{1}{2}at^2$

Motion in two dimensions:

$\mathbf{v} = \mathbf{u} + \mathbf{a}t$

$\mathbf{s} = \mathbf{u}t + \dfrac{1}{2}\mathbf{a}t^2$

$\mathbf{s} = \dfrac{1}{2}(\mathbf{u} + \mathbf{v})t$

$\mathbf{s} = \mathbf{v}t - \dfrac{1}{2}\mathbf{a}t^2$

Index

Index